Social Problems

Social Problems

SIXTEENTH EDITION

Karen Seccombe

William Kornblum
City University of New York Graduate School and University Center

 Pearson

Executive Portfolio Manager: Jeff Marshall
Content Producer: Mary Donovan
Content Developer: Jeremy Judson
Portfolio Manager Assistant: Christina Winterburn
Product Marketing Manager: Candice Madden
Sr. Field Marketing Manager: Kelly Ross
Content Producer Manager: Amber Mackey
Content Development Manager: Brooke Wilson
Art/Designer: Integra Software Services, Pvt Ltd.

Digital Studio Course Producer: Elissa Senra-Sargent
Full-Service Project Management: Integra Software
Services, Pvt Ltd.
Composition: Integra Software Services, Pvt Ltd.
Printer/Binder: LSC Communications, Inc.
Cover Printer: LSC Communications, Inc.
Cover Design: Integra Software Services, Pvt Ltd.
Cover Credit: Riccardo Mayer/Shutterstock

Acknowledgements of third party content appear on pages within the text.

Library of Congress Cataloging-in-Publication Data

Seccombe, Karen, author.
Names: Seccombe, Karen, author. | Kornblum, William, author.
Title: Social problems/Karen Seccombe, William Kornblum.
Description: 16 Edition. | New York, NY: Pearson, [2018] | Revised edition
    of Social problems, [2017]
Identifiers: LCCN 2018042254 | ISBN 9780135164730 | ISBN 0135164737
Subjects: LCSH: Social problems–United States. | United States–Social
    conditions–1980-
Classification: LCC HN59.2 .K66 2018 | DDC 306.0973–dc23
LC record available at https://lccn.loc.gov/2018042254

Access Code Card
ISBN-10: 0-13-521252-9
ISBN-13: 978-0-13-521252-3

Revel Combo Card
ISBN-10: 0-13-546644-X
ISBN-13: 978-0-13-546644-5

Rental Edition
ISBN-10: 0-13-516473-7
ISBN-13: 978-0-13-516473-0

Loose-Leaf Edition
ISBN-10: 0-13-522916-2
ISBN-13: 978-0-13-522916-3

Instructor's Review Copy
ISBN-10: 0-13-524701-2
ISBN-13: 978-0-13-524701-3

Brief Contents

Contents

Special Features

Preface

About This Course

This sixteenth edition of *Social Problems* appears as you are witnessing enormous turmoil in Syria, environmental devastation associated with climate change, continued acts of racism and sexism, growing income inequality, ongoing health care debates, and terrorist acts at home and abroad. In Congress and elsewhere, Republicans warn of an impending debt crisis if public budgets are not cut, while Democrats fear that drastic cuts in spending will curtail the economic recovery and unfairly penalize those in the greatest need of social programs.

As this edition unfolds, the election and rhetoric of the new U.S. president caused more controversy than during any previous administration. There was also a contentious round of midterm congressional and Senate elections to determine party majorities in the Senate and House of Representatives. For many voters, these elections represented a referendum on the Trump administration's wide-ranging policies toward taxes, the environment, education, guns, families, health care, immigration, social welfare programs, and international affairs to name only a few of the major social policy areas that a national election will test.

Does that mean we can expect enormous progress toward solving domestic and global social problems? Unfortunately, this is not likely because the problems discussed in this text have been with us for generations and do not have easy solutions. But no doubt there will be changes in policy based on trends that we can already predict.

Fortunately, for every major social problem there are groups of people dedicated to seeking a solution. Some of them are experts on particular social problems, like the members of the medical profession who confront the tragedies of infectious disease each day, or the teachers who work hard to educate all students, or the scientists who work to better understand climate change and how worst-case scenarios can be avoided. Others are nonprofessionals, often citizens who have decided to devote themselves to doing something about a particular situation or problem. Among these activists are people who have experienced the condition they seek to improve—women who have suffered sexual assault, teens who have been afflicted with gun violence, people who know what it is to be homeless, those who abuse drugs and alcohol and want to help themselves and others, and neighbors confronted with the dumping of toxic wastes. Such groups may include elected officials and other political leaders who are expected to formulate sound social policies to address social problems. This book is written in an effort to make their work more effective and in the hope that some readers will be moved to take up their causes. Karen Seccombe and William Kornblum dedicate it to the citizens of the world who devote some of their precious time on Earth to helping others.

Content Highlights

The overarching goal of this text is to impart a sociological imagination—what students may initially see as individual issues are actually rooted in the social arrangements of society. Many personal troubles are really social problems, at least in part, and these require social solutions to be resolved. This sixteenth edition uses four main themes to guide students as they learn to apply the sociological imagination. These themes include (1) using an empirical approach; (2) linking individual experience with social structure; (3) recognizing that social inequality contributes to social problems; and (4) using a comparative approach. Each of these themes are discussed in the opening chapter, revisited throughout the text, and then highlighted again in the concluding chapter and Epilogue.

Social Problems has been designed and written to be as helpful as possible to both students and professors. Each problem is discussed in a well-organized and clear manner with personal vignettes and current examples. The treatment of each problem is analytical as well as descriptive and includes the most up-to-date examples and research findings available.

Each chapter begins with learning objectives and a personal opening vignette and photo designed to grab student interest. Important terms within the chapter are bold-faced and listed at the end of the chapter with their definitions. In addition, feature box discussions in each chapter deal with current controversies or interesting solutions. *A Personal View* feature boxes are first-person accounts, and include such topics as personal experiences with racism, illegal immigration, sex trafficking, poverty, fatherhood, and unemployment. *A Closer Look* feature boxes examine a problem that has been in the recent public spotlight, such as racial profiling, the outsourcing of jobs, droughts and water usage, and myths about poverty, and show how controversies over the problem are addressed by research. Chapters also include *A Global View* feature boxes that discuss a particular social problem from a global perspective, such as maternal and child health, world population growth, climate change, female genital mutilation, or education in less developed countries.

In keeping with the book's effort to explore different solutions to social problems, there is a section at the end of each chapter called *Going Beyond Left and Right*. Its purpose is to help students think critically about the partisan debates over the problems discussed in the chapter they have just read. This section includes a survey so that students can actively participate and take a stand on current social issues.

New to This Edition

The sixteenth edition of *Social Problems* continues to include the voice of co-author Karen Seccombe, who began her collaboration with the last edition. She brings a fresh perspective to an already solid text. Not only have the data been updated, but so are the compelling issues that students will enjoy learning about. Think of this as a *new* edition reflecting current events relevant to today's students, rather than a tired sixteenth edition, recycling old news in the same old ways.

Each chapter has been revised with chapter objectives and current examples that resonate with students, such as marijuana use, same-sex marriage, sexual assault and harassment, excessive police force against unarmed blacks, climate change, and terrorism. Throughout the text, greater emphasis is given to signature concepts such as sex, gender, race, class, human rights, and globalization.

The reception given to previous editions of *Social Problems* by both students and colleagues has been very encouraging, and many of their suggestions have been incorporated in this most recent revision. This sixteenth edition is both comprehensive and up-to-date with current data and detailed discussion of real-world events. The aim is to retain the book's emphasis on the sociological analysis of social problems, as well as the policies designed to alleviate or eliminate them. This text brings these issues alive through both personal vignettes and empirical data. Although policies change continually, we have attempted to update the discussions of policy to reflect the most recent thinking about solutions to social problems, using the most current data, ideas, and examples available.

- **Chapter 1**, Sociological Perspectives on Social Problems, introduces four main themes that run throughout the text to enhance students' sociological imagination: (1) Using an Empirical Approach; (2) Linking Individual Experience with Social Structure; (3) Recognizing That Social Inequality Contributes to Social Problems; and (4) Using a Comparative Approach. The primary goal is to encourage students to think sociologically about the complex world around them, rather than to simply memorize a collection of random facts. Toward this end, students are introduced to sociological theories and research methods.

- **Chapter 2**, Problems of Health and Health Care, has been significantly expanded to examine the inequities and high cost of health care. Coverage includes the Affordable Care Act (ACA) and Republican attempts to dismantle the program. New material has been added on the cultural and demographic factors affecting health and health care, such as obesity, smoking, and an aging population. As with other chapters, students are encouraged to think sociologically, and research and theory are emphasized.

- **Chapter 3**, Problems of Mental Illness and Treatment, is unique among social problem texts. This chapter covers important issues related to mental illness and its treatment. This edition emphasizes that mental illness is a continuum. Though many people only think of the most extreme cases as mental illness, such as schizophrenia, the reality is that more common issues such as bulimia, anorexia, ADHD, and depression are also forms of mental illness. This chapter contains expanded coverage of suicide in the United States and worldwide. The chapter also contains new information on PTSD, homelessness among those with mental illness, and current issues surrounding deinstitutionalization.

- **Chapter 4**, Alcohol and Other Drugs, contains many new features. First, it more thoroughly discusses alcohol and drug use among specific groups within the population. It also provides a detailed description of each of the more commonly used drugs. It elaborates on the social problems associated with alcohol and drug use, such as health issues, crime, and the consequences of driving while impaired. The chapter also contains a new section on the effects of alcohol on families, including codependency, enabling behaviors, and roles that children often adopt to cope with their parents' alcohol use.

- **Chapter 5**, Crime and Violence, contains the most up-to-date statistics from the FBI and other national data sources. It also has expanded coverage of hate crimes and mass shootings, and contains a new section on gender-based violence. Included is a policy discussion of gun control that presents a solid discussion of the issues involved. As is the case in the other chapters, the theoretical perspectives of Functionalism, Conflict Theory, and Symbolic Interactionism are compared and contrasted.

- **Chapter 6**, Poverty amid Affluence, expands the discussion of the causes and consequences of poverty for both children and adults. Issues related to nutrition and food insecurity, inadequate housing, and health and well-being have been added. The chapter now contains a more thorough discussion of welfare programs and puts a "human face" on poverty—showing that poverty is much more than mere statistics.

- **Chapter 7**, Racism, Prejudice, and Discrimination, provides recent data to demonstrate the changing racial composition of the United States. Recent research findings and current examples show that racism continues to persist in a wide variety of situations. Content on institutional discrimination includes new information on education, income, housing, and the criminal justice system, including the death penalty and wrongful executions. The chapter poses many critical thinking questions, encouraging students to engage in the material.

- **Chapter 8**, Sex and Gender, focuses on sexism, male hegemony, and inequality in the United States and internationally. New to this edition is extensive coverage of female genital mutilation, sexist standards of beauty for women, sexual assault, and women's experiences in the labor force. A policy discussion of the Women's Movement has also been included. Throughout, the chapter highlights that gender and gender stereotypes are issues of concern for both women and men because both have been limited by them.

- **Chapter 9**, An Aging Society, examines the structural and individual-level changes that accompany an aging population. Along with the most recent statistics about the growth of the elderly population around the world and in the United States, the chapter contains new coverage of family issues, same-sex elders, long-term care, and death with dignity. This chapter also contains important international data on the quickly aging world, and the tremendous repercussions for both developed and developing nations. It is designed to encourage students to engage with the world's changing demographics.

- **Chapter 10**, Changing Families, has been significantly revamped to identify the changing norms in marriage and intimate relationships, such as the rise in cohabitation, the legalization of same-sex marriage, and the more equitable, but still gendered, division of household labor. There is a new comparison of conservative, liberal, and feminist reactions to these changes. The chapter also reviews two critical issues in considerable depth: violence (among intimates and child abuse) and divorce. As with all chapters, the data and examples are updated and contemporary.

- **Chapter 11**, Problems of Education, contains new data throughout, along with a heightened discussion of differences in education across racial and ethnic groups and the unique barriers that specific groups face. The chapter contains new international comparisons in educational achievement. There is a greater focus on current challenges in providing high quality education to all students, including in early childhood. The most recent data are used, and students are encouraged to reflect upon how the major theoretical traditions view educational issues.

- **Chapter 12**, Problems of Work and the Economy, contains several new or heightened discussions, including Americans' views of the economy and recession, global markets and sweatshops, and the effects of the changing economy on American workers, such as the growth

in contingent jobs, the erosion of the purchasing power of the minimum wage, and the movement to raise the minimum wage to $15 an hour. This chapter has been revised with students in mind, thinking about their trajectory after college.

- **Chapter 13**, Population and Immigration, contains recent data on worldwide population trends. The chapter contains new information on rising expectations around the world and the realities of factors such as literacy, energy use, and food distribution and hunger. New information has been added on government population control efforts, comparing and contrasting China and Japan. Coverage of immigration under President Trump's administration has been expanded significantly, including a discussion of DACA, the federal policy regarding those unauthorized immigrants who entered the United States as children.

- **Chapter 14**, The Environment, has been substantially updated. There is expanded coverage of environmental stress, including more contemporary and detailed coverage of climate change, air pollution, water pollution, solid waste, and toxic wastes. Environmental racism is discussed. The latest scientific evidence is presented in a clear fashion, readily accessible to students. It also raises the question as to whether it is actually too late to save the environment, a concern that will resonate with many students. This chapter addresses these issues in a serious yet optimistic manner.

- **Chapter 15**, War and Global Insecurity, has been revised given the state of the world in late 2018 as the book goes to press. Well-known recent terrorist attacks in the United States and abroad are discussed, and students are introduced to the major current terrorist groups. This chapter also includes new sections on genocide and on sexual violence as a war tactic. These issues highlight the importance of the sociological imagination; while war is experienced on a personal level, it is also a social problem requiring large-scale social solutions.

The text also concludes with a new short chapter, an Epilogue, that summarizes the four main themes using cutting-edge examples: (1) using an empirical approach; (2) linking individual experience with social structure; (3) recognizing that social inequality contributes to social problems; and (4) using a comparative approach. The goal of the Epilogue is to help students review and integrate what they have learned throughout the course of 15 chapters. We've made sure that the book does not just *end*, leaving students hanging about the meaning and relevance of sociology, but, rather, reinforces the sociological imagination.

Throughout the text, statistical material, figures, tables, and photos have been updated, content is current, and recent research has been cited throughout. The *Social Policy* sections incorporate recent cutting-edge programs and proposals. Timely feature boxes have been designed to enhance student interest and encourage critical thinking.

Revel™

Revel is an interactive learning environment that deeply engages students and prepares them for class. Media and assessment integrated directly within the authors' narrative lets students read, explore interactive content, and practice in one continuous learning path. Thanks to the dynamic reading experience in Revel, students come to class prepared to discuss, apply, and learn from instructors and from each other.

Learn more about Revel

www.pearson.com/revel

Revel for *SOCIAL PROBLEMS*

Providing educational technology for the way today's students read, think, and learn, Revel is an interactive learning environment that offers a fully digital experience. It uses frequent updates of articles and data to illustrate the current state of society. Students can interact with multiple types of media and assessments integrated directly within the authors' narrative:

- Chapter-opening **Current Events Bulletins** feature author-written articles that put breaking news and current events into the context of sociology. Examples include the latest information on gun violence in our schools and the debate over gun control; racism and the royal wedding of Prince Harry and Meghan Markle; and the latest social policy discussions on climate change.

- The *Pearson Original* docuseries videos highlight stories that exemplify and humanize the concepts covered in sociology courses. These videos illustrate a variety of social issues and current events, bringing key topics to life for students while creating opportunities to further develop their understanding of sociology. Therefore, students not only connect with the people and stories on a personal level, but also view these stories and individuals with greater empathy all while contextualizing core course concepts. These videos are incorporated into the chapters and can also be easily accessed from the instructor's Resources folder within Revel.

- **Interactive maps, figures, and tables** feature Social Explorer technology, which allows for real-time data updates and rollover information to support the data

and show movement over time. PowerPoint presentations with every Social Explorer Visualization can be accessed from the instructor's Resources folder within Revel.

- **Interactive Surveys** also feature Social Explorer technology. Students are invited to take a short survey related to the chapter content. They can then compare their views to those of other adults based on large surveys with a nationally representative sample (e.g., The Gallup Poll) and see how their views conform or deviate from others. Surveys include topics such as attitudes toward gender equality; health care and the Affordable Care Act; gun control; raising the minimum wage to $15 an hour; Affirmative Action; the use of torture in interrogations; and explanations for poverty.

- **Slide Show** interactives enable students to see and read about multiple perspectives of a select global social problem in slide-show format and then answer a critical thinking question to promote self-reflection on causes and solutions. For example, students can quickly learn about who the global victims of terrorism are by clicking through a scrollable set of images depicting a Boston Marathon bombing victim, the aftermath of a Syrian barrel-bomb attack, the World Trade Center tower on 9/11, and Ethiopian Christians mourning the death of their congregants at the hands of ISIL. Students are then given an opportunity to compare and contrast traditional war and terrorism.

- **Assessments** tied to primary chapter sections, as well as full chapter exams, allow instructors and students to track progress and get immediate feedback.

- **Integrated Writing Opportunities**: To help students reason and write more clearly, each chapter offers three varieties of writing prompts:

  - **Journal prompts** at the end of each major section ask students to consider critical issues that relate to topics at the module level.

  - **Shared writing prompts**, linked to each chapter's conclusion, encourage students to consider how to address challenges described in the chapter. Through these prompts, instructors and students can address multiple sides of an issue by sharing their own views and responding to each other's viewpoints.

  - **Essay prompts** are from Pearson's Writing Space, where instructors can assign both automatically graded and instructor-graded prompts. Writing Space is the best way to develop and assess concept mastery and critical thinking through writing. Writing Space provides a single place within Revel to create, track, and grade writing assignments, access writing resources, and exchange meaningful, personalized feedback quickly and easily to improve results. For students, Writing Space provides everything they need to keep up with writing assignments, access assignment guides and checklists, write or upload completed assignments, and receive grades and feedback—all in one convenient place. For educators, Writing Space makes assigning, receiving, and evaluating writing assignments easier. It's simple to create new assignments and upload relevant materials, see student progress, and receive alerts when students submit work. Writing Space makes student work more focused and effective with customized grading rubrics they can see and personalized feedback. Writing Space can also check students' work for improper citation or plagiarism by comparing it against the world's most accurate text comparison database available from Turnitin.

Revel Combo Card

The Revel Combo Card provides an all-in-one access code and loose-leaf print reference (delivered by mail).

Supplements

Make more time for your students with instructor resources that offer effective learning assessments and classroom engagement. Pearson's partnership with educators does not end with the delivery of course materials; Pearson is there with you on the first day of class and beyond. A dedicated team of local Pearson representatives will work with you to not only choose course materials but also integrate them into your class and assess their effectiveness. Our goal is your goal—to improve instruction with each semester.

Pearson is pleased to offer the following resources to qualified adopters of *Social Problems*. Several of these supplements are available to instantly download from Revel or on the Instructor's Resource Center (IRC); please visit the IRC at **www.pearsonhighered.com/irc** to register for access.

- **TEST BANK** Evaluate learning at every level. Developed by author, Karen Seccombe, and reviewed for clarity and accuracy, the Test Bank measures this material's learning objectives with multiple-choice and essay questions. You can easily customize the assessment to work in any major learning management system and to match what is covered in your course. Word, Black-Board, and WebCT versions are available on the IRC, and Respondus versions are available on request from **www.respondus.com**.

- **PEARSON MYTEST** This powerful assessment generation program includes all of the questions in the Test Bank. Quizzes and exams can be easily authored and saved online, and then printed for classroom use, giving you ultimate flexibility to manage assessments anytime and anywhere. To learn more, visit **www.pearsonhighered.com/mytest**.

- **INSTRUCTOR'S RESOURCE MANUAL** Create a comprehensive roadmap for teaching classroom, online, or hybrid courses. Designed for new and experienced instructors, the Instructor's Resource Manual includes learning objectives, lecture and discussion suggestions, activities for in or out of class, research activities, participation activities, and suggested readings, series, and films as well as a Revel features section. Available within Revel and on the IRC.

- **POWERPOINTS** In order to support varied teaching styles while making it easy to incorporate dynamic Revel features in class, two sets of PowerPoint Presentations are available for this edition: (1) A set of accessible lecture PowerPoint slides outline each chapter of the text. (2) An additional set of the lecture PowerPoint slides includes LiveSlides, which link to each Social Explorer data visualization and interactive map within the Revel product. These presentations are available to adopters in electronic formats at the Instructor's Resource Center (**www.pearsonhighered.com/irc**) or in the Instructor Resources Folder within the Revel product.

About the Authors

Karen Seccombe is a proud community college graduate, receiving the mentoring and support needed to continue her education in sociology and social work. She earned her BA degree at California State University, Chico; her MSW in Social Work at the University of Washington; and her PhD at Washington State University, in Pullman. Karen is the author of several books, including, *So You Think I Drive a Cadillac?* (4th edition); *Families and Their Social Worlds* (4th edition); *Exploring Marriages and Families* (3rd edition); *Families in Poverty*; and *Just Don't Get Sick*, with co-author Kim Hoffman, which won Honorable Mention from the Pacific Sociological Association.

Karen's research focuses on the health and well-being of poor and vulnerable families. She has been a professor at the University of Alaska, University of Florida, and Portland State University in Oregon. She is a Fellow in the National Council on Family Relations and is active in the American Sociological Association and in the Pacific Sociological Association. She is a Fulbright Scholar and taught Health Policy in Hangzhou, China. She also recently taught in the Semester at Sea program, a shipboard community of nearly 600 students and 50 faculty and staff, traveling around the world to Japan, China, Vietnam, Myanmar, India, South Africa, Ghana, and Morocco. While the ship was at sea, Karen taught Marriage and Family Relationships, Gender and Society, and Social Problems, enriching her courses with the in-port opportunities she and her students experienced. Karen is married to Richard Meenan, a health economist, and has two high school-age children, Natalie and Olivia, and two Australian Shepherds, Bart and Stella. She enjoys traveling the world, hiking, cycling, and relaxing with her pack in the San Juan islands off the coast of Washington. She wants to hear from students and faculty—she aims to please—so please send any comments her way: karen.s.meenan@icloud.com.

Acknowledgments

Revising and updating a social problems textbook is a formidable task, and we learned a great deal in the process. Social Problems is a broad field with many critical issues that change rapidly. This edition has benefitted from the reviews of many sociologists, all of whom have contributed useful comments and suggestions which they will see here in this edition. We want to thank the following:

Diane Lindley, *The University of Mississippi*
Patricia Sawyer, *University of Bridgeport*
Judith Kirwan Kelley, *Curry College*
Henry Borne, *Saint Mary's College*
Evita Bynum, *The Catholic University of America*
Monica Michael, *Cornerstone University*
Maria Cuevas, *Yakima Valley College*
Michael Polgar, *Penn State University*

Many thanks are due to the keen publishing specialists who contributed their talents and energy to this edition. Jeremy Judson worked tirelessly as the developmental editor to ensure this text was organized and expressed ideas with fluidity—always offering timely ideas and good suggestions to enhance the overall content. Thanks, J! We would also like to thank Ohlinger Studios—Beth Jacobson, Director of Development; Jennifer Jacobson, Senior Managing Editor; Brooke Wilson, Managing Editor; Erin Bosco, Program Manager; Rebecca Favorito, Project Manager; Amy Gibbons, Digital Media Manager; Brooks Hill-Whilton, Rights and Permissions Manager.

Finally, because a book is never a solo venture, it's important to acknowledge the assistance of my (Karen's) friends and fellow Bookies in the community of Friday Harbor who offered support along the way and who actually offered *new* books to read that have nothing to do with sociology! In particular, Richard, Natalie, Olivia, Bart, and Stella Meenan—my crazy pack—have my eternal gratitude.

Chapter 1
Sociological Perspectives on Social Problems

Stocktrek Images, Inc./Alamy Stock Photo

 ## Learning Objectives

1.1 Explain the sociological imagination.

1.2 Discuss the definition of a social problem.

1.3 Compare and contrast the three main sociological perspectives on social problems.

1.4 Describe the process that reveals the natural history of social problems.

1.5 Review the four themes of the text.

1.6 Assess the social policy debates between conservatives and liberals.

I live in Fullerton, a suburb about 20 to 40 minutes from Los Angeles, depending on traffic. I like where I live. I'm close to beaches, mountains, and even the desert (although I've only been to Joshua Tree National Monument once). All are only an hour or two drive away. But there is one big problem—we don't have a lot of water for the millions of people who live around here. We have droughts sometimes, and the last one was kinda scary. I saw pictures that showed our reservoirs were really low, and the mountains didn't have a lot of snow. We get our water from the mountain snowpack, so naked mountains mean big trouble! Our teachers at school were warning us that we must conserve water. We were told to take 5-minute showers, and were showed ways to save water as we brushed our teeth. It was weird, as I haven't really thought about water as something that we could actually run out of. I turn on the faucet and water flows, right? Well, apparently, not necessarily. My parents scared me because last spring they hired someone to rip out our grass and plant "drought tolerant plants," whatever that means. No grass? How am I supposed to kick around the soccer ball around this cactus? But my parents explained that we must now pay extra for water, and even pay a fine if we use too much, and it is expensive. My mom said that we are not supposed to water our yard very often or else we have to pay a fine, and these plants do well without a lot of water. Fine, but five-minute showers? "Get real," I told my mom. But then she told me about Cape Town, in South Africa. It's a nice city, and looks like home in a way, but they are totally running out of water! Is that even possible? I looked it up on the Internet (I was sure my mom was making it up), but it's true! They could actually be running out of water!

—Shelby, age 14

Record droughts in California, gun violence at schools, unarmed blacks being killed by police officers, sexual assaults on college campuses, hurricanes battering the Gulf Coast and Puerto Rico, Islamic terrorists, record social inequality, gun violence in our schools, and millions of Americans without health insurance. In such difficult times, Americans may rightly wonder whether we are capable of successfully addressing our most severe problems, let alone the world's problems. This question is one that will arise in specific ways throughout this text's chapters, but you will also see that there is little to be gained by giving in to failure. The history of efforts to address issues of environmental degradation, health problems, crime, racism and sexism, terrorism, poverty, and access to health care presents many bright spots and evidence that the more everyone understands the problems and the more citizens become engaged in seeking solutions, the more successfully society will address social problems.

The United States and other Western nations are experiencing more conflict about how to address social problems than was true in the decades after World War II. Back then, after the devastation and collective sacrifices of World War II, there was more consensus that government should play an important role in providing a "social safety net" for society's members who lacked the means to provide an adequate level of living for themselves and their children. Today, there is widespread debate about public versus private responsibility for addressing issues such as poverty, ill health, and environmental degradation. The ongoing "culture wars," as today's politically ideological divisions and debates are often called, make it far more difficult for people to arrive at a broad consensus about which social policies and programs are most effective for dealing with major social problems. This text applies a social-scientific approach to these problems, which can lead to progress in understanding their causes and arriving at policies to address them. As part of this strategy, every chapter in this text ends with a discussion of how social policies at different levels of government and in the private sector can address specific social problems.

The Sociological Imagination

1.1 Explain the Sociological Imagination.

We live in a world of more than 7.6 billion people, and we share a society with hundreds of millions. Despite the enormity of humankind, most people think of themselves as unique individuals and as having distinctive experiences like no other. However, many of their personal experiences are not unique or exceptional. Instead, they are patterned and shaped by **social structure**, which is the organized arrangements of relationships and institutions that together form the basis of society. For example, how has your sex influenced your life experience? Has being male or being female influenced your choice of a college major or your hobbies, interests, and relationships? Has your sex influenced your willingness to take drugs, commit crime, or enlist in the army and go to war? Has it influenced whether you have been sexually assaulted or battered by a partner? Perhaps another way of framing this question is how would your life be different if you were the "opposite sex"? As you can see, there is a relatively organized set of arrangements associated with your sex.

Taking another example, how has your family affected you? You may have grown up with one parent, two parents, or with no parents at all. How did your family arrangement affect your financial well-being, your social capital, and overall opportunities? If your mother used drugs or alcohol, if your father was in jail, or if an uncle sexually abused you, how do you think those experiences may have affected your life? Families are a primary social institution in all societies and have a profound influence on personal experiences. The feature box *A Personal View: "Running Away to My Future"* offers an example of the ways in which early family life can shape adulthood.

social structure

The organized arrangements of relationships and institutions that together form the basis of society.

A Personal View

Running Away to My Future

Viktor Pravdica/Alamy Stock Photo

Jody is a vibrant 27-year-old single mother who has a bright future ahead of her after a rocky start in life. She was awarded a $7,500 annual scholarship that will help her to attend a four-year university next fall. The scholarship award committee noted "her steadfast determination and her potential to make a difference." These words are an apt description.

Jody was born to a single mother who was poor and addicted to drugs. As a young child, Jody bounced from one home to another, often sleeping on the couch of her mother's latest boyfriend. Nourishing food was scarce, and Jody often went to school hungry. Her mother failed to fill out the forms for the school lunch program, but the school staff could see that Jody was hungry in the morning and let her eat breakfast with the other students who needed it. After school, Jody usually went home to an empty house, left on her own to do homework and make dinner.

Jody loved school, and diligently did her homework every day. School was her refuge. Because she excelled at school, was rarely absent or tardy, and completed her homework, the school assumed that Jody's home life was fine.

As the years went by, Jody did her best to hide the consequences of her family's poverty. She shopped for clothes at the Goodwill when she had a little extra money and hunted for stylish clothes that would not reveal her secret. But one night her mother's latest live-in boyfriend crawled into bed with Jody, who was by then a budding 16-year-old girl, and tried to sexually assault her. Jody screamed, hit him, and ran out of the room, stumbling over her passed-out mother in the living room. Jody vowed never to go back home as long as he was living there. When she confronted her mother the next day, her mother insisted that the boyfriend was staying, and it was Jody who could leave.

Jody took some of her mother's drug money, which amounted to a few hundred dollars, a few clothes, and ran away. With her money, she bought a sleeping bag and supplies to camp out under a bridge with other homeless people. She got a job at a fast-food restaurant making minimum wage. All the while, she continued to go to school, cleaning herself up and washing her hair in the restroom at work. Despite her hardship, she graduated from high school with a B average.

Community college was her next step, but by this time, the stress of homelessness, a dead-end job, and schoolwork were taking their toll. She suffered from depression, which caused her to make several risky choices. She became pregnant. The father did not stick around, and the thought of raising a child in her circumstances depressed her even more. Jody decided to give the baby up for adoption. She cried for weeks before and after her decision but knew in her heart it was the right thing to do. However, by this time, Jody was severely depressed, had dropped out of school, lost her job, and was begging on the street. She lived this way for several years, begging and earning just enough to buy food. Begging meant giving up her pride, but she said that part of living in poverty is blocking out how others might judge you.

By the time Jody was 22, she became pregnant a second time. However, on this occasion, she was determined to keep her baby and do whatever it would take to provide a good home. She sought out social service agencies and asked them for help. A counselor located low-income housing, arranged for medical care so Jody could get the depression medicine she needed, set her up with a part-time job, and helped her enroll back into community college. Jody began to flourish. She loved being a mother and felt that her son gave her life true meaning. She graduated from her community college with honors, and at the advice of the college's financial aid office, applied and received a scholarship to complete her degree. As she describes it, "When I left home at 16, I had no idea that I was running away to my future. With the help that others have offered, I can do this."

Critical Thinking

Using a sociological imagination, how were Jody's choices and constraints shaped by larger social forces? Why do most people consider poverty a social problem rather than simply a personal experience of a few people like Jody?

What Do You Think?

Evaluate your social class standing when you were a child. For example, did your parent(s) go to college? Did your parent(s) have a steady job? What type of house did you grow up in? Now describe how this social class standing has influenced your lifestyle and choices today.

Using a sociological imagination reveals general patterns in what otherwise might be thought of as simple random events. C. Wright Mills stressed the importance of understanding the relationship between individuals and the society in which they live (Mills, 1959). Problems such as poverty, divorce, substance abuse, crime, and child abuse are more than just personal troubles experienced by a few people. They are issues that affect large numbers of people and originate in society's institutional arrangements. In other words, individual experiences are linked to the social structure.

Peter Berger elaborated on these ideas in his 1963 book *Invitation to Sociology*. Although we like to think of ourselves as individuals, much of our behavior (and others' behavior toward us) is actually patterned on the basis of what social categories we fall into, such as age, income, race, ethnicity, sex, and physical appearance. For example, men and women behave differently for reasons that often have nothing to do with biology. Many of these patterns are socially produced. In other words, boys and girls, men and women, are each taught and encouraged to think of themselves differently from one another and to behave in different ways. Society lends a hand in shaping people's lives. Why are over 85 percent of students in Bachelor of Science in Nursing (BSN) programs female (National League for Nursing, 2018)? This demographic fact is obviously not the result of some biological imperative, some quirk of the occupation itself, or some random event. Rather, society even has a hand in shaping something as seemingly personal and individual as the choice of a college major.

Émile Durkheim (1897) conducted an early study of suicide, documenting how social structure affects human behavior. At first glance, what could be more private and individualized than the reasons that surround a person's decision to take his or her own life? The loss of a loving relationship, job troubles, financial worries, and low self-esteem are just a few of the many reasons that a person may have for suicide. Yet looking through official records and death certificates, Durkheim noted that suicide was not a completely random event and that there were several important patterns worthy of attention. He found that men were more likely to kill themselves than were women. He noted that Protestants were more likely to take their lives than were Catholics and Jews. He found that wealthy people were more likely to commit suicide than were the poor. Finally, it appeared that unmarried people were more likely to kill themselves than were married people.

Although his study was conducted over 100 years ago, recent research indicates that these patterns persist. Suicide today is a major social problem, with about 40,000 individuals taking their lives each year. It is the tenth leading cause of death for all Americans, and the second leading cause for youths ages 10 to 34 (Centers for Disease Control and Prevention, July 19, 2016).

The sociological imagination draws attention to the fact that seemingly private issues are often public ones (Mills, 1959). Moreover, when these issues affect the quality of life for a large number of people, they are called social problems.

What Is a Social Problem?

1.2 Discuss the definition of a social problem.

When enough people in a society agree that a condition exists that threatens the quality of their lives and their most cherished values, *and* they agree that something should be done to remedy that condition, sociologists say that the society has defined that condition as a **social problem**. In other words, the society's members have reached a consensus that a condition that affects some people is a problem for the entire society, not just for those who are directly affected. Figure 1–1 illustrates trends in the issues considered to be the top five social problems between 2001 and 2018: the economy, unemployment, the government, health care, and immigration (Gallup, 2018; Riffkin, 2015; Smith and Saad, 2016). As you can see, there is a fair amount of fluctuation in opinion. For example, during the recession, the economy and unemployment were considered the most important social problems. Today, government itself is seen as number one. Today's top social problems are explored in the slideshow, *"Where People Stand on Social Issues."*

social problem

Widespread agreement that a condition threatens the quality of life and cherished values and that something should be done to remedy that condition.

You will see that for every social problem, arguments arise about the nature of the problem, its severity, and the best remedies—laws, social programs, or other policies—to address it. There must be enough consensus among people in a society that a problem exists for action to take place, but consensus on a problem does not indicate consensus on the solution. For example, most Americans are concerned about crime, but what to do about it is wide open for discussion. Some people favor mandatory sentencing for specific crimes, while others feel that a judge or jury should have some discretion. Some people support the death penalty for heinous crimes, while others oppose the death penalty and believe that life in prison without parole is the most appropriate punishment. Moreover, this text will also show that not all people have an equal ability to define social problems and to propose remedies; those with power often have more say in the matter and are listened to most closely.

Social problems are often closely interrelated. Crime, poor school performance, poverty, lack of medical care, unsafe working conditions, violence, drug abuse, environmental degradation, and many other behaviors or situations that we commonly think of as social problems rarely exist in isolation. And for any

Figure 1–1 Most Important Problems Facing the United States by Percentage, 2001–2018

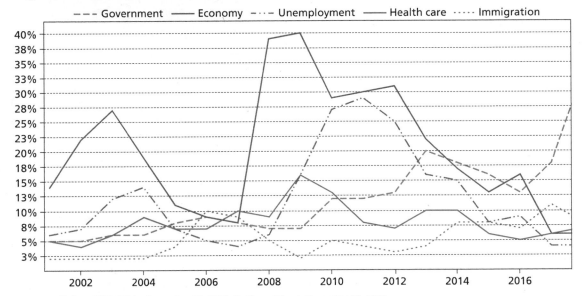

SOURCES: Gallup, 2018; Riffkin, December 14, 2015; Smith and Saad, December 19, 2016.

Where People Stand on Social Issues

Surveys based on representative samples of adults in the United States provide an important gauge of where people stand on social issues. A recent Gallup Poll survey reports that the top social problems in American society today are considered to be the government, economy, immigration, health care, and unemployment, shifting somewhat in the ranking over the past couple of decades. This slide show looks at these issues.

VisualField/Getty Images

The most recent national sample of adults ranked government first in a list of social problems. The majority of both conservatives and liberals say that they often or always do not trust the federal government, and that they feel angry toward it. The level of agreement is striking, given that these two groups see the role of government very differently.

stevecoleimages/Getty Images

Many Americans are concerned about health care. They see rapidly escalating costs and worry about a lack of access as fewer employers offer health insurance as a fringe benefit. The Affordable Care Act (ACA) was created during President Obama's administration to decrease these problems and has met with some success. However, the ACA has experienced political backlash from Republican lawmakers as they have attempted to dismantle it.

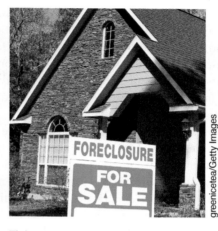

greenicetea/Getty Images

The economy, broadly defined, is also considered a top social problem, although the percentage of persons who rank it at or near the top has declined as the economy has improved in recent years. Housing is an example of an economic problem that affected millions of people. When housing prices began to tumble in the height of the recession, many people found that they owed more on their house than it was worth. Some people could no longer afford to make the payments and their house went into foreclosure. In 2008, there were nearly 4 million homes in foreclosure. By 2018, just a decade later, that number dropped to 577,000.

CrowdSpark/Alamy Stock Photo

Immigration is also ranked by Americans as a pressing social problem. However, the exact nature of the problem and what to do about it are not clear-cut. For example, the majority of Americans say that immigration actually strengthens our country through immigrants' hard work and talent. And most Americans believe that immigrants who live in the United States illegally should be eligible for citizenship if certain requirements are met, especially for those who were brought here as children and who qualify for the program, Deferred Action for Childhood Arrivals (DACA).

Jim West/Alamy Stock Photo

Unemployment, as a problem, was highly ranked during and immediately after the recession as more people realized that it is more than just a personal problem. At the height of the recession, when the national unemployment rate was over 10 percent, the federal government extended the number of weeks a person could collect unemployment. That policy reflected the idea that unemployment is a social problem, not simply an individual issue.

Critical Thinking

Why do you think that these five social problems were rated as the most significant? What changes would you make in this list, and why?

one of these problems, the causes, responsibilities, and solutions are vigorously debated. Are we responsible, some ask, for the sins of others? For example, are not many people poor because they choose to drop out of school or have a baby before they are financially prepared to do so? Or are many people poor because of the erosion of the purchasing power of the minimum wage and social conditions like racism and sexism? These and similar arguments assert not only the causes of social problems but also what should be done about them. People may agree that certain conditions are social problems. Most members of society agree that these conditions ought to be remedied through intentional action. However, people disagree about, and politicize, what the causes are and what the precise intentional action should be.

For instance, many Americans are appalled at the level of gun violence in their nation, but many others are equally appalled at the prospect of more government restrictions on their freedom to buy and use guns as they wish. Clearly, recognition that a social problem exists is far different from arriving at a consensus about a cause and a solution to the problem.

It is worth noting that the idea that a society should intervene to remedy conditions that affect the lives of its citizens is a fairly recent innovation. Until the eighteenth century, for example, most people worked at exhausting tasks under poor conditions for long hours; they suffered from severe deprivation all their lives, and they often died young, sometimes of terrible diseases. But no one thought of these things as problems to be solved. They were accepted as natural, inevitable conditions of life. It was not until the so-called "enlightenment" of the late eighteenth century that philosophers began to argue that poverty is not inevitable, but a result of an unjust social system. As such, changing the system itself through means such as redistribution of wealth and elimination of inherited social status could alleviate many problems.

Sociological Perspectives on Social Problems

1.3 Compare and contrast the three main sociological perspectives on social problems.

Everyone has opinions about the causes of social problems and what should be done about them. In addition to Sociology, other disciplines in the social sciences are concerned with the analysis of human behavior, and sociologists often draw on the results of their research. The work of historians, for example, is vital to an understanding of the origins of many social problems. Anthropologists look at other societies and offer contrasting views of how humans have learned to cope with various kinds of social problems. Perhaps the greatest overlap is between sociology and political science, both of which are concerned with the development of social policies to curb social problems. Other social-scientific approaches to the study of social problems are described in Table 1–1.

Contemporary sociology is founded on three basic perspectives, or sets of ideas, that offer theories about why societies hang together and how and why they change. These perspectives are not the only sociological approaches to social problems, but they can be extremely powerful tools for understanding them. Each of these perspectives—(1) functionalism, (2) conflict, and (3) symbolic interactionism—gives rise to a number of useful and distinctive approaches to the study of social problems, as identified in Table 1–2. The following sections explore these three approaches, using criminal deviance as an example to show the unique contributions of each perspective.

Table 1–1 Other Approaches to the Study of Social Problems

History

History is the study of the past. However, historical data can be used by sociologists to understand present social problems. In studying homelessness, for example, historians would focus on changes in how people obtained shelter in a society and what groups or individuals tended to be without shelter in different historical periods.

Cultural Anthropology

Cultural anthropologists study the social organization and development of smaller, nonindustrial societies, both past and present. Because cultural anthropology is closely related to sociology, many of the same techniques can be used in both fields, and the findings of cultural anthropologists regarding primitive and traditional cultures shed light on related phenomena in more complex, modern societies. An anthropological study of homelessness would look closely at one or a few groups of homeless people. The anthropologist might be interested in how the homeless and others in their communities understand their situation and what might be done about it.

Psychology and Social Psychology

Psychology focuses on human mental and emotional processes, primarily on individual experience. Rooted in biology, it is more experimental than the other social sciences. An understanding of the psychological pressures that underlie individual responses can illuminate social attitudes and behavior. Thus, a psychologist would tend to study the influences of homelessness on the individual's state of mind or, conversely, how the individual's personality and ways of looking at life might have contributed to his or her situation.

Social psychology involves the study of how psychological processes, behavior, and personalities of individuals influence or are influenced by social processes and social settings. It is of special value for the study of social problems. A social psychologist would be likely to study how life on the streets damages the individual in various ways.

Economics

Economists study the levels of income in a society and the distribution of income among the society's members. To understand how the resources of society—its people and their talents, its land and other natural resources—can be allocated for the maximum benefit of that society, economists also study the relationship between the supply of resources and the demand for them. Confronted with the problem of homelessness, an economist would tend to study how the supply of and demand for different types of housing influence the number of homeless people in a given housing market.

Political Science

Political scientists study the workings of government at every level of society. As Harold Lasswell (1941), a leading American political scientist, put it, "Politics is the study of who gets what, when, and how."[1] A political scientist, therefore, would be likely to see homelessness as a problem that results from the relative powerlessness of the homeless to influence the larger society to respond to their needs. The political scientist would tend to focus on ways in which the homeless could mobilize other political interest groups to urge legislators to deal with the problem.

---

[1]Lasswell, H. D., 1941. "The Garrison State." *American Journal of Sociology*, 46:455–468.

1.3.1 The Functionalist Perspective

From the day a person is born until the day that person dies, he or she holds a position—a **status**—in a variety of groups and organizations. In a hospital, for example, the patient, the nurse, the doctor, and the orderly are all members of a social group concerned with health care. Each of these individuals has a status that requires the performance of a certain set of behaviors, known as a **role**. Taken together, the statuses and roles of the members of this medical team and other teams in hospitals throughout the country make up the social institution known as the health care system. A **social institution** is a relatively stable structure of statuses and roles devoted to meeting the basic needs of people in a society. The health care system is an institution; hospitals, insurance companies, and private medical practices are examples of organizations within this institution.

The **functionalist perspective** looks at the ways major social institutions like the family, the military, the health care system, and the police and courts actually operate. According to this perspective, the role behavior associated with any given status has evolved as a means of allowing a social institution to fulfill its function in society. Thus, the nurse's role requires specific knowledge and behaviors that involve treatment of the patient's immediate needs and administration of care according to the doctor's orders. The patient, in turn, is expected to cooperate in the administration of the treatment. When all members of the group perform their roles correctly, the group is said to be functioning well.

status

A social position.

role

The performance of a certain set of behaviors that go with a status.

social institution

A more or less stable structure of statuses and roles devoted to meeting the basic needs of people in a society, for example, the health care system.

functionalist perspective

A way of thinking that considers the way major social institutions such as the family, the military, the health care system, and the police and courts actually operate.

Table 1–2 Major Sociological Perspectives on Social Problems

Perspective	View of Society and Social Problems	Origins of Social Problems	Proposed Solutions
Functionalist	Views society as a vast organism whose parts are interrelated; social problems are disruptions of this system. Also holds that problems of social institutions produce patterns of deviance and that institutions must address such patterns through strategic social change.	Social expectations fail, creating normlessness, culture conflict, and breakdown. Social problems also result from the impersonal operations of existing institutions, both now and in the past.	Engage in research and active intervention to improve social institutions. Create new organizations to address social problems.
Conflict	Views society as marked by conflicts due to inequalities in class, race, ethnicity, gender, age, and other divisions that produce conflicting values. Defines social problems as conditions that do not conform to society's values.	Groups with different values and differing amounts of power meet and compete.	Build stronger social movements among groups with grievances. The conflicting groups may then engage in negotiations and reach mutual accommodations.
Symbolic Interactionist	Holds that definitions of deviance or social problems are subjective; separates deviant and nondeviant people not by what they do but by how society reacts to what they do.	Society becomes aware that certain behaviors exist and labels them as social problems.	Resocializes deviants by increasing their contacts with accepted patterns of behavior; makes the social system less rigid. Changes the definition of what is considered deviant.

In a well-functioning group, there is general agreement about how roles are to be performed by each member. These expectations are reinforced by the society's basic values, from which are derived rules about how people should and should not behave toward one another in different situations. The Ten Commandments, the Golden Rule, the Bill of Rights, and the teachings of all the world's religions are examples of sets of rules that specify how people should behave in different social roles.

But if a society is made up of groups in which people know their roles and adhere to the underlying values, why does that society have social problems like crime and warfare? From the functionalist perspective, the main reason for the existence of social problems is that societies are always changing and having to adapt to new conditions; failure to adapt successfully leads to social problems.

The early French social theorist Émile Durkheim observed that changes in a society can drastically alter the goals and functions of human groups and organizations. As a society undergoes a major change—say, from agricultural to industrial production—the statuses people assume and the roles they play also change, with far-reaching consequences. Thus, for example, the tendency for men and women from rural backgrounds to have many children, which was functional in agrarian societies because it produced much-needed farmhands, can become a liability in an urban-industrial society, where housing space is limited and the types of jobs available are constantly changing. From the standpoint of society's smooth functioning, it can be said that the roles of the father and mother in the rural setting that stresses long periods of childbearing and many children become dysfunctional in an urban setting. Currently developed nations, such as the United States, are undergoing another radical change moving from an Industrial to an Information/Service age. We are beginning to witness the economic consequences of this, such as the closing of manufacturing plants, outsourcing jobs, and a 24/7 economy, all which we explore in Chapter 12.

Wars; colonial conquest; disease and famine; population increases; changing technologies of production, communication, or health care—all these major social forces can change societies and thereby change the roles their members are expected to perform. As social groups strive to adapt to the new conditions, their members may feel that they are adrift—unsure of how to act or troubled by conflict over how to perform as parents or wage earners or citizens. They may question the values they learned as children and wonder what to teach their own children. This condition of social disequilibrium can lead to an increase in social problems like crime and mental illness as individuals seek their own, often antisocial, solutions to the dilemmas they face.

CRIMINAL DEVIANCE: A FUNCTIONALIST VIEW   From the functionalist perspective, all societies produce their own unique forms of crime and have their own ways of responding to them. Of course, sociologists recognize that there are causes within the individual that help explain why one person becomes a criminal while another, who may have experienced the same conditions, does not. But sociologists dig deeper. For the sociologist, using the functionalist perspective, an important question may be why particular crimes are committed and punished in some societies and not in others. Why is it that until quite recently a black man who was suspected of making advances to a white woman was often punished more severely than a black man who was suspected of stealing? Why was the theft of a horse punishable by immediate death on the early western frontier?

The functionalist answer is that societies fear most the crimes that seem to threaten their most cherished values, and individuals who dare to challenge those values will receive the most severe punishment. Thus, the freedom to allow one's horses to graze on common land was an essential aspect of early western frontier society that was threatened by the theft of horses. The possibility that a white woman could entice a black man and that their relationship could be interpreted as anything other than rape threatened the foundations of the American racial caste system, which held that blacks were inferior to whites. In both cases, immediate, sometimes brutal, punishment was used to reinforce the central values of the society.

SOCIAL PROBLEMS AS SOCIAL PATHOLOGY   In the late 1800s and early 1900s, functionalist theorists regarded crime and deviance as a form of "social disease" or social pathology. This view was rooted in the organic analogy that was popular at the time. Human society was seen as analogous to a vast organism, all of whose complex, interrelated parts function together to maintain the health and stability of the whole. Social problems arise when either individuals or social institutions fail to keep pace with changing conditions and thereby disrupt the healthy operation of the social organization; such individuals or institutions are considered "sick" (hence the term *social pathology*).

Today most sociologists reject this notion and believe that the social-pathology approach is not very useful in generating empirical research; its concepts of sickness and morality are too subjective to be meaningful to many sociologists. It attempts to apply a biological analogy to social conditions even when there is no empirical justification for doing so. Modern functionalists do not focus on the behaviors and problems of individuals, per se; instead, they see social problems as arising out of the failure of institutions like the family, the schools, and the economy to adapt to changing social conditions.

SOCIAL-DISORGANIZATION THEORY   Rates of immigration, urbanization, and industrialization increased rapidly after World War I. European immigrants, rural whites, and southern blacks were often crowded together in degrading slums and had trouble learning the language, manners, and norms of the dominant urban culture. Many of those who managed to adjust to the city were discriminated against because of their religion or race, and others lost their jobs because technological advances made their skills obsolete. Alcoholism, drug addiction, mental illness, crime, and delinquency rates rose drastically as people tried to cope with these conditions. As sociologists began to question whether the social-pathology viewpoint could adequately explain the widespread existence of these social problems, they developed a new concept that eventually became known as social-disorganization theory to explain a wide variety of social problems.

This theory views society as being organized by a set of expectations or rules. **Social disorganization** results when these expectations fail, and it is manifested in three major ways: (1) normlessness, which arises when people have no rules that tell them how to behave; (2) culture conflict, which occurs when people feel trapped by contradictory rules; and (3) breakdown, which takes place when obedience to a set of rules is not rewarded or is punished. Rapid social change, for example, might make traditional standards of behavior obsolete without providing new standards, thereby giving rise to normlessness. The children of immigrants might feel trapped between the expectations of their parents and those of their new society—an example of culture conflict. And the expectations of blacks might be frustrated when they do well in school but encounter job discrimination; their frustration, in turn, might lead to breakdown.

Monkey Business/Fotolia

A group of teenagers experience a sense of normlessness. They are neither adults nor children, and our culture has unclear expectations for people in this age group. They are told to go to high school, get good grades, play sports, and go to college. But this path is not of interest to all adolescents.

The stress experienced by victims of social disorganization may result in a form of personal disorganization such as drug addiction or crime. The social system as a whole also feels the force of disorganization. It may respond by changing its rules, keeping contradictory rules in force, or breaking down. Disorganization can be halted or reversed if its causes are isolated and corrected.

social disorganization

The result when rules break down; it is manifested in three major ways: normlessness, culture conflict, and breakdown.

MODERN FUNCTIONALISM: BUILDING INSTITUTIONS In this text, you will see many instances in which social-disorganization theory has been used to explain social problems. A more modern version of the functionalist perspective attempts to show how people reorganize their lives to cope with new conditions. Often this reorganization results in new kinds of organizations and sometimes in whole new institutions. This research focus is known as the institutional approach, or **institution building** (Caplan, 2005). Research on how to improve the organization of public schools to meet new educational demands is an example.

institution building

A modern version of the functionalist perspective, which attempts to show how people reorganize their lives to cope with new conditions.

1.3.2 The Conflict Perspective

By no means do all sociologists adopt the functionalist view of society and social problems. A **conflict perspective** claims that the functionalist idea (that social problems can be corrected by reforming institutions that are not functioning well) is misleading because it ignores dimensions of power. The conflict perspective is based on the belief that social problems arise out of major contradictions in the way societies are organized, contradictions that lead to conflict between those who have access to the good life and those who do not. This perspective owes much of its early development to the writings of Karl Marx (1818–1883), the German social theorist who developed many of the central ideas of modern socialism.

In the *Manifesto of the Communist Party* (Marx and Engels, 1848), *Capital* (Marx, 1867), and other works, Marx attempted to prove that social problems such as unemployment, poverty, crime, corruption, and warfare are not usually the fault of individuals or of poorly functioning organizations. Instead, he argued, their origins may be

conflict perspective

A way of thinking that is based on the belief that social problems arise out of major contradictions in the way societies are organized, contradictions that lead to large-scale conflict between those who have access to the good life and those who do not.

found in the way societies arrange access to wealth and power. According to Marx, the social problems of modern societies arise from capitalism. An inevitable outcome of capitalism is class conflict, especially conflict between those who own the means of production (factories, land, and so forth) and those who sell their labor for wages. In such a system, workers are exploited by their bosses, for whom the desire to make a profit outweighs any humanitarian impulse to take care of their employees.

In the capitalist system as Marx described it, the capitalist is driven by the profit motive to find ways to reduce labor costs—for example, through the purchase of new machinery that can do the work of several people or by building factories in places where people will work for less money. These actions continually threaten the livelihood of workers. Often, they lose their jobs, and their lives are thrown into disarray. Sometimes they resort to crime or even begin revolutions to overturn the system in which they are the have-nots, and the owners of capital are the haves. In general, for Marx and modern Marxian sociologists, social problems may be attributed to the ways in which wealth and power become concentrated in the hands of a few people and to the many forms of conflict engendered by these inequalities.

Marxian conflict theory can be a powerful tool in the analysis of contemporary social problems. To illustrate this point, the following section looks at how this theory explains criminal deviance in societies like the United States.

DEVIANCE: A MARXIAN CONFLICT VIEW Marxists believe that crime and deviance do not occur merely because such organizations as the police and the courts function in certain ways or do not function as they were intended to. Instead, Marxian theorists believe such situations are a result of differences in the power of various groups or classes in society. For example, top organized-crime figures have the money and power to influence law enforcement officials or to hire the best attorneys when they are arrested. Street drug dealers, in contrast, are relatively powerless to resist arrest. Moreover, they serve as convenient targets for an official show of force against drug trafficking. From the Marxian perspective, the rich and powerful can determine what kinds of behaviors are defined as social problems because they control major institutions such as the government, the schools, and the courts. They are also able to shift the blame for the conditions that produce those problems to groups that are less able to defend themselves, namely, the poor and the working class.

Scholars who adopt a Marxian perspective tend to be cautious of proposals to reform existing institutions. Since they attribute most social problems to underlying patterns of class conflict and power differentials, they do not believe that tinkering with existing institutions such as prisons and courts can address the basic causes of those problems unless issues related to power and inequality are addressed. Usually, therefore, their research looks at the ways in which the material conditions of society, such as inequalities of wealth and power, seem to account for the distribution of social problems in a population. Or they conduct research on social movements among the poor and the working class to understand how those movements might mobilize large numbers of people into a force that could bring about major changes in the way society is organized.

VALUE CONFLICT THEORY The Marxian theory of class conflict cannot explain all the kinds of conflict that occur around us every day. In families, for example, conflicts may range from seemingly trivial arguments over television programs to intense disputes over issues like drinking or drug use; in neighborhoods, conflicts may occur between landlords and tenants, between parents and school administrators, or between groups of parents who differ on matters of educational policy such as sex education or the rights of female athletes. Such conflict often focuses not on deep-seated class antagonisms but on differences in values. For most feminist groups, for example, abortion is a social problem if women cannot freely terminate a pregnancy. In contrast, many religious groups define legal abortion as a social problem. The debate over legalization versus criminalization of abortion reflects the conflicting values of important groups in society.

Value conflict theorists define social problems as conditions that are incompatible with group values.[2] Such problems are normal, they add, because in a complex society there are many groups whose interests and values are bound to differ. According to value conflict theory, social problems occur when groups with different values meet and compete. Returning to the example of criminal deviance, value conflict theorists would say that deviance from society's rules results from the fact that some groups do not agree with those rules and therefore feel free to break them if they can. For example, whenever a society prohibits substances like alcohol or drugs, some groups will break the rules to obtain the banned substance. This conflict stimulates the development of criminal organizations that employ gangsters and street peddlers to supply the needs of those who deviate. The underlying cause of the problem is conflicting values concerning the use of particular substances.

From the value conflict viewpoint, many social problems need to be understood in terms of which groups hold which values and which groups have the power to enforce them against the wishes of other groups. Once these distinctions have been determined, this approach leads to suggestions for adjustments, settlements, negotiations, and compromises that will alleviate the problem. These suggestions, in turn, may result in new policies, such as civilian review boards, arbitration of disputes, juvenile drug courts, and changes in existing laws to reflect a diversity of opinions (Larana, Johnston, and Gusfield, 1994).

THE IDEA OF A "CULTURE WAR" IN THE UNITED STATES When headlines claim conflict between different political parties, religious groups, or communities about gun violence, same-sex marriage, abortion, or any number of issues that arouse people's moral passions, it is easy to agree with some commentators that these conflicts are evidence of a "culture war." This supposed broad conflict over deeply held values is said to sway elections and determine the fate of many social policy issues, from gun control to "morning-after pills" to prevent pregnancy, and much more.

Americans are becoming increasingly polarized with respect to social issues (Kiley, 2017). An overwhelming majority (86 percent) of Americans say conflicts between Democrats and Republicans are either strong or very strong, according to a recent Pew Research Center survey. This is greater than the 65 percent of Americans who see strong or very strong conflicts between blacks and whites, and 60 percent who see them between the rich and the poor (Gramlich, 2017).

1.3.3 The Symbolic Interactionist Perspective

Why do certain people resort to crime while the vast majority seeks legitimate means to survive? A functionalist would point out that individuals who do not adhere to society's core values or who have been uprooted by social change are most likely to become criminals. When they are caught, their punishment reinforces the desire of the majority to

There has been increasing polarization in recent years over most political, social, and economic issues. Liberals and conservatives seem to be going in completely different directions.

Jane/Fotolia

[2]Rubington, E. & Weinberg, M. S. 1971. *The study of social problems: five perspectives.* Oxford: Oxford University Press.

conform. But this explanation does not help us understand why a certain individual or group deviates.

Conflict theorists explain deviance as the result of conflict over access to wealth and power or over values. But how is that conflict channeled into deviant behavior? Why do some groups that experience value conflict act against the larger society while others do not? Why, for example, do some gays come out publicly while others hide their sexual preference? Presumably, both groups know that their sexual values may conflict with some people of the larger society, but what explains the difference in behavior? The conflict perspective cannot provide an adequate answer to this question.

The **symbolic interactionist perspective** offers an explanation that gets closer to the individual level of behavior by looking at the symbols people use in everyday interaction—words, gestures, appearances—and how these symbols are interpreted by others. People's interactions with others are based on how these symbols are interpreted.

Research based on this perspective looks at the processes whereby different people become part of a situation that the larger society defines as a social problem. The interactionist approach focuses on the ways in which people take on the values of the group of which they are members. It also explores how different groups define their situation and in so doing "construct" a version of life that promotes certain values and behaviors and discourages others.

A key insight of the interactionist perspective originated in the research of W. I. Thomas and his colleagues in the early decades of the twentieth century. In their classic study of the problems of immigrants in the rapidly growing and changing city of Chicago, these pioneering sociologists found that some groups of Polish immigrant men believed it would be easier to rob banks than to survive in the mills and factories, where other immigrants worked long hours under dangerous conditions. The sociologists discovered that the uneducated young immigrants often did not realize how little chance they had of carrying out a successful bank robbery. They defined their situation in a certain way and acted accordingly. "Situations people define as real," Thomas stated, "are real in their consequences" (Thomas and Znaniecki, 1922).[3] Thus, from the interactionist perspective, an individual's or group's definition of the situation is central to understanding the actions of that individual or group.

Another early line of interactionist research is associated with Charles Horton Cooley and George Herbert Mead. Cooley, Mead, and others realized that, although we learn our basic values and ways of behaving early in life, especially in our families, we also participate throughout our lives in groups made up of people like ourselves; these groups are known as peer groups. From these groups, we draw much of our identity and our sense of who we are, and within these groups, we learn many of our behaviors and values. Through our interactions in peer groups—be they teams, adolescent friendship groups, or work groups—we may be taught to act in ways that are different from those our parents taught us. Thus, when interactionists study social problems like crime, they focus on the ways in which people are recruited by criminal groups and learn to conform to the rules of those groups.

LABELING: AN INTERACTIONIST VIEW OF DEVIANCE Labeling theory is an application of the interactionist perspective that explains certain kinds of social deviance. Labeling theorists think the label "deviant" reveals more about the society applying it than about the act or person being labeled. In certain societies, for example, concern about the environment is far more accepted than it is in the United States. Labeling theorists suggest there are groups and organizations in American society that benefit from labeling environmental activists as deviant— the fossil fuel industries, for

symbolic interactionist perspective

A way of thinking that offers an explanation that gets closer to the individual level of behavior by looking at the symbols people use in everyday interaction—words, gestures, appearances—and how these symbols are interpreted by others. People's interactions with others are based on how symbols are interpreted.

---

[3]Thomas, W.I., & F. Znaniecki. 1922. *The Polish Peasant in Europe and America.* New York: Knopf.

example. In short, labeling theory separates deviant and nondeviant people, not by what they do but by how society reacts to what they do.

According to labeling theorists, social problems are conditions under which certain behaviors or situations become defined as social problems. The cause of a social problem is simply society's awareness that a certain behavior or situation exists. A behavior or situation becomes a social problem when someone can profit in some way by applying the label "problematic" or "deviant" to it. Such labeling causes society to suffer in two ways. First, one group unfairly achieves power over another; "deviants" are repressed through discrimination, prejudice, or force. Second, those who are labeled deviant may accept this definition of themselves, and the label may become a self-fulfilling prophecy. The number and variety of deviant acts may be increased to reinforce the new role of deviant. A person who is labeled a drug addict, for example, may adopt elements of what is popularly viewed as a drug addict's lifestyle: resisting employment or treatment, engaging in crime, and so on. Sociologists term this behavior **secondary deviance**.

According to labeling theory, the way to solve social problems is to change the definition of what is considered deviant. It is thought that the acceptance of a greater variety of acts and situations as normal would automatically eliminate concern about them. Decriminalization of the possession of small amounts of marijuana for personal use is an example of this approach.

Labeling theory is only one of numerous applications of the interactionist perspective to social problems. Another common approach focuses on the processes of socialization that occur in groups and explores the possibility of resocialization through group interaction—as occurs, for example, in groups such as Alcoholics Anonymous. At many points, this text will discuss situations in which intentional resocialization has been used in efforts to address social problems.

THE SOCIAL CONSTRUCTION OF SOCIAL PROBLEMS The interactionist perspective also contributes to what is known as the **social construction** approach to social problems. This approach argues that some claims about social problems become the dominant discourse, while other claims get little or no attention. Powerful people and institutions in society shape our perceptions about social problems and, more generally, our understanding of the social world. The press, television, radio, universities and colleges, government agencies, and civic voluntary associations are examples of institutions that often have a stake in defining what social problems are, how they come about, or what should be done about them. Journalists, television commentators, editorial writers, professors who take public stands on issues, scientists who appear before the cameras, and many other lobbyists and "opinion makers" are in fact involved in selecting some claims and rejecting others. In so doing, they "construct" the way we think about the issues (Griswold, 2012).

Consider an example: The tobacco industry knew that smoking caused cancer and other serious health problems, yet continued to encourage people to smoke through their strong media campaigns, campaign contributions to public officials, and political lobby. The tobacco industry is very powerful, and their dominant claims about smoking being harmless overshadowed the scientific claims about the health hazards associated with tobacco. They successfully encouraged people to see smoking as sophisticated, mature, liberating, and "cool." Do you remember "Joe Camel," or the cigarette targeted to women—Virginia Slims—with their slogan, "You've come a long way, baby"?[4] It took many years to shift the dominant discourse about tobacco, so that now most people recognize its dangerous effects.

secondary deviance

A state in which a person who is labeled "deviant" may then adopt elements of what is popularly viewed as a deviant lifestyle.

social construction

The process by which some claims about social problems become dominant and others get little or no attention; these claims develop through the activities of actors and institutions in society that shape our understanding of the social world more generally.

What Do You Think?

Identify a current social problem, and, using a social construction approach, describe how the media, certain people with power, and specific social institutions have framed this problem.

---

[4]Virginia Slims Cigarette, Virginia Slims.

The Natural History of Social Problems

1.4 **Describe the process that reveals the natural history of social problems.**

To readers of daily websites and news sites, and to faithful watchers of television news, social problems may often resemble fads. People hear a great deal about a particular problem for a while, and then it fades from public attention, perhaps to reappear some time later if there are new developments in its incidence or control. With AIDS, crack cocaine, driving while intoxicated, serial killers, financial scandals, racial violence, terrorism, and so many other problems demanding attention, it is little wonder that the focus on any given subject by the press and the public tends to last only a few days or weeks.

To a large extent, the short attention span of the media can be explained by the need to attract large numbers of viewers or readers; the media can be expected to be rather fickle and to constantly pursue stories that will capture the public's attention. However, sociologists distinguish between the nature of media coverage of a social problem and the way a problem is perceived by the public and political leaders. They have devoted considerable study to the question of how social problems develop from underlying conditions into publicly defined problems that engender social policies and sustained social movements. This subject is often referred to as the "natural history" of social problems.

natural history approach

The idea that social problems develop in a series of phases or stages.

Early in the twentieth century, sociologists recognized that social problems often seemed to develop in a series of phases or stages. They called the study of this process the **natural history approach** because their effort was analogous to the work of biologists who study the development of a great many individual organisms to chart the stages of development of a species (Edwards, 1927; Park, 1955; Shaw, 1929; Wirth, 1927). But whereas sociologists recognize that social problems often follow certain regular stages of development, they also know that there are many deviations from the usual sequence.

In a useful formulation of the natural history approach, Malcolm Spector and John Kitsuse (1987) outlined the following major stages that most social problems seem to go through.

- *Stage 1—Problem definition.* Groups in society attempt to gain acknowledgment by a wider population (and the press and government) that some social condition is "offensive, harmful, or otherwise undesirable." These groups publicize their claims and attempt to turn the matter into a political issue.
- *Stage 2—Legitimacy.* When the groups pressing their claims are considered credible and their assertions are accepted by official organizations, agencies, or institutions, there may be investigations, proposals for reform, and even the creation of new agencies to respond to claims and demands.
- *Stage 3—Reemergence of demands.* Usually, the original groups are not satisfied with the steps taken by official agencies; they demand stronger measures, more funding for enforcement, speedier handling of claims, and so on. They renew their appeals to the wider public and the press.
- *Stage 4—Rejection and institution building.* The complainant groups usually decide that official responses to their demands are inadequate. They seek to develop their own organizations or counterinstitutions to press their claims and enact reforms.

This natural history approach can be applied to the idea that the easy availability of guns—especially handguns, automatic rifles and pistols, and assault weapons—contributes to higher murder rates. In the 1980s, musician John Lennon of the Beatles and President Ronald Reagan were victims of gun violence. Lennon was killed, and while President Reagan escaped serious harm, the bullets hit his press secretary, James Brady, who suffered a serious head injury and permanent disability.

Incidents like these, and many more, *defined the problem* of violence as being due to the easy availability of guns. This definition gained credibility and *legitimacy* as citizen groups pressed their lawmakers for gun control legislation. The Brady Bill, for example, was passed and required identity checks for gun purchasers and a ban on certain types of assault weapons. However, the National Rifle Association and other groups argued that guns are not the problem. The issue is mental illness, they claimed, and legal gun owners should not be denied their rights because a few mentally ill people do the wrong thing.

Meanwhile, by the 1990s, mass shootings began to occur in public venues. Over the past several decades, there have been many of these horrific shootings. Sandy Hook Elementary School: 26 elementary students, teachers, and staff were killed. Virginia Tech University: 56 were killed or injured. Outside a Safeway shopping area where Congresswoman Gabriella Giffords was speaking: 19 people were injured or killed. An Army base in Texas: 43 people were killed or injured. Forty-nine people were killed in an Orlando nightclub. Fifty-eight people were killed while attending a music festival in Las Vegas. Seventeen students were killed at their high school in Parkland, Florida. These acts of violence have led to a *reemergence of demands* for more stringent gun control legislation. Gun control advocates have made their appeals publicly but are growing frustrated by what they see as an inadequate response from the government. They are *rejecting and building their own institutions* to push their agendas and enact reforms.

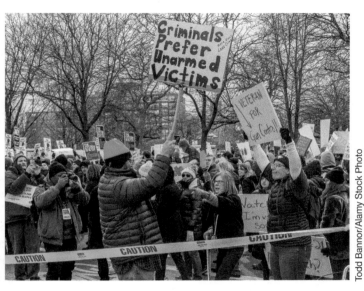

Gun regulation advocates confront a pro-gun counter protester at one of the March for Our Lives protests held throughout the United States, in 2018. In Chicago, thousands of gun control advocates marched in support of increased gun regulation.

Themes of This Text

1.5   Review the four themes of the text.

This text will introduce you to a wide variety of social problems experienced in American society today. However, you will learn more than a collection of random facts. Four themes are woven throughout the chapters to organize the discussion of social problems. These themes suggest that social problems can best be understood by (1) using an empirical approach; (2) linking individual experiences with social structure; (3) recognizing that social inequality contributes to social problems; and (4) acknowledging that understanding social problems requires a comparative perspective. Each of these themes is discussed below.

1.5.1   Using an Empirical Approach

A sociological understanding of social problems demands that one move beyond personal opinion and instead use an **empirical approach**, which is a method that answers questions through a systematic collection and analysis of data. Granted, you may have commonsense ideas about social problems based on personal experience or habits, religious teachings, cultural customs, or societal laws. Because virtually everyone has some experience with social problems, they may think they are experts on the topic.

Historically, the commonsense view of violence among intimates was that it was okay for husbands to beat their wives—within reason. Supposedly, the term "rule of thumb" arises from the belief that the switch that a husband used to beat his wife should be no wider than his thumb. But common sense changes over time. Today, it is against the law in the United States for husbands to hit their wives (and vice versa). However, violence against an intimate partner is not illegal in many parts of the world. There, common sense suggests that violence can be justified, and the husband has the prerogative to hit his wife, although again, usually within "reasonable" limits (e.g., a husband may beat, but not kill, his wife). The World Health Organization

empirical approach

A method that answers questions through a systematic collection and analysis of data.

Todd Bannor/Alamy Stock Photo

takes violence against women very seriously. A study of 24,000 women in 10 countries found that the prevalence of physical and/or sexual violence by a partner varied from 15 percent in urban Japan to 71 percent in rural Ethiopia, with most areas being in the 30 to 60 percent range (Garcia-Moreno et al., 2015; World Health Organization, 2017).

If common sense is subject to historical and cultural whims, then what can researchers depend on to help them understand family dynamics? Sociologists use an empirical approach in collecting and analyzing data. The goals of empirical research can include the following.

- *Describe some phenomenon*   (e.g., how many women have been physically assaulted by someone close to them; how does this number compare with the number of men who are assaulted by their partners each year; how do abused women and men interpret the reasons for the assault)
- *Examine the factors that predict or are associated with some phenomenon*   (e.g., what factors are associated with violence among intimates; what factors predict whether a victim will report the assault to the police)
- *Explain cause-and-effect relationships or provide insight into why certain events do or do not occur*   (e.g., what is the relationship between alcohol and violence among intimates; what is the relationship between attitudes of male dominance and domestic violence)
- *Understand the meanings attached to behavior or situations*   (e.g., how do people interpret their roles as victims or perpetrators)

Empirical research has shown that violence is a serious and pervasive social problem. Global estimates published by the World Health Organization indicate that about 1 in 3 (35%) women worldwide have experienced either physical and/or sexual intimate partner violence or nonpartner sexual violence in their lifetime (World Health Organization, 2017). The U.S. is not far behind (Smith et al., 2017). Men can also be victims, although they tend to be victims of the less severe types of violence.

How can a sociological perspective help people who are battered by their partners? Family scholars conduct basic and applied research to understand the phenomenon, striving to reveal information about the incidence, predictors, social factors associated with violence, the experience of violence, and possible solutions. Psychologists, social workers, and politicians could use this information to develop programs to prevent violence, assist victims, and treat the perpetrators. Intimate partner violence is a social problem, not simply an individual one, and the goal is to uncover the social patterns that underlie it.

Sociologists and other social scientists use a variety of methods to collect and analyze data. A full discussion of these methods is beyond the scope of this text. However, Table 1–3 summarizes six primary methods of collecting data, outlining their strengths and weaknesses. These methods include surveys, in-depth interviews, experiments, focus groups, observational study, and secondary analysis.

Some researchers focus on **quantitative methods** in which data are collected that can be measured numerically. Examples are found in surveys, experiments, or doing further analyses on available government statistics (such as from the U.S. Census Bureau or U.S. Department of Justice) or another source (such as the United Nations). This research yields percentages and other statistics that can be easily interpreted.

Others use **qualitative methods** that focus on narrative description with words rather than numbers to analyze patterns and their underlying meanings. Examples of qualitative research methods include in-depth interviews, focus groups, observational studies, and in-depth analysis using narrative documents such as letters or diaries. Qualitative research does not usually offer statistics but can reveal a rich description and understanding of some phenomena.

quantitative methods

A research strategy in which data can be measured numerically.

qualitative methods

A research strategy that focuses on narrative description with words rather than numbers to analyze patterns and their underlying meanings.

Violence among intimates is a serious social problem affecting millions of women and men. Sociological research provides a window into this phenomenon, including how often it occurs, who is most likely to be victimized, what types of violent acts are most common, and the effectiveness of different programs and policies to help victims.

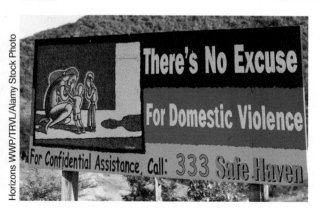

Horizons WWP/TRVL/Alamy Stock Photo

Table 1–3 Six Research Methods: A Summary

Method	Application	Advantages	Limitations
Survey	For gathering information about issues that are not directly observed, such as values, opinions, and other self-reports. Can be conducted through mail or telephone or administered in person. Useful for descriptive or explanatory purposes; can generate quantitative or qualitative data.	Sampling methods can allow researcher to generalize findings to a larger population. Can provide open-ended questions or a fixed response.	Surveys must be carefully prepared to avoid bias. There is a potential for a low return or response rate. Can be expensive and time-consuming. Self-reports may be biased.
In-depth Interview	For obtaining information about issues that are not directly observed, such as values, opinions, and other self-reports. Useful for getting in-depth information about a topic. Conducted in person, conversation is usually audiotaped and later transcribed. Generates qualitative data.	Can provide detailed and high-quality data. Interviewer can probe or ask follow-up questions for clarification or to encourage the respondent to elaborate. Can establish a genuine rapport with respondent.	Expensive and time-consuming to conduct and transcribe. Self-reports may be biased. Respondent may feel uncomfortable revealing personal information.
Experiment	For explanatory research that examines cause-and-effect relationship among variables. Several types: classical experimental design and quasi-experimental designs based on degree of controlling the environment. Generates quantitative data.	Provides greatest opportunity to assess cause and effect. Research design relatively easy to replicate.	The setting may have an artificial quality to it. Unless the experimental and control group are randomly assigned or matched on all relevant variables, and the environment is carefully controlled, bias may result.
Focus Groups	For obtaining information from small groups of people who are brought together to discuss a particular topic. Often exploratory in nature. Particularly useful for studying public perceptions. Facilitator may ask only a few questions; goal is to get group to interact with one another. Generates qualitative data.	Group interaction may produce more valuable insights than individual surveys or in-depth interviews. Researcher can obtain data quickly and inexpensively. Good for eliciting unanticipated information.	Setting is contrived. Some people may feel uncomfortable speaking in a group and others may dominate.
Observation	For exploratory and descriptive study of people in a natural setting. Researcher can be a participant or nonparticipant. Generates qualitative data.	Allows study of real behavior in a natural setting. Does not rely on self-reports. Researchers can often ask questions and take notes. Usually inexpensive.	Can be time-consuming. There could be ethical issues involved in certain types of observation studies, namely, observing without consent. Researcher must balance roles of participant and observer. Replication of research is difficult.
Secondary Analysis	For exploratory, descriptive, or explanatory research with data that were collected for some other purpose. Diverse. Can be large data sources based on national samples (e.g., U.S. Census) or can be historical documents or records. Generates quantitative or qualitative data, depending on the source of data used.	Saves the expense and time of original data collection. Can be longitudinal, with data collected at more than one point in time. Good for analyzing national attitudes or trends. Makes historical research possible.	Because data were collected for another purpose, the researcher cannot control what variables were included or excluded. Researcher has no control over sampling or other biases in the data.

None of these methods are inherently better or worse than the others. The method used depends on the research questions that are posed. For example, if you want to better understand what family life was like in the nineteenth century, you would not want to conduct a survey today. How would people who are alive today best inform you of what happened 150 years ago? Obviously, the best method would be to conduct a further analysis of documents that were written during that period. Diaries, letters or other lengthy correspondence between people, and other such qualitative data could help you understand the common everyday experiences within families. Likewise, you could analyze quantitative data from historical records to get an aggregate picture about, for example, immigration trends, age at first marriage, or the average length of time between marriage and first birth. Census records; birth, marriage, and death registers; immigration records; slave auctions and other transactions; church records; newspapers and magazine articles; employment ledgers; and tax records can also provide insight into the family lives of large numbers of ordinary people.

However, if you want to assess today's opinions or behaviors, perhaps a survey or in-depth interviews would be best. You may want to ask the same questions of everyone in your sample and offer a standard set of answers from which they can choose,

What Do You Think?

If you were conducting a study about violence, would you prefer qualitative or quantitative methods, and why? What could you hope to learn?

such as "Have you ever been hit by a spouse or partner?" (yes, no). "If yes, would you say you have been hit 1–5 times, 6–10 times, more than 10 times?" You can easily quantify this information. Or, if you are interested in broader questions that allow each person in your study to elaborate in his or her own words (such as "How did you come to the decision to leave the violent spouse or partner?"), you would likely use in-depth interviews, which then yield qualitative data.

1.5.2 Linking Individual Experiences with Social Structure

As the sociological imagination has revealed, most people are so embedded in their own lives that they fail to see the connections between their personal experiences and broader social concerns. By extension, many people perceive the lives of others around them also in this way: He's unemployed, and therefore he must not be working hard enough to get a job. She is stressed out from combining work and family, and therefore she needs better time management skills. He committed a crime; therefore, he should go to prison. Social scientists suggest that the best way to truly understand social problems is to see the connections between social structure and personal experience. Therefore, the second theme of this text emphasizes that, while people may initially think of experiences solely in personal terms, their experiences are shaped in large part by the social structure in society, which, as you recall, is the organized arrangements of relationships and institutions that together form the basis of society.

For example, many people are concerned about the number of poor single-parent households headed by women. People often wonder why women do not marry the men who father their children. Terry Lynn is one of these women, and if you look closer, you can see that her life choices are grounded in a social context.

Terry Lynn is a single mother who has never married and is raising a daughter alone, with the temporary help of cash welfare assistance (Seccombe, 2015). She is a shy young woman, yet at the same time, she is eager to tell her story. Terry Lynn works part-time at a bowling alley, a good job considering her weak reading and writing skills. She takes the bus to work, and various shifts sometimes keep her at work well into the night. She is savvy about the additional help she needs to support her child, and therefore deliberately keeps her employment hours below a certain threshold so that she and her daughter will continue to qualify for a childcare subsidy. Even at the age of 24, Terry Lynn knows that providing quality daycare for her daughter is vital. She and her daughter live with a sister in a cramped, rundown, two-bedroom apartment in an unfashionable part of town. The furniture is secondhand, and the couch is threadbare. Nonetheless, Terry Lynn is proud of herself and her daughter for "making it" on their own. You may wonder where the child's father is. He comes around now and then, she says, usually when he wants money or sex from her. Does Terry Lynn ever plan to marry him? Her answer is a definite "No."

Single-parent households have been blamed extensively for a wide variety of social ills. They are far more likely than other families to be poor (Semega, Fontenot, and Kollar, 2017). Why are so many women, especially poor and low-income women like Terry Lynn, having children without marrying their children's fathers?

You might be tempted to look at individual-level factors and ask what is happening within intimate relationships, specifically the couple's values and choices. Certainly, these are important; but many people have found that poor women seem to value marriage quite highly. In fact, if anything, perhaps they value it *too* highly. They believe that their own relationships will never meet the "gold standard" they have set for themselves, such as a partner with a steady job, the chance to own their own home, and a

Terry Lynn represents one of the millions of women raising children alone without significant contribution from the child's father. Would she want to marry him? Her answer is a definite "No." If he doesn't do much for her now, she doesn't think he will do much for her if she married him either.

reasonably lavish wedding ceremony. As a result, they shy away from marriage (Edin and Kefalas, 2005; Seccombe, 2015).

Therefore, you would need to look at structural factors to explain why poor women have children outside of marriage but are often hesitant to marry their partners. William Julius Wilson has suggested that the high unemployment rate of inner-city ur-ban dwellers contributes to their low marriage rate. In his well-known books, *The Truly Disadvantaged* (Wilson, 1987) and *When Work Disappears* (Wilson, 1996), Wilson pointed out that many poor women see marriage to inner-city men as risky because the men cannot support families on their meager wages (Wilson, 1987, 1996). Furthermore, as factories and businesses move out to the suburbs or overseas, unemployment and pov-erty escalate. Consequently, there is a shortage of employed men whom these women see as good marriage prospects. Wilson shows that our changing economy (a structural condition) has a substantial effect on individual relationship choices.

In addition to high unemployment, or perhaps interrelated with it, there are many other structural reasons why poor women often do not marry when they have children. For example, homicide, violence, drug addiction, and incarceration have all taken a tremendous toll on poor men, especially poor black men. In Terry Lynn's case, the father of her child was unemployed and had been in and out of jail, so she did not see him as a reliable "good catch." Although she cared for him, why would she want to marry him?

It is critical to move beyond just an individual perspective to really understand single parenthood among the poor. Social problems may be personally experienced, but they exist in a social context.

1.5.3 Recognizing That Social Inequality Contributes to Social Problems

A third theme of this text is that social inequality is a critical organizing feature in society and contributes mightily to social problems. Most Americans believe that the United States provides nearly equal opportunities for everyone. However, as detailed in upcoming chapters, American society is highly stratified based on economics, power, and social status. Americans fantasize that they can be anything they want to be, but really there is little substantial upward (or downward) social mobility. People usually live out their lives in generally the same social class in which they were born. Families pass on their wealth and social capital (or their lack of it) to their newest members, and this practice perpetuates social inequality. For example, because of the U.S. inheritance laws, affluent parents can distribute their wealth to their children after their death. Relatively little of the wealth is taxed and redistributed, as is the case in other countries. Consequently, some of America's richest people have only marginal employment histories. They do not need to work for a living, yet others who work relentlessly, often in the unglamorous but growing service sector, find no real route to a better life. Their wages are low; they may not receive health insurance or other benefits; and they live on the margins, only one paycheck away from impov-erishment. What type of wealth or social capital do these parents have to pass on to their children?

Inequality is woven into many basic social structures and institutions, and this inequality contributes to social problems, including poor health, immigration, mental illness, crime, poor race relations, overpopulation, violence among intimates, school dropout rates, war, discrimination against women, and environmental degradation.

For example, blacks, Hispanics, and American Indian/Alaska Native youths are less likely to finish high school than are their Asian and white counterparts. This ed-ucational disparity has serious long-term economic consequences, leading to higher poverty rates and more economic stress. But *why* are some groups more likely to quit high school?

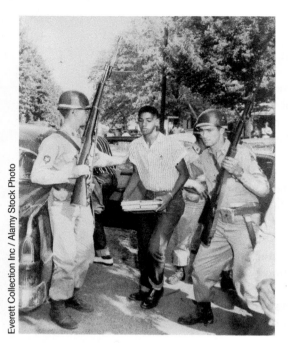

A black student is escorted to a waiting car by National Guard troops enforcing school integration in 1956.

One structural reason has to do with the quality of schools. Traditionally, schools reflect the socioeconomic and racial profile of the surrounding neighborhood; therefore, most schools have a long history of segregation. Desegregation effectively began with the Supreme Court's 1954 ruling in *Brown v. Board of Education of Topeka, Kansas*, which was based on the argument that segregation had negative effects on black students even when their school facilities were equal to those of white students. But many schools remained highly segregated because white or upper-income families transferred to private schools. Moreover, politicians often gerrymandered districts to change school attendance boundaries (Chang, 2018; Richards, 2014). Consequently, today's typical minority student attends school with fewer whites than his or her counterpart did in 1970 (Fiel, 2013).

Another structural reason has to do with the quality of the teachers in the schools. A teacher is estimated to have two to three times the impact of any other school factor on student performance on reading and math tests (RAND Education, 2012). Schools with large numbers of low-income and minority students are more likely than other schools to have teachers who have fewer years of experience, lower licensure exam scores, and lower student test score gains (Goldhaber, Lavery, and Theobald, 2015). Also, classrooms are often segregated into achievement levels, racial composition, and socioeconomic composition, and it is the teachers with less experience who tend to be assigned to the most challenging classes (Kalogrides and Loeb, 2013; Kalogrides, Loeb, and Béteille, 2013).

Patterns of social inequality filter down and shape all components of life—including educational achievement. This text examines the assumptions, values, and ideologies that are used to justify or explain social inequality and how inequality contributes to social problems.

1.5.4 Using a Comparative Perspective

The final theme of this text focuses on the importance of learning about other cultures and other historical periods to better understand American social problems. In the past, it was easier to ignore what was happening in the world beyond U.S. borders, but now, societies are becoming increasingly interconnected. New technologies, immigration, commerce across borders, and greater ease in world travel have increased visibility, and the United States can no longer remain isolated. Societies see other ways of doing things and sometimes adopt pieces of another's culture. One can now travel to many distant parts of the world and still find American fast food, such as McDonald's or Kentucky Fried Chicken. Likewise, the United States also has adopted foods and cultural artifacts from other countries. Tacos and pizza are staples in our diets today, but once were considered exotic or regional ethnic food. Social problems, too, move beyond borders. As shown in the box *A Global View: "World Population: 7.6 Billion and Counting,"* we are all affected by unchecked population growth.

Just as with culture, it is easy to ignore history and focus only on the here and now, yet many of our current social problems are rooted in the traditions of the past. For example, to better understand the current and heated debate over abortion, one should be aware that at one time religious groups did not oppose abortion, including the Catholic Church. Likewise, to truly understand the high rate of divorce in the United States, one should be aware of the ways in which the current notion of love, which evolved in the eighteenth century, changed the entire basis on which mates were chosen, and thereby increased the likelihood of couples ending an unhappy marriage (Coontz, 2005).

Everett Collection Inc / Alamy Stock Photo

A Global View

World Population: 7.6 Billion and Counting

Design Pics Inc/Alamy Stock Photo

As this feature box is being written on July 11, 2018, at 7:57 p.m., 7,635,277,683 people live on planet Earth. Is this a lot of people? Actually, all these people could fit into an area the size of Los Angeles if they squeezed together. So space is not really the problem. The real issue is one of resources: food, water, energy, and overall use of environmental resources. How can all these people feed themselves nutritious food, drink clean water, heat their homes, drive to work, and dispose of their wastes? This question is an important one, and many people suspect that Earth has already exceeded its carrying capacity.

The United States overuses Earth's resources, given the size of its population. Americans use a higher proportion of natural resources and live less sustainably than people in any other country. Americans have a uniquely high standard of living and have come to expect that cheap food, clean water, and gasoline will be available to us whenever we want it. Now, unsurprisingly, other countries want this standard of living, too. But Earth would be in especially bad shape if everyone on Earth lived like an American.

Take energy, for example. Americans constitute 5 percent of the world's population, but they consume 24 percent of the energy. On average, one American uses as much energy as 2 Japanese, 6 Mexicans, 13 Chinese, 31 Indians, 128 Bangladeshis, 301 Tanzanians, and 370 Ethiopians (Mindfully. org, 2015). All the energy that Americans use pollutes the air, water, and soil. It also heats up the atmosphere. But China is right there with Americans, and in fact the Chinese have eclipsed Americans in the use of fossil fuels. The Chinese do, however, have almost five times the population of the United States, so, per person, they still use considerably less than do Americans.

So, what does this mean? Simply put, the example that Americans have set will be copied by other countries around the world. Can Earth support this many people if they live so unsustainably? How many people are we talking about? It's now 8:05 p.m., and Earth's count is up to 7,635,278,747. In other words, in just 8 minutes, Earth's population grew by over a thousand people.

Critical Thinking

What do you think is the carrying capacity of Earth? If you think Earth has surpassed its carrying capacity, what do you propose be done about it? If you think that Earth has not surpassed its carrying capacity, when do you think that might happen, and with what effects?

A **comparative perspective** helps enlighten a current situation because it reveals alternative social arrangements and presents new ways to frame an issue or policy solution. A comparative perspective offers an opportunity for reflection. Nonetheless, this reflection doesn't always mean that we radically change our policies or ways of doing things, but instead, helps us understand, culturally, why we do what we do. For example, some people are concerned about the "demise" of marriage and families: people marry later or not at all, people divorce and remarry, children are raised in stepfamilies, same-sex couples can now legally wed—all changes that will be discussed in Chapter 10. A comparative perspective can show us how marriages and families are constructed elsewhere. For example, in many parts of the world, an arranged marriage is the norm.

As another example, how can a comparative perspective help people understand the nature and role of adolescence in U.S. culture? This concern is an important one because it is well known that adolescents commit a disproportionate number of crimes, experience higher-than-average unemployment, and face a host of other social problems, such as teen pregnancy or drug use.

comparative perspective

A process to learn about other cultures and other historical periods to better understand social problems within one's own culture.

A comparative perspective shows that adolescence, as it is known today, is largely a new social construction, originating in the West in the late nineteenth century as a result of newly created child labor laws and the changing nature of the labor market (Leeder, 2004; Mintz, 2004). Until then, children's labor was needed on farms and even young teenagers were considered mini-adults. However, with urbanization and industrialization in the late nineteenth century, a movement arose to increase the protection of young people. Social reformers known as "child savers" were particularly interested in developing social programs that were age-based and targeted toward children. Compulsory education increased the length of time children spent in school until well into their teenage years. Adolescence became a new period of transition between childhood and adulthood, but without clear-cut norms about what to expect during this period. By the twentieth century, the concept of adolescence as a separate stage of life had taken hold, and it now represents a substantial component of popular culture segregated from adult-oriented culture. Unique clothing, music, and food are directly marketed toward this relatively new consumer group. Nonetheless, it is not completely clear what the developmental tasks of this age group are and how adolescents can best serve the needs of society. Separating adolescents from adults, while giving them an unclear or unknown set of developmental tasks, has not necessarily served adolescents well. This may be part of the reason that adolescence and young adulthood are expanding, with large numbers of people living with their parents well into their mid- to late-twenties (Cohn and Passel, 2018).

How do other cultures construct this age period, and how do adolescents engage in society? How are these social constructions related to the level of technology or wealth in a society? A comparative perspective can shed light on our social problems and new ways to eliminate them.

What Do You Think?

Have you had the opportunity to travel to other cultures? If so, did you see anything that the United States could learn from?

Social Policy

1.6   Assess the social policy debates between conservatives and liberals.

Much of the research conducted by sociologists is designed to provide information to be used in formulating social policies as well as in evaluating existing policies and suggesting improvements and new directions. **Social policies** are formal procedures designed to remedy a social problem. Generally, they are designed by officials of government at the local, state, or federal level, but they can also be initiated by private citizens in voluntary associations, by corporations, and by nonprofit foundations.

1.6.1 Social Policy Debates

There is generally a good deal of debate about social problems and any proposed social policy. Much of the debate consists of discussion and analysis of how well a proposed policy appears to address the problem. Such analysis tends to be considered technical in the sense that, although there is general agreement on the need to address the problem, the debate hinges on the adequacy of the proposed means to achieve the agreed-on ends. Increasingly, however, policy debates have become ideological rather than technical, and in the United States, such debates frequently pit conservatives against liberals.

Generally, conservatives believe in limited government, free markets, individual liberty, personal responsibility, and a strong national defense. They believe the role of government should be to provide people the freedom necessary to pursue their own goals. Conservative policies generally emphasize empowerment of the individual to solve social problems, and they usually seek to limit the involvement of government in the solutions. Conservatives believe private firms, governed by the need to compete

social policies

Formal procedures designed to remedy a social problem; can be designed by officials of government at the local, state, or federal level or by private citizens in voluntary associations, by corporations, and by nonprofit foundations.

in markets and make profits, are the best type of organization for coping with most social problems.

In contrast, liberals tend to believe that government has a responsibility to address social problems. Liberals consider government action necessary to achieve equal opportunity and to protect civil liberties and human rights. Liberals are cautious of the dominance of the market (and, hence, the profit motive) and believe that it can be unfair and exploitive to certain groups in society. Therefore, the free market needs to be regulated to protect consumers, employees, and the environment, according to liberals. While liberals do not abdicate personal responsibility, they believe that the government has a responsibility to provide a structure that is fair to all.

Throughout the twentieth century and into the twenty-first, the government's role in attempting to solve social problems has increased steadily, despite the ideological stands of various administrations. For example, America's role as a world military power, along with new problems of terrorism, has required the continual expenditure of public funds on military goods and services. These costs have increased dramatically with every war and every major change in military technology. Similarly, the fight against drug commerce has added greatly to the cost of maintaining the society's judicial and penal institutions. Every function of government has a similar history of escalating costs because of increases in the scale of the society or the scope of the problem.

1.6.2 Future Prospects

At this writing, the nation's voters have an increasingly ideological approach to social problems, sometimes at the expense of understanding and using empirical research. For example, public attitudes about climate change have become increasingly contentious (Funk and Kennedy, 2017; Pew Research Center, 2017). Despite near scientific consensus that the Earth's climate is changing rapidly due to the emissions of fossil fuels related to human use, 29 percent of adults believe that climate change is mostly caused by natural patterns in the Earth's environment (Saad, 2017). Even among young people who will experience the most severe effects during their lifetime of any group, only 57 percent agree that "global warming will seriously threaten one's way of life" (Jones, 2014).[5] Furthermore, opinions about climate change are largely split along political party lines, with Republicans far more likely than Democrats to deny climate change or attribute it to natural patterns, consistent with their views towards government regulation and individual liberty (Brenan and Saad, 2018). Only 18 percent of Republicans say that they are "very concerned" about climate change or global warming as compared to 66 percent of Democrats (Norman, March 17, 2017).

This conflict is typical of many current controversies over the best ways to handle social issues, with conservatives stressing private or market solutions and liberals calling for public or government actions. These conflicting approaches are discussed in the Social Policy sections that conclude each chapter of this text.

Climate change is one example of division between conservatives and liberals on important social problems. Many conservatives deny that the problem exists or suggest that any change is due to natural fluctuations in the Earth's temperature. The preponderance of scientific research, however, disputes this view.

— CLIMATE CHANGE ? NOW, THAT'S CRAZY TALK !

Sylvie Bouchard/Fotolia

---

[5]Jones, J. M. "In U.S., Most Do Not See Global Warming as Serious Threat," *Gallup* (March 13, 2014).

Going Beyond Left and Right

Sociologists conduct research to provide critical information about social problems, including crime, social inequality, mental illness, racism, environmental degradation, and a host of other important issues. This information, gleaned from research, can then be used to formulate policies and to create programs to help solve social problems, or at least minimize their effects. This is the ideal. The reality, however, is more complicated. People often bring their own set of values and beliefs—which may have little to do with scientific facts—into play as they conceptualize a problem or think of solutions. In fact, the values and beliefs that contradict scientific evidence have even been given a nickname—"alternative facts." Sociology is a fascinating field because it uses empirical methods to collect and analyze real information about the issues that we all care about and about which we all have opinions. People feel strongly about social problems and their solutions. These feelings are increasingly becoming ideologically polarized.

Summary

1.1 Explain the sociological imagination.

The sociological imagination suggests that many of our personal experiences are patterned and are shaped by social structure. Using a sociological imagination reveals general patterns in what otherwise might be thought of as simple random events. Problems such as divorce, substance abuse, crime, and child abuse are more than just personal troubles experienced by a few people. They are issues that affect large numbers of people and originate in society's institutional arrangements. In other words, individual experiences are linked to the social structure.

1.2 Discuss the definition of a social problem.

When enough people in a society agree that a condition exists that threatens the quality of their lives and their most cherished values, *and* they agree that something should be done to remedy that condition, sociologists say that the society has defined that condition as a social problem. Society's members have reached a consensus that a condition that affects some people is a problem for the entire society, not just for those who are directly affected.

1.3 Compare and contrast the three main sociological perspectives on social problems.

Contemporary sociology is founded on three basic perspectives, or sets of ideas, that offer theories about why societies hang together and how and why they change. These perspectives are not the only sociological approaches to social problems, but they can be extremely powerful tools for understanding them. Each of these perspectives—functionalism, conflict theory, and symbolic interactionism—gives rise to several useful and distinctive approaches to the study of social problems.

1.4 Describe the process that reveals the natural history of social problems.

Most social problems go through four major stages: (1) problem definition; (2) legitimacy; (3) reemergence of demands; and (4) rejection and institution building.

1.5 Review the four themes of the text.

This text has four themes: (1) a sociological understanding of social problems demands that one move beyond personal opinion and instead use an empirical approach, which is a method that answers questions through a systematic collection and analysis of data; (2) while people may initially think of experiences solely in personal terms, this text will show the importance of linking individual experience with social structure; (3) social inequality is a critical organizing feature in society and contributes to social problems; (4) it is important to learn about other cultures and other historical periods to develop a better understanding of American social problems today.

1.6 Assess the social policy debates between conservatives and liberals.

Debates about many social problems are becoming increasingly polarized. Conservatives believe in limited government, free markets, individual liberty, personal responsibility, and a strong national defense. In contrast, liberals believe government has a responsibility to address social problems and consider government action necessary not only to achieve equal opportunity but also to protect civil liberties and human rights.

Chapter 2
Problems of Health and Health Care

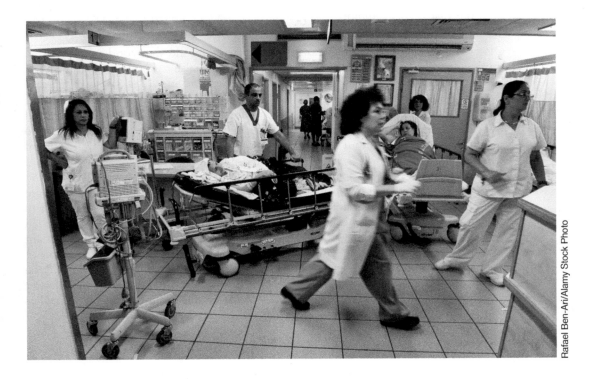

∨ Learning Objectives

2.1 Describe health care as a global social problem.

2.2 Identify the scope of health care problems in America.

2.3 Discuss Americans' unequal access to health care.

2.4 Review the reasons for the high costs of health care.

2.5 Summarize the ethical issues surrounding health care.

2.6 Classify explanations for health care problems.

2.7 Identify key issues in social policy, including the Affordable Care Act.

My son Marcus was complaining about a stomachache, and I just didn't take it very seriously. He's seventeen, and I figured he could just deal with it. But when he started to cry, I knew something was up. I can't remember when it was the last time he cried over pain—maybe when he broke his arm in fifth grade? But, a stomachache? I don't have any insurance so what am I supposed to do? I didn't want to pay for an emergency room visit over just a stomachache. I figured it would go away as they usually do. But as the night went on, I could tell that something was really wrong. He was rolling on the floor in pain, and at one point he seemed to be even losing consciousness. This had to be far more than just a stomachache, so I ended up taking him to the emergency room. It's a good thing I did because after they examined him they told me that his appendix had burst. Poisons were spewing through his body. The doctor told me that if I had waited much longer Marcus could have died. I feel horrible—risking my only son's life because I don't have any money to pay the bill. I know it sounds crazy, but I just didn't know what to do. I don't have any insurance.

Over the past few years, Americans and observers around the world witnessed the implementation of historic legislation to reform the health care system in the United States. After decades of mounting health care costs and increases in the number of people without access to health care, the U.S. Congress passed a compromise reform plan, the Patient Protection and Affordable Care Act (ACA), that promised to add at least 32 million people to those with health care insurance, people like Marcus who have often suffered without it. After a period of intense campaigning by President Obama and his supporters, and equally intense campaigning by ACA opponents, a bitterly divided Congress finally passed the historic health care reform bill in 2010 to be implemented over the next several years. Few legislators or American voters were entirely pleased with the reforms, but the bill culminated many decades of effort to bring the U.S. health care system closer to those of other developed nations to which we often compare ourselves. However, in 2018, under the administration of President Trump, much of the "meat" of the ACA has been stripped away, and the number of people without health insurance is expected to skyrocket. We will examine this issue later in this chapter. But first, let's introduce the various ways in which health and inequalities of access to adequate health care are serious social problems on a global as well as national level.

Health Care as a Global Social Problem

2.1 Describe health care as a global social problem.

The lack of adequate health measures presents a variety of social problems everywhere. In affluent regions like Western Europe, North America, and Australia, problems associated with physical health often involve reducing unequal access to high-quality health care while controlling health care costs. In impoverished regions where high-quality medical care is often lacking, social problems associated with physical health are even more profound: the spread of infectious diseases, high rates of infant and maternal death, low life expectancy, scarcity of medical personnel and equipment, and inadequate sewage and water systems.

It is true that in the past half-century life expectancy has increased in most regions of the world. These improvements often reflect better water and sewage systems and adequate child vaccination programs. But recent reviews of the global health situation indicate that continued improvements in public health systems and in delivery of medical services will be necessary, especially in poor regions, if these gains are to continue (United Nations Development Programme, 2018).

The United Nations rates nations based on a series of indicators of health, education, equality of political participation, and many other factors. The nations are then grouped into high, medium, and low levels of human development for purposes of

Health Care Needs in Less Developed Countries

Less developed countries face considerably different health issues, or face health issues on a significantly different scale than what is found in more developed nations. People in less developed countries fight for basic survival daily: access to food, clean water, and shelter. These pictures reveal some of the many issues faced by people in developing countries.

Michele Burgess/Alamy Stock Photo

Jeoffrey Maitem/Getty Images

fine art/Alamy Stock Photo

This woman from rural Ghana, Africa, is 38 years old. Her life has been hard, and she has faced a number of health issues. She bore six children, only four of whom lived past the age of ten, and she had no prenatal care during her pregnancies. She has rarely been to a doctor and has never been to a dentist.

This little girl of 16 months cries while she is measured for signs of malnutrition. Regular natural disasters in the Philippines, an overreliance on rice, and a lack of breastfeeding have left Filipino children some of the most malnourished in Asia. Over 7 percent of children in the Philippines suffer from acute malnourishment.

Sanitation standards are not the same throughout the world. This dirty squat toilet represents facilities available in many countries, and there are others in the world who would consider themselves lucky to have even this.

QASSEM ZEIN/Stringer

Mehedi Hasan/Alamy Stock Photo

A wounded man lies in a hospital bed in Baghdad after a night of fighting, the victim of a bomb. The ongoing violence has left two of his cousins dead and several others wounded. Many developing nations are engaged in violence that kills, maims, and terrifies men, women, and children.

This woman travels miles to collect water from this canal that she uses for drinking, cooking, and bathing. Access to clean drinking water is a serious social problem, and viruses and worms contained in dirty water kill millions of people every year.

Critical Thinking

What is the United States' responsibility to assist people in developing countries with the health crises they face? Should we be providing more aid? How will we ensure that aid gets to the people who really need it? Or should Americans focus on problems in our own country and let other countries take care of their own problems?

Table 2–1 Health Indicators for Selected Nations, 1970–2017

	Female Life Expectancy at Birth (years)		Infant Mortality Rate (per 1,000 live births)	
	1970	2017	1970	2017
Highly developed (1st world)				
United States	75	81	20	6
Sweden	77	84	11	3
Argentina	70	80	59	10
Costa Rica	68	83	58	8
Less developed (2nd world)				
Hungary	72	79	36	4
Mexico	64	79	79	18
China	61	78	85	10
India	47	70	130	37
Developing (3rd world)				
Nepal	41	71	156	32
Nigeria	42	54	120	69
Sierra Leone	35	52	206	92

SOURCES: Population Reference Bureau. 2018. "2017 World Population Data Sheet With Focus on Youth." Retrieved 2 April 2018 (www.prb.org/2017-world-population-data-sheet/).; World Bank. 2018. "Life Expectancy at Birth, Female (Years)/Data." Retrieved 2 April 2018 (data.worldbank.org/indicator/SP.DYN.LE00.FE.IN?end=2015&start=1970).

life expectancy

How long a person can expect to live, it is usually calculated at birth.

infant mortality

The number of deaths of children in their first year of life, for every 1,000 live births.

What Do You Think?

Realistically, what can be done about global health disparities? And if help is possible, why hasn't it been provided, or has it?

comparison. The numbers in Table 2–1 indicate how much or how little improvement various nations have made in two key health indicators: **life expectancy**, which is defined as how long a person can expect to live and is usually calculated at birth, and **infant mortality**, which is the number of deaths in a child's first year of life, for every 1,000 live births (Population Reference Bureau, 2018).

Life expectancy is highly correlated with a society's quality of health care. As a population's health improves because of better medical care and improved living conditions, the average age to which its members live (i.e., the life expectancy of the population) rises dramatically. For example, Table 2–1 indicates that a person born in Sierra Leone in 2017 (the most recent year for which international comparisons are available) can expect to live only about 52 years; in contrast, a person born in the United States in 2017 can expect to live about 81 years. Differences in life expectancy between developed (sometimes referred to as "industrialized") and less developed (sometimes referred to as "nonindustrialized") nations are largely due to the increasing chance that people in developed nations will survive the childhood diseases and parasites that cause such high death rates in less developed nations.

Table 2–1 also shows the wide gap between these countries in infant mortality rates, the most important comparative indicator of health. In Sierra Leone, the infant mortality rate is 92 per 1,000 live births, almost three times the rate in Nepal, 15 times the rate in the United States, and 30 times the rate in Sweden.

Infant mortality rates and life expectancy are highly correlated with the number of health care professionals in a society, which serves as a measure of the quality of the health care available to its members. However, other factors besides the availability of health care professionals may affect a population's health. In the world's poorest regions, malnutrition, a decline in breastfeeding, and inadequate sanitation and health facilities are associated with high mortality. Poor maternal health and lack of prenatal care contribute even more to persistently high rates of infant mortality and other poor birth outcomes. The feature box *A Global View: "Fistulas"* explains how obstructed labor can not only lead to infant death but also leave the woman with a hole between her vagina and bladder (or rectum), otherwise known as a fistula (The Fistula Foundation, 2018; World Health Organization, January, 2018a).

A Global View

Fistulas

Beza was a small Ethiopian girl of 15 when she married her husband. She had seen him only once before her wedding day, but they had never spoken to one another. Her father told her he was a good man, and so she quit school to become his wife. Five months later Beza was pregnant and she felt a combination of excitement and dread. She didn't see a doctor during her pregnancy because she had no money and the doctor was too far away. When labor began, she lay on the floor of the hut, but the pain was more than she could bear. Labor lasted for three days, but the baby wouldn't come. Finally, on the fourth day, with the help of a neighbor woman, the baby was delivered, but he was dead. As she healed from this trauma she noticed that she was leaking urine and had no ability to control it. Unknown to her at the time, the obstructed labor tore a hole in the tissue between her vagina and bladder. The smell was foul, and she was self-conscious about wetting herself. Her husband wanted nothing more to do with her—she killed his baby, as he saw it, and God was now punishing her—and he kicked her out of their home. She went back to live with her parents, but they too felt shame, so they built a hut for her in the back of their house where she could live, alone.

A story like this one plays out at least 100,000 times every year. Beza suffers from a fistula, a hole between her vagina and bladder caused by the many days of obstructed labor when the pressure of the baby's head against her pelvis cut off blood supply to delicate tissues in the region. The dead tissue falls away, and Beza is left with a hole between her vagina and her bladder. Some women also have a hole between their vagina and rectum as well. This hole results

in permanent incontinence of urine and/or feces. The World Health Organization estimates that approximately 2 million women have untreated fistulas.

Fistulas are most prevalent in sub-Saharan Africa and Asia. They once were present in the United States but were largely eliminated in the latter nineteenth century with improved obstetric care and the use of C-sections to relieve obstructed labor. Yet, nearly half of women in developing countries give birth without any trained personnel, and when complications arise no one is available to assist the woman, leading to injuries such as fistula. Hospitals and personnel who can help them are often hundreds of miles away, and poor roads or a lack of transportation make travel difficult or impossible.

The majority of women who develop fistulas, like Beza, are abandoned by their husbands and ostracized by their communities because of their incontinence and foul smell. They fear going out in public because of the chronic leaking and smell.

The cause of fistulas may be obstructed labor, but the root causes are crushing poverty and the low status of girls and women. In developing nations, poverty and malnutrition stunt growth; a girl's skeleton, including her pelvis, does not fully mature. This stunted condition can contribute to obstructed labor, and therefore a fistula. Couple this condition with very early marriage and childbearing, and we can see why fistulas are an epidemic in the developing world. Very little money is spent on women's reproductive health care; women's needs are low priority.

Yet, fistulas can be treated. A fistula can be easily closed with surgery, and the patient has a good chance of returning to a normal life with full control of her bodily functions. The cost of the surgery is about US$450, which includes the operation, high-quality postoperative care, and even a new dress and bus fare home. The Addis Ababa Fistula Hospital in Ethiopia has treated more than 20,000 women over the past several decades. Their cure rate is over 90 percent.

As for prevention, ready access to emergency obstetric care such as a Caesarean section when complications arise could easily eliminate fistulas, as would delaying the age of first pregnancy. The bottom line for prevention is placing a greater value on women's lives.

SOURCES: Adapted from The Fistula Foundation, 2018; World Health Organization, January, 2018.

Critical Thinking

Why do you think that so little attention has been given to this issue? Is the silence related to culture, shame, patriarchy, economics, or other factors? How are these factors sociological issues? Pretend you have unlimited resources and are asked by the World Health Organization to develop a program to curb, treat, and/or eliminate fistulas. What would your program look like? Be sure to address the root cause.

Celia Mannings/Alamy Stock Photo

The Scope of Health Care Problems in America

2.2 **Identify the scope of health care problems in America.**

Although the health of Americans is vastly superior to most developing nations, it is relatively poor as compared to peer developed nations, such as Canada or countries in Western Europe. A primary reason our country's health registers so badly is that our low-income and minority populations have such poor health. Our comparatively poor health in the United States is due largely to two social conditions: (1) growing inequality and (2) lifestyle problems. Poverty and inequality are associated with lack of health insurance and lack of access to high-quality medical care. Problems in the way we live include sedentary occupations; fattening, nonnutritious foods; and lack of proper exercise, all of which contribute to the high incidence of obesity, heart disease, and other ailments. Environmental pollution and cigarette smoking contribute to the high incidence of respiratory disease and cancer. There can be little doubt, however, that many of our health problems are aggravated by the kind of medical care that is—or is not—available.

medical sociology

The subfield of sociology that specializes in research on the health care system and its impact on the public, especially access to health care.

Medical sociology is the subfield of sociology that specializes in research on the health care system and its impact on the public, especially access to health care (Weiss and Lonnquist, 2015; Weitz, 2017) and the evolution of health care institutions (Starr, 2010). In describing problems of physical health, sociologists are particularly interested in understanding how a person's social class (as measured by income, education, and occupation) influences his or her access to medical care and its outcome. Sociologists also work with economists and health care planners in assessing the costs of different types of health care delivery systems.

Medical sociologists often point out that health care institutions themselves are the source of many problems we associate with health in the United States. They emphasize that the health care system has evolved in such a way that doctors maintain private practices while society supports the hospitals and insurance systems that allow doctors to function (Weitz, 2017). In other words, American health care never developed as a purely competitive industry or a regulated public service. Instead, as we will see shortly, it became a complex institution comprising many private and public organizations.

As great strides were made in the ability to treat illnesses—especially with antibiotics—and to prevent those illnesses through improved public health practices, some doctors began to develop narrow specialties and to refer patients to hospitals with special facilities. This practice created a situation in which specialized doctors and hospital personnel became highly interdependent, and family doctors and preventive medical practices suffered in comparison (Starr, 2010). All efforts to change our health care system, to make it less costly, more efficient, or more humane, must deal with the power of insurance companies, doctors, and other health care providers, power that derives not from their wealth or their ownership of health care facilities but from their mode of relating to one another and to the public. This power is a subject that will become clear after discussing some of the specific problems of American health care.

The range of situations in which health care can be viewed as a social problem is extremely wide. At the micro, or individual, level, where family and friends are affected, such problems comprise issues such as whether the correct medical treatment is being applied, whether an elderly parent should be placed in a nursing home, or whether life support should be terminated. But as the sociological imagination reveals, people's experiences are influenced by larger forces that act throughout society and touch the lives of millions. These forces are the structural problems of health care. At the personal level, individuals may worry about care for elderly loved ones, but at the structural level the issue is how effectively health care is distributed among all people (including the elderly and the poor) and what can be done to improve the delivery of needed medical services.

This section explores several aspects of American health care that contribute to social problems at both the personal and structural levels. Unequal access to health services, the high cost of health care, and our own behaviors and use of technology are among the problems that must be addressed if more Americans are to receive more and better health care.

Unequal Access to Health Care

2.3 Discuss Americans' unequal access to health care.

When we compare ourselves with other advanced industrial nations, the United States is doing a relatively poor job of providing health care for its population. More affluent individuals and families tend to get excellent care in the most up-to-date facilities, and they tend to say that they are satisfied with their care. Low-income persons, in contrast, often have difficulty accessing basic health care, let alone more specialized care.

To a large extent, health care as a social problem can be viewed in terms of unequal access to health care services. Marcus, introduced in the opening vignette, suffered unnecessary pain and almost died because his family had no health insurance. Unfortunately, he is not alone. Many Americans have trouble getting the health care they need when they are ill because they are without health insurance. In 2010 there was an all-time high of 50 million Americans—over 15 percent of the population—without insurance, although that number has declined since then to 29 million in large part because of the Affordable Care Act, as shown in Figure 2–1. A decline is good news, but still, how could so many people be uninsured in a country as wealthy as the United States?

The short answer to this question is that the United States has traditionally had a **fee-for-service health care system**; in other words, if you get sick or injured, you must pay for medical care; the cost is not rolled into taxes. Other countries roll the price of health care into their taxes so that there is little or no additional cost when a person is sick or injured.

During World War II, when wage freezes were in effect, some large companies decided to offer health insurance as a fringe benefit of the job, and why not? Insurance

fee-for-service

A type of health care system in which patients are expected to pay directly for their own medical care; the cost is not rolled into taxes.

Figure 2–1 Number of Uninsured in the United States (millions), 2000–2017

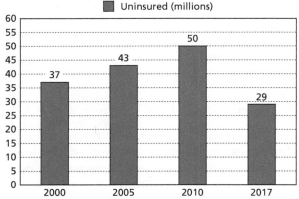

SOURCES: Garfield and Young, 2015; Berchick, Hood, and Barnett, 2018.

was cheap to purchase because health care costs were relatively inexpensive, and few drugs were available. To compete for labor, medium-sized and small businesses also decided to get into the act (Blumenthal, 2006).

By the 1950s and 1960s, Americans began to equate health insurance with employment: you get a job and you get insurance. Americans forgot that this connection began through a simple historical accident (i.e., war-induced wage freezes led employers to offer health insurance instead), and they also forgot that no other developed nation ever tied health insurance to employment. In all developed nations (and many less developed ones), access to health care is a guaranteed right of citizenship, much like education or access to police protection. The result is that many Americans likely took jobs, or stayed in a job, simply because they needed the health insurance the job provided.

However, by the 1970s and 1980s, health care costs began to rise substantially. Small businesses were the first to say, "Hey, we cannot afford this." Today, companies of all sizes are dropping health insurance coverage completely or asking workers to pay more of the costs of the insurance plan. Only 53 percent of firms offered health insurance to employees in 2017, down from 60 percent in 2011 (Henry J. Kaiser Family Foundation, 2017b). Clearly, the connection between health insurance and employment is eroding.

Well, then, why not just purchase insurance yourself if you cannot get it from an employer? Many people in America cannot afford to purchase health insurance privately because the average price of family coverage is now almost $19,000 per year (Kaiser Family Foundation and Health Research and Educational Trust, 2017). Also, until the ACA went into effect, just because a person applied for insurance there was no guarantee that he or she would be granted coverage; many people were turned down by insurance companies because of a preexisting condition. Moreover, although the ACA expanded **Medicaid** coverage (the federal-state health care program for certain categories of low-income people) in those states that opted in, even today most low-income Americans do not qualify for Medicaid.

The consequences of being without insurance can be devastating (Foutz et al., 2017). Compared with those who have insurance, people without health insurance:

- are twice as likely to postpone seeking health care, are over four times as likely to forgo needed care and are more than twice as likely to have a needed prescription go unfilled.
- pay large sums of their own money for their limited care, thereby reducing the amount of money for food, heat, and other necessities. One-third of uninsured patients and half of low-income uninsured patients say that doctors make them pay upfront before any health care is rendered. Medical bills are a major financial hardship, and they contribute to debt and bankruptcy.
- are less likely after an accidental injury to receive any care, are twice as likely to receive no recommended follow-up care, and are more likely to report not fully recovering.

Medicaid

The federal-state health care program for certain categories of low-income people.

What Do You Think?

(1) Why do you think the U.S. health care system is so complicated? (2) What ideas do you have for making the system less complicated?

Cartoonresource/Fotolia

Henry was suspicious of the job offer right from the beginning.

Unlike most countries, U.S. health insurance is designed to be a fringe benefit provided by employers. From the employers' perspective, the costs of health insurance are expensive and therefore many employers are reducing benefits or eliminating them altogether. It is as though they are saying, "You can have a salary, or you can have benefits. You choose."

2.3.1 Profile of the Uninsured

In 2016 approximately 29 million Americans were uninsured. This represents a significant decline in the number of people without insurance, largely because of changes in health care policy. A decline is something to celebrate. However, 29 million people still represents a substantial portion of the American population. Who are these people? Some of the answers may surprise you.

Figure 2–2a Characteristics of the Non-Elderly Uninsured: Family Work Status, 2016

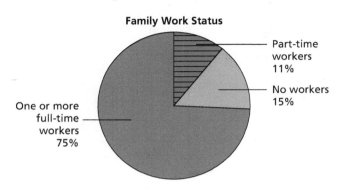

Figure 2–2b Characteristics of the Non-Elderly Uninsured: Family Income based on Federal Poverty Line (FPL), 2016

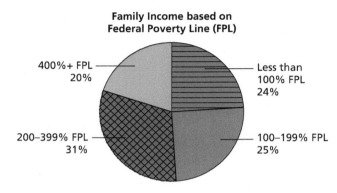

Figure 2–2c Characteristics of the Non-Elderly Uninsured: Race, 2016

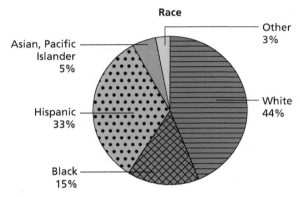

SOURCE: Data from Foutz, J., et al. (December 14, 2017) "The Uninsured: A Primer - Key Facts about Health Insurance and the Uninsured Under the Affordable Care Act," Kaiser Family Foundation.

First, three-quarters of the uninsured are in families where one or both parents are employed full-time, as shown in Figure 2–2a (Foutz et al., 2017). Another 11 percent have a family member who is employed part-time. Their employers do not provide insurance for the worker or his or her dependents, and it costs too much for the family to purchase insurance privately. Only 15 percent of those who are uninsured are also unemployed.

Second, as you can see in Figure 2–2b, the incomes of uninsured Americans are quite varied. While many uninsured persons are poor with incomes at or only slightly above the official poverty line, about 20 percent of those who are uninsured have incomes four times the poverty level, or about $100,000 a year for a family. Even these relatively well-off families may not have insurance through their employer, and feel that paying nearly $19,000 for their own insurance is cost prohibitive. So, while it is fair to say that many uninsured people have lower incomes, certainly not all do (Foutz et al., 2017).

Finally, Figure 2–2c shows that non-Hispanic whites make up the largest uninsured group, but minority groups, especially Hispanics, are overrepresented among those who are uninsured given their size in the population (Foutz et al., 2017). Taken together, these findings are particularly disturbing because low-income people and racial and ethnic minorities tend overall to be in poorer health and therefore need to have good access to health care services (National Center for Health Statistics, 2017).

2.3.2 Inequalities of Race and Ethnicity

Race and ethnic differences in health are well-documented, and several examples of these health disparities are noted in Figures 2–3a, 2–3b, and 2–3c. Perhaps the most obvious sign of health status can be illustrated by life expectancy—on average, how long

Figure 2–3a Major Health Indicators, by Race and Ethnicity: Life Expectancy in Years, 2015

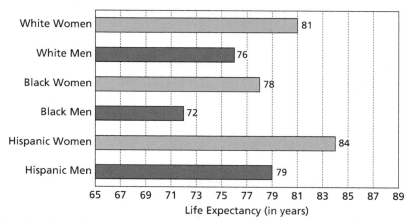

SOURCE: Data from National Center for Health Statistics, 2017.

Figure 2–3b Major Health Indicators, by Race and Ethnicity: Infant Mortality Rate, 2014

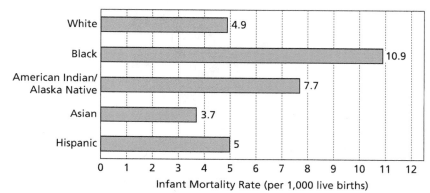

SOURCE: Data from National Center for Health Statistics, 2017.

Figure 2–3c Major Health Indicators, by Race and Ethnicity: Percent Reporting Fair or Poor Health (Self-Assessment), 2016

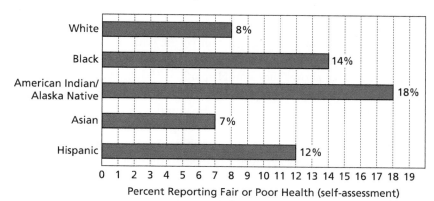

SOURCE: Data from CDC/National Center for Health Statistics, March 30, 2018.

a person born today can expect to live. A comparison of life expectancy for Hispanics, whites, and blacks reveals that Hispanics have the longest life expectancy, with whites and blacks trailing behind. The largest gap—seven years on average—is between Hispanic and black men. The gap between Hispanic and black women is only slightly smaller at six years (National Center for Health Statistics, 2017). Blacks suffer disproportionately more from almost every illness than do whites, and because they are less likely to have been immunized, they suffer higher rates of death from infectious diseases. Blacks are also far more likely to be victims of lethal violence. In addition, the infant mortality rate for blacks is more than twice that for Asians, whites, and Hispanics. Finally, Native Americans and blacks are more likely than other groups to rate their health as only fair or poor (National Center for Health Statistics, 2017).

Some people are surprised to learn that the life expectancy of Hispanics is so high and that their infant mortality is so low, given higher-than-average levels of poverty, prejudice, and discrimination. Yet, as we make these sweeping generalizations about groups such as *"Hispanics"* or *"Asians,"* it is important to remember that significant differences exist within broad racial or ethnic categories, as discussed in *A Closer Look: "Disparities in Hispanic Health Care."* After all, these broad ethnic categories represent diverse groups with distinct cultures. Nevertheless, most data sources lump groups together under these types of umbrella categories.

A Closer Look

Disparities in Hispanic Health Care

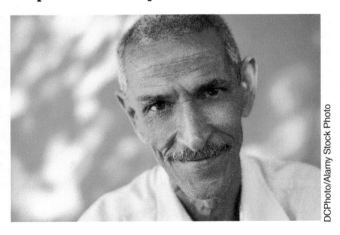

DCPhoto/Alamy Stock Photo

What is behind the statement that Hispanics in the United States live longer, on average, than do whites? Or that Hispanics are almost twice as likely as whites to lack health insurance? The answer to these questions requires that we explore the meaning of the term Hispanic. Often, social categories that lump together large numbers of quite diverse people can mask important trends. In the case of Hispanics, further analysis of the Hispanic subgroups in the United States reveals great variations in rates and sources of health insurance.

Coverage differs substantially among the major Hispanic groups in the United States. Cuban Americans, the majority of whom live in Florida and have been in the United States since the 1960s if not earlier, have by far the highest rates of job-based or other private insurance. Cuban Americans, on average, enjoy a high standard of living. Puerto Ricans, like Cuban Americans, also are quite likely to have insurance, but they have high rates of public government insurance (Medicaid and Medicare) because they are American citizens working in poorly paid jobs with long histories of job discrimination. People of Central American or Mexican descent also have low rates of job-based insurance, but, unlike Puerto Ricans, have extremely high rates of being uninsured. Some of these Hispanics are undocumented and therefore not eligible for public government programs, or they have relatives who are undocumented and therefore fear that claiming benefits could hurt these relatives. The label Hispanic (or Latino) covers groups that are so diverse that it makes almost no sense to lump them together. Theoretically, Hispanic refers to people who trace their ancestry to Spain or Latin America. In reality, it includes people with roots all over the world who have widely different social, cultural, and economic patterns. These patterns help to explain their disparities in health and access to health care. These same concerns can be applied to Asian groups, who share few social and economic characteristics, yet are usually lumped together as one homogenous statistical group.

Critical Thinking

List the different groups classified as Hispanic and Asian. Can you identify ways in which they are culturally different? For example, describe any differences in food, language, or values. Do you think it is racist to lump groups together? Why or why not?

The most comprehensive recent research on inequalities in health care shows that, even with equivalent insurance, racial and ethnic minorities are likely to receive less or inferior care compared with whites, especially for the following conditions:

- *Heart disease.* Blacks are less likely to receive advanced heart treatments; 13 percent fewer undergo coronary angioplasty and one-third fewer undergo bypass surgery.
- *Asthma.* Among preschool children hospitalized for asthma, only 7 percent of black and 2 percent of Hispanic children, compared with 21 percent of white children, are prescribed routine medications to prevent future asthma-related hospitalizations.
- *Breast cancer.* The length of time between an abnormal screening mammogram and the follow-up diagnostic test to determine whether a woman has breast cancer is more than twice as long in Asian American, black, and Hispanic women as in white women.
- *Human immunodeficiency virus (HIV) infection.* Blacks with HIV infection are less likely to be on antiretroviral therapy and less likely to be receiving protease inhibitors than are other people with HIV.
- *Nursing home care.* Asian American, Hispanic, and black residents of nursing homes are all far less likely than white residents to have sensory and communication aids such as glasses and hearing aids (Altman, 2014; Unger and O'Donnell, 2014).

2.3.3 Inequalities of Social Class

From a socioeconomic point of view, there is a strong relationship between having a low income and a higher rate of illness, as is shown in Figure 2–4 (National Center for Health Statistics, 2017). The wealthier people are, the more likely they are to feel, and to be, healthy. For example, only 3 percent of those with household incomes of $100,000 a year or more report that their health is only fair or poor, as compared to 18 percent of those earning less than $35,000—a sixfold difference.

Having a low income affects health from the time of birth. The high rate of infant mortality among poor people is due to several factors associated with poverty. Inadequate nutrition appears to account for the high death rates among the newborn children of low-income mothers. The babies most at risk are those with a low birth weight. Among the causes of low birth weight are the low nutritional value

Figure 2–4 Major Health Indicator, by Income: Only Fair or Poor Health (Self-Assessment), 2016

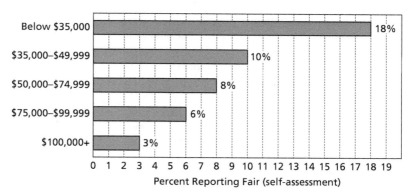

SOURCE: Data from CDC/National Center for Health Statistics, March 30, 2018.

of the mother's diet, smoking or other drug use by the mother during pregnancy, and lack of prenatal care. After the neonatal period (the first three months), the higher rate of infant death among infants living in poverty is linked with a greater incidence of infectious diseases. Such diseases, in turn, are associated with poor sanitation and lack of access to high-quality medical care, as well as with drug use in some cases.

The High Cost of Health Care

2.4 Review the reasons for the high costs of health care.

Unequal access to health care is related to its cost which, in the past several decades, has been very high. In fact, because of the rapidly increasing cost of medical care in recent years, the U.S. health care system is often said to be in crisis. Problems such as containing hospital expenses and the costs of new diagnostic technologies, the cost of prescription drugs, the effects of malpractice lawsuits, and problems with managed care and other medical insurance systems are all specific aspects of the general crisis in health care economics in the United States. Other nations have some of the same problems and some different ones, depending on how they fund their health care systems, but this analysis focuses primarily on conditions in the United States.

In 2017, U.S. health care spending reached $3.5 trillion, or about $10,500 per person (Centers for Medicare and Medicaid Services, 2018). Yet, most Americans are likely to spend an even higher proportion of their incomes on health care in coming years. Declining personal incomes due to global wage competition; dwindling government resources at the state and federal levels; the steady arrival of new drugs, new procedures, and advanced technologies; the continued profit motive in providing health care; and the difficulty of persuading people to change risky behaviors continue to make health care unaffordable for many people. As shown in Figure 2–5, even people with health insurance are concerned about the high cost of health insurance, copayments, and deductibles. The problem is that, even with insurance, many people must pay large sums of money for care.

Figure 2–5 Among the Insured, the Percent Who Find It Difficult to Afford...

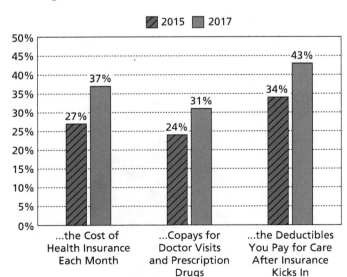

SOURCE: Based on DiJulio, B. et al. "Data Note: Americans' Challenges with Health Care Costs," Henry J. Kaiser Family Foundation (March 2, 2017).

What are the consequences of medical debt?

Jackie, age 51, went for a routine checkup and mammogram, and the doctor was concerned about a lump in one of her breasts. Further tests revealed cancer. As Jackie tells it, she is not sure which caused her greater stress, the cancer or the continuous flow of medical bills demanding immediate payment, which she refers to as "a complete nightmare." Jackie has insurance, but it covered only part of her very expensive and lengthy treatment. To help cover costs, she withdrew $48,000 out of her retirement account; it had taken her over 11 years to save that amount, and the withdrawal left her without any retirement cushion. But the bills continued to mount and the creditors began to call day and night, hounding her for payment. She sold her car and earned $14,000 for it, and the money went straight to medical bills. At one point, things were so dire that Jackie wondered whether she should go without treatment, risking possible death, but instead, a friend suggested that she ask her mortgage company whether they would revise her loan and lower the monthly payment on her house. They turned her down, and Jackie subsequently skipped a few payments. The skipped payments resulted in foreclosure proceedings. Jackie hoped she would be better able to pay past debts, as well as her ongoing care, if she didn't pay the mortgage so, as she put it, "I let them take the house."

Jackie's story reveals that there are many consequences to the high cost of medicine and medical debt, including damaged credit, economic deprivation, depleted savings and other long-term assets, and housing instability. Some people file for bankruptcy, and others are forced to go without the care they need. These consequences can lead to grave emotional distress (Pollitz et al., 2014).

Specifically, what about health care costs so much? Many salient facts about and trends in health care costs can be gleaned from a careful look at Figure 2–6 (Centers for Medicare & Medicaid Services, 2018). Notice that the largest expenditures are for hospital care and physicians' clinical services.

2.4.1 Hospitals

Until the mid-1980s, hospital costs rose at a dramatic pace, primarily because hospitals had little incentive to keep costs down. This situation was aggravated by health insurance programs like Blue Cross, which enabled hospitals to raise their fees almost at will. Expensive medical technologies are another important factor in the increase

What Do You Think?

Why do you think medicine costs so much? This situation hasn't always been the case. Brainstorm to come up with at least five reasons why health care is so expensive. Then compare your answers with those provided in the text.

Figure 2–6 Distribution of National Health Expenditures, by Type of Service (in Billions), 2016

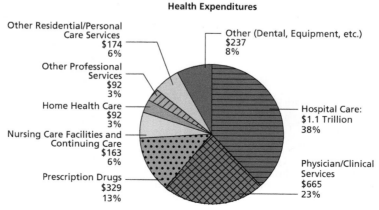

Health Expenditures

Other Residential/Personal Care Services $174 6%

Other Professional Services $92 3%

Home Health Care $92 3%

Nursing Care Facilities and Continuing Care $163 6%

Prescription Drugs $329 13%

Other (Dental, Equipment, etc.) $237 8%

Hospital Care: $1.1 Trillion 38%

Physician/Clinical Services $665 23%

SOURCE: Based on Centers for Medicare & Medicaid Services, January 8, 2018.

in hospital costs, as is the aging of the population, which increases the demand for hospital services.

In recent years, the rate of increase in hospital costs slowed somewhat, largely because of improvements in the efficiency of hospital administration that have been brought about largely by federal and state legislation. One technique used to reduce the level of hospital costs is to lower the average length of hospital stays. Some critics argue that patients are pushed out too early. Stories have circulated in the media of hospitals bussing patients out of the area to avoid further costs (Hubert, Reese, and Sanders, 2013). In addition, many procedures that previously were performed on an inpatient basis have been moved to outpatient and office settings. Other factors in the reduction of the overall level of hospital care are greater use of second opinions and an increase in care by nonhospital providers such as nursing homes and home health agencies.

Unfortunately, these various measures to control costs have not been successful. And as more patients are treated outside of hospitals or stay in hospitals for shorter periods, the costs of home care of the ill are rising rapidly. Another problem is that severe measures to reduce hospital costs disproportionately affect the poor and the elderly, who are more likely to suffer from chronic illnesses that may require hospitalization. These and similar situations illustrate the tendency of cost-control efforts in one area to result in higher costs elsewhere, and they provide an argument for comprehensive reform of the nation's health care system.

2.4.2 Physicians

During much of the twentieth century, a shortage of physicians, together with an increasing demand for medical services, helped doctors command high fees. The supply of doctors has grown significantly since 1950, but this growth has not necessarily led to improved access to medical care or to lower costs. Understanding the distribution of physicians will indicate why. People living in cities and suburbs can find both general and specialized medical care. These places also tend to be more attractive than rural locales to physicians. Even in densely settled urban areas, poor sections may have too few practicing physicians. As a result, physicians who engage in private practice tend to be clustered in metropolitan and wealthier suburban areas, producing shortages elsewhere. For example, there are roughly 31 physicians for every 10,000 people in urban areas, but only 13 per 10,000 people in rural areas. And those 13 physicians are highly dispersed (National Rural Health Association, 2018).

Contrary to what many Americans believe, the share of health care dollars that goes to doctors and clinical services has remained relatively steady over recent years, but they are and will remain a significant share of the nation's health care expenditures. An important component of these services is the cost of medical specialization. Less than one-third of physicians are general practitioners, and the remainder are specialists (Agency for Healthcare Research and Quality, 2014). One reason for the high degree of specialization is the rapid increase in medical knowledge, which means that physicians can become especially competent only in limited areas. Another reason is that high-quality medical care often requires the availability of specialists. The fact remains, however, that specialists command more income than doctors who engage in primary care. A specialist's income may be double or triple that of a general practitioner, although some effort is being made to limit Medicare and Medicaid payments to specialists while increasing payments made to primary care practitioners. Specialization also increases costs in another way; patients must consult several physicians for a variety of ailments instead of one physician for all of them. Visiting several different specialists multiplies the cost of treatment many times, whereas a primary care practitioner can coordinate care for the patient, resulting in greater continuity and ultimately better care.

2.4.3 Malpractice

One factor in the high cost of physicians' services is the cost of malpractice insurance. Fees vary but range from around $9,000 a year for a general practitioner in the South, to over $100,000 for an OB-Gyn in the Northeast (Gallagher Health Care, December, 2017). Malpractice litigation has become more frequent for several reasons. Ineffective health insurance programs play a significant role. If more people were adequately covered, they would be less likely to go to court to recover their health care costs. The increasing sophistication of medical technology also plays a part in the rise of malpractice litigation. Although recent advances enable doctors to perform treatments that once would have seemed miraculous, the treatments can be more hazardous for the patients if they are performed incorrectly or without sufficient skill and care. Public expectations about the powers of modern medicine also increase the likelihood of malpractice suits.

2.4.4 Medical Technologies

Steadily improving medical technologies, many of which can prolong life, are another reason for high medical costs. The list of advanced medical technologies that did not exist a few decades ago is impressive. It includes invasive cardiology (e.g., open heart surgery and angioplasty), renal dialysis, noninvasive imaging (e.g., sonograms, CAT scans, and MRI imaging), complex infertility treatments, organ transplantation, intra-ocular lens implants, motorized wheelchairs, and biotechnologies that are yielding new but costly drugs. Although some technologies may reduce the costs of health care, most studies indicate that they have caused total health care spending to rise because they are very expensive to purchase and operate, and are overused (Clemens, 2017; Henry J. Kaiser Family Foundation, 2012; Rosenthal, 2014). For example, the Hastings Institute, a nonpartisan health research organization, claims that new or increased use of medical technology is responsible for at least 40 to 50 percent of the annual rise in health care costs. Although medical technology and expertise have dramatically advanced, it has not necessarily resulted in a higher quality of life for patients.

2.4.5 Prescription Drugs

The cost of prescription drugs is a large and growing factor in the high cost of health care. The amount of money spent on prescription drugs in the United States far exceeds that in all other countries, largely driven by brand-name drug prices that have been increasing in recent years at rates far beyond the consumer price index (Kesselheim, Avorn, and Sarpatwari, 2016). Even generic drugs, which consumers turn to because of their cost savings, have skyrocketed in price (Hirst, 2014; Wouters, Kanavos, and McKee, 2017). Throughout the industrialized world, advances in pharmaceutical research and technologies are bringing new and more effective drugs to market each year. These remedies often result in major savings for employers and individuals when measured in terms of lower rates of absence from work. But their costs threaten to accelerate the rate of increase in overall medical expenses. Total spending for prescription drugs increased over the past decade, due especially to the demand for new drugs to combat depression, allergies, arthritis, hypertension, and elevated cholesterol. In most other developed nations, the national government negotiates drug prices with drug companies to ensure lower costs for consumers. However, in the United States, the government only gets involved in drug price negotiations associated with federal health programs, such as Medicare or Medicaid. For most people who get insurance through an employer, purchase it privately, or have no insurance (and therefore have to pay the full cost for prescription drugs themselves), there is no federal negotiation, and drug companies are generally free to set their own pricing. Although drug companies say that the prices are justified by the high cost of drug development, there is no evidence of an association between research costs and prices; rather, prescription drugs are priced in the United States primarily on the basis of what the market will bear (Kesselheim, Avorn, and Sarpatwari, 2016).

2.4.6 Demographic Factors

Another set of explanations for the high cost of American health care can be traced to demographic factors. Among the primary demographic factors influencing the cost of health care is the aging of the U.S. population, a phenomenon that is mirrored in many parts of the world but is particularly salient in Western urban industrial nations. Although the rapid increase in the older population—people 65 years or older—will be discussed more fully in Chapter 9, let me say here that they number over 50 million people (Administration on Aging, 2017). They represent about 1 in every 7 Americans. Projections suggest that the number of elderly will almost double to approximately 98 million by 2060.

Why is the number of older people in our society growing so quickly? The rapid aging of the U.S. population is being driven by two realities: First, Americans are living longer than in previous decades and, given the post–World War II baby boom, there are proportionately more older adults than in previous generations. Many Americans are now living into their seventies, eighties, and beyond. The leading edge of the baby boomers reached age 65 in 2011, launching an unparalleled phenomenon in the United States. Now, each and every day for the next 20 years, roughly 10,000 Americans will celebrate their sixty-fifth birthdays. By 2030, when the last baby boomer turns 65, the demographic landscape of our nation will have changed significantly.

The second reason for the large growth in older persons is that the baby boom cohort, the generation of Americans born in the 15–20 year period after World War II, is reaching old age. As this large segment of the population passed through the life span, it exerted a strong influence on national social issues—school shortages when they were young, social activism when they were college-age, and the growth of suburbia when they wanted to raise families. Now entering their retirement years, they are becoming more concerned about health care and income security. Members of this cohort are living longer than previous generations and are likely to require costly medical services as they encounter the chronic illnesses of old age. The resulting pressure from the large number of elderly challenges the Social Security and Medicare systems

Marie and Gabrielle are twins celebrating their birthday. People who live to be 100 years old, centenarians, used to be rare, but that is no longer the case. However, these two may be the oldest twins on record.

NICOLAS LAMBERT/AFP/Getty Images

(Greenwald, Copeland, and VanDerhei, 2017; Henry J. Kaiser Family Foundation, 2017a). Even more striking, the number of people often referred to as the "oldest-old"—those people age 85 and over—are the fastest growing age cohort in the United States. Today they number about 6.54 million, but in 2050, they are estimated to number about 14.6 million (Administration on Aging, 2017). It is these older people who will likely consume a great deal of costly health care in their last years of life.

2.4.7 Cultural Factors

In addition to demographics, cultural factors also contribute to the high cost of health care in the United States. Cultural factors refer to specific ways of life, beliefs, and norms of behavior that may contribute to health or illness. Cultural factors that raise the cost of health care in the United States include aspects of lifestyle such as heavy use of tobacco and alcohol; unhealthy diet; high stress; and sedentary activities like driving, using computers and phones, and watching television and, at the opposite extreme, high-risk activities that increase the likelihood of broken bones and orthopedic surgery. The discussion here highlights several of these specific important factors that affect our health and well-being and contribute to health care costs.

OBESITY   It is strange to think that many people around the world are very sick or even dying because of lack of food, while here in the United States our trouble is that we consume too much food. Obesity is a social problem. It affects many people and has serious consequences not only for the individuals involved but also for society as a whole.

For adults, overweight and obesity ranges are determined by using weight and height to calculate a number called the "body mass index" (BMI). For most people, BMI correlates with their amount of body fat.

- An adult who has a BMI between 25 and 29.9 is considered overweight.
- An adult who has a BMI of 30 or higher is considered obese.

See Table 2–2 for an example of BMI calculation (CDC, 2016).

Today, about 71 percent of Americans age 20 and over are overweight, including about 38 percent who are obese (National Center for Health Statistics, 2017). Among children, one-third are overweight, and 17 percent are obese (Fryar, Carroll, and Ogden, 2016). However, we have not always been such an overweight group. In the past several decades, obesity has become much more prevalent among Americans than it was during the mid-twentieth century.

Why are people obese? It may seem obvious—people eat too many high calorie foods. But obesity is also related to a sedentary lifestyle. Some people talk about genetics as a probable cause. Genetic changes in human populations occur too slowly to be responsible for the obesity epidemic. Further evidence against genetics is the fact that while first-generation immigrants who come to the United States usually have normal weight, second-generation Americans are often overweight or obese. Nevertheless, the variation in how people respond to the environment that

Table 2–2 An Example of Calculating BMI to Determine Weight Category

Height	Weight Range	BMI	Considered
5'9"	124 lb or less	Below 18.5	Underweight
5'9"	125 lb to 168 lb	18.5 to 24.9	Healthy weight
5'9"	169 lb to 202 lb	25.0 to 29.9	Overweight
5'9"	203 lb or more	30 or higher	Obese

NOTE: BMI (body mass index).

SOURCE: Based on CDC, June 16, 2016.

promotes physical inactivity and intake of high-calorie foods suggests that genes do play a role in the development of obesity. Obesity may also be related to illness (e.g., Cushing disease) and medication taken (e.g., steroids, some antidepressants) (CDC, 2018c).

Obesity is a social problem because of the widespread nature of the epidemic, its considerable financial costs, the toll it takes on health, and the connections between obesity and food production and distribution in our country. Major health and social impacts of obesity include the following:

Obesity is a unique problem found primarily in developed countries. While many people in the world struggle to find enough food, Americans in particular face an obesity epidemic.

- Obesity increases the risk of illness from about thirty serious medical conditions.
- Obesity is associated with increases in deaths from all causes.
- Earlier onset of obesity-related diseases such as type 2 diabetes is being reported in obese children and adolescents.
- Obese individuals are at higher risk for impaired mobility.
- Overweight or obese individuals experience social stigmatization and discrimination in employment and academic situations.

The CDC estimates that about 280,000 Americans die each year as a direct consequence of obesity, although the immediate causes of death are quite varied. Heart disease, diabetes, and stroke are especially prevalent consequences of obesity. Second only to smoking as a cause of illness and death, obesity, like smoking, is directly related to trends in individual behavior—and, many critics would add, to the influence of corporations that market unhealthy foods to eager consumers. Conditions of overweight and obesity and their associated health problems have a significant economic impact on the health care system. Medical costs associated with overweight and obesity conditions may involve direct and indirect costs. Direct medical costs may include preventive, diagnostic, and treatment services related to obesity. Indirect costs relate to illness and mortality costs. Illness costs are defined as the value of income lost from decreased productivity, restricted activity, absenteeism, and bed days. Mortality costs are the value of future income lost by premature death (CDC, 2018c).

SMOKING On January 11, 1964, Luther L. Terry, M.D., the ninth Surgeon General of the United States, released the first report on the health consequences of smoking: Smoking and Health: Report of the Advisory Committee of the Surgeon General of the Public Health Service. That report marked a major step in reducing the adverse impact of tobacco use on health worldwide by highlighting its many dangers and addictive qualities. The tobacco companies fought long and hard to discredit these findings (Proctor, 2012). Some catchy slogans they came up with to promote their products include the following (Stanford Research into the Impact of Advertising, 2014):

- "Smoke like a chimney? Who cares? Your mouth will taste clean as a whistle"[1]
- "We don't try to scare you with medical claims"
- "Sensitive throats welcome Luckies"
- "Inhale to your heart's content"
- "More doctors smoke Camels than any other cigarette"

And perhaps the most famous slogan targeted women, tying smoking to liberation: "You've come a long way, baby."

---

[1]Stanford Research into the Impact of Tobacco Advertising. 2014. "Slogans." Retrieved from (tobacco. stanford.edu/tobacco_main/slogans.php).

More than fifty years have now passed since that seminal report was published. During this period, over 30 Surgeon General's reports have offered the latest available scientific evidence to demonstrate the negative health consequences of smoking and involuntary exposure to tobacco smoke. The conclusions from these reports have evolved from a few causal associations in 1964 to a robust body of evidence documenting the irrefutable health consequences from both active smoking and exposure to secondhand smoke across a wide range of diseases and vital organ systems. Smoking is a leading contributor to lung cancer, heart disease, stroke, chronic obstructive pulmonary disease, premature and low birth weight babies, diabetes, and many other cancers and illnesses (American Cancer Society, 2018; American Lung Association, 2018; CDC, February 20, 2018b).

In a nutshell, smoking kills. Worldwide, smoking kills more than 7 million people each year. More than 6 million of those deaths are the result of direct tobacco use while around 890,000 are the result of non-smokers being exposed to second-hand smoke (World Health Organization, March, 2018b). In the United States, tobacco is responsible for almost 500,000 deaths per year, and more than 16 million are living with a disease caused by smoking (CDC, Feburary 20, 2018b).

Despite denials by the tobacco industry, people gradually listened to the official reports and public service announcements highlighting the dangers of smoking. The share of the adult population who smoke declined from 42 percent to 16 percent during the 52-year period between 1964, following the first report by the Surgeon General, and 2016. Men were the first to decrease their smoking behaviors, and then women followed. Today there are more former than current smokers; however, the decline has slowed in recent years. Smoking remains popular among specific groups, as revealed in Table 2–3. In particular, men, Native Americans, those people with lower levels of income, adults between ages 25 and 64, and those who live in the Midwest are most likely to smoke (CDC, February 15, 2018a).

Table 2–3 Who Is Most Likely to Smoke? (2016)

Sex	
Male	18%
Female	14%
Race/Ethnicity	
White	17%
Black	17%
Hispanic	11%
American Indian/Alaska Native	32%
Asian	9%
Age	
18–24	13%
25–44	18%
45–64	18%
65+	9%
Poverty Status	
At or Above Poverty Level	14%
Below Poverty Level	25%
Region	
Northeast	13%
Midwest	19%
South	17%
West	13%

SOURCE: Data from CDC, February 15, 2018.

Smoking remains the leading high-risk behavior associated with poor health, untimely death, and extremely high health care costs. In fact, smoking-related illness in the United States costs more than $300 billion each year, including nearly $170 billion for direct medical care and over $156 billion in lost productivity, including $5.6 billion in lost productivity due to secondhand smoke (CDC, November 16, 2017).

Most smokers begin as adolescents (CDC, March 26, 2018d). In consequence, many health experts consider preventing tobacco use among young people, or getting them to quit, to be among the nation's most important health challenges. School programs and public service announcements are specifically designed to target youth. Efforts have been somewhat successful, with smoking rates among young people declining significantly over the past couple of decades. However, it remains that 8 percent of high school students smoked cigarettes at least once within the past 30 days, and 20 percent have used some type of tobacco product during this period (e.g., electronic cigarettes, cigars, or smokeless tobacco). This use by young people is not surprising given the tremendous marketing efforts targeted at them. In 2015, tobacco companies spent $8.9 billion marketing cigarettes and smokeless tobacco in the United States. This amount translates to more than $24 million each day, or about $1 million every hour (CDC, November 16, 2017).

RISKY BEHAVIORS AND COSTLY PROCEDURES Costly injuries due to skiing, rock climbing, mountain biking, skateboarding, and roller blading are associated with higher-income adolescents and young adults. Sports injuries are only one of many examples reflecting how features of American culture drive up the cost of medical care and health insurance. American culture, more than those of other highly developed societies, emphasizes seeking the most up-to-date medical treatments, whether those treatments have proven helpful. Bone marrow transplants to fight advanced cancers, hormone replacement therapy for women after menopause, and the indiscriminate use of MRI or CAT scans are all examples of expensive procedures or practices that increase costs for all health care consumers. At the same time, Americans have shown great reluctance to support any health care system that would limit their ability to seek whatever medical treatment they desire; this mindset drives up the cost of insurance and means that people who are less able to pay medical bills will postpone important preventive treatments.

What Do You Think?

Do you know someone who smokes? How does he or she justify it, given the scientific evidence outlining the health dangers?

Ethical Issues

2.5 **Summarize the ethical issues surrounding health care.**

As medical technology has improved, and life-prolonging procedures have become more available and dependable, many complex ethical issues have arisen, and our society is only beginning to grapple with them. For example, some new technologies, such as heart and kidney transplants, are extremely costly and cannot be provided to all patients who might benefit from them. Thus, the question arises of how to choose the patients who will undergo these procedures.

The availability of life-prolonging equipment and procedures has also given rise to new questions about the meaning of life and death. State legislatures across the country have been debating the question of whether death occurs when the heart stops beating or when the brain stops functioning. Courts have been required to decide whether patients should have the right to die by terminating life-prolonging treatments.

2.5.1 End-of-Life Issues

Few aspects of health care are as fraught with emotion and confusion as those dealing with how and under what circumstances loved ones die. On one side of the issue are people who believe in the "right to die." Many people have concerns about how they will

euthanasia

The painless killing of a patient suffering from a terminal illness or irreversible coma.

die and suggest that the emphasis by medicine and society on intervention and cure has sometimes come at the expense of good end-of-life care. They claim that people should be able to commit suicide and have others assist them in doing so. **Euthanasia** refers to the painless killing of a patient suffering from a terminal illness or irreversible coma.

Michigan doctor Jack Kevorkian became the personification of the right-to-die issue when he helped a 54-year-old woman with Alzheimer's disease kill herself, using an intravenous device that allowed the patient to receive a lethal drug by pressing a button. The doctor was arrested and charged with first-degree murder; later the charges were dropped, but the doctor was ordered to refrain from using the suicide device in the future. Kevorkian continued to defy the authorities in Michigan and eventually was sentenced to a term in prison. Although many doctors and health authorities condemned the practice at the time, Kevorkian's sensational methods brought the right-to-die issue to national attention.

Today Oregon, Montana, Vermont, Washington, Hawaii, California, Colorado, and Washington D.C. have laws that permit some form of physician-assisted suicide. It's estimated that only a couple of thousand people have used this option. The American College of Physicians oppose physician-assisted suicide, stating instead, "Society's focus at the end of life should be on efforts to address suffering and the needs of patients and families, including improving access to effective hospice and palliative care"[2] (Sulmasy and Mueller, 2017). Nonetheless, physician-assisted suicide has the support of more than two-thirds of American adults, including 81 percent of adults under age 35 (Dugan, 2015).

As the populations of the urban industrial nations continue to age and given the appearance of ever more sophisticated methods for prolonging life, the number of ethical, legal, and technical questions about life's end grows. Imagine that your elderly parent has had a stroke. Doctors express little hope that consciousness can be restored or that life-support systems could be removed without causing death. This scenario is not a rare situation. Unless your family and the terminally ill parent have prepared **advance directives** (a written statement that explains the patient's wishes for medical care should the person be unable to communicate them to the physician) for dealing with the situation, much agony and prolonged suffering can ensue for everyone concerned. Advance directives have two parts: a living will, which tells doctors and hospitals how the patient wants to be cared for should he or she become terminally ill, and a health care proxy, which designates an advocate, usually a close family member, who can make sure that those wishes are honored.

advance directive

A written statement that explains the patient's wishes for medical care should the person be unable to communicate them to the physician.

Explanations of Health Care Problems

2.6 **Classify explanations for health care problems.**

Why do we have such difficulty improving the quality of health care services and providing more equal access to them? The explanations offered by medical sociologists depend to a large extent on the perspective from which they view the problem. Conflict theorists, for example, tend to view the problem as an inherent feature of tensions associated with capitalism: The poor get less medical care because they get less of everything in American society. Those who approach this question from a functionalist perspective have sought the answers in medicine's development into a complex and costly social institution. And from an interactionist perspective, many problems of health care in the United States and other highly developed nations can be traced to cultural factors, including the way people are taught to interact with one another. (See Figure 2–7.) In this section, each of these approaches to the explanation of health care problems is briefly discussed.

---

[2]Sulmasy, L. S. and Mueller, P. S. (2017) "Ethics and the Legalization of Physician-Assisted Suicide: An American College of Physicians Position Paper," *Annals of Internal Medicine,* 167(8):576–578.

Figure 2–7 Three Approaches to Explaining Social Problems in Health

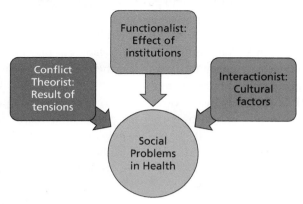

2.6.1 Class and Class Conflict

Sociologists often point out that social class, measured by the income and wealth a household has at its disposal, goes a long way toward explaining the types of illnesses experienced by members of that household and the kinds of health care they receive. We have already suggested that lack of access to good health care causes higher rates of illness and death among those who are poor. Until the early twentieth century, the ill health of poor people was caused largely by infectious diseases. Today, medical science can control and cure such diseases much more effectively, with the result that, by themselves, those diseases no longer account for tremendous differences in health between those who are poor and those who are not. Instead, the chief obstacles to good health in developed nations are lack of access to good health care, inadequate knowledge about health, failure to take preventive medical action, and delay in seeking treatment, all of which are especially prevalent among poor people (Weitz, 2017).

In fact, as control of chronic diseases like cancer becomes more important, the differences between the health of those who are poor and those who are not are likely to increase; that is, poor people will still have higher rates of illness and death than people who are not poor because of their relative lack of access to high-quality health care.

In a classic analysis of the relationship between social class and ill health, Lee Rainwater (1974) introduced the idea that lack of access to health care is not the only factor that affects the health of poor people: Just being poor promotes poor health. Poor people, for example, cannot afford to eat properly, so they are likely to be weak. They often live in the most polluted areas and hence are susceptible to respiratory diseases. Because they cannot afford proper housing, they are exposed to disease-carrying refuse and rodents. Perhaps most important, their lives are filled with stress due to constant worry about getting enough money to pay for necessities. Such long-term stress can cause both physical and mental illness. Being poor also makes it difficult to react to minor signs of ill health. A cough is likely to be dismissed if one does not have enough to eat; only a much worse cough will prompt a visit to a clinic, and by then it may be too late. Poor people also seem to feel middle-aged earlier than those who are not poor.

Social scientists who see class conflict as a basic cause of social-class differences in health and unequal access to health care are skeptical of the increasing privatization of the American health care system. They point out that, as public hospitals are replaced by hospitals run for profit, there is a tendency to avoid treatment of less profitable patients (Wangsness, 2009).

Studies have shown that, as more hospitals are managed by for-profit corporations (as opposed to the public sector), they are indeed more likely to be concerned about earning money and less concerned with providing medical care for patients, particularly those less likely to be able to pay, who require more expensive treatments such as drug counseling, suicide prevention, and AIDS therapy (Ferdinand, Epane, and Menachemi, 2014; Kutscher, 2014). Both public and private hospitals share the duty to accept all patients who require emergency care, but private hospitals can decide to eliminate their emergency facilities altogether, and the requirement for emergency care does not extend to nonemergencies.

Social scientists who view health care problems from a conflict perspective often explain the outcomes of conflicts over medical policy in terms of conflict between classes. For example, in an early study of the social, political, and psychological impact of AIDS in America, Dennis Altman (1987) showed that, as long as AIDS was perceived as a disease of homosexuals and intravenous drug users, members of the middle and upper classes did not put pressure on the government to invest heavily in its treatment and cure. Altman and others have pointed out that, because AIDS strikes disproportionately at less advantaged citizens and members of minority groups, it is often thought of as "their" disease, which was especially true in the beginning years of the epidemic.

2.6.2 Institutions and Health Care

Functionalist explanations of health care problems focus on features of health care institutions themselves. Sociologists with this institutional orientation point out that every society is faced with the problem of distributing health care services among its members. The United States uses a marketplace approach, which views health care as a commodity subject to the demands and spending power of consumers. Canada, by contrast, views health care as an entitlement of citizenship and extends full coverage to all its legal residents (HealthCanada, April 4, 2018).

There are several functionalist arguments for why a service that has come to be viewed as a basic human right, such as health care, should not be treated as a commodity:

- *Information.* A consumer is not in a position to shop for medical treatment in the same way that one shops for other products or services because the need for such treatment cannot be evaluated by the consumer.
- *Product uncertainty.* The consumer does not have sufficient knowledge to judge the effectiveness of sophisticated treatments.
- *Norms of treatment.* Health care is provided under the control of a physician. A patient does not direct his or her own treatment.
- *Lack of price competition.* Prices for doctors' services are not advertised and are not subject to true competition.
- *Restricted entry.* There are numerous barriers to entry to medical school. Many qualified applicants are turned down because of a limited number of places.
- *Professional dominance.* Many health care services restricted to physicians could be performed by trained technicians. This restriction has created a monopoly.
- *Misallocated supply.* An abundance of specialists encourages the use of expensive and sophisticated treatments when simpler ones would be just as effective.

2.6.3 Health and Social Interaction

The relatively poor health of Americans is due in part to features of our lifestyle, including sedentary occupations, nonnutritious diets, lack of proper exercise, environmental pollution, and cigarette smoking (Weitz, 2017). But if activities like smoking are detrimental to health, why do people engage in them? Interactionist explanations of social problems related to health care often draw on studies of patterns of sociability (i.e., interaction among people in groups) and the ways in which people are socialized in different societies and communities. Features of a society's lifestyle, such as smoking, drinking, and diet, are deeply ingrained in the way people interact with one another. Very often we eat, drink, or smoke as much to be sociable as to sustain ourselves.

Excessive eating, leading to obesity, and high rates of alcohol consumption are among the health problems related to patterns of sociability in an affluent society. But as noted earlier, the most pervasive and serious problems are created by smoking. In addition, women may expose unborn infants to the negative effects of smoking, especially low birth weight.

Interactionist perspectives on issues like smoking and health typically focus on the way communications (e.g., advertising images and messages) seek to connect the use of tobacco with particular lifestyles. For example, vaping advertisements targeted to young adults are often sleek and glamorous, showing independent and free thinkers as they vape.

It is helpful to think of the major sociological perspectives as conceptual tools to be used in analyzing a complex social problem such as the prevention and treatment of physical illnesses. No single perspective explains all the important issues, but together they go a long way toward a full explanation. The functionalist view is most helpful in pointing out how social institutions like hospitals should function, why they do not function effectively, and how they could be improved. The conflict perspective allows for more insight into the influence of inequalities of wealth, education, and power on access to and quality of health care. The interactionist perspective points to the way differences in people's perception of social conditions such as the obesity epidemic influence their behavior toward others, as explored in *A Personal View: "My Experience with Obesity."*

Kim Steele/Alamy Stock Photo

Interactionists are interested in how messages are communicated. Not only do tobacco companies try to create visual images (e.g., smoking as glamorous, or smokers as "cool"), the government tries to create visual images as well. The words "slow" and "painful" have been deliberately chosen by the U.S. Surgeon General to make a larger impact.

A Personal View

My Experience with Obesity

Daisy-Daisy/Alamy Stock Photo

I was a very pudgy kid. I didn't know I was overweight until I went to school. Until then I was happy and enjoying all the rich and sugary foods my momma would make. "These will taste yummy," she used to say, as we devoured two dozen chocolate chip cookies in one sitting. Momma was obese, weighing in at more than 300 pounds. But I never noticed. She was what you might call a binge eater. She said it calmed her nerves. And I learned this habit early in life.

By the time I went to kindergarten I weighed nearly 80 pounds. I was much heavier than any other child, but I continued not to notice. I did see that I was the slowest one at PE, and I seemed to huff and puff more than the others, but I didn't give it much thought. That is, until Brian Hemling, the class clown, called me "fatso" when I stood in line to get a drink of water. "Hey fatso, don't drink all the water. Save some for the rest of us." He laughed, and soon several other kids joined in. I felt so embarrassed. I knew what the word fat meant; I just hadn't noticed that I fit the description. But that day changed my life, and not for the better.

Instead of being the happy child I used to be, I began a slow descent into depression. I hated school. A few people were mean to me, but most just ignored me. I didn't have any friends. I was always the last one picked for a team in PE, or the last one picked as a square-dancing partner in third grade. When the teacher decided to start assigning partners, all the boys had their eye on me, hoping that I would be assigned to someone else.

I consoled myself with food. This was easy to do because my momma continued to have fattening foods around the house, and together we would binge on what was available. A large bag of potato chips? No problem. I'd wash it down with a coke and ice cream. Of course, this only made my weight continue to skyrocket.

When I was in seventh grade I had to go to the doctor to get a physical for summer camp. I hadn't been to the doctor in years, and I was embarrassed to take off my clothes in front of her. At this point I weighed almost 190 pounds. But the doctor saw my shyness and was actually really kind about it. However, she also told me directly that I was overweight and needed to be on a special weight loss program. She asked a lot of questions: What foods does my mom buy? What do we eat for dinner? Do we eat in front of the TV? What do I snack on? She called my mother into the room to discuss diet, exercise, and fitness. Then she made us agree to sign me up for a special class designed to help teens with weight loss. This day also changed my life, this time for the better.

I met new friends from the class and was now no longer lonely. Together we had weekly weigh-ins that were made into celebrations, not punishments. We socialized outdoors and exercised: We hiked, biked, and swam our way to fitness. We took cooking classes; if our parents didn't want to cook healthy foods, then we would do it ourselves. It worked! The pounds came off, and within eleven months I was down to my desired weight.

Fortunately, my mom supported my changes, although she did not incorporate them for herself. She remains obese, and now has diabetes, among other health problems. Her feet swell badly, which makes daily life difficult for her. Even working her eight-hour day is tough, and she has missed a lot of work because of her health. I wish she would get serious about losing weight.

—Elise, Age 18

Critical Thinking

Why is there stigma surrounding obesity? Is obesity seen as a medical problem or a personal failing?

Social Policy

2.7 **Identify key issues in social policy, including the Affordable Care Act.**

All developed nations are having difficulty coping with the demands on their health care systems, demands brought on by aging populations with more chronic illnesses. None of them has found easy solutions or avoided the need for compromises and less-than-perfect solutions. But in the United States—as compared with Canada, France,

Germany, England, and the Scandinavian nations—there is an even greater lag in arriving at reforms of health care institutions that address the major problems.

2.7.1 Health Care Reform in the United States: The Affordable Care Act (ACA)

With health costs spiraling upward far faster than the rate of inflation and the number of uninsured steadily increasing, there has long been debate about what to do. President Obama was not the first to tackle health care reform, but in 2010 he was successful in signing into law the **Affordable Care Act (ACA)**. Nicknamed "Obamacare," the ACA mandated the first major overhaul of the U.S. health care system since the creation of Medicare and Medicaid in 1965.

The ACA is complex, but Table 2–4 outlines some of the major provisions (Henry J. Kaiser Family Foundation, 2015).

As soon as the bill was passed, several important measures took immediate effect. Adults and children who were previously denied coverage due to preexisting conditions became eligible for access to health care. Children up to age 26 could stay on their parents' health insurance plan. Small businesses that offer insurance to their employees got a 35 percent tax credit from premiums paid, making it much easier for many small businesses to afford health insurance for their employees.

Other components of the ACA were incorporated more slowly. By 2014, the ACA was in full effect, increasing the number of persons with health insurance by millions. The number of people without insurance fell from 50 million in 2010 to 29 million in 2017. The ACA modeled the strategy of the successful Massachusetts health care system, which requires all citizens to have medical insurance. This individual mandate helps to keep the overall costs down by requiring a very large pool of both healthy and sick people to have insurance. If only a few very sick people had insurance, for instance, health care costs would soar trying to cover their costs. Therefore, in 2014, an IRS penalty of $750 per individual or 2 percent of income—whichever is greater— went into effect for any citizen not covered by an employer or a public plan such as Medicaid or Medicare, and who chooses not to purchase health insurance.

Despite bringing health insurance to millions of people, the program remained somewhat controversial, with Republicans vowing to repeal it; a chant that became especially pronounced during the 2016 Presidential election. "Repeal and Replace" was the Republican slogan, although it was not clear what the ACA was supposed to be replaced with.

One reason for the unpopularity of the ACA is that many people do not know that Obamacare and the ACA are the same thing. A recent survey with a nationally representative sample of adults found that 35 percent of respondents either thought

Affordable Care Act (ACA)

Legislation developed by President Obama and passed in 2010 that is the first major overhaul of the U.S. health care system since the creation of Medicare and Medicaid in 1965.

Table 2–4 Key Components of the Affordable Care Act (ACA)

- Most individuals were required to have health insurance by 2014.
- Individuals without access to affordable employer coverage will be able to purchase coverage through a health insurance exchange with "credits" available to make coverage more affordable to some people.
- Small businesses will be able to purchase coverage through a separate exchange.
- Employers will be required to pay penalties for employees who receive credits.
- New regulations will be imposed on health plans that will prevent health insurers from denying coverage to people for any reason, or for charging higher premiums based on health status or sex.
- Young adults will be allowed to stay on their parents' plan until they are 26 years old.
- Medicaid will be expanded to 133 percent of the federal poverty level (roughly $15,000 for an individual and $30,000 for a family of four).

SOURCE: Based on Henry J. Kaiser Family Foundation, 2015.

The Affordable Care Act (ACA) became highly politicized, with Republicans vowing to repeal it. Since President Trump's election, several of the basic tenets have been eroded, even though the ACA remains.

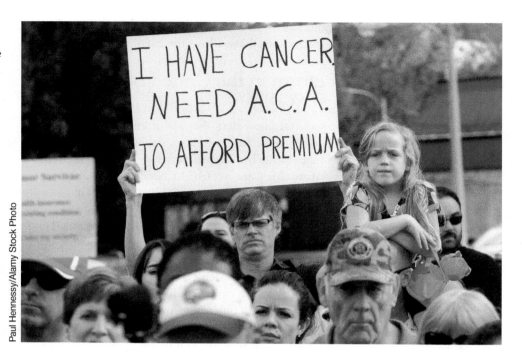

Paul Hennessy/Alamy Stock Photo

What Do You Think?

Give an example of the arguments made by people who (a) think the ACA goes too far, (b) support the ACA, and (c) think the ACA does not go far enough.

Obamacare and the ACA were different policies (17 percent) or did not know whether they were the same or different (18 percent). This confusion was more pronounced among people ages 18 to 29 and among those who earned less than $50,000—two groups that would be significantly affected by repeal. When respondents were asked what would happen if Obamacare were repealed, even more people were stumped. Approximately 45 percent did not know that the ACA would be repealed. In other words, many people denigrated Obamacare but supported the basic tenets of the ACA (Dropp and Nyhan, 2017; Linkins, 2017).

One of President Trump's signature issues during the campaign was to repeal the Affordable Care Act and replace it with an alternative. Trying to make good on that promise, President Trump turned to health care soon after the election but learned that devising an insurance program that both reduces cost *and* reduces the number of Americans who are uninsured is trickier than it seemed. The "Repeal and Replace" mantra turned into just "repeal," but this approach never quite got off the ground. All Democrats and a few Republicans opposed President Trump in eliminating the ACA, and many Americans joined in at town hall meetings around the country to tell their Congressperson to leave their health insurance alone. Consequently, anticipating failure, the Republican plan to repeal the ACA was never brought to Congress for a vote.

Since that time, however, President Trump and the Republican-led Congress have chiseled away at the ACA. For example, they have done away with the individual mandate requiring people to have (or purchase) health insurance. But this is at the heart of keeping costs controlled and increasing access to health care. The administration has also proposed to expand the availability of short-term health plans that do not guarantee minimum benefits or prohibit discrimination against consumers with preexisting health problems. While this may sound good at first ("they will be cheap"), it will again encourage healthier people to opt out of the system, leaving fewer people and those who are the sickest in the insurance pool. This would raise premiums and reduce access to care.

2.7.2 Future Prospects

single-payer

A healthcare system that is financed by taxes and covers the costs of essential healthcare services.

Senator Bernie Sanders, Vermont, has energized the conversation about health care by calling for a "single-payer" health care system, sometimes referred to in the United States as "Medicare for All." **Single-payer** is a health care system that is financed by taxes and covers the costs of essential health care for all residents including doctor, hospital, preventive, long-term care, mental health, reproductive health care, dental, vision, prescription drug, and medical supply costs. The costs are covered by a single government system. Supporters, such as the Physicians for a National Health Program (2016) argue that the program would be funded by the savings obtained from replacing today's "inefficient, profit-oriented, multiple insurance payers with a single streamlined, nonprofit, public payer, and by modest new taxes based on ability to pay."[3] It is likely that 95 percent of all households would save money. Patients would no longer face financial barriers to care such as co-pays and deductibles and would regain free choice of doctor and hospital. Doctors would regain autonomy over patient care. The only real losers, they say, are insurance companies, pharmaceutical companies, and other for-profit medical industries because they have an economic self-interest in keeping the status quo.

Going Beyond Left and Right

The broad sociological issue here is how to improve health care institutions to provide the best possible care for the greatest number of people. Most medical sociologists do not agree that health care should be treated as a commodity that is available in higher amounts and quality to those most able to afford it. But this position does not mean that they believe a single-payer system could be imported to the United States without a great deal of effort and compromise. Any attempt to reform the health care system generates intense political debate and lobbying efforts, either in Congress or in state legislatures. This has most certainly been the case with the ACA.

Summary

2.1 Describe health care as a global social problem.

The lack of adequate health measures presents a variety of social problems to societies everywhere. In affluent regions of the world, problems associated with physical health often involve reducing unequal access to high-quality health care while controlling health care costs. In impoverished regions where high-quality medical care is often lacking, social problems associated with physical health are even more profound: the spread of infectious diseases, high rates of infant and maternal death, low life expectancy, scarcity of medical personnel and equipment, and inadequate sewage and water systems.

2.2 Identify the scope of health care problems in America.

Health care is considered a social problem when members of a society have unequal access to health care institutions and when its cost is too high for people to afford. Medical sociology is the subfield of sociology that specializes in research on the health care system and its impact on the public, especially access to health care and the evolution of health care institutions.

2.3 Discuss Americans' unequal access to health care.

Access to health care is distributed very unequally in the United States. The use and availability of health care are directly related to socioeconomic class and race. People in the lower classes tend to have higher rates of untreated illnesses and disabilities and higher mortality rates for most diseases than do people in the middle and upper classes.

2.4 Review the reasons for the high costs of health care.

Unequal access to health care is related to the cost of obtaining it. Health care costs have risen significantly. The costs of hospital care, physician fees, medical technology, and prescription drugs are major contributors to the high cost of American health care. Population demographics are changing, and the number of people who are elderly and need chronic care is increasing. Cultural factors that raise the cost of health care in the United States include aspects of lifestyle such as heavy use of tobacco and alcohol, unhealthful diet, and lack of exercise. Obesity is a major health problem in the United States and other affluent nations.

---

[3]"What is Single Payer?," Physicians for a National Health Program (2016). Retrieved from http://www.pnhp.org/facts/what-is-single-payer.

2.5 Summarize the ethical issues surrounding health care.

As medical technology has improved and life-prolonging procedures have become more available and dependable, many complex ethical issues have arisen, and our society is only beginning to grapple with them. One example is end-of life issues and the dilemmas surrounding "death with dignity."

2.6 Classify explanations for health care problems.

Conflict theorists believe social class goes a long way toward explaining the types of illnesses experienced by members of a household and the kinds of health care they receive. Functionalist explanations of health care problems focus on features of health care institutions themselves. The interactionist perspective on health care problems points to the role of lifestyle features such as poor diet, lack of exercise, and smoking–including passive smoking (breathing air that contains cigarette smoke).

2.7 Identify key issues in social policy, including the Affordable Care Act.

In March 2010, Congress passed important health care reform legislation called the Affordable Care Act. It is designed to reduce the number of uninsured Americans and to lower health care costs. Under President Trump the program is being dismantled.

Chapter 3
Problems of Mental Illness and Treatment

Catchlight Visual Services/Alamy Stock Photo

Learning Objectives

3.1 Identify the ways that mental illness is a social problem.

3.2 Discuss the social construction of mental illness.

3.3 Assess inequality and differences in mental illness.

3.4 Compare treatment options for mental illness.

3.5 Explain the institutional problems of providing treatment and care.

3.6 Analyze the policy implications of the Affordable Care Act, and their aftermath, for mental illness.

I have had issues with my weight since high school. I was your average nerdy 15-year-old, and I felt hopelessly inadequate. I felt like every girl at school was prettier than I was and more popular. I was painfully shy. I was self-conscious about everything and felt like people were laughing at me behind my back.

I cannot remember how I first heard about throwing up. But I do remember the first time I did it. I was depressed, and had eaten a bag of potato chips, and I wondered if I could do it. I made my way to the bathroom, and I was sweating as I approached the toilet, lifting the seat. I looked at the toilet bowl for ... I'm not sure how long. But then I pulled my hair back, knelt over the toilet, stuck my finger down my throat, and gagged myself until I threw up. I was scared, started to cry, and felt more depressed than ever. I crawled into bed even though it was barely eight o'clock. A month or more passed until I tried it again.

That was eight years ago, and now, I can't seem to stop myself. I throw up at least twice a day. I eat only foods that will come up easily. I eat slowly and chew every bite carefully. It's like a ritual. I count the number of chews. I have a roommate so I have to be careful around her. I only eat alone. I don't like anyone to see me eating. And then, when I'm ready, I purge.

I know this is wrong, but I can't stop. It's all I think about ... when can I eat ... what should I eat ... I need to get rid of what I ate. It's constant. I know this can be dangerous, and I feel so out of control.

mental health

A state of well-being in which the individual realizes his or her own abilities, can cope with the normal stresses of life, can work productively and fruitfully, and is able to contribute to his or her community.

mental illness

A mental, behavioral, or emotional disorder (excluding developmental or substance abuse disorders), diagnosable currently or within the past year and of sufficient duration to meet diagnostic criteria specified within the fifth edition of the *Diagnostic and Statistical Manual of Mental Disorders (DSM-V).*[2]

Any Mental Illness (AMI)

A mental, behavioral, or emotional disorder.

Serious Mental Illness (SMI)

A mental, behavioral, or emotional disorder resulting in serious functional impairment, which substantially interferes with or limits one or more major life activities.

All people have days in which they feel blue, depressed, or anxious. However, for most people, these emotions are fleeting, and for the most part, their **mental health** is good, which is defined by the World Health Organization as "a state of well-being in which the individual realizes his or her own abilities, can cope with the normal stresses of life, can work productively and fruitfully, and is able to make a contribution to his or her community."[1] In other words, despite a brief episode of feeling blue, most people continue to get up in the morning, go to work, take care of a family, and maintain social roles (World Health Organization and the Calouste Gulbenkian Foundation, 2014).

Yet, for some people, this level of functioning is not possible. One of every five Americans age 18 and older has suffered, or continues to suffer, from some form of **mental illness**, defined by the National Institute of Mental Health as (National Institute of Mental Health, November, 2017a):

- A mental, behavioral, or emotional disorder (excluding developmental or substance abuse disorders); and
- Diagnosable currently, or within the past year; and
- Of sufficient duration to meet diagnostic criteria specified within the fifth edition of the *Diagnostic and Statistical Manual of Mental Disorders (DSM-V).*

There are two general categories of mental illness. The first is referred to as **Any Mental Illness (AMI)**, which is defined as a mental, behavioral, or emotional disorder. AMI can vary in impact, ranging from no impairment to mild, moderate, and even severe impairment. The second category, **Serious Mental Illness (SMI)**, is defined as a mental, behavioral, or emotional disorder resulting in serious functional impairment, which substantially interferes with or limits one or more major life activities (National Institute of Mental Health, November, 2017a).

Forty-five million adults in the United States suffer from AMI, which is roughly 18 percent of the adult population. As you can see in Figure 3–1, women are significantly more likely to suffer mental illness than are men. Also, younger people are more likely to suffer mental illness than older age groups, although, if those age 70 and over were put in their own group, they would show higher rates of mental illness. Mental disorders are the leading cause of disability for people ages 15 to 44 in the United States and throughout the world (World Health Organization, 2012). To complicate matters, nearly half of those with any mental disorder meet the criteria for two or more disorders.

---

[1]WHO (2001a). Strengthening mental health promotion. Geneva, World Health Organization (Fact sheet, No. 220).

[2]National Institute of Mental Health, November, 2017a.

Figure 3–1 Past Year Prevalence of Mental Illness Among U.S. Adults, by Sex, 2016

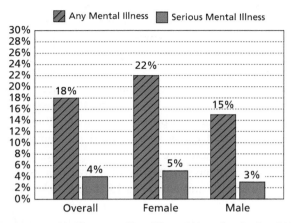

SOURCE: National Institute of Mental Health. 2017a. "Mental Illness." November. Retrieved 23 February 2018 (www.nimh.nih.gov/health/statistics/mental-illness.html).

Many people believe that mental illness is rare. They see mental illness as something that happens only to people with life situations very different from their own, and they believe it will never affect them. People with this perception of mental illness are usually thinking of SMI, such as bipolar disorder or schizophrenia. These disorders are not very common, occurring in only about 4 percent of Americans. Women and younger people have the highest rates of SMI. Unfortunately, at least a third of these individuals are not being treated for their illness (National Institute of Mental Health, November, 2017a).

However, other forms of mental illness also exist. Many millions of women, men, and children suffer from depression, anxiety, seasonal affective disorder, obsessive-compulsive disorder, dementia, attention deficit disorder (ADD) and attention deficit hyperactivity disorder (ADHD), autism spectrum disorder, and panic or eating disorders. These types of conditions are far more common than bipolar disorder or schizophrenia, and they are also considered types of mental illness (National Alliance on Mental Illness, 2015; National Institute of Mental Health, 2018).

In 2008, Congress mandated that mental illnesses be covered under existing health insurance plans just as physical illnesses are covered. But that legislation did not address the needs of the uninsured, and a sizable number of persons suffering from mental illness do not have insurance. The Affordable Care Act (ACA) passed by the U.S. Congress in 2010 expanded coverage, and no longer allowed insurers to deny coverage to someone with a pre-existing condition. In other words, the ACA expanded parity to a much wider pool, making it possible for millions more people to obtain the same coverage for substance abuse disorders and major mental illnesses as they would for heart disease or cancer. However, with the dismantling of the ACA under President Trump, greater numbers of people will lose their health insurance coverage and will go without mental health treatment. This issue will be examined later in this chapter.

Around the world, mental illness is a profoundly underestimated social problem. Globally, it is estimated that 300 million people suffer from depression alone (World Health Organization, April, 2017). While basic physical health has improved worldwide, mental health has remained stagnant or has deteriorated. Funding is low or nonexistent in many countries due to the lack of understanding of mental illness and the stigma associated with it.

What Do You Think?

Close your eyes and picture a person who is "mentally ill." Carefully describe that person in detail. Do you picture a person who suffers from the more extreme forms of mental illness, or do you picture a person who suffers from the more common and less extreme forms?

Mental Illness as a Social Problem

3.1 Identify the ways that mental illness is a social problem.

Until the mid-twentieth century, a large proportion of people who were classified as mentally ill and admitted to mental hospitals were actually suffering from physical ailments like epilepsy and brain tumors. Today, researchers are learning about the biological origins of many mental illnesses, including schizophrenia, autism, and depression. Genes play a role, as do hormones. As researchers discover the biological bases of some mental illnesses, they also gain information about the social conditions associated with mental illness, such as physical abuse, neglect, and stress. The specific relationships between biological factors and certain types of mental illness are considered in detail in psychology and genetics courses. In this text, it is enough to be aware that mental illness, whatever its causes, is a source of serious social problems not only because of the number of people affected but also because of the consequences of mental illness to both the individual and society, and the extent to which social institutions are strained by efforts to care for people with mental illness.

The mental disorders that cause severe social problems are generally among the most extreme forms. Of these, the most sensational are those that threaten the social order—for example, severely mentally ill individuals who become serial killers. Unfortunately, there are many examples to choose from. The gunman Nikolas Cruz, who slaughtered 17 high school students and staff at a high school in Parkland, Florida, in 2018, had a known mental illness. In another highly publicized and horrific case in 2015, an airline copilot who apparently suffered from mental illness deliberately crashed the airliner he was piloting in France, killing himself and 149 other people on board. When the captain left the cockpit for a presumably brief bathroom visit, copilot Andreas Lubitz apparently locked the captain out of the cockpit and then activated a control causing the plane to descend toward rugged terrain. The plane dropped for about eight minutes from its cruising altitude of 38,000 feet before crashing. The authorities said that the flight recording indicated pounding on the cockpit door, Lubitz's steady breathing, and eventually, screaming passengers. He suffered from a mental illness that he kept secret from his employer.

Certainly not all people who suffer serious mental illness are dangerous people or mass murderers. The number of individuals who do such things may be very small, but they constitute an especially serious social problem because they are so violent and irrational. These events receive international attention.

More widespread, but perhaps less threatening to public safety, are individuals with mental illnesses who cannot care for themselves without specialized attention. They may be indigent and homeless, napping on park benches, wandering the streets, and sleeping under bridges. Many cities consider these mentally ill people a public nuisance rather than as people in critical need of medical attention.

For individuals with mental illness, their problems pose difficult personal challenges. They may experience symptoms such as unimaginable fear, uncontrollable hallucinations, panic, crushing sadness, wild elation, roller-coaster mood swings, compulsive eating and then bingeing, exhaustion, and the inability to perform their social roles. For society as a whole, this group's illnesses present a range of social problems: stress in family life, heavy demands on health care institutions, moral and ethical problems (e.g., whether to permit the plea of insanity in criminal cases), and the cost of treatment to society. All of these social problems can be aggravated by the social stigma attached to mental illness, sometimes even by physicians themselves (Chiles, Stefanovics, and Rosenheck, 2017). It can be said that those who have mental illness suffer twice: They suffer from the illness itself, then they suffer rejection, as if their illness were their own fault. Social stigma is not nearly as likely for physical illness, and this factor alone qualifies mental illness for special consideration in the study of social problems.

A distressing aspect of the general problem of mental illness is the social impact of **deinstitutionalization**, or discharging patients from mental hospitals directly into the community. Some of these patients are not able to function as normal members of society, and the consequences can be painful both for them and for those who come into contact with them. For example, some severe disorders such as bipolar disorder, schizophrenia, and dissociative disorder are chronic conditions that must be managed

deinstitutionalization

The act of discharging patients from mental hospitals directly into the community.

with medication. Unfortunately, some people with those disorders find it difficult to manage staying on the medications, which creates a vicious cycle. It has been difficult to develop (or consistently fund) effective means of treating such individuals outside mental hospitals.

Policymakers at every level of society look to sociologists and other social scientists for basic research on the causes of mental illness and on the effects of major policy initiatives like deinstitutionalization or community treatment, as well as for recommendations on how to deal with trends in mental illness. Thus, in addition to sponsoring research on medical approaches to treatment and rehabilitation, the National Institute of Mental Health funds studies of the social epidemiology of mental illness—a concept that includes not simply its distribution in the population but also its impact on families, communities, and welfare institutions, as well as its relation to problems of homelessness and social dependency.

3.1.1 Sociological Perspectives on Mental Illness

Why is sociology interested in mental illness and mental health? Isn't that the domain of psychology? Sociologist Blair Wheaton (2001) reminds us that the social environment is both a starting point and a carrier of mental health or illness. Secondly, the variation in mental health has specific social consequences for our institutions and our society.

In studying social problems related to mental illness, basic sociological perspectives can help clarify the relevant issues and explain some aspects of the origins of mental disorders. The interactionist perspective focuses on the social construction of mental illness, that is, on how our definitions of "normal" and "deviant" behavior in social situations lead to definitions of mental disorders. To a large extent, the definition of mental illness is the province of psychologists and psychiatrists. Their diagnoses result in labels like "schizophrenic" or "depressed." Research by sociologists who have studied the interactions among people who are thought of as mentally ill suggests that such a label may cause one to define oneself as ill and to behave in ways that confirm the self-definition.

Conflict theorists tend to focus on how mental illness may be associated with deprivation and inequality, including unequal access to appropriate care. The emergence of a two-class system of mental health care in the United States is a central concern of this sociological perspective. Typically, more affluent patients with less severe mental illnesses receive higher quality private care, whereas severely ill patients, often reduced to poverty by their illnesses, are shunted into budget-starved public institutions.

From a functionalist perspective, mental illnesses constitute a social problem because they challenge our ability to provide effective treatment. This challenge is especially evident in societies marked by rapid social change, those in which people do not have long-standing attachments to others in their immediate social surroundings or are often separated from their families, or those in which systems of treatment have been changing rapidly and it is not clear how people with mental disorders should be helped.

What Do You Think?

If you were going to study the topic of mental illness, which sociological perspective would you likely use, and why?

3.1.2 Suicide and Mental Illness

As I write, I can see the lower floors of the Empire State Building from my office window. Yesterday afternoon, a junior at Yale University threw himself from the building's 86th floor. Leaving a note of apology in his dorm for his loved ones, he came to New York, proceeded to that upper floor, climbed over a spiked barrier, and leaped to his death. His was the thirty-fourth such suicide since the building opened in 1931 (William Kornblum).

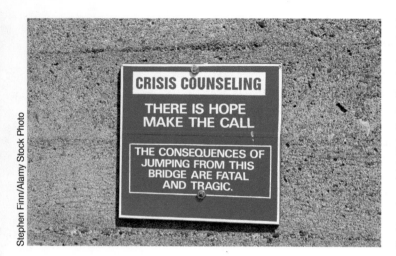

About 44,000 people each year in the United States kill themselves. Suicide is among the leading causes of death in the United States, especially among men.

Every 13 minutes, someone commits suicide in the United States. Suicide is the tenth leading cause of death in the United States, with 44,000 people killing themselves every year (and one million attempts). The rate of suicide, especially among teenagers and young adults, has been increasing steadily since 1950 and is now the second leading cause of death among younger people ages 15 to 34 (Centers for Disease Control and Prevention, 2015; National Institute for Mental Health, November, 2017b).

Men and women approach suicide differently. Women attempt suicide more often than do men, but men are much more likely to actually kill themselves, as shown in Figure 3–2. Women may attempt suicide as a cry for help, and they often use methods that are less lethal (poisoning, 30 percent) than those used by men (guns, 56 percent) (National Institute for Mental Health, November, 2017b).

The World Health Organization estimates that around the world, about 800,000 people take their own lives every year, and 75 percent of these suicides occur in developing countries (World Health Organization, 2018). The link between suicide and mental disorders (in particular, depression and alcohol use disorders) is well established. Depression can be brought on by chronic anxieties over money and loss of work and by marital discord. Initial depression often engenders further depression or abusive behavior and substance abuse, which can accelerate a downward spiral toward suicide. Among the elderly, loss of mental capabilities (dementia) is associated with depression and suicidal tendencies.

But not all suicide is related to mental illness. Many suicides happen impulsively in moments of crisis, causing a breakdown in the ability to deal with life stresses such as financial problems, a relationship breakup, or chronic pain and illness. People commit suicide to avoid severe embarrassment, to escape debt, to express strong political protest, and to avoid severe suffering due to physical illness. In addition, experiencing conflict, disaster, violence, abuse, or loss, and a sense of isolation are strongly associated with suicidal behavior. Suicide rates are also high among vulnerable groups who experience discrimination, for example, refugees and migrants; indigenous peoples; lesbian, gay, bisexual, and transgender (LGBT) persons; and prisoners. In other words, the reasons for suicide are similar from country to country, although some may have greater importance in a particular society due to economic, social, or cultural considerations.

Figure 3–2 Suicide Rates for Males and Females in U.S., by Age

SOURCE: National Institute of Mental Health. 2017b. "Suicide." Retrieved 22 February 2018 (www.nimh.gov/health/statistics/suicide.shtml#part_154969).

The Social Construction of Mental Illness

3.2 **Discuss the social construction of mental illness.**

When sociologists say that mental illness is socially constructed, they are highlighting aspects of those illnesses that help define how both the mentally ill and "normal" people behave. The usefulness of this approach becomes clear if we consider some alternative views of mental illness. In this section, you will get a brief orientation to three different explanations of mental illness: (1) the medical model, which asserts that mental illness is a disease with physiological causes; (2) the deviance approach, which asserts that mental illness results from the way society treats people considered mentally ill; and (3) the controversial argument that mental illness is not a disease but a method governments use to define certain people as being in need of isolation and "treatment." You will also begin to see how sociologists use all three of these explanations as they consider mental illness.

3.2.1 The Medical Model

The most familiar school of thought holds that a mental disorder should be viewed as a disease with biological causes. That is, a mental disorder is primarily a disturbance of the normal personality that is analogous to the physiological disturbance caused by physical disease. It can be remedied primarily by treating the patient. Once this treatment has been done, the patient will be able to function adequately.

Research in the biological sciences, especially genetics, has uncovered strong evidence to support biological explanations of mental illnesses like schizophrenia, bipolar disorder, childhood autism, senility, and even alcoholism (covered more in Chapter 4). In addition to disorders that are classified as mental illnesses, a host of other mental disabilities can appear at birth, for example, Down syndrome, cerebral palsy, and brain damage caused by birth trauma; such disorders present unusual and difficult challenges to those afflicted by them. Other disorders do not become apparent until children are somewhat older, perhaps school age. The box *A Personal View: "My Brain Works Differently"* is based on an interview with Marshall, an 11-year-old boy who has been diagnosed with attention deficit disorder.

Research on the medical model of mental disorders arose in reaction to the earlier notion that mentally disturbed people are mad or "possessed" and should be locked up, beaten, or killed. This move away from that earlier notion made possible serious investigation of the causes and cures of mental disorders and was responsible for the development of virtually all the systems of mental health care and therapeutic treatment in existence today—systems that are still largely in the hands of medically oriented personnel. It has helped reduce the stigma and shame of mental disorder because, after all, "illness can happen to anyone."

Nevertheless, the concept of mental disorder as a disease has certain disadvantages. Because it concentrates on individuals and their immediate environment (often their childhood environment), it tends to disregard the wider social environment as a possible source of the problem. In addition, especially for hospitalized patients, the medical model can lead to impractical criteria of recovery—people may have gained considerable insight into their inner tensions but are still unable to function adequately when they return to the outer tensions of home, job, or society. It is also true that many mental illnesses, which may or may not be caused by an individual's physiology, may be brought on, alleviated, or worsened by conditions in that person's social environment.

A Personal View

My Brain Works Differently

Nicholas Burningham/Alamy Stock Photo

I'm 11 years old and for as long as I can remember, I've had two sides to myself. I'm told that I'm very smart and creative. But I also have to work really, really hard at things that seem much easier for other kids, like memorizing and paying attention.

Here's an example: In math, science, and art, I can figure things out faster than other kids. Like when my teacher tells us a new way to add fractions, it seems obvious to me but not to other kids. But when I'm trying to listen to someone talking or lecturing, my mind starts to wander.

Yesterday when my science teacher was talking about plants, it made me think about what I was going to plant in my garden next year. And that made me think about a new kind of chili pepper that I'm going to try to plant for my dad because he likes spicy things. And that made me think about the hot dishes he used to eat when we visited China. And that made me think about the apartment we stayed in when we were in China.

Pretty soon I didn't have a clue as to what the science teacher was talking about. Then she got mad at me for day-dreaming. Sometimes my thoughts help me bring up new ideas that no one else has thought of. But I don't always get what the teacher is saying and she gets mad when she has to repeat herself.

When I'm doing something that's hard for me, like writing, I drift off easily and end up doing it quick so I can do something else that I'm better at. But then I don't get a very good grade on my essay, and I feel bad. The problem is, there are so many fun things to do in my house; things that I think are just as important as writing. I'd rather do chemistry and cooking experiments in the kitchen or try out new kinds of seeds in my garden, or watch the History Channel with my Dad, or solve logic puzzles and games. My mom gets mad at me sometimes because it takes me a long time to do my homework and she has to remind me a lot, "Come on Marshall, stay on task," she says.

Sometimes I have complicated ideas that I can't explain to others. That really frustrates me, and I get upset with the person for not getting it! I guess you could say I cry pretty easily. It's embarrassing, but I just can't help it.

I've tried some medicine to help me with attention. Isn't it weird that they make medicine for that? One helped me concentrate and be more energetic about school. Another helps make me be more optimistic, but when it wears off, I feel less cheerful and drift more. My medicine helps some, but it doesn't completely solve the problem of attention. I still have to work at it, and sometimes I still drift off even with the medicine.

Medicine doesn't really help the problems I have memorizing and studying for tests. My tutor suggested that I draw pictures when I'm memorizing facts for my history test. When we were studying the Lewis and Clark expedition in history, I drew a picture of a canoe, an Indian feather, and bison. That helped me remember those things for an exam. But it takes too long to study like that, so I wasn't able to get to everything and I got a bad grade. Sometimes it makes me want to give up when I realize how much harder I have to work at things that are not that hard for other kids. But my mom and dad told me that I'm smart; it's just that my brain works differently.

—Marshall, age 11

Critical Thinking

Drawing on the sociological imagination introduced in Chapter 1, the chapter "Sociological Perspectives on Social Problems," analyze whether Marshall's concerns are a personal issue or a social problem.

3.2.2 Mental Illness as Deviance

Scientists do not know precisely what interactions among the multitude of physical and social conditions that affect human beings may cause mental illness in some cases or lead to remission or recovery in others. We do know, however, that the way a mentally ill person is treated once the illness has been diagnosed can have a lasting impact on that person's behavior and on his or her chances of leading a happy and productive life.

The concept of mental disorder as a disease holds that something about a person is abnormal and that the fundamental problem lies in his or her emotional makeup, which was twisted, repressed, or otherwise wrongly developed because of genetic or chemical factors or events early in life. Although this theory seems to explain some mental disorders, many observers believe other factors need to be considered, especially the constant pressure exerted by modern society. Out of this broader effort has developed the view that mental disorder represents a departure from certain expectations of society—that it is a form of social deviance.

In this connection, the idea of residual deviance is useful. According to Thomas Scheff (1963), who formulated the concept, most social conventions are recognized as such, and violation of those conventions carries fairly clear labels: People who steal wallets are thieves, people who act haughtily toward the poor are snobs, and so on. But there is a large residual area of social convention that is so completely taken for granted that it is assumed to be part of human nature. To use Scheff's example, it seems natural for people holding a conversation to face each other rather than to look away. Violation of this norm seems contrary to human nature.

Scheff (1963) suggests that residual deviance occurs in most people at one time or another and usually passes without treatment. What causes it to become a mental disorder in some cases is that *society decides to label it as such.* When this labeling happens, the role of "mentally ill person" is suggested to the deviant individual. Because such people are often confused and frightened by their own behavior—as well as by other people's reactions to their behavior—during a time of stress, they are likely to be particularly impressionable and may accept the role suggested to them. Once they take on this role, it becomes difficult for them to change their behavior and return to their "normal" role.

If this labeling process is what occurs, then mental disorder may actually be a result of the attempts to respond to deviance. By treating a patient in a separate institution, the mental health profession certifies that the individual is indeed a patient and that he or she is mentally ill. The point of this concept of mental disorder as deviance is thus that the disorder may be a function not only of certain individuals' inability to comply with societal expectations but also of the label attached to those who deviate.

3.2.3 Problems in Living

A third approach to understanding mental disorder has been offered by Thomas Szasz, a psychiatrist who has generated considerable controversy by contending that mental illness is a myth. Although this view is not widely accepted, it does call attention to the relationship between diagnosis and repression. Szasz does not claim that the social and psychological disturbances referred to as mental illness do not exist; rather, he argues that it is dangerously misleading to call them illnesses. Instead, he believes, they should be regarded as manifestations of unresolved problems in living.

The significance of Szasz's basic argument is that it concerns justice and individual freedom. As he sees it, a diagnosis of mental disorder involves a value judgment based on the behavioral norms held by psychiatrists. Referring to certain behaviors as illnesses allows doctors to use medicine to correct what are essentially social, ethical, or legal deviations. This approach is not only logically absurd, Szasz contends, but also dangerous.

Szasz (2003) believes that individual liberty can be unwittingly sacrificed through too great a concern for the "cure" of "mental illness." This issue has come to the fore in connection with the forcible removal of homeless individuals from city streets. The presence of homeless people, who are often shabby and dirty and may behave in bizarre ways, offends "normal" citizens. As we will see later in the chapter, the interpretation of this lifestyle as a sign of mental illness has been used to justify the involuntary placement of the homeless in shelters or hospitals, where they are out of sight. We will also see that sensational crimes by mentally ill people, such as incidents of sudden violence in which schizophrenic individuals push unsuspecting pedestrians off train platforms, along with public concern about links between mental illness and violent crimes in schools, have produced renewed efforts to enforce mandatory institutionalization (Salize, Schanda, and Dressing, 2008).

3.2.4 The Social Construction Process

When sociologists speak of the social construction of mental illness, they incorporate all three approaches into their explanations. They recognize that there is often a biological basis for mental illness. In fact, medical and genetic discoveries are making possible more effective treatments. But social-scientific research also finds that mental illness is often aggravated by the fact that mentally ill people are defined and treated as social deviants. Sociologists therefore also study instances in which the label of mental illness is a convenient way of ridding society of people who are troublesome. Most important, sociologists recognize that the classification of mental illnesses and decisions about how they should be treated is determined by how we think about the causes, consequences, and possibilities of treating mental disorders. Even the diagnosis of mental illness requires the emergence of a common set of perceptions among mental health professionals, a point that becomes clear if you look in more detail at the problems of diagnosis.

3.2.5 Classification of Mental Disorders

Clinicians and researchers need a common language to discuss mental disorders. It is impossible to plan a consistent program of treatment for a patient without an accurate diagnosis, and it is impossible to evaluate the effectiveness of various forms of treatment without clearly defined diagnostic terms.

In 1973, to deal with these problems the American Psychiatric Association (APA) embarked on a controversial and ambitious revision of its manual of mental disorders. The new manual, released in 1980 and referred to as the *Diagnostic and Statistical Manual of Mental Disorders*, third edition, or simply as *DSM-III*, represented the work of hundreds of scientists and professionals in the field of mental health care. A revised edition, *DSM-IV*, was published in 1994, and the most recent revision, *DSM-V*, appeared in 2013 (American Psychiatric Association, 2015).

Widely regarded as a major advance in the scientific description and classification of mental disorders, the *DSM-III* had a significant impact on treatment when released.

There are many kinds of mental illnesses. Some are relatively common, such as depression and anxiety, while others occur much less frequently, such as schizophrenia or psychosis. How do mental health practitioners keep track of the different types of illnesses? One important way is by consulting the *Diagnostic and Statistical Manual of Mental Disorders*.

Dule964/Fotolia

Among other things, it made an important contribution to the separation of mental disorders from behaviors (such as homosexuality) that deviated from societal norms at the time but were not a result of mental illness. In general, however, the manual continues to represent the illness model. To a large extent, it seeks to attribute mental dysfunctions to physiological, biochemical, genetic, or profound internal psychological causes.

The *DSM-V* contains several changes. For example, autism spectrum disorder (ASD) is a new *DSM-V* name that reflects a scientific consensus that four previously separate disorders are actually a single condition with different levels of symptom severity. ASD now encompasses the previous *DSM-IV* autistic disorder (autism), Asperger's disorder, childhood disintegrative disorder, and pervasive developmental disorder not otherwise specified.

Several familiar terms are no longer used in *DSM-V*, such as *neurosis*, the older term for a wide range of disorders in which the individual suffers from severe anxiety but continues to attempt to function in the everyday world. The new classification system replaces this term with more specific ones such as *affective disorder, anxiety disorder, somatoform disorder*, and *psychosexual disorder*.

3.2.6 Diagnosis or Label?

Just as some physical illnesses may be culturally defined, so may certain mental disorders. The medical model assumes that patients present symptoms that can be classified into diagnosable categories of mental illness. But there is a growing belief that at least some psychiatric diagnoses are pigeonholes into which certain behaviors are placed arbitrarily. According to labeling theorists, the diagnosis of schizophrenia has been especially subject to misuse. Although there is little agreement about its origins, causes, and symptoms, it is the most commonly used diagnosis for severe mental illness. To labeling theorists, this trend suggests that diagnoses of mental illnesses tend to reflect cultural values, not scientific analysis. People are not "schizophrenic" in the sense that they manifest definite symptoms; instead, their behavior violates society's norms and expectations. A person who sees visions might be considered perfectly normal, even admirable, in many cultures, although in the United States he or she would probably be regarded as disturbed.

The problem with labeling people as mentally ill is threefold: It makes us perceive certain behaviors as "sick," something to be eliminated rather than understood; it gives public agencies the right to incarcerate people against their will simply for not conforming; and it causes those people to define themselves as rule breakers and undesirables and allows them to fulfill that image. Many studies have demonstrated the influence of societal factors on the diagnosis of mental illness as well as the vagueness of such diagnoses. Rosenhan (1973), in a classic study that will be described more fully later in the chapter, found that psychologists and psychiatrists on the staffs of several mental hospitals were unable to determine accurately which of the people they interviewed were mentally healthy and which were mentally ill. Despite the undeniable influence of labeling on the diagnosis and treatment of mental illness, recent large-scale research has shown that interviewers with basic training in the diagnosis of mental illness can spot people with serious mental disorders like schizophrenia and severe depression quite accurately. Such research is vital to our knowledge of the extent of mental illness in a population.

3.2.7 Post-Traumatic Stress Disorder

Even when research findings are available and widely publicized, there is no guarantee, especially with mental illnesses, that effective action will follow. A case in point is the gap that existed until quite recently between what is known about the incidence of mental illness among soldiers who have witnessed violent death and traumatic pressures on battlefields and the provision of adequate mental health services for them.

Once minimized as shell shock or combat fatigue, and frequently confused with cowardice or weakness, post-traumatic stress disorder (PTSD) has always been a consequence of war. Now, mental health researchers understand that an individual may develop PTSD after witnessing or experiencing any traumatic event. Service members are particularly vulnerable because they are often at high risk for death or injury. They may see others hurt or killed. They may have to kill or wound others. They are on alert around the clock. These and other factors can increase their chances of having PTSD or other mental health problems. Symptoms of this disorder may be quite severe and can include flashbacks, nightmares, feelings of detachment, irritability, trouble concentrating, sleeplessness, and in the most extreme cases, suicide (Schoenbaum et al., 2014; U.S. Department of Veterans Affairs, 2017).

The treatment of soldiers with PTSD may improve because of recent studies of the mental health needs of soldiers returning from Iraq and Afghanistan. One large survey of nearly 2,000 recently returned service men and women, from all service branches, components, and unit types found that nearly one-third met the criteria for PTSD (RAND Center for Military Health Policy Research, 2008). Only about half of returned soldiers with symptoms of PTSD sought help. A partial reason for soldiers failing to seek care is a scarcity of providers in many regions of the country (Brown et al., 2015). But another important reason for failing to seek care is more social in nature. Military service members report barriers to seeking care that are associated with fears about the negative consequences of using mental health services. Many feel that seeking mental health care might have negative effects on career prospects or cause coworkers' trust to decline.

Because of these findings, the U.S. Department of Defense has begun administering mental health questionnaires to all soldiers after they have returned home. The Army Study to Assess Risk and Resilience in Service members (STARRS) is the largest study of mental health risk and resilience ever conducted among military personnel. The Army STARRS investigators are looking for factors that help protect a soldier's mental health and factors that put a soldier's mental health at risk (Kessler et al., 2017).

Certainly, soldiers are not the only ones who suffer from PTSD. Much has been written about those who survive violent crime, such as sexual assault (Boyle, 2017). Another example of PTSD that has been largely ignored is that of the young schoolchildren who were going to school near the 9/11 terrorist attacks in New York City. As the box *A Closer Look: "9/11 and Schoolchildren"* shows, many children suffered from PTSD in the aftermath of the attacks, yet most of these children received no counseling to help them deal with the trauma they experienced.

Inequality, Conflict, and Mental Illness

3.3 **Assess inequality and differences in mental illness.**

Sociologists and experts on mental health care have continually refined their research concepts and tools to trace the relationships between mental illness and inequalities of social class, race, ethnicity, gender, age, and other dimensions of social inequality. Sociologists are interested in the relationship between social factors like poverty and the incidence of mental disorders. Is mental disorder associated with social class and with conflicts over the distribution of social rewards? Does it occur more frequently in urban centers than in rural areas or suburbs? In what population groups is it most prevalent? Would changes in social conditions prevent or alleviate certain mental disorders?

3.3.1 Incidence Versus Prevalence of Mental Disorders

Epidemiologists—social scientists who study the course of diseases in human populations—make a distinction between the incidence of a disease or disorder and its prevalence in a given population. Incidence and prevalence are important concepts

epidemiologists

Social scientists who study the course of diseases in human populations.

A Closer Look

9/11 and Schoolchildren

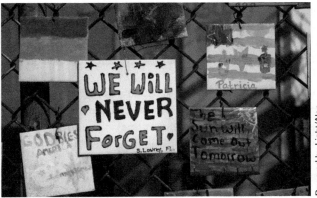

Powered by Light/Alan
Spencer/Alamy Stock Photo

Many people who watched in horror as the World Trade Center towers became a flaming death scene, later experienced symptoms of post-traumatic stress disorder (PTSD)—sleeplessness, attention problems, depression, recurring nightmares, and more—for days, weeks, or even months after the event. But children in New York City were especially prone to suffer one or more symptoms of PTSD long after the event. What follows are segments of the testimony of psychiatrist Christina W. Hoven, who directed a study for the New York Department of Education of children's lingering psychological difficulties because of their experiences on 9/11.

"To better appreciate the complexity and challenges faced by the New York City Board of Education, I want to identify a few issues that contributed to our conceptualizing the study the way we did, that is, to view the aftermath as a probable citywide phenomenon, not just a Ground Zero event:

1. There are approximately 1.2 million children enrolled in the New York City public schools.
2. Approximately 750,000 of them take public transportation every day, including subways, buses, and boats, passing through tunnels and going over bridges on their way to school.
3. Whereas only 35,000 people reside in the area surrounding Ground Zero, more than twenty times that number commute there to work each day. Similarly, the schools near Ground Zero, especially the specialized middle and high schools, are attended primarily by students living outside that area, coming every day from each of the boroughs of NYC.[3]

Briefly summarizing our findings, we observed throughout the City a higher than expected prevalence of a broad range of mental health problems or psychiatric disorders among NYC public schoolchildren. It is estimated that as many as 75,000 (10.5%) New York City public schoolchildren in grades 4 to 12 have multiple symptoms consistent with post-traumatic stress disorder (PTSD); and that 190,000 (26.5%) have at least one of the seven assessed mental health problems (excluding alcohol abuse).

NYC public school students were exposed to the effects of the attack in different ways. Almost all the students in Ground Zero, and two-thirds of children in the remainder of the City, experienced some type of personal physical exposure to the attack, such as being near the cloud of smoke and dust, having fled to safety, having had difficulty getting home that day, and/or continuing to smell smoke after 9/11.

Having a family member exposed to the attack—that is, having a family member killed, injured, or in the World Trade Center at the time of the attack but who escaped unhurt—was more frequent among students in schools outside of Ground Zero than among students in schools near Ground Zero.

We know that previous exposure to trauma elevates an individual's response to any new trauma. We found that nearly two-thirds (64%) of New York City public schoolchildren had been exposed to one or more traumatic events *before* 9/11, including seeing someone killed or seriously injured, [or] seeing the violent/accidental death of a close friend or family member. Again, a disproportionate number of the children with previous exposure go to schools outside of the Ground Zero area.

Exposure to the media was also very high; almost two-thirds (62%) of the surveyed population spent a lot of their time learning about the attack from television....Rates of the other psychiatric disorders [estimated for the city's 1.2 million children from random sample surveys] were as follows:

- 8 percent with major depressive disorder (MDD);
- 10 percent with generalized anxiety disorder (GAD);
- 12 percent with separation anxiety disorder (SAD);
- 9 percent with panic attacks;
- 11 percent with conduct disorder;
- 5 percent with alcohol abuse (grades 9–12 only).

All of these reported mental health problems were determined to be associated with impairment; that is, they were so severe as to indicate a need for immediate further assessment and appropriate intervention. Yet, at least two-thirds of children with probable PTSD following the 9/11 attacks have not sought any mental health services from school counselors or from mental health professionals outside of school."

Source: Hoven et al., 2005.

Critical Thinking

Why do you think that most of the children with probable PTSD from the 9/11 attack have not received any counseling inside or outside of school? Can you identify any structural reasons rather than just personal ones?

[3]Based on Hoven et al., (2005) "Psychopathology among New York city public school children 6 months after September 11," *Arch Gen Psychiatry*, 62(5):545–52.

in studying how mental illness is related to social variables such as inequality, race, gender, and age. The *prevalence* of mental illness usually refers to the estimated population of people suffering from one or more mental illnesses at any given time. The term *incidence* refers to the number of new cases of mental illness diagnosed each year. The prevalence rate of schizophrenia for example, is about five in 1,000. This means that five out of every 1,000 persons have been diagnosed with schizophrenia. These individuals may have been diagnosed recently or many years ago. In contrast, the incidence of schizophrenia per year is only about .20 to .70 per 1,000, meaning that fewer than 1 person out of 1,000 people is diagnosed over a recent one-year period (Messias, Chen, and Eaton, 2007).

The study of incidence and prevalence of mental illness is complicated by the difficulty of determining an accurate calculation of mental disorders. We can count the number of patients in mental hospitals and, somewhat less accurately, those receiving treatment in clinics and other outpatient facilities. It is far more difficult to obtain reliable statistics on the number being treated in private practice. Moreover, an indeterminate number of people who would qualify as having a mental illness are not under treatment at all. Consequently, any statistics on treated mental illness must be viewed as only a very rough estimate of the total number of people suffering from these problems.

Despite these difficulties, sociologists have reached several tentative conclusions about the relationship between mental disorders and patterns of inequality in a society. It should be noted that research on the impact of inequality is often conducted from a conflict perspective. Conflict theorists call attention to the ways in which inequalities of wealth and power produce inequalities in access to effective treatment for mental disorders. Underlying these inequalities is class conflict. For instance, the poor demand more services and better care from public institutions, while those who are better off believe the poor bring their troubles on themselves and do not deserve expensive care facilities and treatment programs. Conflict theorists also emphasize that poverty itself is a social problem that can produce severe stress in those who experience it. Life in poverty is associated with higher exposure to crime and violence, which adds to the stress of everyday life. In some individuals, such extreme stress can precipitate mental illness (Madsen, Nyberg, Hanson, and Ferrie, 2017; Toussaint, Shields, Dorn, and Slavich, 2016).

3.3.2 Social Class and Mental Illness

Long before sociologists began to make systematic studies of social conditions and mental disorders, the connection between the two had been recognized. It was only in the 1930s, however, that serious sociological study of this relationship began, and although the research results are not in perfect agreement, they offer some useful information.

One pioneering study (Faris and Dunham, 1938) investigated the residential patterns of 35,000 hospitalized mental patients in Chicago. The highest rates of mental illness were found near the center of the city, where the population was poor, of very mixed ethnic and racial background, and highly mobile. Although this number included many cases of organic psychosis due to syphilis and alcoholism in the skid row districts, it also included a significantly high rate of schizophrenia throughout the area. Conversely, the lowest rates of mental disorder were found in stable, higher-status residential areas.

Another classic study, the Midtown Manhattan Study, went beyond treatment to include a random sample of 1,660 adult residents of midtown Manhattan (Srole et al., 1978). The researchers found that almost 23 percent were significantly impaired in mental functioning, including many people who were not under treatment. One of the factors investigated was socioeconomic status, not only that of the subjects but also that of their parents. Among subjects considered seriously impaired in mental functioning, the percentage with lower-class parents was twice the percentage of those with upper-class parents. This finding suggests that socioeconomic status is correlated with the mental health of children.

Modern studies continue to find that mental illness is more common at the lowest socioeconomic level than at higher levels (Meyer, Castro-Schilo, and Aguilar-Gaxiola, 2014; Rubin and Stuart, 2018). The research does not indicate, however, whether individuals with mental illness were originally in the lowest social class or whether they drifted down to it as the condition worsened. In other words, the studies fail to make clear whether low socioeconomic status is primarily a *cause* or an *effect* of serious mental illness.

Some researchers reject a poverty or social-stress hypothesis as an explanation of the preponderance of mental illness in the lower classes. Instead, they propose the **drift hypothesis**, which holds that social class is not a cause but a consequence of mental disorder (Cockerham, 2014; Hurst, 2013). In this view, people with mental disorders tend to be found in the lower classes because their illness has prevented them from functioning at a higher social class level, and they have "drifted" downward to a lower class. Despite the disagreement over cause and effect, most sociologists recognize that social class and mental illness form a vicious cycle, as shown in Figure 3–3.

drift hypothesis
A concept that argues that social class is not a cause but a consequence of mental disorder.

3.3.3 Race and Ethnicity

Rates of mental illness differ among most racial and ethnic groups with multi-racial groups, American Indians, Alaska Natives, and Whites experiencing more mental illness than other groups, as shown in Figure 3–4 (National Institute of Mental Health, November, 2017a). But are the differences due to race or ethnicity per se, or can they be explained in terms of social class or some other social factor? For example, American Indians, Alaska Natives, and persons who are White are more likely to have access to health insurance than other groups, and therefore, perhaps they are more likely to be identified as having a mental illness.

However, there is also some evidence that the experience of racial discrimination heightens stress and contributes to mental health problems (Hudson, Neighbors, Geronimus, and Jackson, 2016; Russell, Clavel, Cutrona, Abraham, and Burzette, 2018). A recent study based on data from over 4,000 African Americans and Caribbean blacks

Figure 3–3 The Cycle of Poverty and Mental Disorders

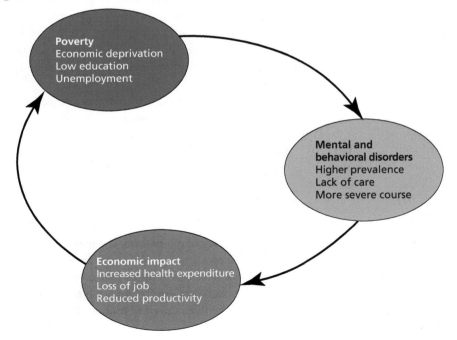

Figure 3–4 Past Year Prevalence of Mental Illness Among U.S. Adults, by Race and Ethnicity, 2016

SOURCE: National Institute of Mental Health. 2017a. "Mental Illness." November. Retrieved 23 February 2018 (www. nimh.nih.gov/health/statistics/mental-illness.html).

suggests that perceived experiences of discrimination in the form of disrespect and condescension (e.g., receiving poorer service at a store) do not by themselves increase risk for most mental disorders. However, hostile and character-based discrimination (e.g., threats and harassment) in combination with disrespect and condescension does seem to place African American and Caribbean black adults at considerable risk for mental health problems (Clark et al., 2015).

3.3.4 Sex

Overall, men and women have different rates of mental illness for certain conditions. It appears that women are more likely to experience depression, anxiety, eating disorders, and phobias, whereas men are more likely to suffer from autism and schizophrenia. Famous women are increasingly speaking out about their mental health issues in efforts to help others, including, Beyoncé, Miley Cyrus, Demi Lovato, Gwyneth Paltrow, Selena Gomez, and J.K. Rowling. Some illnesses are unique to women, such as post-partum depression and peri-menopause related depression.

Women are more likely than men to be diagnosed with depression, and because this disorder is the most common form of mental illness, it is worthy of extended discussion. Efforts to explain this difference in depression are ongoing as researchers explore many potential causes and contributing factors to women's increased risk for depression. It is likely that genetic, biological, chemical, hormonal, environmental, psychological, and social factors all intersect to contribute to depression (Albert, 2015; Leupp, 2017; National Institute of Mental Health, 2015; World Health Organization, 2018; Yucel, 2017):

- *Genetics.* If a woman has a family history of depression, she may be more at risk of developing the illness. However, depression can also occur in women without family histories of depression, and women from families with a history of depression may not develop depression themselves. Genetics research indicates that the risk for developing depression likely involves the combination of multiple genes with environmental or other factors.

- *Chemicals and Hormones.* Modern brain-imaging technologies such as magnetic resonance imaging (MRI) have shown that the brains of people suffering from depression look different from those of people without depression. The parts of the brain responsible for regulating mood, thinking, sleep, appetite, and behavior do not appear to function normally. In addition, important neurotransmitters—chemicals that brain cells use to communicate—appear to be out of balance. But these images do not reveal *why* the depression has occurred. Scientists are also studying the influence of female hormones, which change throughout life. Hormones directly affect the brain chemistry that controls emotions and mood.

- *Premenstrual Dysphoric Disorder.* Some women may be susceptible to a severe form of premenstrual syndrome called premenstrual dysphoric disorder (PMDD), which is associated with depression, anxiety, irritability, and mood swings the week before menstruation and that interferes with their normal functioning. Women with debilitating PMDD do not necessarily have unusual hormone changes, but they do have different responses to these changes. They may also have a history of other mood disorders and differences in brain chemistry that cause them to be more sensitive to menstruation-related hormone changes. Scientists are exploring how the cyclical rise and fall of estrogen and other hormones may affect the brain chemistry that is associated with depressive illness.

- *Postpartum Depression.* Women are vulnerable to depression after giving birth, when hormonal and physical changes and the new responsibility of caring for a newborn can be overwhelming. Many new mothers experience a brief episode of mild mood changes known as the "baby blues," but some will suffer from postpartum depression, a much more serious condition that requires active treatment and emotional support for the new mother. Postpartum women are at an increased risk for several mental disorders, including depression, for several months after childbirth. Women who experience postpartum depression often have had prior depressive episodes. Some experience it during their pregnancies, but it often goes undetected.

- *Menopause.* Hormonal changes increase during the transition between premenopause to menopause, which is called perimenopause. While some women may transition into menopause without any problems with mood, others experience an increased risk for depression, even among women without a history of depression. However, depression becomes less common for women during the postmenopausal period.

- *Stress.* Stressful life events such as trauma, loss of a loved one, a difficult relationship, or any stressful situation—whether welcome or unwelcome—often occur before a depressive episode. Gender-specific risk factors for common mental disorders that disproportionately affect women include gender-based violence, socioeconomic disadvantage, low income and income inequality, low or subordinate social status and rank, and unremitting responsibility for the care of others, including children and aging parents, often while maintaining a job. Stress associated with these factors may trigger a depressive episode. A positive relationship exists between the frequency and severity of such social factors and the frequency and severity of mental health problems in women. Severe life events that cause a sense of loss, inferiority, humiliation, or entrapment can predict depression. However, it is unclear why some women faced with enormous challenges develop depression and some with similar challenges do not.

- *Gender Bias.* Gender bias occurs in the treatment of psychological disorders. Doctors are more likely to diagnose depression in women compared with men, even when they have similar scores on standardized measures of depression or present with identical symptoms. Women are more likely to be prescribed mood-altering psychotropic drugs. Gender differences exist in patterns of help-seeking for psychological

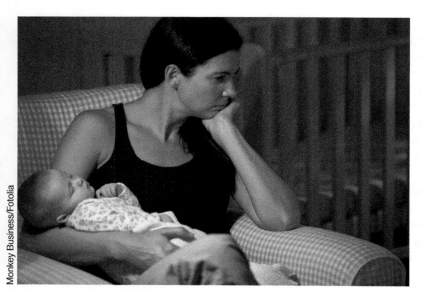

Because of hormonal changes and fluctuations during and after pregnancy, some women experience depression while pregnant or, more commonly, experience depression after the baby is born. Stress likely also plays a significant role. Ask any parent about the work involved in caring for a new baby. Most of this work is taken on by the mother, rather than shared equally between mother and father.

disorder. Women are more likely to seek help from and disclose mental health problems to their primary health care physician while men are more likely to seek specialist mental health care and are the principal users of inpatient care.

Despite the greater focus on women, it is important to recognize that depression, anxiety, and other mental illnesses also affect many men. Prince Harry of England is outspoken with respect to mental health issues, serving as an important role model. Prince Harry was only 12 years old when the car carrying his mother, Princess Diana, crashed in a Paris tunnel in 1997. The Prince spent much of the following two decades—through the conspiracy theories, endless investigations, and royal family concerns—remaining mostly silent about her death, living his daily life as though all was well. He finished school, joined the British army and went to Afghanistan, watched his brother marry, and became an uncle. This was his public side. However, emotionally he was in turmoil. As he now explains it, at royal engagements he was sometimes overcome by a "fight or flight" sensation. He often felt angry, as if he were "on the verge of punching someone," but didn't understand why this was happening. Today, with the help of family, friends, and a therapist, he uncovered the mystery. "I can safely say that losing my mum at the age of 12, and therefore shutting down all of my emotions for the last 20 years," Harry said, "has had a quite serious effect on not only my personal life but my work as well."[4] All the grief that he never processed began to pour out. He now actively speaks out on mental health issues and, along with his brother, Prince William, and sister-in-law, Princess Kate, has created the Heads Together charity to raise funds and increase awareness of mental health issues.

3.3.5 Age

In contrast to most severe and disabling physical diseases, many mental illnesses begin early in life, as shown in Figure 3–5. Twenty-two percent of young adults between the ages of 18 and 25 have experienced some form of mental illness, and 6 percent have experienced a serious mental illness. Anxiety disorders such as panic attacks often begin in late childhood, eating and mood disorders in late adolescence, and substance abuse disorders in the early 20s. Overall, it is estimated that nearly one child in five is affected by some form of mental disorder (Perou et al., 2013). Mental disorders can therefore be thought of as the chronic diseases of the young.

Young people with mental disorders experience disability when they are in the prime of life, when they would normally be most productive, whereas extremely disabling physical illnesses like heart disease and cancer tend to strike adults in the later years of their working lives. The risk of mental disorders declines as people mature out of the high-risk age range. However, elderly people have increasing rates of depression after age 70, which is often due to loss of loved ones and to physical conditions such as progressive dementia manifested in Alzheimer's disease (National Institute of Mental Health, 2015).

The mental problems among the oldest-old population are a growing concern for researchers and policymakers and for millions of elderly people and their families. Alzheimer's disease, a degenerative brain disorder that destroys memory, has

---

[4]Furness, H. (19 April 2017) "Prince Harry: I sought counselling after 20 years of not thinking about the death of my mother, Diana, and two years of total chaos in my life" *The Telegraph UK*.

Figure 3–5 Past Year Prevalence of Mental Illness Among U.S. Adults, by Age, 2016

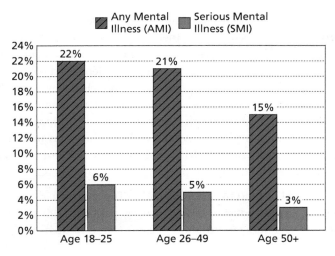

been increasing in prevalence (Alzheimer's Association, 2018). Recent progress in research and development of treatments for depression and possible treatments for Alzheimer's is encouraging, but the problems brought on by mental illnesses among the elderly are likely to increase as the elderly population grows, a subject to which you will return in Chapter 9.

Methods of Treatment

3.4 **Compare treatment options for mental illness.**

The treatment of mental disorders has undergone enormous changes in the past century and remains one of the most controversial aspects of mental health in all societies. This section reviews the major approaches to the treatment of mental illness and changes in mental health institutions. It will show that, although there has been a great deal of progress in treating mental illness, many problems remain, especially in creating and maintaining effective institutions for the treatment and care of the mentally ill (Cockerham, 2014).

The two major approaches to the treatment of mental disorders are medical treatment and psychotherapy. Although these approaches are sometimes used simultaneously, they involve different groups of mental health professionals, and therefore run the risk that the diagnosis and treatment are not properly coordinated. This may be particularly problematic if the patient lacks health insurance or does not have a specific primary provider. In this section, we briefly review the most important methods of treatment. We will begin with medical approaches.

3.4.1 Medical Approaches to Treatment

Medical treatments can help control most mental illnesses. These treatments are provided by physicians, including psychiatrists. Medications can play an important part in a treatment plan. The general consensus is that medicines are usually more effective when combined with psychotherapy. In some cases, medication can reduce symptoms so that other methods of a treatment plan can be more effective. A medication may alleviate some significant symptoms of major depression, and then psychotherapy can help the patient change negative patterns of thinking (National Alliance on Mental Illness, 2018).

What Do You Think?

Why do we know so little about what causes mental illness? When you compare mental illness across different groups, such as age or sex or race, do you think the causes of mental illness differ across these groups?

HISTORY OF MEDICAL APPROACHES   Before the late 1930s, severe psychosis was treated in a variety of ways: by confining the patient in a straitjacket; by administering sedatives; by wrapping the patient in moist, cool sheets; or by immersing the patient in a continuous flow tub for hours at a time (Sheehan, 1982). Then a more drastic treatment was introduced: electroconvulsive therapy in which an electric shock produces a convulsion and brief unconsciousness. This frightening and dangerous treatment has produced dramatic results with deeply depressed patients and some schizophrenics. However, the effects tend to be temporary, and it is not clear how much brain damage the treatment causes. Moreover, it often results in long-term memory loss.

In the 1940s and early 1950s, shock treatment was used extensively, sometimes in coercive and excessive ways (Squire, 1987). The procedure was modified in the mid-1950s and made somewhat safer, but in the 1960s and 1970s, it fell into disfavor as drug therapies became increasingly popular.

COMMON MEDICAL APPROACHES TODAY   The primary medical approach to managing mental illness today involves treating patients with a variety of drugs, ranging from mild tranquilizers to antidepressants and antipsychotic agents. Of all the recent innovations in drug therapy, the administration of antidepressants and antianxiety medications has had the greatest impact and has relieved severe and debilitating symptoms in millions of people. The current standard of treatment involves a drug class known as selective serotonin reuptake inhibitors (SSRIs). Scientists believe that depression can be triggered by a lack of the chemical serotonin, and these drugs essentially maintain higher levels of serotonin in the brain to correct the issue. In other words, these medications work by influencing the brain chemicals regulating emotions and thought patterns.

Prozac was the first SSRI, marketed in the 1980s. Newer related drugs have been developed and are advertised regularly on television with the brand names of Celexa, Wellbutrin, Cymbalta, and Abilify. Treatment typically consists of pills or capsules taken daily. A few medications are available as liquids, as injections, or as tablets that dissolve in the mouth.

In addition to these antidepressants, the development of antipsychotic drugs has made it possible to control the most incapacitating aspects of schizophrenia and paranoia. These medications reduce or eliminate the symptoms of psychosis (delusions and hallucinations) by affecting the brain chemical called dopamine. Newer, second-generation, or atypical antipsychotics can also treat acute mania, bipolar disorder, and treatment-resistant depression. Consistent use of these drugs often permits the patient to control his or her illness, allowing a normal life.

One of the challenges associated with drugs, however, is that mental illness is person-specific, and it is therefore important to find just the right drug that helps each person individually. There is not one drug that works for all people who suffer from a particular condition. Therefore, patients and providers work together, sometimes by trial and error, to find the correct treatment plan. It is generally believed that drugs should be used in conjunction with some other form of therapy for optimum results.

3.4.2 Nonmedical Forms of Treatment

There are many nonmedical forms of treatment for people with mental illness. Some are provided alone, and others are provided in conjunction with drug therapy. Of these nonmedical treatments, psychotherapy is most common.

psychotherapy

Interaction between a patient and a therapist or among patients in groups that is intended to foster insight and change.

PSYCHOTHERAPY   Patients who undergo **psychotherapy** are helped to understand the underlying reasons for their problems so that they can try to work out solutions. The process involves some form of interaction between the patient and the therapist or among patients in groups. Among the major forms of psychotherapy are psychoanalysis, client-centered therapy, cognitive behavioral therapy, and various other types of therapy and support groups (American Psychological Association, 2018; National Alliance on Mental Illness, 2018). There are a variety of types of psychotherapy. Three of the most common types of psychotherapy are described in the following list:

- *Psychoanalysis.* Developed by Sigmund Freud in the late nineteenth century, psychoanalysis seeks to uncover unconscious motives, memories, and fears that prevent the patient from functioning normally. Patients may use various methods of exploration and discovery, including dreams and free association.
- *Client-centered therapy.* This approach was developed by Carl Rogers in the 1940s, and emphasizes current problems rather than unconscious motives and past experiences. The patient sets the course of the therapy, while the therapist provides support.
- *Cognitive behavioral therapy (CBT).* This approach is associated with psychiatrist Aaron Beck from the 1960s. During CBT a therapist will actively work with a person to uncover unhealthy patterns of thought and how they may be causing self-destructive behaviors and beliefs. By addressing these patterns, the person and therapist can work together to develop constructive ways of thinking that will produce healthier behaviors and beliefs. For instance, CBT can help someone replace thoughts that lead to low self-esteem ("I can't do anything right") with positive expectations ("I can do this most of the time, based on my prior experiences").

In therapy and support groups, people attempt to solve their problems through interaction with one another. Support groups are composed of people who have experienced the same problems as the other participants, such as Alcoholics Anonymous, Overeaters Anonymous, and Gamblers Anonymous.

INEQUALITY AND PSYCHOTHERAPY Racial and ethnic minority populations, and those who are poor, underutilize mental health services even when controlling for the type of disorder and clinical need. One reason for their lower use of services is their lower perceived need (Villatoro, Mays, Ponce, and Aneshensel, 2018). Other reasons include a lack of health insurance and access to care. For example, among nonelderly adults with any mental illness and serious mental illness, those with Medicaid or private insurance are almost twice as likely to receive treatment as are those without insurance (Henry J. Kaiser Family Foundation, November 27, 2017).

However, despite health care providers' professional ideal of equality and fairness, research indicates that patients' social and demographic characteristics influence the health care encounter, as shown in Chapter 2. Less is known about the ways in which bias and outright discrimination influence patients' access and treatment of mental health care (Mays, Jones, Delaney-Brumsey, Coles, and Cochran, 2017).

A recent study investigated the effect of mental help seekers' race, class, and gender on the accessibility of psychotherapists (Kugelmass, 2016). Three hundred and twenty psychotherapists each received voicemail messages from one black middle-class and one white middle-class help seeker, or from one black working-class and one white working-class help seeker, requesting an appointment. Social class was conveyed in these calls by differing vocabulary and grammar. Race was communicated through racially distinct names and linguistic styles, including Black English Vernacular. The caller left a message requesting an appointment, which therefore required the psychotherapist to return the call. The results of this study are shown in Figure 3–6. As we can see, middle-class help seekers had appointment offer rates almost three times higher than their working-class counterparts. Race differences

Figure 3–6 Percentage of Therapy-Seeking Calls That Elicited At Least One Appointment

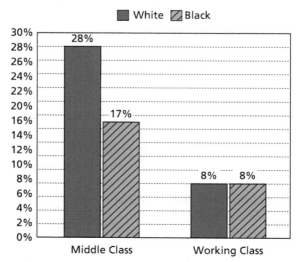

SOURCE: Kugelmass, H. "Sorry, I'm Not Accepting New Patients" An Audit Study of Access to Mental Health Care, *Journal of Health and Social Behavior*, vol. 57, no. 2, (June 1, 2016) pp. 168–183.

emerged only among middle-class help seekers, with blacks considerably less likely than whites to be offered an appointment.

OTHER APPROACHES Drugs and psychotherapy are two important treatment approaches, but there are others as well. Exercise is recommended for people who suffer from many mental illnesses. Research shows that exercise and physical activity can prevent or delay the onset of different mental illnesses, and they also have therapeutic benefits when used as sole or secondary treatment (Harvey et al., 2018; McCash and Abraham, 2018; Zschucke, Gaudlitz, and Ströhle, 2013). Many people who have anxiety, depression, eating disorders, dementia, or schizophrenia receive significant relief from physical activity. On a neurochemical and physiological level, several acute changes occur during and following bouts of exercise. Animal studies found exercise-induced changes in different neurotransmitters such as serotonin and endorphins that relate to mood and positive effects of exercise on stress reactivity. Potential psychological reactions associated with exercise include changes in body image, overall health attitudes, and behaviors; the potential for increased feelings of mastery and social reinforcement; and improved coping strategies, or simple distraction from personal problems.

Social support is another key factor in treating mental illness and is an important tool of recovery (Rueger, Malecki, Pyun, Aycock, and Coyle, 2016; Werner-Seidler, Afzali, Chapman, Sunderland, and Slade, 2017). A study of 153 persons ages 16 to 84 with serious mental health illnesses found that having a strong social support network, the size of the network, and engaging in social activities were related to higher scores on a commonly used "recovery assessment scale" (Hendryx, Green, and Perrin, 2009). The nature of the activities (more/less social, more/less physically active, inside/outside the home) was not important; rather, activities of any type were related to recovery. Furthermore, engagement in activities was more important as levels of social support declined. The results of this study suggest that both social support and activities may promote recovery, and that for persons with poor social support, engagement in a variety of individualized activities may be particularly beneficial.

What Do You Think?

Have you or someone you know closely ever suffered from a mental illness? If so, did this person receive any type of treatment? Describe the treatment. Do you think it helped? Why or why not?

Treating Mental Illness

There are many ways to treat mental illness. Unlike physical illnesses, which are more likely to be predictable across patients, mental illness and its treatment are very individualized. What works for one person does not necessarily work for another person, even if both are thought to suffer from the same disorder.

Piggu/Fotolia

One of the more common treatments for mental disorders is drugs. However, the commonly used medicines work differently on people with the same condition. Sometimes people must try several before they find the one that works well for them. Drugs are not without their controversies, but millions of people say they have been helped by them.

Dmitriy Shironosov/Alamy Stock Photo

Psychotherapy is an important source of treatment and is generally advised even if drugs are the primary treatment. Here, a woman seeks help for her obsessive-compulsive disorder that involves repetitive and compulsive thoughts and behaviors.

Riccardo Meloni/Fotolia

Social support from family or friends is also a key factor keeping many mental illnesses at bay and is an important tool of recovery from mental illness. Getting involved in social activities is also helpful, although many mental illnesses such as depression, phobias, or anxiety may keep people from socializing.

Wavebreak Media ltd/Alamy Stock Photo

Physical exercise is another nonmedical type of treatment that has had some success in preventing or treating mental illness, especially those disorders that are less severe. Exercise has positive effects both physiologically, such as by releasing endorphins, and socially by increasing a sense of mastery.

Hitdelight/Fotolia

Critical Thinking

Using the sociological imagination, explain why mental health and mental health treatments are not simply personal problems.

Socializing with others can happen in many ways. This man receives support, warmth, and love from his border collie, "Zeke."

Institutional Problems of Providing Treatment and Care

3.5 **Explain the institutional problems of providing treatment and care.**

The forms of treatment described earlier are carried out in a variety of settings. Psychotherapy generally occurs in settings such as psychologists' offices. Medical treatments, in contrast, may require either outpatient or inpatient care. Some patients are so seriously ill that they cannot be cared for outside a hospital or clinical setting. In this section, we discuss issues related to the care of the mentally ill in hospitals and other institutions (Beam, 2003; Keene, 2013; Payne, 2009).

3.5.1 Mental Hospitals

Alvaro German Vilela/Fotolia

This woman is a patient in one of the remaining mental hospitals. She has a history of hurting herself, and in this picture she is wearing a straitjacket.

In the late nineteenth and early twentieth centuries, care for patients with mental illness usually involved mental hospitals. The general thought was that mentally ill people should be isolated in institutions to receive appropriate treatment, and for their own safety and the safety of others. The number of mental hospitals and institutions increased substantially during this period.

Also, the smaller nuclear family was less well equipped during this period to care for its disabled members and began to look to the state for assistance (Curtis, 1986). Institutions like mental hospitals were developed to meet this need. In such institutions, those with mental illnesses were to be sheltered from a hostile world, kept from harming themselves or others, and given help and treatment. Hospitals were built in secluded spots and surrounded by high walls and locked gates. Within the walls, all the patient's needs were to be met. But the purpose of the hospital was not merely to protect patients from society and, if possible, to cure them; it was also to protect society from the patients. The old stereotype of the "raving lunatic" persisted, and eventually, security came to be considered more important than therapy.

For the sake of economy and efficiency, a system of enormous hospitals developed, each housing several thousand patients and staffed largely by aides whose main job was to keep things quiet on as low a budget as a state legislature could decently supply. Staffing these hospitals was a perennial problem. Salaries were usually low; working conditions were unattractive or discouraging; and well-trained personnel were almost irresistibly tempted away by private hospitals, clinics, or private practice, where the rewards, both monetary and in terms of visible therapeutic achievement, were much greater. Consequently, public institutions depended heavily on less-trained personnel, particularly attendants or nursing aides. The hospital building often fell into disarray without adequate funds for maintenance. They were usually crowded and dirty, with an air of despair.

There is evidence that hospitalization may not always be the best solution to mental illness, even in good hospitals. Long-term studies have shown that patients who do not improve enough to be discharged within a short period are likely to remain hospitalized for a very long time, if not indefinitely. This effect is due in part to the inadequacies of the hospital. It also seems to be a consequence of hospitalization itself, a position taken by Erving Goffman (1961). Goffman developed the concept of the **total institution**, which is defined as a place of residence and work where many like-situated individuals are cut off from the wider society for an appreciable period

total institution

A place of residence and work where many like-situated individuals are cut off from the wider society for an appreciable period of time and together lead an enclosed life.

of time and together lead an enclosed life. Mental hospitals are an example of a total institution, as are prisons and religious convents.

Goffman (1961) regarded the mental hospital as a prime example of a total institution. His field research and work in mental hospitals convinced him that because inmates are constantly subject to its control, the hospital profoundly shapes their sense of self. In general, mental hospitals downgrade patients' desire for self-esteem and emphasize their failures and inadequacies. Uniform clothing and furniture, a regimented routine, and the custodial atmosphere of the hospital make patients docile and unassertive. Because the psychiatric approach requires cooperation, staff members often encourage patients to view themselves as sick and in need of help. Any act of self-assertion or rebellion may be interpreted as further evidence of illness, and patients will be expected to take that view of themselves. Release from the hospital is often contingent on the patient's accepting, or appearing to accept, the official interpretation of his or her hospital and prehospital life. Goffman concluded that, in most cases, there is a high probability that hospitalization will do more harm than good.

Goffman has received heavy criticism, particularly for not having conducted enough empirical research on enough hospitals to determine whether all mental hospitals could be called total institutions. Moreover, although Goffman's view has had a great influence on the way people think about mental hospitals (and prisons), he is accused of having been influenced by the literary power of his ideas and images rather than by the force of empirical data (McEwen, 1988; Scull, 1988).

The classic study by Rosenhan (1973) illustrates the conditions prevailing in many mental hospitals. This research project involved eight "normal" people, or pseudopatients, who were admitted to several mental hospitals and diagnosed as schizophrenics. Their only symptom was a fabricated one: They said that they had heard voices on one occasion. Although the pseudopatients spent some time in the institutions and were recognized as normal by their fellow inmates, the staff continued to think of them as schizophrenic. Some were released with the diagnosis of "schizophrenia in remission," and none was ever thought to be cured. In a follow-up study, a hospital that had heard of these findings was informed that over a period of three months some pseudopatients would attempt to gain admission to the hospital, and staff members were asked to judge which applicants were faking illness. Over the three-month period at least 41 patients were judged to be pseudopatients. In fact, none of those patients was faking.

The results of this study were widely cited as supporting the labeling theory in that the diagnosis of illness—or health—was applied regardless of the actual condition of the patient. But also of interest here is what the pseudopatients observed while in the hospital. As much as possible, staff members were separated from patients by a glass enclosure; psychiatrists almost never appeared on the wards. When pseudopatients approached staff members with questions, the most common response was to ignore the questions or mumble something—avoiding eye contact with the patient—and quickly move on. Patients were sometimes punished excessively for misbehavior, and in one case, a patient was beaten. Overall, the atmosphere for patients was one of powerlessness and depersonalization.

3.5.2 Community Psychology

Three societal and scientific changes occurred in the mid-twentieth century that questioned whether institutionalizing those who were mentally ill was the best approach.

- *The development of psychiatric drugs* during the 1950s treated many of the symptoms of mental illness. The mental hospitals began using the new drugs in the

1950s. As a result, thousands of patients who had been assaultive became docile. Many who had spent their days screaming subsided into talking to themselves. In addition, the revolution went far beyond hospital care. New "wonder drugs" like Thorazine made it possible to release hundreds of thousands of hospitalized patients (Sperry, 1995), who were supposed to receive outpatient treatment in their own communities.

- *Society accepted that the mentally ill needed to be treated* instead of simply locked away.
- *Federal funding such as Medicaid and Medicare* went toward community mental health centers instead of mental hospitals. Medicaid, a health care program for those who are poor, and Medicare, a health care program for the elderly, were established in the mid-1960s, and became an important funding mechanism for mental health care. Money was primarily spent on outpatient care rather than on mental hospitals.

To show how much treatment approaches have changed, in 1955 there were 560,000 public mental hospital beds in the United States, amounting to about 340 beds per 100,000 population. That number has shrunk considerably to only 35,000 beds today, or just 11 beds per 100,000 population (Treatment Advocacy Center, 2015). Today there is a shortage of psychiatric beds (Torrey, 2016). As a result, hospital emergency rooms are often crowded with psychiatric patients. In addition, large numbers of former patients are in jail or prisons or are homeless (Treatment Advocacy Center, 2015).

community psychology

The idea of easily accessible, locally controlled facilities that could care for mentally ill people in their own communities.

The **community psychology** movement arose from two basic sources: (1) awareness that social conditions and community resources must be considered in dealing with individual mental health problems; and (2) the idea that psychologists or psychiatrists should be able to contribute to the understanding and solution of social problems. The guidelines laid down for the centers provided for a wide range of mental health care in the community and for coordination with, and consultative assistance to, other community agencies.

The Community Mental Health Centers Construction Act set up a sophisticated support system to aid newly released patients, many of whom need considerable help in relearning the skills of everyday life and social interaction. The cornerstone of this system is the **halfway house**, a small residential community in which ex-patients are helped to make the transition from the hospital to normal life. They may receive therapy from a psychiatrist, they may be trained for a job and helped to obtain or keep one, and they are able to practice fitting into a community in which behavior is not subject to hospital regulations.

halfway house

A small, privately run residential community, usually located in an urban area, in which ex-patients are helped to make the transition from the hospital to normal life.

Under optimal conditions, halfway houses can provide high-quality care; however, a variety of obstacles have prevented them from meeting the needs of many discharged mental patients. Operating somewhat in a vacuum—with little working relationship with the state mental hospitals from which they receive patients— many halfway houses soon found themselves with far more patients than they had staff or facilities to handle. In addition, halfway houses and other community mental health centers face an enormous funding problem. As a result, halfway houses and other community mental health facilities have found it difficult to meet the growing demand for services (Mental Health America, 2018; National Council for Behavioral Health, 2017).

To effectively address the needs of people with mental illness, a variety of institutions and approaches, all working together, are required. Schools, hospitals, families, community centers, and law enforcement agencies need to become more aware of mental health problems and how to deal with them. In affluent nations, including the United States, one reason that so many cases of mental disorder go untreated is the lack of coordination and failure to overcome problems of stigma, discrimination, and lack of support in the person's social environment.

3.5.3 Deinstitutionalization and Homelessness

The preceding section noted that, beginning in the mid-1950s, large numbers of mental patients were deinstitutionalized, or released from mental hospitals, based on the belief that psychiatric patients would have a higher quality of life if treated in their communities rather than in mental hospitals.

Throughout the 1960s and 1970s it was hoped that reductions in the hospital population would be accompanied by reductions in the incidence of mental disorders. This hope proved to be in vain. Released from institutions, many persons who were mentally ill found that they had no place to go. Many did not have relatives who would take them in, and they did not have resources for housing. Far from decreasing, the incidence of mental disorders increased. At the same time, the funding of community mental health centers was cut back.

Geoff Smith/Alamy Stock Photo

Not all homeless people are mentally ill, but it is estimated that at least a quarter of homeless men and nearly two-thirds of homeless women do suffer a serious mental illness. Deinstitutionalization has released many mentally ill people who would otherwise be in mental hospitals. Is this policy a good one or a bad one?

The presence of mental patients among the homeless is due partly to their tendency to congregate in central-city neighborhoods, which are unable to provide the services they need. It has also been caused, in part, by the passage of laws originally designed to protect the rights of the mentally ill. Because only patients who are demonstrably dangerous may be involuntarily committed to mental hospitals, most mentally ill patients receive only brief, episodic care. Chronically mentally ill people who are not dangerous to themselves or others are released into the community. Some find housing in single-room occupancy (SRO) hotels or cheap rooming houses, but these forms of housing are far less available today than they were in the 1950s and 1960s because landlords have either abandoned them or converted them into condominiums. As a result, mentally ill people often end up on the streets.

On a given night, about 550,000 people are homeless (U.S. Department of Housing and Urban Development, 2018). Somewhere between a quarter and a third of homeless persons have a serious mental illness (SMI) that may be untreated (Treatment Advocacy Center, 2018). Other persons who are homeless may not suffer from an SMI but are individuals or families who have been caught in either a cycle of unemployment or low-paying, dead-end jobs that fail to provide the means to get off the streets.

Homelessness usually is the final stage in a long series of crises and missed opportunities, the result of a gradual process of disengagement from supportive relationships and institutions. The situation is especially severe for those who have an SMI. They are isolated. Family members and friends have become tired and discouraged or are unable to help. Social workers are overburdened and cannot give them the attention they need, and the mentally ill themselves cannot communicate their needs adequately.

Because of experiences like these, the homeless, especially those who have an SMI, tend to be afraid of strangers, which is one reason they often reject offers of shelter and efforts to help them. The fear experienced by some homeless people is so great that it can be overcome only with enormous effort and patience. It should also be pointed out, however, that mental illness can be a consequence of homelessness as well as a cause of it. People who lose their homes suffer severe stress. They experience hunger, lack of sleep, and physical illnesses. In addition, they are "disorganized, depressed, disordered ... immobilized by pain and traumatized by fear"[5] (Kozol, 1988).

What Do You Think?

Compare and contrast how a functionalist, conflict theorist, and symbolic interactionist would look at the issue of mental illness and homelessness.

---

[5]Kozol, J. "The Homeless and Their Children," *The New Yorker*, January 25, 1988, p. 65.

Social Policy

3.6 **Analyze the policy implications of the Affordable Care Act, and their aftermath, for mental illness.**

Before parity legislation passed during the George W. Bush administration in 2008, it was common for insurance companies to impose a lifetime limit of benefits for mental illness of $50,000, whereas the limit for physical health care might range from $750,000 to $1 million. Yet some feared that an unintended consequence of parity legislation would be that insurance companies would drop mental health coverage altogether, which would reduce the number of people covered by any form of mental health insurance.

The 2010 Affordable Care Act (ACA) moved further toward parity for mental disorders and for those who suffer from them. By disallowing the insurance company practice of denying coverage for family members with prior illnesses, physical or mental, it ensures that millions of Americans will be eligible for coverage and treatment. This development can both reduce human suffering and reduce the federal deficit because the sooner mental illness is treated, the lower the cost to society in the long run. The ACA also moved toward an investment in a national system of electronic health records giving mental health professionals improved capability to follow patients who move from one neighborhood or city to another and to continuously update their medical records so that everyone in the treatment network of a given individual can be kept current.

Nonetheless, President Donald Trump and the Republican Congress have attempted to dismantle the ACA, seeing it as ineffective and failing to rein in health care costs. The precise consequences of this for mental health coverage remain to be seen. However, it is expected that dismantling the ACA will result in more people losing insurance coverage or purchasing so-called "junk insurance" policies that are less expensive, but contain high deductibles and large co-payments, leaving people with inadequate physical and mental health coverage (Abelson, 2017).

An important problem in caring for those with mental illnesses is the lack of coordination of treatment, exacerbated by having no or inadequate insurance. Because the mental health care field is divided between therapists and medical practitioners, there is a widespread tendency to see psychotherapy and medical treatment as mutually exclusive. Yet a patient who is on medication needs to take the medicine in the prescribed dosage at the correct intervals. It follows that there must be a high level of coordination of treatment between social workers, therapists, and others in the patient's social world on one hand, and the clinical personnel who prescribe medication and decide whether patients should be hospitalized on the other.

Without coordination of care, people suffering from mental disorders often do not follow their medication regimes, or they may fail to get treatment as their conditions change, or in many instances they may fail to receive any treatment at all. Individualized treatment for mental illnesses can be complicated and require close coordination between patients and health care professionals. Some mental disorders can result in extremely high costs to the individuals involved and their families, as well as to society at large, when treatment is delayed or uncoordinated and intermittent. Bipolar disorder, for example, is the most expensive mental health care diagnosis, both for patients with the illness and for their health insurance plans, and it is the sixth most frequent cause of disability worldwide.

All untreated mental illness costs money. Although precise numbers are hard to pin down, it is estimated that untreated mental illness costs the U.S. economy at least $105 billion annually in lost earnings each year in absenteeism and reduced worker productivity (Giang, 2012). Millions of dollars more are spent on costly emergency room visits and additional doctor bills. The Affordable Care Act is moving toward an investment in a national system of electronic health records that should give mental health professionals improved capability to follow patients who move from one neighborhood or city to another and to continuously update their medical records so that everyone in the treatment network of a given individual can be kept current.

3.6.1 Future Prospects

President Trump has voiced the need for increased mental health services in the wake of the epidemic of mass shootings. After the 2018 high school shooting in Parkland, Florida, President Trump pointed to inadequate mental health treatment, rather than guns, as the cause of the shooting. His 2019 budget proposal indicates there are a few areas where he would like to boost mental health resources. The biggest injection of funding—$8.6 billion—would go toward the Department of Veterans Affairs to improve intervention for at-risk veterans. The budget also adds $1 million to the Children's Mental Health Services program, a small increase to their budget this year which was funded at $119 million. However, President Trump's proposed budget also slashes spending for the Substance Abuse and

Mental illness can be controlled. With the right treatment, people who have a mental illness can lead happy, healthy, and productive lives.

Mental Health Administration by $665 million. Additionally, the National Institute of Mental Health would see a 30 percent reduction in funding—a half a billion dollar decrease—in 2019 (Romo, 2018). President Trump's proposed budget is only a starting point; the final budget will surely be a compromise between the President and both Republicans and Democrats in Congress.

Going Beyond Left and Right

Whose responsibility is it to assist those with mental illness? This question may not give rise to as many moral, ideological, or political debates as some other social problems, but there are controversies nonetheless. Concern about mental illness is reemerging because of its connection with gun violence. It is easy to stereotype those persons who suffer from mental illness as deviant or dangerous. If mental illness is only identified by its most serious forms, then it is not surprising that such stereotypes exist. However, mental illness encompasses several disorders that range in severity, including attention deficit disorder, depression, anxiety, seasonal affective disorder, obsessive-compulsive disorder, dementia, autism spectrum disorder, panic disorders, bulimia, and anorexia, among others.

Summary

3.1 Identify the ways that mental illness is a social problem.

Mental illness is a social problem because of the large numbers of people who suffer emotionally and physically from mental disorders. Mental disorders are the leading cause of disability for people ages 15 to 44 in the United States and throughout the world. Mental illness is also a social problem because of the potential harm caused by

people with unchecked serious mental illness, such as the mass shootings in schools.

3.2 Discuss the social construction of mental illness.

When social scientists say that mental illness is socially constructed, they are highlighting aspects of those illnesses that help define how both the mentally ill and "normal" people behave. There are three main approaches to constructing mental illness: (1) the medical model, which asserts that mental illness is a disease with physiological causes; (2) the deviance approach, which asserts that mental illness results from the way people considered mentally ill are treated; and (3) the controversial argument that mental illness is not a disease but a method governments use to define certain people as being in need of isolation and "treatment."

3.3 Assess inequality and differences in mental illness.

Sociologists and experts on mental health care have continually refined their research concepts and tools to trace the relationships between mental illness and inequalities of social class, race, ethnicity, gender, age, and other dimensions of social inequality. There are significant differences among these groups. Women are far more likely than men to suffer from depression and anxiety, while men are more likely to suffer from autism or attention deficit disorder. Differences are likely due to a combination of genetic, hormonal, and social factors.

3.4 Compare treatment options for mental illness.

The treatment of mental disorders has undergone enormous changes. The primary medical approach to managing mental illness today involves treating patients with a variety of drugs, ranging from mild tranquilizers to antidepressants and antipsychotic agents. The primary nonmedical approaches include psychotherapy, exercise, and social support. Although these approaches are sometimes used simultaneously, they involve different groups of mental health professionals, who often have difficulty coordinating the diagnosis and treatment of their patients.

3.5 Explain the institutional problems of providing treatment and care.

Mental hospitals and institutions were the primary method of dealing with persons with mental disorders until the mid-twentieth century. The development of drugs and a growing concern that large mental hospitals were essentially warehouses brought a reconsideration of how to best treat mentally ill people. Beginning in the mid-1950s, large numbers of mental patients were deinstitutionalized, or released from mental hospitals, based on the belief that psychiatric patients would have a higher quality of life if treated in their communities rather than in mental hospitals. The goal was to help these people through community mental health centers; however, some mentally ill persons are homeless and do not get the care they need.

3.6 Analyze the policy implications of the Affordable Care Act, and their aftermath, for mental illness.

The Affordable Care Act (ACA) helps people with mental illnesses because they can no longer be denied coverage for prior mental illnesses by insurance companies. The ACA increased insurance coverage and treatment for millions of Americans. Nonetheless, the ACA is politically controversial, and President Trump and the Republican-led Congress have made attempts to repeal it. This, along with the increase in the availability of so-called "junk insurance," is likely to decrease the number of people eligible for mental health coverage.

Chapter 4
Alcohol and Other Drugs

Backyard Productions/Alamy Stock Photo

 ## Learning Objectives

4.1 Discuss the nature of the problem associated with alcohol and drugs, including definitions, abuse, and addiction.

4.2 Identify the perceptions toward alcohol and drinking patterns.

4.3 Assess several social problems related to alcohol.

4.4 Describe the effects of alcohol on the family.

4.5 Compare treatment options for alcoholism.

4.6 Summarize the most commonly used drugs that are abused.

4.7 Identify some of the patterns, problems, and treatments associated with drug abuse.

4.8 Review policy considerations of drug laws and enforcement.

Yeah, I like to get high. So what? How is it any business of yours? I'm basically a law-abiding citizen, but now and then I like to cut loose. A little Oxy never hurt anybody. The high makes me feel strong, powerful, on top of my game. I buy some on payday from a friend who gets it from the doctor for back pain. She says her back is good enough and sells it on the side. I don't see how I could ever become addicted. I have a great Friday and Saturday night with my buddies, and then I'm done for a week until next payday. Or sometimes I skip a payday if my money needs to go somewhere else. Like, I'm saving for a snorkeling trip to Mexico, and that definitely cuts into my Oxy money. I've never had any problems with using it, except when one guy last summer tried to steal some from me. That pissed me off and we roughed each other up a little. But he apologized, and quickly left the house after I bloodied his nose, and I haven't seen him around since. One of my buddies got a small inheritance from his grandmother when she died, and he bought four new tires for his car and I swear he spent the rest on drugs. He's off the deep end, using every day. Well, I don't think I'll be getting any inheritances in the near future so I'm safe.

People use drugs, including alcohol, to ease pain, increase alertness, relax tension, lose weight, gain strength, fight depression, feel "high," and prevent pregnancy. Americans of all ages and at all socioeconomic levels consume vast quantities of chemical substances every year. Most of these drugs are socially acceptable, and most people use them for socially acceptable purposes. Alcohol is a drug, as are caffeine and nicotine; these substances are commonly and widely used as aids to sociability and ordinary activity. But some drugs and some users of drugs are socially defined as unacceptable, and it is these drugs and users that constitute the drug problem.

The uses and abuses of alcohol and other drugs are discussed together in this chapter for several reasons. Through its personal and social effects, alcohol abuse is as harmful as the abuse of less socially accepted drugs. Moreover, many drugs, including alcohol, offer satisfactions that make them attractive to many people, but they can be habit forming, sometimes with destructive consequences to both users and nonusers; thus, there are controversies over the causes, consequences, and moral implications of their use. Efforts to control drug use—particularly the "War on Drugs" that has been a cornerstone of American social policy against substance abuse for over 40 years—are increasingly controversial among political leaders and social scientists because of their seeming failure.

Strategies of interdiction and control are often associated with other social problems, such as violence, racism, and crime. Drastic measures to prevent drug cultivation and importation can also have negative effects on democratic institutions, both in the United States and abroad, with little evidence of success in diminishing drug supplies. Moreover, despite the nation's huge investments in anti-narcotics policies, experts on addiction continually find that alcohol abuse is more prevalent and damaging to individuals and society than any other form of substance abuse.

Abuse of alcohol and other drugs is a growing problem throughout the world. Alcohol addiction has been a long-standing problem, but addiction to opiates and cocaine is a growing problem in many countries, including the United States, China, Latin America, Russia, and many countries in Eastern Europe. Civil strife in drug-producing nations like Colombia and Afghanistan has multiple causes, but the importance of world drug markets as a cause of violence in these and other nations is undeniable. However, in its most recent survey of world drug use, the United Nations found that Americans use more drugs than people in other countries (United Nations Office on Drugs and Crime, 2017). Americans are also more likely to die from drug-related illness. Although this chapter focuses primarily on alcohol and drug problems in the United States, much of what is learned in this nation also has a bearing on drug issues in other nations.

The Nature of the Problem

4.1   Discuss the nature of the problem associated with alcohol and drugs, including definitions, abuse, and addiction.

From a pharmacological viewpoint, a drug is any substance, other than food, that chemically alters the structure or function of a living organism. A definition this inclusive, however, encompasses not only medicines but also a huge range of substances from vitamins and hormones to herbs, snake and mosquito venom, antiperspirants, insecticides, and air pollutants. Obviously, this definition is too broad to be of practical value. Definitions that depend on context are more useful. In a medical context, a drug may be any substance prescribed by a physician or manufactured expressly to relieve pain or to treat and prevent disease. In a socio-logical context, which is of most interest here, the term **drug** denotes any chemical substance that affects physiological functions, mood, perception, or consciousness; has the potential for misuse; and may be harmful to the user or to society. In addi-tion to the illegal drugs that attract so much attention such as cocaine or marijuana (although in some states marijuana is legal), many pharmaceutical drugs, such as Oxycontin or Adderall, are abused as well (National Institute on Drug Abuse, January 2018a).

drug
Any chemical substance that affects physiological functions, mood, perception, or consciousness; has the potential for misuse; and may be harmful to the user or to society.

Although the sociological definition is more satisfactory for our purposes than the original, much broader one, it omits the social bias that has traditionally deter-mined what substances are *labeled* drugs. When members of a society have used a habit-forming substance for long periods, that substance may not be classified as a drug in that society, even if it has been proven to be harmful. Alcohol, caffeine, and tobacco (nicotine) are examples of such substances that we usually do not think of as drugs.

4.1.1 Subjective and Objective Dimensions

Like so many other social problems, drug use has both objective and subjective dimensions. The *objective aspect* is the degree to which a given substance causes physiological, psychological, or social problems for the individual or the social group—the family, the community, or the entire society. The *subjective aspect* is how people perceive the consequences of drug use and how their perceptions result in social action concerning drug use (such as norms, policies, laws, and programs).

Of course, these subjective perceptions may be based on objective evidence, but very often they are based on past practices and combinations of scientific and folk wisdom about a given substance. Aspirin, for instance, is one of the most widely used drugs in the United States. From an objective standpoint, we know that aspirin can cause ulcers, gastrointestinal bleeding, and other ailments. But most Americans believe—this is the subjective aspect—that aspirin is a harmless drug that is danger-ous only when taken in massive doses. Thus, aspirin use is part of our overall drug problem in objective terms but not in subjective terms. For many Americans, the same failure to allow objective facts to shape subjective perceptions is true in the case of al-cohol, which will be discussed later in the chapter.

Other drugs are part of the social problem of drug use because they are perceived as problems, even if the way they are used by certain people is not problematic in objective terms. Marijuana is an example. Objectively, there is little evidence that marijuana users damage themselves psychologically or physiologically, although researchers believe marijuana may decrease the user's motivation to concentrate and learn complex material. Yet the subjective view of many Americans, especially those in policymaking positions, is that marijuana is a dangerous drug. This subjective viewpoint is incorporated into laws against marijuana use, and these laws, in turn, foster the illegal traffic in marijuana.

The discrepancy between the subjective viewpoint and objective reality comes to prominence quite often in U.S. political affairs. In 1992, former U.S. President Bill Clinton's admission that he had tried marijuana as a student but had not inhaled be-came the subject of innumerable jokes during the presidential election campaign. The question of whether George W. Bush had used cocaine as a young man while "sowing his wild oats" was a persistent issue during the 2000 presidential primaries. President Obama, who admitted to trying marijuana as a younger man, received much less attention for it. Was the question even asked of President Trump? Nothing objectively has changed about marijuana between President Clinton's and President Trump's tenure. Yet, subjective views have changed considerably. In 2012, Colorado and Washington became the first states to vote to legalize marijuana for recreational purposes. Since then, seven more states and Washington, DC, have followed—although Vermont and DC, while allowing marijuana possession and growing, have continued to bar sales for recreational purposes.

The point is that some drugs are treated as social problems within our society's dominant system of norms and institutions, but concerns about others are shifting. Meanwhile, other drugs, such as alcohol, caffeine, and nicotine, are not really defined as social problems even though in objective terms their harmful consequences have been fully documented (Centers for Disease Control and Prevention, January 25, 2017d).

4.1.2 Abuse and Addiction

The difficulty of separating the subjective and objective dimensions of drug use causes a great many problems of definition for experts in the field. The term drug abuse is widely used, but it can refer to many things. First, it may refer to the objectively harmful consumption of drugs that are subjectively approved of, such as alcohol and tranquilizers. Second, it also refers to the use—in any amount—of drugs that are subjectively disapproved of, such as marijuana, even if the objective facts about their effects in certain dosages do not indicate that they are particularly harmful. Third, almost all strongly addicting drugs, such as heroin or methamphetamine, are harmful both to the user and to society at any level of use and are usually included under the term drug abuse.

Despite this ambiguity, the National Institute on Drug Abuse continues to support the use of the term *drug abuse*, and we will use it in this chapter—except that we define **drug abuse** as both the use of socially unacceptable drugs and/or the excessive or inappropriate use of acceptable drugs in ways that can lead to physical, psychological, or social harm.

The term **addiction** is also used rather loosely, but in fact it is a complex phenomenon that involves the drug user's physical and psychological dependence, the type of drug, and the amount and frequency of use. Physical dependence occurs when the body has adjusted to the presence of a drug and will suffer pain, discomfort, or illness—the symptoms of withdrawal—if its use is discontinued. Psychological dependence occurs when a user needs a drug for the feeling of well-being that it produces and the person may become anxious or agitated when the drug is unavailable.

It is important to note that not all drug use is considered abuse in the sense that it impairs health. A person who is suffering from an illness that requires treatment with morphine might be addicted but would not be considered an abuser. However, there can be no doubt that some drugs are not only physically addicting but also dangerous to society because they compel their users to seek ever larger quantities to maintain a high.

These highly addictive drugs can be a major social problem in that thousands of otherwise productive people may disappear from the labor market or become involved in an underground drug economy. The classic example is the city of Shanghai before the Chinese Communist revolution of 1949. It has been estimated that almost 500,000 residents of Shanghai were addicted to opium and had to spend hours in smoking dens each day. Earlier in the twentieth century, thousands of Americans were addicted to a form of opium known as laudanum, which they used for headaches and menstrual cramps. Today, opioid addiction is wreaking havoc on many lives and communities in pockets within the United States.

What Do You Think?

Do you think that marijuana for personal use should be legal in the United States? Why or why not? What about more harmful drugs, such as alcohol, caffeine, and nicotine? Why do you think that some of these drugs are legal, while others are not?

---

drug abuse

The use of socially unacceptable drugs and/or the excessive or inappropriate use of acceptable drugs in ways that can lead to physical, psychological, or social harm.

addiction

A complex phenomenon that involves the drug user's physical and psychological dependence, the type of drug, and the amount and frequency of use.

However one ultimately defines abuse and addiction, mere knowledge of patterns of use in the general population at a given moment and over time is an essential starting point. This point is where social-scientific data play an important role. Large, national surveys of alcohol and drug use by adults and teens are carried out by professional social scientists. They also assess the incidence of mental illness and its relationship to drug and alcohol-related disorders. At their most basic level, these surveys establish the prevalence and incidence of alcohol, tobacco, and illegal drug use in the general population. As discussed in Chapter 3, prevalence refers to the estimated population of people living with a given condition, and incidence refers to the number of new cases.

Table 4–1 shows the proportion of high school seniors who have ever used a particular substance and those who have used it over the past month (Johnston et al., 2018). These data are from a large-scale annual survey, *Monitoring the Future*, which has been surveying high school seniors since 1975, and which included eighth and tenth graders beginning in 1991. Students are given a self-administered questionnaire (to encourage honesty) about their substance use. This survey is an essential barometer of drug use among young Americans. Like all surveys, however, it has its limitations; in particular, it does not sample young people who have dropped out of school, an important population in the study of drug use.

As shown in the table, nearly half of high school seniors report having used an illicit drug sometime in their life, and one-quarter report that they have used one over the past month. Marijuana and alcohol are the most commonly used drugs, although the number of high school seniors who have used prescription drugs has increased significantly from previous survey years. Vaping is also increasing in popularity; in fact it was not even included in the annual survey until 2015.

Drug prevalence data are especially helpful in comparing the popularity of specific drugs in a population or a segment of a population, such as teenagers. Questions from the *Monitoring the Future* survey that ask about the use of any illegal drugs over the lifetime, as reported in Figure 4–1, are especially helpful in tracking trends in drug consumption over time.

Table 4–1 Lifetime Prevalence Rates of Use of Different Drugs among High School Seniors, 2017

Substance	Ever Using Drug	Used during Past Month
Any Illicit Drug	49%	25%
Any Illicit Drug Other Than Marijuana	20%	6%
Marijuana	45%	23%
Prescription Drugs	17%	5%
Cocaine	4%	1%
Hallucinogens	7%	2%
Heroin	0.7%	0.2%
Inhalants	5%	0.8%
Ecstasy/MDMA	5%	1%
Amphetamines	9%	3%
Alcohol	62%	33%
Cigarettes	27%	10%
Any Vaping	36%	17%

SOURCE: Based on Johnston, L.D., P.M. O'Malley, R.A. Miech, J.G. Bachman, & J.E. Schulenberg. 2015. Monitoring the Future National Survey Results on Drug Use: 1975–2017: Overview, Key Findings on Adolescent Drug Use. Ann Arbor: Institute for Social Research, The University of Michigan.

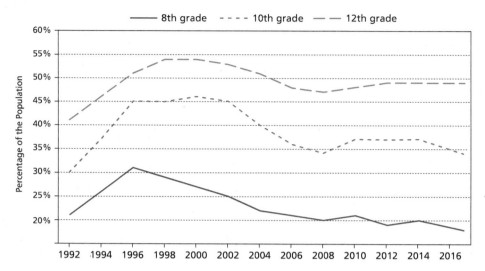

Figure 4–1 Trends in Lifetime Prevalence of Any Illegal Drug, 8th, 10th, and 12th Graders, 1992–2017

SOURCE: Based on Johnston, L.D., P.M. O'Malley, R.A. Miech, J.G. Bachman, & J.E. Schulenberg. 2015. Monitoring the Future National Survey Results on Drug Use: 1975–2017: Overview, Key Findings on Adolescent Drug Use. Ann Arbor: Institute for Social Research, The University of Michigan.

What Do You Think?

Why do you think that drug use among teenagers has stabilized since 2008? Consider economic, social, and cultural reasons.

The figure shows the trends among eighth-, tenth-, and twelfth-grade students between 1992 and 2017. Eighteen percent of eighth graders reportedly have tried an illicit drug, as have 34 percent of tenth graders and 49 percent of twelfth graders. Drug use by teenagers decreased significantly between the late 1990s and mid-2000s. Rates climbed somewhat in 2008, but have since stabilized (Johnston et al., 2015).

Alcohol Use, Abuse, and Alcoholism

4.2   Identify the perceptions toward alcohol and drinking patterns.

Because alcohol is the most commonly used drug and can do substantial harm to individuals, families, and communities, this section focuses on several aspects of alcohol use and abuse. There is wide variation in how much people drink. Figure 4–2 breaks down the adult population into ten groups called deciles and examines how much each group drinks in an average week. As you can see, 40 percent of adults do not drink at all, and most groups drink very little. However, the top group—the top-drinking 10 percent of the population—consume an average of almost 74 drinks a week, or more than 10 drinks a day. The second highest group averages over two drinks a day (Ingraham, 2014).

4.2.1 Perceptions of Alcohol Use, Abuse, and Alcoholism

In our society, people have mixed feelings about alcohol. On one hand, alcohol creates warmth and high spirits and promotes interpersonal harmony and agreement ("Let's drink to that"). It has long been used in informal rituals (Christmas eggnog) and formal rites (wine as the blood of Christ) and has been important in the economies of many nations. The growing and harvesting of grapes, grain, and other crops used to produce alcoholic beverages, as well as the brewing, fermenting, distilling, and sale of alcoholic beverages, provide employment, trade, and tax revenues. On the other

Figure 4–2 Average Number of Drinks Per Person Consumed Weekly by Decile, Adults Age 18 and Over, 2014

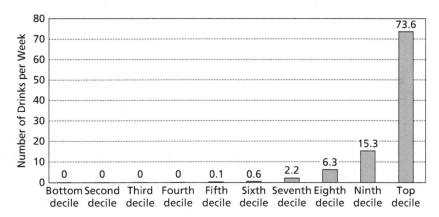

SOURCE: Based on Ingraham, C. 2014. "Think You Drink a Lot? This Chart Will Tell You." *Washington Post.* 25 September. Retrieved 15 April 2015 (www.washingtonpost.com/blogs/wonkblog/wp/2014/09/25/think-you-drink-a-lot-this-chart-will-tell-you/).

hand, the problems created by the abuse of alcohol are staggering. They include public drunkenness and disorderly behavior, traffic and industrial accidents, poor social functioning, broken marriages, child abuse, and aggravation of existing conditions such as poverty, mental and physical illness, and crime (National Institute on Alcohol Abuse and Alcoholism, June 2017).

Over 15 million Americans age 12 and over suffer from **Alcohol Use Disorder (AUD)**. To be diagnosed with AUD, individuals must meet certain criteria outlined in the *Diagnostic and Statistical Manual of Mental Disorders (DSM)*. Under *DSM–5*, the current version of the *DSM*, anyone meeting any two of the 11 criteria during the same 12-month period receives a diagnosis of AUD. The severity of AUD—mild, moderate, or severe—is based on the number of criteria met (Substance Abuse and Mental Health Services Administration, September, 2017):

1. spent a lot of time engaging in activities related to alcohol use
2. used alcohol in greater quantities or for a longer time than intended
3. developed tolerance
4. made unsuccessful attempts to cut down on use
5. continued use despite physical health or emotional problems associated with alcohol use
6. reduced or eliminated participation in other activities because of alcohol use
7. experienced withdrawal symptoms when cutting back or stopping use
8. problems at work, home, and school because of alcohol use
9. regularly using alcohol and then doing something physically dangerous
10. repeated trouble with the law because of alcohol use
11. continued use of alcohol despite problems with family or friends

Some, but certainly not all, people with AUD are addicted to alcohol. Those people who are physically addicted are considered alcoholics and have the following four symptoms of **alcoholism**.

- *Craving.* An uncontrollable urge for intoxication.
- *Loss of Control.* Not being able to stop drinking once drinking has begun.
- *Physical Dependence.* Acute withdrawal symptoms including uncontrollable trembling, nausea, rapid heartbeat, and heavy perspiration.
- *Tolerance.* The need to drink greater amounts of alcohol to get high.

Alcohol Use Disorder (AUD)

Individuals must meet certain criteria outlined in the *Diagnostic and Statistical Manual of Mental Disorders (DSM)*. The severity of AUD—mild, moderate, or severe—is based on the number of criteria met.

alcoholism

The state of being addicted to alcohol with the following four symptoms: craving, loss of control, physical dependence, and tolerance.

Alcohol plays a prominent role in our society. Most people drink only occasionally and have only a couple of drinks at a time. However, for a small but significant portion of the population, alcohol poses a large problem and interferes with the rest of life: work, school, family, and other social roles.

Oddly, the problems associated with AUD—chronic inebriation, vagrancy, missed days of work, not fulfilling family obligations—seem to arouse less interest and concern than the abuse, or even the use, of other drugs. Alcohol is thoroughly integrated into Western culture. It is adapted to our complex lifestyle because, in addition to relieving tension and reducing sexual and aggressive inhibitions, alcohol seems to facilitate interpersonal relations, at least superficially, whereas other drug experiences, even in groups, are often highly private.

The perception of alcohol as a social problem varies with changes in American culture and increased knowledge about the effects of alcohol use. According to some sociologists, in the early decades of the twentieth century, alcohol was a symbol that masked the larger social conflict between the working class, with its large immigrant component, and the upper class, which sought to control the workers and increase their productivity (Szasz, 1992).

In recent years, the American public has become more aware of the dangers associated with drinking—for example, the extensive damage it can cause to a developing fetus and the high correlation between highway accidents and driving while intoxicated. In the United States, alcohol is implicated in about 20 percent of all fatal highway accidents (National Highway Traffic Safety Administration, January, 2018), approximately one-third of all homicides, and 20 to 25 percent of drownings and boating deaths (Centers for Disease Control and Prevention, May 15, 2014a). These problems have led to crusades against excessive drinking rather than against alcohol itself. Both the Highway Safety Council and the Council for Accident Prevention note significant declines in traffic deaths due to drinking and in-home accidents associated with alcohol consumption. These decreases seem to indicate that crusades against excessive drinking are having an impact, and their success will surely reinforce efforts to educate the public about its risks.

4.2.2 Alcohol Abusers and Alcoholics

Several factors seem to be related to whether, how much, and in what ways an individual uses alcohol and becomes an alcohol abuser or alcoholic. Among these factors are biological and socioeconomic factors, gender, age, religion, and cultural influences. Of particular interest are genetics, sex, and age.

GENETICS Alcoholism and alcohol abuse appear to be due in part to biological factors and genetics, although the precise details are not yet known (National Institute on Alcohol Abuse and Alcoholism, 2015; Tawa, Hall, and Lohoff, 2016). How do researchers detect this? One mechanism is to study people who were adopted or who are twins (Verhulst, Neale, and Kendler, 2015). Adoption studies allow researchers to separate the effects of genetic and environmental factors because adoptees receive their genetic heritage from one set of parents and their rearing environment from another set. The degree to which adoptees resemble their biological relatives is a direct measure of genetic influence. Conversely, the degree to which adoptees resemble their adoptive relatives is a measure of the influence of family environment. Five adoption studies of alcoholism in males and four studies in females have included adequate sample sizes to evaluate genetic influences on alcoholism. In all five studies of male adoptees, participants with a biological family history of alcoholism were at significantly higher (i.e., 1.6 to 3.6 times greater) risk for alcoholism than were participants without a family history of alcoholism. This finding suggests that genetics contributes substantially to the risk for alcoholism among males. The studies of female adoptees, in contrast, obtained mixed results, with only two of the four studies finding a significantly increased risk of alcoholism among females with a biological family history of alcoholism compared with females with a negative family history. These results provided some evidence of possible sex differences in heritability but are inconclusive because of the small numbers of alcoholic female adoptees in the studies (Prescott, 2003).

So far, researchers who study the genetic factors linked to alcoholism are able to explain about half the risk for alcoholism faced by any given individual (Verhulst, Neale, and Kendler, 2015). Therefore, genes are important, but do not alone determine whether someone will become an alcoholic. Environmental factors, as well as gene and environment interactions, account for the remainder of the risk (Chartier, Karriker-Jaffe, Cummings, and Kendler, 2017).

Nonetheless, neurological studies show that brain function is often different in alcohol abusers and their children. Studies of alcoholism and biogenetic factors also indicate that some ethnic groups, particularly Native Americans, have lower tolerances for alcohol than other groups do, putting them at greater risk for alcoholism, and that some Asian populations have highly negative physiological reactions to alcohol, which tend to diminish their risk of becoming alcoholics.

SEX   Compared with women, men are more likely to drink alcohol, drink in larger quantities, and have more difficulty with their drinking, as indicated in Table 4–2. Sixty-one percent of men report having consumed an alcoholic beverage over the last month, as compared with 51 percent of women.

Sex differences in body structure and chemistry, however, cause women to absorb more alcohol and take longer to break it down and remove it from their bodies (i.e., to metabolize it). In other words, after drinking equal amounts, women have higher alcohol levels in their blood than men, and the immediate effects of the alcohol occur more quickly and last longer. One reason is that, on average, women weigh less than men. In addition, alcohol resides predominantly in body water, and pound for pound, women have less water in their bodies than men do. Other biological differences, including hormones, also may contribute. These differences also make women more vulnerable to alcohol's long-term effects on their health, including higher rates of liver damage, breast cancer, and heart disease (National Institute on Alcohol Abuse and Alcoholism, June, 2017; Wilsnack, Wilsnack, and Kantor, 2014).

Recent decades have seen a significant increase in alcohol abuse and alcoholism among adult women. Women are increasingly likely to be arrested for drunk driving and are showing up in emergency rooms dangerously drunk (Glaser, 2013). For both sexes, social factors—the presence of alcoholism in the family, childhood

Table 4–2 Sex Differences in Alcohol Consumption, 2015

	Women	Men
Drank Alcohol in the Last Month	51%	61%
Engaged in Binge Drinking in the Last Month	22%	32%
Engaged in Heavy Alcohol Use in the Last Month	5%	10%
Had Alcohol Use Disorder (AUD) in the Last Year	4%	8%
Had AUD and Received any Treatment in the Last Year	5%	7%

SOURCE: Data from National Institute on Alcohol Abuse and Alcoholism. 2017. "Alcohol Facts and Statistics." June. Retrieved 28 February 2018 (www.niaaa.nih.gov/alcohol-health/overview-alcohol-consumption/alcohol-facts-and-statistics).

unhappiness, and trauma—are important influences. But for women, increasing rates of alcohol abuse and alcoholism seem to go beyond these traditional factors. Some suggest it is related to their greater freedoms in society as compared to previous generations—working and having a career, going to school, and remaining single—while others focus on the increased stress in women's lives as the culprit (Glaser, 2013). Today's women are supposed to "have it all"—a strong education, an exciting career, and a happy family life, and many choose to unwind from this stress with alcohol. Interestingly, it is upper-middle-class women and lower-middle-class men who are more likely to drink heavily.

Yet the statistics on female alcoholism may be misleading. As women have become more visible in society, their drinking patterns have become more visible. Perhaps researchers are only now learning to identify the female alcoholic, and many women may still be hiding their drinking problems at home. Moreover, even if there has been an increase in alcoholism among women, it remains true that women have far fewer drinking problems than men do.

A special issue among women involves drinking alcohol while pregnant. Alcohol can disrupt fetal development at any stage during a pregnancy—including at the earliest stages before a woman even knows she is pregnant. Alcohol passes easily from a mother's bloodstream into her developing baby's blood. Alcohol present in a developing baby's bloodstream can interfere with the development of critical organs and body parts, including the brain, leading to **fetal alcohol spectrum disorders (FASD)**, which are a group of conditions that can occur in a person whose mother consumed alcohol during pregnancy. These effects can include physical abnormalities and problems with cognition, behavior, and learning that last a lifetime. Prenatal alcohol exposure is the leading preventable cause of birth defects in the United States (Centers for Disease Control and Prevention, June 6, 2017c).

It is not known precisely how much alcohol must be consumed during pregnancy for these results to occur, so pregnant women are advised to avoid alcohol entirely. Because the fetus is small, its blood-alcohol content will be much higher than that of the mother. A woman may hardly notice the effects of her drinking, but meanwhile her fetus is getting drunk.

fetal alcohol spectrum disorders (FASD)

A group of conditions that can occur in a person whose mother consumed alcohol during pregnancy. These effects can include physical abnormalities and problems with cognition, behavior, and learning that last a lifetime.

AGE Heavy drinking among men is most common at ages 21 to 30; among women, it occurs at ages 31 to 50. Nonetheless, drinking by teenagers and young adults is among the most serious aspect of alcohol use as a social problem, especially because so many lives are needlessly ended by alcohol-related deaths and because patterns of adult alcohol use are established during the teenage and young-adult years. Alcohol is by far the most frequently used illicit drug among teenagers, and it is consumed far more often than nicotine or marijuana (Johnston et al., 2018).

Many teenagers drink alcohol. The popularity of alcohol among young people is attributed to many factors, including the difficulty, expense, and danger of obtaining other drugs, and the manufacture and advertisement of alcoholic products that are especially appealing to the young, such as sweet wines and alcoholic beverages that resemble popular drinks such as lemonade. Drinking among young people can also be construed

A number of high-profile and well-funded research studies monitor alcohol use among teens and young adults because they are more likely than those in other age groups to binge drink, which contributes to a host of social and health problems.

Wavebreakmedia Ltd UC29/Alamy Stock Photo

as a rebellion against the adult world—an attempt to assert independence and imitate adult behavior. Some authorities believe strict regulations on drinking only make it more appealing. Moreover, prohibition of drinking by the young is extremely difficult in a society in which alcohol is widely used and relatively easy to procure.

When teens and young adults do drink, they often consume large amounts of alcohol. **Binge drinking** is defined as a pattern of drinking that brings blood alcohol concentration levels to 0.08 g/dL. This form of drinking amounts to a consumption of five or more drinks in a single session for males and four or more drinks for females. Binge drinking is a particularly dangerous behavior pattern because it can contribute to violence, auto accidents, and other major problems. Yet, more than half of the alcohol consumed by adults in the United States is in the form of binge drinks, as is about 90 percent of the alcohol consumed by youth under the age of 21 (Centers for Disease Control and Prevention, June 7, 2017a).

Because binge drinking is found most commonly among young adults, it has been studied intensely by two nationwide surveys. The first one, the *Monitoring the Future* survey, introduced earlier in this chapter, is conducted by the Institute of Survey Research at the University of Michigan. The second survey, the *Harvard School of Public Health College Alcohol Study* (CAS), is based on 50,000 college students attending 120 universities around the country. From these data, we know that, among high school students, binge drinking is on the decline, from about 32 percent of students acknowledging binge drinking over a two-week period in 1998 to less than 20 percent today (Johnston et al., 2018). The CAS survey of college students reports higher levels of binge drinking, with 43 percent of students reporting binge drinking at least once in a two-week period (Wechsler and Nelson, 2008).

binge drinking

A pattern of drinking that brings blood alcohol concentration (BAC) levels to 0.08 g/dL. Although the quantity of alcohol required to reach this level can vary, in general it amounts to a consumption of five or more drinks in a single session for males, and to four or more drinks for females.

What Do You Think?

Why do many young college people binge drink? What are some of the consequences of binge drinking? Design a program to help combat binge drinking on your college campus.

Alcohol-Related Social Problems

4.3   Assess several social problems related to alcohol.

Excessive use of alcohol contributes to many different social problems: accidental injury, sexual assault, murder, family violence, divorce, suicide, ruined health, fetal harm, and many more. The United States spends approximately $249 billion annually on problems related to excessive drinking (Centers for Disease Control and Prevention, June 7, 2017a). In this section, we briefly describe a few of these problems.

4.3.1 Health

Alcohol contributes to 88,000 deaths per year in the United States (Centers for Disease Control and Prevention, 2013). On average, alcoholics can expect to live 10 to 12 fewer years than nonalcoholics.

There are several reasons for this shortened life span. Alcohol contains a high number of calories and no vital nutrients. Thus, alcoholics generally have a reduced appetite for nutritious food and inevitably suffer from vitamin deficiencies; as a result, their resistance to infectious diseases is lowered. Drinking can also damage the heart, causing problems such as stroke, high blood pressure, arrhythmias (irregular heartbeat), and cardiomyopathy (stretching and drooping of the heart muscle). Over a long period, large amounts of alcohol also destroy liver cells, which are replaced by scar tissue; this condition, called cirrhosis of the liver, is the cause of tens of thousands of deaths each year in the United States. Other problems associated with the liver may include steatosis (fatty liver), alcoholic hepatitis, or fibrosis. Heavy drinking also contributes to the incidence of cancer, especially cancers of the mouth, esophagus, throat, liver, and breast.

DON'T EVEN THINK ABOUT IT

Solomonjee/Fotolia

Drivers under the influence of alcohol kill about 10,000 people a year. This number, while very high, represents a decline over the past couple of decades, and is due to many factors, including an increase in the drinking age, more effective law enforcement, and widespread educational campaigns to highlight the risks of driving while intoxicated.

Mothers Against Drunk Driving (MADD)

A nonprofit organization working to protect families from drunk driving and underage drinking through education and support of victims and survivors.

4.3.2 Drinking and Driving

After a hard night of partying, Nate hopped in his car for the drive home. "I'll drive slowly," he told himself, assuming that he could outwit the effects of six beers on his system. He was not successful. He didn't see the stop sign and ran right through it, totally oblivious. But he did feel the bump a minute later—"What was that?" He got out of the car, still wobbly, and saw that he had hit a cat, a black and white kitten, whose tuxedo face was now covered in blood and whose body was twisted in an awful position. He prayed the cat was dead so it wouldn't suffer, and he was thankful that he didn't hit a person. Two weeks later, he received a photo ticket in the mail, showing his car running the stop sign. He stared at the ticket, his stomach clenching, realizing that he could have paid far heavier penalties for driving while drunk.

There is a significant connection between alcohol use and vehicular accidents. Drivers whose alcohol level is over the legal limit of .08 are involved in nearly a third of traffic fatalities, accounting for 10,076 deaths in 2013 (National Highway Traffic Safety Administration, January, 2018). Body weight, length of time between drinks, type of alcohol, fatigue level, and medications or other drugs can all affect a person's blood alcohol level, so there is no set amount of alcohol that determines the legal limit. The good news, however, as you can see in Figure 4–3, is that there has been a steady decline in the rate of alcohol-related fatalities, down to about 10,300 in 2015 (Centers for Disease Control and Prevention, June 16, 2017b).

These declines can be attributed to low rates of drinking by high school students and young adults, greater awareness of the consequences of drunk driving, more rigorous social policies (e.g., raising the drinking age to 21 in all states), and enforcement of those policies. In particular, as states have adopted more uniform laws about driving under the influence of alcohol, and as more funding has been devoted to enforcement of these laws, declines in alcohol-related driving fatalities are evident.

State police and other authorities credit much of this success to the activities of **Mothers Against Drunk Driving (MADD)**, a nonprofit organization working to protect families from drunk driving and underage drinking through education and support of victims and survivors. Candy Lightner founded MADD in 1980 after the death of her 13-year-old daughter Cari in California. Cari was walking to a school carnival when a drunk driver struck her from behind. The driver had three prior drunk driving convictions and was out on bail from a hit-and-run arrest two days earlier. Her daughter was not alone. Nearly 17 percent of the 200 children who are killed by alcohol-impaired drivers each year are children who are struck down while walking or riding their bicycles (National Highway Traffic Safety Administration, 2016).

4.3.3 Crime

At least one-third of crimes are committed by someone under the influence of alcohol. Some of these crimes are relatively minor offenses such as disorderly conduct or vagrancy. In arrests for serious violent crimes, drunkenness generally does not appear in the charges, although alcohol often contributes to criminal acts. Based on victim

Figure 4–3 Fatalities and Fatality Rate per 100 Million Vehicle Miles Traveled (VMT) in Alcohol-Impaired-Driving Crashes, 2004–2015

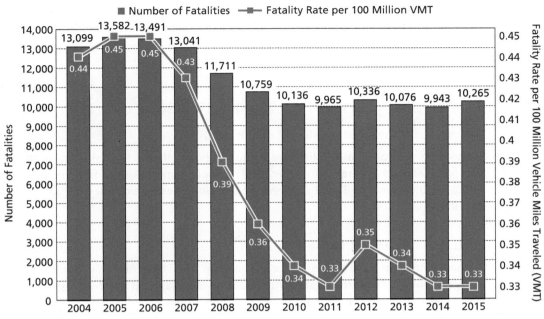

SOURCE: National Highway Traffic Safety Administration. "Traffic Safety Facts 2016 Data: Alcohol-Impaired Driving." U.S. Department of Transportation, Washington, DC; 2017 Retrieved 16 April 2018 (https://crashstats.nhtsa.dot.gov/Api/Public/ViewPublication/812450).

reports, alcohol use by the offender was a factor in (National Council on Alcohol and Drug Dependence, Inc., 2015a):

- 37 percent of rapes and sexual assaults (much higher among college students),
- 15 percent of robberies,
- 27 percent of aggravated assaults, and
- 25 percent of simple assaults.[1]

Sexual assault is a pervasive problem in society, and it is especially prominent on college campuses, where most assaults involve alcohol use by the perpetrator, victim, or both (Behnken, 2017; Testa and Cleveland, 2017; Tyler, Schmitz, and Adams, 2017). Roughly 1 in 5 females and 1 in 71 males will experience sexual assault while in college (Krebs et al., 2009). It is estimated that about 80 percent of victims and perpetrators know each other to some degree. They may be so-called "friends," classmates, acquaintances, or roommates. Drinking parties are a staple at most colleges and universities, and while alcohol does not cause rape per se, it does reduce inhibitions, thereby leading to vulnerable situations, aggressiveness and hostile masculinity, and inappropriate behavior. Sexual assault and rape will be discussed more fully in the next chapter.

Likewise, in many homicide cases, alcohol is found in the victim, the offender, or both. A significant percentage of male sex offenders are chronic alcoholics or were drinking at the time of the offense. The reasons for the high correlation of drinking with arrests for serious violent crimes are not fully understood. It has been pointed out that alcohol, by removing some inhibitions, may cause people to behave in unaccustomed ways. Also, as with other drugs, the need to obtain the substance may lead to theft or other property crimes and sometimes to violent crimes like armed robbery. Since chronic alcoholics may be unable to hold steady jobs, their financial difficulties are compounded, perhaps increasing the temptation to commit crimes. Also, the values and self-image of chronic heavy drinkers tend to change as their condition worsens. They are more likely to associate with delinquents or criminals, which may lead them to commit criminal acts themselves.

---

[1]National Council on Alcohol and Drug Dependence, Inc., 2015.

What Do You Think?

Identify a research question or hypothesis related to alcohol use and/or abuse that a functionalist, a conflict theorist, and an interactionist might pose. How are these research questions or hypotheses different from one another?

In addition to its link with serious crimes, alcoholism creates another problem; it places a major strain on the law enforcement system, which must process large numbers of petty offenders. Arrests, trials, and incarcerations of offenders cost taxpayers billions of dollars each year. And many of these arrests involve a small segment of the community—the neighborhood drunk or derelict who may be repeatedly arrested and imprisoned briefly over the course of a year.

Effects of Alcoholism on the Family

4.4   Describe the effects of alcohol on the family.

If the only victims of alcoholism were the alcoholics themselves, the social effects would be serious enough. However, other people, especially the families of alcoholics, also suffer. The home can become a chaotic battlefield, affecting all family members.

4.4.1 Consequences for Adults

Alcohol abuse can leave a marriage or relationship very shaky or may cause it to break up completely because the relationship usually centers around the drinking member: his or her moods, health, feelings, work situation, stresses, and coping. The needs of the other spouse or partner and the needs of the children are ignored or subsumed under the needs of the alcoholic.

Two common interrelated sources of marital conflict are financial and work issues. Alcohol is expensive—and can cost upwards of thousands of dollars a year. At the same time, many alcoholics find it difficult to keep a job, or they are absent from work frequently, missing out on pay after their sick-leave benefits expire.

Spouses and partners deal with alcoholism in several ways. **Codependency** refers to a relationship pattern in which a person assumes the responsibility for meeting others' needs, often to the detriment of their own needs. Codependency is far more than simply caring for another person. Instead, codependent people lose their own sense of identity and awareness of their own feelings. They take too much responsibility for their addicted spouse or partner. Usually, a codependent person engages in **enabling behaviors**. They will do things to cover for, support, and enable the alcoholic to continue to drink. For example, the codependent person might call an employer to claim that the drinker is sick when he or she is actually suffering from a hangover, might buy alcohol for the drinker, might excuse the drinker from doing domestic chores or participating in family life, might make up excuses to the children as to why their parent is not fulfilling his or her roles in the family, or might in other ways send messages to the drinker that it is okay to continue drinking.

codependency

A relationship pattern in which a person assumes the responsibility for meeting others' needs, often to the detriment of their own needs.

enabling behaviors

Behaviors that a codependent person will do to cover for, support, and enable an alcoholic to continue to drink (or to enable another type of abuser to continue toxic behaviors).

4.4.2 Consequences for Children

Alcohol abuse in a family can strain children's lives. Children in families where one or both parents abuse alcohol are more likely to have problems with depression, aggression, peer relationships, delinquency, school performance, and emotional issues as compared with their peers whose parents do not have problems with alcohol. These problems stem from the painful emotional climate, dysfunction, and turmoil in the home (Dayton, 2011). Their environment is often unpredictable, chaotic, and filled with broken promises. Children may be asked to keep inappropriate secrets (e.g., "Don't tell Mommy that you saw Daddy drinking");

A Personal View

"My Dad Is an Alcoholic"

Monkey Business/Fotolia

My dad is an alcoholic. There, I said it. Do you know that this is the first time that I have talked about this issue to someone outside my family? He gets drunk every night after work, "I think I'll have a little scotch," he says, even when he is finishing a huge bottle. I hate it when he asks me to make him a drink.

I'm too ashamed to admit to my friends that my dad is an alcoholic, but they probably know because he is often drunk when they come over. And he gets loud when he is drunk. I don't even like my friends to come to my house anymore; I'll make excuses why it would be better for me to go over to their houses or meet somewhere else. My sister, Rachel, doesn't bring her friends over either. One time Dad made a crude sexual joke in front of one of her friends, and that was that. She got mad at him and yelled, and he slapped her hard

in front of her friend. He apologized the next day, as he usually does, but I don't think she will ever forgive him. She told me she hates him.

I just try to stay out from under his radar. I do really well in school so he doesn't have any reason to bother me. I like the attention that I get from my teachers. They all think I'm really smart. I'm not so sure I'm smart, but it makes me feel good that they think so.

I tried talking to Mom about his drinking and how Rachel hates him, but my mom just said that it's natural for girls and their fathers to fight. She doesn't see the problem. It's weird. Sometimes she will come to Rachel and me at night crying about his drinking, but then at other times when we bring it up, she'll say "Oh, it's not that big of a deal." She even sometimes does both in the same conversation! A couple of weeks ago, Mom came to us crying and saying that she couldn't take it anymore, and a minute later, when Rachel said that she couldn't take it anymore either, Mom gave her a mean look and said, "Don't talk about your father like that! He's doing the best he can." It's like Mom just snapped. She can say it, but we can't. I hate what my dad is doing to my family.

—Chris, age 13

Critical Thinking

When a parent is an alcoholic, other members of the family often play specific roles related to the alcoholism. What roles do you see being played out in this family?

to live by arbitrary and rigid rules (e.g., going to bed unusually early so parents can drink); and to cope with chronic disappointment (e.g., parents making promises that they repeatedly do not keep). Many children in this kind of environment receive inadequate nurturing. Unlike a spouse who can choose to leave the situation, children in dysfunctional families are trapped. They cannot leave. Instead, they often play one of several roles to cope:

- *Chief Enabler.* A child may put aside his or her own personal feelings and become increasingly more responsible for control of the alcoholic and the family.
- *Family Hero.* This child tries to better the family situation by succeeding in the environment outside the home, such as school. Often, this behavior is a cry for positive recognition for the family or to increase self-worth.
- *Scapegoat.* Not willing to work as hard as the hero for recognition, the scapegoat pulls away in a destructive manner, bringing negative attention to the family.
- *Lost Child.* This child takes care of his or her personal problems quietly and avoids trouble. Often ignored by the family, this child faces problems inward, and is often lonely and quietly suffering.

- *Mascot.* To deal with personal pain and loneliness, this child is charming and funny in times of stress. This behavior relieves pain for some family members, but does not really help the mascot.

Many children experience long-term effects of their parent's alcohol abuse. They may have little grasp of what is considered "normal" family behavior. Many suffer from low self-esteem, have trouble forming and maintaining close relationships, and experience other emotional difficulties (Kaplan, Nayak, Greenfield, and Karriker-Jaffe, 2017; Park and Schepp, 2015).

The feature box, *A Personal View: "My Dad Is an Alcoholic,"* chronicles a teenage boy's family life in which his father is an alcoholic. Can you identify the roles played out in the family?

Treatment of Alcoholism

4.5 Compare treatment options for alcoholism.

There are several treatment options for alcoholism, including rehabilitation, Alcoholics Anonymous, Antabuse, and other programs. These approaches differ from one another; there is not one option that is right for everyone.

4.5.1 Rehabilitation

Alcoholism is increasingly viewed as an illness with a variety of psychological and physiological components; therefore, it is possible to rehabilitate, but not completely cure, many alcoholics (Brick, 2004). A variety of nonpunitive attempts have been made to assist alcoholics in overcoming their addiction or habituation and to help alcoholism-prone individuals handle disturbing emotions and anxieties. The Comprehensive Alcohol Abuse and Alcoholism Prevention, Treatment and Rehabilitation Act of 1970 created the National Institute on Alcohol Abuse and Alcoholism to coordinate federal government activities. It also created the National Advisory Council on Alcohol Abuse and Alcoholism to recommend national policies. The act also provided grants to states for the development of comprehensive programs for alcoholism, for specific prevention and treatment projects, and incentives for private hospitals that admit patients with alcohol-related problems.

Traditionally, hospitals offered little beyond the "drying out" and release of alcoholic patients; they might treat a specific medical problem caused by alcohol but not alcoholism itself. The American Hospital Association now advocates hospital alcoholism programs and is attempting to utilize the resources of general hospitals in community treatment programs.

4.5.2 Alcoholics Anonymous

Some of the most impressive successes in coping with alcoholism have been achieved by Alcoholics Anonymous (AA). The effectiveness of this group in helping individual alcoholics is based on what amounts to a conversion. Alcoholics are led to this experience through fellowship with others like themselves, some of whom have already mastered their problem while others are in the process of doing so. In 2017, there were more than 118,000 AA groups throughout the world, with over 2.1 million members (Alcoholics Anonymous, June, 2017).

The organization insists that drinkers face up to their shortcomings and the realities of life and, when possible, make amends to people they have hurt in the past. The movement also concentrates on building up alcoholics' self-esteem and reassuring them of their basic worth as human beings. Since its founding in 1935, the group has developed a technique in which recovered alcoholics support and comfort drinkers who are undergoing

Alcoholics Anonymous (AA), founded in 1935, has over 2 million members. The cornerstone of AA is a 12-step program based on faith in a "higher power."

rehabilitation. This support is also available during crises when a relapse seems likely, and on a year-round basis through meetings that the alcoholic may attend as often as necessary.

AA has created special groups to deal with teenage and young adult drinkers. It has also established programs to aid nonalcoholic spouses and the children of alcoholics. Alateen is for young people whose lives have been affected by someone else's drinking. The alcoholic need not be a member of AA for relatives to participate in these offshoot programs, which developed out of the recognition that an entire family is psychologically involved in the alcohol-related problems of any of its members.

It appears that AA is the most successful large-scale program for dealing with alcoholism; it estimates its membership at over 2 million. According to the AA 12-step credo, it is essential for addicts to acknowledge their lack of control over alcohol use and to abstain from all alcoholic beverages for the rest of their lives. This approach sees alcoholism as an allergy in which even one drink can produce an intolerable reaction—a craving for more.

The voluntary nature of the program probably contributes to its success; however, it is unlikely that this approach, with its insistence on total abstinence, could be applied successfully to all alcoholics. In particular, alcoholics who reject the spiritual tenets of AA, which teach the recovering alcoholic to seek help from a "higher power," whatever that may mean to the individual, would not identify with many aspects of the AA approach. Alcoholics who are unwilling to accept these tenets can find programs that are related to the 12 steps of the AA program but eliminate the spiritual aspects.

4.5.3 Antabuse

Antabuse, a prescription drug, sensitizes the patient in such a way that consuming even a small quantity of alcohol causes strong and uncomfortable physical symptoms. Drinkers become intensely flushed, their pulse quickens, and they feel nauseated.

Before beginning treatment with Antabuse, the alcoholic goes through a process to **detoxify** (keep off alcohol until none shows in blood samples) his or her body. Then the drug is administered to the patient along with doses of alcohol for several consecutive days. The patient continues to take the drug for several more days, and at the close of the period another dose of alcohol is administered. The trial doses of alcohol condition the patient to recognize the relationship between drinking and the unpleasant symptoms. (Similar treatment programs depend on different nausea-producing drugs or electric shock to condition the patient against alcohol; this process is known as **aversion therapy or behavior conditioning**).

Antabuse (or Disulfiram) has gained only limited acceptance in the treatment of alcoholics. Critics claim that its effect is too narrow and that this approach neglects the personality problems of the drinker. They also maintain that the drug does not work for people who are suspicious of treatment or who have psychotic tendencies.

detoxify

To keep a person off alcohol or another substance until none shows in blood samples.

aversion therapy/behavior conditioning

A form of treatment that applies nausea-producing drugs or electric shock to condition the patient against alcohol.

4.5.4 Other Programs

A problem drinker or alcoholic who receives help while at home and on the job usually responds better than one who is institutionalized. Community care programs treat these problem drinkers, as well as their families, to improve their self-image and enhance their sense of security within the family.

Employee assistance programs, a relatively new development, have demonstrated considerable effectiveness in treating problem drinkers in the workplace. Their success depends on their availability on a scheduled basis and during crises, on the maintenance of absolute confidentiality, and on the development of rapport between the counselor and the patient as they explore underlying psychological problems such as loneliness, alienation, and poor self-image. Also important is the patient's desire to remain in the community and to continue working.

Illegal Drug Use and Abuse

4.6 **Summarize the most commonly used drugs that are abused.**

Although alcohol currently has a secure place in American social policy, it was made illegal during the Prohibition era in the early twentieth century. How does society respond to other drug use? The major categories of illegal drugs are constantly changing as culture and customs change. In eighteenth-century England, the use of tobacco was forbidden; anyone found guilty of consuming it could be punished by extreme measures such as amputation or splitting of the nose. In the United States, cocaine was introduced to the public early in the twentieth century as an additive to a new commercial soft drink, Coca-Cola.

Today the use of illegal drugs embraces an extremely diverse set of behaviors, ranging from recreational use of marijuana to heroin addiction. The most commonly used drugs today, in addition to alcohol, are marijuana, prescription drugs or cold medicines (for nonmedical purposes), hallucinogens (such as LSD), cocaine, inhalants, MDMA (which often goes by the names of Ecstasy or Molly), methamphetamine, crack cocaine, and heroin (National Institute on Drug Abuse, 2018c). Opioids have come under increasing scrutiny because of the large numbers of people who have become quickly addicted to them, which will be discussed later in this chapter.

The percentage of people ages 12 and over and those between the ages of 18 and 25 who have reported using these drugs at some point during the past year is reported in Table 4–3. Use ranges from a third of young adults using marijuana to less than

Table 4–3 Percentage of Persons Age 12 and Older and Ages 18–25 Who Have Used a Drug in the Past Year, 2016

	Age 12 and Older	Ages 18–25
Marijuana	14%	33%
Prescription Drugs/Psychotherapeutics	7%	15%
Hallucinogens	2%	7%
Tranquilizers/Sedatives	3%	6%
Cocaine	2%	6%
MDMA (Ecstasy/Molly)	0.9%	4%
Inhalants	0.6%	1.4%
Methamphetamine	0.5%	0.8%
Heroin	0.4%	0.7%

SOURCE: National Institute on Drug Abuse. 2017c. "Trends & Statistics: Costs of Substance Abuse." April. Retrieved 28 February 2018 (www.drugabuse.gov/related-topics/trends-statistics).

1 percent trying heroin (National Institute on Drug Abuse, April, 2017c). Next, we'll discuss each of these drugs, concluding with a section on the recent opioid crisis.

4.6.1 Marijuana

Marijuana refers to the dried leaves, flowers, stems, and seeds from the hemp plant, *Cannabis sativa*. The plant contains the mind-altering chemical *delta-9-tetrahydrocannabinol* (THC) and other related compounds.

Like alcohol, marijuana is a social drug, one that is often used in social gatherings because it is thought to ease or enhance interaction. Because the use of marijuana is widespread and there is little evidence that it has detrimental long-term effects or leads to the use of stronger drugs, the federal government has shifted its enforcement efforts to the more clearly addicting drugs. About half of states now allow small amounts of marijuana to be used for medicinal purposes, such as helping with nausea.

As of mid-2018, nine states—California, Colorado, Washington, Oregon, Nevada, Vermont, Massachusetts, Maine, and Alaska—have legalized small amounts of marijuana for personal use. In contrast, being caught with any marijuana in Arizona is a felony. Under President Obama, federal prosecutors were discouraged from bringing charges wherever marijuana is legal under state law. However, President Trump rescinded this policy in his first few days in office, creating some confusion surrounding whether it is legal to sell, buy, or possess marijuana in those parts of the country where state and federal law conflict (Savage and Healy, 2018). This could be a problem for Republicans facing reelection battles in states with legal marijuana.

Is marijuana harmful? Many people compare it to alcohol, which, although legal, does have some harmful side effects, especially with heavy use. Marijuana use directly affects the brain—specifically the parts of the brain responsible for memory, learning, attention, decision making, coordination, emotions, and reaction time. Developing brains, like those in babies, children, and teens, are especially susceptible to these adverse effects of marijuana. Long-term or frequent marijuana use has been linked to increased risk of psychosis or schizophrenia in some users (Volkow et al., 2016; Fibey et al., 2014).

Proponents of marijuana point out that the prohibition of marijuana takes a financial and social toll on society, and that enforcement is inherently biased. They point to the medicinal properties of marijuana and point out that it is less toxic than alcohol.

4.6.2 Abuse of Prescription Drugs

Abuse of prescription drugs is becoming an ever more serious form of drug use and addiction. Opium-derived pain medicines such as Oxycontin and Vicodin; benzodiazepine tranquilizers such as Valium and Xanax; sedatives and sleeping pills such as Ambien and the barbiturates; and prescription amphetamines, often dispensed as diet pills, are among the most frequently abused of the widely available but heavily controlled prescription drugs. Pain relievers, which, because they are derived from opium, are among the most addictive prescription drugs, are also the most commonly abused.

Most adults over age 40 who abuse or become addicted to prescription drugs first used the drug under a physician's supervision. But young adults and adolescents tend to obtain the drugs through friends and street dealers. The National Institute on Drug Abuse reports that since the early 1990s, abuse of prescription-type drugs has "escalated substantially" across the nation, especially among people between the ages of 12 and 25 (National Institute on Drug Abuse, January, 2018a). The agency also warns that use of multiple drugs, known as polydrug use, is extremely common among abusers of prescription drugs. The mixing of drugs for nonmedical recreational use has risks that are dangerously underestimated by users.

4.6.3 Hallucinogens

Hallucinogenic compounds found in some plants and mushrooms (or their extracts) have been used—mostly during religious rituals—for centuries. While the exact mechanisms by which hallucinogens exert their effects remain unclear, research suggests that these drugs work, at least partially, by temporarily interfering with neurotransmitter action or by binding to their receptor sites. Some hallucinogens also cause users to feel out of control or disconnected from their body and environment (National Institute on Drug Abuse, January, 2016c).

Unlike most other drugs, the effects of hallucinogens are highly variable and unreliable, producing different effects in different people at different times. This changeability is mainly due to the significant variations in amount and composition of active compounds, particularly in the hallucinogens derived from plants and mushrooms. Because of their unpredictable nature, the use of hallucinogens can be particularly dangerous even though there is little evidence of hallucinogens being habit forming.

4.6.4 Cocaine

Cocaine is a powerfully addictive stimulant drug made from the leaves of the coca plant native to South America. It produces short-term euphoria, energy, talkativeness, and a feeling of increased intellectual power. Cocaine is a strong central nervous system stimulant that increases levels of the neurotransmitter dopamine in brain circuits regulating pleasure and movement. Normally, dopamine is released by neurons in these circuits in response to potential rewards (like the smell of good food) and then recycled back into the cell that released it, thus shutting off the signal between neurons. Cocaine prevents the dopamine from being recycled, causing excessive amounts to build up in the synapse, or junction between neurons. This buildup amplifies the dopamine signal and ultimately disrupts normal brain communication. It is this flood of dopamine that causes cocaine's characteristic high.

Crack cocaine is a form of cocaine that can be smoked rather than ingested through the nasal passages. Commercial cocaine is "cooked" with ether or bicarbonate of soda to form a "rock" of crack. When it is smoked, crack produces an instant and extremely powerful rush that tends to last only about 15 minutes and to cause a strong desire for another rush. This form of cocaine is therefore highly addicting. Crack is more expensive than cocaine in its powder form, and its use is often associated with an expensive lifestyle. Perhaps for this reason, some athletes, movie stars, and politicians who previously used cocaine have become addicted to crack, with disastrous consequences in some cases.

With repeated use, cocaine can cause long-term changes in the brain's reward system as well as other brain systems, which may lead to addiction. With repeated use, tolerance to cocaine also can develop; many cocaine abusers report that they seek but fail to achieve as much pleasure as they did from their first exposure. Some users will increase their dose in an attempt to intensify and prolong their high, but this practice can also increase the risk of adverse psychological or physiological effects (National Institute on Drug Abuse, June, 2016b).

4.6.5 Inhalants

Many products readily found in the home or workplace—such as spray paints, markers, glues, and cleaning fluids—contain volatile substances that have mind-altering properties when inhaled. People do not typically think of these products as drugs because they were never intended for that purpose.

Abusers of inhalants breathe them in through the nose or mouth in a variety of ways (known as "huffing"). They may sniff or snort fumes from a container or dispenser (such as a glue bottle or a marking pen), spray aerosols (such as computer

Legalizing Marijuana

Americans are ambivalent about marijuana. In the 1960s, the drug was popular among college students and other people "rebelling" against the norms of society. Today, as research shows the health effects of marijuana are significantly less serious than those of other drugs, including alcohol, many people are wondering why it is still illegal and lumped together with other "illicit" drugs.

Marijuana is the most commonly used illicit drug, tried by nearly half the population ages 12 and over. It is one of the few drugs whose use has been increasing in recent years.

There has been a move to allow marijuana to be used for medical purposes when prescribed by a physician. People who suffer from cancer or other painful illnesses, or whose medical treatment causes nausea, may find significant relief from their symptoms from marijuana. Currently, only about half of the states allow marijuana for medicinal purposes.

Some advocates of marijuana go even further to suggest that it should be legal. Nine states have legalized small amounts of marijuana for personal use.

Other people oppose legalizing marijuana. They believe that it is a powerful drug with harmful side effects for the person using it and for society. Jeff Sessions, the U.S. Attorney General, has said that good people don't smoke marijuana.

Some people oppose legalizing marijuana because they are concerned that it will lead to using other, more dangerous drugs. The popular view that marijuana is a stepping stone or gateway to stronger drugs is not supported by research. It may be true that most people who abuse drugs first use alcohol and marijuana, but only a small percentage of people who use these drugs go on to use more dangerous and addicting drugs.

Critical Thinking

Reflecting on the four themes of this text—the importance of using an empirical approach, linking individual experiences with social structure, understanding that social inequality contributes to social problems, and acknowledging that understanding social problems requires a comparative perspective—how do each of these themes inform your understanding of drug and alcohol use?

cleaning dusters) directly into their nose or mouth or place a chemical-soaked rag in their mouth. Abusers may also inhale fumes from a balloon or a plastic or paper bag. Although the high produced by inhalants usually lasts just a few minutes, abusers often try to prolong it by continuing to inhale repeatedly over several hours.

Most abused inhalants depress the central nervous system in a manner not unlike alcohol. The effects are similar—including slurred speech, lack of coordination, euphoria, and dizziness. Inhalant abusers may also experience light-headedness, hallucinations, and delusions. With repeated inhalations, many users feel less inhibited and less in control. Some may feel drowsy for several hours and experience a lingering headache. Long-term use can damage the heart, liver, and muscles and can cause anemia and nerve damage (National Institute on Drug Abuse, February, 2017a).

4.6.6 MDMA

MDMA (3,4-methylenedioxy-methamphetamine), popularly known as ecstasy or, more recently, as Molly, is a synthetic mind-altering drug that has similarities to both the stimulant amphetamine and the hallucinogen mescaline. It produces feelings of increased energy, euphoria, emotional warmth and empathy toward others, and distortions in sensory and time perception. MDMA was initially popular among white adolescents and young adults in the nightclub scene or at "raves" (long dance parties), but the drug is now used by a broader segment of the population.

MDMA is taken orally, usually as a capsule or tablet. The popular term *Molly* (slang for "molecular") refers to the pure crystalline powder form of MDMA, usually sold in capsules. The drug's effects last approximately 3 to 6 hours, although it is not uncommon for users to take a second dose of the drug as the effects of the first dose begin to fade. It is commonly taken in combination with other drugs.

MDMA acts by increasing the activity of three neurotransmitters—serotonin, dopamine, and norepinephrine. The emotional and pro-social effects of MDMA are likely caused directly or indirectly by the release of large amounts of serotonin, which influences mood. The surge of serotonin caused by taking MDMA depletes the brain of this important chemical, however, causing negative after-effects—including confusion, depression, sleep problems, drug craving, and anxiety—that may occur soon after taking the drug or during the days or even weeks thereafter (National Institute on Drug Abuse, October, 2016a).

"Meth" can be used in a number of ways. Many people prefer to inject it into their veins because it produces an intense euphoria almost instantaneously.

4.6.7 Methamphetamine

Methamphetamine (also called meth, crystal, chalk, and ice, among other terms) is an extremely addictive stimulant drug. It takes the form of a white, odorless, bitter-tasting crystalline powder. Methamphetamine is taken orally, smoked, snorted, or dissolved in water or alcohol and injected. Smoking or injecting the drug delivers it very quickly to the brain, where it produces an immediate, intense euphoria. Because the pleasure also fades quickly, users often take repeated doses, in a "binge and crash" pattern (National Institute on Drug Abuse, February, 2017b).

Methamphetamine is causing widespread concern among law enforcement officials and medical professionals. It is often manufactured in makeshift "super laboratories" in Mexico or the United States, but it can also be manufactured in people's homes and garages using inexpensive over-the-counter drugs. At present, methamphetamine is making headlines and appears to be gaining in popularity among teenagers and young adults, especially in rural areas and small towns throughout the nation. Because the drug can be produced using some over-the-counter cold remedies, these cold medicines have been pulled from the market.

4.6.8 Heroin

Heroin is an opioid drug that is synthesized from morphine, a naturally occurring substance extracted from the seedpod of the Asian opium poppy plant. Heroin can be injected, inhaled by snorting or sniffing, or smoked. All three routes of administration deliver the drug to the brain very rapidly. Most heroin users experience a sudden, intense feeling of pleasure; others may feel greater self-esteem and composure. But because heroin slows brain functions, the addict becomes lethargic after the initial euphoria (National Institute on Drug Abuse, January, 2018b).

Heroin has a very high risk for addiction, which can be characterized by uncontrollable drug-seeking no matter the consequences. The notorious relationship between crime and heroin addiction results not from the influence of the drug, per se, but from the suffering caused by the lack of it: Addicts avoid withdrawal symptoms at all costs.

A person addicted to heroin frequently suffers from malnutrition, as well as from hepatitis, AIDS, and other infections caused by intravenous injection of the drug. In communities where heroin addicts are numerous and visible, there is often conflict over the advisability of providing free needles so that addicts will not be forced to share illegally purchased hypodermics and risk the mixing of blood that may contain the HIV virus.

What Do You Think?

What types of drugs were popular in your high school? What was the general attitude toward these drugs and their health risks?

Patterns, Problems, and Treatment

4.7 Identify some of the patterns, problems, and treatments associated with drug abuse.

People who abuse drugs face many of the same issues as those who abuse alcohol (and some people abuse both simultaneously). But there are also substantial differences between who uses drugs, the problems they can bring, and treatment options.

4.7.1 Patterns of Drug Use

The study of drug use in the United States is a social-scientific undertaking of great magnitude. The data come from two major sources. The first source includes reports from public and private agencies that deal with arrest, hospitalization, treatment, or legal matters. These reports offer important evidence about trends in drug use among individuals arrested for crimes or admitted to hospital emergency rooms. But they do not tell us very much about the distribution of drug use in the general population. This information is obtained from large-scale national surveys, the second source.

The annual survey of 16,000 high school seniors that was mentioned earlier, *Monitoring the Future*, gives a glimpse of drug (and alcohol) use among teenagers. Another important survey is the National Household Survey on Drug Abuse, which is sponsored by the National Institute on Drug Abuse, and which focuses on adults. Other surveys that collect information on various aspects of substance use and abuse are quite common, but these two allow researchers to track patterns of use from year to year.

WHO USES DRUGS? Data from the national surveys indicate that drug use among Americans has stabilized or is declining somewhat, except for a few drugs, most noticeably marijuana. As shown in Figure 4–4, after a decline in the early 2000s, marijuana use began to increase by the mid-2000s. By 2016, there were more than 20 million people who had used it in the past month—about 8.9 percent of people ages 12 and over.

Surveys of drug use over time also provide information about its distribution by sex, socioeconomic status, and racial or ethnic background (Newcomb, Birkett,

Figure 4–4 Percentage of Persons Age 12 and Older Who Have Used Drugs Over the Past Month, 2002–2016

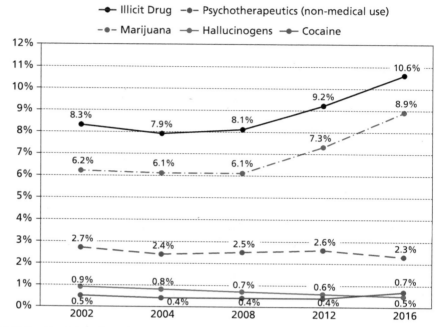

Legend:
- Illicit Drug
- Psychotherapeutics (non-medical use)
- Marijuana
- Hallucinogens
- Cocaine

Illicit Drug: 8.3% (2002), 7.9% (2004), 8.1% (2008), 9.2% (2012), 10.6% (2016)

Marijuana: 6.2% (2002), 6.1% (2004), 6.1% (2008), 7.3% (2012), 8.9% (2016)

Psychotherapeutics: 2.7% (2002), 2.4% (2004), 2.5% (2008), 2.6% (2012), 2.3% (2016)

Hallucinogens: 0.9% (2002), 0.8% (2004), 0.7% (2008), 0.6% (2012), 0.7% (2016)

Cocaine: 0.5% (2002), 0.4% (2004), 0.4% (2008), 0.4% (2012), 0.5% (2016)

SOURCE: National Institute on Drug Abuse. 2017c. "Trends & Statistics: Costs of Substance Abuse." April. Retrieved 28 February 2018 (www.drugabuse.gov/related-topics/trends-statistics).

Corliss, and Mustanski, 2014). Men are more likely to use drugs, and they use more of them than do women. Drug use is found in all socioeconomic groups, although the type of drug used differs substantially due to the cost of the drug and the culture surrounding its use. For example, the abuse of prescription drugs is more likely to occur among the middle classes and those with more money because of the cost of the drugs or the likelihood of having health insurance to help pay for the drugs. Drug use is higher among Native Americans and blacks, least common among Asians, with whites and Hispanics falling somewhere between. Young adults use drugs more frequently than those who are older; however, drug use among older people is increasing.

HOW DOES DRUG USE SPREAD? Most sociologists and social psychologists agree that drug use is a learned behavior that spreads through groups of peers who influence one another. In a pioneering study, Howard S. Becker (1963) traced the career of a marijuana user, showing that users must learn how to smoke the drug and identify their reaction to it as pleasurable. If they are unable to make this identification, they stop using the drug. They also gradually learn that the social controls that work against marijuana use—limited supplies, the need to maintain secrecy, and the definition of drug use as immoral—either do not apply to the peer group or can be circumvented.

Drug use is high among young people ages 18–24. The peer group is an important influence on whether a young person will use drugs.

Monkey Business/Fotolia

The most important direct influence on drug use is that of the peer group (Sellers, O'Brien, Hernandez, and Spirito, 2018). However, other factors set the stage for involvement in drug-using peer groups, including the individual's socioeconomic status and neighborhood environment and the influences of family, religion, and school. Drug use is more likely when a young person has problems in school, or when the family is forced to live in a neighborhood where young people have ready access to drugs (Green et al., 2010). If the individual's social milieu contributes significantly to drug use, what effect might a change in milieu have? Most U.S. soldiers who were addicted to heroin in Vietnam were generally able to kick the habit rather easily when they returned home, which shows that people can abstain from an extremely addicting drug when their social milieu no longer supports it. This is also an example of the phenomenon that drug researchers term "maturing out," that is, the tendency of drug users to decrease their use of drugs of all kinds, including alcohol, beginning in their late 20s (Han, Gfroerer, and Colliver, 2010).

4.7.2 Problems Associated with Drug Abuse

A wide number of social and health problems are associated with drug abuse. Here we will examine two: crime and the spread of HIV.

CRIME Images of drugs and crime abound in the media. Popular television shows, such as *NCIS*, illustrate how drugs and crime are interrelated. However, the nature of drug-related crimes varies with the type of drug involved. Neither marijuana nor low-to-moderate use of barbiturates are likely to promote violence. Users of other drugs, such as heroin, crack cocaine, or methamphetamine, in contrast, seem disproportionately involved in crime. The connection of these drugs with crime occurs because people who abuse these drugs can rarely support their habit on their own without resorting to crime. In addition, many abusers already have a criminal history (National Council on Alcohol and Drug Dependence, Inc., 2015b,c).

The crimes committed to support a drug habit tend to be money-seeking crimes such as burglary, prostitution, and shoplifting. Although these crimes may provide 40 to 50 percent of the addict's income for drug purchases, one study estimated that almost half the annual consumption of heroin in New York City is financed by selling the drug itself along with the equipment needed to inject it. All these crimes, considered nonviolent in themselves, nevertheless are often accompanied by violence such as muggings or armed robberies.

Jail or prison time alone has little effect on the reduction of drug addiction or in promoting recovery. Sixty to 80 percent of those who abuse drugs commit a new crime (typically a drug-driven crime) after release from jail or prison (National Council on Alcohol and Drug Dependence, Inc., 2015b,c). Incarceration without access to treatment or without specific plans for treatment after the person's discharge is not particularly effective.

DRUG USE AND AIDS A primary means by which AIDS spreads among heterosexual populations is the sharing of needles and syringes by intravenous drug users. Public health officials were slow to realize the extent of AIDS transmission among intravenous drug users. Hence, they were also slow to initiate educational and other programs that might hinder the spread of the disease in this population.

Efforts to reach addicts must overcome several obstacles. Because their activity is illegal, addicts are reluctant to come forward to be tested for AIDS. Public health workers lack credibility in the eyes of addicts but attempts to employ ex-addicts in outreach programs have had more success. Needle exchange programs have been tried successfully in many cities. The World Health Organization sponsored a study of HIV prevalence in 103 cities throughout the world. In 36 cities with needle exchange programs, HIV infections declined by 19 percent annually, but in 67 cities without such programs infection rates increased by 8 percent each year (Campbell, 2005). Remarkable results like these provide strong support for needle exchange and other "harm reduction" programs that seek to reduce the ravages of drug addiction. However, public opposition to programs that appear to condone drug use limits their impact.

4.7.3 Treatment of Drug Abuse

Efforts to rehabilitate those who abuse drugs have been impeded by the notion that "once an addict, always an addict." Until recently, statistical evidence supported this belief, and the prospects for returning addicts to normal living were bleak. However, drug use spreads through the peer group and may be reversed with a change in social milieu. And drug use does not necessarily follow a predictable course from experimentation to addiction; instead, it encompasses a wide range of behaviors that may include experimentation, occasional use, regular use, and heavy use. These behaviors stem from the interaction of many complex factors, and efforts to rehabilitate addicts have not always addressed all of them. Two types of treatment programs are discussed here: therapeutic communities and methadone maintenance.

THERAPEUTIC COMMUNITIES Therapeutic communities are a way to attack the high relapse rate of addicts who are detoxified and returned to the larger society. They enable individuals to reenter social life gradually and at their own pace. This controlled reentry reduces the shock of moving from a protective institutional environment to the much greater freedom of the outside world.

Phoenix House operates one of the most highly developed therapeutic community programs around the country. In the Phoenix program, addicts who have completed their treatment are transferred to a Re-Entry House for gradual reintegration into everyday life. Educational facilities are part of the program and include training in vocational skills and preparation for entry into other educational programs.

The Phoenix House approach rests on two key precepts: that addicts must assume responsibility for their own actions and that treatment should address psychological as well as physical difficulties. Phoenix House relies on ex-addicts, who are often more effective in breaking through the barriers of isolation and hostility. In addition, ex-addicts provide living proof that addiction can be overcome. In operation since 1968, the Phoenix House program has helped many addicts recover permanently.

METHADONE MAINTENANCE Methadone, a synthetic narcotic, has been tested extensively and is now used regularly in treatment programs for heroin addicts. In prescribed amounts, it satisfies the addict's physical craving, preventing the agonizing symptoms of withdrawal. Although it does not produce a high, methadone is addicting and therefore offers not a cure but a maintenance treatment for addicts who do not respond to other types of therapy.

Many people, including addicts themselves, believe methadone keeps addicts dependent on drugs and hence is useful only for a short time while the addict is weaned from heroin. Methadone treatment can be regarded as a form of social control imposed by the dominant culture. The substance is legally available only through approved programs, which require addicts to report to the treatment center for their daily dosage. Nonetheless, these ambivalent attitudes toward methadone treatment do not seem to deter potential clients.

Social Policy

4.8 **Review policy considerations of drug laws and enforcement.**

Social policies that address drug and alcohol abuse take two main forms. One consists of control strategies—that is, attempts to help individuals or groups control their own behavior—coupled with efforts to build local institutions (e.g., residential treatment centers) that provide helping services. The second is law enforcement, meaning attempts to tighten the enforcement of existing laws or to enact new laws designed to deal with the problem more effectively. Control strategies such as rehabilitation and other efforts were discussed earlier in the sections on treatment, and this section focuses on law enforcement.

4.8.1 Law Enforcement

One approach to a problem like drug abuse is to crack down on the sale or use of the drug. This rationale was used for Prohibition, an era in which the manufacture, sale, or transportation of alcoholic beverages was banned beginning in 1919 by an amendment to the U.S. Constitution. Although Prohibition was repealed in 1933, the attitudes that gave rise to this approach are still in evidence. Chronic drinkers are still thrown in jail to dry out; people are still arrested in most states for possession of a single marijuana cigarette; drug addicts still receive heavy jail sentences. In many places "treatment" is simply incarceration.

Yet, repeated arrests of chronic alcoholics or drug abusers merely perpetuate a revolving-door cycle. Offenders are arrested, processed, released, and then arrested again, sometimes only hours after their previous release. Each such arrest, which involves police, court, and correctional time, is expensive and may contribute to the labeling process in which an excessive drinker becomes an alcoholic and behaves accordingly.

It is also important to note law enforcement approaches can differ considerably depending on the type of drug involved. For example, response to the opioid crisis is markedly different from that of crack cocaine just a few decades ago. Some have alleged that the difference in the two approaches is tantamount to racism, as described in the feature box, *A Closer Look: "Can Drug Policies Be Racist?"*

4.8.2 Drug Law Reform

Many observers believe that revising drug laws so that they deal with issues more realistically and consistently can ease the drug problem. The most insistent demands for reform have focused on marijuana. It is considered unfair to classify marijuana with the far more dangerous hard drugs, and even people who do not favor legalization of marijuana may support reductions in the penalties for its possession and sale.

The legalization of marijuana for medical uses has created a major rift between states and the federal government. Marijuana can significantly reduce the pain and nausea associated with cancer, cancer treatments, and other serious illnesses. Critics see the use of marijuana for medicinal purposes as a first push toward legalizing marijuana more generally. After some states objected to this push, in 2005 the Supreme Court, in a 6 to 3 ruling, decided that doctors can be barred from prescribing marijuana for patients. The ruling gave clear precedence to federal antidrug legislation over "medical marijuana" laws passed by the states. Yet, the number of states allowing marijuana to be used for medical purposes, as well as allowing it for personal use, is quickly growing.

Regarding other drugs, some experts advocate revision of drug laws and, in some cases, propose outright legalization. One argument for the legalization of heroin is that it would drive down the price of the drug so that addicts would no longer be compelled to engage in crime to support their habit. The British system is cited in support of this position. The British view drug addiction as a disease that requires treatment, and they regulate the distribution of narcotics through physicians and government-run clinics. This system does not give addicts unlimited access to narcotics, but it eases the problem of supply. Those who oppose this approach fear that it might tempt people to experiment with drugs.

A Closer Look

Can Drug Policies Be Racist?

Opioid use and abuse has reached epidemic proportions—over 40,000 deaths were attributed to opioids alone in 2016. That comes to 116 deaths each day (U.S. Department of Health and Human Services, 2018). Faced with a rising national wave of opioid addiction and its consequences, families, law enforcement, and political leaders of all persuasions are joining one another to speak with moving compassion about real people crippled by addiction. Today, police chiefs facing heroin addiction in their communities are responding not by invoking a drug war, but by trying to save lives and get people into rehabilitation so that they can get the help they need. Addiction is couched as a public health problem. The national plan to fight opioid addiction is largely geared toward prevention, treatment, and recovery. One other important fact is worthy of mention—most opioid users are white and at least middle class.

There was no such compassion for the victims of the crack cocaine epidemic that swept the country thirty years ago. Instead of concern, we felt scorn and asked for punishment. Politicians in both parties spoke of "super predators"—young faceless poor black men who elicited little sympathy. We heard of crack babies and shameless black mothers who put their "high" above their families' well-being. There was little talk about the problems these addicts faced: their stresses, lack of jobs, or poverty. The fight against crack cocaine was deemed a war on drugs rather than a public health effort, and the federal drug czar of the time announced that the war would be fought primarily by spending more on law enforcement personnel and building prisons. Mandatory minimum prison sentences sent hundreds of thousands of poor, young black men to prison for non-violent drug offenses. Fueled by the media, popular opinion supported these efforts; there was little compassion or empathy toward those who were addicted.

It seems that the framing of a drug problem is more sympathetic, and the response is much more oriented toward help when the addicted are white and middle class than when they are black and poor. When white people are affected, addiction becomes a "disease." This likely reflects the fact that most legislators are white and upper class. They know people who are affected by opioids—their neighbors, friends, or family members. The epidemic feels real to them. However, when the poor black community was primarily afflicted, it was easy for legislators to blame the victim; to think that "those people" are immoral and responsible for their own problems.

Yes, drug policies can be racist.

Sources: (Baker, 2017; Lopez, 2017; U.S. Department of Health and Human Services, 2018)

Critical Thinking

What are the causes of the opioid crisis, and in what ways are these causes similar or different to the crisis involving crack cocaine? Which approach to fighting drug use makes most sense to you: treatment or incarceration? Many people, mostly black men, are still in prison for their involvement with crack cocaine, while whites are getting treatment instead of prison for their involvement with opioids. What should be done about this, if anything?

Issues of foreign policy complicate the problem of enforcement at the national level. Through economic and military aid, the United States supports the governments of countries that are major suppliers of illegal drugs, particularly Colombia, Peru, and Bolivia. It has been suggested that the United States should suspend foreign aid to governments that do not cooperate with efforts to stop the flow of drugs into the U.S. market. Other suggestions include imposing trade sanctions on those countries or reducing military assistance.

An issue that has generated a great deal of controversy is the testing of public employees for drug use. Appeals court rulings have reversed lower court decisions that such testing violates the Fourth Amendment to the Constitution, which protects citizens against "unreasonable searches and seizures." Many private firms are imposing drug (including alcohol) testing on employees in sensitive positions.

4.8.3 Future Prospects

It is difficult to bring about change in drug policies in the United States. No elected official wants to look "soft" on drugs, even if most constituents ask for a softer approach. Nearly half of American adults say that they have tried marijuana (Swift, 2017). The majority of Americans now favor legalizing marijuana for personal use, as illustrated in Figure 4–5 (McCarthy, 2017). As you might expect, there is a difference between Republicans (51 percent) and Democrats (72 percent) in the support for legalizing marijuana, but a majority of both groups now support legalization. Nonetheless, right now many elected officials who oppose legalization see the political stakes as being too high for them to reconsider their stance. However, this may change in the near future if the number of Republicans and Democrats who support legalization continues to rise. This is certainly an issue to watch.

Figure 4–5 Americans' Views on Legalizing Marijuana, 1969–2017

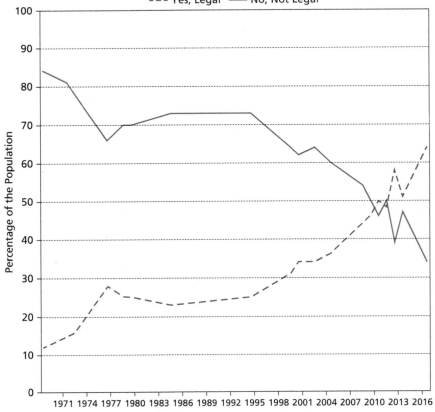

SOURCE: Based on McCarthy, J. (Oct. 25, 2017) "Record-High Support for Legalizing Marijuana Use in U.S.," Gallup.

Going Beyond Left and Right

Is there really a difference between the views of those on the left and those on the right about drug and alcohol use and abuse? In fact, there are many differences, although there are no monolithic views on either side of the political spectrum. Too many people have had direct experiences with drug and alcohol use, and too many people have had problems for this issue to be a partisan one.

Summary

4.1 Discuss the nature of the problem associated with alcohol and drugs, including definitions, abuse, and addiction.

Like so many other social problems, drug use has both objective and subjective dimensions. The term *drug abuse* is widely used, but it can refer to many things. In this chapter, the term *drug abuse* is defined as both the use of socially unacceptable drugs and/or the excessive or inappropriate use of acceptable drugs in ways that can lead to physical, psychological, or social harm. The term *addiction* is often used rather loosely, but in fact is a complex phenomenon that involves the drug user's physical and psychological dependence, the type of drug, and the amount and frequency of use.

4.2 Identify the perceptions toward alcohol and drinking patterns.

In our society, people have mixed feelings about alcohol. Despite high rates of alcohol consumption by some people, the problems associated with alcohol abuse—especially chronic inebriation, vagrancy, missed days of work—arouse less interest and concern than the abuse, or even the use, of other drugs. Several factors seem to be related to whether, how much, and in what ways an individual uses alcohol and becomes an alcohol abuser or alcoholic. Among these factors are biological and socioeconomic factors, gender, age, religion, and cultural influences.

4.3 Assess several social problems related to alcohol.

Excessive drinking contributes to health problems, accidental deaths and injury through drunk driving, and crime. Alcohol is a factor in 88,000 deaths per year; Mothers Against Drunk Driving (MADD) has waged a large campaign to reduce the number of drivers who are impaired; and about one-third of all crimes are committed by someone under the influence of alcohol.

4.4 Describe the effects of alcohol on the family.

Alcohol abuse can leave a marriage or relationship very shaky or may cause it to break up completely because the relationship usually centers on the drinking member and his or her moods, health, feelings, work situation, stresses, and coping. Partners and children often take specific roles within the family to cope with living with the alcoholic and engage in enabling behaviors.

4.5 Compare treatment options for alcoholism.

There are several treatment options for alcoholism, including rehabilitation, Alcoholics Anonymous, Antabuse, and other programs. Rehabilitation is often done through hospitals and clinics, allowing a person to "dry out" while under care. Alcoholics Anonymous focuses on fellowship with others like themselves, some of whom have already mastered their problem while others are in the process of doing so. Antabuse, a prescription drug, sensitizes the patient in such a way that consuming even a small quantity of alcohol causes strong and uncomfortable physical symptoms.

4.6 Summarize the most commonly used drugs that are abused.

In addition to alcohol, the most commonly abused drugs include marijuana, prescription medicines, hallucinogens, cocaine, inhalants, MDMA, methamphetamine, and heroin.

4.7 Identify some of the patterns, problems, and treatments associated with drug abuse.

Data from national surveys indicate that drug use among Americans has stabilized or is declining somewhat—except for a few drugs, most noticeably, marijuana. Drug use is higher among males, Native Americans, and young adults. Drugs are associated with several social problems, including crime and the spread of HIV. There are several treatment options, including therapeutic communities and methadone maintenance.

4.8 Review policy considerations of drug laws and enforcement.

Social policies that address drug and alcohol abuse take two main forms. One consists of control strategies—that is, attempts to help individuals or groups control their own behavior—coupled with efforts to build local institutions (e.g., residential treatment centers) that provide helping services. The second is law enforcement, meaning attempts to tighten the enforcement of existing laws or to enact new laws designed to deal with the problem more effectively. It is extremely difficult to bring about change in drug policies or create a more relaxed enforcement of certain policies. No elected official wants to look as though he or she is "soft" on drugs.

Chapter 5
Crime and Violence

Ian Allenden/Alamy Stock Photo

 ## Learning Objectives

5.1 Describe the nature of crime and crime statistics, including police discretion and problems of accuracy.

5.2 Compare different types of crimes and the people who commit them.

5.3 Evaluate biological explanations for crime and violence.

5.4 Contrast the sociological explanations for crime and violence.

5.5 Identify ways to control crime and violence.

5.6 Explain the policy considerations surrounding gun control.

Clay just got himself in big trouble. Never one to do very well in school, and tired of being a loner, 16-year-old Clay has been hanging around a group of older kids who think school is a waste of time and would rather hang out on the streets. He looks up to these kids, "Man, they do want they want to do . . . they don't just go with a crowd and stay in school because they are supposed to . . . they think for themselves," he says. One day, they decided to dare one another to break into a house in the neighborhood and steal some small items that they could easily pawn, "You know, jewelry and stuff like that, nothing too big or fancy." Clay wasn't very sure about this idea; he had never done anything like this before. But he didn't want his new friends to think poorly of him so he remained quiet. They walked by a few houses, but something didn't look right in them. Maybe someone was home, or a dog was barking, or a radio was on. Finally, they found a house that looked empty, and it had a side window sized just right for one of the smaller guys to crawl through. After his friend made it inside and opened the door for the rest of the group, the search began for jewelry, prescription drugs, silverware, and other small items. Clay even found a stash of money, at least a hundred dollars' worth! All seemed cool. As they were leaving and about to jump into the car, a neighbor yelled at them, "Hey, what are you doing? What's going on?" They sped away, but apparently the neighbor had a good look at the license plate. Eventually, the police caught up with all of them, and now they all face counts of burglary. Clay, along with the others, will face jail time.

Americans consistently rank crime as among the most serious social problems in the United States. Depending on their concerns about issues such as health care or the state of the economy, they may rank any of these problems as more serious at a given moment. But for many decades, crime has been ranked at or very near the top of the list of major social problems. Yet, at the same time, crimes have actually decreased in number. The overall rate of violent crime has been cut in half since 1994, and the decline in property crimes comes close to that.

While these numbers are quite encouraging, it is also true that the United States has far higher rates of crime than do most other developed nations. It also is a leader in rates of imprisonment of its citizens, despite falling crime rates.

This chapter examines these and other trends in crime and violence more fully. You will see that there is a good deal of argument among experts about whether these trends are likely to continue. One reason for the disagreement is that it is difficult to measure actual crime rates. An annual survey of U.S. households by the U.S. Department of Justice asks respondents detailed questions about their experiences with crime. This survey reveals that the actual rates of violent personal and property crime are two to three times higher than the official rates reported to the police. Many victims do not report crimes to the police because they believe nothing can be done.

The Nature of Crime and Crime Statistics

5.1 Describe the nature of crime and crime statistics, including police discretion and problems of accuracy.

There is no single, universally agreed-on definition of crime. In the words of one of the world's foremost historians of crime, the late Sir Leon Radzinowicz, crime

is something that threatens serious harm to the community, or something generally believed to do so, or something committed with evil intent, or something forbidden in the interests of the most powerful sections of society. But there are crimes that elude each of these definitions and there are forms of behavior under each of them that escape the label of crime. The argument that crime is anything forbidden, or punishable, under the criminal law is open to the objection that it is circular. But at least it is clear cut, it refers not to what ought to be but to what is, and it is an essential starting point.

(Radzinowicz and King, 1977, p. 17)[1]

According to this argument, a **crime** is any act or omission of an act for which the state can apply sanctions. This definition is most frequently used to define crime and the one we will use in this chapter. However, keep in mind that what activities constitute crime are subject to changing values and public sentiments; moreover, as you will see shortly, factors such as police discretion play a major role in the interpretation of certain behaviors as crimes.

The **criminal law** in any society prohibits certain acts and prescribes the punishments to be meted out to violators. Confusion frequently arises because, although the criminal law prescribes certain rules for living in society, not all violations of social rules are violations of criminal laws. A swimmer's failure to come to the aid of a drowning stranger, for example, would not constitute a criminal act, although it might be considered morally wrong not to have done whatever possible to save the victim, short of risking one's own life.

Many acts that are regarded as immoral are ignored in criminal law but are considered civil offenses. Under **civil law**—laws that deal with noncriminal acts in which one individual injures another—the state arbitrates between the aggrieved party and the offender. For example, civil law is involved when a person whose car was destroyed in an accident sues the driver responsible for the accident to recover the cost of the car. The driver at fault is not considered a criminal unless he or she can be shown to have broken a criminal law, for instance, to have been driving while intoxicated.

crime

Any act or omission of an act for which the state can apply sanctions.

criminal law

The practice wherein society prohibits certain acts and prescribes the punishments to be meted out to violators.

civil law

Laws that deal with noncriminal acts in which one individual injures another.

5.1.1 Police Discretion

In addition to problems of definition, such as ambiguity about whether loitering is a crime, certain other factors contribute to the difficulty of knowing what crimes are committed in a particular society. A significant factor is the role of police discretion (Brown, 1988). In practice, the definition of criminality changes according to what the police believe criminal behavior to be. Given the thousands of laws on the books, police officers have considerable discretion about which laws to ignore, which laws to enforce, and how strongly to enforce them. This discretionary power, in turn, gives them many opportunities to exercise their own concept of lawful behavior in decisions about what complaints merit attention, whom they should arrest, and who should be released (Lee, Vaughn, and Lim, 2014).

In a classic study of two groups of adolescents in the same high school, William Chambliss (Chambliss, 1973) examined how the biases of the local police affected their treatment of middle- and lower-class delinquents. A group of middle-class boys (the Saints) had been truant almost every day of the two-year period during which they were studied. They drove recklessly, drank excessively, and openly cheated on exams. Yet only twice were members of the Saints stopped by police officers; even then, nothing appeared on their school records. The members of the other group (the Roughnecks) all came from lower-class families. Unlike the Saints, who had cars and could "sow their wild oats" in parts of town where they were not known, the Roughnecks were confined to an area where they could be easily recognized; they therefore developed a reputation for being delinquent.

The demeanor of the two groups of boys differed markedly when the police apprehended them. The Saints, who were apologetic, penitent, and generally respectful

---

[1]Radzinowicz, L. & King, D. F. S. (1977) *The Growth of Crime: The International Experience.* New York: Hamilton.

What Do You Think?

The study involving the Roughnecks and the Saints was conducted over 40 years ago. Describe how things have changed, or how they have remained the same.

of middle-class values, were treated as harmless pranksters. The Roughnecks, who were openly hostile and disdainful toward the police, were labeled deviant. These results demonstrate that factors such as low income, unemployment, or minority status are not the only ones that have a bearing on the commission of juvenile crimes. Although these factors did account for a higher rate of detection and punishment, the rates of actual misbehavior in Chambliss's study were virtually the same for both groups. Differences in the official records of the two groups reflect the discretionary power of the police (Chambliss, 2000).

5.1.2 Problems of Accuracy

Another issue that contributes to the problem of determining the level of crime in a society is that police statistics depend on police reports, which in turn depend on the level and quality of police personnel in a given area. Because police are assigned to lower-income communities in greater numbers, there is a tendency for police records to show higher crime rates for those communities and lower rates for more affluent areas.

If official data on crime are less than fully accurate on a local level, it is possible that similar problems undermine the accuracy of national crime statistics. One standard index of criminal activity in the United States, the Uniform Crime Reports (UCR), is a national database of nearly 18,000 city, university and college, county, state, tribal, and federal law enforcement agencies voluntarily reporting data on crimes brought to their attention. Since 1930, the FBI has administered the UCR Program and continued to assess and monitor the nature and type of crimes committed. The program's primary objective is to generate reliable information for use in law enforcement administration, operation, and management (Federal Bureau of Investigation, 2017). Criminologists, sociologists, legislators, municipal planners, the media, and other students of criminal justice use the data for varied research and planning purposes (Federal Bureau of Investigation, 2017).

The UCR supplies demographic data as well, such as the racial and economic profiles of people arrested for crimes such as murder, rape, assault, and robbery. Data support the long-held assumption that minority group members and poor people are more likely than nonminority and wealthier individuals to be involved in crimes. Yet it must be remembered that UCR statistics cite only individuals who are apprehended. If adult offenders in middle- and upper-class groups are less likely to be caught or punished, like the Saints in the Chambliss (1973) study, then UCR-based data become inaccurate. Because those data do not profile those who successfully evade apprehension and prosecution, the UCR fails to reveal the entire range of criminal activity in the United States.

Acting on this idea, researchers attempted to devise other ways of tracking criminal activity. Self-report studies, such as the National Crime Victimization Survey (NCVS) sponsored by the U.S. Department of Justice, ask respondents detailed questions about their experiences with crime, whether or not the crime was reported to the police. Whereas higher crime rates occur among minorities and poor people when judged by UCR data, self-reporting techniques indicate that rates of criminal activity are more similar among people of different racial or income groups than originally imagined (Dunaway et al., 2000).

Although they cover a set of similar crimes, the UCR and the NCVS differ in significant ways. First and foremost, the programs serve different purposes. The UCR Program's primary objective is to provide a reliable set of criminal justice statistics for law enforcement administration, operation, and management. The Department of Justice established the NCVS to provide previously unavailable information about crime (including crime not reported to police), victims, and offenders (Planty, Langton, and Barnett-Ryan, 2014).

Table 5–1 Number of Violent Crimes, and Rate of Violent Crime per 100,000 People, 1994, 2000, 2016

Year	Number of Violent Crimes	Violent Crime Rate (per 100,000 people)
1994	1,857,670	714
2000	1,425,486	507
2016	1,248,185	386

SOURCE: Data from FBI Uniform Crime Reports, 2017a.

Table 5–2 Number of Property Crimes, and Rate of Property Crime per 100,000 People, 1994, 2000, 2016

Year	Number of Property Crimes	Property Crime Rate (per 100,000 people)
1994	12,131,873	4,660
2000	10,182,584	3,618
2016	7,919,053	2,451

SOURCE: Data from FBI Uniform Crime Reports, 2017a.

With these caveats in mind, according to the UCR there has been a steady decline in the number and the rate (which is adjusted for the size of the population) of violent crime. This decline is shown in Table 5–1. For example, the rate of violent crimes has dropped by nearly half between 1994 and 2016, from 714 to 386 crimes per 100,000 people in the population (FBI Uniform Crime Reports, 2017a).

The UCR also reported that the number of property crimes has been decreasing substantially, as reported in Table 5–2. Property crimes include burglary, larceny-theft, and motor vehicle theft. Property crimes since 1994 have dropped 40 percent. These numbers are somewhat surprising because, even during severe economic recession, property crime continued to decline.

As expected, the data supplied by the NCVS shows that crime is more prevalent than depicted in the UCR. For example, while the UCR reported 1,248,185 violent crimes reported to the police in 2016, as shown above, the NCVS indicates that 3,629,180 individuals claim to have been victims of violent crime that year. Table 5-3 indicates the percentage of victimizations that were reported to the police in 2016. As you can see, people are least likely to report rape and thefts (Morgan and Kena, December, 2017).

Table 5–3 Percentage of Victimizations That Are Reported to the Police, 2016

Type of Crime	Percent
Violent Crime	**42%**
Rape	23%
Robbery	54%
Assault	42%
Intimate Partner Violence	47%
Property Crime	**36%**
Household Burglary	50%
Motor Vehicle Theft	80%
Theft	30%

SOURCE: Morgan, R. E. & Kena, G. (December 2017) Criminal Victimization, 2016. U.S. Department of Justice, Office of the Justice Programs, Bureau of Justice Statistics. NCJ 251150.

Types of Crimes and Criminals

5.2 Compare different types of crimes and the people who commit them.

This section reviews several major types of crimes and criminals. These categories include (1) violent personal crimes such as murder; (2) property crimes such as theft; (3) occupational crimes, which are sometimes nicknamed white-collar crimes and include acts such as embezzlement for personal gain; (4) corporate crimes, which can include offenses such as defrauding employees or falsifying company records; (5) organized crime, which might include global crime syndicates; (6) public-order crimes such as gambling or prostitution; (7) hate crimes, which are the commission of a traditional offense like murder, arson, or vandalism with an added element of bias; and (8) gender-based violence (slow to be recognized as hate crimes), which are offenses such as sexual assault or sex trafficking that are targeted primarily toward women. Note that these are not official classifications used by the FBI but are useful here as a point of discussion.

5.2.1 Violent Personal Crimes

Violent personal crimes include rape, assault, robbery, and various types of homicide—acts in which physical injury or death is inflicted or threatened. Their frequency within the U.S. population is shown in Figure 5–1, represented as a rate per 100,000 people. As you can see, the most serious crimes occur less frequently than those that are less serious. For example, the murder/homicide rate in 2016 was 5.3 per 100,000 people, while the rate for aggravated assault was over 248 per 100,000 people (FBI Uniform Crime Reports, 2017a).

Although robberies and assaults occur most often between strangers, rapes and murders are very often perpetrated on "friends," acquaintances, or relatives. For example, federal sources reveal that at least 80 percent of rape victims know their attacker—an issue that will be explored more fully in Chapter 8—and about 75 percent of all solved homicides involve victims who are related to or acquainted with their assailants (Breiding et al., 2014; National Institute of Justice, 2017; Smith et al., 2017).

According to the U.S. Department of Justice, **rape** refers to "the penetration, no matter how slight, of the vagina or anus with any body part or object, or oral penetration by a sex organ of another person, without the consent of the victim."[2] Given this definition, men can be raped as well. Rape is still rape if the victim was drunk, high, drugged, or passed out and unable to consent. Many rape victims fail to report the crime because they feel shame or perceive threats from the perpetrator (Munzer, Fegert, Ganser, Loos, Witt, and Goldbeck, 2016).

Criminal homicide takes two forms: **murder** is defined as the unlawful killing of a human being with malice aforethought; **manslaughter** is unlawful homicide without malice aforethought. In practice, it is often difficult to distinguish between them. Someone may attack another person without intending to kill, but the attack may result in death. Depending on the circumstances, one case might be judged to be murder and another to be manslaughter. Often the deciding factor is the extent to which the victim is believed to have provoked the assailant. In this discussion of violence, we will use the term *murder* for both

rape

Penetration, no matter how slight, of the vagina or anus with any body part or object, or oral penetration by a sex organ of another person, without the consent of the victim.

murder

Unlawful killing of a human being with malice aforethought.

manslaughter

Unlawful homicide without malice aforethought.

The murder rate in the United States has been declining for many years; however, it remains among the highest of any developed nation.

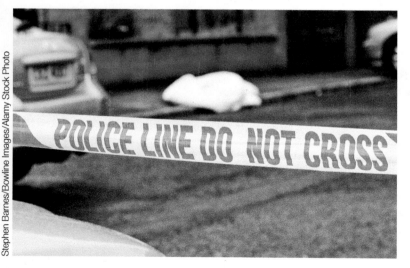

Stephen Barnes/Bowline Images/Alamy Stock Photo

---

[2]U.S. Department of Justice, January, 2012.

Figure 5–1 Violent Crime Rate, per 100,000 People, 2016

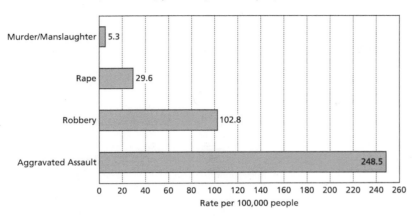

SOURCE: Based on FBI Uniform Crime Reports, 2017a.

terms without distinguishing the degree of malice aforethought, as does the FBI when they record statistics.

Paradoxically, most murderers do not have a criminal record. Of course, there are those who use actual or threatened violence as tools in a criminal career, but these individuals are exceptions. As a rule, professional criminals try to keep murder to a "necessary" minimum because of the "heat" it would bring from the law. Instead, most murderers do not see themselves as real criminals, and until the murder occurs, neither does society.

Murder does, however, follow certain social and geographic patterns. Guns tend to be the weapon of choice: guns were used in more than 70 percent of all murders. The FBI reports that murders occur most often in large cities. There are also regional differences; for example, murder is more likely to occur in the southern United States, even though it is one of the more rural parts of the country (FBI Uniform Crime Reports, 2017a). This tendency seems to be a result of the culture of the region, which tends to legitimize personal violence and the use of weapons, coupled with high levels of gun ownership. For example, in Louisiana, which has a murder rate that is four times the national average, almost half of all households own at least one gun. In contrast to Louisiana, in Hawaii, which has a murder rate only about half of the national average, less than 10 percent of households have guns (Violence Policy Center, 2015).

Men are more likely to commit murder than are women. Men are socialized to be more violent than women and may have more experience with guns because of recreation or military use. Most of the time, the killer and the victim are of the same race. Approximately 85 percent of white murder victims were slain by white offenders, and about 90 percent of black victims were slain by black offenders (FBI Uniform Crime Reports, 2017a). For black men in the United States, the chances of living beyond age 40 are worse than in the poorest nations of the world, mainly because of the toll taken by gun violence.

More significant than the demographic characteristics of murderers and their victims is the relationship between them. Several studies have indicated that this relationship is generally close; often the victim is a member of the killer's family or is an intimate partner. This is especially true for women—over half of women who are murdered are killed by an intimate partner (Petrosky et al., 2017).

Overall, murder and other violent crimes have been on the decline over the past several decades. Despite this progress, the level of deadly violence remains higher in the United States than in any other urban industrial nation (United Nations Office on Drugs and Crime, 2013), as illustrated in Map 5–1. Although rates of interpersonal violence are higher in some poorer nations that are riddled with gang or drug violence, no major industrialized nation has murder rates as high as those in the United States.

Map 5–1 Homicide Rates, by Country or Territory, 2012 or Latest Year

Homicide rate
- 0.00 – 2.99
- 3.00 – 4.99
- 5.00 – 9.99
- 10.00 – 19.99
- 20.00 – 29.99
- > = 30.00
- WHO estimates
- No data available

SOURCE: United Nations Office on Drugs and Crime, 2013.

The widespread availability of guns and the contribution of drugs to violence are important factors in this situation, but those who study the problem also point to the pervasiveness of violence in our culture. Increasingly frequent incidents of aggressive driving, often referred to as "road rage," increases in fights at sports events and school outings, high rates of family violence, and outbreaks of deadly violence in workplaces have drawn attention to the underlying levels of interpersonal violence.

5.2.2 Property Crimes

Like violent crime, property crimes have also declined over the past decades. Property crimes include acts of theft, vandalism, check forgery, shoplifting, arson, burglary, and auto theft. Many of these crimes are impulsive and rather unsophisticated, with the offenders lacking the skills of the professional criminal. Because occasional offenders commit their crimes at irregular intervals, they are not likely to associate with habitual lawbreakers. Nonprofessional shoplifters, for example, view themselves as respectable law-abiders who steal articles from stores only for their own use. They excuse their behavior claiming that what they steal has relatively little value and that the "victim" is usually a large, impersonal organization that can easily replace the stolen article. Neither nonprofessional shoplifters nor nonprofessional check forgers are likely to have a criminal record for other types of activities. Like vandals and car thieves, they usually work alone and are not part of a criminal subculture; they do not seek to earn a living from crime.

Some people who commit property crimes, however, are more professional in nature and may be embedded in a criminal subculture. They have a more sophisticated operation and may have a network of scouts to help avoid detection, and a middle-man to help transfer the stolen goods.

One type of crime has gained widespread attention in recent years—**identity theft**. Although the FBI and the Bureau of Justice Statistics have a unique category for such crimes, for the sake of discussion here, it makes sense to think of identity

identity theft

Stolen identity, which can then lead to a misuse of a credit card, bank account, or other theft.

theft as a type of property crime. The type of property stolen is an identity, which can then lead to a misuse of a credit card, bank account, or other theft. In 2014, Target announced that personal contact information for 110 million customers had been compromised. The method used was not particularly inventive; someone installed malware in Target's security and payments system designed to steal every credit card used at the company's 1,797 U.S. stores.

No one knows exactly how widespread this form of theft is, but an estimated 17.6 million Americans—about 7 percent of U.S. residents age 16 or older—were victims of identity theft in 2014 (Bureau of Justice Statistics, 2015). Most victims (86 percent) experienced the misuse of an existing credit card or bank account. About 4 percent of victims had their personal information activity stolen and used to open a new account or for other fraudulent activity.

The widespread use of online databases has given computer hackers an incentive to work with conventional criminals to "phish" through millions of online computers in search of openings that will enable them to invade private and corporate computers and steal identity data. As widespread as this computer "phishing" has become, however, experts on identity theft point out that even more identity information is obtained through old-fashioned means like stolen wallets, lost identification cards, and rummaging through trash bins. Nevertheless, much of the effort to develop ways of fighting identity theft focuses on increasing security for critical databases in government and the corporate sector (U.S. Department of Justice, 2015). The U.S. Department of Justice offers tips for avoiding identity theft, listed in Table 5–4.

5.2.3 Occupational (White-Collar) Crimes

The phenomenon of occupational crime was defined and popularized by sociologist Edwin H. Sutherland, first in a 1940 article and then in his 1961 book *White Collar Crime*. Sutherland analyzed the behavior of people who break the law as part of their normal business activity for personal gain: corporate directors who use their inside knowledge to sell large blocks of stock at tremendous profits, accountants who juggle books to conceal the hundreds of dollars of company funds that they have pocketed, executives who use the company for money laundering, and rank-and-file employees who slowly and quietly embezzle money. Such acts do not raise as much attention in society as other types of property crimes. They may not come to the criminal courts, and even if they do, they are rarely judged as severely as other kinds of criminal activities. Since Sutherland first described it, the category of occupational crime has broadened to include both individuals committing illegal acts in the course of their

Table 5–4 SCAM to Avoid Becoming a Victim of Identify Theft or Fraud

S	Be **stingy** about giving out your personal information to others unless you have a reason to trust them. Adopt a "need to know" approach to your personal data. If someone you do not know calls you on the phone asking for your personal data, such as a request for funds for a charity event, ask him or her for a written request. If the person refuses, hang up.
C	**Check** your financial information regularly, and look for what should be there, for example, monthly statements from credit card companies itemizing every transaction. Also look for what should not be there, such as unauthorized purchases or credit cards that you did not request.
A	**Ask** periodically for a copy of your credit report. Your credit report should list all bank and financial accounts under your name, and it will provide other indications of whether someone has wrongfully opened or used any accounts in your name.
M	**Maintain** careful records of your banking and financial accounts. Even though financial institutions are required to maintain copies of your checks, debit transactions, and similar transactions for five years, you should retain your monthly statements and checks for at least one year, preferably longer.

SOURCE: U.S. Department of Justice, 2015.

jobs and entire corporations circumventing the law. It has come to include acts such as embezzlement, fraud, false advertising, violations of labor laws, insurance fraud, money laundering, and black-market activities.

The occupational offender is far removed from the popular stereotype of a criminal. Few people imagine that a lawyer or stockbroker is likely to engage in illegal activities. Because of their respectable appearance, it is difficult to think of these offenders as criminals. In fact, occupational offenders often consider themselves respectable citizens and do everything possible to avoid being labeled as lawbreakers—even by themselves.

Sutherland's theory of differential association asserts that occupational criminality, like other forms of systematic criminal behavior, is learned through frequent direct or indirect association with people who are already engaging in such behavior. (We discuss this theory later in the chapter.) Thus, people who become occupational criminals may do so simply by going into businesses or occupations in which their colleagues regard certain kinds of crime as the standard way of conducting business.

One well-known example of white-collar crime, and perhaps the most expensive, involves a man named Bernard Madoff. Wealthy investors gave him millions of dollars to invest for them in his trading accounts. But he never invested their money. He was paying earlier investors with money he was collecting from the new ones who flocked to his legendary brokerage firm. Madoff was known to pay "safe returns, 10 percent, give or take," year after year, not the higher but more fickle interest rates of hedge funds. When the mortgage bubble burst in 2008, many rich people found themselves short of funds and began asking Madoff for amounts that he could not deliver. Shortly thereafter, facing complete ruin, he gave himself up to the authorities. Investors, including many universities, foundations, and nonprofit organizations, lost an estimated total of $52 billion. Madoff is now serving a life sentence in federal prison. His type of investment fraud is called a Ponzi scheme after one of the earliest known such swindles. Charles Ponzi brought the idea to America from Europe in the 1920s, telling investors he was buying international stamps that would appreciate in value. Instead, he used new money to pay off earlier investors and to support his lavish lifestyle. All Ponzi schemes will eventually fail, but along the way, many people lose a great deal of money. It must be said, however, that investors in Ponzi schemes almost always have the hope of unrealistic gain, which makes them prone to be taken in (Matulich and Currie, 2008).

5.2.4 Corporate Crimes

Related to white-collar crime are corporate crimes, that is, crimes that are committed by a corporation or an individual working on behalf of an organization (rather than an individual working on his or her own behalf), usually for monetary gain. Corporate crime may include acts such as defrauding of employee pension plans, clandestine environmental pollution, illegal labor practices, falsification of company records, price-fixing, antitrust violations, or bribery of public officials. Recent disclosures of corporate crime in the tobacco and food industries commanded large headlines and large lawsuits. The financial and housing crises of the mid-2000s also have a basis in corporate crime. Former Attorney General Eric H. Holder proclaimed in 2015, "We have never hesitated to investigate and prosecute any individual, institution or organization that attempted to exploit our markets and take advantage of the American people."[3] He made this claim when the Justice Department announced that Standard & Poor's (the ratings agency) had agreed to pay $1.4 billion to settle civil charges that it inflated ratings on mortgage-backed securities at the heart of the financial crisis (Stewart, 2015). But who are the specific individuals involved? As is often the case with corporate crimes, low-level employees are charged with crimes, but higher-level executives manage to skirt prosecution.

---

[3]"Remarks for Attorney General Eric Holder Press Conference Announcing Settlement with S&P," Washington, February 3, 2015.

A researcher from the University of Virginia law school analyzed 303 cases with corporations from 2001 to 2014 in which companies avoided guilty pleas by paying fines and agreeing to other measures. His results are found in his book *Too Big to Jail* (Garrett, 2014). It would seem obvious that *individuals* actually committed the crimes, since corporations are legal entities and cannot be charged unless their employees engaged in wrongdoing. Yet the researcher found that individuals were charged in only 34 percent of the cases. And of those, only 42 percent received any jail time.

One particularly grievous case involves Pfizer, the large pharmaceutical company that has a string of nonprosecution agreements and guilty pleas. In the most recent instance, Pfizer paid $2.3 billion, including a criminal fine of $1.2 billion, for bribing doctors to prescribe an off-label painkiller and an antipsychotic drug. None of its senior executives have ever been charged or convicted (Garrett, 2014).

In another recent case, Tyson Foods entered into a deferred prosecution agreement and paid a $4 million fine after disclosing what would seem to be a clear-cut case of bribery at its Mexican subsidiary. Yet no individuals were charged or even named. Meanwhile, the highest-ranking executive involved took early retirement and got a send-off of $1 million in cash, a multi-million dollar consulting deal, reimbursement of his country club dues, and use of the corporate jet (Stewart, 2015).

The Wells Fargo scandal involved the creation of millions of fraudulent checking and savings accounts. The bank admitted that 3.5 million accounts were opened in their customers' names between 2009 and 2016 without the consent of the customers. Wells Fargo employees moved funds from their customers' existing accounts into the newly created accounts without their customers' knowledge or consent. The phony accounts, opened with their customers' real money, earned the bank unwarranted overdraft and other fees and allowed bank employees to boost their sales figures, leading to higher commissions and bonuses. Also without their customers' knowledge or consent, Wells Fargo employees submitted applications for 565,443 credit card accounts in their customers' names. Unlike most other corporate crimes, in which a certain few are doing bad things, these actions were widespread at the bank, with thousands of employees engaged in secretly creating fraudulent new bank and credit card accounts. Over 5,000 Wells Fargo employees have been fired, including the CEO, and the bank's once-sterling industry reputation lies in tatters. The company ended up paying $185 million to regulators and settled a class-action lawsuit for $142 million (Egan, 2017; Sweet, 2017).

5.2.5 Organized Crime

Organized crime includes many types of criminal organizations, from large global crime syndicates that originated in Sicily and Italy (the Mafia) and, more recently in Mexico and Central and South America, to smaller local organizations whose membership may be more transient (World Economic Forum, 2016). Many benefits of globalization such as easier and faster communication, movement of finances, and international travel, have also created opportunities for transnational organized criminal groups to flourish, diversify, and expand their activities (United Nations Office on Drugs and Crime, 2018).

The groups that we usually think of as representing organized crime tend to be large and diversified regional or national units. They may organize initially to carry on a particular crime such as drug trafficking, extortion, prostitution and human trafficking, or gambling. Later, they may seek to control this activity in a given city or neighborhood, destroying or absorbing the competition. Eventually, they may expand into other types of crime, protecting their members from arrest through intimidation or bribery of public officials (Salinger, 2004).

Unlike other types of crime, organized crime is a system in which illegal activities are carried out as part of a rational plan devised by a large, often global organization that is attempting to maximize its overall profit. There is no single structure under which

Examples of Corporate Crime

Corporate crimes are those crimes that are committed by a corporation, or an individual working on behalf of a corporation, for monetary gain. When caught, the corporation may have to pay a fine, which often is little more than a slap on the wrist, or underlings are punished while key executives go free. This slideshow illustrates some recent examples of corporate crime in the United States.

Thousands of construction companies broke employment laws and cheated on their taxes to gobble up a slice of the federal stimulus money that kept the building industry afloat during the recession. Thousands of companies avoided state and federal taxes, cheated vulnerable workers, and undercut law-abiding competitors.

An investigation by the New York State attorney general's office into store-brand supplements being sold at Walmart, Walgreens, GNC, and Target found that many did not contain the herbs shown on their labels and some included potential allergens not identified in the ingredients list.

Pfizer, a large pharmaceutical company, has had repeated violations and many nonprosecution agreements that resulted in large fines. However, to a multibillion-dollar company, the fines are relatively minor.

Wells Fargo bank employees opened millions of checking and savings accounts and submitted credit card applications for unsuspecting clients. They made millions of dollars in overdraft penalties and other fees.

Critical Thinking

What type of penalties should be levied on corporations that are found guilty of committing high-level crimes? Is fining the corporation sufficient? Why or why not?

Former U.S. Attorney General Eric Holder takes a question during a news conference to make a major financial fraud announcement in 2015 at the Justice Department in Washington, D.C. Ratings agency Standard & Poor's (S&P) agreed to pay a $1.37 billion fine to resolve allegations that S&P had engaged in a scheme to defraud investors in structured financial products known as Residential Mortgage-Backed Securities (RMBS) and Collateralized Debt Obligations (CDOs).

Mario Tama/Getty Images

Scott Olson/Getty Images

digitallife/Alamy Stock Photo

Oli Scarff/Getty Images

Alex Wong/Getty Images

groups function—they vary from hierarchies to clans, networks, and cells, and may evolve into other structures. These groups are typically insular and protect their activities through corruption, violence, international commerce, complex communication mechanisms, and an organizational structure exploiting national boundaries (FBI, 2018).

To operate most efficiently, organized crime relies on the division of labor in the performance of numerous diverse roles. Within a typical organized crime syndicate in a large metropolitan area, there will be groups in the stolen car and parts business, others in gambling, and still others in labor rackets. In each of these and other businesses, there will be specific occupations such as enforcer, driver, accountant, lawyer, and so on. Another major feature of organized crime is that the crime syndicate supplies goods and services that a large segment of the public wants but cannot obtain legally. Without the public's desire for gambling or drugs, for example, organized crime's basic means of existence would collapse.

A large and growing source of revenue for organized crime focuses on human trafficking, particularly selling and buying women and girls for sexual servitude. Millions of girls and women have been forced into sexual slavery, although not all of this is related to organized crime, of course. Human trafficking is discussed in depth later in this chapter.

Drug trafficking is organized crime's other important source of revenue. Its direct dealings in narcotics tend to be limited to imports from abroad and wholesale distribution. The United Nations Convention on Transnational Organized Crime identified cybercrime, identity-related crimes, trafficking in cultural property, environmental crime, piracy, organ trafficking, and fraudulent medicine as new and emerging crimes of concern. The emergence of these new crime types gives rise to the need for law enforcement response to adapt its efforts and capacities accordingly (United Nations Office on Drugs and Crime, 2018).

It is particularly hard to fight organized crime, for several reasons. A major one is the difficulty of obtaining proof of syndicate activities that will be accepted in court. Witnesses rarely come forward; either they fear retaliation or they themselves are too deeply implicated. Since the top levels of the syndicate's hierarchy are so well insulated from those below them, witnesses are rarely able to testify against them. Documentary evidence is equally rare, since the transactions of organized crime are seldom written down. Finally, corruption of government officials hinders effective prosecution of organized crime.

Despite these obstacles, in recent decades the FBI has made immense progress in its battle against organized crime; today, numerous reputed syndicate leaders are under indictment or in jail. Experts credit this breakthrough to several factors, the most prominent of which is that the FBI now devotes about one-quarter of its personnel to combating organized crime. Other important factors are using undercover agents in long-term investigations, pooling the resources of agencies that formerly competed with one another, and giving the FBI jurisdiction in narcotics cases. Especially significant has been the use of sophisticated surveillance techniques and computer technology. The witness protection program, in which witnesses are offered new identities, support, and protection in moving away from their organized-crime contacts, has also proven successful in several instances.

5.2.6 Public-Order Crimes

In terms of sheer numbers, public-order offenders constitute the largest category of criminals; their activities far exceed reported crimes of any other type. Public-order offenses include prostitution, gambling, use of illegal substances, drunkenness, vagrancy, disorderly conduct, and traffic violations. These offenses are often called "victimless crimes" because some people believe that they cause no harm to anyone but the offenders themselves (although prostitution is being reevaluated as a victimless crime as connections to human trafficking become clearer). Society considers these crimes because they violate the order or customs of the community.

Public-order offenders usually do not consider themselves criminals or view their actions as crimes. The behavior and activities of prostitutes and drug users, however, tend to isolate and segregate them from other members of society, and these individuals may find themselves drawn into criminal roles.

Prostitution is a particularly relevant example of public-order crime because of the way young women (and young men or adolescents) are exploited by older adults in the sex trade, both in the United States and in developing countries (Kristof and WuDunn, 2009, 2014). Prostitution is illegal everywhere in the United States except in some counties of Nevada. There is little pressure on other states to follow Nevada's example; however, proponents of legalization claim that prostitution will continue to exist regardless of the law and that recognizing this fact would bring many benefits: Legalization would make prostitutes' incomes taxable; it could eliminate or reduce the frequent connection of prostitution with crime and government corruption; and health regulations for prostitutes could be enacted and enforced, reducing the incidence of sexually transmitted diseases. They argue that prostitution is a victimless crime and that the legalization of brothels would result in a reduction of streetwalking and public solicitation, which disturb residents of the neighborhoods where they occur.

However, others say that prostitution does indeed have a victim: the prostitute (Matthews, 2015; Menaker and Franklin, 2018). Many prostitutes have been trafficked for sex and are not working of their own free will. Prostitutes do not keep most of the money they earn, and they are subject to manipulation, violence, and the control of a pimp. Those against legalized prostitution also believe that society is the ultimate victim of prostitution and that legalization would not necessarily remove the prostitute from exploitation by pimps or organized crime figures. Moreover, legalizing prostitution might make it seem increasingly normative, which might encourage more young women to enter "the life" and encourage more men to exploit these women. Many opponents of legalization support decriminalization, meaning that, while not legal, prostitutes should not be considered criminals.

5.2.7 Hate Crimes

> Marcus was attacked by a group of white supremacists, targeted simply because he was black and walking in "their" neighborhood.

> Colton was accosted by a group of men shouting "Die faggot," as he was leaving a gay bar. They chased Colton down as he tried to run away and they stabbed him.

> Mohammad had his car spray-painted with the word "terrorist" while it was parked at the mall.

> Lindsey walked up to a Sikh teen in the school hallway and said, "I'm going to cut your hair!" The Sikh teen replied, "For what? It is against my religion to cut my hair!" Lindsey replied, "I don't care," and later snuck up behind the Sikh teen and cut the victim's hair.

A hate crime is a traditional offense like murder, arson, or vandalism with an added element of bias. For the purposes of collecting statistics, the FBI Uniform Crime Reporting (UCR) Program collects hate crime data regarding criminal offenses motivated, in whole or in part, by the offender's bias against a race, religion, disability, sexual orientation, ethnicity, gender, or gender identity (FBI Uniform Crime Reports, 2017b). Only recently has the FBI begun keeping data on crimes motivated by bias related to gender (sex) and gender identity (transgender and gender nonconforming). Because determining the offender's subjective motivation is difficult to do, bias is to be reported only if investigation reveals sufficient objective facts to lead a reasonable person to conclude that the offender's actions were motivated, in whole or in part, by bias.

Figure 5–2 Types of Hate Crimes (**N** = 7,321), 2016

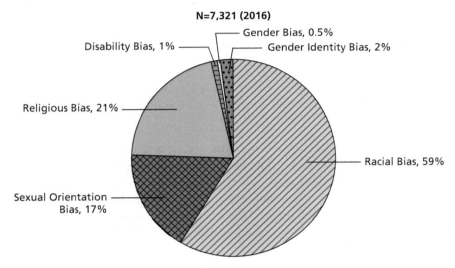

N=7,321 (2016)

Gender Bias, 0.5%

Gender Identity Bias, 2%

Disability Bias, 1%

Religious Bias, 21%

Racial Bias, 59%

Sexual Orientation Bias, 17%

SOURCE: Based on FBI Uniform Crime Reports, 2017b.

In an exhaustive study of hate crimes, the FBI concluded that 59 percent of such incidents in 2016 were racially motivated, 21 percent were motivated from religious biases, and 17 percent resulted from bias toward sexual orientation, as shown in Figure 5–2. Almost two-thirds of hate crimes are against people; the other third involve crimes against property, such as vandalism against a house or car. Of those crimes against people, intimidation was the single most frequently reported hate crime offense, but simple assault and aggravated assault were not far behind (FBI Uniform Crime Reports, 2017b).

The FBI investigated the types of crimes that we now call hate crimes as far back as World War I; however, the FBI began to look at the issue more closely after the Civil Rights Act of 1964 was passed. This legislation moved the protection of civil rights from a local to a federal function. In particular, the murder of civil rights workers Andrew Goodman, James Chaney, and Michael Schwerner in Mississippi in June 1964 provided the impetus for a stronger federal effort to protect and foster civil rights for black Americans. The case was called MIBURN (for Mississippi Burning), and became the largest federal investigation ever conducted in Mississippi. Three years later, seven men were convicted of conspiring to violate the civil rights of the murdered civil rights workers and were sentenced to prison.

Even when hate crimes do not result in murder and mayhem, these criminal acts reveal hatreds and violent propensities that go far beyond what we usually see in violent or property crimes. Hatred of gays or people of other races and religions is widespread in all societies; the propensity to express it through violent acts tends to be a phenomenon primarily of youth and young adults. Nevertheless, the emotions that motivate the deeds are taken from the adults who socialize young people.

5.2.8 Gender-Based Violence

Cutiyo lives in a camp for internally displaced persons (IDPs) with her four children near Somalia's capital city, Mogadishu. Last night, she heard a woman being attacked, and the screams brought back the trauma of her own experiences of rape. Cutiyo believes that rape has become more pervasive at the camp and the situation for women and girls has deteriorated since she herself was first raped two years ago. "When we saw someone, we used to say, 'How are you.' Now when we see each other we ask, 'Were you raped today?'" The first time Cutiyo was raped she was asleep in her makeshift shelter with two of her youngest children. "The men took turns raping me while one of them stood guard outside. There were five of them. I struggled and screamed, but no one came to help me. My children were terrified." The next day, as word of the assault spread, the camp manager came to check on her and took her to the police station. As she explained the details of the assault, she got sick and vomited. They told her to go home and forget about the assault, but before they let her go, they made her clean the floor. She never returned to the police station to pursue the case. She was afraid the assailants would come after her and "do something worse." Four months later, Cutiyo was raped again at night in her tent by a different gang of assailants. Two months after that, her oldest daughter was raped. She was eleven years old.

Violence is a widespread problem around the world, and women and girls are overwhelmingly its victims. Because violence against women and girls is so common, it is often described as **gender-based violence**, defined by the United Nations General Assembly as any act of gender violence that results in or is likely to result in physical, sexual, or psychological harm and suffering to women, including threats of such acts, coercion, or arbitrary deprivations of liberty, whether occurring in public or private life.

Gender violence would include, among other things:

gender-based violence

Any act of gender violence that results in or is likely to result in physical, sexual, or psychological harm and suffering to women, including threats of such acts, coercion, or arbitrary deprivations of liberty, whether occurring in public or private life.

- Intimate partner violence
- Sexual abuse
- Forced prostitution
- Female genital mutilation
- Rape
- Honor killings
- Selective malnourishing or infanticide of female children

Gender-based violence is an epidemic and occurs in both developed and developing nations (Kristof and WuDunn, 2009; United Nations Population Fund, 2017). It causes more death and disability in women between the ages of 15 and 44 than cancer, malaria, traffic accidents, and war combined. Human Rights Watch, the World Health Organization, the United Nations, and Amnesty International are international organizations dedicated to protecting the human rights of people around the world, and report that many countries have horrendous records on addressing violence against women and girls. For example, in sub-Saharan Africa, many women are infected with HIV and will eventually die because the government has failed in any meaningful way to condemn, criminalize, or prosecute violence against women in the home. In Niger, which has one of the highest rates of child marriage in the world, three-quarters of girls between the ages of 20 and 24 were married by their eighteenth birthday, and usually not by choice (UNICEF, 2017). In Somalia, rape is so common that it has been reported as "normal" (Human Rights Watch, 2014). Women in Ecuador face prison sentences of one to five years for securing an abortion that results from a rape (Human Rights Watch, 2013). Global estimates published by WHO indicate that more than 1 in 3 (35 percent) women worldwide have experienced either physical and/or sexual intimate partner violence or nonpartner sexual violence in their lifetime (World Health Organization, November, 2017).

human trafficking

The illegal and highly profitable business of recruitment, transport, or sale of human beings into all forms of forced labor and servitude.

Another important form of gender-based violence found all over the world is **human trafficking**, which is the illegal and highly profitable business of recruitment, transport, or sale of human beings into all forms of forced labor and servitude (United Nations Office on Drugs and Crime, 2018b; U.S. Department of State, 2017). Perhaps 20 to 30 million adults and children are in forced labor or sexual servitude at any given time, although precise numbers are impossible to know. It is estimated that at least 70 percent of persons trafficked are women and girls.

Some victims are forced into manual, military, or domestic labor, but most become sexual slaves. They are coerced, kidnapped, sold, deceived, or otherwise trafficked into sexual encounters, as illustrated in the story of Anu and Reeta in the box *A Global View: "Anu and Reeta."* Increasingly around the world, girls are sought out in the mistaken belief that they are less likely to be HIV-positive. In reality, they are most vulnerable to HIV infections because their bodies are physically unready for sex and may tear more easily. Sex trafficking victims are exposed to pelvic inflammatory disease, HIV/AIDS, and other sexually transmitted infections. Human traffickers may force pregnant victims to undergo abortions, usually in unsafe conditions, posing further trauma and health risks. In addition to physical harm suffered, the range of recurrent emotional and psychological abuse victims often experience can lead to a host of disorders, such as anxiety, depression, and panic attacks. In addition to injuries and disease associated with multiple sexual encounters, they become dangerously attached to pimps and brothel operators and become financially indebted to them. Moreover, they may become addicted to drugs that have been given to subdue them. If women and children do manage to escape and return to their families, they may be rejected because of the stigma associated with prostitution.

Human sex trafficking is not only slavery but also big business (Kristof and WuDunn, 2009, 2014). In fact, it is the fastest-growing business of organized crime and among the largest criminal enterprise in the world. Most sex trafficking is international, with victims taken from places such as South and Southeast Asia, the former Soviet Union, Central and South America, and other less developed areas. They are then moved to more developed nations, including Asia, the Middle East, Western Europe, and North America, including the United States (United Nations Office on Drugs and Crime, 2018b; Walker-Rodriguez and Hill, 2011).

Sexual trafficking results from a broad range of factors, including poverty, inequality, and economic crises. Globalization has triggered an influx of money and goods to certain groups, further aggravating disparities between rich and poor and promoting new levels of consumerism. Influenced by patriarchal norms in which women and girls are disvalued, some families sell their daughters to traffickers or put them in vulnerable positions as domestic workers in far-off urban locations. Husbands, who have virtually complete control over their wives, may sell or "rent" them out for money.

Another example of a gender-based crime is **nonconsensual pornography (NCP)**, commonly known as "revenge porn" and has been referred to as the cyberwar against women. NCP is defined as the nonconsensual distribution of private, sexually explicit images, which can be distributed through social media networks, messaging platforms, and websites. The photo or video may have been taken voluntarily (i.e., by the person pictured—a selfie—or by a friend or significant other) or involuntarily (i.e., by a voyeur or a hidden camera placed to capture a sexual encounter), and then shared with others without consent. NCP can be motivated by revenge, a desire to make money, blackmail, or so-called "entertainment." Laws around revenge pornography have not yet kept up with the ease of transmitting images across the web. As this book goes to press, Congress is considering whether NCP should be a federal crime; currently it falls to state statutes, which vary considerably. As of 2017, 38 states and the District of Columbia have specific laws outlawing distribution of revenge porn. However, revenge porn laws are still relatively new and the laws are continuing to develop (FindLaw, 2018; Morris, November, 2017).

Why do some people commit crimes, and others don't? Here we will look at a variety of explanations, framing them under the headings of (1) biological explanations; and (2) sociological explanations of crime.

nonconsensual pornography (NCP)

The nonconsensual distribution of private, sexually explicit images, which can be distributed through social media networks, messaging platforms, and websites. It is often referred to as "revenge porn."

A Global View

Anu and Reeta

Sudip Pokhrel/Alamy Stock Photo

For millions of people, Bombay is a city of dreams. It was the land of plenty, where the rich people lived. Among these people who harbored such ideas were Anu and Reeta, who were two teenage mountain girls from a small mountainous village about 105 kilometers northwest of the Nepalese capital, Kathmandu. Life was very difficult in their poor village where hardship, starvation, and scarcity were a villager's daily way of life. Sensing that their only hope was to run away, one spring day the two girls left their village along with a group of other young girls and two men. Their journey brought them to a large market center for hand-made woolen carpets. Anu and Reeta got jobs in one of these factories and joined other carpet weavers, most of whom had come from the mountain regions to start a new life.

After about three months, an old woman who lived in Bombay offered to take them there. For the girls, it was as if their dreams had come true! The silk sarees and golden ornaments of the women returning from Bombay, and most of all their prestige, had made a deep impression on Anu and Reeta.

They eagerly agreed to go with the woman on the trip, having no idea what was in store for them. After many days of travel, when the girls were lost and confused, the woman sold them to an infamous brothel in Calcutta for 25,000 rupees each. Anu and Reeta were imprisoned by the man who bought them and were beaten, raped, and tortured. Once "broken," they were forced to become sex slaves in one of the largest red-light areas in the world, where dozens of young girls are brought every day through trickery, just like Anu and Reeta. Most of the 40,000-plus prostitutes in this area of Calcutta are from Nepal.

After three cruel years of being forced to service men sexually, a seemingly magical change happened in their lives. Two of their regular customers rescued and married them. As it turned out, little changed in their lives; their husbands brought "customers" home and insisted that Anu and Reeta have sex with them. Their husbands beat and tortured their wives if they refused and kept all the money earned for themselves.

One day, Anu's husband told her they were leaving to go to Bombay. This long-held dream was now a nightmare because it separated her from her best friend, Reeta. Anu begged to stay put, but her husband ignored her pleas. After arriving in Bombay, her husband immediately sold her to a brothel for 12,000 rupees in another large red-light area in Asia, harboring around 100,000 prostitutes. Her husband disappeared. Anu met several other Nepali women in the brothel where she lived and worked and learned that all of them had a more or less similar story to tell.

Anu spent about 18 months in a dark room of this brothel receiving, on the average, four or five customers daily. She was let out of the room for only 20 minutes a day for "exercise." Anu was forced to entertain all types of customers, regardless of what they wanted from her. For her services, she received nothing but two meals a day and, occasionally, small tips given to her by kind customers. Bombay, once her land of dreams, was now nothing more than the dark room and filth of the brothel area.

She became infected with several sexually transmitted diseases and was admitted to a hospital where she was treated for several months. A sympathetic doctor was able to get her released from the brothel, realizing that Anu was dying and had little time left to live.

She returned to her village after leaving the hospital, now having been gone for almost five years. Some of her relatives sympathized with her and her tragic situation and took her in. Others were less sympathetic but left her alone. She died soon after.

As for Reeta, no one knows what happened to her.

Critical Thinking

Why didn't Anu and Reeta simply leave the brothel in Calcutta if they were unhappy there? If you were in Anu's position, what would you have done differently, if anything? What can be done to eliminate human trafficking?

Biological Explanations of Crime

5.3 **Evaluate biological explanations for crime and violence.**

A medieval law stated that "if two persons fell under suspicion of crime, the uglier or more deformed was to be regarded as more probably guilty" (Ellis, 1914; quoted in Wilson and Herrnstein, 1985, p. 71).[4] This law and others like it illustrate the age-old and deep-seated belief that criminality can be explained in terms of certain physical characteristics of the criminal. An example of this point of view is the theory of crime advanced by an Italian physician, Cesare Lombroso, in the late nineteenth century. Lombroso was convinced that there is a "criminal man," a type of human being who is physically distinct from ordinary human beings. He believed, in short, that there was such a thing as a "born criminal." Although this explanation was wrong, it served to initiate scientific inquiry into the causes of crime.

In the twentieth century, Lombroso's theory and other biologically based explanations of crime were discredited and supplanted by sociological theories. However, some theorists (e.g., Wilson and Herrnstein, 1985) defend the identification of biological characteristics that appear to be predisposing factors in criminal behavior rather than full explanations of it. They believe certain inherited traits, such as an extra Y chromosome or a particularly athletic physique, may be correlated with a greater-than-average tendency to engage in criminal behavior. Research on the possibility of a link between criminality and an extra Y chromosome has consistently failed to demonstrate such a relationship.

5.3.1 Biology, Violence, and Criminality

Is violence simply part of human nature? With the growth of sociobiologists and evolutionary pscyhologists in the mid-twentieth century, this question has been fiercely debated (Winking, 2018). These perspectives are based on the premise that some behaviors (social and individual) are at least partly inherited and can be affected by natural selection (Miczek, 2001). Because violence is such a common occurrence, some social scientists have argued that human aggressive tendencies are inherent or instinctual. Harvard biologist E.O. Wilson referred to warfare as "humanity's hereditary curse" (Taylor, 2016).[5] According to this view, it is our forms of social organization that help to keep violent tendencies under control.

Other experts argue that aggression is natural, but violence is not. In an exhaustive review of research on the causes of interpersonal violence, a panel of experts convened by the National Academy of Sciences concluded that there is no solid evidence to support the early neurological or biological explanations of violent behavior among men. The panel did note, however, that findings from studies of animals and humans point to several features of the nervous system as possible sources of such explanations and recommended continued research (Reiss and Roth, 1993).

In her response to the report, Dorothy Nelkin (1995), a well-known evaluator of scientific panels, argued that "biology is not destiny" and "it is not necessary to explain through biology why a child exposed to poverty and racism might become violent."[6] The real source of violence, she believes, can be found in the growing inequality in the United States and other societies. More modern social scientists agree with the beliefs that the causes of crime and violence are rooted in our social structure, and social inequality is a prime suspect (Coccia, 2017; Metz and Burdina, 2018). This argument is an important sociological viewpoint, to which we will return in later chapters.

---

[4]Ellis, 1914; quoted in Wilson, J. Q., & Herrnstein, R. J. (1985) *Crime and human nature: The definitive study of the causes of crime.* New York: Simon & Schuster (p. 71).

[5]Taylor, S. (Sept. 25, 2016) "How Natural is War to Human Beings?: The Case for a Peaceful Past," *Psychology Today.*

[6]Nelkin, D. "Biology Is Not Destiny," *New York Times* (1995 September 28); p. A27.

5.3.2 Sex Differences and Crime

Women and men are equally likely of being crime victims (Morgan and Kena, December, 2017). However, men are far more likely than women to commit crimes (based on arrest data). Indeed, sex is one of the most obvious correlates of criminality. Women commit about 20 percent of violent crimes, and 38 percent of property crimes (FBI Uniform Crime Reports, 2017a).

What explains sex differences in crime rates? Different arrest rates for men and women may be a result of biological differences between men and women, along with different patterns of socialization, as discussed in Chapter 8. On average, males are biologically more aggressive than females. Higher levels of testosterone and androgens play a large part in this aggression.

However, in our society, men have been raised to be more aggressive than women, and they have therefore been more likely to commit certain crimes. Women generally have been regarded more protectively by the police and the courts; therefore, they have been less likely to be arrested and, if arrested, less likely to be punished severely, especially if they are wives and mothers. Despite the persistent sex differences in arrest numbers, the number of crimes committed by women has increased substantially over the past several decades.

Sociological Explanations of Crime

5.4   Contrast the sociological explanations for crime and violence.

Demographic factors do not offer a complete explanation of who commits, or who is a victim of, crime. Statistics do not, for example, explain why some juveniles and young adults drift into long-term criminal careers or why some young people never commit crimes. Nor do they tell us why some individuals, such as white-collar criminals, begin breaking laws during adulthood and middle age. Thus, in addition to demographic analyses of crime, sociologists have proposed several theoretical approaches to explain why some people become criminals and others do not.

The first theoretical approach discussed here has evolved from conflict theory; it claims that most crime is either a form of rebellion by disadvantaged groups or a form of illegal exploitation by the rich and powerful. A second approach, derived from the functionalist perspective, holds that crime stems from the uncertainty about norms of proper conduct that accompanies rapid social change and social disorganization. A third major explanation applies the interactionist perspective to the study of how people drift toward criminal subcultures and become socialized for criminal careers.

5.4.1 Conflict Approaches

Conflict theorists identify inequalities of wealth, status, and power as the underlying conditions that produce criminal behavior. The groups in society that are more disadvantaged than other groups, such as the poor and racial minorities who experience discrimination, are thought to be likely to rebel against their situation. Criminality, in this view, is one way in which disadvantaged individuals act out their rebellion against society.

The cast of *Orange Is the New Black*, the popular television show that profiles female inmates in a women's federal prison. The lead character, Piper Chapman, is a woman in her thirties who is sentenced to prison after being convicted of a decade-old crime of transporting money for her drug-dealing girlfriend.

Splash News/Alamy Stock Photo

INEQUALITY AND CRIME   As noted earlier in the chapter, official statistics show a high incidence of crime among members of the lower socioeconomic classes. Those statistics have fueled a sociological debate over the relationship between social class and criminality. For much of the twentieth century, many sociologists believed that people in lower socioeconomic classes were more likely than those in higher classes to commit crimes. Current research suggests that crime is distributed among all the social classes, but arrests are most often made in lower-class neighborhoods and prosecuted most strictly where defendants have limited access to legal help (Sanchez-Jankowski, 2008). While that finding may be true, social inequality—that is, the gap between haves and have-nots in a society— seems also to produce its own incentives for crime (Coccia, 2017; Metz and Burdina, 2018).

CROSS-CULTURAL RESEARCH   The United States has experienced tremendous increases in economic inequality in the past several decades. In comparison with other advanced nations to which it compares itself, the United States has developed one of the largest gaps between the rich and the poor segments of its population. Worldwide, there is a correlation between social inequality and homicide rates. This correlation does not prove that inequality causes homicide, but it suggests that the anger and resentment of people who do not share in the benefits of a rich society often find violent, even murderous, ways to vent their frustrations (Daly, 2016; Enamorado et al., 2014; Wilkinson and Pickett, 2010). In the nations of the former Soviet Union, or in Mexico and several countries in Central and South America for example, there have been rapid increases in poverty and in the number of wealthy individuals, many of whom have made their fortunes in connection with organized crime or other criminal activity. This rapid social change, in which it is no longer clear what the rules of behavior are or whether laws will be enforced, tends to produce lawlessness, corruption, and crime.

RACE, ETHNICITY, AND CRIME   Study of crime based on official data shows that blacks are overrepresented among those who are arrested, convicted, and imprisoned. Blacks represent 38 percent of arrests for violent crime, and 28 percent of arrests for property crime, despite being only 13 percent of the population (FBI Uniform Crime Reports, 2017a).

It is possible that the overrepresentation of blacks in official crime statistics is partly due to greater surveillance of black communities by the police and to the greater likelihood that blacks who commit crimes will be arrested and imprisoned. The famous cases of Trayvon Martin, a 17-year-old African American in Florida, who was fatally shot by George Zimmerman, a neighborhood watch volunteer; Freddie Gray, a 25-year-old black man from Maryland who died of a spinal injury while in police custody; Michael Brown, a young unarmed black man who was shot and killed by a white police officer in Ferguson, Missouri; and Eric Garner in New York City who, while selling untaxed cigarettes, was placed in a chokehold by a white police officer, which resulted in Garner's death, demonstrate the likelihood that race continues to be an influencing factor in how blacks are treated by the police.

However, victimization surveys show that police and court bias cannot be the sole cause of high rates of crime among blacks. Blacks are far more likely than whites to be victims of crime, and it is unlikely that these higher victimization rates are caused by whites who enter black neighborhoods to commit crimes.

A more plausible explanation is the disproportionately high percentage of blacks in the lower classes that, as you saw earlier, is associated with higher crime rates. Research by William Julius Wilson (1996) points to the growing isolation of some black communities from sources of jobs and income. This trend is especially marked in and around cities that have lost large numbers of manufacturing jobs, which once provided a relatively decent livelihood for black and other minority workers. In communities where legal employment is in short supply, people often turn to illegal activities. Another key social factor that contributes to higher crime rates is racial discrimination (Burt, Lei, and Simons, 2017; Sykes, Piquero, and Gioviano, 2017).

5.4.2 The Functionalist View and Anomie Theory

Functionalists focus on issues to explain crime that are different from those proposed by conflict theorists. Anomie theory, also known as the goals-and-opportunities approach, is favored by many scholars who seek explanations of crime. Robert K. Merton (1968) argued that a society has both approved goals and approved ways of attaining them. When some members of the society accept the goals (e.g., home ownership) but do not have access to the approved means of attaining them (e.g., earned income), their adherence to the approved norms is likely to be weakened, and they may try to attain the goals by other, socially unacceptable means (e.g., fraud). In other words, criminal behavior occurs when socially approved means are not available for the realization of highly desired goals.

Anomie, the feeling of being adrift that arises from the disparity between goals and means, may vary with nationality, ethnic background, bias, religion, and other social characteristics. Some societies emphasize strict adherence to behavioral norms—the case in Japan, for example—and for those societies, the degree of anomie may be fairly low. Other societies place relatively more emphasis on the attainment of goals and less on their being attained in socially approved ways. Merton (1968) maintains that the United States is such a society. Identifying anomie as a basic characteristic of U.S. society, he lists several kinds of common adaptations. One of these, innovation, consists of rejecting approved practices while retaining the desired goals, which seems to characterize the behavior of certain lower-class gang members who have adopted socially approved goals but have abandoned socially approved methods of attaining them.

This rejection of approved practices occurs widely in groups with the greatest disjuncture among goals, norms, and opportunities. In this country, anomie of this type is most often found among those who have the greatest difficulty in obtaining a good education or training for high-paying jobs, particularly members of disadvantaged minority groups. Higher crime rates among such groups are not automatic, but they can happen when society erects barriers to the attainment of valued goals. If more attainable goals were set for people in lower socioeconomic classes, presumably there would be less disjuncture between goals and means and hence less anomie. For example, if low-cost rental housing were more widely available as a goal, more poor

anomie

The feeling of being adrift that arises from the disparity between goals and means.

Anomie is a feeling of being lost or adrift that can result from the disparity between goals and means. Jackson wants a better life than the one he was dealt, but how does he get there?

Paolese/Fotolia

people could see how even low-wage jobs would improve their lives. When only luxury homes are available (and shown as models on television), then poor people sense the futility of conventional jobs or other approved means.

Research has provided some support for the premise on anomie (Schaible and Altheimer, 2016), although there are types of crimes that it fails to explain adequately, such as assault for purposes other than monetary gain. This inability of the theory to explain certain crimes is related to the question most frequently raised about Merton's theory: Are financial success and material possessions only middle-class goals? Do members of the lower classes have different values and aspirations? Many sociologists believe that people in the lower classes tend to hold two sets of beliefs simultaneously. That is, they share the norms and values of the larger society but are forced to develop standards and expectations of their own so that they can deal realistically with their particular circumstances. For example, people in the lower classes share the view with the affluent that crime is bad, but they lack conventional means to attain goals such as secure jobs. They may consider illegal "hustles" as an alternative means to some goals, especially when these crimes seem justified by the behavior of others outside their communities whom they observe buying drugs or sex or other illicit goods and services. It is not surprising, therefore, that studies have supported Merton's view that anomie, rather than poverty itself, is a major cause of crime and delinquency.

5.4.3 Interactionist Approaches

Interactionist explanations of criminal behavior focus on the processes by which individuals internalize the norms that encourage criminality. This internalization results from the everyday interaction that occurs in social groups. Interactionist theories differ in this respect from anomie theory, which sees criminal behavior as the result of certain aspects of social structure or from conflict theory which sees income inequality as the primary culprit of crime. Two examples of interactionist theories of criminality are (1) Edwin Sutherland's theory of differential association and (2) the subcultural approach to the study of juvenile delinquency.

DIFFERENTIAL ASSOCIATION   Introduced by Sutherland in 1939, the approach known as **differential association**, with some later modifications, still seems to explain the widest range of criminal acts. According to this theory, criminal behavior is a result of a learning process that occurs chiefly within small, intimate groups—family, friends, neighborhood peer groups, and the like. The lessons learned include both the techniques for committing crimes and, more importantly, the motives for criminal behavior. Law is defined not as a set of rules to be followed but as a hindrance to be avoided or overcome (Dobrow, 2015).

differential association

A theory that suggests that criminal behavior is a result of a learning process that occurs chiefly within small, intimate groups—family, friends, neighborhood peer groups, and the like.

People internalize the values of the surrounding culture, and when their environment includes frequent contact with criminal elements and relative isolation from noncriminal elements, they are likely to become delinquent or criminal. The boy whose most admired model is another member of his gang or a successful neighborhood pimp will try to emulate that model and will receive encouragement and approval when he does so successfully.

DELINQUENT SUBCULTURES AND CONFLICTING VALUES   Subcultural theories of criminality view criminal behavior as *normal* learned behavior. These theories of crime focus on the content of learned behavior rather than the process of learning that behavior. Subcultural theories tend to focus on class and ethnic subcultures, including lower social class and inner-city communities (Black, 2014).

The issue of status is especially relevant to the study of delinquent subcultures. Albert K. Cohen (1971), for example, viewed the formation of delinquent gangs as an effort to alleviate the difficulties that gang members encounter at the bottom of the status ladder. Gang members typically come from working-class homes and find themselves measured, as Cohen put it, with a "middle-class measuring rod" by those who control access to the larger society, including teachers, businesspeople, the police, and public officials. Untrained in "middle-class virtues" such as ambition, ability to defer gratification, self-discipline, and academic skills, and therefore poorly prepared to compete in a middle-class world, they form a subculture whose standards they can meet. This delinquent subculture, which Cohen described as nonutilitarian, malicious, and negativistic, "takes its norms from the larger culture, but turns them upside down. The delinquents consider something right, by the standards of their subculture, precisely because it is wrong by the norms of the larger culture" (p. 28).[7]

Other sociologists do not believe that the formation of delinquent subcultures is a frustrated reaction to exclusion by the dominant culture. Instead, they see delinquency as a product of lower-class culture. For example, Miller used lower-class culture to explain delinquent behavior among lower-class youths, stating that deviance is normative in lower-class cultures. In his classic study of street gangs, Miller identified six "focal concerns" of lower-class culture that often lead to the violation of middle-class social and legal norms (2001):

- *Trouble.* Trouble is important to the individual's status in the community, whether it is seen as something to be kept out of or as something to be gotten into. Usually there is less worry about legal or moral questions than about difficulties that result from the involvement of police, welfare investigators, and other agents of the larger society.
- *Toughness.* Toughness comprises an emphasis on masculinity, physical strength, and the ability to "take it," coupled with a rejection of art, literature, and anything else that is considered feminine. This concept is partly a reaction to female-dominated households and the lack of male role models both at home and in school.
- *Smartness.* In the street sense of the term, smartness denotes the ability to outwit, dupe, or "con" someone. A successful pimp, for example, would be considered smarter than a bank clerk.
- *Excitement.* To relieve the crushing boredom of ghetto life, residents of lower-class communities often seek out situations of danger or excitement, such as gambling or high-speed joyrides in stolen automobiles.
- *Fate.* Fate is a major concern because lower-class citizens frequently feel that important events in life are beyond their control. They often resort to semi-magical resources such as "readers and advisers" to change their luck.
- *Autonomy.* Members of this group are likely to express strong resentment toward any external controls or exercise of coercive authority over their behavior. At the same time, however, they frequently seem to seek out restrictive environments, perhaps even engineering their own committal to mental hospitals or prisons.

What Do You Think?

Pick a specific type of crime, and compare and contrast what a conflict theorist, a functionalist, and a symbolic interactionist would see as the causes of that crime. What would they see as a solution to that crime?

Research by Gerald Suttles (1970) and Elijah Anderson (1992) on the street-corner culture of delinquents and other groups provides evidence of continuity in these values. Anderson, for example, writes that lower-class life has an internal coherence that is seldom appreciated by the casual observer. Both researchers show that teenagers and young adults in lower-class street corner groups make careful distinctions based on trust and confidence. They may be labeled street people by the larger society, but among themselves, they continually rank each other according to notions of respect and trust derived from their life on the street.

---

[7]Cohen, A. K., (1971) *Delinquent Boys: The Culture of the Gang.* New York; London: Free Press.

Controlling Crime

5.5 Identify ways to control crime and violence.

Efforts by the police, courts, and other agencies to control crime need to be understood as part of society's much larger system of social control. In its broadest sociological sense, **social control** is the capacity of a social group, which could be an entire society, to regulate itself according to a set of "higher moral principles beyond those of self-interest" (Janowitz, 1978, p. 3).[8] The Ten Commandments are a good example of what is meant by such values as they are translated into norms of everyday life. All of a society's ways of teaching the young to conform to its values and norms (i.e., socialization), together with the ways in which people in a society reward one another for desired behaviors, contribute to social control. But every society also includes members who deviate from its norms, even strongly held norms like the prohibition against murder or thievery.

Techniques of social control range from informal processes such as gossip, ridicule, advice, and shunning to the formal processes embodied in the actions of the police, courts, corrections officers, and others who work in the criminal-justice system and in related systems such as the mental-health and juvenile-justice systems. It is important to recognize that, without the great array of informal controls that exist in every community and society, none of the formal systems would be of much use. If the police and the courts and other formal institutions of social control are at all effective, it is because most people are law-abiding and these institutions need deal with only a relatively small minority (which may still be a very large number in absolute terms).

Most formal systems of social control rely on coercion rather than on reward. Surely this approach is true of courts and prisons. However, it is not true entirely; even in a prison or other correctional facility, a person can be rewarded for behavior that is defined as positive and as having favorable consequences for the individual and for society. The fact that coercion and punishment often far outweigh persuasion and reward reflects the different goals society has incorporated into its institutions of criminal law, that is, police, prosecution, and corrections (Garland, 2005).

social control

The capacity of a social group, which could be an entire society, to regulate itself according to a set of higher moral principles beyond those of self-interest.

Jason O. Watson (USA: California photographs)/Alamy Stock Photo

Prison is primarily designed to punish lawbreakers. The thought is that, if the punishment is severe enough, it will deter others from engaging in criminal behavior.

---

[8]Janowitz, M. (1978) *The Last Half-Century: Societal Change and Politics in America.* Chicago: University of Chicago Press.

In examining how these formal institutions of social control operate (and sometimes fail to operate), it is important to remember that formal efforts to control crime can be classified under three headings: (a) retribution-deterrence; (b) rehabilitation; and (c) prevention.

5.5.1 Retribution-Deterrence

Retribution and deterrence—"paying back" the guilty for their misdeeds and discouraging them and others from committing similar acts in the future—have historically been the primary focus of efforts to control crime. Although retribution no longer follows the "eye for an eye, tooth for a tooth" formula (in which in earlier times slanderers had their tongues cut out, thieves had their hands amputated, and rapists were castrated), today's retributive orientation can be seen in public demands for longer sentences for such crimes as murder.

The punishments meted out to murderers, forgers, and other offenders are meant to serve several purposes. Besides the often-cited goals of preventing crime and rehabilitating offenders, punishment serves to sustain the morale of those who conform to society's rules. In other words, law-abiding members of society demand that offenders be punished partly to reinforce their own ambivalent feelings about conformity. They believe that, if they must make sacrifices to obey the law, then someone who does not make such sacrifices should not be allowed to "get away with it." Even those who view criminals as sick rather than evil, and who call for the "treatment" of offenders to correct an organic or psychological disorder, are essentially demanding retribution.

Some criminologists, such as James Q. Wilson (1977, 1993), have suggested that society needs the firm moral authority derived from stigmatizing and punishing crime. Although Wilson grants that prisoners must "pay their debts" without being deprived of their civil rights after release from prison and without suffering the continued indignities of parole supervision and unemployment, he stresses the moral value of stigmatizing crime and those who commit it: "To destigmatize crime would be to lift from it the weight of moral judgment and to make crime simply a particular occupation or avocation which society has chosen to reward less (or perhaps more) than other pursuits. If there is no stigma attached to an activity, then society has no business making it a crime" (1977, p. 230).[9]

Laws that establish penalties for crimes are enacted by the states and by the federal government. But concern for the rights of citizens who face the power of the state to enforce laws and inflict punishment is a prominent feature of the U.S. Constitution. The Fourth Amendment guarantees protection against "unreasonable searches and seizures"; the Fifth Amendment guarantees that citizens shall not be compelled to testify against themselves, be tried more than once for the same crime (double jeopardy), or be deprived of due process of law; the Sixth Amendment guarantees the right to a public trial by an impartial jury, the right to subpoena and confront witnesses, and the right to legal counsel; the Eighth Amendment prohibits "cruel and unusual punishment" and "excessive" bail or fines.

It is important to note these points because they are at the heart of conflicts about how fairly laws are enforced and how impartially justice is meted out. In the controversy over capital punishment, for example, opponents argue that it has become a form of cruel and unusual punishment. Others argue that because those who are condemned are often unable to afford adequate counsel, they have been deprived of their rights under the Sixth Amendment. Whatever one believes about such controversies,

---

[9]Wilson, J. Q. (1977) *Thinking about Crime.* New York: Vintage Books.

it is clear that the Constitution establishes the basis for protection of individual rights, but also leaves much discretion to citizens and lawmakers to establish the ground rules for how justice is to be carried out.

The role of the sociologist in these debates is to help establish a scientific basis for decision making. Empirical data collected by social scientists and government statisticians can be used to compare homicide rates in states that have the death penalty and states that do not. When this comparison is done, the results provide dramatic support for the contention that the death penalty does not deter murderers. As a form of retribution, it may allow victims' family members to feel that justice has been done, but the data show that murder rates in states like Texas and Louisiana, where the death penalty is legal and executions routine, remain higher than average despite capital punishment.

5.5.2 Rehabilitation

The idea of rehabilitating offenders rests on the concept of crime as a social aberration and the offender as a social misfit whose aberrant behavior can be modified to conform to society's norms—in other words, "cured." Yet, there are no clear guidelines concerning the form of rehabilitation that will be most effective with a particular kind of offender. Rehabilitation usually includes varying amounts of counseling, educational and training programs, and work experience. In the past, the most successful programs have been those that prepare criminals to enter the world of legitimate work and help them secure and hold jobs after incarceration. However, such ambitious programs are unlikely to be implemented on a large scale.

By the 1990s, both the ideal and the practice of rehabilitation in prisons and among paroled offenders had reached a low point in what has historically been a cyclical process. Efforts to institute rehabilitation programs often follow efforts to increase the severity of sentencing. When it is shown that longer sentences and harsher punishment do not prevent crime or repeated offenses, society tends to shift toward efforts to rehabilitate criminals (Conklin, 2007).

Studies of **recidivism**—the tendency that a former inmate will break the law after release and be arrested again, indicate that almost half of federal offenders are rearrested within five years after release (Markman, Durose, Rantala, and Tiedt, 2016). There is no conclusive evidence that any program is 100 percent successful in reducing recidivism. All that can be said is that some of the rehabilitation experiments undertaken to date—in particular, those that help with the re-entry process, and include extensive job training, job placement, housing, and a social support group—have been more successful than others (James, 2015).

The nature of the prison system itself is a major hindrance to rehabilitative efforts. As a "total institution" prisons remove offenders from virtually all contact with society and its norms, then subject them to almost continual contact with people who have committed crimes ranging from petty larceny and fraud to homosexual rape and murder (Garland, 2005). Sometimes, inmates are abused by their guards. Within prison walls, offenders are punished by being deprived of liberty, autonomy, heterosexual contacts, goods and services, and the security normally obtained from participation in ordinary social institutions. At the same time, prisoners create a social order of their own. Adherence to the norms of prison life, which may be necessary for both mental and physical well-being, further separates inmates' goals and motivations from those of the larger society and makes it more difficult for them to benefit from whatever rehabilitative measures are available.

The most common type of rehabilitation program consists of work training. However, prison work is generally menial and largely unsatisfying, involving jobs such as kitchen helper or janitor. The difficulty of rehabilitating offenders in prison

recidivism

The tendency that a former inmate will break the law after release and be arrested again.

has led to various attempts to reform them outside prison walls. Perhaps the oldest and most widely used system of this kind is the work-release program, in which prisoners are allowed to leave the institution for part of the day or week to work at an outside job. Although this type of program was first authorized in Wisconsin in 1913, it has become widely used only since the mid-1950s. Today, many states and the federal government have authorized various kinds of work-release programs.

In general, work-release programs seem to work well (Bales et al., 2015). Besides removing convicts from the criminal society in the prison, work-release programs reimburse the state for some of the costs of supporting them and allow the prisoners to support their dependents, thereby helping them stay off public assistance programs. In addition, a work-release program is a practical step toward reintegrating offenders into society because many of those who successfully complete the program retain their jobs after release, or at least have a job history to offer potential employers. In fact, in a classic study, Martinson (1972) found that the most effective single factor in rehabilitating offenders is a program of training for work following release; work during the prison term itself; and above all, job placement and training during probation.

5.5.3 Prevention

The idea of preventing crime and delinquency before they occur is an attractive one, but like rehabilitation, it is difficult to implement. Crime prevention is customarily defined in three different ways: (1) the total of *all influences* and activities that contribute to the development of a nondeviant personality; (2) attempts to deal with *specific conditions* in a person's environment that are believed to lead to crime and delinquency; and (3) specific services or programs designed to prevent *further* crime and delinquency.

Programs based on the first definition include measures designed to improve the social environment, such as improved housing and job opportunities for those who live in low-income neighborhoods. Although one of their goals may be the reduction of crime and delinquency in the target area, it is rarely their primary goal. The most positive results are found in evaluations of Job Corps and other education, job training, and social skills programs in which young people at risk are given a chance to leave their neighborhood peer groups.

The second definition includes efforts based on Sutherland's theory of differential association (Sutherland and Cressey, 1960), such as efforts to reduce children's exposure to the antisocial and/or illegal activities of people around them, to improve their family life, and to create a viable and conforming social order in the community itself. Several projects of this sort have been attempted; some, like the Chicago Area Project, have had notable success. The Chicago Area Project was an early prevention program established in the mid-1930s in the Chicago slums, where immigrant families were no longer able to control their children because of a weakening social order. The project sought to develop youth welfare programs that would be viable after the project leaders had left, assuming that local youths would have more success than outside workers in establishing recreation programs, community improvement campaigns, and programs devoted to assisting youths and adults who were returning to the community after release from prison. The project not only demonstrated the feasibility of using untrained local youths to establish welfare programs but also indicated a possible decrease in the delinquency rate (Kobrin, 1959). This model has been used successfully in many communities to diminish gang violence.

Finally, most crime prevention programs attempt to work within the third definition—prevention of further delinquency and crime. They include not only well-established approaches such as parole, probation, and training schools but also more experimental programs. It is difficult to compare these approaches with those attempted under the other two definitions because they deal with quite different sets of circumstances.

What Do You Think?

Develop a crime prevention program based on at least one of the three dimensions listed above. What theory best informs your program: conflict theory, functionalism, or symbolic interactionism?

Social Policy

5.6   Explain the policy considerations surrounding gun control.

The fact that violent crimes and property crimes have declined in recent years has finally been noted by many Americans, who report being less fearful and concerned about crime than they were just ten years ago (Brenan, 2017; Gallup, 2017). Yet others are convinced that violence is on the rise. This widespread misperception may be partly the result of sensational episodes of violence that dominate cable television stations, the fact that more people are incarcerated than ever before, as well as a widespread fear of identity theft, which polls show is the crime that is currently most feared. This persistent fear despite the facts likely influences attitudes toward gun ownership and gun control.

5.6.1 Gun Control

Over the past several decades, discussions have been increasingly heated between those calling for stricter federal supervision of the purchase and sale of firearms, and those who believe that Americans have the right to own guns with minimal interference from the government. **Gun control** is a broad term that covers any sort of restriction on what kinds of firearms can be sold and bought, who can possess or sell them, where and how they can be stored or carried, what responsibilities a seller has to vet a buyer, and what obligations both the buyer and the seller have to report transactions to the government. Often, the term is used to cover related matters, such as limits on types of ammunition and magazines, or other technology, like the type that enables guns to fire repeatedly (Pérez-Peña, 2015). In recent years, gun control debates have focused primarily on background checks for buyers, allowing people to carry weapons in public, waiting periods to purchase a gun, and whether to allow the possession of assault rifles.

Some gun control measures are already in effect. In 1993, in response to what had come to be perceived as a national epidemic of gunshot injuries and deaths, as well as the earlier shooting of President Reagan and his press secretary James Brady, Congress finally passed the Brady Act and other legislation to limit the access of felons to handguns and assault weapons. Federal law also prohibits certain people from owning firearms, including those with certain kinds of criminal records or mental illness, drug addicts, immigrants without legal status, veterans who left the military with a dishonorable discharge, and anyone with a permanent restraining order, among others. Federal law requires that licensed gun dealers conduct a background check, through a database run by the FBI, to see if the potential buyer is among those prohibited from owning a gun.

These laws sound restrictive. So, then, what is the issue?

- Many guns are not purchased from licensed dealers. They are purchased from small-scale sellers, including many who do business at gun shows, and these sellers are not required to do background checks. This is the so-called "gun show loophole."
- The data on individuals who are barred from owning guns—those with certain kinds of criminal records or mental illness, drug addicts, immigrants without legal status, veterans who left the military with a dishonorable discharge, and anyone with a permanent restraining order, among others—are woefully incomplete.

gun control

Restrictions on what kinds of firearms can be sold and bought, who can possess or sell them, where and how they can be stored or carried, what responsibilities a seller has to vet a buyer, and what obligations both the buyer and the seller have to report transactions to the government. It may also cover related matters, such as limits on types of ammunition and magazines, or other technology.

Demonstrators take part in a rally against gun violence and ask for stricter policies regarding who can buy guns and where guns can be purchased. The rally in New York City is a combined effort of health care providers, victims and their families, youth organizations, union members, and faith leaders.

John Moore/Getty Images

- Mental illness can be difficult to document. While the law prohibits gun possession by a person "adjudicated as a mental defective" by a court or other authority, most people with serious mental illness never receive such adjudication. Most mass shootings have been carried out by people who were recognized by those around them as being deeply disturbed, yet were able to own guns legally.
- From 1994 to 2004, federal law also banned the sale of many types of assault rifles and high-capacity magazines, but the law expired and has not been renewed.
- Most gun control laws exist at the state level, and these vary substantially from one state to the next. For example, in Rhode Island, any person with a concealed carry permit can bring a gun onto the grounds of a public school, but next door in Massachusetts, written permission from school officials is required—and rarely given.

What are the arguments of those on each side of the debate? For those who oppose gun control, the debate often comes down to the Second Amendment, whose eighteenth century context and language have been endlessly parsed and debated: "A well regulated militia being necessary to the security of a free state, the right of the people to keep and bear arms shall not be infringed."[10] Gun rights advocates say that means an *individual* right to gun possession, while gun control advocates say it means the people's *collective* right, through a militia. Gun rights advocates, led by the National Rifle Association (NRA), see weapon possession as a matter of individual rights. With the recent media attention around mass shootings, the NRA has become more vocal in their campaign that "guns don't kill . . . people do."[11] Gun rights advocates say that people have the right to arm themselves for hunting, self-defense, sport—or just because they want to (Parker et al., 2017; Pérez-Peña, 2015; Pew Research Center, 2017). They also suggest that more guns make society safer because gun violence can be intercepted when it occurs. For example, President Trump has suggested that training and arming specific teachers at schools will make the schools safer.

In contrast, those who favor stricter gun control measures point to the number of people killed by gun violence. According to the Centers for Disease Control and Prevention, over 36,000 people were killed by guns in 2015 alone, which represents a significant increase from the year prior (Murphy et al., November, 2017). Most gun control advocates do not ask that guns be banned. Instead, they suggest that fewer guns, better records on who has them, and some restrictions on purchase, possession, and storage would still allow law-abiding people to have firearms, while resulting in far fewer deaths (Parker et al., 2017; Pérez-Peña; Pew Research Center, 2017). They are becoming increasingly angry at politicians who fear crossing the NRA's agenda.

5.6.2 Future Prospects

The shootings at Virginia Technical University in Blacksburg in 2007, Sandy Hook Elementary School in 2012, a concert in Las Vegas in 2017, and Marjory Stoneman Douglas High School in Parkland, Florida, in 2018, among many other mass shootings, led to renewed calls for better enforcement of existing laws requiring background checks for gun buyers. But even these devastating mass murders did not result in a rush by our politicians to change gun laws. They tend to fear the influence of gun advocates. Changing gun laws may require a cultural shift on gun usage much like there was for cigarette smoking. What was once viewed as an individual right is now seen as infringing on the rights of others.

Opponents of gun control legislation include the NRA, one of the most powerful and outspoken interest groups in the nation. The NRA draws much of its strength from areas of the nation where hunting is popular and where there is a strong feeling

---

[10]The Second Amendment (Amendment II) to the United States Constitution, December 15, 1791.
[11]National Rifle Association (NRA).

that people need to protect themselves and their families. Members of the NRA claim that gun control measures would violate the "right to bear arms" that is contained in the Second Amendment to the United States Constitution. This position is a strong one—and one that most political leaders are unwilling to challenge directly. Opponents of gun control claim that the decision to commit murder has nothing to do with possession of a gun; a killer can stab, strangle, poison, or batter a victim to death. Gun control, therefore, would make little difference.

Although this argument sounds logical, it ignores the lethal potential of guns, which are about five times more likely to kill than knives (the next most commonly used murder weapon), according to those who advocate greater controls and protections against guns. And since most murders are spontaneous results of passion rather than carefully planned acts, it follows that the easy availability of guns is likely to increase the death rate in criminal assaults. In most cases, murders are a result of three factors: impulse, the lethal capacity of the weapon, and the availability of the weapon. Limiting guns would eliminate or at least reduce the latter two factors.

Going Beyond Left and Right

No one likes crime, except perhaps the criminals themselves. All Americans are concerned about crime and violence, regardless of political persuasion. However, what differs is the opinion on the best ways to tackle crime and violence in the community. Some people oppose gun restrictions and see gun ownership as a potential solution to crime, while others believe that access to guns is itself a cause of crime, particularly violent crime.

While the political debate continues, it is important to evaluate the data provided by sociologists, criminologists, and other social scientists to inform social policy. In addition to data about the number of gun deaths per year, or the number of guns in circulation, it is also essential to establish the mood of the general public.

Summary

5.1 Describe the nature of crime and crime statistics, including police discretion and problems of accuracy.

A crime is any act or omission of an act for which the state can apply sanctions. According to the Uniform Crime Reports (UCR) of the Federal Bureau of Investigation (FBI) there has been a steady decline in the number and the rate of violent and property crime in the United States. However, exact statistics are difficult because of ambiguity about whether certain acts are crimes, police discretion regarding what laws to ignore and which ones to enforce, and reporting accuracy.

5.2 Compare different types of crimes and the people who commit them.

Violent personal crimes include rape, assault, robbery, and various types of homicide—acts in which physical injury is inflicted or threatened. Occasional property crimes include vandalism, check forgery, shoplifting, and some kinds of automobile theft. White-collar crimes are those in which people break the law as part of their normal business activity. Corporate crimes are committed by a corporation or an individual working on behalf of an organization (rather than an individual working on his or her own behalf), usually for monetary gain. Organized crime is a term that includes many types of criminal organizations, from large global crime syndicates to smaller local organizations whose membership may be more transient. Public-order offenses include prostitution, gambling, use of illegal substances, drunkenness, vagrancy, disorderly conduct, and traffic violations. Hate crimes include traditional offenses such as murder, arson, or vandalism with an added element of bias against a race, religion, disability, sexual orientation, ethnicity, gender, or gender identity. Gender-based violence includes acts likely to result in physical, sexual, or psychological harm and suffering to women, including threats of such acts, coercion, or arbitrary deprivations of liberty, whether occurring in public or private life.

5.3   Evaluate biological explanations for crime and violence.

Early criminologists proposed that crime and violence had a biological basis in some people; however, most experts now argue that, although aggression is natural, violence is not. Men commit far more crime than do women, which may be explained by men's greater level of aggression and the different ways that men and women are socialized.

5.4   Contrast the sociological explanations for crime and violence.

Conflict theory proposes that most crime is either a form of rebellion by members of disadvantaged groups or a form of illegal exploitation by those who are rich and powerful. The functionalist perspective holds that crime stems from the uncertainty about norms of proper conduct that accompanies rapid social change and social disorganization. The interactionist perspective tends to focus on the study of how people drift toward criminal subcultures and become socialized for criminal careers.

5.5   Identify ways to control crime and violence.

Efforts by the police, courts, and other agencies to control crime include (a) retribution and deterrence, (b) rehabilitating offenders, and (c) crime prevention.

5.6   Explain the policy considerations surrounding gun control.

Over the past several decades, discussions have been increasingly heated between those calling for stricter federal supervision of the purchase and sale of firearms, and those who believe that Americans have the right to own guns with minimal interference from the government.

Chapter 6
Poverty amid Affluence

Jeff Swensen/Getty Images

∨ Learning Objectives

6.1 Discuss the extent of social inequality in the United States.

6.2 Recognize the importance of wealth.

6.3 Summarize how poverty is measured, and identify who are poor.

6.4 Compare and contrast Marxian and Weberian approaches to social stratification and class.

6.5 Identify the consequences of poverty for children and adults.

6.6 Analyze the individualistic, structural, and cultural explanations for poverty.

6.7 Assess the implications of social policy in terms of welfare reform.

Sheila could be considered "poster material" for poverty. Unlike the popular stereotypes, she is not a teenager, she is not lazy, she is not unwilling to work, and she doesn't have eight children by eight different fathers. Instead, she is a quiet, unassuming 32-year-old, trying to raise her 10-year-old daughter on her own after her husband walked out on them. He pays no child support and never has, and she has great difficulty supporting her daughter on the meager income she earns from her housecleaning job. Sheila and her daughter live in a small, dank, one-bedroom apartment "on the other side of the tracks," as it is known to those in the relatively well-off community. Her daughter never invites over friends from school; she is too embarrassed for them to see her home. They have a car, but it is 16 years old, and it often doesn't work. Right now it needs a new battery, but there is no money to buy one, so it sits in the driveway while they both walk to where they need to go. Once payday comes again, they will have a little extra money to ride the bus, shaving hours off their commute time.

A few years ago, Sheila turned to welfare programs for financial help. She received $241 a month for the two of them, about $300 in food stamps, and the security of having Medicaid if a health problem arose. But she is no longer eligible for welfare because she no longer meets the strict time limits and work requirements of the program. Instead, she makes do on her waitressing job that pays minimum wage plus tips. Her daughter now rakes leaves on weekends and turns her money over to her mother to help pay the rent.

As Sheila tells it, there is always a stressful undercurrent in their lives. Will they have enough money to live on? Will they be able to pay their rent or have to risk eviction? Will they ever be able to fix their car? Despite her careful planning, something unexpected comes up almost every month. Last month, both of them needed winter coats, and even the used ones at the Goodwill set them back $30. Now her daughter has outgrown her athletic shoes, and Sheila shudders when she thinks how much they may cost. To make up the difference in the budget this month, she decided to turn the heat down in the house to 58 degrees. They simply cannot afford both heat and shoes.

The stress of not having enough money is always gnawing at Sheila, and she believes it is responsible for her poor health. She has seen a doctor to find what is ailing her, but they cannot pinpoint the problem. It is probably stress, they tell her. Sheila knows that a better-paying job would alleviate this stress, but her reading, writing, and math skills are low, typical for someone who did not complete high school. Sheila has always worked, usually at housekeeping or waitressing jobs, and has always been poor. But she values education, and knows that it is her daughter's ticket out of poverty. "Do good in school," she tells her daughter.

In the United States and throughout the world, the gap between those who are rich and those who are poor is widening. Of the 7.6 billion people on the planet, nearly 11 percent, or 800 million people, are so poor that they must subsist on the equivalent of two dollars a day or less (The World Bank, 2017a). Although poor people in the United States, including Sheila and her daughter, do not routinely face starvation like poor people might elsewhere, the decline in their nutrition, health, and overall well-being is of serious concern. Many Americans go to bed hungry; live in substandard, rat-infested housing; and live in neighborhoods that are too dangerous to go outside. This level of poverty and social inequality, challenging enough on its own, can also contribute to a wide array of other social problems.

Why does poverty exist? What can people do about it? This chapter offers many different explanations for the persistence of poverty amid growing affluence. It also highlights the wide ideological differences in policies proposed for dealing with poverty. You might wonder how something that is so obviously harmful could have solutions that are so controversial.

By almost any standard measure, the United States ranks as one of the wealthiest nations in the world. Its gross domestic product (GDP)—the total market value of all final goods and services produced within the United States in one year—was over $19 trillion at the end of 2017 (U.S. Department of Commerce, January 26, 2018). Dividing the GDP by the total population to derive the per capita GDP (a crude but commonly used measure of the comparative wealth of nations) shows that the United States ranks well above most other countries, with a GDP of about $60,000 per person.

Most other advanced industrial nations such as France, Germany, Denmark, and the United Kingdom fall below this figure by $10,000 or more, although a few countries such as Iceland and Luxembourg have GDPs per person higher than the U.S. (International Monetary Fund World Economic Outlook Database, 2018). Meanwhile, many countries in Africa have a GDP of less than $1,000 per person. Since a large part of this money goes for food, many people around the world have very few financial resources.

You will see in this chapter that the gap between those who are rich and those who are poor has widened all over the world. In the world today, there are a record-breaking 2,089 billionaires and 36 million millionaires, but there are hundreds of millions of homeless people (Credit Suisse, 2017). While hunger and malnourishment are widespread in the developing world, Americans spend upwards of $66 billion per year on ways to lose weight and to lower their caloric intake (Market Data Enterprises, 2017). These growing disparities between rich and poor throughout the world have direct effects on the situation of the poor population in the United States because many jobs are "exported" to countries where extremely poor people will accept work at almost any wage. The increase in world poverty also contributes to environmental degradation and political instability and violence, which drain resources that might be used to meet a nation's domestic needs. *A Global View: "Adeola's Story"* gives a glimpse into these multiple harsh consequences of poverty.

In the United States, the standard of living for most Americans has been declining, while the concentration of wealth in the hands of a few fortunate people has been expanding (Stone, Trisi, Sherman, and Horton, 2017; Thompson and Smeeding, 2014). As you read this chapter, you will first look at the extent of social inequality in the United States. Then you will discover some of the consequences of the inequality that characterizes U.S. society. Finally, the chapter will present several theories to explain the presence of poverty in one of the world's most affluent nations and some social policies designed to reduce or eliminate poverty.

Although this chapter focuses on poverty in the United States, you will have a chance to also make appropriate comparisons to other countries. However, it is important to note that the experience of poverty is based on conditions in one's own society. People like Sheila and her daughter feel poor (or rich) with reference to others around them, not with reference to very poor or very rich people elsewhere in the world. The experience of living in the United States as a teenager in a family for which every penny counts—there is rarely enough money for new clothes or a family car or out-of-town trips—can be as emotionally difficult to bear as life in poverty anywhere. An American who is poor draws little comfort from the fact that poor people in the United States are relatively better off than poor people in Bangladesh.

Social Inequality: The Haves and the Have-Nots

6.1 **Discuss the extent of social inequality in the United States.**

Although equality of opportunity is a central value of U.S. society, equality of outcome is not. In other words, most Americans believe everyone should have the same *opportunity* to achieve material well-being, but they do not object much to inequality in the *actual situation* of different groups in society. The middle-class standard of living is portrayed over and over again in media representations of American lifestyles. But this image ignores both the handful of extremely rich Americans and the tens of millions who share only minimally in the nation's affluence. To observe inequality and understand its impact, you need only compare a few aspects of the lives led by the affluent and the poor in our society.

A Global View

Adeola's Story

Adeola, who is only 13, is already known as a thief in his rural community located in northern Nigeria. He steals whatever he can: fresh eggs from the neighbors' chickens, vegetables from the gardens, or trinkets from old ladies at the Saturday market that he can later sell for a profit. When people see him, they shoo him away like he is a fly—annoying but inevitable. But when they catch him stealing, they often let him keep some of the goods, even though they tell him, "Adeola! Stop that! Thieving is no way to live!"

They tolerate some of Adeola's antics because he is responsible for taking care of his younger sister and brother, who are only 10 and 7 years old. They are three of the millions of children who have been orphaned by AIDS (see Figure 6–1). Like most of the other orphans, Adeola and his siblings live in sub-Saharan Africa, which is notoriously poor and ravaged by HIV and AIDS. Their father died last year from the disease that everyone whispers about, but won't discuss aloud. Their mother soon fell weak and died earlier this year. Adeola, the dutiful older brother, quit school when his father became too ill to work and tended to their small farm. But, now with his mother gone too, keeping up the farm is too much for him, and there is no money to invest in new crops. Instead, to provide for himself and his siblings, he steals what he can. But the community is poor, and therefore Adeola, like the rest of the community, struggles for the basics of food, shelter, and clothing.

Poverty is especially severe in rural areas of Nigeria, where up to 80 percent of the population lives below the poverty line. The country's rural women and men who are poor depend on agriculture for food and income. About 90 percent of Nigeria's food is produced by small-scale farmers who cultivate small plots of land and depend on

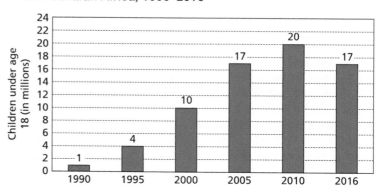

Figure 6–1 Increase in Children Orphaned by AIDS in Sub-Saharan Africa, 1990–2016

Y-axis: Children under age 18 (in millions)

- 1990: 1
- 1995: 4
- 2000: 10
- 2005: 17
- 2010: 20
- 2016: 17

NOTE: "Orphaned" includes children who lost at least one parent to an AIDS-related cause.
SOURCES: UNICEF, July 2017.

rainfall rather than irrigation systems. The poorest groups barely eke out a subsistence living and are often low on food. Drought, deforestation, and overgrazing are ongoing problems. Rural infrastructure in Nigeria has long been neglected. Investments in health, education, and water supply have been focused largely on the cities. As a result, the rural population has extremely limited access to services such as schools and health centers, and about half of the population lacks access to safe drinking water. This neglect affects agricultural production. The lack of rural roads impedes the marketing of agricultural commodities, prevents farmers from selling their produce at reasonable prices, and leads to spoilage. The farmers' isolation also limits their access to new equipment and technology, further reducing their yields.

The productivity of the rural population is further hindered by ill health, particularly HIV and AIDS, tuberculosis, and malaria. Parents become ill and either can no longer care for their crops or die, leaving hungry children like Adeola and his siblings in their wake.

SOURCES: International Fund for Agricultural Development, 2014; UNICEF, July 2017.

Critical Thinking

Why should Americans be concerned about poverty in developing nations like Nigeria? If countries like Nigeria are so poor, why do they continue to engage in risky behaviors such as unprotected sex, which jeopardizes their livelihood (and lives) even further?

The affluent live longer and better and can afford the best medical care in the world, the finest education, and the most elegant possessions (Bor, Cohen, and Galea, 2017; Elgar, Gariépy, Torsheim, and Currie, 2017; Stanford Center on Poverty and Inequality, 2017). In addition, by discreetly influencing politicians, police officers, and other public officials to promote or defend their interests, they can obtain social preference and shape government policies. This capacity to purchase both possessions and influence gives those who are extremely wealthy a potential power that is grossly out of proportion to their numbers.

For those who are poor, the situation is reversed. Although America's poor people seldom die of starvation and generally have more resources than the hopelessly poor populations of the developing world, they lead lives of serious deprivation compared with others in their own culture. This relative deprivation profoundly affects the style and quality of their lives. It extends beyond the mere distribution of income and includes inequality in education, health care, police protection, job opportunities, legal justice, housing, and many other areas. Poor people require more medical treatment and have longer and more serious illnesses. Their children are more likely to die than those who are more affluent, and their life expectancy is below the national average. They are more apt to live in deteriorating neighborhoods located near toxic waste sites. Given their despair, they are more likely to become criminals or juvenile delinquents, and they contribute more teenage pregnancy, alcoholism, and violence to U.S. society than any other socioeconomic group.

What Do You Think?

Why are poor people more likely to have a mental illness than those who are not poor? What is the cause and what is the effect? That is, does poverty contribute to mental illness, or does mental illness contribute to poverty?

Those Who Are Rich

6.2 Recognize the importance of wealth.

What does being "rich" mean? It is more than just the size of a paycheck that makes a person rich because many rich people do not even work or have salaries. Instead, it is important to consider **net worth**, a frequently used measure of wealth, which refers to the value of savings and checking accounts, real estate, automobiles, stocks and bonds, and other assets (minus debts). Inequality, when considered in terms of net worth, is staggering: 1 percent of all households hold over one-third of all personal wealth. The distribution of income, just one slice of wealth, is also unequal: The wealthiest 20 percent of households receive roughly 52 percent of all income (average $213,941), while the poorest 20 percent receive less than 4 percent (average $12,943), as shown in Tables 6–1 and 6–2 (Semega, Fontenot, and Kollar, 2017). And the gap between the haves and have-nots has widened over the past several decades (Stone, Trisi, Sherman, and Horton, 2017).

net worth

For a person or entity, the value of savings and checking accounts, real estate, automobiles, stocks and bonds, and other assets (minus debts).

Table 6–1 Share of Income Received by Each Fifth and Top 5 Percent of Households, 1990, 2000, 2016

	1990	2000	2016
One-fifth with lowest income	4%	4%	4%
Next lowest one-fifth	10%	9%	9%
Middle one-fifth	16%	15%	14%
Next highest one-fifth	24%	23%	23%
One-fifth with highest income	47%	50%	52%
Top 5 percent	19%	22%	23%

SOURCE: Semega, J. L., K. R. Fontenot, and M. A. Kollar, 2017. "Income and Poverty in the United States: 2016." Current Population Reports. P60–259. September. Washington, DC: U.S. Census Bureau.

Table 6–2 Mean Household Income Received by Each Fifth and Top 5 Percent, 2016

Lowest One-Fifth	$12,943
Next Lowest One-Fifth	$34,504
Middle One-Fifth	$59,149
Next Highest One-Fifth	$95,178
Highest One-Fifth	$213,941
Top 5 Percent	$375,066

SOURCE: Semega, J. L., K. R. Fontenot, and M. A. Kollar, 2017. "Income and Poverty in the United States: 2016." Current Population Reports. P60–259. September. Washington, DC: U.S. Census Bureau.

A debutante and guests attend the Sixtieth International Debutante Ball at the posh Waldorf-Astoria hotel in New York. She and her guest typify the upper class, and, like most people, tend to socialize with other people who are of similar economic standing.

welfare state

A type of country in which a significant portion of the GDP is taken by the government to provide certain minimum levels of social welfare for those who are poor, elderly, or disabled, among others.

What Do You Think?

Do you know anyone from a household who would be classified in the top 5 percent in terms of wealth, or would you classify yourself as being in that group? Does that person (or do you, if applicable) stay separate from others in lower-income groups?

The United States has a long history of attempting to redistribute wealth through taxation and other policies. These policies have been instituted for three reasons: (1) Those who are wealthy get more out of the economic system and can afford to pay more taxes; (2) the wealthy have a greater investment in the economic system and should pay more to maintain it; and (3) redistributing some income from the rich people to the poor people is fair and just in a democratic society. Ideas such as these led to the establishment in the 1930s of President Franklin D. Roosevelt's New Deal, which, together with the Great Society legislation proposed by President Lyndon B. Johnson in the 1960s, created most of this country's welfare institutions and programs.

The United States is considered a **welfare state**, meaning that a significant portion of the GDP is taken by the government to provide certain minimum levels of social welfare for those who are poor, elderly, disabled, and vulnerable in other ways. In a welfare state, governments at all levels attempt to smooth out the effects of recessions through programs such as unemployment insurance, and the transfer of some wealth from the rich segments of the population to the poor segments through programs like Medicaid or through cash welfare, known as Temporary Assistance to Needy Families (TANF). However, these programs are often stigmatized, and those who receive them are looked down upon (Cohen, Krumer-Nevo, and Avieli, 2017; Seccombe, 2015).

In general, the competition for resources—not only income and wealth but also what money can buy (e.g., exclusive vacations, comfortable housing, top-quality education)—heavily favors those who are rich. For example, people in upper income brackets have many legal ways to avoid taxes. If they purchase real estate, they can obtain substantial tax reductions for mortgage interest payments at the same time that the property is increasing in value. President Trump's tax plan, passed in late 2017, will also be of greater benefit to those who are wealthy, as compared to those who are middle or lower income (Tax Policy Center, November 20, 2017).

Several other aspects of the welfare state's programs have escaped stigmatization. These programs have been nicknamed "wealthfare," and consist of subsidies for rich people. For example, government import–export policies are designed to protect certain industries such as textiles or steel and the jobs of their employees from foreign competition. However, when the government limits imports of a certain product, competition is stifled and consumers must pay the prices demanded by domestic manufacturers. Similarly, when the government agrees to rescue failing corporations, as it has done with railroads, banks, and aerospace companies, the owners of substantial portions of the corporations' capital are most likely to benefit. It can be argued that the poor segments of the population are relative losers in these situations since, as a result, less government money is available for social programs. Likewise, when government revenues are raised through such means as sales taxes on gasoline, those with less money effectively bear a greater share of the burden because the proportion of tax they pay is higher relative to their smaller incomes than it is for those who are rich. Corporations are heavy users of the nation's resources but pay a declining share of taxes to help support roads, education, improvements in air quality, and the like. Figure 6–2 shows this decline, expressed as a percentage of the nation's GDP from 1942 to 2016. As you can see, during World War II, corporate income taxes equaled about 7 percent of GDP, but have been declining since then. During the 1950s through 1970s, corporate taxes averaged around 3 or 4 percent of GDP. Today, they hover around less than 2 percent. Who is picking up the slack?

Figure 6–2 Corporate Income Taxes as a Percentage of Gross Domestic Product, 1942–2016

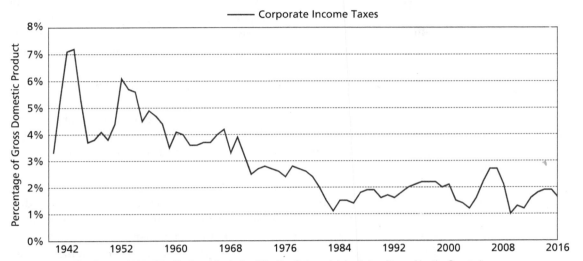

SOURCE: Tax Policy Center. 2017. "Distributional Analysis of the Tax Cuts and Jobs Act as Passed by the Senate." 4 December. Retrieved 4 February 2018 (www.taxpolicycenter.org/publications/distributional-analysis-tax-cuts-and-jobs-actpassed-senate/full).

Those Who Are Poor

6.3   **Summarize how poverty is measured, and identify who are poor.**

Although those who are rich are able to take advantage of various ways of improving their situation, those who are poor face an entirely different set of circumstances. *Poverty* is a deceptively simple term to define. Certainly those who are poor have less money than other people. In addition, the money they do have buys them less. Poor people must often purchase necessities as soon as they have cash (e.g., when a welfare check or paycheck arrives). They cannot shop around for sales or bargains, and they can be taken advantage of by shopkeepers who raise their prices the day welfare checks are delivered. When they buy on credit, poor people must accept higher interest rates because they take longer to pay and are considered poor credit risks. Inflationary price increases affect poor people first, and more severely. The cost of essential consumer goods may rise suddenly (e.g., when energy costs increase as a result of a crisis in the Middle East), but the wages of the lowest-paid people and government income assistance payments rise slowly if at all.

For most people, poverty simply means not having enough money to buy things that are considered necessary and desirable. Various formal definitions of poverty have been offered. John Kenneth Galbraith (1958) stressed the sense of degradation felt by those who are poor and concluded that "people are poverty stricken when their income, even if adequate for survival, falls markedly behind that of the community" (p. 245). Poverty may mean a condition of near starvation, bare subsistence, or any standard of living measurably beneath the national average. A generally agreed-on, scientifically based, and more specific definition of *poverty* is needed to deal more effectively with poverty as a social problem.

The Poverty Line

Official U.S. government definitions of poverty are based on the calculation of a minimum family food budget. The U.S. Department of Agriculture regularly prepares estimates of the cost of achieving a minimum level of nutrition, based on average food prices. It is assumed that an average low-income family must spend one-third of its total income on food; thus, by multiplying the family food budget by three, the government arrives at a poverty income that can be adjusted for the number of people in the household and for changes in the cost of food. The official measure is also corrected at least annually for changes in the cost of living as measured by the consumer price index (CPI). In 2016, this inflation-corrected, official poverty line for a family of four was $24,563. By this measure, 40.6 million people, or 12.7 percent of the U.S. population, were below the poverty line as shown in Figures 6–3a and 6–3b (Semega, Fontenot, and Kollar, 2017). This 2016 measure represents an improvement from recent years as the country slowly pulled out of a recession.

This official poverty measure was developed in 1965 by Mollie Orshansky, an economist at the Social Security Administration, who reasoned that the primary measure of the adequacy of a person's level of living is food consumption. However, although this definition was accepted as the official means of establishing a poverty line, there has been continuing controversy and debate over definitions of poverty and their implications for social policy.

Some conservative social scientists and policymakers are critical of the way poverty is measured. In particular, they have argued that if benefits provided to poor people, such as reduced-price school lunch programs, Medicaid, and subsidized housing, are included in the calculation of income, then the extent of poverty is much less than is generally believed. These differences in measurement could

Figure 6–3a Number of People in Poverty, 1959–2016 (Millions)

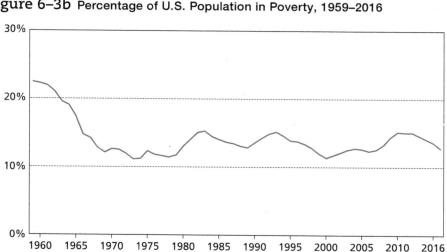

SOURCE: Semega, J. L., K. R. Fontenot, and M. A. Kollar, 2017. "Income and Poverty in the United States: 2016." Current Population Reports. P60–259. September. Washington, DC: U.S. Census Bureau.

Figure 6–3b Percentage of U.S. Population in Poverty, 1959–2016

SOURCE: Semega, J. L., K. R. Fontenot, and M. A. Kollar, 2017. "Income and Poverty in the United States: 2016." Current Population Reports. P60–259. September. Washington, DC: U.S. Census Bureau.

affect whether millions of Americans are classified as being above or below the official poverty line.

But those who believe that existing poverty measures actually underestimate the size of the poor population also have strong arguments on their side. First, when the poverty line was first created, it averaged about half the median income of Americans; however, it has eroded and now only represents about one-third of the median household income. In addition to the cost of food, other costs such as childcare, home heating, and housing also have increased substantially over the past few decades. In other words, not only are there more poor people than officially counted, these people are considerably poorer than those who were counted decades ago.

Second, there is the argument that taxes, alimony, out-of-pocket health care expenses, and many work-related expenses should be excluded from the income figures used to determine poverty status because this money cannot be used to purchase food and other necessities of life.

Third, the official poverty definition does not take into account regional differences in the cost of living and therefore neglects hundreds of thousands of poor people in high-cost cities like Washington, D.C., while overestimating the number of poor people in smaller towns, where the cost of living is lower. Finally, many researchers and advocates for poor people note that the poverty threshold is extremely low and that people living above that level are still quite poor.

When the poverty formula was first developed, conveniences such as telephones and indoor plumbing were not necessarily part of Americans' expectations of a minimally adequate level of living. And at that time, far fewer children lived with only one parent and far fewer women were employed. Childcare, a significant expense for most working families (and essential if a single parent is to work), was not the major and necessary expense it is today. With these factors in mind, many suggest that the poverty line is far too low, and underrepresents the real number of needy people in America.

Who Is Living in Poverty, and Why?

The 12.7 percent of the population living in poverty represents many people across different types of family structures, races, ages, and personal situations, as shown in Table 6–3. For many people, poverty is a short-term event caused by a single, temporary crisis, for example, an unexpected job loss, an accident or illness, or a divorce. For

Table 6–3 People and Families in Poverty (13 Percent of Total Population) by Selected Characteristics, 2016

Characteristic	Percent in Poverty
Age	
Under 18	18%
18–64	12%
65 and over	9%
Race	
White (Non-Hispanic)	9%
Black	22%
Asian and Pacific Islander	19%
Hispanic	19%
Family Type	
Married Couple	5%
Female-Headed	27%
Male-Headed	13%

SOURCE: Semega, J. L., K. R. Fontenot, and M. A. Kollar, 2017. "Income and Poverty in the United States: 2016." Current Population Reports. P60-259. September. Washington, DC: U.S. Census Bureau.

others like Sheila, introduced in the opening vignette, poverty is a longer-term event. Both situations can cause suffering and hardship, and it is estimated that about half of Americans will experience a bout of poverty sometime in their lives. The following sections take a closer look at who is living in poverty and why.

SINGLE-PARENT FAMILIES Of all children under the age of 18 in the United States, 18 percent are living in poverty. Put another way, almost one child in five lives in a family with a household income so low that they are considered poor. The situation is especially common for children in single-parent families headed by women. Today, over one-quarter of female-headed families live below the poverty threshold (Semega, Fontenot, and Kollar, 2017).

One reason for such high levels of poverty among these families is the decrease in subsidies for low-income children and their mothers. For example, food assistance benefits from SNAP (formerly known as the Food Stamp Program) are the nation's most important anti-hunger program. It helps more than 40 million low-income Americans afford nutritional food each month. Two-thirds of SNAP benefits go to families with children. While benefits are modest, they can make a real difference in alleviating hunger and food insecurity, and improving quality of life.

> *Some nights were really hard. The hunger would be gripping my stomach and all I could think about was food. We just didn't have enough of it at the end of the month. Simple as that. What we did have we gave to the little ones because you can't let babies go hungry. (Tania, age 15)*

SNAP funding has been substantially reduced over the past several years. In late 2013, the amount of SNAP money received by a family of four dropped from $668 to $632 a month (Sherter, 2013). Thirty-six dollars a month may not sound like much, but these critical dollars can make the difference between a child getting enough food to eat and going hungry. Yet the 2013 cuts are small compared to President Trump's 2018 budget, which proposed to cut SNAP by more than $193 billion over the next 10 years. This amounts to a 25 percent cut, accomplished through a cost shift to states, cutting eligibility for millions of households, and reducing the size of benefits for hundreds of thousands more (Dean, 2017). The declines in food aid to poor children highlight the stark differences between the United States and most other affluent nations in the efforts made at the national level to combat child poverty.

CHILDREN Nearly one out of five American children lives in poverty. The United States leads all affluent nations in the proportion of its children it allows to live in poverty, according to a recent UNICEF study (UNICEF Innocenti Research Centre, 2013), as illustrated in Figure 6–4. Of 35 nations reviewed by UNICEF, only Romania has a higher percentage of children in poverty (internationally defined as living in a household below half of the median income). Why does the United States fare so poorly? Most other affluent industrial nations have far more effective and generous social safety nets, welfare systems that assist significant proportions of children and their families in their efforts to escape poverty (Bogenschneider, 2014; Midgley, Dahl, and Wright, 2017).

Most industrial nations do a far better job helping parents in low-income families obtain quality childcare services that will allow them to work steadily while their children are adequately cared for. In the United States, in contrast, childcare is often a major obstacle for low-income single mothers who want to work and could be successfully employed. Their jobs may have split shifts or night hours, which make it difficult to find and afford childcare (Laughlin, 2013; Seccombe, 2015). The stress and fatigue associated with nonstandard hours or evening and night shifts may adversely affect parenting, contributing to less responsiveness and sensitivity toward the children (Kaiser, Li, and Pollmann-Schult, 2017). Several researchers reviewed 23 studies on this topic that were published between 1980 and 2012. Of these, 21 reported

What Do You Think?

Why do you think that other countries are more helpful to their low-income families than the United States is to its? Do you think the United States should be more like those countries, or should those countries be more like us?

Figure 6–4 Relative Child Poverty Rates, Percentage of Children Aged 0-17 Living in Households with Equivalent Incomes Below 50% of National Median

SOURCE: UNICEF Innocenti Research Centre. 2013. "Child Well-Being in Rich Countries: A Comparative Overview." Report Card 11. April. Retrieved 26 February 2014 (www.unicef-irc.org/publications/pdf/rc11_eng.pdf).

a significant relationship between nonstandard work schedules and adverse child developmental outcomes, such as lower cognitive development, behavioral problems, depression, and child obesity (Li, Johnson, Han, Andrews, Kendall, Strazdins, and Dockery, 2014). Yet, quality childcare for children, especially poor children, is crucial to their social and cognitive development. Substandard childcare, in contrast, can have devastating and long-lasting results (Friedman-Krauss, Barnett, and Nores, 2016; Landry et al., 2014).

A study by the National Institute of Child Health and Human Development illustrates this point. Researchers had tracked more than 1,300 children since 1991. The results showed that obedience and academic problems among children who received low-quality care in their first 4½ years of life persisted through their fifteenth birthdays. Researchers and experts who commented on the study agreed that these results point to the likelihood of lifelong problems, which would include higher than expected rates of school failure and dropping out, higher rates of incarceration, and greater likelihood of teenage parenthood (Stein, 2010).

Father involvement and child support enforcement are other major areas of concern for poor mothers struggling to work and raise children simultaneously. Noncustodial parents (who are mostly fathers) have a legal responsibility to support their children. In the past, these payments were arranged privately between the parents, and not surprisingly, the amount of these awards varied widely. More recently, the federal government has mandated child support and will prosecute a person who willfully avoids paying, but still, the data remain unimpressive. Too often, men are unwilling or unable to pay court-ordered child support payments. Only about half of custodial parents have some type of formal agreement or court award (Grall, 2016). Children without the protection of a legal child support order receive little, if anything,

Figure 6–5 Level of Child Support Payment Among Custodial Parents with a Formal Agreement or Court Order, 1995, 2005, 2015

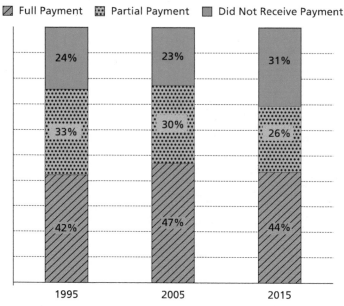

SOURCE: Grall, T. S. 2018. "Custodial Mothers and Fathers and Their Child Support: 2013." Current Population Reports. U.S. Census Bureau. P60–255. January. Retrieved 18 August 2016 (www.census.gov/content/dam/Census/library/publications/2016/demo/P60-255.pdf).

from their noncustodial parent. Some of these noncustodial parents offer occasional in-kind benefits instead, such as food, transportation, or household supplies (Kane, Nelson, and Edin, 2015). Among those who do have a legal child support order, less than half of custodial parents receive the full amount of the award, as shown in Figure 6–5 (Grall, 2018).

MINORITY GROUPS It should be noted that although whites are by far the largest group among poor families, blacks and Hispanics are overrepresented, given their size in the population. For example, about 22 percent of blacks and 19 percent of Hispanics have incomes below the official poverty level, compared with about 9 percent of the non-Hispanic white population and 10 percent of Asian Americans. In other words, a larger proportion of the black and Hispanic populations have incomes below the poverty level than do whites and Asian Americans, but in terms of actual numbers of individuals, more whites can be counted as being in poverty (Semega, Fontenot, and Kollar, 2017).

Several factors are thought to be responsible for the lower earning power of blacks and Hispanic workers and their higher rates of poverty. Among the most important are low wages, discrimination, and educational deficits. The proportion of people of black or Hispanic background working at low-wage and minimum-wage jobs is higher than the proportion of whites in such jobs. The federal minimum wage was raised from $5.15 per hour to $7.25 per hour in three increments beginning in 2006, but has now fallen far behind the poverty threshold. Twenty-nine states have set a minimum wage higher than the federal threshold (National Conference of State Legislators, January 2, 2018).

The discrimination experienced by blacks, Chicanos, Puerto Ricans, Native Americans, and other minority groups in housing, education, and health care exacerbates the effects of low income. In fact, discrimination often accounts for their inability to find higher-paying employment. Members of these groups often pay higher rents and live in dilapidated or deteriorating dwellings, and the quality of predominantly minority schools is often inferior to that of predominantly white schools. In

What Do You Think?

Asian Americans have been nicknamed "model minorities." Why are they so financially successful compared with other minorities?

these and other areas, the disparity between blacks and whites in both opportunity and treatment is evident.

THOSE WITH DISABILITIES Americans have an ambivalent attitude toward poverty (Jansson, 2012). We recognize that poor people are not always responsible for their situation, yet those who must turn to public assistance (sometimes referred to as the "dependent poor") are often pictured as lazy, shiftless, or dishonest. Their private lives are scrutinized because those who have more money are often suspicious of them and worry that they may be taking advantage of the rest of society.

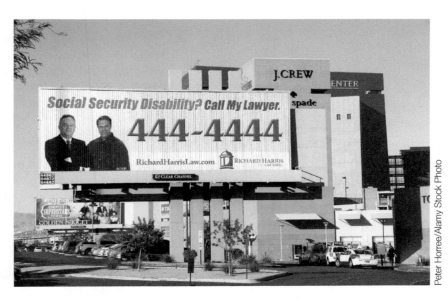

However, a significant proportion of those who are poor are people who have struggled with disabilities from childhood. A serious disability may beget poverty because jobs are limited and other aspects of life may be hampered. However, poverty itself may beget further disabilities, especially in children. Although disabilities are not unique to poor families, children in low-income households are more likely to be chronically ill or disabled because of the environmental risks of substandard housing and low-income neighborhoods and because of deficiencies in nutrition and health care. Moreover, childhood disability not only correlates highly with later adult dependence, but also can create extreme hardship for single parents already burdened by the basic effects of poverty.

Many people who are poor have disabilities that prevent them from working full- or even part-time.

Event Poverty

Some families are prone to what is known as *event poverty*. In the event of illness, loss of one of the jobs, marital discord, or pregnancy, for example, the family could easily lose half its income and then plunge well below the official poverty level. When a manufacturing plant or other place of employment closes abruptly, hundreds of workers may be thrown out of work. Or a family may become impoverished because of high medical bills (we will return to this subject shortly) or, as Americans have seen so dramatically in the last decade, because they have lost everything in a storm or other natural disaster. The following sections discuss some of the events and situations that can lead to poverty.

A SEVERE RECESSION The recession that began in 2008 has largely abated at this writing in late 2018 as unemployment remains at a low of 4 percent. Nonetheless, many people lost their homes to foreclosure, used their retirement savings to live on, racked up tremendous credit card debt, and ran up expensive health care bills. Many of these people are still trying to catch up to where they were financially prior to the recession. Moreover, good-paying union and manufacturing jobs continue to decline, while lower-paying service jobs grow. Many jobs now require a college degree as simply an entrance requirement for consideration.

Take a moment to consider some of these financial problems and related issues in more depth. "Rhonda" is one of many people who are looking for a good job with good pay (Seccombe, 2015). She has a high school diploma, but does not have a college degree. She is a single mother, and would like to raise her young son Bobby without relying on government assistance. Rhonda, who wants a permanent full-time job but has been stymied by the tremendous growth in part-time, temporary positions, explains (Seccombe, 2015, p. 177):

What Do You Think?

Do you know anyone who has experienced event poverty? If so, how did it effect him or her?

Hopefully I can get me a job. A permanent job. My sister's trying to get me a job where she works. I put my application in last week. And it would be a permanent job. When you go through those agencies, it's just temporary work. It's just whenever they need you, and it's unfair too. Every job I've found is through this temporary agency, like Manpower, but it's only temporary. And they cut my check and my food stamps, and when my job ends, it's like you're stuck again. So I'm trying to find a permanent steady job. But it's hard around here. I've been out looking for work, and hoping that something comes through.

Rhonda may be surprised to learn that temporary agencies prospered during the recent recessionary economy. Manpower is one of the largest private employers in the United States. Rhonda's experience with temporary agencies is not unique, however, and the success of these agencies reflects the growing divide between the haves and the have-nots.

IMMIGRATION Immigration is a different kind of life event that may be associated with poverty or with efforts to escape from it. Although it is important to remember that the majority of Hispanics and Asians are neither impoverished nor immigrants, poor people from Mexico and South and East Asia are among the largest immigrant groups today (Lopez and Radford, 2017). Many live in the poorest city neighborhoods and rural counties. Most of the adults work full-time, often in the lowest-paying and most undesirable jobs. Most lack health insurance, and many fear that changes in welfare laws will make it impossible for them to send their children to school or to receive the same benefits as others who pay taxes.

The issue of whether poor and unskilled immigrants drive down the wages of those who are working and poor and represent a burden to taxpayers generates a great deal of controversy. Politicians who wish to capitalize on the resentment some Americans already feel toward immigrants often use this argument. For example, President Trump has criticized immigrants on numerous occasions, suggesting that many are criminals. He has proposed building a wall to protect the border. In a similar vein, Arizona passed a law giving police authorization to check on the immigration status of anyone they reasonably suspect of being in the United States illegally. The failure to carry identification of one's legal status would be a crime. Opponents argue that such a law violates civil liberties and encourages racial profiling.

working poor

Individuals who, within a year, spent at least 27 weeks in the labor force (working or looking for work), but whose incomes fell below the official poverty level.

LOW WAGES We see poor people working all around us, in restaurant kitchens, on landscaping crews, installing roofs in the hot sun, and taking care of our loved ones. According to the U.S. Department of Labor, the "**working poor**" are individuals who spent at least 27 weeks in the labor force (working or looking for work), but whose incomes fell below the official poverty level. Of all the people in the labor force for at least 27 weeks, about 9 million people, or almost 6 percent of the nation's labor force, are working at wages so low that they remain below the official poverty threshold (Bureau of Labor Statistics, 2017).

The situation of those who are working and poor has deteriorated over the past few decades. There are several reasons for this downhill slide, including technological changes that eliminate certain kinds of jobs, globalization (which exports jobs to lower-wage regions of the world), the stagnation of the minimum wage, and the reluctance of the middle and upper classes to share their wealth with less fortunate members of society.

UNEMPLOYMENT OR LIMITED PART-TIME WORK In addition to those who are working but cannot escape from poverty because of low wages, some people in the United States either are working part-time or are out of the labor force and receiving minimal benefits. These people live on a bare-bones budget and have difficulty providing for even the basics in life. Their numbers are growing at a rapid rate. Sociologists often consider "extremely" poor people or households to be those living at 50 percent of the poverty threshold, which would amount to roughly $12,000 a year for a family of four or about $6,000 for one person. Using this definition, over 18 million Americans, 6 million of whom are children, live in extreme poverty (Semega, Fontenot, and Kollar, 2017).

Poverty and Social Class

6.4 **Compare and contrast Marxian and Weberian approaches to social stratification and class.**

In every society, people are grouped according to their access to the things that are considered valuable. This phenomenon is **social stratification**—a pattern in which individuals and groups find themselves in different positions in the social order, positions that enjoy varying amounts of access to desirable goods and services.

The stratification of individuals and groups according to their access to various occupations, incomes, and skills is called social **class stratification**. A social class is a large number of people who have roughly the same degree of economic standing; to varying degrees, depending on the culture, people may enter or leave a given class as their economic fortunes change. Marxian social theory emphasizes a form of this stratification. For Marx and his followers, the basic classes of society are determined by ownership or nonownership of the means of production of goods and services. The owners are called capitalists, and those who must sell their labor to the capitalists are the workers.

Marx referred to members of capitalist societies who are poor and not in the labor force as the **lumpenproletariat**. This class is made up of people at the margins of society who either have dropped out of the capitalist system of employment or have never been part of it at all. Marx thought of the lumpenproletariat as comprising the criminal underworld, street people, the homeless, and all the other categories that make up the marginal members of humanity. He believed capitalism would always impoverish the working class because the owners of capital would seek to exploit the workers to the fullest extent possible, and as a result, the lumpenproletariat would expand and become ever more dangerous to the stability of capitalist societies.

The German sociologist and historian Max Weber was critical of the Marxian perspective. Weber accepted most of the Marxian analysis of economic classes, but he did not believe capitalism would inevitably cause the expansion of the lumpenproletariat. Moreover, he pointed out that other valued things besides wealth are distributed unequally in modern societies. For example, status (or prestige) and power are both highly valued, and their distribution throughout society does not always coincide with the distribution of wealth. People who have made their money recently, for example, are often accorded little prestige by capitalists who made their money much earlier.

In their studies of the American system of social stratification, social scientists have developed a synthesis of the Marxian and Weberian approaches. They have devised designations like upper class, upper middle class, middle class, working class, and

social stratification

A pattern in which individuals and groups find themselves in different positions in the social order, positions that enjoy varying amounts of access to desirable goods and services.

class stratification

The stratification of individuals and groups according to their access to various occupations, incomes, skills, and opportunities.

lumpenproletariat

Members of capitalist societies who are poor and not in the labor force, according to Karl Marx.

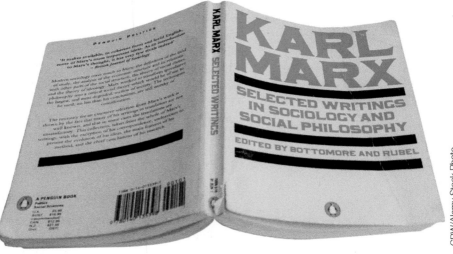

The writings of Karl Marx continue to be widely read today.

poor class, which combine the Marxian concept of economic class with the Weberian concept of status.

Sociologists have pointed out that the ways in which people distinguish among these class levels have both *objective dimensions*, which can be measured by quantifiable variables such as income or by membership in certain clubs, and *subjective dimensions*, which are the ways in which individuals evaluate themselves and others (and the way they feel about people in the various objective classes). Objectively, Americans base their estimations of social class position more or less on the Marxian model. Major employers, powerful political leaders, and very wealthy people are assigned to the upper class. Managers of large firms and relatively well-off people with successful businesses and professional practices (e.g., physicians) are in the upper middle class. People who are employed as middle-level managers and averagely paid professionals (e.g., teachers) are in the middle class. People who earn lower salaries or depend on hourly wages make up the working class (e.g., janitors). People who lack steady work or drift back and forth between legitimate employment and other ways of obtaining income are considered the poor class.

The subjective dimension of social class becomes evident when people are asked to identify the class to which they belong. For example, the proportion of people who classify themselves as poor is considerably lower than the proportion that is classified as such by the Census Bureau. Part of the reason for this difference is the stigma associated with poverty. Many poor people have low-paying jobs and hesitate to identify themselves as poor even when they are; instead, they place themselves in the working class.

All of these social class categories are extremely difficult to define precisely. The designations "middle class" and "working class" are especially problematic. In the booming 1950s and 1960s, when the GDP doubled each decade, it appeared that the distinctions between the working and middle classes were becoming blurred and meaningless. For a period of about 20 years, more people shared in the benefits of expanding wealth. Lower-income workers were adopting lifestyles that seemed to make them indistinguishable from the middle class of salaried employees and professionals. In that period, only the extremes of social stratification were easy to identify: the wealthy at the top and the poor at the bottom. Otherwise, the incomes of most Americans were giving them access to what sociologist David Riesman called the "standard package" of goods and services available in a wealthy society (Riesman, Glazer, and Denney, 1950). That package included a home, a car, and consumer goods such as TV sets, air conditioners, and washing machines (Blumberg, 1980).

The growing strength of labor unions allowed workers to bargain for higher wages and better benefits than ever before. The growth of public educational institutions made education available to more people and provided training for new jobs and professions. Social welfare programs like Social Security, workfare, food stamps, Medicare and Medicaid, affirmative-action programs, youth programs, unemployment insurance, and many other kinds of government support seemed to offer the hope that the degree of inequality in American society would be reduced still further. However, events of recent decades have reversed the trend toward greater affluence for all, and the gap between those who are poor and those who are affluent has increased. Further discussion of this subject will continue in later sections of the chapter.

Consequences of Poverty

6.5 **Identify the consequences of poverty for children and adults.**

Poor families face a higher degree of stress, disorganization, and other problems in their lives. Poverty is difficult for everyone, but weighs especially heavily on children's physical, social, and emotional health.

How Poverty Can Affect Children

Poor children are vulnerable. They tend to exhibit more antisocial behavior and are more likely to drop out of school or become teenage parents, are more likely to suffer from depression, and are in poorer health (National Center for Health Statistics, 2017). Naturally, not all poor children suffer these outcomes; many poor children are the models of success. However, they are more likely than other children to face a host of serious challenges. How does poverty exert its influence? Figure 6–6 summarizes the pathways through which poverty hurts children. Poverty contributes to:

- Inadequate health and nutrition
- Lower-quality home environment
- Parental stress and mental health problems
- Fewer resources for learning
- Housing problems
- Poor-quality neighborhoods

INADEQUATE HEALTH AND NUTRITION   Research is clear about the relationship between poverty and health. Poverty puts the health of children at risk in many ways, including the likelihood of having low birth weight, which in turn increases chances of serious chronic and acute illness, along with emotional and behavioral problems (National Center for Health Statistics, 2017). Children who are poor may also receive inadequate food and nutrition. Over 12 percent of households experienced **food insecurity** at some point in 2016, defined by the United States Department of Agriculture (USDA) as not having enough nourishing food available on a regular basis. Seventeen percent of households with children experience food insecurity (Coleman-Jensen, Rabbitt, Gregory, and Singh, 2017). Children suffer the immediate pain of hunger and the longer-term consequences of malnutrition. They run the risk of more frequent colds, ear infections and other infectious diseases, impaired brain function, and stunted growth, and they are more vulnerable to lead poisoning and other environmental toxins and suffer from a variety of behavioral, emotional, and academic problems (Gundersen and Ziliak, 2015; Johnson and Markowitz, 2017; Shankar, Chung, and Frank, 2017).

food insecurity

A condition, defined by the United States Department of Agriculture (USDA), as not having enough nourishing food available on a regular basis.

LOWER-QUALITY HOME ENVIRONMENT Warm loving relationships with parents, in conjunction with rich opportunities for learning, help children thrive. The Home Observation of the Measurement of the Environment (HOME) is a widely used interview and observation tool assessing parent–child interaction. The HOME shows that poverty has a significant negative effect on the quality and stimulation of the home environment (Crosnoe, Leventhal, Wirth, Pierce, Pianta, and NICHD Early Child Care Research Network, 2010; Yeung, Linver, and Brooks-Gunn, 2002). A landmark study published in 1995 showed that, in high-poverty households, children were exposed to an average of 30 million fewer words by age three than were their middle-income peers (Hart and Risley, 1995). More recently, a study of the linguistic capabilities of very young children found that by only 18 months, children from poor backgrounds knew 60 percent fewer words compared to children from middle-income backgrounds (Fernald, Marchman, and Weisleder, 2013). Obviously, parents cannot teach their children what they themselves do not know. There are also other differences. For example, parents who are poor are less nurturing and more authoritarian, and they use more inconsistent and harsh physical discipline.

PARENTAL STRESS AND MENTAL HEALTH PROBLEMS What else about an impoverished family environment increases the likelihood of negative outcomes for children? Parents living in poverty face a high level of stress, depression, and mental health problems related to their situation. For example, high levels of male unemployment are significantly associated with child abuse and deprivation. While

Figure 6–6 Pathways from Poverty to Adverse Child Outcomes

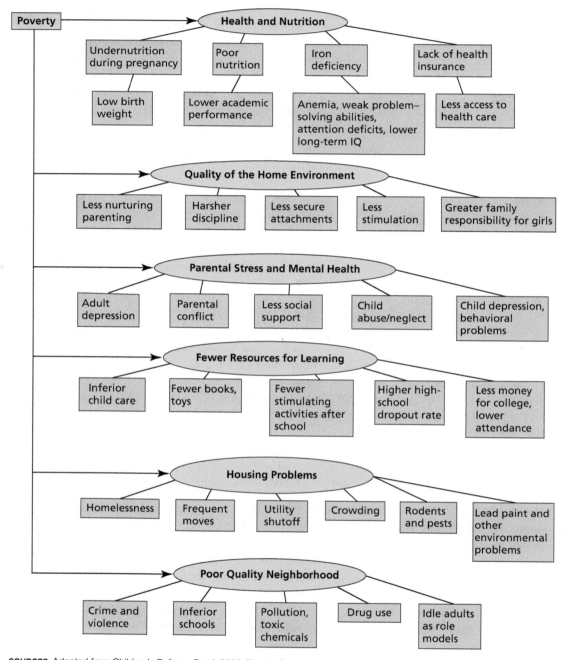

SOURCES: Adapted from Children's Defense Fund, 2005; Brooks-Gunn and Duncan, 1997; and Seccombe, *Families and Their Social Worlds*, 3e. © 2016 Pearson.

child abuse occurs in many different types of households, poor children have a higher probability of being abused, neglected, and more severely injured by abuse than do children in more affluent households (Bywaters, Bunting, Davidson, Hanratty, Mason, McCartan, and Steils, 2016; Centers for Disease Control and Prevention, 2015).

FEWER RESOURCES FOR LEARNING In every respect, poor children get less education than those born into more affluent families. They receive fewer years of schooling, have less chance of graduating from high school, and are much less likely to go to college. On average, children living in poverty have fewer resources for learning in the home, including books and educational toys. Therefore, high-quality childcare and preschool programs become very important to helping them overcome the disadvantages in their home environment. Unfortunately, childcare and preschool are very expensive, and few subsidized spots are available. Full-time childcare can easily cost over $15,000 per year for each child (Child Care Aware of America, 2017). Consequently, many children living in poverty start school academically behind their peers (Hair, Hanson, Wolfe, and Pollak, 2015). This disadvantage often continues throughout life. Generally, children who are poor receive lower grades and lower scores on standardized tests, they are less likely to finish high school, and are less likely to attend or graduate from college than are other children (Federal Interagency Forum on Child and Family Statistics, 2014). The low educational attainment of poor children tends to perpetuate poverty. In general, those who are less educated have lower incomes, less secure jobs, and more difficulty in improving their economic condition (Tamborini, Kim, and Sakamoto, 2015). Children of parents with less than a high school education generally do not do as well in school as children whose parents have completed high school (Child Trends Data Bank, September, 2016). Thus, the cycle in which poverty and education are linked may be passed from one generation to the next if interventions are not available.

HOUSING PROBLEMS The 2017 fair market rent for a two-bedroom apartment, according to the U.S. Department of Housing and Urban Development, was $764 in Wichita, $944 in Phoenix, $1,232 in Chicago, and $1,295 in Miami (U.S. Department of Housing and Urban Development, 2017). Because many poor people cannot afford these levels of cost, they end up living in housing that is overcrowded, infested with vermin, in need of major repairs, lacking basic plumbing facilities, without needed appliances, and inadequately heated (Siebens, 2013). For example, Table 6–4 compares the likelihood of some of these deficits among those with household incomes in the lowest quintile (20 percent of the population) versus the highest quintile. As the table shows, families with the lowest incomes are far less likely to have appliances such as clothes washers, dishwashers, or computers in the home; are more likely to have housing with pests or in poor repair; and are more likely to live in unsafe homes or neighborhoods.

Many children who are poor experience frequent moves, live in crowded conditions, or have utilities in their homes shut off. It is difficult to do homework when there are no lights in your home. Some poor families are homeless. Over 550,000 people were homeless on any given night in early 2016, according to research compiled by the U.S. Conference of Mayors (2016). This is a significant decline since the recession because the economy has improved; nonetheless, housing remains elusive for many of the poorest members of our community. People who live in their cars while they work at jobs that

Table 6–4 Comparisons of Home and Neighborhood by Income

	Lowest Quintile	Highest Quintile
Appliances Lacking in Home		
Clothes washer	31%	4%
Dishwasher	55%	10%
Computer	47%	4%
Housing Condition		
Pests	13%	6%
Dissatisfied with repair of home	10%	3%
Dissatisfied with overall housing	6%	1%
Neighborhood Conditions		
Stay at home for safety	16%	5%
Consider home safe	1%	4%
Consider neighborhood safe	3%	11%

SOURCE: Siebens, J. 2013. Extended Measures of Well-Being: Living Conditions in the United States. U.S. Census Bureau. Report P70–136.

A Personal View

"All I Want Is a Fish"

When I was a little girl, I always wanted a pet. I begged my mom to get a dog. I knew someone who had one, and I thought it would be cool to have one too. My mom looked at me as if I was crazy. "How am I supposed to feed you AND a dog?" she shrieked. "I can feed one of you, but I can't afford to feed you both. So you choose."

I knew that she meant what she said. We didn't have much money, and after paying rent on our trailer and trying to scrape up the money to pay the utility bill, there just wasn't much left over. Sometimes we'd keep the trailer ice cold in the winter to save money. At night, Mom and I slept together to stay warm. I know Mom even sold her food stamps a few times to gather up a little more cash. We ate noodles for a week, but at least it was hot, filled our bellies, and it paid our bills for the month.

I hated always scrimping on things. Kids at school would tease me sometimes because of the clothes I wore. Hey, those clothes were not the latest style, but that coat kept me warm anyway. But really, I just wanted to be like every other girl at school—having new shoes now and then, feeling pretty, and having a friend. It's no fun being poor. People notice what you're wearing, or where you're living, or what you're eating for lunch, and it's embarrassing. But I didn't talk about these things with Mom much. She said it gave her migraines.

That's why I wanted a pet. Mom never let me play outside in our neighborhood—it's too dangerous—and I was lonely cooped up in the house alone when she worked. I wanted someone to cuddle, to talk with, someone who would not judge me, and would think I was beautiful. I imagined that a dog would offer these things. But every time I asked her about it, Mom would give me that look, and start talking about food again—how much I eat, how much a dog eats.

Finally it came to me—a fish! They don't eat much, do they? Really, how much can those tiny little grains of food cost? One of those little containers must last a whole year. So I begged mom for a fish—someone whose container I could cuddle, who I could talk with, someone who would not judge

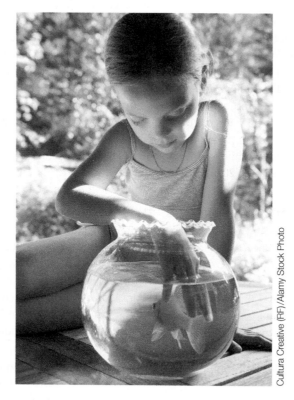

Cultura Creative (RF)/Alamy Stock Photo

me, and who would think I was beautiful. Again, all my mom could talk about was the stress of it all and my constant begging for things she could not afford. "But please Mom," I pleaded. "All I want is a fish."—Cassandra

Critical Thinking

As you think about the poverty pathways, which specific ones come to mind as you read this short story? What makes child poverty a social problem rather than an individual one for this particular family?

What Do You Think?
Create a program to help eliminate or decrease the effects of poverty on children. How would you intervene in each of these pathways?

do not pay enough for them to afford local housing are homeless—so are people sleeping over the warm air of exhaust grates in the alleys of urban office buildings. Women seeking safety from abusive spouses by sleeping with their children in a local women's shelter may have a home, but during the time they are in the shelter, they too are homeless. As these examples suggest, it is extremely difficult to actually count those who are homeless or even to adequately describe all the forms homelessness can take.

POOR-QUALITY NEIGHBORHOODS Children living in poverty are increasingly isolated from those who are not poor in their communities, and they tend to live in inner cities where violence, crime, truancy, loitering, and a sense of despair predominate (Children's Defense Fund, 2014). Guns kill nearly 1,300 children and teens each year, and nearly 6,000 are treated for gunshot wounds (Fowler, Dahlberg, Haileyesus, Gutierrez, and Bacon, 2017). Guns are the third leading cause of death among children. They are the leading cause of death among young blacks ages 15 to 34 (Children's Defense

Fund, 2014). "All I Want Is a Fish" reveals how these different pathways of poverty play out in a child's life. As you read Cassandra's simple story of wanting a pet, put yourself in her shoes and visualize her experience.

Consequences of Poverty for Adults

The effects of poverty on the lives of children are clear; similarly, the potentially harmful health effects of poverty on adults are also numerous. For example, adults living in poverty have significantly higher morbidity (sickness) and a lower life expectancy than other adults (National Center for Health Statistics, 2017). They are more likely to work in dangerous occupations and live in unsafe neighborhoods, and their homes are more likely to be located near toxic sites.

One issue with far-reaching consequences for families is that men and women living in poverty are less likely to marry (Edin and Kefalas, 2005; White and Rogers, 2000). Poverty undermines economic security and makes men less attractive marriage partners. For example, Wilson (1987) suggests that the key factor in explaining the falling marriage rate among inner-city blacks is their declining employment opportunities as jobs move to the suburbs or overseas.

Poverty also undermines marital stability and leads to greater marital conflict. Poverty increases stress or depression, which can then lead to anger, resentment, and hostility between partners, and difficulties among children (Conger and Conger, 2008; Haushofer and Fehr, 2014; Jackson, Trail, Kennedy, Williamson, Bradbury, and Karney, 2016).

Why Does Poverty Persist?

6.6 **Analyze the individualistic, structural, and cultural explanations for poverty.**

Many theories are offered to explain the nature of poverty and account for why so many people are impoverished in the United States. Here we will discuss individualistic, structural, and cultural explanations.

Individualistic Explanations

"Rags to riches" stories are popular in the United States. Americans like to believe that anyone can pull him- or herself up by the bootstraps with hard work, and that people in the United States can be anything they want to be. From that perspective, it follows that those who are poor, particularly welfare recipients, are blatant examples of those who have failed to work hard. An individualistic explanation argues that poverty is primarily the result of laziness or lack of motivation, and those who are poor generally have only themselves to blame. It asserts that the United States is largely a land of meritocracy, and that hard work will reap social and financial rewards.

Individualistic explanations are popular in America. There is great ambivalence toward those who are poor (Godfrey and Wolfe, 2016; Homan, Valentino, and Weed, 2017). People who are more likely to espouse individualistic explanations are white, live in the southern and north-central regions of the United States, are older than 50, and have moderate levels of education. Perhaps surprisingly, even welfare recipients tend to denigrate those who are poor. They distance themselves from other people on welfare, despite the fact that their circumstances are not altogether different (Seccombe, 2015). As "Sheri," a 27-year-old mother of three who had received welfare for seven years, said:

> *I think a lot of them are on it just to be on it. Lazy. Don't want to do nothing. A lot of them are on it because a lot of them are on drugs. Keep having kids to get more money, more food stamps. Now that's abusing the system. And a lot of women are abusing the system.*

Growing Up Poor

Poor children are vulnerable. They face many challenges as they grow. This slideshow illustrates some of the difficulties of growing up poor.

Hunger and malnutrition are not just problems in the developing world. Many American adults and children are also food insecure and are at risk for a number of health problems. Here, people are handed bread during a food distribution by a local food bank.

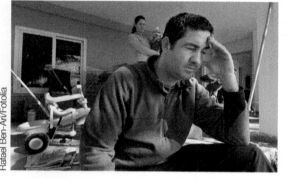

Parents living in poverty face a high level of stress, depression, and mental health problems related to their situation. Finding enough money for food, shelter, and clothing is a constant struggle.

Poor children generally have fewer resources for learning. There are fewer books available at home, and they are less likely to go to preschool because of the cost. Consequently, many children who are poor begin school already academically behind their peers.

This 3-year-old and her mother just received shoes and school supplies during a charity event to help more than 4,000 underprivileged children at a mission in the Skid Row area of Los Angeles. Skid Row contains one of the largest populations of homeless people in the United States. This mother and her daughter stay at a shelter when room is available, but must often resort to staying under bridges.

Children play in a neighborhood with abandoned buildings, pawnshops, and used needles and condoms in the empty lots. Some of the parents refuse to let their children go out and play after school. "I don't want trouble," one mother says.

Critical Thinking

Of all these possible difficulties that children who are poor face, which do you think are most serious, and why? Can you identify any solutions to these problems?

Structural Explanations

Structural explanations attribute poverty to the functioning of the dominant institutions of society, such as markets and corporations. In contrast to individualism, a social structural explanation assumes that poverty is a result of economic or social imbalances within the social structure that restrict opportunities for some individuals. For example, the U.S. economy has been changing over the last several decades, resulting in erosion of the purchasing power of the minimum wage, a growth in low-paying service jobs, and job relocation from inner cities to the suburbs. Although low wages may be enough to support a single person, a family trying to make ends meet would be living near or below the poverty threshold. Moreover, low-wage jobs often fail to provide families with important benefits like sick leave, health insurance, or retirement benefits. Other societal issues, such as sexism, racism, and segregation, cause disparities in education, employment, and income.

Individualistic explanations are popular in American society. Many people believe that anyone can be rich if he or she is willing to work hard, and that the poor have primarily themselves to blame.

Closely related are those structural explanations that emphasize the dual market for labor. In studies of the migrations of blacks and other groups to the cities, sociologists have found that there is a dual labor market in which favored groups are given access to the better jobs—those that offer secure employment and good benefits. Other groups, usually minority groups and migrants, are shunted into another segment of the labor market in which the jobs pay extremely poorly and offer no security or benefits (Elger, 2015; Wilson, 1987).

These inequalities are social problems, not simply personal ones. People may find themselves vulnerable because of their social location and relationship to the social structure. A changing economy, a drive for profit inherent in capitalism, racism, sexism, and an eroding safety net have greater deleterious effects on some than on others. One woman highlights the value of this safety net as she compares what is available to families in Hungary with what is available to those in the United States.

I am an American and my husband is Hungarian, and we made a deliberate choice to have our children in Hungary. I'm happy to live here because the benefits for families surpass those of just about any other country I've heard of. For example, when I had a baby, my maternity leave was three years. She went to daycare and preschool, which are free. Elementary school has optional aftercare if you want it. Most schools also offer wonderful activities after school, like music lessons, dance, computer clubs, and sports. All families receive a monthly family supplement grant until the child turns 18. The more children, the larger the grant. When the child turns six, we get an additional $100 or so at the beginning of each school year to cover school supplies. All children have medical coverage through the age of 18, or even longer if they are in college. Pediatricians make house calls—just try to find that in the U.S.! A friend of mine has a child with a disability and she receives the minimum wage to stay home and take care of him. When you compare Hungary with the U.S., there is no question that the U.S. needs more generous benefits for families. Sometimes I get homesick, but then I think of my overworked, stressed-out friends back home and think: No way. I think parents everywhere should have the same opportunities we've got here in Hungary to make life easier for families.

Her point is that families need programs and policies in place to remain socially and economically healthy. Families without these benefits are more likely to slip into poverty.

Cultural Explanations

Cultural explanations of poverty are based on the interactionist perspective in sociology. In this view, people become adapted to certain ways of life because of the way they were raised, including adapting to poverty.

Proponents of the cultural approach argue that a "culture of poverty" arises among people who experience extended periods of economic deprivation. Under these conditions, new norms, values, and aspirations emerge and eventually become independent of the situations that produced them, so that eliminating the problem does not eliminate the behaviors that have been developed to deal with it. The result is a self-sustaining system of values and behaviors that is handed down from one generation to the next (Bell, Fosse, Lamont, and Rosen, 2015; Lewis, 1968; Murray, 1984).

The idea that there is a culture of poverty that arises among chronically poor individuals and families is controversial. William J. Wilson (1987), a noted expert on inner-city poverty, rejects the concept, claiming that it is a general label that does not fit in many instances. But he recognizes that long spells of poverty may have long-term consequences for children and grandchildren. He attributes this decline in family norms to the despair felt by those living in poverty, especially impoverished men. This despair also leads to higher rates of suicide, homicide, incarceration, and addiction, which in turn decrease the pool of eligible men in poor communities.

Overall, he suggests that poor people in inner-city ghettos and elsewhere share the same values and express the same aspirations as more affluent Americans, but their confidence in attaining them is greatly diminished by their negative life experiences. They may develop certain styles of language and expression that look like a separate culture to outsiders, but these differences, according to Wilson, hardly qualify as a culture of poverty.

Sociologist Herbert J. Gans (1995) is also critical of the culture-of-poverty thesis. Gans stresses the heterogeneity of those who are poor, noting that some are in families that have been poor for generations, while others are poor only periodically; some have become so used to coping with deprivation that they have trouble adapting to new opportunities; and some are beset by physical and emotional illnesses. He is critical of the idea that culture is holistic, that no element of it can be changed unless the entire culture is altered. Instead, he argues that behavior results from a combination of cultural and situational influences.

Gans (1995) maintains that the ultimate solution to the problem of poverty lies in discovering the specific factors that constrain those who are poor as they react to new opportunities when these opportunities conflict with their present cultural values. He believes that Americans must examine the kinds of changes needed in our economic system, social order, and power structure and in the norms and aspirations of the affluent majority that permit a poor class to exist. These themes will all emerge again in considerations of social policy and poverty.

Social Policy

6.7 **Assess the implications of social policy in terms of welfare reform.**

As is evident throughout this chapter, the extent of poverty in the world's most affluent society is a matter of continuing controversy, and so are the questions of what can be done about it. These questions are intimately bound up with attitudes toward those

What Do You Think?

Which of these three explanations for persisting poverty makes the most sense to you, and why? Do you think most people your age feel as you do?

A Closer Look

Myths about Poverty in the United States

As if they did not have enough to cope with, those who are poor are often stigmatized as lazy, dishonest, and unable to help themselves. In fact, as you have seen, people living in poverty are an extremely diverse population, and many are among the hardest-working people in the nation. Here are seven common myths and the facts that debunk them:

Myth 1: The vast majority of those living in poverty are blacks or Hispanics. Poverty rates are higher among blacks and Hispanics than among other racial/ethnic groups, but they do not make up the majority of the poor. Non-Hispanic whites are the most numerous racial/ethnic group in the poverty population.

Myth 2: People are poor because they do not want to work. Half of those who are poor are not of working age: Many living in poverty are under age 18, and another group is age 65 and older. Is expecting them to work realistic? As for adults, many do have jobs but earn below-poverty wages. Numerous individuals who are poor cannot work because of a serious disability or because they must care for family members.

Myth 3: Poor families are trapped in a cycle of poverty that few escape. The poverty population is dynamic—people move in and out of poverty every year. Less than 15 percent of those who are poor remain in poverty for five or more consecutive years.

Myth 4: Welfare programs for those who are poor are straining the federal budget. Social assistance programs for low-income families and individuals accounted for less than 12 percent of federal expenditures. A much larger share of the budget goes to other types of social assistance (such as Social Security), which mainly go to middle-class Americans.

Myth 5: The majority of people who are poor live in inner-city neighborhoods. Less than half of the people in poverty live in central-city areas, and less than one-quarter live in high-poverty inner-city areas. Over one-third of those who are poor live in the suburbs, and more than one-fifth live outside metropolitan areas.

Myth 6: People who are poor live off government welfare. Under the new rules for public assistance, which require welfare recipients to work after two years of public assistance, welfare itself accounts for a diminishing proportion

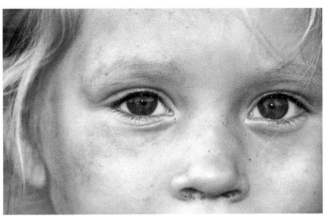

Steluta Sabau/Fotolia

of the income of adults who are poor. Well over half of the income received by adults in poverty comes from wages or other work-related activity. Perhaps the most pernicious myth about those who are poor is that they do not share the work ethic of the middle class—that they are lazy or shiftless and would much rather be on welfare than work. Many studies have shown that people living in poverty have a strong work ethic and regret being on welfare (Seccombe, 2015). The research indicates that, in terms of life goals and willingness to work, there are no differences between those who are poor and those who are not; the differences are that those who are poor lack opportunities and confidence to succeed, and hence, they accept welfare or low-wage work as a necessity.

Myth 7: Most of the people who are poor are single mothers and their children. Female-headed families represent less than half of those who are poor. About a third of those in poverty live in married-couple families.

Critical Thinking

How many of these myths did you believe before reading this chapter? Why are these myths so widespread? What myths exist about people who are rich? Do these myths tend to be more positive, negative, or about the same as the ones that attempt to describe those who are poor? As a budding sociologist, how do you interpret any differences in the myths?

who are poor: Are the poor to blame for their own poverty? Do they avoid work? Would providing more jobs for the poor do any good? One's views on these issues have a lot to do with one's opinions about government intervention on behalf of the poor. Many myths surround poverty, and these are summarized in *A Closer Look: "Myths about Poverty"* in the United States.

Many people believe that those who are poor are largely to blame for their own poverty (Seccombe, 2015; Smith, 2017). The argument goes this way: As a group, most

---

Table 6–5 Reasons for Poverty, 2013

Which of the following reasons do you think is most responsible for the continuing problem of poverty?

Reason	Percentage
Too much government welfare that prevents initiative	24%
Lack of job opportunities	18%
Lack of good educational opportunities	13%
Breakdown of families	13%
Lack of work ethic	10%
Lack of government funding	4%
Drugs	3%
Racial discrimination	2%
Other	4%
All reasons equally	8%
Not sure	1%

SOURCE: McClam, E. 2013. "Americans Blame Poverty on 'Too Much' Welfare, NBC/WSJ Poll Shows." thegrio.com. 6 June. Retrieved 1 March 2015 (thegrio.com/2013/06/06/americans-blame-poverty-on-too-much-welfare-nbcwsj-pollshows/).

---

of those who are poor are unemployed. They are responsible for their own condition because they will not work. If they could be persuaded to work for a living or were forced to take jobs, poverty could be eliminated. What we have now is a group of free-loaders who are getting by on welfare, and welfare does more harm than good. One national survey asked adults (McClam, 2013), "Which of the following reasons do you think is most responsible for the continuing problem of poverty: lack of government funding and programs, the lack of job opportunities, racial discrimination, the break-down of families, drugs, the lack of a work ethic, the lack of good educational opportunities, or too much government welfare that prevents initiative?" Which answer do you think scored the most votes? See Table 6–5 for the answer.

The inaccuracy of this argument is evident when one examines the data on poverty and work. Many families in poverty, including those on welfare, do work, often full-time, but minimum wage does not pull a family out of poverty. Moreover, other people who are poor cannot work because of physical or mental problems or because they are children or elderly. Welfare and other antipoverty programs help to keep many families safe and secure, although they do not cover the true extent of need (Jusko and Weisshaar, 2014).

Reform of "Welfare as We Know It"

In 1996, Congress passed the Personal Responsibility and Work Opportunity Reconciliation Act, more widely known as "welfare reform." This landmark legislation targets the parents of children in households whose incomes fall below the poverty line. Poor parents who were formerly entitled to monthly payments or assistance are now required to obtain jobs or enroll in work training programs to qualify for supplemental assistance through their state governments. These state payments are subsidized by federal government grants. Few policy changes have received more attention or generated more confusion or ideological controversy.

Advocates of welfare reform, including both Republicans and Democrats, point to a dramatic decline in the number of people, especially female single parents, receiving various types of "welfare" payments under the Temporary Assistance to Needy Families (TANF) program after welfare was reformed. Since the passage of welfare reform, many people have left welfare, usually for low-wage work. From

Figure 6–7 Number of Families Receiving Cash Welfare Benefits for Every 100 Families with Children in Poverty

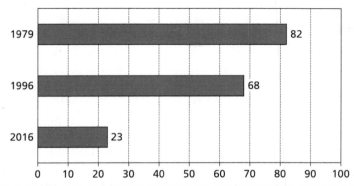

SOURCE: Floyd, I., L. Pavetti, and L. Schott. 2017. "TANF Reaching Few Poor Families." Center for Budget and Policy Priorities. 13 December. Retrieved 30 January 2018 (www.cbpp.org/research/family-income-support/tanf-reaching-few-poorfamilies).

1994 to 2017, national caseloads fell by two-thirds, declining from 5 million to about 1.1 million families (Administration for Children and Families, Office of Family Assistance, 2017). Advocates of welfare reform also cite abundant examples of people who have succeeded in finding real employment. The individuals showcased are ones who have gained greater self-esteem and pride from their jobs.

However, have these far-reaching changes actually improved the lives of poor families? Although declining caseload numbers are often seen as a sign of success, families leaving welfare for work are not necessarily better off financially (Mitchell and Pavetti, 2018; Trisi and Pavetti, 2012). Commonly, families have difficulty paying their rent or utilities; have experienced bouts of food insecurity (i.e., they did not have money to purchase food for their family) or used a food bank; and have no reliable transportation, making it more difficult to work or take children to school. In the past, these vulnerable families could rely on TANF, but with the reforms of the 1990s, receiving this support is often no longer the case. As Figure 6–7 reveals, for every 100 families with children in poverty, only 23 of them even receive TANF benefits, a significant decline from the time before welfare was reformed. In many states the situation is even more dire; in 13 states fewer than 10 percent of poor families with children receive TANF (Floyd, Pavetti, and Schott, 2017). Are these children really better off now that their parent (or parents) work? If so, it's not by much. They are still in poverty.

Part of the reason that families leaving welfare sometimes fare poorly is that many face one or more significant barriers to securing employment. The most common work barriers that TANF recipients face include low levels of education and a lack of work experience, mental and physical health challenges, and the necessity to care for a child with special needs. Other TANF recipients report domestic violence, which can make it difficult to work, and some have criminal records, which can severely limit work opportunities.

Another reason that families remain poor is that the work they find is often of a temporary nature with low pay. For 86 percent of families leaving TANF, their earnings were below the poverty level (Mitchell and Pavetti, 2018). Additionally, work also comes with new expenses, such as childcare or additional laundry expenses.

So what is the truth about welfare reform? The answer is that there is no single truth. Instead of a national program and set of policies dealing with cash assistance, the United States now has 51 different systems across all states and the District of Columbia. This hodgepodge makes it extremely difficult to analyze which mix of financial incentives, work supports, and work obligations is most effective (Schott and

Nito/Fotolia

Families who leave welfare for work usually earn low pay, and at the same time, they may lose critical benefits that helped them make ends meet. To save costs, some skimp or go without food.

Floyd, 2017). Different state policies are still being evaluated. Positive claims based only on reduction of the welfare rolls should never be taken as the full measure of the program's success.

It is important to remember that the United States also attempts to provide a safety net of social insurance programs for *all* taxpayers and their dependents, not only those who are already quite poor. Some social insurance programs are intended to compensate for loss of income, regardless of income level or need. Through unemployment insurance, for example, cash benefits are paid for short periods to insured workers who are involuntarily unemployed.

Other forms of social insurance include workers' compensation programs, which provide wage replacements to insured workers who suffer occupational injuries, and veterans' compensation plans, which issue benefits to disabled veterans to make up for their loss of earning potential. Social Security payments to elderly people also fall into this category. Cash income-support programs are provided for unemployable people, those who are not covered by any form of social insurance, and those with special needs, such as veterans.

Other programs provide "goods and services," such as food, housing, and health care, rather than income. These programs include public housing and urban renewal, health plans like Medicare and Medicaid, and food supplements like the commodity distribution program (which distributes surplus farm products to poor households). You could even say that police and fire departments are a form of social insurance; we pay taxes for these programs, and they are there for us if we need them.

However, note that the specific programs that those who are poor use (e.g., Medicaid) are likely to be stigmatized, whereas the program that cuts across income levels (e.g., Medicare) is not stigmatized.

Future Prospects

One example of a sound social policy with the potential to offset poverty is the Earned Income Tax Credit (EITC), which is a refundable federal tax credit for low-income workers and their families. It has been hailed as a boon to low-income workers, in effect raising their pay by up to several dollars per hour. In essence, it's a cash subsidy for low-income workers.

To qualify for the credit in the 2017 tax year, working families with children must have annual incomes below about $39,600 to $53,999 (depending on marital status and the number of dependent children). Also, working-poor people without children who have incomes below about $15,000 ($20,600 for a married couple) can receive a very small EITC.

The EITC is applauded for lifting millions of adults and children out of poverty each year. It also rewards employment because it offers a supplement to wages for qualifying low-income workers. The EITC makes it easier for families to transition from welfare to work. It can tribute to basic necessities, enable families to make special needed purchases, or build a savings cushion.

Yet, at the same time, the EITC has less of an impact on poverty than it could. It is a once-a-year tax credit, unlike the monthly assistance offered in most other developed nations. Furthermore, the EITC offsets only some of the taxes paid. In that sense, its ability to augment wages is limited.

In looking towards the future, the EITC's usefulness could be enhanced if it followed a model more closely related to other developed nations. Families with children in Canada and Western Europe, for example, receive a modest monthly stipend to help offset some of the costs of raising children. Children are recognized as a valuable resource for the entire community, not just for the children's parents, and therefore the community contributes to the costs of raising them. A monthly stipend, rather than a once-a-year tax credit, would help to ensure that children's basic needs are taken care of on a regular basis.

Going Beyond Left and Right

Why is a person poor? Another side to this question asks why a person may be rich. These are important questions because the discourse forms the basis for many policy decisions. Are poor people primarily lazy, content to live off the public dole? If so, then policy makers will be inspired to cut benefits for those they see as "able-bodied" and impose work requirements. For example, President Trump has discussed implementing work requirements for those seeking Medicaid. Or, are people primarily poor because of circumstances beyond their control? If so, policymakers will create programs that attempt to level the playing field and eliminate discrimination and other social inequalities. Clearly, the public discourse is important. What do you think? Why is a person poor? Conversely, why are they rich?

Summary

6.1 Discuss the extent of social inequality in the United States.

Although the United States ranks among the wealthiest nations in the world, many Americans are living in poverty. In the past several decades, the gap between those who are rich and those who are poor has widened.

6.2 Recognize the importance of wealth.

The United States has a long history of attempting to re-distribute wealth through taxation and other policies. In so doing, however, it has actually provided more opportunities for those who are rich to get richer than for those who are poor to escape from poverty.

6.3 Summarize how poverty is measured, and identify who are poor.

Just under 13 percent of Americans live below the official poverty line, which is a significant improvement from a decade ago, when the recession was in full force. Those who are poor include children, elderly people, single mothers, ill or disabled individuals, students, and people who work either full- or part-time at poverty-level wages.

6.4 Compare and contrast Marxian and Weberian approaches to social stratification and class.

The stratification of individuals and groups according to occupation, income, and skills is called class stratification. The Marxian view of stratification holds that classes are determined by economic measures. This view has been supplemented by those of Weber and his followers, who pointed out that other valued things besides wealth, such as status and power, are distributed unequally in modern societies. American society can be divided into five main classes: the upper class, the upper middle class, the middle class, the working class, and the poor class.

6.5 Identify the consequences of poverty for children and adults.

Consequences of poverty can be severe, especially to children, and include poor health and unequal access to health services, substandard home environment, parental stress, inadequate education, substandard housing and homelessness, and neighborhoods of poor quality.

6.6 Analyze the individualistic, structural, and cultural explanations for poverty.

Individualistic explanations for poverty place the blame on the person; structural explanations of poverty attribute it to dominant social institutions; and the cultural explanation holds that extended economic deprivation creates a culture of poverty with its own norms and values.

6.7 Assess the implications of social policy in terms of welfare reform.

The 1996 welfare reform bill requires able-bodied recipients to enroll in a training program or find work. Evaluations of the new system find that more parents are working, but are not necessarily better off.

Chapter 7
Racism, Prejudice, and Discrimination

dsteller/Getty Images

 Learning Objectives

7.1 Describe the growing diversity of the American population.

7.2 Sequence the continuing struggle for minority civil rights.

7.3 Explain the social construction of minority groups.

7.4 Contrast racism, prejudice, and discrimination.

7.5 Summarize the origins of prejudice and discrimination.

7.6 Identify examples of institutional discrimination.

7.7 Discuss some of the consequences of prejudice and discrimination.

7.8 Analyze the policy of affirmative action.

Michael Brown was an unarmed black teenager in Ferguson, Missouri, who was shot and killed by a white police officer. What do we know about this case? Brown and his friend were walking down the street on a Saturday afternoon. According to Brown's friend, a police officer drove up to them and said "get the f—k on the sidewalk" and then braked in front of Brown. The officer threatened to shoot, then fired multiple shots, and Brown ran for his life. At one point Brown stopped, with his hands up in surrender, yelling "I don't have a gun, stop shooting!" But Brown was then shot and collapsed to the ground. Other witnesses corroborated that Brown had his hands up while the police officer shot at him repeatedly. The police, in contrast, tell a different story. They say that a fight broke out after the police officer asked the two boys to step aside. The gun went off in the police car. The officer was not indicted. A few months after Brown's death, Eric Garner, a black man, died in New York after a police officer put him in a chokehold, despite the fact the New York City Police Department prohibits the use of chokeholds. Garner was accused of selling single cigarettes from packs without tax stamps. When the police officer took Garner's wrist behind his back, Garner swatted his arm away. The officer then put his arm around Garner's neck and pulled him backwards onto the ground. After releasing his arm from Garner's neck, the officer pushed Garner's head into the ground while four other officers moved to restrain Garner, who repeated "I can't breathe" eleven times while lying face down on the sidewalk. Garner lost consciousness, and officers turned him onto his side to ease his breathing while waiting seven minutes for an ambulance to arrive. Garner remained lying on the sidewalk the entire time. The police contend Garner was not put in a headlock and that no choking took place. The officer was not indicted. And then there is the story of Freddie Gray in Baltimore . . . The stories go on and on.

In many ways, the United States prides itself on its ethnic and racial diversity and on the progress it has made since the Civil War toward greater tolerance and racial harmony. The election of Barack Obama in 2008 was rightfully marked as a historic first of which the nation could be proud. The global response to Obama's victory was amazement that a nation that had fought a civil war largely over slavery could have come so far.

However, the realities of partisan politics, ecological disasters, international conflicts, and signs of racism have lowered the sense of optimism. Americans' worries about race relations are at an all-time high, as shown in Figure 7–1 (Swift, 2017). In 2001, over one-quarter of respondents to a Gallup poll reported that they worried a "great deal" about race relations. By 2010, early in Barack Obama's presidency, the percentage who expressed a "great deal" of worry about race relations hit an all-time low of 13 percent, a trend that began near the end of the George W. Bush presidency. The level of

Figure 7–1 Race Relations Worries in U.S. at Record High, 2001–2017

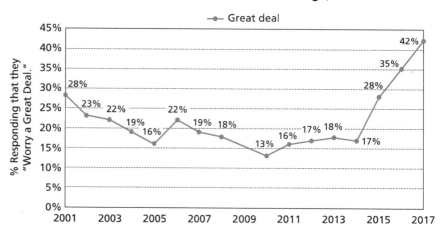

SOURCE: Based on Swift, A. (March 15, 2017) "Americans' Worries About Race Relations at Record High," Gallup. Retrieved from http://news.gallup.com/poll/206057/americans-worry-race-relations-record-high.aspx.

worry about this issue stayed relatively low until 2015, and then began to climb sharply. This surge in worry about race relations likely stems from the racial tensions and public discussion sparked by high-profile police incidents with unarmed black men, and the public's response. In 2017 concern is at an all-time high, likely fueled by President Trump's derogatory racial comments and concern over immigration.

It is important to note that the United States has made significant progress in addressing social problems related to racial inequality over the past century. In the early twentieth century, the United States was still characterized by deep racial and ethnic divisions. Its educational and economic institutions were marked by sharp patterns of racial and ethnic exclusion, its communities rigidly segregated along racial lines. Indeed, when he surveyed the situation of prejudice and discrimination in the 1930s and 1940s, the eminent Swedish social scientist Gunnar Myrdal called the situation of "poor and suppressed" minorities in the land of freedom and opportunity "the American dilemma." Although much has changed since that time, racial and ethnic prejudice is still a significant social problem in many areas of American life.

A More Diverse Nation

7.1 **Describe the growing diversity of the American population.**

Anyone who takes a quick look at the United States cannot help but notice the nation's diversity. An assortment of ethnic restaurants is available from which to choose, within schools many languages may be spoken, and a trip to the mall reveals people dressed quite differently from one another. The United States is quickly becoming more diverse every year due to immigration patterns and birthrates among specific groups, as shown in Figure 7–2. Currently, a little more than one person in three is a member of a minority group, but in Hawaii, New Mexico, California, and Texas, minorities outnumber whites. However, by 2060 minority groups are likely to comprise about 56 percent of the U.S. population. The percentage of blacks and American Indians will remain relatively stable, Asian Americans and Pacific Islanders will nearly double but remain a small group, and the growth of Hispanic groups will be considerable. Although now making up 17 percent of the population, Hispanics are expected to grow to 29 percent by the year 2060 (Colby and Ortman, 2015; Kaiser Family Foundation, 2018).

What Do You Think?

What types of cultural changes do you expect in American society in the future as whites become the minority in number? Do you believe that these potential cultural changes will be good or bad (or neutral) for America, and why?

Figure 7–2 U.S. Population by Race and Ethnicity, 2016, 2060

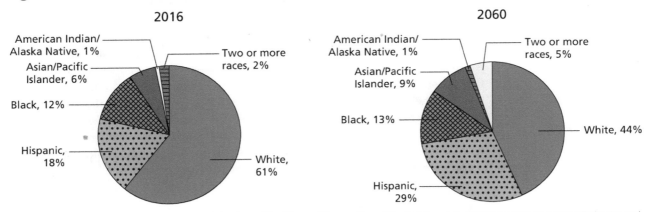

SOURCE: Colby, S. L., and J. M. Ortman. 2015. "Projections of the Size and Composition of the U.S. Population: 2014 to 2060: Population Estimates and Projections." Current Population Reports, 25–1143. March. U.S. Census Bureau. Retrieved 9 March 2015 (www.census.gov/content/dam/Census/library/publications/2015/demo/p25-1143.pdf).; Kaiser Family Foundation, 2018.

The Continuing Struggle for Minority Civil Rights

7.2 Sequence the continuing struggle for minority civil rights.

Although the constitutional bases for racial equality were established in the 1860s and 1870s with the ratification of the Thirteenth, Fourteenth, and Fifteenth Amendments, it was not until the mid-twentieth century that the rights guaranteed by these amendments began to be exercised effectively (Parrillo, 2019; Schaefer, 2019). Starting with Supreme Court decisions that affected specific, small areas of life, black Americans began to work their way toward equality. A major legal breakthrough came in 1954 with the historic decision in *Brown v. Board of Education of Topeka* that "separate educational facilities are inherently unequal."[1] The Supreme Court later applied this "separate cannot be equal" doctrine to a wide range of public facilities.

The Civil Rights Act of 1964 was another important step. Unlike the civil rights acts passed in 1957 and 1960, the 1964 act provided a means for fighting discrimination in employment and public accommodations and for denying federal funds to local government units that permitted discrimination. Eventually, the comprehensive Voting Rights Act of 1965 followed, as well as a federal prohibition against housing discrimination in the Civil Rights Act of 1968. Subsequent affirmative-action orders by President Lyndon B. Johnson aided the enforcement of these new laws; in addition, the Johnson administration set up new programs, such as the Head Start preschool program, to counter the effects of discrimination.

But in 1964, when the discrepancy between legal equality and actual inequality was clear, the impatience of some American blacks developed into anger, and in August 1964, a riot erupted in Watts, a black section of Los Angeles. By the time the wave of violent protest set off by the Watts riot subsided, it had struck almost every major urban center in the country. In 1967, after especially destructive riots in Newark and Detroit, President Johnson appointed the National Advisory Commission on Civil Disorders to investigate the origins of the disturbances and to recommend ways to prevent or control them in the future. Its findings suggested that there had been very little change since Gunnar Myrdal's early study. Describing the basic causes of the civil disorders, the commission stated,

> *The first is surely the continuing exclusion of great numbers of Negroes from the benefits of economic progress through discrimination in employment and education, and their enforced segregated housing and schools. The corrosive and degrading effects of this condition and the attitudes that underlie it are the source of the deepest bitterness and at the center of the problem of racial disorder. (p. 203)*

The commission concluded that "our nation is moving toward two societies, one black, one white—separate and unequal" (p. 1).[2]

Although the situations of other minority groups—Native Americans, Chicanos (Mexican Americans), Hispanic Americans (especially Puerto Ricans and Cubans), Asian Americans, and some white ethnic groups—have received less intensive study, they are similar to that of black Americans. One form of discrimination to which members of other groups are particularly vulnerable is harassment at the voting booth, largely because of some individuals' inadequate command of English. The 1975 extension of the Voting Rights Act attempted to alleviate this problem by requiring cities with sizable "language minority" populations to provide bilingual ballots in elections; it also permanently banned the use of literacy tests as a prerequisite for voting.

---

[1] *Brown v. Board of Education of Topeka,* 347 U.S. 483 (1954). US Supreme Court.

[2] National Advisory Commission on Civil Disorders. 1968. *Report of the National Advisory Commission on Civil Disorders.* Washington, DC: U.S. Government Printing Office.

Over the past few decades there has been an influx of immigrants not only from Spanish-speaking countries, but also from Asian countries, especially Korea, Vietnam, Cambodia, India, and Pakistan. The experiences of these immigrants have shown that small groups with education, business experience, and some funds, coupled with cultural values that stress family cohesion and extremely hard work, have less difficulty in adapting to their new environment. In contrast, large populations that gather in concentrated settlements, as Vietnamese immigrants have done in Texas and California, have been targets of racial hostility. Thus, it appears that the larger a group and the more segregated it is, the more hostility it encounters.

In the same vein, Stanley Lieberson (1990) argued that when an immigrant group is small, it is relatively easy for it to develop an occupational niche or specialty, as the Greeks and the Chinese have done in the restaurant industry. He cites a study showing that 15 percent of Greek immigrants were working in the restaurant industry and 9 percent of Swedish immigrants were carpenters. But when an immigrant population grows, it becomes far more difficult for the group to retain control of an occupational niche and expand it enough to accommodate newcomers. Later arrivals, therefore, are more dependent than earlier immigrants on the general labor market.

The terrorist attacks on the United States in 2001 showed quite vividly how national and world events can quickly change the fortunes of particular minority groups. According to the U.S. Commission on Civil Rights, Ohio Advisory Committee (2001),

> *For those of Middle Eastern descent or appearance, September 11 ushered in fear of reprisal and concern for personal safety. Some Muslims, Arab Americans, and Southeast Asians have paid a high price for sharing a similar appearance or cultural and religious background of the accused terrorists. In the months after the attacks, reports of harassment and assaults against these groups soared, as did complaints of workplace bias and allegations of racial profiling by law enforcement and airline personnel.*[3]

The situation of immigrant groups highlights the problems of minority status in the United States. But before discussing these problems in detail, it is important to gain a clearer understanding of the meaning of the term *minority* as it is commonly used today.

The Social Construction of Minorities

7.3 **Explain the social construction of minority groups.**

One often hears the claim that, due to immigration and differences in the birthrates of various groups within the population, the United States is rapidly becoming a "nation of minorities." This claim refers especially to the increasing numbers of Hispanics, Asians, and other groups, but it does not address the more important sociological aspects of the term *minority*. From the standpoint of social problems, minorities are those groups that do not receive the same treatment as others in society. But how and why does such a situation come about? Arriving at answers to these questions depends on understanding three terms that are central to the discussion: *racial minorities, ethnic minorities*, and *assimilation*.

Racial minorities are groups of people who share certain inherited characteristics, such as eye folds or brown skin. Most experts believe that the biologically determined racial groups into which humanity is divided—Caucasoid, Mongoloid, and Negroid—are strictly social categories and that the actual hereditary differences among them are meaningless. This perspective is known as the "social constructionist" explanation for the existence of racial minorities. Race is a socially constructed concept in that people take what are rather trivial biological distinctions and "construct" ideas about more general differences among groups. Historically, when it is convenient for those in power to do so, they have used socially constructed ideas about racial superiority and inferiority to justify slavery or other extreme forms of racial dominance.

racial minorities

Groups of people who share certain inherited characteristics.

---

[3]U.S. Commission on Civil Rights, Ohio Advisory Committee. 2001. Briefing on Civil Rights Issues Facing Muslims and Arab Americans in Ohio Post-September 11. 14 November. P.203, 1.

ethnic minorities
Groups of people who share cultural features, such as language, religion, national origin, dietary practices, and a common history, and who regard themselves as a distinct group.

Ethnic minorities are made up of people who share cultural features, such as language, religion, national origin, dietary practices, and a common history, and who regard themselves as a distinct group. Ethnicity represents culture, whereas race attempts to represent biological heritage. Thus, a black woman who recently moved to the United States, and grew up in Jamaica, is not really an African American in terms of ethnicity. Her race may be the same as that of an African American (i.e., Negroid), but her cultural heritage is likely to be very different.

This distinction causes some confusion. For example, the U.S. Census Bureau classifies all blacks according to their race—black—not by their ethnicity. Some people, however, use the term *African American* rather than *black* because they are interested in the uniquely African American experience. Likewise, the U.S. Census Bureau often classifies all Hispanics by race—separating white Hispanics from black Hispanics—but generally ignores ethnicity—Mexican American, Puerto Rican, Cuban American—which masks the rich diversity found among Hispanic groups that may have little or nothing to do with skin color or language. After all, how much do Mexican Americans and Cuban Americans really have in common? Other times, the U.S. Census Bureau will single out Hispanics as one ethnic group, combining black and white Hispanics and masking the diversity within these groups.

They, too, have been victims of socially constructed ideas about superiority and inferiority. For example, 6 million Jews were killed by the Nazis because of the socially constructed ideas about them: Jews were thought not only to have abhorrent religious views, and too much economic and political influence, but also to be biologically distinct. From this perspective, there was a biological component to the struggle between Jews and everyone else, and the only way to win the struggle was to exterminate all Jews.

Since this time, there have been other cases of genocide with the intention of eliminating ethnic groups, including Cambodia, Rwanda, Serbia, Syria, and Myanmar. In Rwanda, it is estimated that anywhere from 500,000 to 1,000,000 people were slaughtered in a 100-day period from April 7, 1994, to mid-July of that year. The Hutu majority, incited by top government officials to kill all Tutsi, brutally murdered their neighbors and fellow villagers with machetes and other weapons. Seventy percent of all Tutsi living in Rwanda were killed as the world watched in horror, too stunned to intervene. Former President Bill Clinton referred to America's lack of intervention as one of his biggest regrets while in office.

Syria has been engaged in civil war since 2011. What began as a democratic uprising against President Bashar al-Assad's regime has transformed into a violent struggle between local, national, regional, and international forces, in which the Syrian government, extremist groups, and outside actors perpetrate atrocities against civilians as a systematic strategy of war. The conflict in Syria has cost the lives of nearly 500,000 people, displaced more than half the country's population, and involved numerous crimes against humanity. Syrians are being subjected to starvation, exposure, preventable diseases, and lack of medical care; to enforced disappearances; to chemical weapons attacks—which are banned under international law—and to torture, rape, and killings. When people are forced to leave the country where they live like this, they become known as refugees. The conflict in Syria has caused one of the largest refugee movements in recent history. The rapidly rising number of Syrian refugees is over 5.5 million, and another 6.1 million are internally displaced (The U.S. Holocaust Museum, March, 2018).

The plight of the Rohingya in Myanmar (formerly called Burma) is gaining international attention for the atrocities being committed against this largely Muslim group (Al Jazeera News, 2018; Kristof, 2018; McCain and Jolie, 2018). In 2017 over 700,000 Rohingya fled the country to Bangladesh after being targeted by the military for systematic killing, torture, arson, gang rape, and other mass atrocities amounting to ethnic cleansing. They are denied food and medical care. Two-thirds of the refugees are women and girls; the men have been killed. They live in squalid and violent camps. Girls are vulnerable to forced early marriage to "save" them

Suvra Kanti Das/Alamy Stock Photo

At least 700,000 Rohingya have fled persecution in Myanmar and entered Bangladesh to escape systematic killings, torture, rape, arson, and other forms of violence. Yet, they are largely unwelcome in Bangladesh and live in crowded camps lacking basic necessities.

from assault or are tricked into jobs in brothels. The United Nations has said that the situation bears the markings of "genocide," and several world leaders have declared it "ethnic cleansing." The late Republican Senator John McCain and actress Angelina Jolie, a seemingly unlikely pairing, have worked to bring attention to the tragic situation, and pleaded for the United States to take the lead in stopping the violence and safeguarding the rights and freedoms of all Burmese people.

It should be noted that the term *minority* as used by sociologists does not refer to a group's numerical size in the population. For example, blacks in South Africa are a minority, even though they make up 90 percent of the population. All minority groups have their own special characteristics, but the following characteristics are sociologically significant (Feagin, 2013; Simpson and Yinger, 1985):

- Minorities are subordinate segments of a complex society.
- Minorities tend to have special physical or cultural traits that are seen as undesirable by the dominant segments of the society.
- Minorities develop a group consciousness or "we feeling."
- Membership in a minority is transmitted by a rule of descent—one is born into it—which can impose the minority status on future generations even if by then its special physical or cultural traits have disappeared.
- Members of a minority, whether by choice or by necessity, tend to marry within their group.

Sometimes members of either a racial or an ethnic minority slowly cease being "different" by taking on the characteristics of the mainstream culture. This process is called **assimilation**. Members of a minority group may adapt their own unique cultural patterns to those of the majority, or intermarry, and over time the group ceases to be singled out as a minority. Many Caucasian immigrant groups in the nineteenth century fit this pattern: The Irish, Greeks, or Italians may have been considered distinct groups, living in their own enclaves, speaking their own language, and eating traditional foods. But over time they assimilated, and today they do not receive a lot of attention for being an ethnic group. It is easier for Caucasians to assimilate because they usually do not have distinctive physical features.

There is no clear-cut distinction between who constitutes a majority or a minority group; rather, any given group can be placed at some point along a continuum of "minorityness." Sociologist Michele Lamont (2003) compared racism in the United States and France, two highly developed nations, and asked the question, "Who counts as

assimilation

A process through which a racial or an ethnic minority group slowly ceases being "different" by taking on the characteristics of the mainstream culture.

What Do You Think?

Assimilation is controversial. Is it a good idea for all Americans to eventually look and sound alike, or should Americans keep their distinct racial and ethnic differences? Which view would make a stronger America in your opinion, and why?

'them'?"[4] Lamont interviewed 150 white, working-class men living in the suburbs of Paris and New York. Instead of asking directly about racism, respondents were asked to describe the kinds of people they like and dislike, the kinds of people they feel similar to and different from, and the types of people to whom they feel inferior or superior. The Americans were much more likely than the French to mention race or skin color as a deciding factor. In particular, blacks emerged most often as the group disdained by the white New Yorkers as "them"; yet in France, blacks were not of concern. The French "them" were Muslim immigrants (Lamont, 2003).

Subordinate status is the principal characteristic of a minority group. Once established, however, the dominant–subordinate relationship is not fixed for all time. Either through the efforts of the subordinate group itself or because of changing legal or economic conditions, power relationships can be altered. You can see in American society, for example, that women are not as subordinate as they were only a generation ago. Similarly, in southern counties where blacks considerably outnumber whites, extensive voter registration has enabled blacks to become politically significant. On a broader scale, most of the former colonial areas of Africa and Asia are now independent nations, and some countries that formerly lacked influence, such as China, are now world powers.

Despite these examples of long-term change, it is usually very difficult for members of a subordinate group to attain a share of power and influence. The dominant group naturally wants to protect its privileged position. Among the weapons it uses to do so are prejudice and discrimination.

Defining Racism, Prejudice, and Discrimination

7.4   Contrast racism, prejudice, and discrimination.

racism

Behavior, in word or deed, motivated by the belief that human races have distinctive characteristics that determine abilities and cultures.

Racism is behavior, in word or deed, that is motivated by the belief that human races have distinctive characteristics that determine abilities. Racists believe in this erroneous concept of race; they also believe that their own race is superior and therefore ought to dominate or rule other races. Racism may be an attribute of an individual, or it may be incorporated into the institutions (social structures and laws) of an entire society. Nazi Germany, South Africa under apartheid, and the United States before the civil rights era of the mid-twentieth century are examples of societies and nations that incorporated racist beliefs within their social institutions. Societies that have attempted to eliminate racism from their institutions continue to struggle with the legacies of their racist histories.

prejudice

An emotional, rigid attitude toward members of the subordinate group.

Prejudice is an emotional, rigid attitude toward members of the subordinate group. But while prejudices are attitudes, not all attitudes are prejudices. Both share the element of *pre*judgment—the tendency to decide in advance how to think about a situation or event. Unlike other attitudes, however, prejudice involves an emotional investment that strongly resists change. Prejudiced people tend to be so committed to their prejudgments about a particular category of people that even in the face of rational evidence that the prejudgment is wrong, they will maintain their prejudice, even defend it strongly, and denounce the evidence.

It is important to note that prejudice need not always involve antipathy. One can be prejudiced in favor of a person or group, with a similar degree of disregard for objective evidence. Prejudice is based on attitude; it is a tendency to think about people in a categorical, predetermined way: *My daughter Ashley has a new boyfriend, a Chinese boy. He's a good catch. You know how smart those Chinese people are.*

---

[4]Lamont, M. (2003). "Who Counts as 'Them': Racism and Virtue in the United States and France." *Contexts 2* (4):36–41.

Discrimination is the differential treatment of individuals considered to belong to a particular social group. To treat a member of a subordinate group as inferior is to discriminate against that person. Members of the dominant group tend to use one standard of behavior among themselves and a different standard for any member of a subordinate group.

Discrimination is overt behavior, although it may sometimes be difficult to observe—as in tacit agreements among real estate agents to steer members of minority groups to certain blocks or neighborhoods. To justify the behavior to themselves, people tend to rationalize it by claiming that those whom they discriminate against are less worthy of respect or fair treatment than people like themselves. Moreover, people tend to be ethnocentric—to see their own behavioral patterns and belief structures as desirable and natural and those of others as less so.

It may be easy to say that discrimination is a thing of the past, but it would be untrue, as shown in Figure 7–3. A recent survey asked a representative sample of white and black persons about their experiences with discrimination. Have people acted as if they were suspicious of you, or that you weren't smart? Have you been treated unfairly in hiring, pay, or promotion? Have you been unfairly stopped by police? As you can see in the Figure, blacks are five to six times more likely than whites to say that these things have happened to them (Pew Research Center, June, 2016).

Sociologists and others have conducted many natural experiments and found that, despite what people say they would do, many do discriminate. Discrimination occurs among employers (Milkman, Akinola, and Chugh, 2014; Quillian, Pager, Hexel, and Midtbøen, 2017); on eBay auctions in which an iPod held by a white hand received 21 percent more offers than one held by a black hand (Doleac and Stein, 2013); by service workers who may give black customers less than optimal service (Brewster, Brauer, and Lynn, 2015); and landlords posting on Craigslist who were less

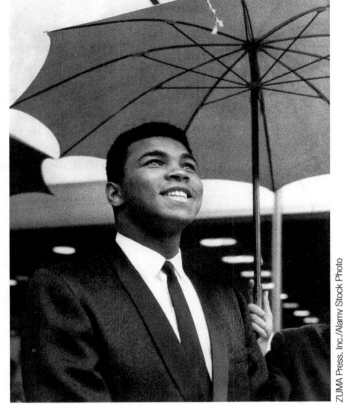

Cassius Clay (now known as Muhammad Ali) won the 1964 World Heavyweight Boxing Championship. Despite the honor, he was routinely denied service in restaurants for being black.

discrimination

The differential treatment of individuals considered to belong to a particular social group.

Figure 7–3 Who Experiences Discrimination?

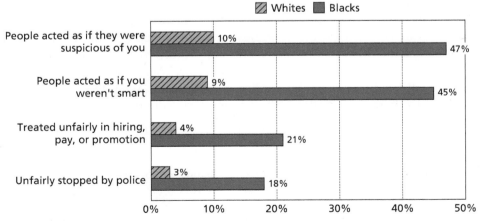

SOURCE: Based on "On Views of Race and Inequality, Blacks and Whites Are Worlds Apart," *Social Demographic Trends*, Pew Research Center (June 27, 2016). Retrieved from http://www.pewsocialtrends.org/2016/06/27/on-views-of-race-and-inequality-blacks-and-whites-are-worlds-apart/st_2016-06-27_race-inequality-overview-09/.

likely to respond to e-mails with stereotypical black-sounding names than to their white counterparts (U.S. Department of Housing and Urban Development, 2013).

Even highly educated persons exhibit racism. In academia, college professors report incidents of racial and ethnic discrimination by their peers and administration (Zambrana et al., 2017). Our state legislators are less likely to respond to constituents with black-sounding names than to those with white-sounding names (Butler and Brockman, 2011). Physicians have described black patients—regardless of their education and income levels—as less intelligent, less educated, more likely to abuse alcohol and drugs, less likely to follow medical advice, and less likely to participate in rehabilitation than white patients (Williams and Wyatt, 2015). Perhaps it's not surprising that discrimination itself contributes to racial disparities in health care and higher death rates among minorities from cancer, heart disease, diabetes, and HIV infection (Cloustin, Rubin, Phelan, and Link, 2016; Colen, Ramey, Cooksey, and Williams, 2017).

Prejudice and discrimination are closely related, and both are often present in a given situation. But this pairing is not always the case. Robert Merton (1949) outlined four possible relationships between prejudice and discrimination: unprejudiced and nondiscriminatory (integration), unprejudiced and discriminatory (institutional discrimination), prejudiced and nondiscriminatory (latent bigotry), and prejudiced and discriminatory (outright bigotry) (see Table 7–1). Although it is possible to be both completely free of prejudice and completely nondiscriminatory—or to be a complete bigot—most people fall somewhere between these two extremes. It is possible to be prejudiced against a particular group but not to discriminate against it; it is also possible to discriminate against a particular group but not be prejudiced against it.

The builders of a new, expensive cooperative apartment house may not be personally prejudiced against Arabs, but they may refuse to sell apartments to Arab families (i.e., they may discriminate against Arabs) out of fear that the presence of Arab families would make it more difficult to sell the remaining apartments. This example is a clear case of institutional discrimination (the lower-left cell in Table 7–1). Or the reverse may occur: In a corporation that holds a government contract, and hence is subject to federal equal employment opportunity regulations, the personnel director may be very prejudiced personally against blacks but may hire a black woman as a management trainee—that is, not discriminate—to comply with the law. This behavior is an example of latent bigotry (the upper-right cell).

Suppose the builders were confronted with a different situation: a Hispanic family attempting to buy one of their apartments. On the one hand, they might very well discriminate out of both personal prejudice and concern for profits—a case of outright bigotry (the upper-left cell). On the other hand, there can be situations in which legal controls prevent latent bigotry from affecting such behaviors as the sale of a house to a Hispanic family, but those controls cannot prevent social isolation of the family after the sale. These examples illustrate the difficulty of keeping personal prejudices from leading, sooner or later, to some form of discrimination, particularly if a significant number of people share the same prejudice (Ore, 2006).

Table 7–1 A Typology of Prejudice and Discrimination

Prejudice (the Attitude)	Discrimination (the Behavior)	
	Yes	No
Yes	Outright bigotry	Latent bigotry
No	Institutional discrimination	Integration (both psychological and institutional)

SOURCE: Based on Merton, R. K. (1949) *Social Theory and Social Structure.* Glencoe, Ill.: Free Press.

Origins of Prejudice and Discrimination

7.5   Summarize the origins of prejudice and discrimination.

Although prejudice and discrimination are weapons used by a dominant group to maintain its dominance, sometimes they are used unconsciously. Do patterns of prejudice and discrimination result from the aggregation of individual attitudes and behaviors, or do prejudice and discrimination arise from the society? In fact, neither argument excludes the other; both are possible.

7.5.1 Prejudice and Discrimination in the Individual

Prejudice and bigotry may manifest in individuals in several ways. Two are discussed below: frustration-aggression, and projection.

FRUSTRATION-AGGRESSION   At one time or another, most human beings feel frustrated. They want something, but because of events or other people they cannot get it. This can lead to anger and to aggression, which may be expressed in any of several ways. The most obvious way is to strike at the source of the frustration, but often that action is impossible; frustrated individuals may not know the source, or are subjectively unable to recognize it, or are in a position in which they cannot risk such an action. Whatever the reason, the results are the same: They are unable to vent their anger on the real source of their frustration.

Instead, the aggression is often directed at a safer and more convenient target, usually one that somewhat resembles the real source of the frustration. In other words, the aggression is displaced onto a scapegoat. When this displacement is not limited to one person but is extended to include all similar people, it may produce prejudice.

For example, suppose a middle-aged man who has been working for 20 years at the same job is told by his young supervisor that his job will soon be eliminated because of automation. The man is understandably angry and frightened. But if he were to vent his aggression on the supervisor, he would almost certainly be fired. That evening, as he is telling his woes to friends at the local bar, a young man comes in for a beer. The middle-aged man accuses the youth, and "all you lazy kids," of being a good-for-nothing and ruining the country, and only the intervention of the bartender prevents him from assaulting the young man.

It is clear that this man has displaced his aggression toward his young supervisor onto all young people. Rather than deal with the supervisor and the whole range of factors that led to the elimination of his job, he blames the problems of the country on young people; that is, he uses them as a scapegoat.

PROJECTION   Another source of prejudice and discrimination is **projection**. Many people have personal traits that they consider undesirable. They wish to rid themselves of those traits, but they cannot always do it directly—either because they find the effort too difficult or because they are unable to admit to themselves that they possess those traits. They may relieve their tension by attributing the unwanted traits to others, often members of another group. This behavior makes it possible for them to reject and condemn the traits without rejecting and condemning themselves. Since the emotional pressures under-lying projection can be very intense, it is difficult to counter them with rational arguments.

An often-cited example of projection is white attitudes toward black sexuality. Historically, many whites saw blacks as extremely promiscuous and uninhibited in their sexual relations, and there was much concern about protecting white women from sexual attacks by black men. Actually, it was white men who enjoyed virtually unlimited sexual access to black women, particularly slaves. White society, however, regarded overt sexuality as unacceptable, and it is likely that white men felt some guilt about their sexual desires and assaults on black women. To alleviate their guilt, they projected their own lust and sexuality onto black men—a much easier course than admitting the discrepancy between their own values and behavior.

projection
The act of attributing the un-wanted traits of oneself onto others.

Protesters in California demonstrate against illegal immigration and amnesty for undocumented immigrants. The frustration-aggression perspective suggests that the real frustration among protesters is a lack of jobs with good pay and benefits. The protesters use illegal immigrants as a scapegoat.

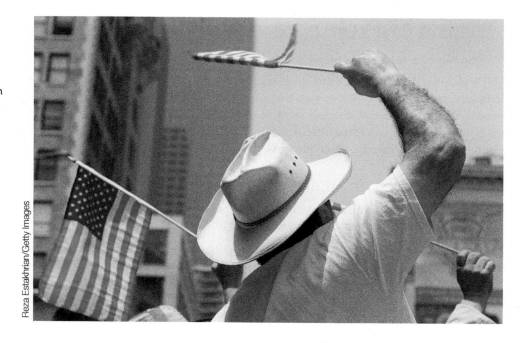

Reza Estakhrian/Getty Images

7.5.2 Prejudice and Discrimination in Social Structures

Looking at individuals does not fully explain why certain groups face prejudice and discrimination. To understand this behavior, you will need to look at larger social processes.

POLITICAL DOMINANCE AND ECONOMIC EXPLOITATION In many societies, the demand for more than the available supply of certain goods gives rise to a competitive struggle, which usually results in the dominance of one group and the subordination of others. Even if the initial competition is for economic goods, the contest is ultimately a struggle for power and hence, a political process. Once established, political dominance is likely to be reinforced by economic exploitation. Slavery and serfdom are the most obvious forms of exploitation, but "free" workers may also be exploited. Migrant farmworkers are an example. They work in dirty jobs in the hot sun, stooped over for hours, and receive low pay and no benefits.

Economic exploitation is one form of discrimination practiced by the dominant group against a subordinate group. Historically, the subordinate group has consisted of unskilled workers. In the case of blacks, for example, unskilled jobs were plentiful and available (at low wages) before the 1940s. With the development of protective labor legislation (e.g., minimum wage, antidiscrimination, and workers' compensation laws), employers could no longer use the subordinate group as a source of cheap labor. Blacks were then systematically denied jobs as white-dominated unions maintained control over skilled jobs and employers sought cheaper unskilled labor by transferring basic manufacturing operations abroad (Sears, Sidanius, and Bobo, 2000).

A recent example involves the change in the policy of the U.S. Census under President Trump that would include questions about citizenship, something that was dropped from the Census more than 50 years ago. At first glance we might think, well, why not ask about citizenship? The problem is that the Census is designed to be a *count* of people, and the federal government allocates billions of dollars to regions based on the count of people who live there. For example, school funding may increase or decrease because of how many young people live in a certain area. If people who are undocumented are asked about their citizenship, it is likely that they will not fill out the form for fear of exposing their status, which could lead to deportation. And since those who are undocumented tend to live in certain regions, the count of residents in these regions may be grossly underestimated, thereby curtailing services for all people who live there.

LAWS AND POLICIES   Discrimination can take many other forms. Members of the subordinate group may be legally prevented from owning property or voting or may be terrorized into submission. Some legal forms of discrimination are symbolic measures to keep the subordinate people "in their place," such as the severe immigration control law passed in the Arizona State Legislature in 2010 and signed into law by the state's governor, Jan Brewer. The law, nicknamed the "show me your papers law," requires state troopers to ask for identification and proof of citizenship or legal status in the United States from anyone they stop who, in their judgment, might be an illegal immigrant. It was unclear how a state trooper would make such a judgment, and it was left to the troopers' discretion. After much controversy and court hearings, the law was enforced beginning in 2012. The law is an example of many initiatives in the Southwest that are designed to address what advocates regard as a crime wave by illegal immigrants. In the meantime, one very immediate effect is the rise of protests throughout the nation, and especially in cities with large numbers of immigrants of Hispanic origin. After SB 1070 passed in 2010, two dozen copycat bills were introduced in state legislatures across the country; five passed in Alabama, Georgia, Indiana, South Carolina, and Utah. The ACLU and a coalition of civil rights organizations have filed lawsuits in all six states. Laws inspired by Arizona's SB 1070 invite rampant racial profiling against Latinos, Asian Americans and others presumed to be "foreign" based on how they look or sound.

SOCIAL NORMS   A **social norm** is a commonly accepted standard that specifies the kind of behavior appropriate in a given situation. It is relevant to this discussion because, although it does not clarify why prejudice and discrimination begin, it helps explain how and why they are perpetuated.

Social norms are learned in a process that begins almost at birth. Small children soon learn what kind of behavior elicits the approval of their parents and what kind is likely to elicit a rebuke. The same process continues as they encounter other significant adults. Gradually, children internalize the values and norms of their society. They receive approval from parents and other adults, and later from their peers, when they behave in socially acceptable ways; they experience disapproval when they do not.

A good example of a social norm that pertains to minority–majority relations is **homogamy**, the requirement or expectation that one must marry a person like oneself with respect to such characteristics as religion, social class, and race or ethnicity. This expectation has been a particularly strong norm in the United States for race. The early U.S. censuses included a category called *mulatto* to describe people of multiple races. **Antimiscegenation laws** banning marriage between whites and other races were common well into the latter half of the twentieth century. Racially mixed couples often encountered severe hostility, and many felt compelled to move to places like Greenwich Village in New York City or Hyde Park in Chicago, where there were similar couples and they could feel less "deviant." The U.S. Supreme Court struck down such laws in 1967 in the case of *Loving v. Virginia*; however, Alabama was the last state to formally repeal its antimiscegenation law through a state constitutional amendment as late as 2000.

Today, fifty years after *Loving v. Virginia*, interracial marriage is on the rise. By 2015, 17 percent of newlyweds were interracial couples, and among Asians and Hispanics, that figure is close to 30 percent (Livingston and Brown, 2017). Attitudes toward interracial marriages have become more favorable over the decades, and now only about 9 percent think that it is a bad thing for society (Livingston and Brown, 2017). The norm of homogamy is far weaker today than it was even a generation ago. Younger adults have grown up in an environment immersed with multicultural images including those in music, art, sports, and television. They saw a biracial man as president when many of them were

social norm
A commonly accepted standard that specifies the kind of behavior appropriate in a given situation.

homogamy
The expectation that one must marry a person like oneself with respect to such characteristics as religion, social class, and race or ethnicity.

antimiscegenation laws
Laws banning marriage between whites and other races.

Ethnic and Racial Stereotypes

Stereotypes are exaggerations of some small element of truth, grossly distorted and taken out of context. They are usually negative in nature, but not always. Nonetheless, whether positive or negative, stereotypes are harmful because they treat people as one homogeneous group and ignore personality and other individual differences.

9 Lives Illustration/Shutterstock

Asian Americans are stereotyped as smart and as having professional, well-paying careers. Although the median income of Asians is the highest among all racial and ethnic groups, it is not fair to say that all Asians are doing well financially. Many Asians, especially those from Vietnam, Cambodia, and Laos, work in poorly paid service work or in factories.

Anton Lunkov/Shutterstock

The image of the Mexican bandit, wearing a sombrero, red bandana, a vest, and boots with spurs is widespread. The "Frito Bandito" was a classic image in advertising. However, most Mexican men do not look like this, are definitely not bandits, and could be highly offended by the stereotype.

Robert Miu/Shutterstock

patrimonio designs ltd/Shutterstock

yuriytsirkunov/Shutterstock

One of the many stereotypes about blacks, especially black men, is that they are good in sports. Yes, a look at professional sports teams usually shows an overrepresentation of blacks, but that observation is a far cry from assuming that most blacks are good athletes. Black people come in all shapes, sizes, and abilities.

Stereotypes of Native Americans are less than flattering. Images like this one do not represent the lives of Native Americans, and yet, these images are common, including as mascots for sports teams. Many teams have changed their mascots, but others such as the Washington Redskins, have resisted changes despite some degree of public outcry.

Stereotypes also abound regarding white people; they have the world in the palm of their hands! However, race and ethnicity are also interwoven with class and sex. Rich white men may be overrepresented among the powerful, but poor whites, and poor white women in particular, generally do not have the same opportunities.

Critical Thinking

What other racial or ethnic stereotypes exist? Make a list of stereotypes for each primary racial and ethnic group. Compare and contrast these stereotypes: Is the list longer for some groups than others? Do some groups have more positive (or negative) stereotypes than other groups?

still children. On the contrary, older Americans grew up with the notion that segregation was normal, justifiable, and the appropriate way for Americans to live their lives. Even so, the views of many elderly persons have evolved over time.

STEREOTYPES Still another source of prejudice and discrimination is **stereotyping**, or attributing a fixed and usually unfavorable or inaccurate conception to a category of people. Whereas social norms are concerned primarily with behavior and only indirectly with attitudes, stereotyping is a matter of attitude.

Usually a stereotype contains (or once contained) some element of truth, but it is exaggerated, distorted, or taken out of context. We tend to perceive and understand things in categories and apply the same mental process to people. We build up mental pictures of various groups, pictures made from overgeneralized impressions and selected bits of information, and then use them to define all members of a group regardless of their individual differences. Thus, we come to assume that all Native Americans are alcoholics, all women are emotional, all African Americans are good at sports, all residents of Appalachia or the Ozarks are hillbillies, all Puerto Ricans are short, all Italians are gangsters, all Jews are religious, all Asians are smart, all Swedes are blond, all Frenchmen are amorous, all old people are senile, and so forth. None of these generalizations will stand up to even perfunctory analysis, yet many people habitually use them in thinking about minority groups. The slide show, *"Ethnic and Racial Stereotypes,"* reveals some common stereotypes about racial and ethnic groups.

stereotyping

Attributing a fixed, and usually unfavorable or inaccurate, conception to a category of people.

Institutional Discrimination

7.6 **Identify examples of institutional discrimination.**

If discrimination is a socially learned behavior of members of dominant groups, designed to support and justify their continued dominance, it is reasonable to expect that it will be built into the structure of society. When members of a society are socialized to believe that certain groups are naturally to be treated as inferiors, it would seem perfectly reasonable to formulate public policies and build public institutions that discriminate against them.

To some extent, this type of socialization is exactly what has happened in the United States. When many Hispanics, blacks, Native Americans, Asians, women, and members of other minority groups are not treated fairly, it is not necessarily because of the conscious prejudices of individual public officials. It often is not a case of "I don't like your kind, so I am not going to hire you." There are laws in place designed to protect people from discrimination of that nature.

These laws are not always successful, however, as evidenced by the 37,000 individual filings of discrimination based on race or national origin to the U.S. Equal Employment Opportunity Commission in 2017. As you can see in Table 7–2, these types of filings have remained about level since 2000 (U.S. Equal Employment Opportunity Commission, 2018). Nonetheless, there is another type of discrimination that is even more difficult to prove.

Table 7–2 Number of Individual Filings of Discrimination Based on Race or National Origin, 2000, 2017

	2000	2017
Race	28,945	28,528
National Origin	7,792	8,299

SOURCE: U.S. Equal Employment Opportunity Commission. 2018. "Statistics." Retrieved 15 March 2018 (www.eeoc.gov/eeoc/statistics/index.cfm).

As a Native American student in the public school system in Oklahoma, I always felt a bit offended when we celebrated Columbus Day, or when we learned that Columbus "discovered" America. Oh really? My forbearers were here long before Columbus sailed over in his funky boats. Yes, Columbus opened up North America for white people, but he also brought death and destruction to MY people. I didn't like celebrating that.
—*Tiva, 18-year-old recent high school graduate*

institutional discrimination

An unconscious result of the structure and functioning of the public institutions and policies themselves.

Institutional discrimination is an unconscious result of the structure and functioning of the public institutions and policies themselves. It often goes unnoticed by the dominant group because it is woven into the cultural fabric of society. Our culture celebrates Christopher Columbus; Southern culture celebrates the Confederate flag (although as of July 2015 it no longer flies over the statehouse in South Carolina); and Mississippi and Alabama continue to celebrate Robert E. Lee (the leader of the Confederate army) on the same day as the Martin Luther King Jr. federal holiday, despite the obvious conflict of interest. Practices such as these are rarely noticed as racist or discriminatory until a crisis occurs, such as the gunning down of nine black church-goers in South Carolina in 2015, which began the national outcry to remove the Confederate flag from South Carolina's state capital.

Racial profiling provides another example. It refers to the practice—by law enforcement personnel, security agents, or any person in a position of authority—of disproportionately selecting people of color for investigations. To a large degree, racial profiling is a form of institutional discrimination because police or intelligence organizations unfairly single out certain groups, distinguished by racial characteristics, in seeking to enforce rules or laws. From the authorities' viewpoint, this behavior may be justified by the belief that their suspicions correspond to realistic probabilities of wrongdoing by members of those groups. Thus, after 9/11, Arab Americans and Indian American Sikhs wearing turbans—in fact, anyone with swarthy skin and a beard—have been far more likely than lighter-skinned individuals to be searched at airports.

Racial profiling has also been a major subject of controversy among blacks and other people of color who are disproportionately stopped while driving and searched for possible drug possession. According to the theory among law enforcement personnel, such people are more likely than others to be involved in drug use and drug dealing (Epp, Maynard-Moody, and Haider-Harkel, 2014). Others argue that racial profiling is justified because the facts show that blacks and Hispanics are indeed disproportionately more likely to drive fast and to be carrying drugs than whites. But as we see in *A Closer Look: "Driving while Black,"* the best research on this issue to date has convinced judges in many courts that indeed racial profiling violates the civil rights of innocent people and must be curtailed.

Since it would be difficult to discuss all categories of institutional discrimination against all minority groups, this discussion focuses on four major categories: education, housing, employment and income, and social justice.

7.6.1 Education

Americans take public school systems very seriously. Undoubtedly, one reason is that, in this country, education has generally been seen as the road to social and economic advancement. It is almost an article of faith that American children should get more education than their parents and achieve higher social and economic status.

Since the 1940 census, which was the first to ask about educational attainment, the average number of years of school completed by all Americans has increased steadily, and the educational gap between racial and ethnic groups has declined considerably (McFarland, Cui, and Stark, 2018; Musu-Gillette et al., 2016; Snyder, de Brey, and Dillow, 2018). Despite these gains, members of minority groups remain less likely to finish high school or attend college than are whites, as shown in Figure 7–4 (Snyder, de Brey, and Dillow, 2018). The figure reports the percentage of persons age 25-29 who have (a) completed high school or higher; and (b) completed a bachelor's degree or higher.

A Closer Look

Driving while Black

Many blacks assert that they are unfairly singled out for traffic stops and other investigations, which, if initiated because of their race, are violations of their civil rights. Data from studies that have been done on who is stopped by the police tell identical stories: Racial minorities are stopped at significantly higher rates than whites. A survey of 2,329 drivers in and around Kansas City sheds light on this issue (Epp, Maynard-Moody, and Haider-Harkel, 2014). The data collected allowed the researchers to distinguish between two types of stops—those stops to enforce traffic safety laws such as speeding, and those stops designed to investigate the driver. One of the researchers' key findings is that these two types of stops differ from start to finish. Traffic safety stops are based on clear violations of the law, and the officer tends to quickly issue a ticket or warning, and the driver is let go. Investigatory stops last much longer. The officers drag out the stop as they ask questions, try to look inside the vehicle, and seek consent for a search.

The researchers found that in traffic safety stops, being black had no influence. Blacks were not more likely than whites to be stopped for clear traffic safety law violations. But in investigatory stops, the issue is *who you are* rather than *what you have done* and being black is a primary factor in the likelihood of being stopped. For example, the researchers found that a black man age 25 or younger had a 28 percent chance of being stopped for an investigatory reason over the course of the year, while a similarly aged white man had only a 12.5 percent chance. Police in investigatory stops tend to pull over young people, but a black man must reach age 50 before his risk falls below that of a white man under age 25. Overall, black drivers are nearly three times more likely than whites to be subjected to investigatory stops.

Being black is also the primary influence on how far police officers pursue their inquisition in these investigatory stops. Black drivers were five times more likely than whites to be subject to searches. One man, "Billy," explained how he was pulled over on his way to a job interview by a highway patrolman for speeding even though he was going only two miles over the speed limit. The trooper made Billy get out of his car and put his hands on the hood while the trooper searched the car. Finding nothing, the trooper explained that the reason why he checks the car is because the police have been having problems with people trafficking drugs up and down the highway—the assumption being that it is okay to stop a black person because of the (extremely slim) chance that he will be smuggling drugs. This stop was not Billy's only time being pulled over. On another occasion, Billy, his wife,

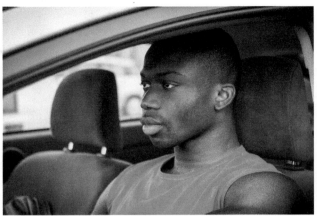

Stefano Cavoretto/Alamy Stock Photo

and his cousin were stopped while on their way to visit an ill relative and their rental van was searched for drugs by a sheriff's deputy.

It comes as no surprise that black people view investigative stops more harshly than whites. These stops impart feelings that the police are trying to hurt racial minorities, not help them. Investigative stops like Billy's undermine confidence in the policy, which is why three times as many blacks as whites responded in the survey that you cannot always trust police to do the right thing. Likewise, black respondents were five times more likely than whites to agree with the statement, "The police are out to get people like me."

As the discriminatory practice of investigative stops comes to light, many people are demanding change. New York City is taking a close look. A judge there ruled that New York City's stop and frisks, as practiced, violate the Constitution. She ordered that police be better trained in what kinds of justifications for these stops are constitutional, and all police officers must explain, in writing, any stops of this nature that they instigated. She also appointed a lawyer to monitor the police department's implementation of these directives. At this writing, her decision was suspended by the appellate court.

Critical Thinking

Have you, or someone you know, ever been stopped by the police for an investigative issue? If you answered yes, do you believe your race or ethnicity was a factor? What information would you need to help you decide whether race was, or was not, a factor? Can you identify other social institutions in which discrimination is likely to occur?

Figure 7–4 Percentage of Persons Ages 25–29, By Selected Levels of Educational Attainment and Race/Ethnicity, 2006 and 2016

SOURCE: Based on Snyder, T. D., de Brey, C., & Dillow, S. A. (2018). *Digest of Education Statistics 2016*, NCES 2017-094. National Center for Education Statistics.

In an important early study of how minority achievement in education and in the labor force is related to parents' wealth, Dalton Conley (1999) found that the level of education of one's parents and their net worth (not only income but also the total of all owned assets, or wealth) are the two best predictors of the quality of higher education their children will receive. Since black students tend to come from far less wealthy homes than white students do, their ability to go to the prestigious universities and colleges that produce the most entrants into the professions and the world of finance and business is far more limited. Consequently, although as we have seen blacks and other minority persons increase their educational attainment substantially, their inability to pay the costs of an elite higher education presents a major barrier to their full equality in a labor market that demands increasingly sophisticated skills and in which success often hinges on personal contacts established in college.

There is no doubt that the more highly educated usually receive substantially higher salaries than those with less education (Bureau of Labor Statistics, October 24, 2017). However, blacks and Hispanics at all levels of education earn less than their white counterparts. Figure 7–5 compares the median annual earnings of full-time workers age 25–34 by their educational levels (National Center for Education Statistics, February, 2018). The figure shows that whites earn the most money at lower levels of education (high school diploma or less), and Asians earn the most at higher levels of education. Meanwhile, blacks and Hispanics earn significantly less than whites or Asians at all levels of education.

One explanation for these differences in educational achievement and earnings is the quality of schooling that different groups experience. Throughout the United States, school administrations are under pressure to raise standards and increase performance, especially in underachieving schools. These schools are often found in

Figure 7-5 Median Annual Earnings of Full-Time Year-Round Workers, Age 25-34, by Educational Attainment and Race/Ethnicity, 2015

SOURCE: National Center for Education Statistics. 2018. "Digest of Education Statistics: 2016." February. Retrieved 15 March 2018 (nces.ed.gov/programs/digest/d16/).

communities with high proportions of low-income black and Hispanic households. The causes of this situation and policies to address it have been hotly contested issues. Relevant here is the issue of minority segregation and poor schools, along with the retreat from policies to achieve school desegregation.

In its 1954 *Brown v. Board of Education* decision, the Supreme Court mandated integration "with all deliberate speed" but was vague on actual remedies to be used. The decision effectively wiped out **de jure segregation**—segregation required by law—and by finding that "separate but equal" schooling was inherently unequal, it set in motion decades of sporadic efforts to achieve more racially balanced classrooms. To do so, states and municipalities had to address **de facto segregation**, segregation resulting from housing patterns, economic inequalities, gerrymandered school districts, and the departure of middle-class families from communities with increasing rates of minority households and poor or mediocre schools.

Throughout much of the 1970s and 1980s, busing of students, primarily minority students, to schools outside their neighborhoods was the primary remedy for desegregation. Today, however, busing is largely considered to have been a failure. White families tend to move to suburban areas, leaving minorities behind in the central cities. At the same time, no alternative strategies have been implemented to achieve school desegregation. Demands for higher standards and higher achievement are not generally matched with increases in funding for schools in lower-income minority neighborhoods. Public schools in the United States are typically funded from local property taxes or local levies, so wealthier communities can afford to pay higher salaries to teachers and hire more experienced teachers than can financially strapped inner-city schools.

A study by the Civil Rights Project on school desegregation found that resegregation of the races is increasing. Between 1988 and 2013, the share of intensely segregated nonwhite schools more than tripled, rising from 6 percent to 18 percent of all public schools (Orfield, Ee, Frankenberg, and Siegel-Hawley, 2016). The situation among Hispanic students is even more alarming. In the southern, northeastern, and western United States, almost half of all Hispanic school children attend a school

de jure segregation

Segregation that is required by law.

de facto segregation

Segregation that is not required by law, but results from housing patterns, economic inequalities, or gerrymandered school districts.

What Do You Think?

Describe the level of de facto segregation in the neighborhood in which you grew up. What specific factors contributed to its racial and ethnic makeup?

School busing was a common method of school integration in the 1970s and 1980s. Children were bussed from one school to another so schools would have racial parity. However, the result was "white flight"; white families moved out to the suburbs to avoid busing. The program was disbanded by the 1990s, but segregation along racial and ethnic lines, especially with respect to social class, continues.

referred to as "intensely segregated," meaning that fewer than 10 percent of the students at the school are white. This segregation has accelerated rather than declined, especially in the western United States where the majority of Hispanic children live (Orfield, Frankenberg, Ee, and Kuscera, 2014).

What is the "big deal" about segregated schools? Schools that serve predominately black and Hispanic students, particularly those who are from lower-income families, usually offer fewer resources for learning while also having greater needs (Hanselman and Fiel, 2017; Morris and Perry, 2016; Owens, 2018; Reardon and Owens, 2014). They have a harder time hiring, retaining, and paying good teachers. Classrooms have a higher turnover of students and teachers, a greater number of students with special needs, and less parental involvement. Students have less access to Advanced Placement classes, new books, the latest science equipment, and other resources that cost money. But perhaps most of all, segregated schools deprive both whites and minorities of the opportunity to meet people of other backgrounds to expand their understanding about living in a diverse society (Badger, 2014).

7.6.2 Housing

School desegregation is an extremely difficult issue to address when such a high proportion of minority and nonminority people live in segregated neighborhoods to begin with. Understanding housing patterns is important because declining residential segregation would indicate that minority groups are increasingly able to afford to live in the same neighborhoods. A decline in segregation would also show that majority and minority populations may increasingly prefer (or are indifferent to) living together in the same communities or neighborhoods, and may increasingly share the same cultural values, national identity, and education. Residential integration would suggest a breakdown of majority-minority social and economic divisons (Lichter, Parisi, and De Valk, 2016).

Reviews of residential patterns by the U.S. Census Bureau show that housing segregation has diminished only slightly over the years, and it remains a serious problem (Badger, 2014; Frey, 2015; Logan, 2011). Blacks have become less isolated from Hispanics and Asians over time, but their exposure to whites has changed very little. This situation is true regardless of income. In other words, affluent blacks have only marginally higher contact with whites than do blacks who are poor. Analyses also show that minorities at every income level live in poorer neighborhoods than do whites with comparable incomes (except for the most affluent Asians).

A practice that contributes to high rates of segregation is racial steering, a practice in which real estate brokers refuse to show houses outside of specific areas to minority buyers. Before the landmark judicial decisions of the 1950s, racial steering was enforced through restrictive covenants—agreements among homeowners not to sell their property to people designated as undesirable. Although restrictive covenants are now illegal, racial and ethnic steering still occurs unofficially in many all-white neighborhoods. Because it operates below the surface, with no written agreements, racial steering is difficult to prevent.

Massey and other sociologists who study racial and ethnic segregation assert that more audit research is needed to show lawmakers that racial steering and other forms of discrimination exist and that laws against them must be enforced far more rigorously (Massey and Fischer, 2004). In audit research, a black or minority couple is sent to real estate agents and shown (or not shown) certain types of housing. Then a white couple is sent to the same agents and the results are compared; this process is repeated many times with different agents to determine whether a systematic pattern of discrimination exists.

Today, segregation may be perpetuated or maintained by a series of laws and policies that, on the surface, have little to do with race. For example, suburban density zoning has been shown to directly affect the proportion of minority groups in the neighborhood. Likewise, it is perfectly legal for landlords, real estate agents, and bankers to discriminate against homeowners based on income. But given the lower incomes of blacks and Hispanics, on average, than whites and Asians, class divisions can also easily become racial divisions (Massey and Rugh, 2017).

7.6.3 Employment and Income

Let's say you are a manager for a mid-sized company and you want to hire someone for a job. You receive four interesting applications from the following people: Emily, Greg, Lakisha, and Jamal. Who are you going to call for an interview?

Sociologists at Harvard University sent people to apply for low-wage jobs. The applicants were given identical resumes and similar interview training. The black-sounding applicants were offered jobs much less often than were the white applicants. In fact, blacks with no criminal record were offered jobs at about the same rate as white applicants who had criminal records (Pager, Western, and Bonikowski, 2009).

In another study, people seeking to discuss research opportunities before applying to a doctoral program contacted over 6,500 university professors. The names of the students were randomly assigned to signal sex and race (white, black, Hispanic, Indian, and Chinese), but the students were otherwise identical. The researchers found that university faculty were significantly more responsive to white males than to all other groups. This bias was especially strong in higher-paying disciplines that are dominated by white men but was also found in disciplines that contain higher numbers of women and minorities in them (Milkman, Akinola, and Chugh, 2014).

In fact, another research team conducted a meta-analysis of every available field experiment of hiring discrimination against blacks or Hispanics between 1989 and 2014 (Quillian, Pager, Hexel, and Midtbøen, 2017). Together, these 24 studies represent 55,842 applications submitted for 26,326 positions. The data show that, since 1989 whites receive on average 36 percent more callbacks than blacks, and 24 percent more callbacks than Hispanics. There was no change in the level of hiring discrimination against blacks over the past 25 years, although there was modest evidence of a decline in discrimination against Hispanics. Even accounting for applicant education, applicant gender, study method, occupational groups, and local labor market conditions did little to change the results. In other words, contrary to claims of declining discrimination in American society, levels of discrimination remain largely unchanged, at least at the point of hire.

The idea that work will improve one's social status is deeply ingrained in U.S. culture. The work ethic suggests that, if you really want a job, you can find one, and that, if you work hard, you will make money. The corollary to this idea is the notion that, if you are wealthy, you deserve your wealth because you worked for it, and if you are poor, it is largely because you are lazy or unmotivated (Seccombe, 2015). This view ignores the fact that discrimination is no less prevalent in employment than it is in education and housing, as noted earlier in Table 7–2 which showed 37,000 reports of racial discrimination were brought before the U.S. Equal Employment Opportunity Commission.

One of the most pervasive stereotypes associated with blacks is that they are impoverished. This is a tremendous overgeneralization. The median household income among blacks is about $39,500. Although this is well below the average for a white household ($65,000), it's also far above the poverty level (Semega, Fontenot, and Kollar, 2017). In fact, 41 percent of blacks have household incomes of at least $50,000, and 15 percent of black households earn at least $100,000. Income data for black married couples show special promise.

This means that many blacks are entering the world of the middle class, having worked themselves up from the working or lower classes. Most of these younger blacks did not have parents from whom they could inherit money or receive extensive financial assistance; therefore, they have fewer assets than whites. U.S. Census Bureau data reveal extensive differences in assets between blacks and whites, which have clear impacts on family consumptive patterns, family values, and family relationships. For example, only 42 percent of black adults own their own home, compared to 73 percent of whites (U.S. Census Bureau, July 27, 2017). Moreover, white families have at least ten times the assets of black families, and the gap has become wider since the recession (Dettling, Hsu, Jacobs, Moore, and Thompson, 2017). These discrepancies are due to a variety of factors: (1) blacks fared worse during the recession than did whites; (2) whites are more likely to draw upon the assets of their parents through an inheritance or loan to be able to afford a home, car, or other high-ticket item; (3) whites have an easier time obtaining mortgage loans from banks; (4) homes in predominantly white neighborhoods appreciate in value more rapidly than do homes in predominantly black neighborhoods; and (5) blacks have lower retirement savings (Brooks, 2017; Oliver and Shapiro, 2006).

What Do You Think?

What amount and types of assets do you think you will inherit from your parents? How will these assets shape your future?

7.6.4 Justice

Philosopher and social theorist Cornel West (1994) recounts an all-too-familiar tale of the daily injustices faced by racial and ethnic minorities. While driving to a college lecture, he remembers, "I was stopped on fake charges of trafficking cocaine. When I told the police officer I was a professor of religion, he replied, 'Yeh, and I'm the Flying Nun. Let's go, nigger!'" (p. xv).[5] Such degrading experiences with the police and other street-level authorities enrage members of minority groups who know that those with less power receive worse treatment in the justice system. This kind of treatment is seen in the recent publicized cases of unarmed black men being mistreated, even to the point of death, by police officers, as shown in the opening vignette.

The U.S. system of justice is based on two premises that are relevant to this issue: (1) justice is blind; that is, racial, ethnic, economic, or social considerations are irrelevant in the eyes of the law, and (2) any accused person is considered innocent until proven guilty in a court of law. But do these assumptions apply equally to everyone?

As noted in Chapter 5, minority groups are overrepresented in official arrest records, and it seems probable that in general they are more likely to be arrested and charged with a crime, regardless of whether they are guilty. The higher arrest rates among minorities are partly due to the higher arrest rates among the poor in general (who, as noted earlier, include a disproportionate number of minority group members), but there is considerable evidence that discrimination plays a role in who is arrested. For example, although black and white persons use drugs at about

---

[5]West, C. (1994) *Race Matters*. New York: Vintage.

similar rates, the imprisonment for blacks on drugs charges is six times that for whites (NAACP, 2018). After arrest, the obstacle of the bail system must be overcome. It is here that the criminal justice system may be most discriminatory. To begin with, bail involves money; those who have it can usually arrange to be released after arrest and await their trial in freedom, subject only to the limitations of the bail agreement. Those who do not have money are punished, in effect, because of the long delay between arrest and trial in many jurisdictions (particularly in big cities). They are compelled to wait in jail until their case comes up. Even those who can pay bail can rarely afford costly legal counsel, and those who are detained have little opportunity to prepare a defense. This inequality in the administration of justice extends to the sentencing process. Although blacks and Hispanics account for less than a third of the population, they make up almost 60 percent of the prison population (NAACP, 2018).

Racial differences do not stop there, however. They continue into the more extreme realms within our criminal justice system.

RACIAL INEQUALITIES IN CAPITAL PUNISHMENT The U.S. Supreme Court banned the death penalty for many decades, in part, because of the recognition that the effects of prejudice and the inability to afford good legal counsel would discriminate against minority defendants. In 1977, however, the Court reversed its position and the death penalty was reinstated. There have been nearly 1,500 executions since that time. The number of executions peaked in 1999 with 98 executions, but has been declining since, with 23 executions in 2017. Roughly 2,800 people are currently on death row, which includes 53 women (Death Penalty Information Center, February, 2018).

The issue of racial bias in the sentencing and the application of the death penalty cannot be ignored. Figures 7–6a and 7–6b show the racial and ethnic background of defendants who have been executed and those who are currently on Death Row. As you can see, while the majority of people executed are white, blacks are greatly over-represented, given their size in the population. The situation for blacks is even more extreme among those on death row.

Some people argue that this racial disparity does not represent bias because black people are overrepresented among those who commit capital crimes. If blacks commit more capital crimes, then it follows that they are put to death at higher rates, the argument goes. However, David C. Baldus, a leading expert on the subject and the author of numerous studies that have influenced the courts, notes, "Some people are being sentenced to death based on race, and I find that morally and legally objectionable" (quoted in Eckholm, 1995, p. B1).[6] For example, consider the following:

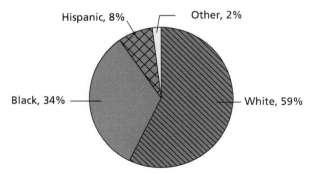

Figure 7–6a Race and Ethnicity of U.S. Defendants Executed, 1976–2017

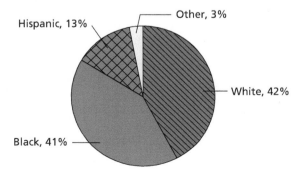

Figure 7–6b Race and Ethnicity of U.S. Death Row Inmates, 1976–2017

SOURCE: Death Penalty Information Center. 2018. "Facts about the Death Penalty." 23 February.

[6]Quoted in Eckholm, E. (1995). "Studies Find Death Penalty Tied to Race Of the Victims," *The New York Times*, p. B1.

Nearly 1,500 executions have occurred since 1977. Roughly 2,800 people are currently on death row. The racial biases in the sentencing and the application of the death penalty cannot be ignored.

- Jurors in Washington State are three times more likely to recommend a death sentence for a black defendant than for a white defendant in a similar case (Beckett and Evans, 2014).
- In Louisiana, the odds of a death sentence were 97 percent higher for those whose victim was white than for those whose victim was black (Pierce and Radelet, 2011).
- A study in California found that those who killed whites were over three times more likely to be sentenced to death than those who killed blacks, and over four times more likely than those who killed Hispanics (Pierce and Radelet, 2005).
- In the case of interracial murders, those cases with a black defendant and a white victim were fourteen times more likely to involve execution than those cases with a white defendant and a black victim (Death Penalty Information Center, February, 2018).

FELONY DISENFRANCHISEMENT In 48 states, people convicted of a felony may lose the right to vote (sometimes permanently), which is known as felony disenfranchisement. With the world's highest rates of imprisonment, the United States is also the world's leader in felony disenfranchisement, a dubious distinction that has an enormous impact on the political fate of minority groups. Because of the dramatic expansion of the criminal justice system in the last 40 years, over 6.1 million Americans are unable to vote due to state felony disenfranchisement policies. Blacks are overrepresented among those unable to vote (The Sentencing Project, June, 2017).

WRONGFUL EXECUTIONS There is also the all-important issue of wrongful executions. No one likes to talk about it, but there have been cases of innocent people—or those whose guilt was in serious doubt—who have been put to death. Blacks are overrepresented in the number of wrongful executions. Some have been exonerated because of DNA evidence discovered later indicating that they were not involved in the crime. Other cases involved witness perjury or misidentification, and false confessions. The "lucky" death row inmates are those who are exonerated and freed before execution, although they were incarcerated an average of 11 years before being freed (Innocence Project, 2018). It is clear that determining guilt or innocence is not an exact science. As said by Freddie Lee Pitts, who was exonerated from Florida's death row for a crime he did not commit, "You can release an innocent man from prison, but you can't release him from the grave" (National Coalition to Abolish the Death Penalty, 2018).[7]

Some Consequences of Prejudice and Discrimination

7.7 **Discuss some of the consequences of prejudice and discrimination.**

The harmful effects of prejudice and discrimination touch all Americans. As the Supreme Court noted in its decision in *Brown v. Board of Education of Topeka*, the lives of

---

[7]National Coalition to Abolish the Death Penalty, 2018.

members of the dominant group are also stunted by the artificial barriers and warped perceptions that such social divisions create. Here, however, we will consider the effects on the subordinate group, since the effects are usually more serious.

What happens to people who must live with the realities of discrimination and the prejudice? First, there are, of course, effects on the individual psychological well-being of minority group members. Second, both individuals and groups develop protective reactions against prejudice and discrimination.

Consider the effects of discrimination on psychological well-being. In his groundbreaking work, *Children of Crisis*, Robert Coles (2003) documented some of the effects on the first black children to attend desegregated schools in the South. These children were subjected to blatant discrimination and bitter prejudice, including mob action against them and their parents. Coles observed the children for several months after desegregation, focusing on how they depicted themselves and their world in drawings. His account of the drawings of one black girl, Ruby, is fascinating. For months Ruby would never use brown or black except to indicate the ground. However, she distinguished between white and black people. As Coles describes:

> *She drew white people larger and more lifelike. Negroes were smaller, their bodies less intact. A white girl we both knew to be her own size appeared several times taller. While Ruby's own face lacked an eye in one drawing, an ear in another, the white girl never lacked any features. Moreover, Ruby drew the white girl's hands and legs carefully, always making sure that they had the proper number of fingers and toes. Not so with her own limbs, or those of any other Negro children she chose (or was asked) to picture. A thumb or forefinger might be missing, or a whole set of toes. The arms were shorter, even absent or truncated. (p. 47)[8]*

A Personal View

Everyday Racism

I've gotten to know my biology lab partner pretty well in high school and we've had some interesting conversations. I think she was trying to show me how cool she is when she said the other day, "I don't know what the big deal is about race; we're all the same." All the same? Oh really? I wanted to tell that girl a thing or two about race. First of all, the simple fact that she can see it as no big deal is an example of white privilege. As a dark-skinned Latina, I don't have that same privilege. I have to think about race every day whether I want to or not. Last week, I went into a grocery store and the clerk at the counter told me I had to leave my backpack at the counter; I saw plenty of other white folks and they were able to keep their purses or backpacks with them. A few months ago when I went to the movies with my older sister, the ticket clerk was speaking very loudly and slowly to us. He assumed that we didn't speak English well! Last year, my older brother was driving home from work and was stopped by the police for no reason at all. They made him get out of his car and they searched his vehicle. He didn't do a thing! I'm guessing they thought he had drugs. Awhile before that, my cousin was stopped by police, and the same thing happened to him. My other brother liked this certain girl and asked her out, but she told him no because her father doesn't want her to date Mexicans. My sister, brothers, and I were all born here! So, when my biology lab partner downplayed race and said

Myrleen Pearson/Alamy Stock Photo

it was no big deal, I debated whether or not to tell her all of this. I ended up keeping quiet, which to be honest, is another example of racism. I was afraid to tell her the truth.

—Gabriela, age 16

Critical Thinking

If you were Gabriela, how would you have responded to her biology lab partner? How would you explain white privilege and racism? How do you think her lab partner would respond?

[8]Coles, R. (2003) *Children of Crisis*, p. 47. New York: Back Bay Books.

At the same time, Jimmy, a white classmate, always depicted blacks as somehow related to animals or extremely dirty and dangerous. However, Coles noted that, over time, blacks' self-image improved, and whites became less prejudiced. For example, after about two years of contact with Ruby and other black children in his school in New Orleans, Jimmy grew less fearful of blacks, and the change was reflected in his drawings. Coles concluded that children were conditioned to fear and distrust members of the other race, but that with continuing friendly contact, these prejudices were broken down. He also found that children eventually helped change their parents' attitudes.

This pioneering work has set the stage for more recent studies that focus on the ways in which racism affects individuals. More recent studies find that people who experience racism are more likely to be depressed and discouraged, have more negative images about their racial or ethnic group, do more poorly in school, and experience greater stress and physical ailments (Banks and Stephens, 2018; Kwate and Goodman, 2015; National Association of School Psychologists, 2012). The feature box, *A Personal View: "Everyday Racism,"* highlights one girl's story about the racism that she experiences and the fact that it can be oblivious to whites.

Those who internalize racism are particularly vulnerable to lower psychological well-being (Banks and Stephens, 2018). **Internalized racism** is the personal conscious or subconscious acceptance of the dominant society's racist views, stereotypes, and biases of one's ethnic group. It gives rise to patterns of thinking, feeling, and behaving that result in discriminating, minimizing, criticizing, finding fault, invalidating, and hating oneself while simultaneously valuing the dominant culture.

One important method for helping to combat internalized racism is **racial/ ethnic/cultural socialization**, which involves teaching children about their cultural heritage, and providing children with the coping skills necessary to develop and maintain a strong and healthy self-image in the face of possible prejudice and discrimination (Derlan, Umaña-Taylor, Jahromi, and Updegraff, 2018). This type of socialization can instill a sense of identity and pride. It teaches children about religious traditions, introduces them to specific types of foods, cultural holidays, languages, or dialects, and imparts a set of values associated with a larger group identity. It also includes teaching the truths about racial and ethnic oppression in society.

In addition to individual responses to prejudice and discrimination, larger group responses also may occur, such as public protest. After the success of the Montgomery bus boycott of 1955 and 1956 (when blacks stopped riding buses until discriminatory seating rules were eliminated), a broad social movement for desegregation emerged. Initially led by Martin Luther King, Jr., the movement was directed against laws that enforced or created a statutory inequality—that is, an obstruction maintained for the purpose of denying minority groups the rights and privileges enjoyed by other Americans. In the 1960s, however, as hopes were high, progress was slow. As white resistance increased, minority protests sometimes took violent forms. Anger, frustration, and rage provoked urban riots across the country. At no time, however, did a majority of blacks approve of the violent protests (National Advisory Commission on Civil Disorders, 1968).

internalized racism

The personal conscious or subconscious acceptance of the dominant society's racist views, stereotypes, and biases of one's racial or ethnic group.

racial/ethnic/cultural socialization

Teaching children about their cultural heritage, and providing children with the coping skills necessary to develop and maintain a strong and healthy self-image in the face of possible prejudice and discrimination.

The Martin Luther King, Jr. Memorial in Washington, D.C., pays tribute to the leader of the modern civil rights movement. He was an advocate for nonviolent, peaceful demonstrations.

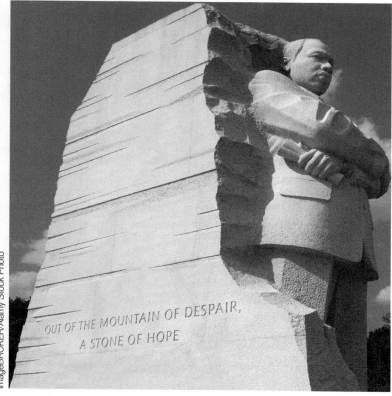

OUT OF THE MOUNTAIN OF DESPAIR, A STONE OF HOPE

imageBROKER/Alamy Stock Photo

Social Policy

7.8 **Analyze the policy of affirmative action.**

Another example of a group response is the development of affirmative action policies. In response to the demands of blacks and other minority groups for a more equal share in the benefits of the American way of life, leaders have instituted various programs to alleviate the effects of prejudice and discrimination. For the most part, these programs tend to have more support among liberals and Democrats, which helps explain why such initiatives tend to wax and wane in different presidential administrations. One of these approaches is affirmative action.

7.8.1 Affirmative Action

Perhaps the most controversial policy designed to redress past institutional discrimination is **affirmative action**. This term refers to policies based on a body of federal law originating in the 1964 Civil Rights Act that bans discrimination based on race, religion, sex, or national origin in areas such as employment, education, and housing (Kelley, 2010; National Conference of State Legislatures, 2014). Affirmative action programs require institutions that have engaged in discriminatory practices to increase opportunities for women and members of minority groups. The policy is controversial because, with the goal of correcting past patterns of discrimination, institutions such as universities and businesses must make special efforts to recruit minority applicants, and those efforts may affect white applicants.

affirmative action

Controversial policies that require institutions that have engaged in discriminatory practices to increase opportunities for women and members of minority groups.

Proponents see affirmative action as proactive measures to remedy inequality, fight discrimination, and have an integrated society with equal opportunities for all members. Opponents believe it is misguided social engineering that uses quotas and preferences to replace qualified people with unqualified minorities and women. They claim it promotes "reverse discrimination," and is harmful to those it is trying to help. In fact, John Roberts, Chief Justice of America's Supreme Court, takes a dim view of affirmative action. "The best way to stop discrimination on the basis of race," he says, "is to stop discriminating on the basis of race" (*The Economist*, 2013).[9]

HISTORY OF AFFIRMATIVE ACTION   Until the mid-1960s, minorities were barred from certain jobs, some universities would not admit them, and many employers would not hire them. The Civil Rights Act of 1964 made discrimination illegal in the workplace, in federally funded programs, and in privately owned facilities open to the public. The original goal of the civil rights movement had been "color-blind" laws; however, many people were concerned that simply ending a long-standing policy of discrimination did not go far enough. One year later, Congress passed the Voting Rights Act, which gave the U.S. Department of Justice the power to take "affirmative" steps to eliminate discrimination. President Lyndon B. Johnson gave the U.S. Department of Labor the responsibility of enforcing affirmative action. In that role, the Labor Department began requiring government contractors to analyze the demographics of their workforce and to take proactive measures to remedy inequalities.

Over time, the U.S. Supreme Court has defined the scope of affirmative action policy through a series of legislative initiatives and decisions. Overall, the Court has upheld the constitutionality of affirmative action in principle but has placed restrictions on how it is implemented. One of the major restrictions on affirmative action has to do with quotas. By way of background, in an effort to enable members of minority groups to receive the same educational opportunities as whites, beginning in 1965 the federal government required schools to establish goals for minority enrollment and in some cases to set quotas that specify the number of minority students

---

[9]"Affirmative Action: Is Affirmative Action a Good Idea?," *The Economist*, 2013.

to be admitted each year. These policies met with considerable opposition. Charging that affirmative action is reverse discrimination, critics focused on the Supreme Court case of Allan Bakke, a white student who was refused admission to the medical school of the University of California at Davis even though his grades were higher than those of many black students who were admitted under an affirmative action program.

TESTING AFFIRMATIVE ACTION IN THE COURTS   Allan Bakke was a 35-year-old white male who applied to a number of medical schools in 1976. He was a strong applicant with a solid grade point average and high test scores but was denied admissions by several universities because of his age (age discrimination was legal at that time). Bakke was also denied entrance to the medical school at the University of California, Davis, for two years in a row, but he noted that several minority candidates were admitted with lower grades or test scores than his. Feeling that this treatment was unfair, Bakke sued the university. He sought an order admitting him on the grounds that the special admissions programs for minorities violated the U.S. and California constitutions and Title VI of the Civil Rights Act. In 1976, the case was argued before the state supreme court. The court at the time was thought to be liberal, and it was assumed that the court would support the university and uphold the idea of special preferential treatment of minorities. However, this action did not occur. The court barred the university from using race in the admissions process and ordered it to provide evidence that Bakke would not have been admitted under a race-neutral program. The university conceded that it could not do so, and the court ordered Bakke's admission.

The story does not end there. The university requested that the U.S. Supreme Court review the case, and in the meantime, halt the order requiring Bakke's admission. In 1978, the majority of the U.S. Supreme Court found that the special quota program, which earmarked a specific number of seats for minorities, did discriminate against Bakke. However, they also ruled that less restrictive programs, such as making race one of several factors in admission, would not be discriminatory. Justice Powell offered the example of the admissions program at Harvard University as one he believed would pass constitutional muster: Harvard did not set rigid quotas for minorities, but actively recruited them and sought to include them as more than a token part of a racially and culturally diverse student body. Although a white student might still lose out to a minority student with lesser academic qualifications, the admissions program at Harvard could theoretically help (or hurt) any student by reviewing other factors that would contribute to a diverse student body, such as the ability to play sports or a musical instrument. The Supreme Court saw no constitutional violation in using race as one of several factors used to enhance diversity. Yet, Justice Powell noted that, because the university had admitted that it could not prove that Bakke would not have been admitted under a race-neutral admissions program, the portion of the California Supreme Court's decision ordering Bakke's admission was upheld. In 1980, Bakke entered medical school, eventually becoming an anesthesiologist.

Several other test cases have redefined the scope of affirmative action. In a 2003 case at the University of Michigan, the Supreme Court ruled that the school's point system that gave minority applicants a better chance of acceptance was unconstitutional. The justices affirmed the law school's more individualized method of reviewing applicants, which allows race to be one of many factors in deciding whom to admit. The point system was considered by the majority of the Supreme Court justices to be too "mechanistic" and was considered tantamount to a quota system.

Opponents were not satisfied and felt the ruling did not go far enough, and in 2006, they put affirmative action to a state vote. The people voted 58% to 42% to amend the state constitution to prohibit preferential treatment in public education, government contracting, and public employment. Groups favoring affirmative action sued to block the part of the law concerning higher education. They noted that the number of minority students admitted to the most selective schools declined in those states that forbid affirmative action. They wanted the Supreme Court to intervene.

In 2014, Michigan was once again in the limelight on affirmative action. The Supreme Court upheld the Michigan constitutional amendment passed in 2006 that banned affirmative action in admissions to the state's public universities. In the 6 to 2 ruling (with Justice Sotomayor and Justice Ginsburg dissenting), the majority claimed that there were no legal grounds for overruling the will of the voters in that state. Their ruling effectively endorsed similar measures in seven other states and may encourage more states to enact measures banning the use of race in admissions. Justice Sotomayor's written dissent touched on the personal importance of affirmative action (Lempert, 2014):

George Wada/Fotolia

> [R]ace matters for reasons that really are only skin deep, that cannot be discussed any other way, and that cannot be wished away. Race matters to a young man's view of society when he spends his teenage years watching others tense up as he passes, no matter the neighborhood where he grew up. Race matters to a young woman's sense of self when she states her hometown, and then is pressed, "No, where are you really from?" regardless of how many generations her family has been in the country. Race matters to a young person addressed by a stranger in a foreign language, which he does not understand because only English was spoken at home. Race matters because of the slights, the snickers, the silent judgments that reinforce that most crippling of thoughts: "I do not belong here."[10]

The arguments continued. In a more recent Supreme Court case, *Fisher v. the State of Texas*, Abigail Fisher sued because she was denied entrance to the University of Texas and claimed that any preference the university gives to minority students is unconstitutional. The Supreme Court handed down a decision in 2016 that rejected this challenge to race-conscious admissions. Justice Kennedy wrote that universities should have substantial leeway in designing their admission programs (Liptak, 2016).

Affirmative action programs have successfully increased the number of minorities in professional positions. Mariana is a second-year law student at the University of California, Berkeley. She graduated in the top 10 percent of her high school class and graduated with a B+ average from a state university in central California that served predominately low-income students, most of whom were first-generation college students. Her goal is to practice family law in minority communities.

What Do You Think?

Referring to Justice Sotomayor's comment, have you ever felt "I do not belong here," for reasons related to race, ethnicity, sex, age, gender orientation, income, or some other reason? How did it make you feel? What did you do about it?

Future Prospects

Despite the legislative challenges, the Supreme Court has established the value of affirmative action programs in schools and work settings. The need is not expected to last forever: "We expect that 25 years from now, the use of racial preferences will no longer be necessary to further the interest approved today," former Justice O'Connor wrote in 2003.[11] Doing the math, this prediction would suggest that affirmative action programs will no longer be needed by 2028. Whether that situation will indeed be the case is a matter of speculation.

---

[10]Lempert, R. (April 25, 2014) "The Schuette Decision: The Supreme Court Rules on Affirmative Action," Brookings. Retrieved from https://www.brookings.edu/blog/fixgov/2014/04/25/the-schuette-decision-the-supreme-court-rules-on-affirmative-action/.

[11]Justice O'Connor (2003), *Grutter v. Bollinger,* 539 U.S. 306. U.S. Supreme Court.

Some suggest that the issue is not race *per se*, but class. An example of race-blind social policy in the interests of increasing diversity and equality of opportunity is the practice recently instituted by Harvard and other private universities of awarding full scholarships to students who have been accepted by the university but whose families earn less than $60,000 per year. Since more minority students than white students fall into this category, this strategy is showing some success at encouraging minority enrollments. Other universities have taken note and now offer similar programs.

No one really knows whether former Justice O'Connor's prediction about affirmative action being unnecessary by 2028 will come true. It does remain, however, that eliminating individual and institutional racism is a very long process.

Going Beyond Left and Right

Where do you stand on these issues? You may be among those who feel that affirmative action programs are a necessary proactive measure to remedy inequality, fight discrimination, and ensure equal opportunities for all. Or, you may be a person who would like to see less racism and discrimination and more equality, but you may also have some concerns about whether affirmative action is reverse discrimination. Others have doubts about any government-sponsored program to deal with inequality. They believe that individuals must stand on their own merit, and sociodemographic background considerations are largely irrelevant.

Summary

7.1 Describe the growing diversity of the American population.

The United States is becoming more diverse due to immigration patterns and birthrates among minority groups. Currently a little more than one person in three is a member of a minority group; however, by 2060, minority groups are likely to comprise about 56 percent of the U.S. population. The percentage of blacks and American Indians will remain relatively stable, Asian Americans/Pacific Islanders will nearly double but remain a small group, and the growth of Hispanic groups will be considerable.

7.2 Sequence the continuing struggle for minority civil rights.

The Thirteenth, Fourteenth, and Fifteenth Amendments to the Constitution were ratified in the 1860s and 1870s, but it was not until the mid-twentieth century that the rights guaranteed by these amendments began to be exercised. It took further legislation, such as the Civil Rights Act passed in 1964, to make discrimination illegal. But the discrepancy between legal equality and actual inequality remains and progress is slow.

7.3 Explain the social construction of minority groups.

There is no clear line between totally dominant and totally minority groups; rather, any given group can be placed at some point along a continuum of "minorityness," and

this continuum can shift historically and cross-culturally. What is defined as a minority group at one point in time, or in one particular culture, may not be seen as a minority elsewhere.

7.4 Contrast racism, prejudice, and discrimination.

Racism is behavior, in word or deed, that is motivated by the belief that human races have distinctive characteristics that determine abilities. Prejudice is an emotional, rigid attitude toward members of the subordinate group. Prejudiced people tend to be so committed to their prejudgments about a certain category of people that, even in the face of rational evidence that the prejudgment is wrong, they will maintain their prejudice, even defend it strongly, and denounce the evidence. Discrimination is the overt differential treatment of individuals considered to belong to a certain social group.

7.5 Summarize the origins of prejudice and discrimination.

The origins of prejudice and discrimination are numerous and complex, and to explain them, it is necessary to consider both the individuals and the structural organization of society.

7.6 Identify examples of institutional discrimination.

Institutional discrimination is an unconscious result of the structure and functioning of the public institutions and policies themselves. It is more difficult to prove than other forms of individual discrimination. There are many types of institutional discrimination, including in education, housing, employment and earnings, and justice.

7.7 Discuss some of the consequences of prejudice and discrimination.

There are two types of general responses to prejudice and discrimination. The first response focuses on the individual, and the second focuses on the larger group's protective reactions against prejudice and discrimination.

7.8 Analyze the policy of affirmative action.

Affirmative action refers to policies based on a body of federal law originating in the 1964 Civil Rights Act that bans discrimination based on race, religion, sex, or national origin in such areas as employment, education, and housing. Affirmative action programs require institutions that have engaged in discriminatory practices to increase opportunities for women and members of minority groups.

Chapter 8
Sex and Gender

Diamondforce/Fotolia

 Learning Objectives

8.1 Analyze the distinction between sex and gender.

8.2 Define traditional gender roles.

8.3 Examine the roots of sexism and inequality.

8.4 Identify several examples of sexism and inequality today.

8.5 Assess the sources of sexism.

8.6 Describe the Women's Movement and its policy agenda.

Joelle Taylor is getting married next month. In the whirlwind of final preparations for a large wedding, she almost forgot about gathering all the documents she will need to revise once she changes her last name to Robson. Joelle Robson! Joelle asked her maid of honor for some assistance in coordinating her name change, knowing that there will be a lot of forms to fill out. Her maid of honor gave her an odd look, and responded "What? You're not going to change your name, are you? That's so old-fashioned . . . so sexist . . . so ugh." Joelle was shocked by her friend's response. Don't all women change their name when they get married? What's the big deal, she wondered? With the help of her maid of honor, Joelle did a little investigating and found that most women today do change their last names when they marry. Joelle also found out that several hundred years ago, married women had no surnames at all. They were simply the wives of so-and-so. By the sixteenth century, women began to routinely take the surnames of their husbands because they were considered his property, and religious doctrine of the time considered husband and wife to be a single person. That single person was the man; the woman could not hold property, vote, or speak out in a public assembly. Legally, wives virtually ceased to exist. In more modern times, most women continued to take their husband's names when they married, but the likelihood of doing so shifted somewhat from one decade to the next. But as if the name change quandary wasn't enough, Joelle's investigation also identified other aspects of weddings and married life that surprised her. Her engagement ring is a carryover from a custom designed to take women off the marriage market; the practice of a father giving his daughter away and handing her to the groom is exactly how it sounds; the tradition of a bride's parents paying for the wedding is reminiscent of dowry; the woman's white wedding dress symbolizes virginity; and her husband's lifting of the veil symbolizes his right to consummate the marriage. "Hmmm," said Joelle, "I just had no idea. Why do these sexist customs persist?"

Personal questions like Joelle's have sociological significance. Have you noticed that most women routinely change their last name when they marry, whereas men virtually never do so? There have been times in history when it was common for women to keep their last names, but in more modern times its popularity comes and goes. Today, about 20 percent who have married in recent years have kept their last name in full, and another 10 percent have retained it in part, such as hyphenating it with their husband's last name (Miller and Willis, 2015; Sifferlin, 2015). The remaining 70 percent have taken their husband's last name and discarded their own. Why do women change their last names when they marry? Some may argue, "It's just easier this way . . .", but look at macro-explanations: Changing of wives' names is a carryover from older patriarchal and patrilineal customs where upon marriage a woman became the legal property of her husband. It was important to name the child after the father so that he could identify and establish "ownership" of his heirs. Surnames (last names) were created to codify inheritance rules and thereby bolster tax revenues (Stevens, 1999; Stoiko and Strough, 2017). But why does the tradition continue today? Much of what people do in marriage is simply done out of habit, even when the tradition has no legal or financial basis. There is a powerful pull toward reproducing tradition. Yet, these persistent traditions tell something about women's continued roles in our society.

Virtually all social institutions—whether political, religious, economic, educational, or familial—differentiate between men and women in fundamental ways. Throughout the world, people are obsessed with perceived sex differences, and these become the basis on which power is distributed. Perceptions about differences between men and women are sometimes used to deny women equal rights under the law or equal opportunities in work or education.

Yes, it is true that over the past several decades women in the United States and around the world have made many notable gains. Rates of literacy are increasing; more women are gaining political rights in more nations; and there is an increasingly active global array of women's organizations working to achieve equal rights and empowerment. In many impoverished regions, it is women who form economic cooperatives, develop women's reproductive health clinics, carry forward the fight for women's political rights, and provide the greatest impetus to positive social change and economic development.

In Western countries, women are increasingly gaining education and entering occupations that were traditionally dominated by men. For example, in the United States over one-third of lawyers and physicians are now women (American Bar Association, 2017; Association of American Medical Colleges, 2016). Moreover, the gap between the earnings of men and women is narrowing. At the end of 2017, the median earnings of women who worked full-time were about 81 percent of those of men, compared with 68 percent in 1985, just a generation ago (Bureau of Labor Statistics, January 17, 2018).

Despite the gains of recent decades, however, sex discrimination and stereotyping continue to limit the opportunities of women. From a global perspective, the extent to which women remain subordinate to men remains a severe obstacle to further development. Women face an array of daunting social problems, including dire poverty, severe lack of rights in many nations and cultures, forced marriage, rape and other violence, enslavement in sex industries, and societal failure to recognize and develop their full human potential (Kristof and WuDunn, 2010, 2014). Globally, women are beset by hunger and violence far more than are men.

This chapter explores the relevance of sex and gender in our lives—within our societies, our culture, our social institutions, and our families and close relationships. Sex and gender are major organizing constructs within societies, cultures, social institutions, and personal relationships. They are critical components of our identity (Rogers and Meltzoff, 2017). You may be thinking that the two concepts are the same, but they are quite different.

Is It Sex or Gender?

8.1 Analyze the distinction between sex and gender.

The term **sex** refers to biological differences and one's role in reproduction, as indicated in Table 8–1. Typically, people think of sex in terms of genitalia: male and female, or man and woman. However, anatomical categories are not always easily identifiable, as is the case with **intersexed** individuals. The ambiguity is often the result of chromosomal or hormonal imbalances during the prenatal stage. It is difficult to get a firm number of intersexed individuals because sexual ambiguities occur along a continuum and not everyone agrees on what exactly constitutes an intersexed person. The frequency of surgery needed to normalize the genital appearance runs about 1 or 2 for every 1,000 births. The genitals are usually surgically reconstructed to adhere to the child's genetic chromosomes, either XX for a female or XY for a male.

In contrast to sex, which is rooted in biology, **gender** refers to the culturally and socially constructed differences between males and females, which are found in the meanings, beliefs, and practices associated with femininity and masculinity. These concepts are learned attitudes and behaviors, not biological or physical qualities. Gender is socially constructed; expectations about gender differ around the globe. People may be born male or female, but they learn the culturally and socially prescribed traits associated with masculine or feminine patterns of behavior.

sex

Biological differences and one's role in reproduction.

intersexed

Individuals with anatomical categories that are not easily identifiable.

gender

The culturally and socially constructed differences between males and females, which are found in the meanings, beliefs, and practices associated with femininity and masculinity.

Table 8–1 Summary of Sex and Gender

Sex
• Biological differences and role in reproduction
• Usually "male" or "female," although some people are intersexed

Gender
• Culturally and socially constructed differences associated with men and women
• "Masculinity" or "femininity" is learned

8.1.1 Gender Is Socially Constructed

In most societies throughout the world today, and certainly throughout history, men and women have been viewed as far more different than alike. Men and women even refer to one another as "the opposite sex." Men are often assumed to be more aggressive, sexual, unemotional, rational, and task-oriented than women, whereas women are assumed to be more nurturing, passive, and dependent. Many social roles played out in families every day reflect these presumed characteristics. For example, research shows that mothers spend far more time than do fathers on childcare, even when both work outside the home for pay, because women are thought to be more innately nurturing (Parker and Livingston, 2017).

However, the suggestion that men and women are the opposite of one another is seriously flawed. Modern social science and biological researchers note that men and women are far more alike than different. Both men and women express aggression, passivity, nurturance, rationality, instrumentality, and other gender-typed behaviors. All people possess both so-called masculine and feminine traits, although to varying degrees.

Expectations about gender are in large part socially constructed (Ward and Edelstein, 2014). They are variable across and within cultures, are historically situated, and reflect broad social patterns. Gender is not completely innate or instinctive. Rather, much of it is socially and culturally produced. A hundred years ago the general consensus was that women were too frail to work outside the home. Exceptions were made for poor or immigrant women, but the popular folklore was that ideally, women were dainty creatures best suited to the confines of the home. Yet, biologically, women are the same today as they were then. Nothing has really changed except for the social construction of gender.

8.1.2 Sex Differences

Even though men and women are far more alike than they are different from one another, it is important to note that the biological differences between men and women extend beyond the ones necessary for reproduction (Fine, 2017; Schmitt, 2017). Although using human subjects in this line of research presents a set of special challenges, many studies suggest that males are biologically stronger, more active, and more aggressive than females, on average. However, in other ways, males are more fragile. Males suffer from a wider variety of physical illnesses; infant mortality rates are higher among males; and their life expectancy is shorter in almost all countries, including the United States (National Center for Health Statistics, 2017; Population Reference Bureau, 2018). Males are afflicted with more genetic disorders and suffer from accidents at a higher rate than do females. Depression, however, is far more common among women, as learned in Chapter 3. Certainly, many men suffer from depression and many women deal with physical illness. However, scientists tend to be interested in statistically typical behaviors rather than exceptions.

There is also some scientific evidence that males and females may solve intellectual problems somewhat differently (Mosley, 2014). Although most research points to no overall differences in average levels of intelligence (measured with IQ tests), men tend to perform better at certain spatial tasks and mathematical reasoning tests. Meanwhile, women tend to outperform men in terms of the precision with which they perform certain manual tasks. Women also tend to excel on tests that measure recall of words or matching items.

What is the cause of these differences? Originally, the assumption was that these were innate biological differences. Then more recently, it was popular to attribute sex differences exclusively, or nearly so, to social learning. The argument was that males and females are treated differently because of sex-typing, and therefore, they come to behave differently and develop different skill sets (Bandura, 1977; Bussey and Bandura, 1999). However, the most recent accumulating evidence now suggests that some cognitive and skill differences may be present at very early ages. These differences may result from hormones such as women's higher levels of estrogen and progesterone and men's higher levels of androgens, including testosterone. Exposure to different hormones begins in the uterus and may have implications for the way the brain is "wired" (McCarthy et al., 2012; Miller and Halpern, 2014). Studies of female fetuses who had been exposed to abnormally large quantities of androgens because of a genetic defect called congenital adrenal hyperplasia (CAH) showed that the girls exposed to CAH as children were more likely to prefer playing with typically masculine toys, such as construction or transportation toys, as compared with the other girls who preferred typically feminine toys (Kimura, 2002).

Although brain research is still in its infancy, there is some evidence that the size, shape, and use of the brain may differ somewhat by sex in regions involved in language, memory, emotion, vision, hearing, and navigation (Becker et al., 2008; Bramble, Lipson, Vashist, and Vilain 2017; McEwen and Milner, 2017). Some studies suggest that women may use more parts of their brain at once, while men are more inclined to have focused responses (Onion, 2005). One study conducted with mice has shown that, as mammals develop in the womb, testosterone and related hormones trigger cell death in some regions of the male brain and foster cell development in other regions (Forger et al., 2004). Removing or adding testosterone in mice shortly after birth causes their brains to develop according to the presence or absence of the hormone, regardless of their sex.

Given these intriguing studies, what is the role of nature versus nurture, and how would this relationship play out in personal relationships, social institutions, cultures, and societies? Social scientists suggest that most sex differences are probably a result of both biological and social influences, with social factors powerfully shaping biological ones (Eliot, 2009; Etaugh and Bridges, 2013; Fine, 2010). This process becomes clear when examining the wide variety of sex and gendered expectations cross-culturally. What one culture defines as distinctly feminine behavior or activities, another culture may see as quite masculine, as the research by the famous anthropologist George Murdock (1949, 1957) has shown. Are females more emotional—or are males? Answers to questions like this one are not universal; they vary across different cultures.

Although all people may possess both masculine and feminine traits, most people display primarily the gendered traits that are associated with their sex in a particular culture. Females are indeed usually more "feminine" and tend to behave in culturally prescribed feminine ways, and males are more "masculine." This tendency is likely due to both the strong cultural messages received throughout our lives as well as various biological forces.

8.1.3   Incongruence between Sex and Gender

Most people (but certainly not all) have a binary view of sex and gender; that is, you are either male and expected to behave in masculine ways or female and expected to behave in feminine ways. An interesting exception to this expectation occurs on a cultural level in Native American culture, in which berdache, or Two-Spirit, men assume a woman's social roles in virtually every respect. They are considered a third gender and not necessarily gay or lesbian.

People who are transgender have an identity that differs from what would be expected based on the sex characteristics with which they are born. Regardless of their physical appearance, inside they feel that they are truly the other sex. Transgender women are not usually as obvious in Western cultures because women are allowed more leeway to behave in traditionally masculine ways, such as wearing men's clothing or acting aggressively.

Transgender issues have been largely ignored historically, but this situation is beginning to change as more transgender people speak out (Platt and Bolland, 2017; Schilt and Lagos, 2017; Winter, Settle, Wylie, Reisner, Cabral, Knudson, and

---

What Do You Think?

How would your life be different if you were the "opposite" sex? Put yourself in the same family and general social setting, but as the opposite of the sex you are now. Describe the changes that might take place.

Olympic champion athlete Bruce Jenner was uncomfortable identifying as a male from earliest memories. She has now transitioned to Caitlyn, and finally feels that she is her authentic self. In contrast, Chastity Bono, the child of famous duo "Sonny and Cher," today identifies as a male living his life comfortably as Chaz.

Baral, 2016). Danica Roem made history, winning election to Virginia's House of Delegates as an openly transgender woman. Caitlyn Jenner, who was a male Olympic athlete in the 1970s, and Chaz Bono, a writer and musician who was the daughter of the famous singers Sonny and Cher, are examples of celebrities who have transitioned. Because of the long-held stigma associated with being transgender, no one knows the exact number of transgender men and women, but about 0.6 percent of the U.S. population, or roughly 1.4 million people *identify* as transgender (Flores, Herman, Gates, and Brown, 2016).

Some transgender individuals harbor a deep sense of discomfort about their sex and wish to live fully as members of the other sex (Shipherd, Green, and Abramovitz, 2010). These persons may undergo sex reassignment surgery and hormone treatments, either male-to-female or female-to-male. The American Society of Plastic Surgeons, which represents 94 percent of all U.S. board-certified plastic surgeons, revealed that members of the organization performed over 3,200 "transmasculine" and "transfeminine" surgeries in 2016, a 20 percent increase over 2015 (American Society of Plastic Surgeons, May 22, 2017). Sex reassignment surgery, however, is expensive, costing at least $100,000 (Taylor, 2015). The preparation is time-consuming and emotionally difficult. Consequently, because of the cost and potential difficulties, most transgender persons go without it.

8.1.4 The Social Evaluation of Sex and Gender

What should be clear by now is that men and women are somewhat different and somewhat alike and that the gendered roles associated with sex are socially constructed and vary not only from one place to another but also from one historical period to another. Why is this information important for the study of social problems?

It is important because societies, cultures, social institutions, and personal relationships *evaluate* these sex and gender differences, and guess what? Women very often come up short. Around the globe, women are often considered "less than" men. Women are trafficked as sex slaves, are mutilated by having their clitorises cut out from their bodies, are denied access to schools, are forbidden the right to vote, are raped on college campuses (among other places), are paid less than men for equal work, are subjected to the rule of their husbands, and are forced to marry, because women have been deemed as less important, less valuable, less intelligent, and less morally righteous than men. *This* oppression is a social problem, indeed.

What Do You Think?

Can you identify a specific personal experience situation in which you felt that men and women (or masculinity and femininity) were evaluated differently? How did this make you feel?

Traditional Gender Roles

8.2   Define traditional gender roles.

In Chapter 7, we suggested that prejudice often becomes the justification for discriminatory behavior. That is, if people believe that a certain group is "inferior" or "different," they can easily justify less-than-equal treatment of its members. It is also suggested that the norms of society are an important source of prejudice and discrimination. If an entire society is prejudiced against a certain group and discriminates against it, then most members of that society will accept such actions as natural and right.

Until the 1960s or so, it was widely accepted that the primary desirable roles for a woman were wife, mother, and homemaker and that her entire life should revolve around these roles. Women were expected to be nurturing and skilled in the emotional aspects of personal relationships. They were considered too delicate to do "men's work" and therefore were legally denied many career and job opportunities. In contrast, men were expected to be leaders and providers, highly rational and able to not let emotions get in the way of action. They were taught to "act like a man" and that "big boys don't cry." These expectations often caused men to deny their emotions and thus made them less able to enjoy many aspects of life in their families and communities. Women and men were thought to be biologically different and hence were treated differently by social institutions—including the government and legal system.

Today many people think of the traditional roles of women and men as outdated. However, as you will see later in this chapter, vestiges of these gendered roles remain. You can see them in personal relationships and in social institutions. Nonetheless, it is also true that in many countries the status of women is far more subordinate than in our own country. Women face substantial restrictions on their lives and may be unable to pursue careers outside the home, make important decisions for their children, or vote. In 2017, Saudi women were finally allowed to drive, Saudi Arabia being the final holdout. This traditional hierarchy is extremely resistant to change. Women and men are shaped by the culture in which they are raised, so that most adults are thoroughly indoctrinated or socialized for the roles their culture has prescribed for them. Change is suspect because it threatens their identity. Sometimes people wonder why women allow themselves to be subordinate, but it is important to understand that they are subject to the same cultural teachings as are men.

However, within this hierarchy there is considerable variation in the types of behavior that are considered appropriate for men and for women. These behaviors often reflect the values of a particular society more than any innate or "natural" qualities. Whereas it was once supposed that behavioral differences between men and women are innate, today it is clear that many of these differences are taught and learned through socialization. And, although it was once believed that there are universal standards of masculine and feminine behavior, in fact the standards vary a great deal among societies.

The Roots of Sexism and Inequality

8.3   Examine the roots of sexism and inequality.

sexism

The entire range of attitudes, beliefs, policies, laws, and behaviors discriminating against women (or against men) on the basis of their sex or gender.

Sexism is the counterpart of racism and ageism, which are discussed in Chapters 7 and 9, respectively. It may be defined as the "entire range of attitudes, beliefs, policies, laws, and behaviors discriminating against women (or against men) on the basis of their [sex or] gender" (Safilios-Rothschild, 1974, p. 1).[1] In this section we describe several factors that contribute to sexism around the world and in the United States.

[1]Safilios-Rothschild, C. (1974). *Women & Social Policy.* Englewood Cliffs, NJ: Prentice Hall, Inc.

8.3.1 Power, Male Hegemony, and Patriarchy

Sociologists who study gender relations call attention to persistent patterns of male dominance throughout the institutions of modern societies. This is known as **patriarchy**, a form of social organization in which men dominate and have power and authority over women. R. W. Connell (1995), for example, has analyzed how dramatic inequalities in the distribution of power in societies often deprive women of opportunities to realize their full potential. Connell's research shows that, wherever possible, males attempt to preserve their hegemony (controlling power) over women. In relations marked by hegemony, domination by one group, class, or sex over another is achieved by a combination of political and ideological means. Although political power or coercion is always important, ideologies can be equally important. In relationships between men and women, these ideologies differ from one culture to another, and can be reinforced by religion. For example, traditional religious texts are filled with passages demeaning women, although their interpretations may be softened in modern-day language. For instance, Christianity teaches patriarchy, as witnessed in the following passages in the New Testament (1 Tm. 2:11–15):

patriarchy

A form of social organization in which men dominate and have power and authority over women.

> Let a woman learn in silence with all submissiveness. I permit no woman to teach or to have authority over men; she is to keep silent. For Adam was formed first, then Eve; and Adam was not deceived, but the woman was deceived and became a transgressor. Yet woman will be saved through bearing children, if she continues in faith and love and holiness, with modesty.[2]

Connell's (1995) work shows that, in much of the industrialized world, men still have much greater access than women to cultural prestige, political authority, corporate power, individual wealth, and material comforts. Individual men or small groups may be confused or insecure about these inequalities. Men with feminist ideals may join with women in rejecting male hegemony. But despite all the recent feminist criticism and despite all the documented struggles by women to assert their equality and make political and economic gains in the workplace, men continue to be dominant. With some notable exceptions (the occasional female boss or political leader), male–female relations are structured so that women are subordinate. This subordination is reinforced by the symbolic equation of masculinity and power.

An unfortunate aspect of ideologies that support male dominance is that even people victimized by them tend to believe that they are true. Thus, many women are prejudicial to other women, undervalue the work of other women, and tolerate, or even encourage the sexual objectification of women (Vaillancourt, 2013). This has been called, "internalized sexism" or "internalized misogyny" (Feltman and Szymanski, 2018; Szymanski and Hendrichs-Beck, 2014).

8.3.2 Stereotyping

As you saw in Chapter 7, one source of prejudice and discrimination is stereotyping—attributing a fixed and usually unfavorable and inaccurate conception to a category of people. Stereotypes often make it easier to justify unequal treatment of the stereotyped person or group.

Women have traditionally been stereotyped as weak, emotional, nurturing, dependent, kind, and good listeners, among many other attributes. Although these might sound a bit outdated, many people believe that women are indeed weaker, more emotional and nurturing, more dependent, kinder, and better listeners than men. However, there is also a set of stereotypes about men that limits their ability to function fully and effectively. Some have argued that, although both boys and girls

---

[2]Scripture quotations are from the Revised Standard Version Bible, copyright © 1989 the Division of Christian Education of the National Council of the Churches of Christ in the United States of America.

Table 8–2 Percent of Men Saying that Men Face a Lot or Some Pressure to Do the Following

	Age 18–36	Age 37–52
Be Willing to Throw a Punch if Provoked	69%	55%
Have Many Sexual Partners	61%	34%
Join in When Other Men Are Talking About Women in a Sexual Way	57%	41%

SOURCE: Data from Parker, K., Horowitz, J., & Stepler, R. (Dec. 5, 2017) "On Gender Difference, No Consensus on Nature vs. Nurture," Pew Research Center.

---

receive gendered messages about how they are supposed to behave, today perhaps boys experience even more pressure to conform to traditional stereotypes than do girls (Kimmel and Messner, 2013). The masculine stereotype is that all men are tough, unemotional, and dominant; yet, however unrealistic and inaccurate this stereotype is, many men (and women) believe it. And, although this may be surprising, younger men buy into many stereotypes more so than older men, as shown in Table 8–2. The masculine stereotype not only limits the freedom of men to engage in any activity or occupation they choose but also limits their personal relationships. They are uncomfortable discussing their feelings with other men, and instead, their relationships are more competitive in nature.

Examples of Sexism and Inequality Today

8.4   Identify several examples of sexism and inequality today.

Sexism is widespread and is found in virtually every society; however, it is obviously more pronounced in some societies than in others. In many places in the world today, women cannot drive, vote, divorce, or own property in their own name. In virtually every society, women's activities and jobs carry less prestige and pay than those that are primarily held by men. Even when men and women work in identical or comparable jobs, women are paid significantly less for their effort overall. Moreover, women are underrepresented in public office, and men primarily make the laws that women must follow, including those on issues that affect women in particular, such as abortion, birth control, or guaranteed family leave. These inequities are justified based on biology ("it's human nature"), religion ("it's God's will"), economics ("that's not a budget priority"), or cultural customs ("that's the way we do things here")—all representative of patriarchy as discussed in the previous section.

We begin this discussion of sexism and inequality by illustrating an extreme example of patriarchy experienced in the world today. Sometimes it is easier to see how patriarchy operates by examining the most glaring example because it is often easier to identify patriarchy elsewhere than it is within our own borders. We will then turn to gendered experiences in the United States and other developed nations: Does patriarchy operate here also?

8.4.1 Female Genital Mutilation

The young girl introduced in *A Global View: "Female Genital Mutilation,"* like 200 million other women and girls, suffers as she tries to recover from the dangerous practice of female genital mutilation (FGM), also known as female genital cutting or female circumcision (World Health Organization, January, 2018). In an excruciatingly painful procedure, often without anesthesia, a woman's clitoris, and possibly also part of her vulva and vagina, are cut and removed with a knife, razor blade, or broken glass. She is then sewn up to ensure virginity for her future husband.

A Global View

Female Genital Mutilation

Shani is a young woman born and raised in a rural village in Egypt. Like most females there, she has undergone female genital mutilation. This is her story.

My genitals were mutilated at the age of nine. I was told by my grandmother that they were taking me down to the river to perform a certain ceremony, and afterwards I would be given a lot of food to eat. As an innocent child, I did not know what was ahead of me and the pain that I would endure for the rest of my life.

Once I entered the secret area behind the bushes, I was taken to a very dark room and was told to undress. I was scared, and therefore just stood there unable to move. But an old woman blindfolded me and stripped me naked. Four strong women carried me to the site for the operation. I was forced to lie flat on my back while two women held tight to each leg, and another woman sat on my chest to prevent my upper body from squirming away. A piece of cloth was forced in my mouth to stop me screaming.

When the cutting began, I put up a big fight. I was genitally mutilated with a blunt penknife. They stabbed and cut and ripped at my body. I was not given any anesthetic in the operation and the pain was terrible and unbearable. I lost a lot of blood and it was everywhere. I kept telling them, "You're going to kill me." Yet those who took part in the operation were happy. They ignored my screams. Some of them had alcohol to drink. I saw a few other women were dancing and singing.

After the operation, they tied my legs together so I could not move. I laid this way for nearly two weeks. The medicine they put on my wound stank and was painful. When I wanted to urinate, I was forced to stand upright. The urine would spray over the wound and would cause agonizing pain all over again. Sometimes I tried not to urinate because of the terrible pain. They did not give me any antibiotics to fight against infection. Afterwards, I hemorrhaged and became anemic. I suffered for a long time from acute vaginal infections.

When I married, my husband had to rip me open again. He tried not to hurt me, but I nearly passed out from the pain. He is a good man, but I hate sex, I'll always hate sex.

DUBAR TOOTA DHAQNA–QABUUN /KITTAANUUN/FAYYAA ISAANII MIIDHUUDHA . AKKANA GOCHUU HAADHIENU !

Per-Anders Pettersson/Getty Images

But I know that it did not have to be this way. I've heard of other girls who were not cut. A health worker came to our village and said that cutting is no good. She urged us to leave our daughters alone. I believe her, and I will try to keep my daughter away from this.

Critical Thinking

Why do women put up with this procedure? Why don't they just say no? What obstacles might the health worker face when she goes into a village or community to tell people that "cutting is no good"? Can you design a public health strategy for eliminating, or at least reducing, female genital mutilation?

Among countries with adequate national data, Somalia, Guinea, Djibouti, and Sierra Leone have the highest prevalence of FGM; at least 90 percent of women ages 15–49 have had their genitals cut, as shown in Figure 8–1. In addition, the practice of FGM and its harmful consequences concern a growing number of women and girls in Europe, North America, Australia, and New Zealand as a result of international migration. It is estimated that about 500,000 women living in Europe have had their genitals cut (World Health Organization, 2011).

In one form of genital cutting, **clitoridectomy**, the clitoris is cut out of the body. In the more extreme form, **infibulation**, the vaginal lips are also cut or scraped away, and the outer labia are stitched together, leaving only a miniscule opening for menstrual blood and urine to escape the body. The procedure is done crudely; a layperson

clitoridectomy

A procedure in which the clitoris is cut out of the body.

infibulation

A procedure in which the clitoris is cut out of the body, the vaginal lips are cut or scraped away, and the outer labia are stitched together, leaving only a miniscule opening for menstrual blood and urine to escape the body.

Figure 8–1 Percentage of Girls and Women Aged 15–49 Who Have Undergone Female Genital Mutilation

SOURCE: Data from "Female Genital Mutilation/Cutting: A Global Concern," (2016) UNICEF.

rather than a physician usually conducts it. One study of nearly 2,000 women living in Egypt who had their genitals cut reports that only 14 percent of the cutting was performed by a doctor (Yount, 2002). In an excruciatingly painful procedure, often without anesthesia, the girl is tied or held down and the instrument used may be a knife, razor blade, or broken glass. Often, the girl's body is stitched together with thorns or catgut, and her knees are bound together for several weeks for the incision to heal itself and not tear open again when she walks.

The health consequences of genital mutilation are swift, long-lasting, and severe, and they include much more than a loss of sexual pleasure. Immediate consequences include possible shock, hemorrhaging, or bleeding to death. Soon afterwards, women face possible pelvic infection, dangerous scarring, and internal pain from urination and menstrual fluids that cannot properly escape the body. As they mature, they may experience infertility, a greater likelihood of miscarriage, recurrent urinary tract infections, anal incontinence, and fissures. Intercourse will be painful, childbirth will be prolonged and obstructed, it is likely that the perineal area will be lacerated, and there is a greater chance of stillborn births (World Health Organization, January, 2018). Many women also experience serious levels of depression, anxiety, and PTSD after FGM (Adelufosi, Edet, Arikpo, Aquaisua, and Meremikwu, 2017).

Why is this practice so popular, and why has it continued for so many years? It is deeply rooted in the patriarchal traditions (rather than religious teachings) in these societies (Panet, 2013). Women are expected to be subject to the social and sexual control of men at all times. They are expected to be virgins at the time of marriage and must remain sexually faithful thereafter. Removing the clitoris, the source of women's sexual pleasure, ensures that they will not experience orgasm, and thus the likelihood of engaging in or enjoying sexual relationships outside of marriage is lessened. Among women whose entire external genital area has been removed, the opening that remains is so small as to forbid penetration. Husbands are virtually guaranteed that their wives are virgins.

FGM persists, and is endorsed, perpetuated, and often conducted by other women, because women's status is low and their options are few. Marriage and motherhood are the primary ways in which women receive recognition. Without marriage, they bring shame to themselves and to their families. Virginity is highly valued, and this procedure helps to ensure that women's sexuality will be muted.

What Do You Think?

How would you develop a campaign to eliminate female genital cutting? Who would you involve, and how would you get your message across? How would you take into account the culture in which people live?

Mothers have been taught to believe that if they do not have their daughter's clitoris removed or have her infibulated, the chances of finding a husband will be reduced considerably and their daughter will bear considerable shame (Yount, 2002).

The good news is that FGM is declining around the world due to public health and education efforts. For example, in Guinea, where FGM is nearly universal among women 15 and older, only about half of girls under 15 have undergone the procedure. While it's likely that some of these young girls will undergo FGM eventually, today many women and men across Africa and the Middle East oppose it. Even in Somalia, where FGM is also nearly universal, a third of women think the practice should end (UNICEF, 2016). A recent survey conducted in Somalia and Ethiopia with nearly 500 students found that 59 percent of boys said that they would prefer to marry a girl who had not undergone this procedure—a step in the right direction because a primary motivation for FGM has been to enhance marriage prospects (Abathun, Gele, and Sundby, 2017).

8.4.2 Sexist Standards of Beauty

After reading about FGM, it's easy to say, "Whew, I'm glad I live in the United States." However, the United States has its own set of patriarchal norms and sexist customs. Do any come to mind? How many U.S. presidents have been women? Vice presidents? Senators? How many heads of Fortune 500 companies are women? How does women's pay compare with men's? Where did you get your last name? How do standards of beauty vary for men and women—some with potentially dangerous or painful repercussions (hint: think cosmetic surgery, breast implants, waxing, or even high-heeled shoes)?

Nearly 1.8 million cosmetic surgery procedures were performed in 2016 (American Society of Plastic Surgeons, 2017). Nearly 90 percent of cosmetic surgery patients are women. Table 8–3 reveals the top five surgical cosmetic procedures in 2016 (American Society of Plastic Surgeons, 2017). All these procedures have declined since 2000 with the exception of breast augmentation, which increased by over 30 percent. These procedures should be cause for concern, as they can have short- and long-term side effects.

There are a variety of reasons that a person might seek cosmetic surgery. The first is the desire to create change because of a birth defect, an accident, or an illness that affects the person's looks. The second reason is to enhance attractiveness in people who feel some aspect of their body could be changed and improved to make them more attractive to others. Women, in particular, fall victim to the idea that they must be "perfect" (however culturally defined). Women who have cosmetic surgery have internalized the media messages about "ideal" women's body image and are dissatisfied with their own bodies (Lee and Clark, 2014). As shown in the slide show, *Beauty Ideas for Women*, what we define as beautiful is socially constructed. There is no one absolute standard of beauty. Instead, beauty standards vary historically and across cultures.

Developed nations such as the United States contain many patriarchal norms and customs. Let's look at another example of sexism—women in the labor force.

Table 8–3 Top Five Surgical Cosmetic Procedures in 2016

Type of Procedure	Number of Procedures
Breast Augmentation	260,467
Liposuction	235,237
Nose Reshaping	223,018
Eyelid Surgery	209,020
Facelift	131,106

SOURCE: Data from 2017 Plastic Surgery Statistics Report, American Society of Plastic Surgeons. Retrieved from https://www.plasticsurgery.org/documents/News/Statistics/2017/plastic-surgery-statistics-report-2017.pdf.

Beauty Ideals for Women

The United States is not the only country that has harsh beauty ideals for women. Historically, and around the world today, women have endured painful procedures and have been maimed in the quest to be beautiful in the eyes of men. As you look at the photos in this slideshow, reflect on the societal pressures that women face to be beautiful.

Print Collector/Getty Images

This woman, like millions of other women in China, was told that big feet are ugly on a woman. To secure a proper husband, she submitted to a procedure that slowly and painfully broke all the bones in her feet, so they could heal in a bent, deformed shape, referred to as "golden lilies" or "bound feet." Throughout the rest of her life, she could barely walk, and her dependency was considered a further attraction.

Elena Lemekhova/Alamy Stock Photo

The goal of this apparatus is to give the impression of an elongated neck, a sign of a woman's maturity and beauty. Girls may begin to wear small coils at the age of 2 and gradually increase the number of coils as they grow older. The weight of the coils will eventually place sufficient pressure on the clavicles to cause them to deform and create an impression of a longer neck.

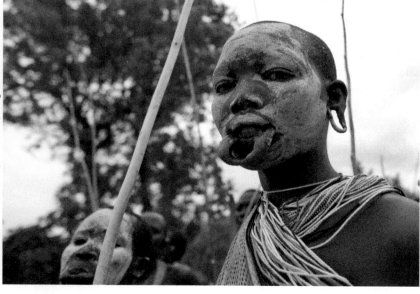

Eric LAFFORGUE/Gamma-Rapho via Getty Images

When a Suri girl in Ethiopia is about to be married, usually in her teens (around 14 or 15), the gap between her lower lip and the flesh below is pierced and gradually stretched. In the beginning a hole is made in the lip with a wooden stick. The stretch continues as successively bigger discs of clay or wood are accommodated by the disfigured lip. Generally, the two lower front teeth are pulled (or knocked) out to aid the process. The final size of the plates determines how many cattle the woman will receive as a dowry, so the more stretched her lip the better, and the more cattle the woman is worth. Some women have stretched their lips to allow plates up to 20 cm in diameter. Having a lip plate is considered a sign of beauty.

Karwai Tang/Getty Images

Singer Taylor Swift illustrates the emphasis on thinness in American culture. The desire to be unnaturally thin is related to a wide variety of dangerous eating disorders among women, including anorexia and bulimia. Why is such extreme thinness considered beautiful?

Tracy Whiteside/Fotolia

Breast augmentation is a leading form of cosmetic surgery. Very few women with low body fat would have large breasts naturally; instead, they are turning to surgery. But surgery is risky, and women could face several side effects. But risks notwithstanding, why do so many women want to add uncomfortable weight onto their bodies? Why do they conform to unrealistic fantasies?

Critical Thinking

Drawing on what you have learned in this chapter, why are standards of beauty for women often so extreme, and why do women go along with these standards?

8.4.3 Women in the Labor Force

In addition to unrealistic standards of beauty, sexism is also evident in women's employment situations. Women are concentrated in lower-status jobs at the low end of the pay scale. The vast majority of retail clerks, typists, and secretaries are women, whereas men account for the largest proportions of corporate directors, white-collar administrators, and blue-collar supervisors (U.S. Department of Labor, October, 2017). Some people may try to claim that these differences are due to men's greater educational attainment. However, that claim is not the case. On average, women have more education than do men.

HISTORY OF WOMEN'S EMPLOYMENT   Today, most women work outside the home for pay, whether or not they are married and whether or not they have children. But this practice has not always been the case. In early colonial America, most families worked closely with the land. Their lives revolved around the seasonal work necessary for farming and ranching. The labor of men, women, and children was needed and was considered invaluable to the success of the family enterprise.

In the nineteenth century, the U.S. economy was evolving from an emphasis on agriculture to an emphasis on industrialization. During this century, work was often done away from home, and people were paid wages for their labor. New industries needed expanding numbers of laborers, so, in addition to recruiting men, factories hired many young, poor, minority, and immigrant women and children. By 1890,

17 percent of women were in the labor force (Coontz, 2000). Much of the work in these factories was dangerous and dirty, and there were minimal occupational safety standards compared to today. Women's roles became increasingly intertwined with class and race: Poor or minority women *had* to work, whereas white middle-class women stayed far away from the outside world of work.

This pattern continued for many years. During the 1940s through the mid-1970s (except briefly during WWII), most employed women were either single, married without children, or had husbands that did not earn enough to support the family. Married mothers worked outside the home in small numbers and tended to organize their labor force participation around childbearing and childrearing. In the 1940s and 1950s, they tried to wait until their children had grown up before returning to work; in the 1960s, mothers tried to wait until their children were in high school; and by the 1970s, it had dropped to when children were in middle school. Nonetheless, the general convention was, unless a mother had to work because of dire economic circumstances, employment was secondary to the bearing and rearing of children.

By the mid-1970s, a new pattern of mothers' labor force participation emerged and has continued today: Over two-thirds of married mothers and three-quarters of unmarried mothers (i.e., never married, divorced, separated, or widowed) are employed for pay (Bureau of Labor Statistics, 2017). However, instead of continuing to adapt work to fit childbearing, the reverse has occurred. Childbearing and childrearing are adapted to fit the demands of work. Families have delayed having children and have had fewer of them, and some women and men have chosen not to have children at all (Martin et al., January 5, 2017). Thus, a macro-level condition of changing norms surrounding women's employment has led to micro-level changes in the structure of families.

Beginning in earnest in the 1970s, Americans have witnessed a restructuring of the U.S. economy. Whereas the country was once heavily dependent on raw materials and manufacturing, today the U.S. economy is heavily geared toward the provision of a wide range of services from medical care to food and entertainment. Real wages (wages after accounting for inflation) have declined, and most families rely on two paychecks to make ends meet.

HOW DO WOMEN WORKERS FARE? How do female workers fare compared with their male counterparts? Table 8–4 reports women's earnings as a percentage of men's earnings among people who work full-time over an entire year (U.S. Department of Labor, October, 2017). The table compares data for whites, blacks, Asians, and Hispanics. As you can see, there has been considerable movement toward greater equality over time, although the gap has remained relatively constant since the early 2000s. The data also reveal that black and Hispanic women earn incomes closest to their male counterparts, whereas the gender gap for whites and Asians is the widest. Why do you think this is the case?

Table 8–4 Women's Earnings as a Percentage of Men's Earnings, 1980–2016

	Total	White	Black	Asian	Hispanic
1980	64%	63%	76%	–	74%
1985	68%	67%	83%	–	78%
1990	72%	72%	85%	–	87%
1995	76%	73%	86%	–	87%
2000	77%	76%	84%	80%	88%
2005	81%	80%	89%	81%	88%
2010	78%	78%	88%	80%	89%
2016	81%	79%	88%	77%	84%

SOURCE: U.S. Department of Labor, Women's Bureau. 2017. "Women in the Labor Force: Data and Statistics." October. Retrieved 14 March 2018 (https://www.dol.gov/wb/stats/stats_data.htm).

Figure 8–2 Women's and Men's Earnings, by Age, 2016

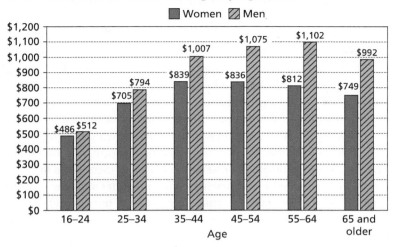

SOURCE: Based on "Women's and Men's Earnings by Age in 2016," Bureau of Labor Statistics, August 25, 2017.

Pay differences continue even among those who are most educated. Women without a high school diploma earn about 77 percent of their male counterparts' salaries, whereas women with advanced degrees earn roughly 75 percent of men's salaries (U.S. Department of Labor, August, 2017). Thus, contrary to what we might believe, the pay gap between men and women who work full-time, year-round, increases rather than decreases with higher educational attainment.

Differences in pay between men and women are smaller among younger workers than they are among those who are older, as shown in Figure 8–2. For example, employed women between the ages of 16 and 24 earn about 95 percent of what men earn; however, the gap widens considerably after that. It is likely that these young adults are working at temporary, service-oriented jobs, and have the lowest levels of education. As men and women finish college, and begin to have children, the pay gap increases.

WHAT ACCOUNTS FOR THESE GENDER DIFFERENCES?   Realistically, differentials could be due to a number of factors. One explanation offered is the different work habits of men and women. For example, among full-time workers, men tend to work a greater number of hours, which could boost pay. But, as a sociologist, look at the social context of this fact—why is it men tend to work longer hours on average? Could it be because women are responsible for the majority of household labor and childcare? Many women might say that they would work longer hours if their spouse or partner made dinner, picked up the kids after school, and did the laundry. We see that, as the division of household labor has become more equitable in recent years, the amount of time women spend working has also increased.

A second explanation for pay differences is labor market segmentation in which men and women usually work in different types of jobs: Women tend to work in less prestigious, nonunionized, and lower-paying jobs. Women are more likely than men to work as secretaries, registered nurses, elementary and middle school teachers, and in service work. To eliminate sex-segregated jobs in the United States, about half of male (or female) workers would have to change occupations.

A third explanation for wage differences is discrimination: Women are paid less for doing the same job as men. In virtually every job category provided by the Department of Labor, men are paid more than women. Even in occupations in which women are the large majority of workers—such as housecleaners, nurses, or clerical workers—men in these occupations earn more, as measured by average weekly earnings for full-time workers and by the earnings ratio, which divides women's earnings by those of men.

What Do You Think?

If young women between the ages of 16 and 24 earn 95 percent of men's wages (while older women earn less), do you think these young women will retain this advantage as they age, or will they see their advantage start to decline?

The differences are particularly striking in occupations such as physicians, lawyers, and judges, which require years of professional education and experience.

Wage and job discrimination are illegal under the Equal Pay Act of 1963 and the Civil Rights Act of 1964, yet they continue to exist (Marken, 2016). Nearly 26,000 charges of sex discrimination were filed with the Equal Employment Opportunity Commission (EEOC) in 2017 (Equal Employment Opportunity Commission, 2017). Google, Uber, Walmart, and the restaurant chain Ruby Tuesday, are among the many employers who have been sued for sex discrimination in recent years. In a major sex discrimination settlement, more than 5,000 women who formerly worked for the Rent-A-Center Corporation of Plano, Texas, the nation's largest rent-to-own company, were awarded a total of $47 million in damages. Over many years, the company had systematically promoted men instead of women, and the women, finding themselves in dead-end jobs, typically left the company and found new jobs with different employers. After a suit was filed with the EEOC, the company eventually settled with the plaintiffs. Unfortunately, however, hundreds of such claims are pending before the Commission, and many others have never been filed because of fear or lack of knowledge on the part of those women who have been discriminated against. But large awards such as the one involving Rent-A-Center serve to remind large employers that such discrimination is illegal.

ROOM FOR IMPROVEMENT It is important to acknowledge that things have changed considerably over the last several decades, and women face fewer obstacles in education and the labor market than ever before. Women receive the majority of bachelor's degrees and are quickly moving to parity in advanced degrees. They are moving into new fields in record numbers—law, business, medicine, and engineering, to name just a few formerly "nontraditional" fields. Is it safe to say then that sexism is a thing of the past? No, not really. For example, a set of researchers used the Implicit Association Test (IAT) to assess gender biases. The IAT measures how quickly a person can pair two concepts, in this case, women and leadership, or men and leadership. The researchers looked for unconscious gender biases in the notion of leadership and then observed whether these biases affect how a person would vote. Despite "political correctness," the average person did indeed find it easier to pair words like *president, governor,* and *executive* with male names. Meanwhile, people were also more likely to pair words like *secretary, assistant,* and *aid* with female-sounding names. It appears that many people had an unconscious gender bias in that they had more difficulty associating leadership positions with women than they did with men (Mo, 2012).

8.4.4 Rape, Sexual Assault, and Harassment

Other forms of sexism are obvious in American culture. Among the most persistent and difficult aspects of sexism are rape, sexual assault, and sexual harassment, introduced in Chapter 5. In 2013 the official legal definition of **rape** was changed from "the carnal knowledge of a female forcibly and against her will," to "penetration, no matter how slight, of the vagina or anus with any body part or object, or oral penetration by a sex organ of another person, without the consent of the victim."[3] This expanded definition now is gender neutral and includes sodomy (oral and anal penetration) and use of an object. Rape is still rape if the victim is drunk, high, drugged, or passed out and unable to consent. Nearly 20 percent of women in the United States report having been raped, as compared with less than 2 percent of men, as shown in Table 8–5 (Smith et al., 2017).

Sexual assault may include rape, but it also includes other types of behavior, such as (1) *unwanted physical contact*—unwanted sexual experiences involving touch but not sexual penetration, such as being kissed in a sexual way, or having sexual body parts fondled, groped, or grabbed and (2) *unwanted noncontact sexual experiences*—unwanted

rape

Penetration, no matter how slight, of the vagina or anus with any body part or object, or oral penetration by a sex organ of another person, without the consent of the victim.

sexual assault

An act that may include rape, but which also includes other types of behavior, such as unwanted physical contact or noncontact, unwanted sexual experiences.

---

[3]"An Updated Definition of Rape," U.S. Department of Justice Archives, U.S. Department of Justice, January 6, 2012.

Table 8–5 Lifetime Prevalence of Unwanted Physical Contact, and Unwanted Noncontact, by Sex

	Women	Men
Rape	19%	2%
Unwanted Sexual Contact	28%	11%
Unwanted Noncontact Sexual Experience	32%	13%
Sexual Coercion	13%	6%

SOURCE: Data from Smith, S. G., et al (2017) "The National Intimate Partner and Sexual Violence Survey: 2010–2012 State Report," National Center for Injury Prevention and Control, Centers for Disease Control and Prevention, Atlanta, Georgia.

experiences that do not involve any touching or penetration, including someone exposing their sexual body parts, flashing, or masturbating in front of the victim, someone making a victim show his or her body parts, someone making a victim look at or participate in sexual photos or movies, or someone harassing the victim in a public place in a way that made the victim feel unsafe.

More than one woman in four has experienced unwanted sexual contact, as has one in nine men, as shown in Table 8–5 (Smith et al., 2017). Noncontact, unwanted sexual experiences have occurred to one in three women, and one in eight men. Another 13 percent of women, and 6 percent of men, report that they have been **sexually coerced**, defined as unwanted vaginal, oral, or anal sex after being pressured in ways that included being worn down by someone who repeatedly asked for sex or showed they were unhappy; feeling pressured by being lied to, being told promises that were untrue, having someone threaten to end a relationship or spread rumors; and sexual pressure due to someone using their influence or authority.

Who is committing these crimes? It varies by the type of crime being committed, as shown in Figure 8–3. This figure includes data from females only and shows that the relationship between the perpetrator and victim tends to differ across these crimes.

sexual coersion

Unwanted vaginal, oral, or anal sex after being pressured in ways that include being worn down by someone who repeatedly asked for sex or showed they were unhappy, feeling pressured by being lied to, being told promises that were untrue, having someone threaten to end a relationship or spread rumors; and sexual pressure due to someone using their influence or authority.

Figure 8–3 Lifetime Reports of Sexual Violence Among Female Victims by Type of Perpetrator

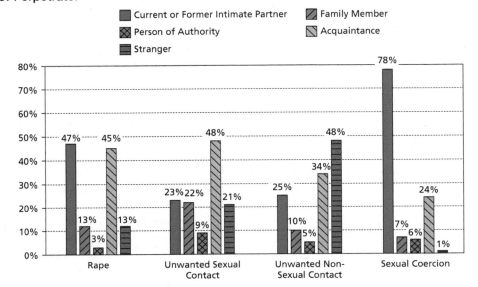

SOURCE: Data from Smith, S. G., et al. (2017) "The National Intimate Partner and Sexual Violence Survey: 2010–2012 State Report," National Center for Injury Prevention and Control, Centers for Disease Control and Prevention, Atlanta, Georgia.

For example, rape is most likely committed by a current or former intimate partner, or by an acquaintance. Unwanted sexual contact is most often committed by an acquaintance, whereas noncontact, unwanted sexual experiences tend to be initiated by strangers (Smith et al., 2017). Sexual coercion tends to be committed by a current or former intimate partner. These crimes are often not reported to the police out of fear or shame.

Rape, sexual assault, coercion, and harassment (which can include sexual contact or noncontact unwanted sexual experience) have a long history but received new attention recently as many prominent men's sexually harassing behavior was exposed, including politicians, actors, and comedians, among others. Anita Hill may have first opened the door to publicly denouncing sexual harassment in 1991, as she charged that Clarence Thomas, who was nominated to the Supreme Court, sexually harassed her. As his former employee and a law professor (currently at Stanford), she claimed that Thomas made lewd and suggestive comments and tried to coerce her into having sex with him. Despite her testimony, he was confirmed as a Justice to the Supreme Court and her allegations were almost forgotten. Today there is a renewed awareness, but social science data, as well as personal testimonies from the #MeToo movement, remind us that these unwanted behaviors have been around for a very long time. As prominent cases of harassment were uncovered, the #MeToo movement was born, representing the plight of the average woman coming forth to tell her story of harassment, assault, and rape by bosses, colleagues, and others.

Nowadays, sexual harassment may occur electronically. This can happen through text messages, email, instant messaging and social networks. It can include verbal threats, images, and as discussed in Chapter 5, revenge porn. A large study by the Pew Research Center based on a representative sample of adults found that half of young women between the ages of 18 and 29 report receiving explicit images that they did not ask for (Duggan, July 11, 2017). A large study of teenagers found that one in four dating teens is abused or harassed online or through texts by their partner (Zweig and Dank, 2013).

Stalking, another type of harassment, has received greater attention since California passed the first anti-stalking law in 1990. **Stalking** consists of repeated and obsessive contact or tracking of another person—attention that is unwanted and causes a reasonable concern for one's safety (Smith et al., 2017). It is a combination of many unwanted acts that, by themselves, are not necessarily abusive—for example, sending flowers or gifts, calling on the telephone, or sending a text or e-mail—but, when taken together may constitute a form of mental abuse. Stalking exists on a continuum. It may be so subtle that the victim is not even aware it is happening or, in contrast, the perpetrator may purposefully try to instill terror in the victim.

THE COLLEGE ENVIRONMENT   College students are particularly vulnerable to rape, sexual assault, harassment, and stalking, in part because of their age, but also because of the group living quarters and the party atmosphere at many universities (Sinozich and Langton, 2014). In a study of female undergraduates, 19 percent, or nearly one in five, experienced attempted or completed sexual assault since entering college. And many of the respondents in this study still had several years of college ahead of them (Centers for Disease Control and Prevention, 2012).

Who is being raped, and who is doing the raping? Among college students, about 80 percent of victims and perpetrators know each other; they are intimate partners, "friends," roommates, acquaintances, and classmates (Sinozich and Langton, 2014). Women are raped by their study partner on the way to the library, by the guy they just met at the party in the dorm, by their roommate's brother, or by the partner they are involved with.

The pioneering work of Mary Koss and her colleagues (Koss and Cook, 1993; Koss, Gidycz, and Wisniewski, 1987) sheds some interesting light on college-age perpetrators. In a survey of 32 college campuses, they found that although fully 12 percent of men had committed acts that would fit the legal definition of rape

What Do You Think?

Have you or someone that you know ever been abused or sexually harassed online? How did you (or they) respond? How does this type of harassment differ from that which is done in person?

stalking

Obsessive contact or tracking of another person—attention that is unwanted and causes a reasonable concern for one's safety.

or attempted rape, only 1 percent thought their actions were criminal. Many made a distinction between "forcing a girl to have sex" and "rape," as though they are different. The law, of course, makes no such distinction. Even today, many men believe in myths about rape (e.g., it's committed by strangers; no woman can be raped against her will), and those men tend to have murkier ideas about what constitutes consent (Shafer et al., 2018).

Oddly, many college women blame themselves for being raped, either wholly or partially (Donde, 2017). One study indicated that rape survivors attributed the most blame to themselves and to society, some blame to the situation, and the least blame to the male involved, even though the majority of women clearly voiced their nonconsent (Cook and Messman-Moore, 2018). They may be more likely to refer to the rape as a "sexual assault" than as an actual rape itself (Donde et al., 2018).

The issue of sexual assault among college students has gained new urgency in recent years as the number of reports of forcible sex offenses on campus has surged, and several cases have received national press. The Obama administration opened civil rights investigations of more than 110 colleges and universities for their handling of sexual violence complaints. Many rape victims fail to report the crime because they feel shame or perceive threats from the perpetrator (Munzer, Fegert, Ganser, Loos, Witt, and Goldbeck, 2016). A 2011 letter from the Office of Civil Rights told campus officials they must respond more promptly to reports of sexual violence and also use a less rigorous standard, known as "preponderance of the evidence," when determining whether an assault occurred. Until that time, many campuses had been using a more stringent standard, known as "clear and convincing." However, the administration of President Trump officially rescinded Obama-era campus sexual assault guidance. Education Secretary Betsy DeVos, along with Republicans and groups that advocate on behalf of individuals' rights, have argued that the guidance amounted to an overreach of federal authority, and could put undue burden on accused students to defend themselves against allegations (Camera, 2017).

What Do You Think?

What is it about a college environment that makes rape and sexual assault so prevalent? What do you think is happening at your college? What can or should be done about it? How can feminist theory or conflict theory guide you?

"DATE-RAPE" DRUGS   Alcohol or drugs are often involved in a sexual assault (Roudsari, Leahy, and Walters, 2009). **Date-rape drugs** such as gamma hydroxybutyrate (GHB), Rohypnol (popularly known as "roofies" or "roofenol"), or ketamine hydrochloride (ketamine) can immobilize a person to facilitate an assault (U.S. Department of Health & Human Services, Office of Women's Health, April 28, 2017). The effects of these drugs cause people to be physically helpless, lose muscle control, feel very drunk, or lose consciousness, and they often can't remember what happened. The drugs usually have no color, smell, or taste and can be easily added to flavored drinks without the victim's knowledge. How can you protect yourself? Don't accept drinks from other people; open containers yourself; keep your drink with you at all times, even when you go to the bathroom; don't share drinks; don't drink from punch bowls or other large, common, open containers because they may already have drugs in them; don't drink anything that tastes or smells strange (sometimes GHB tastes salty); and have a designated nondrinking friend with you to make sure you stay safe.

date-rape drugs

Drugs such as gamma hydroxybutyrate (GHB), Rohypnol (popularly known as "roofies" or "roofenol"), or ketamine hydrochloride (ketamine), which can immobilize a person to facilitate an assault.

Sources of Sexism

8.5   **Assess the sources of sexism.**

We have described some of the causes of the subordination of women and indicated some of the major inequities that women face in our society. In this section, we discuss in some detail the processes by which American institutions reinforce and perpetuate sexism.

8.5.1 Socialization

gender socialization

A process whereby people learn to behave according to the gendered norms of a culture.

If much of gendered behavior is socially constructed and learned, where do people learn it? **Gender socialization** is the process whereby people learn to behave according to the gendered norms of a culture. They are taught the norms associated with being male or female (Ward and Edelstein, 2014). Gender socialization may be a conscious effort such as a teacher criticizing a young girl for being rowdy and "unladylike" in the classroom or scolding a young boy for displaying his emotions because "big boys don't cry." It also may occur on a less conscious level, for example, parents providing different toys for their children—dress-up clothes for their daughters and war toys for their sons. The **agents of socialization**, summarized in Table 8–6, include the people, social institutions, and organizations that teach boys and girls their gendered expectations. Through socialization, people internalize to varying degrees the roles, norms, and values of their culture and subculture, which become their guides to behavior and shape their deepest beliefs.

agents of socialization

The people, social institutions, and organizations that teach boys and girls their gendered expectations.

FAMILY MEMBERS Parents and other family members have the initial responsibility for introducing the gendered norms and expectations of their culture (Endendijk et al., 2013; Halpern and Perry-Jenkins, 2016). They teach a child about what to wear, how to behave, what toys to play with, what the child's status is, and what the overall expectations are for the child. Consciously or not, parents, especially fathers, often treat their sons and daughters differently (Mascaro, Rentscher, Hackett, Mehl, and Rilling, 2017). They hold baby girls more gently and cuddle them more than they do boys. Parents of girls describe their children as more dainty and delicate than do parents of boys, and the choice of dress usually reflects these perceptions. This different treatment might help to explain why many parents hold a specific preference for their child's sex, as discussed in the feature box, *A Closer Look: "A Son or a Daughter?"*

TOYS Children's toys and games are also differentiated on the basis of sex (Jirout and Newcombe, 2015; Sweet, 2014). Toys for boys often emphasize rough-and-tumble play (e.g., sports, guns, vehicles, action figures), whereas toys for girls often focus on quiet or nurturing activities (e.g., dolls, arts and crafts, kitchens and cooking).

An analysis of virtually any children's toy store will reveal that pink aisles specialize in girl toys whereas others are reserved for toys for boys. Toy websites are equally gendered. A toy as seemingly gender-neutral as a bicycle takes on great gender significance by its color: pink for girls, blue for boys. Targeting toys by sex has consequences beyond socialization. Boys are more likely to play with toys that develop spatial intelligence—K'nex, puzzles, Lego bricks—than girls are. Marketing

Table 8–6 Agents of Socialization and How They Work

Family Members
• Parents and other family members have the initial responsibility for introducing the gendered norms and expectations of their culture.

Toys
• Books show boys as leading characters and girls in stereotypical roles; toys are sex-typed.

Schools
• The "hidden curriculum" traditionally encouraged sex-typed behavior and taught girls to fear academic success. However, things are changing, and now girls are experiencing greater success at school than boys. Yet, training for many occupations remains sex-typed.

Peers
• Same-sex play reinforces different interaction styles that carry over into adulthood.

Media
• Television, music videos, and electronic games tend to focus more on boys and present girls in stereotypical and sexist ways.

A Closer Look

A Son or a Daughter?

If you could have only one child, would you prefer to have a son or a daughter?

Kian Khoon Tan/Alamy Stock Photo

Around the world, many couples are answering this question with a resounding "son!" The preference for sons over daughters has dramatically shifted the sex ratio in countries like China and India, where strict birth control is encouraged but patriarchal norms are prominent. Preference for boys is also found in many other cultures throughout the world. This preference could lead to a worldwide shortage of girls now that various techniques for detecting the sex of a fetus can be assessed. But what about the United States? Is there a preference for sons over daughters here?

The Gallup Poll conducts research on a variety of social, economic, and political issues, using large, nationally representative samples of adults in the United States, and the data collected can be compared over time to assess how things are (or are not) changing. Gallup has conducted telephone interviews with over 1,000 adults ages 18 and older, living in all 50 states and the District of Columbia. Americans have been asked about their preferences for a boy or girl—using slightly different wordings over the years—since 1941. The findings are generally consistent: If Americans could have only one child, they would prefer that it be a boy rather than a girl by a

40 percent to 28 percent margin (Newport, 2011). The preference for sons is highest among men, and, rather surprisingly, highest among younger adults. Younger men ages 18 to 49 prefer boys to girls by a 54 percent to 19 percent margin, as you can see in Table 8–7. Republicans, conservatives, and those with less education also tend to prefer a son.

Table 8–7 Preference for a Son versus a Daughter, Responses to *"Suppose you could only have one child. Would you prefer that it be a boy or a girl?"*

	Boy	Girl	Doesn't matter/ Unsure/No opinion
Total	**40%**	**28%**	**32%**
Men	49%	22%	28%
Women	31%	33%	36%
Age 18–29	54%	27%	18%
Age 30–49	39%	27%	34%
Age 50–64	34%	29%	37%
Age 65 and over	31%	29%	40%
Men 18–49	54%	19%	26%
Women 18–49	36%	35%	28%
Men 50 and over	41%	26%	33%
Women 50 and over	25%	32%	42%
Postgraduate	32%	33%	35%
College Graduate	35%	29%	36%
Some College	39%	28%	33%
High School or less	44%	25%	30%
Republicans/Leaners	43%	25%	30%
Democrats/Leaners	39%	33%	28%
Conservative	41%	25%	34%
Moderate	40%	27%	33%
Liberal	36%	37%	28%

However, there is some possibility that these long-held preferences are starting to change. A new study measured that preference in a different way. While having a daughter versus a son used to make American parents more likely to keep having children, presumably to try for a son, now the opposite is true. Having a daughter makes it less likely that parents will keep having children (Miller, 2018).

This trend is certainly one to watch.

Critical Thinking

Why do men most starkly want sons, but women do not seem to care? Why are younger people, who are usually more liberal on social issues, more likely to want sons than are older persons? Do Americans deliberately attempt to select the sex of their child?

hidden curriculum

An undocumented teaching approach that informally teaches gendered norms.

Toys for boys and girls differ and perpetuate gendered stereotypes. Dolls for boys are called "action figures" and usually emphasize toughness, whereas dolls for girls emphasize domesticity.

plays a role. Girl-oriented product lines such as Lego Friends focus on playacting rather than construction; aisles in some toy stores distinguish "building sets" from "girls' building sets" (Jirout and Newcombe, 2015).

SCHOOLS Schools represent a more formal type of socialization. Considering how much time children spend in school, the socialization they receive there inevitably affects how they behave. Daycare centers, preschools, elementary schools, secondary schools, and even college classrooms are important arenas in which gender socialization occurs. Research a decade or two ago revealed that teachers called on boys to answer questions more often than girls and that boys were given more public praise by teachers. The **hidden curriculum** informally teaches gendered norms, and in this case, taught girls that academic achievement could mean forfeiting popularity (Orenstein, 1994). Consequently, although girls tended to excel in elementary school, by the time they reached middle and upper school, they lost confidence and tested more poorly than boys (Kenney-Benson et al., 2006).

But something has changed. In recent years, much emphasis has been placed on ridding the schools of bias against female achievement and gender equality. Today, it appears that many girls and young women have a strong achievement ethic, are doing well in school, and are surpassing boys and young men. More girls apply to, attend, and graduate from college now than boys. For example, 33 percent of males between the ages of 25 and 29 have a bachelor's degree, as compared to 40 percent of their female counterparts (National Center for Education Statistics, 2017). Many college majors, however, remain sex-typed. Students in nursing, elementary education, and social work are overwhelmingly female, whereas students in engineering and computer science are still primarily male.

PEERS Peer groups, an important source of socialization, grow in importance as a child ages (Mulvey and Killen, 2014; Kågesten et al., 2016). However, even young children are socialized by their same-sex peers to conform to traditional gender expectations. Psychologist Eleanor Maccoby (1998), in her seminal study of children's play groups, found that children between the ages of 2 and 3 tend to prefer same-sex peer play groups when provided with the opportunity to do so. She also noted that when girls were playing with other girls, they were as active as were boys playing with other boys. However, when girls were playing with boys, they frequently stood back and let the boys dominate the toys or games. Maccoby speculated that the boys' rougher play and greater focus on competition was unattractive to girls, and girls responded by pulling back rather than by trying to exert their own play style. Maccoby suggests that these peer groups reinforce different interaction styles that carry over into adulthood: Boys' groups reinforce a more competitive, dominance-oriented style of interaction, which carries over into adult male communication patterns that include greater interrupting, contradicting, or boasting. Girls' cooperative groups reinforce a style that contributes to adult female communication patterns, including expressing agreement and acknowledging the comments of others and asking questions rather than making bold pronouncements.

MASS MEDIA   The mass media, including television, radio, and video games, are an important mechanism for socializing children. More than two-thirds of American households play computer or video games; 55 percent of these players are male (Entertainment Software Association, 2018). Video games are an increasing part of children and teen's entertainment, and consumers spent almost $27 billion on games, hardware, and accessories (Entertainment Software Association, 2017). Women and girls are portrayed in these games much less frequently than are men and boys, and when they are included, are often shown in subordinate or "hypersexualized" ways (Near, 2013; Strum, 2016). In videos with ratings of Teen or Mature, women's bodies are often artificially thin with exaggerated breasts. They are also considerably more attractive than most of the male characters and are often portrayed with revealing clothing.

Television also teaches and reflects gendered stereotypes. Boys, especially middle-class white boys, are at the center of most children's television programming, playing the most roles and engaging in the most activity (Gerding and Signorielli, 2014; Sink and Mastro, 2017). Reviews of recent children's television shows reveal that male characters are still more likely than female characters to answer questions, boss or order others, show ingenuity, and achieve a goal. A study of morning commercials showed that half of the commercials targeted to girls spoke about physical attractiveness, whereas none of the commercials targeted to boys mentioned attractiveness (National Institute on Media and the Family, 2009). Incidentally, females are less likely than males to be shown eating, not an insignificant finding given the higher rates of eating disorders among girls and women (National Institute of Mental Health, 2013).

Recent advertising campaigns have sought to attract the growing population of educated females by presenting successful businesswomen and female scientists to endorse products. But the patterns of sexism in advertising remain strong: Sex appeal and sexual stereotypes are still used to sell many products.

Socialization reinforces sexism, as do many social institutions. In particular, organized religion and the legal system contribute to sexism in our society.

8.5.2   Organized Religion

Women attend church more frequently, pray more often, hold firmer beliefs, and cooperate more in church programs than men do (Pew Research Center, April 12, 2016); yet, organized religion is dominated by men (Mills, 1972). In their theological doctrines and religious hierarchies, churches and synagogues tend to reinforce women's subordinate role. Explicit instructions to do so can be found in the Bible: "A woman must be a learner, listening quietly and with due submission. I do not permit a woman to be a teacher, nor must woman domineer over man; she should be quiet. For Adam was created first, and Eve afterwards; and it was not Adam who was deceived; it was woman who, yielding to deception, fell into sin" (Timothy 2:11–15).[4]

Historically, organized religion has reinforced many secular traditions and norms, including the traditional views that men are primary and women secondary, and that a woman's most important role is procreation. In Judaism, women are

---

[4]Timothy 2:11–15, The New English Bible.

required to obey fewer religious precepts than are men because less is expected of them. Orthodox Jewish males recite a prayer each morning in which they thank God that they are not women. The Catholic Church still assumes authority over a woman's sexual behavior, forbidding the use of birth control devices because they prevent reproduction.

In recent decades there have been some changes. The movement to allow women to hold leadership positions in churches and synagogues has had some success: In more liberal denominations (such as Episcopalians, Presbyterians, and Reformed Jews), women may be ordained as ministers and rabbis. Within the Catholic Church, there are groups of women devoted to changing the norm against female priests, but they encounter resistance from traditionalists in the Catholic hierarchy.

8.5.3 The Government and Legal System

There have been many legal barriers to sexual equality throughout history. For example, a 1919 study by the Women's Bureau (a federal bureau created by Congress) found that women were explicitly barred from applying for 60 percent of all civil-service positions, notably those involving scientific or other professional work. Women were placed in a separate employment category, and their salaries were limited. Many labor laws were also implemented for women during the early and mid-1900s, such as those that set shorter work hours, allowed lower wages, regulated how much a woman could lift, and required breaks from work for lunch or bathroom use (Stansell, 2010). These laws were ostensibly to protect women, but in effect kept them from a variety of jobs. As late as 1965, the EEOC stated that laws designed to protect women (but not men) were not discriminatory. Labor laws have now changed, but they have left behind a legacy that says it is okay to treat men and women differently under the law.

As another example, it took until 1938 for a judge to lift the ban on birth control, a ruling that involved Margaret Sanger, a leading crusader for the rights of all women to have access to contraceptives. However, it took until 1965 for the Supreme Court (in *Griswold v. Connecticut*) to guarantee married couples the right to use birth control, ruling that it was protected in the Constitution as a right to privacy. Meanwhile, millions of unmarried women living in 26 states were still denied the right to buy birth control to protect themselves from an unwanted pregnancy. It took until 1972 for the Supreme Court (in *Baird v. Eisenstadt*) to find birth control to be legal for all citizens, regardless of marital status. Again, while laws surrounding birth control have changed, women have more recently fought for their reproductive self-determination.

As a final, more modern-day example, in the United States men are 15 times as likely to be incarcerated as are women. What explains this gap? Is it due to sex differences in the frequency and type of criminal behavior, or are courts or prosecutors treating genuinely equivalent cases differently based on sex? According to research, both are operating. Men do indeed commit a greater number of serious crimes, but women and men who commit identical crimes are treated differently under the criminal justice system, with far greater leniency for women (Starr, 2012). Using information gleaned from four national data sources, Sonja B. Starr, a researcher from the University of Michigan Law School, found that women are twice as likely as men to avoid incarceration if convicted of the same crime. Moreover, if incarcerated, men receive sentences that average 63 percent longer than women do (Starr, 2012). She speculates on the factors that may explain the leniency afforded to women.

> *Girlfriend Theory:* Women might be viewed as minor players—perhaps mere accessories of their male romantic partners. Prosecutors and judges may consider such women less dangerous, less morally culpable.

Parental Responsibilities: Prosecutors and/or judges worry about the effect of maternal incarceration on children, and therefore give women lighter sentences.

Cooperativeness: Female defendants receive leniency because they are more cooperative with the government.

Sympathetic Life Circumstances: Female defendants may be seen as having more troubled life circumstances, such as poverty, mental illness, addiction, and abuse histories. If so, they may be perceived as less morally culpable or as candidates for rehabilitation.

Starr's research allowed her to test these theories statistically. She found that these theories were important and explained part, but not all, of the sex differences in punishments for identical crimes. She speculates that sex discrimination may be a remaining factor due to chivalry, paternalism, and trivializing women.

Social Policy

8.6   **Describe the women's movement and its policy agenda.**

There are many social policies that touch on sex and gender. This section looks at a broad issue, the women's movement, describing its history and policy agenda.

8.6.1   The Women's Movement

The women's movement in the United States was officially founded in 1848, when a women's rights convention held in Seneca, New York, was attended by 300 women and men, many of whom, like Elizabeth Cady Stanton and Lucretia Mott, were active in the abolitionist movement. The Seneca convention endorsed a platform that called for the right of women to vote, to control their own property, and to obtain custody of their children after divorce, all thought to be heresy at the time. After women won the right to vote in the 1920s, considered to be a major political victory, the women's movement receded from public consciousness. This consciousness was awakened again in the 1960s, a decade characterized by considerable activism and numerous social movements.

In 1970, enthusiastic and resolute women march in a parade down Fifth Avenue in New York on the fiftieth anniversary of the passage of the Nineteenth Amendment, which granted women the right to vote.

John Olson/Getty Images

The resurgence of the movement in the 1960s occurred in a context of widespread social change. In 1963, the year in which Betty Friedan's book, *The Feminine Mystique*, appeared, the President's Commission on the Status of Women published its recommendations for equal opportunity in employment. In 1964, Congress passed the Civil Rights Act, which included a provision (Title VII) that made it illegal to discriminate against women in promotion and hiring. But the Equal Employment Opportunity Commission (EEOC), established to enforce Title VII, was unwilling to serve as a watchdog for women's rights. As a result, in 1966, a pressure group, the National Organization for Women (NOW), was founded. Its stated purpose was "to take action to bring women into full participation in the mainstream of American society *now*, exercising all the privileges and responsibilities thereof in truly equal partnership with men."[5]

Attitudes about gender roles have undergone a major transformation since the resurgence of the women's movement. Although as we have seen, significant inequalities and double standards continue to exist, they are far less sharply defined than they were in earlier decades.

8.6.2 Changes in Men's Roles

The issues of women's rights have often eclipsed the need for men to examine and change their own gendered roles. Inspired by the successes of women, however, many men are exploring the roles that have also limited them in the past, and they are discovering a new freedom in moving toward sex-role egalitarianism, as shown in the feature box, *A Personal View: "What Does It Take to Be a 'Good Father'?"* There is evidence of a beginning shift in male gendered roles, especially among educated men in their twenties and thirties. The presence of women in the workforce, especially mothers, is leading to greater egalitarianism as women become breadwinners and men participate more freely (although not equally) in childrearing and housework, as described in upcoming Chapter 10.

As suggested earlier in this chapter, some people suggest that boys experience even more pressure to conform to cultural stereotypes than do girls (Kimmel and Messner, 2013). Girls are allowed more leeway. They can behave in ways that have been considered masculine; for example, there is little social stigma in being a "tomboy," whereas boys are not allowed to behave in ways that are deemed feminine. To be told that "you throw like a girl" or to be labeled a "sissy" (which is the opposite of a tomboy) is tantamount to social suicide. Likewise, women have moved into many occupations traditionally held by men (such as doctor or lawyer), whereas men may still shy away from occupations such as nursing or elementary education, in part because they would feel stigmatized for doing "women's work," and fear that their masculinity will be questioned.

And finally, while women are allowed, even encouraged, to express their emotions, the cultural imperative for men is to remain stoic and strong. Suppressing emotions can lead to problem behaviors among young boys. The use of alcohol and drugs, police detainment, fighting and other acts of aggression against their peers, school suspension, or forcing someone to have sex against their will, are all associated with heightened traditional masculine ideals. Consequently, numerous books have been published over the past decade about the "boy crisis"—how to raise emotionally healthy, well-balanced, and achievement-oriented boys (Slocumb, 2015).

---

[5]Statement of Purpose, The National Organization for Women's 1966 Statement of Purpose, National Organization for Women. Retrieved from https://now.org/about/history/statement-of-purpose/

A Personal View

What Does It Take to Be a "Good Father"?

Sean Prior/Alamy Stock Photo

In this essay, 41-year-old David, father of two, compares what it takes to be a good father today with what it meant for his father's generation.

When I was a young boy living at home with my parents, my father was not very involved in day-to-day activities around the house. We all understood that his job was to earn a living and support us. He did so with gusto and was generally gone from home from 7 in the morning until at least 7 at night, and sometimes all day on Saturdays, too. Sunday was our primary family day, and we usually did something special—took a drive to the beach, visited our relatives, or had a special Sunday dinner. Although my dad wasn't around much, my sisters and I all considered him to be a "good father." When he was at home in the evening after work, usually he was catching up on the evening news on television or reading the newspaper. Sometimes he helped us with our homework, but usually we had it done well before he came home in the evening. My mom always said, "Try not to bother your dad with things like homework. He's tired when he comes home and needs to relax." This is just how it was in the 1960s.

Fast forward to today. I am 41 years old and have two children of my own. I cannot imagine my wife saying to them, "Try not to bother your dad with things like homework. He's tired when he comes home and needs to relax." It just wouldn't happen. Why? First, we both work. Unlike my mom who was a homemaker, my wife Ana is a nurse, and therefore we both need to take care of the children. Second, I actually want to be involved in the day-to-day activities around the house. No offense to my father—I understand that he was just doing what was expected of him at the time—but I want a different path. I don't want to just earn money, but I want to help spend it too! I like hanging out with the kids, helping them with homework, taking them fun places, and watching them grow and become the best they can be. Third, even if I wanted to just be a breadwinner, I don't know whether society would let me do that. I think I would be labeled a "bad father" if I just went to work and then came home and read the newspaper while my wife did all the housework and childcare. Men, at least in my circles, are looked down on if they don't at least help pitch in. In only one generation we have completely redefined what it means to be a "good father."

Critical Thinking

On a societal level, what accounts for the changes in how we define a good father? How do you think David's father would interpret the changes associated with what is expected of fathers? David says, "Men, at least in my circles, are looked down on if they don't at least help pitch in." Do you think that is the case for all men today? What types of men are most likely to agree, and disagree, with David?

8.6.3 Future Prospects

What Jessie Bernard (1987) refers to as the "feminist enlightenment" has made significant progress in recent years. Women throughout the world have benefited in many ways, ranging from improved health and education to expanded economic and political opportunities. Over the past half-century, American women have increased their levels of education, strengthened their position in the labor force, and boosted their economic standing by gaining access to more well-paying occupations (Geiger and Parker, 2018). Globally, more women today can read and write than ever before in history. More women have access to family planning services, giving them increasing control and power over their lives. Where once it was regarded as a private matter, preventing and redressing violence against women and girls is at last on the public policy agenda (U.N. Women, 2015).

Much of this progress can be attributed to the role of the United Nations as a platform for women's issues. These efforts continue to build momentum throughout the developing world. Gender rights are *human rights*, as former Secretary of State Hillary Clinton said in her speech at the United Nations 4th World Conference on Women (Clinton, 2018).

Nonetheless, in no country are women as a group truly equal to men in terms of political power, economic opportunities, and social status. How can this be changed? Laws establishing equal rights for women provide an important basis for demanding and achieving equality in practice. These laws can be a critical reference point for political and cultural struggles, driving changes in social norms, popular attitudes, and policy shifts. But ensuring women's rights requires more than just legal reform. The translation of equality in the law into equality of outcomes is not automatic. Even where gender-equal laws have been put into place, entrenched inequalities, discriminatory social norms, and harmful customary practices, as well as dominant patterns of economic development can undermine their implementation and positive impact (U.N. Women, 2015).

According to the United Nations, the achievement of substantive equality requires action in three interrelated areas (U.N. Women, 2015):

- redressing women's socioeconomic disadvantage
- addressing stereotyping, stigma, and violence
- strengthening women's agency, voice, and participation[6]

Coordinated public action across all three of these dimensions has the potential to make lasting transformations in structures and institutions that constrain women's rights. These are issues for both developed countries, including the United States, and developing countries around the world. Although the particulars differ from country to country, the facts are indisputable: empowering women can have tremendous rewards for the world economy, reducing poverty and social inequality, improving health and well-being, and increasing environmental sustainability (International Monetary Fund, 2016; U.N. Women, 2015, 2017; Worldwatch Institute, 2016).

Going Beyond Left and Right

This chapter has focused on sex and gender issues, highlighting historical and contemporary gendered roles, sexism, and social inequality. The old saying "You've come a long way, baby" could apply to some of the changes that have taken place. In a 1936 Gallup Poll, only 30 percent of Americans said they would vote for a woman for president even if she were qualified for the job and represented their interests. However, in contrast, today almost (but not quite) 100 percent of Americans express a willingness to have a woman in the highest office in the country. Many seemingly radical ideas have now come to pass, or even if they haven't, they don't really seem so radical anymore. They have been embraced by the mainstream. For example, while the fight over equal pay for equal work continues, it would be a lonely person who would stand up and say, "I oppose!"

But how do Americans really feel about gender equality? Do they believe that women have the same equal opportunities as men? Do they think the country has gone far enough in giving women equal rights, or do they think America has gone too far? Who has it easier today, men or women? And finally, affirmative action was introduced in Chapter 7, but it is a set of policies and programs designed to help women as well as racial and ethnic groups.

---

[6]U.N. Women, 2015.

Summary

8.1 Analyze the distinction between sex and gender.

Virtually all social institutions—whether political, religious, economic, educational, or familial—distinguish between men and women in fundamental ways, and these differences become the basis on which power is distributed. The term sex refers to biological differences and one's role in reproduction. Gender refers to the culturally and socially constructed differences between males and females found in the meanings, beliefs, and practices associated with femininity and masculinity.

8.2 Define traditional gender roles.

Until the early 1970s, it was widely accepted that the primary desirable roles for a woman were wife, mother, and homemaker and that her entire life should revolve around them. In contrast, a man was expected to be a leader and provider, a highly rational person who would not let emotions get in the way of action.

8.3 Examine the roots of sexism and inequality.

Sexism is the counterpart of racism and ageism, and it can be defined as the entire range of attitudes, beliefs, policies, laws, and behaviors discriminating against women (or against men) on the basis of their sex or gender. Power, male hegemony, and stereotyping are the roots of patriarchy.

8.4 Identify several examples of sexism and inequality today.

Sexism is widespread and is found in virtually every society. One example of sexism is female genital mutilation, which affects 100 to 140 million women and girls today. Sexism is also evident in the United States. One example of sexism can be seen in the employment status of women. Women workers earn considerably less than men. Other examples of sexism include rape, sexual assault, sexual harassment, and stalking.

8.5 Assess the sources of sexism.

Sources of sexism include gender socialization, which is the process whereby people learn to behave according to the gendered norms of a culture. Agents of socialization that teach people about gender include family members, toys, schools, peers, and the mass media. Organized religion and the government and legal system also reinforce sex and gender inequality.

8.6 Describe the Women's Movement and its policy agenda.

The women's movement in the United States was officially founded in 1848, with a women's rights convention held in Seneca, New York, endorsing a platform that called for the right of women to vote, to control their own property, and to obtain custody of their children after divorce. After women won the right to vote in the 1920s, the women's movement receded from public consciousness until the 1960s. Since then, several laws have passed, the National Organization for Women was created, and many men are also exploring the ways that they have been limited by traditional gender roles.

Chapter 9
An Aging Society

Marmaduke St. John/Alamy Stock Photo

 Learning Objectives

9.1 Evaluate the degree to which aging is a social problem.

9.2 Compare the growth of the elderly population in developed and developing countries and assess the reasons for this growth.

9.3 Discuss the growth in the elderly population in the United States and the consequences of this growth.

9.4 Contrast the physiological, psychological, and social and cultural aspects of aging.

9.5 Analyze the economics of aging.

9.6 Describe the unique issues that families with older members may face.

9.7 Identify the health concerns common among the elderly and describe the primary program that pays for their health care.

9.8 Summarize the Social Security program.

I have a birthday coming up and I'm looking forward to celebrating it with my family and friends. For a while there I didn't really like birthdays. They made me feel old. I remember turning 35 and thinking, "I remember when my parents were this age." It bothered me a lot. I remember turning 50. My youngest child left for college that year. I was an "empty-nester" and entering a new chapter in life. I remember turning 65 and became officially "an elderly person." That one stung. I turned 80 just a few months after Harry died. I felt so old then. But now birthdays make me feel young! I'm going to be 100 years old. This one is particularly special, so all my kids and their young ones will be there. Some are even traveling from as far away as Colorado to come celebrate with me in California. I wish Harry could be here with me, to see me surrounded by our family. I remember the fun and romance we had when we were young! He was a part of my life beginning in high school. We met when a few kids from school gathered for a bonfire at the beach. I miss Harry terribly. We'll be together one day, but not this day. This day is all about me. I hope my hair looks okay. I had it fixed yesterday so I could look my best for the pictures. After all, not everyone gets to turn 100, do they?

One hundred years ago, not many understood a lot about the physical and social aspects of aging. Those who were elderly made up such a small proportion of the population that most researchers did not spend time studying them. Most people assumed that old age meant deterioration. Few people worried about dementia or Alzheimer's disease as we do today; instead, a person who was elderly and seemed deranged was simply called "old," as though senility was automatic.

Today, more people know far more about aging than they did in the past, mainly because more people are entering that age category called "elderly." The demographics of the United States, as well as those around the world, are quickly changing; in fact, the proportion of people classified as elderly within the global population is increasing faster than any other age group (He, Goodkind, and Kowal, 2016). The elderly population is a force to be reckoned with because political clout often accompanies size. Yet, in many ways, aging is a social construction, not simply a biological phenomenon. Yes, everyone grows older, but how aging is defined, how it is perceived by other members of the culture, and the policy implications that come from these definitions and perceptions can vary quite a lot.

In social terms, age is a major factor in determining groupings and role assignments in a society. Age plays a large part in how people feel about themselves and what society expects of them. And the way in which a society thinks about its aged members depends very much on the value its culture attaches to age as opposed to youth. The American culture places a high value on youth and youthful attractiveness; consequently, Americans tend to devalue aging because it is associated with changes in physical appearance that detract from the image of youth.

This chapter examines the demographic changes under way in the United States and around the world. It explores what it means to have increasing numbers of older people in the population. The issues that older people face and how Americans choose to address these issues—retirement, Social Security, widowhood, health, and family caregiving—are bound to become concerns for all members of society.

Aging as a Social Problem

9.1 **Evaluate the degree to which aging is a social problem.**

Why is aging a social problem, you ask? There are two primary reasons. One has to do with social structure. Aging places stress on society as well as on the individual, as we will show later in the chapter. For example, as the American aging population continues to grow, and the country's number of younger workers does not keep up, how will Americans pay for the programs that older people use? Economic programs such as Social Security and health programs such as Medicare are a large and growing part of the federal budget. Are these programs sustainable as is, or will Americans need to make some changes, and if so, what type of changes? Should the country tax workers even more? Should the country cut the funding for these programs? Should society restrict eligibility only to those who are elderly and poor or low-income? Should society raise the age at which people become eligible for these programs? These types of questions show that the large and growing number of elderly persons is a social problem.

The second reason aging can be viewed through a social problem lens involves a more micro, or individual, approach. It has to do with the way that elders live their lives and are treated in society. For example, many elders are widowed, live alone, and experience food insecurity or poor health. In the future, the number of people facing these issues will be quite large. Should Americans try to improve the quality of life for their elderly population, and if so, returning to the issues above, how do they achieve this goal?

9.1.1 Sociological Perspectives on Aging

Aging is often studied from the point of view of one or more of the basic perspectives introduced in Chapter 1. From the functionalist perspective, for example, aging is a problem because the institutions of modern society are not working well enough to serve the needs of those who are dependent and aged. The extended family, which once allowed elders to live out their lives among kin, has been weakened by greater social mobility and a shift to the nuclear family as the basic kinship unit. Those who are elderly are rendered less useful as their functions are replaced by those of other social institutions. As grandparents, for example, older people once played an important part in socializing those who were young, teaching them the skills, values, and ways of life of their people. Now those functions are performed by schools and colleges.

Interactionists take a different view. They see the term *elderly* often used as a stigmatizing label; older people are less valuable because they do not conform to the norms of a youth-oriented culture. Interactionists acknowledge elderly people may be victims of ageism, which comprises forms of prejudice and discrimination that are directed at them not only by individuals but also by social institutions. The remedy, according to interactionists, is to fight ageism in all its forms. *A Global View: "HIV Is Not Just a Young Person's Disease"* shows that ageism prevents many older people from accessing information or treatment about HIV, leading to a growing world health crisis.

Finally, conflict theorists focus on elders' status and power to shape social institutions to meet the unique needs of older persons. In this view, elders must resist the effects of labeling and the loss of their roles by banding together in organizations, communities, and voting blocs that will assert their need for meaningful lives and adequate social services. In this regard, elderly persons have been very successful. They represent a large and relatively organized group. Which legislator, for example, would dare rise up and ask that Social Security or Medicare be eliminated, or even significantly reduced? If any legislator proposed such a thing, they would likely be quickly removed from office. Table 9–1 summarizes the major sociological perspectives on aging.

Table 9–1 Major Sociological Perspectives on Aging

Perspective	Why Aging Is a Social Problem
Functionalist	Social institutions do not adequately serve people as they grow older (e.g., the family is no longer capable of providing adequate care).
Interactionist	The elderly are stigmatized and are victims of ageism because they do not conform to the norms of a culture that emphasizes youthfulness.
Conflict	The problem of the elderly is their relative lack of power; when they organize for political action, they can combat ageism.

A Global View

HIV Is Not Just a Young Person's Disease

Namukasa was born a long time ago—she does not remember when—in the southwest corner of Uganda. She is an old woman, with a wrinkled face and gray hair. She bore six children, and four of them are still alive. They live nearby with their own families and help take care of her. Her husband has long since passed away. One of her daughters died in childhood from a sickness that she is unsure of. Another daughter died from AIDS as a young adult. *That* sickness Namukasa is very sure of. HIV and AIDS are commonplace in Uganda, although no one speaks much of them publicly. It is considered shameful and not something spoken of beyond a whisper in the confines of home.

Namukasa is also infected with HIV. But unlike her daughter who caught the dreaded disease as a young adult, Namukasa caught it as an old woman. She met a man, and he seemed nice enough. She is past the age at which she could get pregnant. If there is no risk of having a baby, why not have sex, she asked herself? Namukasa—old, wrinkled, and gray—now has HIV, which she contracted at the age of 59. She does not want to go to a doctor. "HIV is a young person's disease," she says.

Despite the global attention being paid to HIV and AIDS, most people knew very little about infection among those who are elderly until recently. There is a common misperception that older people are not sexually active; therefore, there is little need for research or programs specifically tailored to older adults. However, 5.8 million people who live with HIV worldwide are age 50 and older (AVERT, 2018). The problem is especially acute in sub-Saharan Africa. Some of these people have had HIV for many years, perhaps their lives have been extended due to antiretroviral therapy, while others, like Namukasa, contracted the disease as an older woman.

Apparently, those who are elderly are indeed sexually active. Because they are beyond the age of reproduction, they often take risks and have sex without using condoms. Furthermore, several biological and cultural factors put older people at an added risk of becoming infected with HIV. The thinning of the vaginal wall after menopause increases the risk of HIV transmission during sex. And practices such as wife inheritance and ritual cleansing, in which a widow is expected to either marry or have sex with relatives of the deceased husband, can increase older women's exposure to the virus.

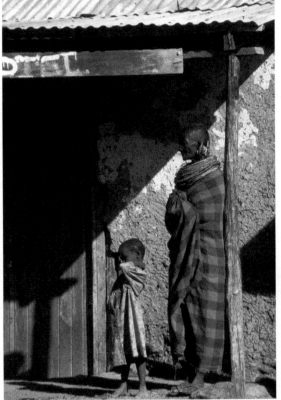

Thomas Cockrem/Alamy Stock Photo

HIV prevention programs must expand to include the considerations and needs of older persons. Ageist stereotypes about sex and those who are elderly must be put aside so that fewer people like Namukasa are infected, and if infected, they receive the treatment they need.

Critical Thinking

Create an HIV/AIDS prevention program that would be targeted toward older people such as Namukasa. What would be the main features of this program? Would it differ from programs targeted toward younger people? How would you market your program? What types of challenges would your program face?

Changing Demographics around the World

9.2 **Compare the growth of the elderly population in developed and developing countries and assess the reasons for this growth.**

What Do You Think?

Do you think those who are elderly have higher status and are treated better in developed or less developed countries?

Learning more about aging is important because the world is in the midst of a powerful revolution—a *demographic* revolution. The changes that an aging population brings will be felt by all of us, from the richest nations to the poorest ones. The world population is aging at an unprecedented rate. The number of people who are age 60 and over is expected to more than double from about 962 million today to 2.1 billion in 2050. It is difficult to imagine, but the number of older people will then exceed the number of children in the world (United Nations, Department of Economic and Social Affairs, Population Division, 2017).

9.2.1 Developed versus Less Developed Countries

Many people assume that this growth in the number of older people is occurring primarily in developed nations like the United States or within Europe. But this assumption is *wrong*. Yes, it is true that most developed nations have a high and growing *proportion* of elderly people in their population, such as Japan with a third of their population 60 or older in 2017. Compare Japan's proportion of elderly people with Qatar and the United Arab Emirates, which are the "youngest" countries, with less than 3 percent of their population age 65 or over (United Nations, Department of Economic and Social Affairs, Population Division, 2017).

Populations of developed countries may have higher *proportions* of those who are elderly, but the actual *numbers* of the elderly in less developed countries are very large, and they are increasing at a staggering rate that far exceeds the rate in developed countries. as you can see in Map 9–1. In many countries, the population of the elderly is expected to double or even triple within a generation, including Singapore, Colombia, Brazil, Costa Rica, the Philippines, Indonesia, Mexico, South Korea, Egypt, Bangladesh, China, and Peru (He, Goodkind, and Kowal, 2016; Population Reference Bureau, 2018).

These countries tend to be poorer and often are without economic or health care provisions for the elderly. The question of how to care for these elders will become one of the most vexing policy issues in the coming decades. The effects will be felt far beyond the borders of individual nations; they will spread throughout the global economy.

THE "OLDEST-OLD" Among the elderly, the largest increase around the world is in the "oldest-old" cohort—those age 80 and over (sometimes defined as age 85 and over). The oldest-old cohort currently constitute about one in five elders, but will grow quickly, given the large number of births in the 1940s and 1950s, and the fact that people are living longer lives due to better nutrition, sanitation, and health care developments. The global population of the "oldest-old" is expected to more than triple between 2015 and 2050, growing from 126.5 million to 446.6 million. The oldest old population in some Asian and Latin American countries is predicted to quadruple by 2050 (National Institutes of Health, March, 2016).

An age of 80 or 85 years used to be considered very old, but now, many people are even living to age 100 or beyond. These people are called centenarians. Even as recently as a generation ago, one rarely met anyone who was 100 or 101 years old. But today it is not uncommon, and it seems like everyone has an old-age story to tell. (Author Karen Seccombe's grandmother lived to be 108 and a half! You can learn more about her life in the Feature Box, *A Personal View: "Celebrating My Grandmother's 105th Birthday."*)

Map 9–1 Percentage of Population Aged 65 and Over: 2015 and 2050

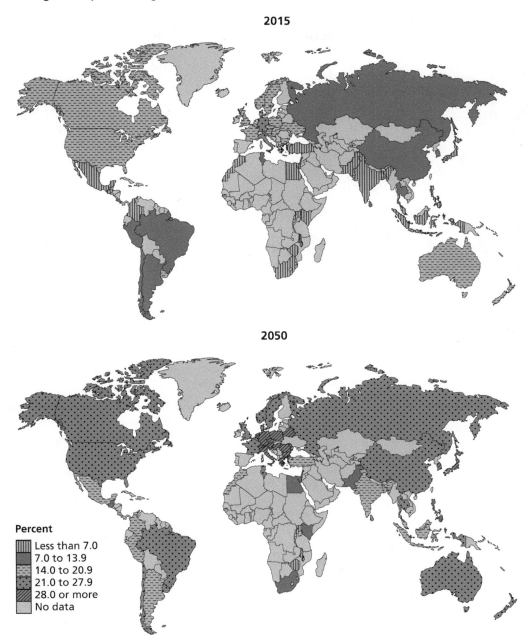

2015

2050

Percent
- Less than 7.0
- 7.0 to 13.9
- 14.0 to 20.9
- 21.0 to 27.9
- 28.0 or more
- No data

SOURCE: He, W., D. Goodkind, and P. Kowal. 2016. "An Aging World: 2015: International Population Reports." P95/16-1. March. Washington, DC: U.S. Census Bureau.

On one hand, it seems that living longer is a good thing because it provides more time for families and loved ones to be together. On the other hand, this unprecedented rise in the number of the oldest-old and centenarians can also be considered a social problem because as more people live to the oldest ages, we will see more chronic conditions such as arthritis, osteoporosis, and dementia. These types of conditions require more medical care and more personal help with cooking, cleaning, bathing, and home repair. Who will provide this care? Most countries have few government agencies or private facilities to provide this care. Furthermore, among the oldest cohorts, most are widowed and an increasing number live alone (United Nations, Department of Economic and Social Affairs, Population Division, 2017). Who then will care for these older people? The clear majority of elderly people around the world will be cared for by their adult children, and chances are, these adult children will be in their sixties or seventies themselves.

A Personal View

Celebrating My Grandmother's 105th Birthday

Karen Seccombe

As more adults are living past 100, many families now are celebrating birthdays that would have been unheard of a generation or two ago. The essay below asks you to ponder what such a birthday could mean.

My extended family gathered in Montana for my grandmother's birthday—who had just turned 105. Yes, you read that correctly—105! We celebrated the marvelous and very long life of this amazing woman. But wait, that was three and a half years ago. She is now over 108! She was born in 1901, and just imagine the changes she has witnessed:

- William McKinley was president of the United States when she was born.
- Henry Ford showcased the first model T for $950 when she was 7 years old.
- World War I began when she was 13.

- Women did not receive the right to vote until she was 19.
- The Roaring Twenties occurred when she was in her twenties.
- World War II, the deadliest war in history, began when she was 38.
- The case of *Brown v. Board of Education*, which decided that separate schools for black children were inherently unequal, was not settled until she was in her fifties.
- Medicare, the health insurance program for those who are elderly, was created when she was 64—just in time!
- Personal computers were not readily available until she was in her eighties.
- Cell phones were not commonplace until she was well into her nineties.
- Her youngest great-grandchild, Olivia, was born when she was 102; her youngest great-great-grandchild (to date), Crosby, was born when she was 107.

Here's to you, Grandma!
Love,
Karen

Note: Karen Seccombe is one of the authors of this textbook. Her grandmother Blanche Coy Seccombe died peacefully at the age of 108 and a half only a few years ago.

Critical Thinking

If you lived to be over 100, what type of social, technological, environmental, and political changes do you think could occur during your lifetime? Do you see these changes as good or bad for society?

9.2.2 Reasons for the Rapid Growth in the Elderly Population

Why is the world's population aging so quickly? There are two primary reasons: (1) people are living longer and (2) fewer babies are being born.

Obviously, the first reason for the rapid growth in the elderly population is that more people are living longer. Life expectancy (how long a person can expect to live) can be calculated at any age, but the most common way is to calculate it from birth: For a girl or boy born today, how long on average can she or he be expected to live? Extraordinary strides have been made in extending life expectancy in much of the world. In 1900, a child born in the U.S. had an average life expectancy of 48 years for males and 51 years for females. In contrast, for a child born in 2018, life expectancy has increased to 83 for males and 87 for females (Social Security Online, 2018). Other countries have made similar advances because of improved nutrition, sanitation, health care, and other scientific discoveries. Infectious diseases such as influenza, smallpox, or measles that killed many people in the past have been controlled in many parts of the world.

However, a few countries have experienced no substantial gains in life expectancy, and others have actually experienced a decline. Most of these countries are in Africa.

The most prominent reason is that HIV/AIDS is still a fatal disease in many African countries and thereby reduces life expectancy. The life expectancy in the U.S. has declined slightly since 2015 (Kochanek et al., December, 2017). The precise reasons are unknown, but the increase in drug-related deaths is a strong possibility (Tinker, 2017).

A second reason for the tremendous growth in the elderly population around the world is a decline in fertility rates; fewer babies are being born. Countries with low fertility rates such as Japan and Western Europe tend to have high proportions of people who are elderly. With fewer births over an extended period, cohorts of older people make up an increasing proportion of the population. Demographers use the term **demographic transition** to refer to the process in which a society moves from a situation of high fertility rates and low life expectancy to one of low fertility rates and high life expectancy.

Figure 9–1 shows population pyramids for Germany and Uganda—countries with among the highest and lowest proportions of elderly—and Mexico, which is somewhere in between, in 1950, 2020, and projections for 2050. The pyramids show the population by age and sex. In 1950, the charts show a pyramid structure: higher numbers of people at the bottom of the age structure, and fewer people at the top. Life expectancy was low, and the number and proportion of those who were elderly in the population were small, particularly in developing nations, such as Uganda and Mexico.

However, 57 years later in 2017, the population distribution in developed nations like Germany had changed. Birthrates were lower; therefore, the pyramid shape has largely disappeared. There is a noticeable "bulge" in the **baby-boom generation** (those born after World War II), who by 2020 were in their fifties and sixties. Yet, looking at Uganda, the pyramid in 2020 looks strikingly like that in 1950. There are many births, and few elderly. Mexico is in between these two extremes. Mexico's population distribution still looks like a pyramid with youth outnumbering elderly, but the gap has begun to shrink.

In another 30 years, projecting out to 2050, patterns are expected to shift as birthrates continue to decline and life expectancy increases. In Germany, the 80 and over group is the largest cohort, far exceeding the number of young children. Mexico's population also ceases to be shaped as a pyramid. Changes can be seen in Uganda as well, although certainly not as dramatic as the other two countries. Births in Uganda are expected to lower somewhat, and more people are living longer (United Nations, Department of Economic and Social Affairs, Population Division, 2017).

9.2.3 Aging and Modernization

Research on nomadic societies has found that, in some situations, especially in times of scarcity or when they impeded the group's mobility, elderly persons were often badly mistreated and even encouraged to die (Hooyman, Kawamoto, and Kiyak, 2015). Explorers and anthropologists have also cited instances of mistreatment in some tribal societies. But in many settled agrarian societies, the status of adults actually increases with age. In many African and Asian nations, for example, decisions about land tenure, kinship, and ceremonial affairs are the province of those who are elderly. In the United States and most Western countries, the productive and cultural roles of those who are aged have been weakened by industrialization and by the migration of family members to cities. In this sense, the problems of those who are aged are part of the larger complex of social changes known as **modernization**, which typically describes three characteristics: (1) the transformation of societies to urbanized and industrialized ways of life based on scientific technologies, (2) individualized rather than communal or collective roles, and (3) a cosmopolitan outlook that values efficiency and progress. Thus, many problems faced by elderly persons in the United States today are social problems that arise from the nature of modern Western society.

Modernization produces far-reaching changes in societies, but clearly, the terms *modernization* and *progress* are not equivalent. With modernization come new social problems and sometimes, new solutions. Modernization is usually associated with increasing length of life, but longer life is a positive change only when the quality of

demographic transition

The process in which a society moves from a situation of high fertility rates and low life expectancy to one of low fertility rates and high life expectancy.

baby-boom generation

The large number of people who were born between the mid-1940s and the early 1960s who are now reaching retirement age.

modernization

Contains three characteristics: (1) the transformation of societies to urbanized and industrialized ways of life based on scientific technologies, (2) individualized rather than communal or collective roles, and (3) a cosmopolitan outlook that values efficiency and progress.

Figure 9–1 Distribution (Percentage) of Population by Sex and Age Group in Germany, Mexico, and Uganda, in 1950, 2020, and 2050

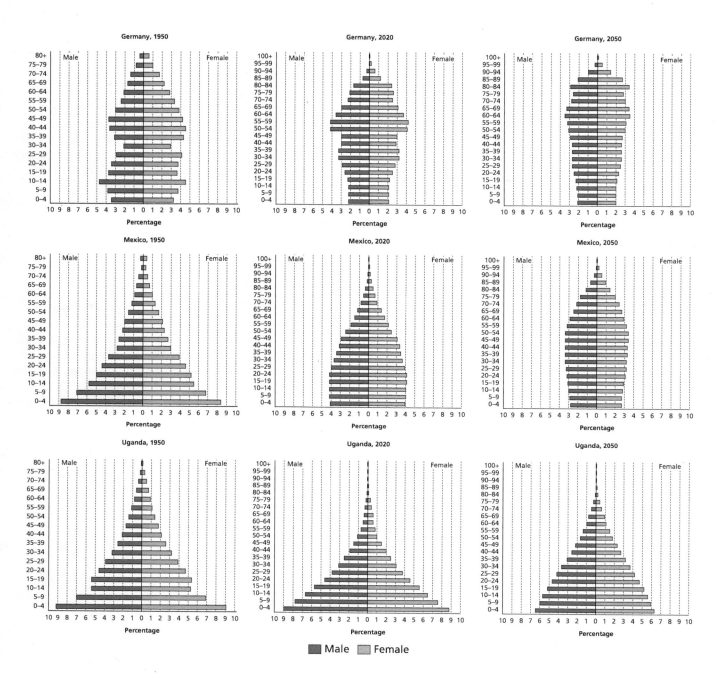

Male Female

SOURCE: United Nations, 2017. World Population Prospects: The 2017 Revision.

life is also enhanced. For many people, however, as the life span increases, so do the pain and suffering associated with old age. As the population of people who were elderly increased, modern societies across the globe began to deal with poverty and illness among their elderly citizens. Pension plans, Social Security, and health care systems were developed to address their needs.

From the earliest periods of human prehistory (before written evidence of human civilization appeared) to the present, the average life expectancy has increased by many decades. In prehistoric times, a person could expect to live into his or her early forties; now, life expectancy is over 80 years in many countries. Great surges in life expectancy occurred with the transition from hunting-and-gathering to agrarian societies, with the development of modern techniques of sanitation and water supply, and with the discovery of the causes of diseases and of antibiotics and techniques for preventing many major illnesses. In the past 20 or 30 years, however, the rate of increase in life expectancy has decelerated. There are biological limits to how long humans can live, and although there may be small shifts in life expectancy in the future, we cannot expect advances at the same rate as in the past indefinitely.

We can expect, however, that the number of older people who are alive but unwell will increase. As more people live longer, the proportion with major medical problems increases, as does the need for costly health care. Although most people wish to live longer lives, the negative side is that many may experience pain and suffering. Thus, society faces an increased need to improve the quality of life of and to find ways to care for a growing number of elderly people who are frail and ill.

The Elderly Population in the United States

9.3 **Discuss the growth in the elderly population in the United States and the consequences of this growth.**

The number of elderly people in the United States is growing rapidly, which is bound to shape our culture, family relationships, and political and economic systems. This next section examines the growth of the elderly population, the consequences of this growth, and some of the challenges that elderly people may face.

9.3.1 Who Are Included in the Elderly Population?

Only a century ago, people did not live very long, even in the United States. Many younger Americans probably spent long portions of their lives rarely seeing a person who was elderly.

More recently, the elderly population in the United States has been increasing almost four times as fast as the population as a whole, and seniors now constitute one of every seven Americans (Administration on Aging, 2017). Today, there are over 50 million people age 65 and older in the United States, and as you can see in Figure 9–2, the numbers are quickly rising. By 2040 there are likely to be another 25–30 million elders, and by 2060 the number could be about 98 million. Much of the growth between 2020 and 2060 in the elderly cohort will occur

The number of elderly people in the United States is strong and growing rapidly. Today there are 50 million people who are age 65 and over, but that number could jump to 98 million by 2060.

John Birdsall/Alamy Stock Photo

Figure 9–2 Number of Persons 65+, 1900–2060, United States (in Millions)

SOURCE: Administration on Aging. 2017. "A Profile of Older Americans: 2017." Retrieved 23 March 2018 (www.aoa.acl.gov/Aging_Statistics/Profile/2016/docs/2016_Profile.pdf).

as the baby-boom generation ages. And like the rest of the world, Americans will see the number of the oldest-old and centenarians increase.

However, not all groups are equally likely to reach old age. Minorities are under-represented in the aging population, in part due to their lower life expectancy. For example, a white girl born today can anticipate living an average of 81 years, 4 years longer than a black girl.

Two-thirds of the elderly live in urban areas, many in central cities. For them, problems of aging are complicated by problems of the urban environment: crime, decaying neighborhoods, the shortage of affordable housing, and congestion. Yet, although most elderly people live in urban areas, they also represent the highest proportion of the population of small towns. This phenomenon is a result of the patterns of migration that have occurred since World War II, when many people moved from farms to small towns. Many of those people are now elderly. In turn, their children have relocated from these small towns to suburbs or cities.

The resulting migration has led to varied concentrations of elderly and younger people in different parts of the nation. Map 9–2 shows the distribution of elderly people throughout the United States. As you can see, certain states such as Kansas, Nebraska, and Florida contain large proportions of elderly people, while other states such as Utah, Illinois, or Georgia have a more youthful population. In counties with high proportions of elderly residents, there is a need for creative entrepreneurs who are willing to help their elderly neighbors remain independent as long as possible.

Yet, not all elderly people have stayed put in small towns. Another important pattern of migration is the movement of retired people to the West and South. As people age, some move to communities where the climate is warmer and an infrastructure of services and institutions (elder-care residential developments, hospitals, and nursing care facilities) exists. In some parts of the United States, such as south Florida and parts of Arizona and southern California, they have become a large group and exert considerable political influence.

Map 9–2 Map of the United States by County: Distribution of Elderly Persons

Legend

- Less than 12.4%
- 12.4 to 14.3%
- 14.4 to 17.7%
- More than 17.8%

SOURCE: U.S. Census Bureau, Census 2010 Summary Fig. 1.

9.3.2 Consequences of the Growth in the Elderly Population

People who were born in the 1940s and early 1950s, the beginning of the baby boom, are now retirement age. As they grow old, physically and socially, their large numbers exert major influences on our society. Among these influences is the likelihood of increased conflict between the generations over scarce public resources. For every federal dollar spent on children, seven dollars are spent on the elderly (Klein, 2013). AARP (formerly called the American Association for Retired Persons) has a very active and well-funded lobbying group, and they spend considerable resources on assuring that the needs and interests of elderly people are well represented in Congress. Is there a parallel organization with similar clout for other age groups? Not really. In these lean times, should the federal government fund programs such as Medicare for elderly people, or should they fund programs such as Medicaid for children (Quadagno, 2002)? As can be seen from their turnout at elections, the elderly population is a political force to be reckoned with. People over age 65 vote at higher rates than does the total voting-age population. Thus, as the population grows older, political leaders will be unable to ignore the power wielded by elderly people at the ballot box.

Another consequence of our changing demographics is the changing cultural attitudes toward youth and old age. For example, think about fashion. I tell my college students that they can thank baby boomers for such things as designer eyewear, spandex in jeans, and comfortable "everyday" walking shoes. These were not readily available before baby boomers made them fashionable. Instead, people wore unattractive glasses ("boys never make passes at girls who wear glasses" was a classic taunt); girls and women wore male Levi denim jeans with unflattering fits; and shoes were not designed for the athleticism of females. But, the large numbers of baby boomers who now need glasses, have expanding waistlines, and have bunions on their feet from poor fitting uncomfortable shoes have demanded change, and the fashion industry listened. The point is that elderly people exert an increasing influence over social policy and popular culture in large part because of their size in the population.

9.3.3 Ageism

Elderly people are growing in numbers and are making their voices heard. Yet, at the same time, many prevalent attitudes in modern society contribute to ageism. Western cultures tend to value youth, associating it with vitality and beauty. This theme is reflected throughout the culture, even in greeting cards that mock older people (Ellis and Morrison, 2005):

- *60?! Don't worry—we're still just kids ... trapped inside the bodies of old people.*
- *There's a reason "sixty" and "sexy" sound alike! The hearing is starting to go.*
- *60 is when you start asking yourself life's big questions. Like "why did I come into this room? I knew a minute ago ..."*[1]

One of these ageist attitudes is the inordinate value placed on youthful looks, especially for women. Older adults do not meet the standards of youthful beauty (Barrett and Toothman, 2017; Clarke, 2017).

Over 1.6 million people age 55 and over had Botox injections in 2016 to ease the wrinkle lines in their faces. Cosmetic surgery is at an all-time high as many older women opt for facelifts or other ways to look younger. As shown in Table 9–2, in 2016

What Do You Think?

We have listed several trends that baby boomers are responsible for, including stretch jeans, designer eyewear, and comfy shoes. Can you think of any others? Are all the trends positive, or are any negative?

---

[1]Ellis, S. R., & Morrison, T. G. (2005). "Stereotypes of Ageing: Messages Promoted by Age-Specific Paper Birthday Cards Available in Canada." Baywood Publishing Company, Inc.

Table 9–2 Surgical Cosmetic Procedures for Persons Age 55 and Over in the United States in 2016

	Number	Share of Total Surgeries
Eyelid Surgery	101,251	48%
Facelift	85,500	65%
Dermabrasion	35,813	41%
Liposuction	24,112	10%

SOURCE: Data from American Society of Plastic Surgeons. 2017. "2016 Plastic Surgery Statistics Report."

alone there were over 100,000 eyelid surgeries, 85,000 facelifts, 35,000 dermabrasions, and 24,000 liposuction surgeries done on people age 55 or older. These procedures cost thousands of dollars and are not without risk, but the quest for a youthful appearance apparently outweighs the cost and risk for many. Ageism as a social problem is also confounded with sexism, the focus of Chapter 8. Feminist social scientists ask, with reason, whether ageism would be the problem it is in American society if men outlived women instead of the reverse (Friedan, 1993).

The mass media play a part in promoting ageism. Just as women and minority groups must contend with negative images in the media, so must older people. Television often portrays the elderly as weak in both body and mind, and as a burden on their relatives—or else as unnaturally wise or kindhearted. Direct-to-consumer advertising on television leaves the impression that all people who are elderly suffer from sexual dysfunction, heartburn, constipation, and arthritis. Given the growth in the elderly population, one would think that images of the elderly would become more positive, but research finds that images are actually becoming more negative (Levy, 2017). Because ageism is so deeply rooted in the social and psychological fabric of our culture, it is extremely difficult to eliminate.

The difficulties of those who are old in modern societies are reflected in the much higher-than-average suicide rate in the elderly population (American Foundation for Suicide Prevention, 2018; CDC, February 5, 2018). Overall, about 13.4 people of every 100,000 kill themselves in a given year, but among the elderly age 85 and over, that figure rises to about 19 people per 100,000 adults in that age group. The suicide rate for persons age 75 to 84 is only slightly less, at about 18.2 per 100,000. Although declining health, loss of status, and reduced income play a part in suicides by the elderly, a lack of relationships with family, friends, and coworkers seems to exert the most consistent influence (Hooyman and Kiyak, 2011). An analysis of suicides by elderly people over a period of nine years in Pinellas County, Florida, indicated that widowed males were more likely to commit suicide than any other group of old people. Elderly women were more likely to have extended family ties, friends, and club memberships that provided social restraints against suicide. Elderly men who enjoyed these kinds of contact were less likely to commit suicide. This finding mirrors the classic finding by Émile Durkheim (1897/1951), one of sociology's founders, that people of any age who lack social attachments are more likely to commit suicide than are people with active social lives among family and friends.

Dimensions of the Aging Process

9.4 **Contrast the physiological, psychological, and social and cultural aspects of aging.**

There are different ways to think about the aging process, including physiological, psychological, and social/cultural aspects. These perspectives on aging are discussed in the following sections.

What Do You Think?

When do you think a person becomes *old*? Is there a specific number that you can cite?

9.4.1 Physiological Aspects of Aging

CHRONOLOGICAL AGING Chronological aging, the simple accumulation of years, is an automatic process. You may have observed, however, that not everyone seems to age at the same rate. Some people look and act middle-aged while still in their twenties, whereas some 60-year-olds radiate the vitality and health that are usually associated with youth. The actual age associated with being "old" has shifted in recent years. As the saying goes, "Sixty-five is the new fifty."

PRIMARY AND SECONDARY AGING There are two categories in the aging process: (1) primary aging, the result of molecular and cellular changes, and (2) secondary aging, which is an accelerated version of normal aging (Whitbourne, 2005) that is caused by environmental factors such as lack of exercise, stress, trauma, poor diet, disease, and even sun exposure.

The effects of primary aging are seen in the characteristics that we associate with advancing years, including gray hair, balding, wrinkles, and increased susceptibility to disease. As the body ages, its systems degenerate. The brain, for example, loses thousands of cells daily from birth onward. Some of the body's organs such as the skin can regenerate their cells, although they do so less effectively with each passing year. Others such as the kidneys lack regenerative powers and eventually wear out. More significant, however, is a general decline in the body's immune defenses, which fight off infections such as pneumonia. As a result, elderly people often die of diseases that would not usually be fatal to younger people (Quadagno, 2002).

Aging is a gradual process; not all the body's systems age at the same rate. The process of decline usually starts relatively early in life. By the mid-twenties, the skin begins to lose its elasticity and starts to dry out and wrinkle; by 30, the muscles have begun to shrink and decrease in strength. As time passes, the capacity of the lungs is reduced, and less and less air is drawn into the body; circulation slows, and the blood supply decreases; bones become brittle and thin; hormonal activity ebbs; and reflexes become slower. This is a natural process. Aging is not a disease, but it does increase susceptibility to disease.

Some researchers are convinced that each of us carries a personal "timetable" for aging within our cells, a timetable controlled by our genes. Others believe that secondary aging factors are also involved. The role of stress is particularly important. One of the most salient age-related changes is the decline in homeostatic capacity—the ability to tolerate stress. This type of decline makes older people more susceptible to stress, and it takes them longer to return to normal after being exposed to a stressful situation.

The reduced capacity to cope with stress is a result of primary aging, but stress itself is an agent of secondary aging. Together, stress and the declining capacity to cope with it may be responsible for many illnesses that plague elderly people. Older people are confronted by numerous stress-producing situations, including widowhood, the

Aging is a gradual process that begins from the day we are born. It happens so slowly that most people almost do not notice it—until they "suddenly" realize that they are old!

Gldcreations/Fotolia

death of friends and family members, and loss of status and productivity. Illnesses such as leukemia, cancer, and heart disease often strike in the wake of stress-producing life changes.

9.4.2 Psychological Dimensions of Aging

The aging process produces not only physical effects but also psychological ones. Self-concept and status are particularly important as aging occurs. One theory observes older people living in a shrinking social environment. Their world grows smaller and smaller as they leave work, as their friends and relatives die, and as their mobility decreases; at the same time, their social status changes and they become less influential.

New roles always require some adjustment, but this adjustment is complicated for the elderly because their new roles are poorly defined; there are few role models or reference groups on which they can pattern their behavior. In our society the labels applied to those who are old are often negative because they are based on an ethic that equates personal worth with economic productivity. However, as the cohort of baby boomers begins to age, their large numbers are commanding changes in the way the elderly view themselves, the way others see them, and the way society responds to them. For example, there has been a tremendous growth of housing communities, senior centers, and social groups that emphasize friendship, fun, and support. Rather than a shrinking world, many look forward to retirement as a new chapter in life, one that can be exciting and full of promise and new experiences.

9.4.3 Social and Cultural Dimensions of Aging: Aged People as a Minority Group

Social gerontologists frequently refer to those who are aged as a minority group, pointing out that the elderly cohort exhibits many characteristics of such groups, as described in Chapter 7. Like members of racial and ethnic minorities, elderly people can be victims of prejudice, stereotyping, and discrimination. However, some social scientists argue that, although elderly people share many characteristics of minorities, they are not a true minority group. Unlike traditional minority groups—such as blacks, Native Americans, and Jews—those who are elderly do not exist as an independent subgroup; everyone has the potential to become old. Some suggest that it would be more accurate to describe the elderly cohort as a "quasi-minority," reflecting their unique position in our society (Quadagno, 2002).

What Do You Think?

How do television and movies portray those who are elderly? Are there differences in the ways that older men and older women are portrayed in the media?

The potential power of this quasi-minority is enormous. They are more politically active than other age groups. For example, 71 percent of persons who are 65 and over voted in the 2016 Presidential election, as compared to only 49 percent of those persons under age 30 (File, May 19, 2017). Likewise, many older persons remain active in voluntary associations well into their eighties. They play a much larger role in organizational life than many younger people assumed (Riley and Riley, 2000).

The Economics of Aging

9.5 Analyze the economics of aging.

Two contrasting images emerge in discussions of the economic conditions and well-being of the elderly. One projects an image of retired tycoons living in mansions on the Florida coast. In stark contrast, the other image projects elders as poor, alone, living in ramshackle housing, and eating dog food to stay alive. Although some elderly people fit each of these stereotypes, the reality is that most are somewhere in the middle of these two extremes.

9.5.1 Income and Assets: How Those Who Are Elderly Fare

The median household income of a person age 65 or older in the United States is about $40,000, which is well above the poverty line, according to Census Bureau data (Semega, Fontenot, and Kollar, 2017). This income comes from several sources (Brandon, 2016).

- *Social Security:* Almost all retirees have Social Security payments, and more than half of retirees depend on them for at least half of their income. One-quarter of retirees depend on a Social Security check for 90 percent of their income.
- *Retirement Benefits:* Pensions, 401(k)s, and other workplace retirement plans provide income to about 45 percent of retirees. This provides about 21 percent of aggregate income for retirees.
- *Continued Work:* Nearly one-third of retirees receive income from employment, and this is an increasing component of financial security in retirement. However, it is primarily young retirees who continue working in some capacity, but again, even older persons are increasingly dependent upon earned income.
- *Asset Income:* The proportion of retirement income that is generated by assets such as interest, dividends, royalties, and real estate has dropped over the years, and now constitutes only about 10 percent of retirement income.

Many Americans are (or should be) concerned about having sufficient income during retirement. About one-third of the workforce has no savings set aside specifically for retirement, and that figure is even higher (37%) among persons aged 45 to 54 who should already have substantial savings (Bloom, 2017). In addition, many Americans cannot necessarily rely on a pension. Employers are moving away from offering pension plans that provide periodic payments over the life of the retiree and his or her spouse. In the early 1990s, about 35 percent of private industry employees had a traditional pension plan from their employer, but today it is down to only 18 percent, and most of these employees work for very large firms or for the government. Instead, employers are either dropping retirement benefits altogether, or moving towards 401(k) plans, which let workers save and invest a piece of their paycheck before taxes are taken out. Employers often chip in money to the plan as well. Taxes aren't paid until the money is withdrawn from the account, which is a nice benefit for workers. However, this type of plan can be risky because investments are never guaranteed, and the stock market can be volatile.

The result is that many elderly people rely primarily, or even exclusively, on Social Security, but this program was never intended to be the major or sole source of retirement income (Waid, 2014). Nearly half of older Americans rely on Social Security for at least 50 percent of their family income, and nearly one elder in four relies on it for at least 90 percent. As a result, many of them are hovering just barely above the poverty line. The Census Bureau may not count them as poor, but for all practical purposes, their lives are quite impoverished.

What Do You Think?

What would a conflict theorist have to say about why so many older people are nearly poor?

9.5.2 Economic Discrimination

With limited pensions and little retirement savings, older people are putting off the age at which they retire. At the same time, older workers can be targets of job discrimination. The U.S. Equal Employment Opportunity Commission received 18,376 complaints of age-based discrimination in 2017 (U.S. Equal Employment Opportunity Commission, 2018).

One method of age discrimination at work is "forced" retirement, which is a life-altering experience with social, economic, and emotional effects. The practice of forced, or mandatory, retirement at a certain age is against the law in most industries (airline pilots, as one example, however, are not covered by this law). Nevertheless, some companies try to circumvent the law and find ways to oust older workers because it gives companies a tool for cutting labor costs. In a tight economy, a company may try to retire its older employees, who earn higher salaries, and replace them with younger workers who usually are paid less.

Older workers may also encounter job discrimination when seeking new employment. The 1967 Age Discrimination in Employment Act is designed to protect workers over the age of forty. Employers can no longer advertise for applicants under a certain age, but a phrase such as "one to three years' experience" accomplishes the same goal of targeting younger workers. When they do obtain interviews, older workers may be rejected as "overqualified," a euphemism for "too old." For these reasons, older unemployed workers remain jobless longer than younger ones.

9.5.3 Multiple Jeopardy

Overall, elderly persons are less likely than any other age group to live in poverty, largely because of income programs such as Social Security (Semega, Fontenot, and Kollar, 2017). Nonetheless, certain groups of elderly persons are vulnerable to becoming impoverished. To be old, female, and black (or Hispanic or Native American) in American society is to experience **multiple jeopardy**—to face more hardships than one would face if one were in just one or two of these categories. The cumulative disadvantages minorities and women have experienced throughout their lives put them at greater risk to live in poverty. For example, because older women's salaries are lower than those of men, their pensions and Social Security benefits are also lower. The Social Security system gives no credit for homemaking, the principal occupation of most women until recent decades. Many employed older women suffer the double burdens of age and sex discrimination. Factor in the disadvantages experienced by most minority groups, and the basis for multiple jeopardy becomes clear.

multiple jeopardy

Having multiple minority statuses that include being old, female, and black (or Hispanic or Native American), which may cause more hardships than a person would face if he or she were in just one or two of these categories.

9.5.4 Retirement

Retirement is a fairly recent concept. Before the advent of Social Security and pension plans, few workers could afford to stop working. As a result, people worked well into old age, perhaps modifying the nature of their work to match their diminished strength.

This is the situation in many less developed countries today. Four conditions must be met for significant numbers of elderly people to be able to withdraw from the labor force (Morgan and Kunkel, 1998):

- A society must produce an economic surplus that is large enough to support its nonemployed members.
- There must be a mechanism in place to divert some of that surplus to the nonemployed members, such as through a pension or government transfer program.
- Nonemployed members should be viewed positively by the rest of society, and their activities or leisure must be seen as legitimate.
- The nonemployed members must have accumulated an acceptable number of years of productivity to warrant support by the other members of society.[2]

These three retired friends have a standing weekly appointment at the beauty shop and then have a lively lunch together. Their leisurely retirement is the envy of people in many parts of the world where stopping work is simply not an option.

---

[2]Morgan, L. & Kunkel, S. (1998) *Aging: The Social Context.* Thousand Oaks, CA: Pine Forge Press.

These conditions materialized in the United States after industrialization during the nineteenth and twentieth centuries. However, today, these four conditions are under threat. The cost of caring for the elderly population—Social Security, health care programs, and private retirement plans—is consuming a greater share of our country's income. Work provides us with more than an income. It is also an important part of our identity. People commonly say, "I *am* a high school teacher," "I *am* a dentist," "I *am* a police officer," as though they *are* the occupation. Retirement is an important event because it not only reduces income but also alters a major identity.

Still, many people eagerly await this change and see retirement as a legitimate, earned privilege. They look forward to extended time with friends and family and having the opportunity to pursue other hobbies and interests. The average age at retirement fell from 69 years in 1950 to 59 years in 2002 but has since risen to age 62. Additionally, the age at which younger people now *expect* to retire is also on the rise, as shown in Figure 9–3 (Riffkin, 2014; Transamerica Center for Retirement Studies, December, 2015).

The rise in the age of retirement is likely due to several factors:

- *Social Security.* Changes to Social Security have created many incentives to continue working and have made work more attractive relative to retirement. For example, the delayed retirement credit, which increases benefits for each year that claiming is delayed between the full retirement age and age 70, has improved incentives to keep working.
- *Improved health and longevity.* Life expectancy for men at 65 has increased about 3.5 years since 1980, and much of the evidence suggests that people are also healthier. The correlation between health and labor force activity is very strong.
- *Pension type.* The shift from a regular pension to 401(k) plans eliminated built-in incentives to retire. Studies show that on average, workers covered by 401(k) plans retire a year or two later than similarly situated workers covered by a defined benefit plan.
- *Less physically demanding jobs.* With the shift away from manufacturing, jobs now involve more knowledge-based activities, which put less strain on older bodies.
- *Decline of retiree health insurance.* Combine the decline of employer-provided retiree health insurance with the rise in health care costs, and workers have a strong

---

Figure 9–3 Trends in Actual and Expected Age at Retirement, 2002–2015 (Age In Years)

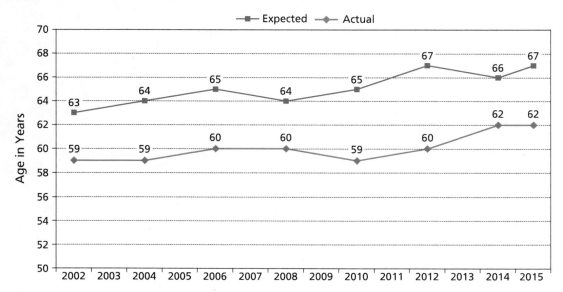

SOURCE: Riffkin, R. 2014. "Average U.S. Retirement Age Rises to 62." Gallup. 28 April. Retrieved 23 October 2014 (www.gallup.com/poll/168707/average-retirement-age-rises.aspx).; Transamerica Center for Retirement Studies. 2015. "The Current State of Retirement: Pre-Retiree Expectations and Retiree Benefits." TCRS 1300-1215. December.

incentive to keep working and maintain their employer's health coverage until they qualify for Medicare at 65.

- *Joint decision making.* More women are working; wives on average are three years younger than their husbands; and husbands and wives usually like to coordinate their retirement.
- *The recession of the 2000s and poor economy.* Some elders sustained significant losses to their retirement funds, lost their jobs, or were forced to take pay cuts during the recession, and now work longer to make up the difference.

We also see that many older workers are now retiring in stages rather than all at once. The recent recession and low interest rates on retirement savings forced many older people to go back to work part-time. Fewer Americans are confident that they will have the necessary money needed for retirement (Employment Benefit Research Institute, 2018).

From the point of view of society overall, large-scale retirement creates social problems because those who are no longer in the labor force are dependent on the wealth produced by those who are still working. Over the next 25 years, the ratio of retirement-age people to working-age adults will increase considerably around the world. In fact, the United States will fare rather better than nations like Japan, Austria, and Germany, where the number of retirees may severely overstretch the ability of the working population to produce adequate surpluses. But even in the United States, the problem of increasing dependency ratios poses a threat to the Social Security and Medicare systems, a problem you will be able to consider further in the social policy section of this chapter.

Family Relationships

9.6 **Describe the unique issues that families with older members may face.**

Having a partner through marriage or cohabitation is an important buffer against loneliness and isolation in old age (Wright and Brown, 2017). Most married older couples have a relationship that has endured many years. Newspapers are full of stories of couples celebrating their fiftieth or sixtieth wedding anniversaries. Together, the couple has faced life and its transitions: the birth of a child, job opportunities, disappointments, the effort to balance work and family, the departure of children from home, and their living as just a couple once again.

Almost three-quarters of men age 65–74 are married, as are more than half of women. However, as people age, the likelihood of being married begins to decline, particularly for women (U.S. Census Bureau, April 6, 2017). Among those age 85 and over, nearly two-thirds of men remain married, compared to only 19 percent of women, as shown in Figure 9–4.

As we age, the likelihood of being married decreases, especially for women, while the likelihood of being widowed increases.

A common misperception about the elderly is that they are no longer sexually active. In the classroom, any discussion of elders' sexuality is largely met with snickers or looks of disbelief. In response to that, I ask students, "Well, at what age do you plan to give up sex?" Then, I hear gasps.

Sexuality remains an essential element of the lives of the elderly (Forbes, Eaton, and Krueger, 2017; Gillespie, 2017; Karraker and DeLamater, 2013). A large majority of elders have a positive view of sexual relationships, and if married or partnered, it's quite likely that they are still sexually active. Although about 70 percent of men over age 70 have some degree of erectile dysfunction (Capogrosso et al., 2013), the availability of Viagra can help a man maintain an erection and be able to experience a full range of sexual intimacy. There has been some concern that drugs such as Viagra may contribute to an increase in HIV among older persons, reported in an earlier feature box (Hillman, 2008; Lin et al., 2017; Paniagua, 1999).

Figure 9–4 Percent of Older Men and Women Who Are Married or Widowed, By Age, 2016

SOURCE: U.S. Census Bureau. "America's Families and Living Arrangements: 2017." 6 April. Retrieved 12 February 2018 (www.census.gov/data/tables/2016/demo/families/cps-2016.html).

AARP conducted a comprehensive survey about sexuality in midlife and beyond, based on a sample of over 1,600 older adults (Fisher, 2010). About half of men and women aged 60–69 reported engaging in sexual touching or caressing at least once per week, and about a quarter reportedly engaged in sexual intercourse at least weekly. Undoubtedly, these numbers would be even higher if we only included men who were married or partnered. Those who do experience a significant decline in sexual activity because of widowhood, or their own or their partner's poor health, often find their situation depressing or frustrating. Most older persons see sexual activity as a critical part of a good relationship.

9.6.1 Lesbian, Gay, Bisexual, and Transgender Couples

When most people think of a person who is lesbian, gay, bisexual, or transgender (LGBT), chances are they do not envision a senior citizen. Nonetheless, roughly 1.5 million persons who are elderly identify as lesbian, gay, bisexual, or transgender (LGBT), and that number may double by 2030 (Sage, 2017). Although they face many of the same issues that other elders face, such as health problems or the need for reliable transportation or housing assistance, they also have many unique concerns (Choi and Meyer, 2016; Fredriksen-Goldsen, Bryan, Jen, Goldsen, Kim, and Muraco, 2017; Fredriksen-Goldsen, 2018).

- LGBT elders are more likely than heterosexual elders to live alone, increasing the chance of loneliness or isolation. LGBT older adults have fewer options for informal care when they need assistance.
- Older gay men are aging in a context sharply shaped by HIV/AIDS. Among LGBT older adults, HIV-positive elders have worse overall mental and physical health, disability, and poorer health outcomes, and a higher likelihood of experiencing stressors as well as barriers to care, than HIV-negative elders.
- LGBT older adults have experienced and continue to experience discrimination due to their sexual orientation and gender identity. Studies find LGBT older adults experienced high rates of lifetime discrimination and physical and verbal abuse in relation to their sexual and gender minority identity. One study found that LGBT

seniors searching for retirement homes experienced unfavorable differential treatment (less housing availability, higher pricing, etc.) compared to non-LGBT seniors.

- LGBT older adults have worse mental and physical health compared to heterosexual older adults. LGBT older adults have higher risks of mental health issues, disability, and higher rates of disease and physical limitation than their heterosexual counterparts.
- Likewise, transgender older adults have significantly higher risk of poor health, disability, depressive symptoms, and stress, as compared with those who are not transgender. Many of these risks are associated with experiences of victimization and stigma.

A study conducted with over 2,400 LGBT older adults age 50 and over reviewed their health status and identified both the risk factors contributing to poorer health and the protective factors to health outcomes. The findings showed that among those in the study group, lifetime victimization, internalized stigma, financial barriers, obesity, and limited physical activity contribute to poor general health, disability, and depression. In contrast, social support and a social network of adequate size served as protective factors, decreasing the odds of poor health, disability, and depression. In other words, those LGBT elders who had strong and extensive support systems were doing better than those without (Fredriksen-Goldsen et al., 2017).

Only recently have same-sex couples been allowed to marry in all states. Until this change, many state and federal programs and laws treated same-sex couples differently from married heterosexual couples. For example, tax laws and other regulations of 401(k)s and pensions discriminated against same-sex partners, costing the surviving partner in a same-sex relationship tens of thousands of dollars a year, and possibly more than $1 million over a lifetime. For example, if a person with a 401(k) pension plan dies, the money rolls over to a *legal spouse* without any tax penalty. However, since gays and lesbians could not legally marry in most states, the surviving partner would have to pay a 20 percent federal tax.

Even basic rights such as hospital visitation or the right to die in the same nursing home as one's partner are regularly denied to unmarried couples. These policies have social, economic, and health consequences for gay and lesbian elders (Human Rights Campaign, 2018). They may hide their sexual orientation from their health care and social service providers out of fear, further compromising their ability to get needed care and assistance. Many gay and lesbian seniors remain hidden, reinforcing isolation and forgoing services they may truly need.

9.6.2 Widowhood

The death of a spouse or partner stands as one of life's most stressful events (Holmes and Rahe, 1967). It often means the loss of a companion and friend, perhaps the loss of income, and the ending of a familiar way of life. Widowhood can occur at any point in the life cycle, but because it is most likely to occur among older people, research tends to focus on that population.

Fifteen million persons are classified as widowed in the United States, and over three-quarters of them are women (U.S. Census Bureau, April 6, 2017). The number of people who have *experienced* widowhood, however, is much larger than that because some have remarried.

Women are more likely to be widowed than are men for three primary reasons. First, mortality rates among females are lower than for males; therefore, they live to older ages. The life expectancy of females at age 65 exceeds that of males of that age by nearly 7 years. Second, wives are typically 2 to 3 years younger than their husbands and consequently have a greater chance of outliving them. Third, widowed women are less likely to remarry than are widowed men. There is a lack of eligible men

Family Experiences of Older People

Family relationships continue into old age and they can grow in size and complexity. This slideshow introduces you to some of the many family experiences of older people.

Anabe and Sani have been married for 58 years. Their love, respect, and romance have never gone out of their relationship, despite the challenges of raising five children.

Rita and Kay have been married for 4 years; however, if you were to ask them when they married, they would tell you it was 32 years ago when they became college sweethearts. State and federal law prohibited them from legally marrying until recently.

Most grandparents report that their relationships with their grandchildren are meaningful and fun. Grandfathers are now more likely to recognize the importance of having close emotional involvement with young children and have opportunities to participate in ways that seemed unavailable to them when they were fathers.

Many older people do not have a spouse, or they may not live near their adult children or grandchildren. Their friends may become "fictive kin." This group of friends meet twice a week to play music at the Senior Center, and they enjoy the camaraderie and friendship that have developed over the years.

Grandparents take on parent-like roles in many parts of the world. This grandmother lives with her son, daughter-in-law, and grandson. Both parents work and lead busy lives, and therefore she gladly considers herself to be her grandson's primary caregiver.

Critical Thinking

How do you think that family relationships in old age differ across social class and race/ethnicity? What might account for any differences?

because cultural norms encourage older men to date and marry younger women, but not the reverse.

You may have heard others suggest that an elderly person often dies soon after his or her spouse dies. "He just gave up ..."; "She died of sadness ..."; "He saw no reason to go on after Rose died...." But is there any truth to this so-called "widow effect"; that is, is there really an increased probability of death among new widows and widowers? Two Harvard sociology professors decided to answer this question by following nearly 4,500 U.S. couples age 67 and older for five years (Elwert and Christakis, 2006). They found some truth to the "widow effect"; the likelihood of death does increase slightly after a spouse dies. The effect, however, does not occur equally among racial and ethnic groups. White men were 18 percent more likely to die shortly after their spouses' deaths, as were 16 percent of white women. But among blacks, a spouse's death had no effect on the mortality of the survivor.

Why would widowhood contribute to an early death for whites, but not for blacks? On marrying, blacks and whites appear to receive many of the same health, financial, and socioemotional benefits, such as emotional support, caretaking when ill, and enhanced social support, so what could account for the variations in the "widow effect"? Research shows that blacks are almost twice as likely to live with other relatives (Cohn and Passel, August 11, 2016; Pew Charitable Trusts, March 2, 2016), are more active in religious groups, and when married are less likely to adhere to a traditional gendered division of labor, which may reduce dependence on a spouse. It seems that blacks may somehow manage to extend the benefits of marriage into widowhood and are therefore less likely than whites to die soon after their spouse passes on (Elwert and Christakis, 2006).

9.6.3 Grief and Bereavement

People handle their grief over the death of a loved one in a variety of ways. Some try to remain stoic; others cry out in despair. Some people fear death, whereas others, perhaps because of a strong religious faith, see it as part of a larger "master plan." Those widows and widowers in poor health at the time of widowhood had significantly higher risks of complicated grief and depression (Utz, Caserta, and Lund, 2012).

One of the more well-known perspectives on death and dying is based on the work of Elizabeth Kübler-Ross (1969). Her work with 200 primarily middle-aged cancer patients suggested five somewhat distinct stages that dying people and their loved ones experience. Although some critics say that not everyone experiences these stages, or in any particular order, Kübler-Ross's work is useful nonetheless. The five stages are:

- *Denial*—Many people first refuse to believe that they or a loved one is dying. They may ask for additional medical tests, desire a second or third opinion, or in other ways deny that death is near.
- *Anger*—When coming to grips with the truth, some people become angry. They may project this anger toward friends, family, people who are well, or medical personnel.
- *Bargaining*—The dying person or loved one may try to forestall death by striking a bargain with God.
- *Depression*—Depression may set in when the dying person or his or her loved ones realize that winning the fight against the illness or disease is not possible. Those who are dying may be depressed over the symptoms of their condition (e.g., chronic pain) or effects of their treatment (e.g., hair loss). As they see and plan for their future, the loss they face can feel overwhelming.
- *Acceptance*—Eventually, a patient and/or loved one may come to accept the approaching death. In this stage, each may reflect on their lives together.[3]

---

[3]Kübler-Ross, E. 1969. *On Death and Dying*. New York: Macmillan.

These five stages are highly individualized. No two people pass through them at exactly the same pace, and many people may go back and forth between stages before finally reaching acceptance.

Health and Health Care among the Elderly

9.7 **Identify the health concerns common among the elderly and describe the primary program that pays for their health care.**

Most elderly people report their health as good or excellent. Only about a quarter assess their health as fair or poor. Elderly men and women report only a small difference in health, and the gap has narrowed in recent years. However, older blacks are more likely to describe their health as only fair or poor than are whites or Asian Americans (National Center for Health Statistics, 2017).

9.7.1 Health Problems

dementia

An overall term that describes a wide range of symptoms associated with a decline in memory or other thinking skills severe enough to reduce a person's ability to perform everyday activities.

Despite various improvements in the general way of life, there is no denying that as people age their health declines in several ways. If people live long enough, everyone is likely to lose some of his or her vision and hearing; to develop chronic conditions such as arthritis, heart disease, or diabetes; and to suffer some degree of memory impairment (National Center for Health Statistics, 2017). The health status of older adults is a result of a complex set of factors, including individual factors such as diet, exercise, and heredity, and structural factors such as socioeconomic status, racism, and access to health care. People may need someone to help with many things that they used to do for themselves: cooking, cleaning, home repairs, and perhaps even personal care.

Researchers have measured the degree of physical impairment by using a common set of activities of daily living (ADLs) such as bathing, dressing, eating, getting into and out of bed, walking indoors, and using the toilet. Instrumental activities of daily living (IADLs) include meal preparation, shopping, managing money, and taking medication. By using a common set of measures, gerontologists can track elders' degree of impairment and can make some comparisons across different samples. Millions of elderly people cannot perform ADLs and IADLs. As people age, they may become more disabled.

9.7.2 Severe Memory Loss

Perhaps one of the most difficult disabilities facing some elders, and those who care for them, is severe memory loss, known as dementia. **Dementia** is not a specific disease. It is an overall term that describes a wide range of symptoms associated with a decline in memory or other thinking skills severe enough to reduce a person's ability to perform everyday activities such as (Alzheimer's Association, 2017a):

- the ability to generate coherent speech and understand spoken or written language;
- the ability to recognize or identify objects, assuming intact sensory function;

Despite images to the contrary, most elderly people are in good health and stay active. This man swims for 30 minutes almost daily, as he has done for years. Community centers often have special exercise programs that cater to elderly people.

ysbrandcosijn/Fotolia

- the ability to execute motor activities, assuming intact motor abilities, sensory function, and comprehension of the required task; and
- the ability to think abstractly, make sound judgments, and plan and carry out complex tasks.[4]

Alzheimer's disease is by far the most common form of dementia, affecting over 5 million persons. It is the seventh leading cause of death for people of all ages and the fifth leading cause of death among people age 65 and over (Alzheimer's Association, 2017a). The disease starts subtly; a person may have difficulty remembering names or recent events. It progresses over the course of years, and later symptoms include impaired judgment; disorientation; confusion; behavior changes; lack of recognition of loved ones; and eventually the inability to walk, speak, and even swallow. Alzheimer's is ultimately fatal. Given the changing demographics of our country, and the growing size of the oldest old cohort, Americans will see a large increase in people with Alzheimer's: 10 million baby boomers are expected to eventually develop it.

Alzheimer's disease takes a large toll on the individual, the family, and the community. Annually, about 16 million caregivers provide 18 billion hours of unpaid care valued at over $230 billion (Alzheimer's Association, 2017a). It also takes a toll on our communities. Alzheimer's cost the nation about $260 billion for health care, long-term care, and hospice for people, and the amount is expected to rise to $1.1 trillion by 2050 as the number of Alzheimer's patients continues to grow (Alzheimer's Association, 2017b). Given that the direct and indirect costs of Alzheimer's and other dementias, not to mention the cost in terms of families' heartache and despair, it is no wonder researchers are vigorously pursuing an agenda of prevention, treatment, and cure.

9.7.3 Medicare

Today, most people in developed countries such as the United States do not encounter the infectious diseases such as tuberculosis or measles that used to be deadly, and if they do, they survive them. Instead, people live longer and become more prone to chronic illnesses such as arthritis, which develop over a long period and are often expensive to treat. Thus, the elderly tend to require increasing amounts of costly medical care.

Because elderly people require more medical care than others, and because the cost of medical care was impoverishing many elderly people, the Medicare program was created in 1965. **Medicare** is a federal health insurance program for people age 65 and older (and for younger people receiving Social Security Disability Insurance payments or suffering from a few specified conditions).

Medicare has kept millions of elderly people from impoverishing themselves to pay for their health care costs by making health insurance far more affordable and available. Because it is a universal program (available to virtually all citizens age 65 and over), rather than a program only for low-income people, it carries no stigma. And because virtually all elderly people qualify, administrative costs are significantly lower than other programs that have stringent income requirements.

Medicare, however, has some problems with it. First, Medicare does not provide elders with "free" health care. It covers most hospital costs but only part of physicians' bills, and the charges that are not covered can quickly become an enormous financial burden. Moreover, most nursing home care is not covered, nor are dental care, hearing aids, eyeglasses, and many other important and often used

Medicare

A federal health insurance program for people age 65 and older (and for younger people receiving Social Security Disability Insurance payments or suffering from specified conditions).

---

[4]Alzheimer's Association, 2017a.

Figure 9–5 Ways in Which Medicare Beneficiaries Supplement Their Medicare

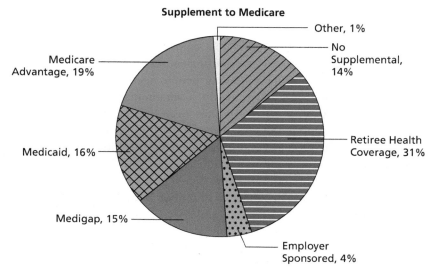

Supplement to Medicare

- Other, 1%
- No Supplemental, 14%
- Medicare Advantage, 19%
- Retiree Health Coverage, 31%
- Medicaid, 16%
- Medigap, 15%
- Employer Sponsored, 4%

SOURCE: Based on McArdle, F., T. Neuman, & J. Huang. 2014. "Overview of Health Benefits for Pre-65 and Medicare-Eligible Retirees." 14 April. Retrieved 26 October 2014 (kff.org/report-section/retiree-health-benefits-at-the-crossroads-overview-of-health-benefits-for-pre-65-and-medicare-eligible-retirees/).

health services. Given high deductibles, co-payments, and payments for things not covered under Medicare, elderly persons spend an average of over $6,000 of their own dollars each year on medical care (Cubanski and Neuman, July 18, 2017). Consequently, most elders have some form of additional insurance, as shown in Figure 9–5, which they often pay for themselves. Only the poorest, about 16 percent, may also qualify for Medicaid, the federal–state health care program designed to serve poor people, regardless of age. Medicaid also covers long-term care, but again, only for those who are poor enough to qualify (McArdle, Neuman, and Huang, 2014).

A second criticism of Medicare is that the health care providers are usually reimbursed by the government at a lower rate than they would be if they were seeing patients with private insurance. Providers complain that reimbursement is too low and cumbersome. They are not required by law to see Medicare patients, and therefore, many providers refuse to do so. Consequently, of those Medicare patients who reported looking for a new primary care physician, 28 percent reported a problem finding one who would see them (MedPAC, 2014).

A third concern of Medicare points to the changing U.S. demographic structure, which has some distressing repercussions for the Medicare program. Medicare is primarily funded through taxes; working people pay taxes today for programs used by those who are elderly today. In the future, as the U.S. population ages, there will be fewer working adults paying taxes relative to the number of elderly people needing Medicare services. There were about 4 workers for each Medicare user in 2001, but there will be only 2.3 workers by 2030 (Heritage Foundation, 2013). This trend coupled with rising health care costs clearly signals that the country faces a serious challenge. The Medicare program cost about $590 billion in 2017 (net of income from premiums), and this cost is estimated to grow to almost $1.2 trillion by 2027 (Cubanski and Neuman, 2017). To deal with this problem, Congress could modify the program in several ways, such as increasing the amount that elders pay by raising deductibles and co-payments, covering fewer services, or even raising the age at which people are eligible for Medicare services, like what has been done with Social

Security. The goal is to keep Medicare solvent well into the future because our society recognizes that the health of seniors is a social concern, not merely an individual problem.

9.7.4 Long-Term Care

As people live longer, and their health deteriorates, many need **long-term care**, which is care for their chronic physical or mental conditions that will likely never go away. How do we care for the growing numbers of elderly people who can no longer care for themselves?

FORMAL CARE Some who are elderly in the United States rely on formal care provided by social service agencies on a paid or volunteer basis. This care could include a variety of types: paid visiting nurses, meals or housecleaning programs, a paid personal attendant, assisted living, or nursing home care.

Assisted-living facilities are a booming business. They vary in scope: Some assisted-living facilities are little more than apartments for seniors with optional food, housekeeping, and entertainment services, and others provide more skilled nursing care. The price varies by geographic location and what services are included, but averages approximately $45,000 per year (Genworth, 2017).

In contrast to assisted living facilities, nursing homes provide the most intensive level of care, at an average cost of about $97,000 per year (Genworth, 2017). They are available for those who cannot be cared for at home because of medical needs and who have likely moved beyond what most assisted-living centers can provide. Few elderly people actually live in nursing homes, although that number rises with age. Most people do not need the intense level of care, cannot afford such care, and would rather be cared for at home.

INFORMAL CARE In contrast to formal care, most elders in the United States rely primarily on informal care, which is unpaid care by someone close to the care recipient, such as a spouse, daughter, daughter-in-law, son, or even a grandchild, friend, or neighbor. These caregivers provide a wide variety of hands-on care, such as cooking, cleaning, bathing, housekeeping, shopping, administering and managing medications, coordinating care with medical providers, and watching over the elderly person to ensure his or her safety and well-being.

Historically, tending to the elderly was the task of daughters or daughters-in-law who were full-time homemakers. As more women work outside the home, they are less available to care for elderly parents and therefore sons or other relatives may chip in. Some of these adult caregivers also have their own children to care for and are therefore described as the **sandwich generation**. Because most adult caregivers are employed, they may make substantial sacrifices at work to accommodate caregiving, including going in work late or leaving early, working fewer hours, taking a leave of absence, turning down a promotion, choosing early retirement, or giving up work completely. Caregivers often spend their own money to provide medicines, groceries, or other supplies to the person they are caring for. Caring for elderly parents or a spouse can be a labor of love, but it's also time-intensive, potentially expensive, and often stressful (Gilhooly, Gilhooly, Sullivan, McIntyre, Wilson, Harding, Woodbridge, and Crutch, 2016; Kim, Dunkle, Lehning, Shen, Feld, and Perone, 2017).

As society continues to age, the United States could benefit from an explicit plan for caring for frail elders. If caregiving is indeed a personal responsibility to be provided by family members, then families should be strengthened by a variety of financial and policy benefits, such as tax credits, paid family leave, free or low-cost senior day care, or respite care. Moreover, although the Family Medical Leave Act allows for 12 weeks of leave from employment to allow a person to care for a sick or disabled

long-term care
Care for chronic physical or mental conditions that will likely never go away.

sandwich generation
Adults who are caring for an aging parent while also caring for their own children under age 18.

What Do You Think?

Look into the future to a time when your parent(s) need long-term care. What will you do? How will this care be provided? Will you rely on formal or informal care, and how will you integrate this care with your own work, family, and leisure?

Vbaleha/Fotolia

Many people no longer want their last living days to be spent in a hospital, hooked up to machines. They would prefer to die at home, which they see as a more dignified way to pass.

hospice

Offers care to a dying person, with the goal of maintaining or improving quality of life; the focus is on caring, not curing.

relative (in qualifying workplaces), the time off is unpaid, which makes it prohibitive for many people.

9.7.5 Death with Dignity

"Death with dignity" has become a popular phrase as people confront the issues of relegating those who are old and those who are terminally ill to institutions and possibly to a life sustained by machines. Often, the use of these technologies prolongs the dying process rather than maintains life.

Although old people have always died, those who are dying have not always been old. Only in recent decades has death occurred mainly among the elderly. Because of this new link between old age and death, the social issues related to death also involve aging. It is becoming increasingly important *how* we die. Dying is not a medical condition; it is a personally experienced, lived condition. And many people are finding that current practices in hospitals and nursing homes offer little possibility of a good and meaningful death.

In contrast, **hospice** offers medical care with a different goal: maintaining or improving quality of life for someone whose illness, disease, or condition is terminal. The focus is on caring, not curing. Each patient's individualized care plan is designed to address the physical, emotional, and spiritual pain that often accompanies terminal illness. Hospice care also offers practical support for the caregiver(s) during the illness and grief support after the death (Hospice Foundation of America, 2014).

Hospices can be located in health facilities made to be as homelike as possible. But increasingly, hospice emphasizes health services at home for those who are dying, including visiting nurses, on-call physicians, and counselors. This kind of service enables many people to live their final days in the familiar surroundings of their own home, surrounded by their loved ones. As reported in Table 9–3, almost half of hospice patients die at home (National Hospice and Palliative Care Organization, 2014). Being at home with one's family seems to provide a greater chance for "death with dignity"; being institutionalized implies loss of control and individuality.

The hospice movement has had an astounding impact on how people actually experience death. Over a third of all deaths in the United States now occur to patients who are in the care of a hospice program, and the total number of patients served either in hospice facilities or hospice home care exceeds 1.5 million.

One of the most unusual episodes in the sociology of old age is the story of Brandeis University professor Morris Schwartz. Much to his surprise, Schwartz became one of the most respected contemporary voices on issues of life and death. And it is all because a former student took the trouble to renew their friendship and to listen to what his former professor had to say, as highlighted in the feature box, *A Closer Look: "Tuesdays with Morrie."*

Table 9–3 Characteristics of Hospice Users

Sex		
	Female	56%
	Male	44%
Age		
	Under 65	17%
	65–74	16%
	75–84	28%
	85+	41%
Race/Ethnicity		
	White	82%
	Black	9%
	Asian/Pacific Islander	3%
	American Indian	0.3%
	Hispanic (either White or Black)	7%
	Multiracial or Other	7%
Location of Death		
	Private Residence	42%
	Nursing Home	17%
	Other Residential Facility	7%
	Hospice Inpatient Facility	27%
	Acute Care Hospital	7%

SOURCE: Data from National Hospice and Palliative Care Organization. 2014. "NHPCO's Hospice Facts and Figures: Hospice Care in America: 2014 Edition." Retrieved 3 March 2014. (www.nhpco.org/sites/default/files/public/Statistics_Research/2014_Facts_Figures.pdf).

A Closer Look

Tuesdays with Morrie

What is it like to spend time with someone who is dying? Newspaper columnist Mitch Albom recounts the time spent with his 78-year-old Sociology professor, Morrie Schwartz, who was dying from amyotrophic lateral sclerosis, otherwise known as ALS.   Albom, a former student of Schwartz, carved out time every Tuesday for several hours to talk to his former professor, and learn from him. He recorded his insights about life and death and compiled them into a book titled *Tuesdays with Morrie*, which became a best seller. It was featured on the *Oprah Winfrey Show*, and a television movie of the story was made. By now the book has reached many millions of people with its message.

Morrie Schwartz had many lessons to teach about confronting death. Chief among them is that there is not always a "happy" ending; death is part of life and must be experienced fully. It is not something to be ashamed of, to be whispered about, as is too often the case. For Schwartz, the end of life is a time to dwell on "love, responsibility, spirituality, awareness."[5] To do so,

[5]Albom, M. (1997) *Tuesdays with Morrie: An Old Man, A Young Man and Life's Greatest Lesson.* New York: Doubleday.

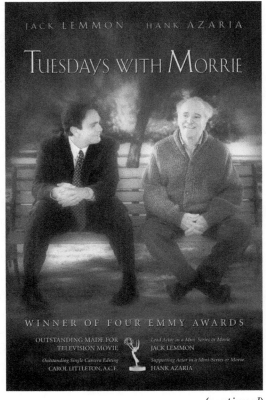

AF archive/Alamy Stock Photo

(continued)

despite his increasing weakness and pain, the former professor surrounded himself with the people and things he loved and, according to Albom, essentially wrapped himself in a cocoon of human activities, conversation, interaction, and affection. He even hosted his own "living funeral" to give his family and himself the rare opportunity to hear and say the things that they all felt needed to be said. Schwartz's criticism of the American way of death was thus countered by his loving and deeply personal example of how death can be dignified, spiritual, and enlightening.

Critical Thinking

Why is death such a difficult issue to confront? This is not the case in all societies. What might account for the differences?

Social Policy

9.8   **Summarize the Social Security program.**

There are many critical social policy issues that are of concern to the elderly, including the quality and cost of Medicare, long-term care, affordable senior housing, and adequate transportation options, to name just a few. Here we will discuss Social Security because it is the largest source of income for those who are elderly.

9.8.1   The History Behind Social Security

The United States is one of over 150 countries that have some sort of financial program for elders. Each program operates somewhat differently but provides at least some financial benefit to help the elderly make ends meet.

In the United States during the late nineteenth and early twentieth centuries, few companies had private pensions for seniors, and the government did not provide public pensions. Consequently, elderly people who could still work usually continued to do so. Public pensions were introduced many times in the U.S. Congress between 1900 and 1935 with no success. But during the Great Depression, it became obvious that those who were elderly could not rely on jobs, private pensions, savings, or their families for financial support. By 1935, unemployment rates among those 65 and older were well above 50 percent (Hardy and Shuey, 2000), and a federal commission determined that nearly half of all seniors in the United States could not support themselves.

The Social Security Act was passed in 1935, creating many kinds of assistance programs. One of them, Old Age, Survivor, and Disability Insurance (OASDI), is the program Americans have come to know as "Social Security." It offered seniors public pensions as a response to the austere poverty that many of them endured. The Social Security system was not designed to be the main source of income. It was originally intended as a form of insurance against unexpected reductions in income due to retirement, disability, or the death of a wage-earning spouse. However, the system has become a kind of government-administered public pension plan. It is now seen as an earned right for seniors, not a form of welfare. Payments from Social Security have successfully reduced the percentage of seniors who are impoverished.

9.8.2   How Social Security Works

OASDI retirement benefits are financed by a tax on earnings up to a certain level that is set by Congress. For the year 2018, that earnings level is $128,400. Any earnings over that amount are not taxed. The tax is paid by both the employee and the employer at a rate of 6.2 percent each (Social Security Administration, 2017). The Social Security tax has been called a regressive tax because it essentially taxes low earners at a higher rate than high earners. For example, say "Bob" earned $128,400 in 2018; therefore, he paid 6.2 percent of his income or $7,961 in Social Security taxes. Meanwhile, "Josie" earned twice that amount, or $256,800, but still paid 6.2 percent only on the first $128,400 she earned, so Josie also paid $7,961. The rest of Josie's income is free of Social Security tax. Thus, Bob paid 6.2 percent of his *total income* in Social Security tax while Josie paid only 3.1 percent on hers. As a higher wage earner, Josie is, in effect, taxed at a lower rate, and as a lower wage earner, Bob is taxed at a higher rate.

Social Security is a major income source for those who are elderly, and for some it is the only source of retirement income. It is guaranteed for life and adjusted for inflation. It serves nearly 60 million retired workers and their dependents at a total cost of about $850 billion a year (DeSilver, 2015). Yet it is important to remember that Social Security serves other groups, too. For example, nearly 11 million disabled workers and their dependents receive Social Security benefits, as do about 6 million survivors (widows, widowers, and their dependents). These groups account for about one-quarter of Social Security beneficiaries. However, these groups are not growing substantially. In contrast, the size of the elderly population is rapidly increasing, thus the attention on that age group.

9.8.3 Future Prospects

The Social Security program is facing an impending challenge that causes many people to wonder if it will be around to help them in old age, as revealed in Figure 9–6. Only 13 percent of retirees and 6 percent of workers in 2017 were "very confident" that Social Security will continue to provide benefits of at least equal value to those today, representing a steep decline in confidence over the past two decades. In contrast, 12 percent of retirees and 20 percent of workers claim that they are "not at all confident" that Social Security will continue to provide benefits at the same level of value.

Figure 9–6 Confidence That Social Security Will Continue to Provide Benefits of At Least Equal Value to Benefits Received by Retirees Today

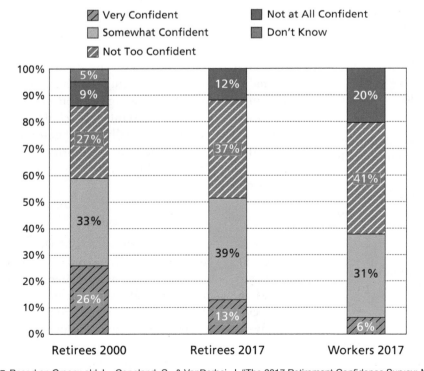

SOURCE: Based on Greenwald, L., Copeland, C., & VanDerhei, J. "The 2017 Retirement Confidence Survey: Many Workers Lack Retirement Confidence and Feel Stressed about Retirement Preparations," EBRI Issue Brief, Number 431 (March 21, 2017).

Their concern stems from the fact that we have an increasing number of people living longer (drawing on Social Security) and have fewer people in the cohort behind them to pay into the system. Thus, over the next two decades as the baby boomers retire, how can Social Security remain solvent? There are several options. First, for younger cohorts among the baby boomers, the retirement age for benefits has been raised to 66 or 67 years (depending on birth date). As we go forward, other sacrifices may be needed to keep the program solvent, such as increasing the tax rate above the current 6.2 percent, eliminating the regressive cap so that all income is taxed instead of just the first $128,400, raising the retirement age even further, or changing Social Security to serve only those who are poor or low income rather than all those who are elderly.

Going Beyond Left and Right

Social Security has the tremendous support of virtually all Americans, regardless of political affiliation, age, ethnicity, or sex. It is an extremely popular program and one that most Americans cannot imagine living without. In a recent poll, 89 percent of adults claimed that Social Security benefits are more important now than ever to ensure that retirees have a dependable income (Tucker, Reno, and Bethell, 2014). Social Security, although originally developed by Democrats and opposed by Republicans, now has widespread support.

Summary

9.1 Evaluate the degree to which aging is a social problem.

Aging is a social problem for two reasons. First, aging places stress on society. For example, as the American aging population continues to grow, and the country's number of younger workers does not keep up, how will Americans pay for the programs that those who are elderly use? The second reason aging can be viewed through a social problem lens involves an individual approach. It has to do with the way that elders live their lives and are treated in society.

9.2 Compare the growth of the elderly population in developed and developing countries and assess the reasons for this growth.

Most developed nations have a high and growing *proportion* of elderly people, but in terms of sheer numbers, most elderly people live in developing nations. People are living longer, and fewer babies are being born.

9.3 Discuss the growth in the elderly population in the United States and the consequences of this growth.

Today, there are over 50 million people age 65 and older in the United States, and the numbers are quickly rising. By 2060, when you are likely to still be alive, the number could be about 98 million. As they grow old, physically

and socially, their large numbers exert major influences on our society.

9.4 Contrast the physiological, psychological, and social and cultural aspects of aging.

There are two categories in the physiological aging process: (1) primary aging, the result of molecular and cellular changes, and (2) secondary aging, an accelerated version of normal aging that is caused by environmental factors. Changing self-concept and status are particularly important as psychological processes as aging occurs. Culturally, social gerontologists frequently refer to the elderly as a minority group who can be victims of prejudice, stereotyping, and discrimination.

9.5 Analyze the economics of aging.

Average income among people who are elderly hovers around $40,000 per year. This income comes from several sources, such as earnings, pensions, or retirement savings, but the largest single source, at nearly 40 percent, comes from Social Security. Earnings comprise about a quarter of the average income of elders, and pensions account for 20 percent. Assets such as stocks, bonds, or income from rented real estate, and other unknown income sources make up the remainder. Those who have multiple areas of vulnerability, for example, being old, female, and members of a minority, are most likely to be poor.

9.6 Describe the unique issues that families with older members may face.

Most elderly people have been married for many years. However, 15 million people are classified as widowed in the United States, and over three-quarters of them are women. The death of a spouse or partner stands as one of life's most stressful events. Widowhood can occur at any point in the life cycle, but because it is most likely to occur among older people, research tends to focus on that population.

9.7 Identify the health concerns common among the elderly and describe the primary program that pays for their health care.

Most elderly people report their health as good or excellent. Despite various improvements in the general way of life, there is no denying that as people age their health declines in several ways, such as losing some degree of vision and hearing. Medicare is the program that helps pay the health costs for people who are elderly.

9.8 Summarize the Social Security program.

The Social Security Act was passed in 1935, creating many kinds of assistance programs. One of them, Old Age, Survivor, and Disability Insurance (OASDI), is the program Americans have come to know as "Social Security." It was not designed to be the main source of income. It was originally intended as a form of insurance against unexpected reductions in income due to retirement, disability, or the death of a wage-earning spouse. However, the system has become a kind of government-administered public pension plan.

Chapter 10
Changing Families

RetroClipArt/Fotolia

Learning Objectives

10.1 Define the term *family* and explain why it is important.

10.2 Identify the functions of families.

10.3 Compare and contrast three perspectives on family change.

10.4 Discuss the changing norms of marriage and intimate relationships.

10.5 Review different types of parenting contexts.

10.6 Explain two types of family problems or challenges: violence and divorce.

10.7 Discuss family policy, using the example of paid family leave.

The cultural imagery of American families that we see on television and throughout the media suggests that "normal" families contain a mom, a dad, and siblings, all of whom are expected to behave toward each other in very specific ways. The problem is this cultural imagery is at odds with the reality of life for many families. This family ideology implicitly denigrates those families whose structure or cultural practices are different, and it contributes to negative self-images and even self-derogation among members of such families, as I found in my research. I conducted interviews with 73 grown children of Korean and Vietnamese immigrants and found that when these young adults contrasted behavior in their immigrant families with mainstream images of normalcy, they interpreted their own family life, as well as that of Asians and Asian Americans in general, as deficient. They emphasized Americanized definitions of love that stress expressiveness, such as the display of affection, sentimentality, and close communication. They downplayed their parents' instrumental style of love emphasized in Asian cultures, such as their material support of children well into adulthood and—in the case of many parents—their decision to immigrate in search of a better life and education for their children. However, because their parents did not conform to Americanized notions of expressive love, these children often described them as distant, unloving, uncaring, and not "normal." This ideology puts immense pressure on many of the children of immigrants in this study to assimilate and encourages some to denigrate their own ethnic family styles as deficient in comparison. As Robert, 24, who emigrated from Korea at age 7, explained, "I still find myself envying white American families and wishing that my family was perfect like theirs. So basically I find myself suckered into this ideal image of the American family. And I realize, sadly, that my family is not the American family and never will be."

—Karen Pyke (referring to Pyke, 2000a, 2000b)

What Is a Family?

10.1   **Define the term *family* and explain why it is important.**

We all probably come from some type of family. Many Americans, especially younger Americans, accept divorce, cohabitation, remaining single, same-sex marriage, and being childfree as legitimate lifestyles, while at the same time, espousing that marriage, children, and a strong family life are important goals toward which they strive (Livingston and Caumont, 2017).

This chapter explores social and cultural aspects of families, describes how they have changed in recent years, and identifies some of the contemporary social problems that they face. But first ask yourself, "What is a family?" Oddly, despite the often-used term, there is no widespread agreement on its definition.

For example, Edward and Ashley, a young couple, have been dating for several years. Two years ago, they moved in together and are saving money to buy their first house. They love each other very much and plan to marry someday. Are they a family? Would your answer be different if I told you that Edward and Ashley had a child together last year? Meanwhile, Jonathon and Martin, an older same-sex couple, have been happily together for the past 30 years but are not married because, until recently, their state did not allow it. Are they a family? Finally, Valeria and David recently married, and each of them has a child from a previous marriage. David's son lives on the other side of the country and has met Valeria's daughter only a couple of times. What are the family lines here? Are David and Valeria's children family to one another?

The U.S. Census Bureau defines a **family** as two or more people living together who are related by birth, marriage, or adoption. This definition remains the basis for many social programs and policies, including employee fringe benefits, such as health and dental insurance or family and medical leaves. However, this official definition does not really reflect the rich diversity of family life today (Amato, 2014). Some people suggest that if people *feel* that they are a family and *behave* as though they are a family, then they should be recognized as such. The focus should be on greater inclusion of

family

Relationships by blood, marriage, or affection, in which members may cooperate economically, may care for any children, and may consider their identity to be intimately connected to the larger group.

What Is a Family?

Families play a primary role in all cultures around the world. Family roles, responsibilities, and even membership may vary from one region to another. For example, the United States and most developed countries recognize grandparents, aunts and uncles, and cousins on both the mother's and father's side of the family—called a bilateral approach to family. However, in many parts of the world, only one side is recognized as kin, either those on the father's side (patrilineal) or those on the mother's side (matrilineal). Despite differences like this, there are many similar functions of families. These functions include the regulation of sexual behavior, reproduction and socializing children, providing a path for inheritance, economic cooperation among members, social status placement, and a mechanism for providing warmth, intimacy, and protection.

Eric Isselée/Fotolia

Families are universal. Although they may vary in size or social roles, they remain a cornerstone of life in all cultures. In less developed countries, families often take the place of social institutions such as schools or health care.

BSIP SA/Alamy Stock Photo

Although the teenage pregnancy rate has been steadily declining, the number of older single parents is on the rise. Adoption is a popular mechanism for having a child, although the number of international adoptions has been declining since 2005.

Scott Griessel/Fotolia

Vitalinka/Fotolia

Family size has been shrinking in the United States. Most American families have only two children. However, unlike some countries such as China and India that put significant pressure on families to remain small to control population growth, American families can be as large or small as desired.

Eugenio Marongiu/Fotolia

About one in five people today say that they do not want to have children. This couple is very happy with one another and their dog, "Scooby." They think of Scooby as part of the family.

Same-sex couples actively sought the right to marry and be recognized as legitimate families in the eyes of the law. Most people now agree with the position that same-sex couples should be allowed to marry and agree with the Supreme Court's decision in 2015 that allowed them to wed.

Critical Thinking

What is your own personal definition of "family"? What factors influence your views? These factors might include religion, culture, personal experience, or your parents' values.

family relationships. This chapter uses a broader and more inclusive definition than that taken from the Census Bureau. Families are defined here as *relationships by blood, marriage, or affection, in which members may cooperate economically, may care for any children, and may consider their identity to be intimately connected to the larger group.*[1]

Why does it matter how we define family? The definition used has important consequences with respect to informal and formal rights (Human Rights Campaign, 2018). For example, neighbors, schools, and other community groups interact with family members differently from ways they interact with other nonrelated groups who live together. Families even get special membership discounts to a wide variety of organizations that roommates or friends do not get. For example, an individual membership to a particular organization may be $25, but a family rate is $30, regardless of family size. However, far more is at stake than simply a few dollars. The agreed-on definition has important consequences that are legally recognized. For example, under most employer insurance plans, only a worker's spouse and legal children can be covered by a health or dental insurance policy. Taxes also favor those who are legally married. It is for these reasons, and many more, that same-sex couples fought for the right to marry.

Functions of Families

10.2 **Identify the functions of families.**

The family is a vital institution in all societies, although the structure of families and what is expected of parents and children varies widely across different cultures and societies. In many parts of the world today parents select their children's spouses, a practice that most people in Western cultures reject. But as you watch the video of Rati and Subas, you may be surprised to see how appreciative young people can be to have their parents choose their spouse. Perhaps even more surprising than the differences found in families from place to place are the *similarities* across families. Structural functionalists often discuss families in terms of the important functions that they serve for individuals and for society at large.

In general, there are at least six universal functions of families, and although they may play out differently from one culture to another, they are regarded as key features of family life.

- *Regulation of Sexual Behavior:* Every culture, including ours, regulates sexual behavior. Cultural norms make it clear who can have a sexual relationship with whom and under what circumstances. One virtually universal regulation around the world is the incest taboo, which forbids sexual activity (and marriage) among close family members. However, the definition of "close family members" differs, although it usually involves at least parents and their children, and siblings.
- *Reproduction and Socializing Children:* For a society to continue, it must produce new members to replace those who die or move away. Families have the primary responsibility for producing the newest members and for teaching them the culture in which they live. Children learn primarily from their families the language, values, beliefs, interpersonal skills, and general knowledge necessary to adequately function in society.
- *Property and Inheritance:* As families moved from a nomadic lifestyle as hunters and gatherers to one based on agriculture, it became possible for the first time for people to accumulate surplus property beyond what was needed for sheer survival. Friedrich Engels (1884/1902) tied the origin of the family to males' desire to

---

[1]Seccombe, K., & Warner, R. L. (2004). *Marriages and Families: Relationships in Social Context.* Belmont, CA: Wadsworth/Thomson Learning.

identify heirs so that they could pass down their property to their sons. Monogamy worked in men's favor. Without it, paternity was uncertain. Therefore, men sought to strictly control women sexually, economically, and socially through marriage.

- *Economic Cooperation:* Adults and children have physical needs for food, shelter, and clothing. Families are the first line of defense for providing these necessities to its members. There is usually a gendered division of labor, with certain tasks primarily performed by men and others by women. However, exactly which tasks are considered masculine or feminine varies from one society to the next.

- *Social Placement, Status, and Roles:* All members of society relate in some way to the basic structure of that society, usually in a way that preserves order and minimizes confusion and conflict. We fit in by way of a complex web of statuses (positions in a group or society) and roles (behaviors that are associated with those positions). Through our families, we are given an identity and position in society. For example, we are born into a certain social class, ethnic or racial group, religious affiliation, or geographic region.

- *Care, Warmth, Protection, and Intimacy:* People need more than food, shelter, and clothing to survive. Families are intended to provide the care, warmth, protection, and intimacy that individuals need. However, cross-culturally, families may give different weights to these features. For example, in many less developed societies, love is not a feature of marriage. Likewise, in more developed countries, families may be less focused on the aspect of protection, leaving that to the local police department.

What Do You Think?

Provide examples of each of these functions in modern American society. How have they changed, if at all, over time?

Perspectives on Family Change

10.3 Compare and contrast three perspectives on family change.

In every recent presidential election campaign, "family values" have been a hot issue, largely because some people are concerned that the family is in a state of decline and facing a great number of social problems (Laplant, 2016), citing "the neglect of marriage," "lack of commitment by men," "the rise in cohabitation," and "fatherless families." Popular television shows, newspapers, and magazines bombard viewers with stories about the demise of the family and the problems families face: single parenthood, juvenile delinquency, teen pregnancy, family breakups. Some refer to the "good old days," when there were fewer problems, life was easier, family bonds were stronger, families had more authority to fulfill their functions, and people were generally happier. People who believe that today's families are being threatened suggest: (1) Americans are rejecting traditional marriage and family life; (2) family members are not adhering to roles within families; and (3) many social and moral problems result from the changes in families.

In contrast to this pessimistic perspective, others remind us that these golden years of the past never really existed. They argue that families have always faced challenges, including desertion, poverty, children born out of wedlock, alcoholism, unemployment, violence, and child abuse (Coontz, 2007). Yet, despite these long-standing problems, attempts to strengthen families through improved social services and financial assistance have been met with resistance. Ensuring that families have adequate childcare, low-cost educational opportunities, jobs with livable wages, health care regardless of cost, and safe housing is at odds with the emphasis on "rugged individualism." Instead, a theme felt by many Americans is that people should "pull themselves up by their own bootstraps."

Families are changing in composition, expectations, and roles. What is causing these changes? Are these changes good or bad? What are the consequences of family change? These questions are hotly debated—a debate that is woven firmly into the U.S. political discourse, as you can see in any nightly news show, from Fox News to MSNBC. Janet Giele (1996) contrasts three conflicting political viewpoints about the causes and consequences of changes in families, as shown in Figure 10–1.

Figure 10–1 Conservative, Liberal, and Feminist Views of Family Change

Conservative

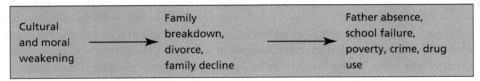

| Cultural and moral weakening | → | Family breakdown, divorce, family decline | → | Father absence, school failure, poverty, crime, drug use |

Liberal

| Changing economic structure | → | Changing family and gender roles | → | Diverse effects: poor v. productive children |

Feminist

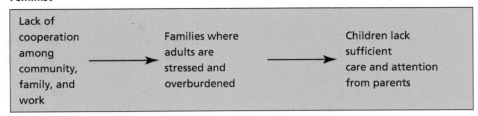

| Lack of cooperation among community, family, and work | → | Families where adults are stressed and overburdened | → | Children lack sufficient care and attention from parents |

SOURCE: Giele, J. Z. 1996. "Decline of the Family: Conservative, Liberal, and Feminist Views." In Promises to Keep: Decline and Renewal of Marriage in America, In D. Popenoe, J. B. Elshtain, and D. Blankenhorn, eds. Lanham, MD: Rowman & Littlefield.

10.3.1 Conservative Perspective

Conservatives express grave concern that changes in family structure put children at risk (Laplant, 2016; Murray, 1984; Wilcox, 2017). They suggest that many challenges families face are linked to cultural and moral weakening. This weakening contributes to father absence and family disorganization through divorce or having children outside of marriage, which ultimately results in greater poverty, crime, drug use, and a host of other social problems.

Conservatives argue that the weakening of the U.S. moral fabric can be traced to the decline of religious practice and affiliation. They suggest that the lack of religious influence has reshaped our cultural norms so that practices such as nonmarital sex, cohabitation, or having a child outside of marriage are no longer seen as immoral. When this shift in norms happens, society witnesses the breakdown of the traditional two-parent family, which conservatives argue is the cornerstone of society. Fathers become increasingly irrelevant in the lives of women and children. Divorce rates and illegitimacy soar. Husbands divorce their wives, leaving their children behind. They form new unions and have additional children, referred to as **multiple partner fertility**, sometimes without providing financially or emotionally for the children they already have. Conservatives suggest that welfare and other social programs actually serve to undermine families, rather than help them, because they make it easy for men to leave their partner and children.

According to conservatives, when families break up and fathers become increasingly marginalized, social problems flourish. Poverty becomes rampant, and children fail to thrive. They do worse in school, and possibly turn to alcohol, drugs, and crime to try to alleviate their suffering. Conservatives suggest that the solution to this downward spiral is to strengthen and support traditional marriage. They propose restoring the ideal of the two-parent family by making other types of families less attractive. For example, the government should minimize its support of single mothers and encourage couples to marry and rely on one another for the care of their children.

multiple partner fertility

Having children with multiple partners.

10.3.2 Liberal Perspective

Liberals also note that families have changed significantly in recent decades, resulting in many challenges. However, liberals suggest that these challenges result from economic and structural adjustments that place new demands on families without offering additional social supports. These changes include the loss of relatively high-paying manufacturing jobs, an erosion of the minimum wage, a decline in employer-sponsored fringe benefits, and a rise in the number of low-paying service sector jobs. These economic circumstances have influenced a number of changes within families. First, there is an increasing need for both husbands and wives to work to support the family. Second, corresponding with dual-earner households, there is a greater need for childcare assistance. Third, because young women are less inclined to marry men with few good economic prospects, there is a rise in cohabitation and having children outside of marriage. According to William Julius Wilson (1996), a scholar and former president of the American Sociological Association, it is partly the lack of jobs in the inner city that drives up the rate of nonmarital births because the men are not considered "marriageable."

The result, according to liberals, is the creation of an underclass. Poor children face extraordinary challenges because they don't have the social supports to weather these changes. Liberals essentially believe in a market economy, but they ask for sufficient social supports to help families in the lower tiers of the economy or those who face other vulnerabilities. Such supports include welfare benefits, job training programs, educational subsidies, expansion of quality childcare programs, and strengthening supports for working families.

10.3.3 Feminist Perspective

The feminist perspective blends elements of both conservative and liberal perspectives. In common with conservatives, feminists share a heightened respect for the often invisible but important caregiving work done in families. With liberals, they share a concern that the changes in economic conditions have had many deleterious consequences for families, particularly those that are most vulnerable. Yet, there are also sharp differences with conservative and liberal perspectives. The feminist perspective criticizes conservatives for exploiting female caregivers, which allows men to be more active in the public realm. Meanwhile, the feminist perspective also criticizes liberals for perpetuating the notion that the best families are those that are somehow self-sufficient.

Feminists attribute the difficulties children face to a lack of cooperation between the community, family, and employers to improve the quality of life. They express concern that a sense of individualism permeates U.S. culture and there is little collective responsibility for one another's welfare. They point to comparative research in other countries that shows that government support for all families causes poverty and its associated problems to plummet, while health, education, and well-being soar. However, in the United States, the lack of collective spirit results in families in which adults feel routinely stressed and overburdened. Although poor families may feel these stresses more acutely than the middle class, all families suffer. Children may suffer because they lack sufficient care and attention from their parents who are expected to fend for themselves with little outside support.

Feminists ask for alternative policies that place higher value on the quality of human relationships. They work for reforms that strengthen neighborhoods and volunteer groups, support caregiving activities, and encourage education and employment among both women and men. They advocate that family policies should be enacted to protect and nurture families, including in the areas of childcare, maternity benefits, health care, work guarantees, and other economic supports. In sum, feminists judge the strength of a family not by its form (dual-parent versus single-parent), but by the social well-being that comes from parents knowing that they have the support necessary to be the best family caregivers and productive workers that they can be (Giele, 1996).

What Do You Think?

Which perspective—conservative, liberal, or feminist—is most popular in our society, and why? Do you think it might vary across social groups, such as by age, education, or sex? Which perspective makes the most sense to you, and why?

Changing Norms of Marriage and Intimate Relationships

10.4 Discuss the changing norms of marriage and intimate relationships.

Many aspects of marriage have changed substantially over the past few decades. For example, fewer people marry, and those who do so marry later and likely cohabit beforehand. Same-sex couples demanded the same right to marry that is afforded to heterosexual couples. Partners are renegotiating their roles with their relationships, including the division of household labor. These issues are discussed in the sections that follow.

10.4.1 The Declining Rates of Marriage

In the United States, most people want to marry and eventually do so. Less than 4 percent of adults remain unmarried throughout their lives. Although the practical necessity of marriage has declined in recent years as more women can support themselves financially and more men know their way around the domestic arena, the symbolic importance of marriage has remained high. Marriage is now a sign of prestige rather than conformity because it often comes *after* a certain level of attainment (after a job, a career, savings, or children) rather than before.

Among the roughly 250 million Americans ages 18 and over, 53 percent are currently married. This represents a significant decline in marriage rates over the past generation. Asian Americans have the highest percentages of married people over age 18 in the population, whereas blacks had the lowest. Figure 10–2 compares the marital status of adults ages 18 and older in 1970 and 2017 (U.S. Census Bureau, May 4, 2018). The figure reveals that the likelihood of being married has declined significantly. Instead, more people report to be never married, divorced, or widowed. In fact, the percentage of the adult population who claim to be divorced is more than triple that in 1970. However, this figure represents a *snapshot* in time; it is likely that most of these unmarried or divorced people will marry.

If the vast majority of people marry eventually, why does it look like so few people are married? One reason is that people are delaying the age at which they marry.

Figure 10–2 Marital Status of U.S. Population 18 Years and Over, 1970 and 2017

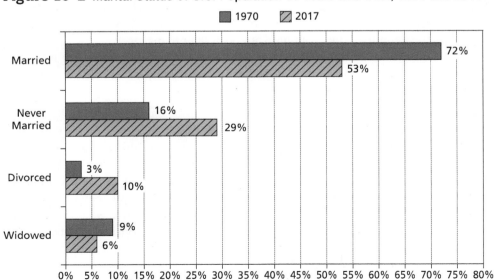

SOURCE: U. S. Census Bureau. May 4, 2018. "America's Families and Living Arrangements: 2017." Retrieved 6 September 2018 (https://www.census.gov/data/tables/2017/demo/families/cps-2017.html).

Figure 10–3 Median Age at First Marriage, 1890–2017

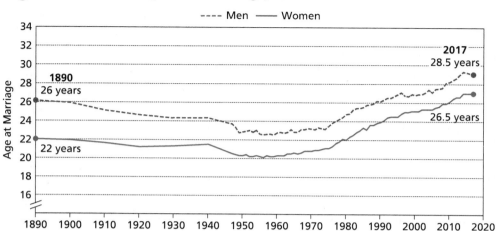

SOURCE: U. S. Census Bureau. May 4, 2018. "America's Families and Living Arrangements: 2017." Retrieved 6 September 2018 (https://www.census.gov/data/tables/2017/demo/families/cps-2017.html).

The average age at which people marry has fluctuated substantially through time. The age at marriage at the end of the nineteenth century was about what it is today. However, ask your grandparents at what age they married, and don't be surprised if it was by age 20 or 21. One psychiatrist wrote in 1953 that "a girl who hasn't a man in sight by the time she is 20 is not altogether wrong in feeling that she may never get married," and therefore, young women set their sights on finding a husband early (Coontz, 2007). Consequently, as shown in Figure 10–3, the age at marriage dropped to an all-time low during the 1950s to 20 years for women (with the greatest number marrying at age 18) and 23 for men (U.S. Census Bureau, May 4, 2018).

Since the 1950s, the age at first marriage has been steadily increasing. Today, the average age for marriage has risen to 27 and 29 years for women and men, respectively, increasing by several years in just a generation, as shown in Figure 10–3 (U.S. Census Bureau, May 4, 2018). For those people with advanced education, the average age is even higher.

The delay of marriage is occurring among all racial and ethnic groups. This delay is likely due to greater educational and economic opportunities, especially for women. As increasing numbers of women go to college, graduate school, or begin careers, they are more likely to postpone getting married and having children. It is not necessarily that marriage is less appealing; it is just more appealing to wait. Women enjoy an annual income premium if they wait until age 30 or later to marry.

Just because people are waiting to marry does not mean that they are not interested in committed relationships. The decline in marriage rates has been accompanied by a rise in unmarried couples living together (Stepler, 2017).

10.4.2 The Rise in Cohabitation

cohabitation

Living with a romantic and sexual partner without being married.

It is tempting to think that the younger generation invented **cohabitation** (living with a romantic and sexual partner without being married), but it has been practiced long before modern times. In the mid-1800s, people may have spoken little of cohabitation, but it was a fact of life for many, especially in rural areas. A couple may have wanted to marry, but perhaps a minister was unavailable, or the couple was waiting until family could arrive for the wedding. Cohabitation was usually considered a temporary state until the couple could marry, and therefore others in the community generally treated them as a married couple (Cott, 2002).

However, as the United States began to develop and urbanize, these reasons for cohabitation became much less relevant. Consequently, cohabitation became less common in the early part of the twentieth century. People who lived together without being married were considered sinful or deviant.

The attitude toward cohabitation changed again in the late 1960s and 1970s, when young people rebelled against established norms and institutions (Popenoe, 2008). This period was one of new freedoms for a large baby-boom youth cohort. It was the era of "sexual revolution," new reliable birth control, and expanded access to education and the workplace for women. People no longer felt the need to marry young. These societal changes may have led people to ask, why not just live together?

Today, the Census Bureau estimates that 8 million U.S. households are maintained by heterosexual cohabiting couples (U.S. Census Bureau, May 4, 2018), more than twice the number in 2000. People who cohabit span all ages, races, and ethnic groups and are found within all social classes.

Fifty years ago, cohabitation was considered by most people to be either immoral or deviant. Today, it is commonplace. Most people have cohabited before marriage, as is the case with this couple as they move into their new home.

Along with changing behavior around cohabitation, there is now a greater acceptance of cohabitation. In a national survey, high school seniors were asked whether they agreed with the statement, "It is usually a good idea for a couple to live together before getting married to find out whether they really get along."[2] Attitudes are considerably more favorable than those of a generation ago, with 71 percent of young men and 67 percent of young women agreeing that cohabitation is a good idea, compared with only 45 and 33 percent, respectively, in the late 1970s (Bachman, Johnston, and O'Malley, 2014). Likewise, the General Social Survey, a large survey based on a nationally representative sample of adults, reports that about half of older adults agree or agree strongly with the statement, "Living together is an acceptable option" (Brown and Wright, 2016).

COHABITATION AND MARRIAGE   More than two-thirds of marriages begin with cohabitation (Copen et al., 2012), but that fact does not necessarily mean that cohabitation leads to marriage. Those are two different issues. In fact, only about half of cohabiting relationships end up in marriage within three years (Goodwin, Mosher, and Chandra, 2010). The others either break up or continue cohabiting.

The belief that living together before marriage is a useful way "to find out whether you really get along" is widespread but not completely accurate. Cohabitation may ease roommate problems, and it may make good financial sense, but is cohabitation a good test for marriage? Interestingly, people who cohabit are actually *more* likely to have unhappy marriages and to divorce (Perelli-Harris, Berrington, Gassen, Galezewska, and Holland, 2017).

There are two possible reasons for the positive relationship between cohabitation and divorce. First, a **selection effect** may be operating, meaning that the cohabitors do not represent a random sample and that the type of person who cohabits may be the same type of person who would be more likely to end an unhappy marriage (Copen et al., 2012; Kuperberg, 2014). For example, someone who values personal freedom may be both more likely to cohabit and more likely to divorce. Or, a less religious person may be more likely to cohabit and more likely to end an unhappy marriage. In other words, it is not the case that cohabitation *causes* the divorce per se; rather, the relationship between cohabitation and divorce is **spurious**, meaning that both cohabitation and divorce are really caused by a third factor—in this case, the high value placed on personal freedom or looser religious values.

The second reason for the relationship of divorce and cohabitation may be cause and effect. Perhaps something about the cohabitation experience weakens a relationship and makes it more prone to divorce. Attitudes and behaviors developed through

selection effect

An effect that occurs when the sample is not random and leads to biased inferences about social processes, such as the relationship about cohabitation and divorce.

spurious

A type of apparent relationship between two variables that is really caused by a third factor.

---

[2]National Center for Marriage and Family Research, 2010.

cohabitation may be at odds with long-term marriage. For example, couples who co-habit are more likely to maintain financial independence and keep their own separate checking accounts (Hamplová, Le Bourdais, and Lapierre-Adamcyk, 2014), possibly emphasizing the couple's degree of separateness and undermining a feeling of unity. It is possible that cohabiting couples are living more like singles, with less of an emphasis on permanence and, therefore, are not really "testing" the relationship as if it were marriage. Consequently, when they do marry, the social expectations that come along with being a husband, wife, son-in-law, and daughter-in-law remain new and uncharted territory.

So, which is it: Is the relationship between cohabitation and divorce a spurious relationship, or does cohabitation really cause divorce? It is likely that both operate to some degree, but the most research supports the notion of the relationship between cohabitation and divorce as spurious.

COHABITATION AND CHILDREN   About 40 percent of cohabiting couples have children under the age of 18 residing in the home, born to one or both partners. This percentage is about the same as the percentage of married couples who have children in the home (U.S. Census Bureau, May 4, 2018). Most often, the children are from one partner's previous union. However, there is a growing trend among many cohabiting couples to have at least one child together, especially among those cohabiting couples with less education (Gibson-Davis and Rackin, 2014).

Whether cohabitation is good or bad for children largely depends on what alternatives exist. Possible living arrangements include living with a single mother, living with a parent and his or her unmarried partner, living with a parent and his or her new spouse (stepparent), living with two cohabiting biological parents, or living with two married biological parents. Children can potentially benefit from living with a cohabiting partner when resources are shared with family members (Forehand, Parent, Golub, and Reid, 2016). For example, a study by sociologists Manning and Brown found that between 7 and 9 percent of children of cohabiting relationships faced high risk (de-fined as experiencing poverty, food insecurity, and housing insecurity) compared with 13 percent of children living with a single mother. Further, only 2 percent of children in mar-ried biological or married stepparent families faced this risk (Manning and Brown, 2006).

The research suggests that, in general, children receive the most economic sup-port and do the best academically and socially when they are reared in households with two married biological parents (Brown, Manning, and Payne, 2016; Rothwell and McEwen, 2017). However, this family structure is not possible for everyone. Moreover, some married-couple households are fraught with conflict. Therefore, embracing only one type of family structure as "best" and others as "less than" is not helpful because all families have their strengths and challenges.

10.4.3 Same-Sex Marriage

Many people see same-sex marriage as one of the most important civil rights issues of our times. The Supreme Court ruled in June 2015 that the right for same-sex couples to marry is protected under the 14th Amendment, citing the clauses that guarantee equal protection and due process. In a close 5-4 decision, the justices outlined several reasons same-sex marriage should be allowed. They wrote that the right to marriage is an inherent aspect of individual autonomy and that gay Americans have a right to intimate association beyond merely freedom from laws that ban homosexuality. Extending the right to marry protects families and the children within them.

The battle to give gays and lesbians the right to marry has been long and steeped in controversy. In 1996, the federal Defense of Marriage Act (DOMA) was passed with bipartisan support and defined marriage as a legal union between one man and one woman. It allowed states to refuse to recognize same-sex mar-riages performed under the laws of other states. In June 2013, the Supreme Court struck down DOMA, saying in a 5 to 4 ruling that the federal government cannot disparage marriages recognized by the states (DeSilver, 2013).

Public opinion has continued to move toward supporting same-sex unions. Today, overall, more than half of Americans now support same-sex marriage. As you can see in Table 10–1, younger adults, Democrats, women, and whites are most likely to express support for marriage equality (Pew Research Center, 2017).

Advocates see same-sex marriage as a civil rights issue: Gays and lesbians should not be discriminated against, and forbidding them to legally wed is an overt form of discrimination. Because they generally do not see homosexuality as a choice, they equate restrictions on same-sex marriage with the restrictions on interracial marriage that were strictly enforced in some states and repealed only a generation ago. Advocates believe that allowing same-sex couples to marry does not harm or diminish heterosexual marriage or hurt society in any way. Pointing to the few countries that do allow gays and lesbians to wed, they note no ill effects. Love and public commitment should be encouraged rather than suppressed.

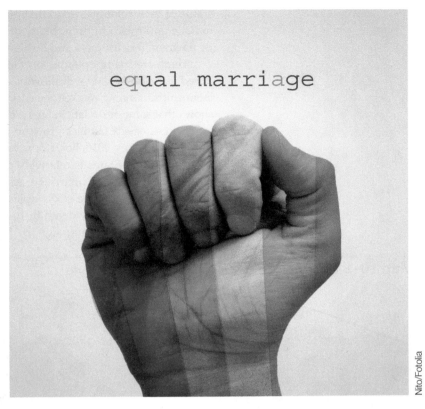

Nito/Fotolia

Public opinion toward same-sex marriage has changed significantly in recent years. In June 2015, the U.S. Supreme Court ruled 5-4 that it is legal for all Americans, no matter their sex or sexual orientation, to marry the people they love.

Opponents' views vary, but some suggest that same-sex marriage is immoral and is in violation of God's teaching. For example, the Catholic Church decries homosexual acts because they do not lead to procreation. Early American antisodomy laws discouraged all forms of nonprocreative sex (including heterosexual oral and anal sex). Islam has a similar view. Other opponents simply suggest that marriage has *always* been defined as between a man and a woman and see no need to change it. In particular, there is some concern that allowing gays and lesbians to wed elevates the

Table 10–1 Percentage of U.S. Adults Who Support Same-Sex Marriage, June, 2017

Total	**62%**
Political Affiliation	
Democrat	76%
Republican	47%
Age	
Millennials born 1981 or later	74%
Generation X born 1965–1980	65%
Baby Boomers born 1946–1964	56%
Silent Generation born 1928–1945	41%
Sex	
Female	64%
Male	60%
Race	
White	64%
Black	51%
Hispanic	60%

SOURCE: Pew Research Center. 2017. "Support for Same-Sex Marriage Grows, Even Among Groups That Had Been Skeptical." 26 June. Retrieved 11 February 2018 (www.people-press.org/2017/06/26/support-for-same-sex-marriage-growseven-among-groups-that-had-been-skeptical/).

status of their relationship to that of a heterosexual couple and legitimizes their right to have and raise children. Many of these opponents support civil unions or domestic partnerships for gays and lesbians, but draw the line at legal marriage.

There are many opinions on the subject, steeped in deeply held values. An often raised question is: How will allowing same-sex couples who are in loving and devoted relationships to marry weaken the social institutions of marriage and family? The research shows that same-sex relationships are as fulfilling as heterosexual ones and that children raised in same-sex families grow up happy and well adjusted (Adams and Light, 2015; Biblarz and Stacey, 2010; Bos, Knox, van Rijn-van Gelderen, and Gartrell, 2016; Farr, 2017).

The United States is relatively progressive with respect to attitudes and policies surrounding same-sex marriage. As shown in Map 10–1, the U.S. is one of only 25 countries in which same-sex couples can legally marry. In contrast, same-sex relationships are punishable by death in 10 countries, and criminalization occurs in 72 countries (Human Rights Campaign, 2018).

Map 10–1 Same-Sex Relationships Throughout the World

Legend:

▨ Same-sex marriage is legal

In several states of Mexico, same-sex couples need to obtain an amparo - which cannot be denied by the courts - before they can wed. The U.K. has marriage equality with the exception of Northern Ireland.

▨ Same-sex marriage is legal, but not enacted

Austria's constitutional court in December 2017 ruled in favor of marriage equality, which will come into effect on or before January 2019.
Taiwan's constitutional court in May 2017 ruled in favor of marriage equality, which has yet to be enacted by the legislature

▥ Same-sex relationship is criminalized

▤ Same-sex relationship is punishable with death penalty

Criminalized in the country and punishable by death in some parts. Also, has laws to inhibit LGBT advocacy.
Criminalized in the country and punishable by death in some parts.

▦ Laws inhibit LGBT Advocacy

☐ Not legal, but not criminalized

SOURCE: Human Rights Campaign. 2018. "Marriage Center." Retrieved 2 February 2018 (www.hrc.org/campaigns/marriage-center).

10.4.4 The Division of Household Labor

The work at home that feeds, clothes, shelters, and cares for family members is just as important as the work that occurs in the labor market. Yet, household labor has been considered "women's work," and not deemed worthy of scientific study until roughly 30 years ago. Since then, a tremendous amount of research has been done to examine who does what in the home, under what circumstances, and why and how housework is embedded in complex family processes.

How is household labor defined? Generally, it refers to unpaid work that is done to maintain family members and/or a home. It usually excludes childcare and other types of emotional labor and caregiving. According to national surveys, the five most time-consuming major household tasks are (1) meal preparation or cooking; (2) housecleaning; (3) shopping for groceries and household goods; (4) washing dishes and cleaning up after meals; and (5) laundry, including washing, ironing, and mending clothes. Coltrane (2000) refers to these tasks as **routine household labor** because they are repetitive and less able to be postponed than are other tasks. Although some people enjoy some or all of these activities, most people say that they do not enjoy routine household work, calling it boring, onerous, and mundane. Other tasks such as gardening, paying bills, household repairs, or servicing the car, called occasional labor, occur less frequently and have more flexibility in timing.

Women do significantly more housework than men. The size of men's and women's contributions vary across studies, but most find that women spend 50–100 percent more time on various household tasks than men do (U.S. Department of Labor, June 28, 2018; Yavorsky, Kamp Dush, and Schoppe-Sullivan, 2015).

For example, in a 2015 study of over 1,200 parents, half of mothers in two-parent households say they do more than their partners in this area, compared with 32 percent of fathers who say their wives or partners do more. For their part, fathers are more likely to say they and their partners share household chores and responsibilities about equally: More than half (56%) say this is the case, while 46% of mothers agree (Pew Research Center, 2015). Data from the American Time Use Study, published by the U.S. Department of Labor, indicates that women spend about twice as much time on household chores as do men, as shown in Table 10–2.

The answer to who does what with respect to childcare isn't much different from housework regarding division of work (Pew Research Center, 2015; U.S. Department of Labor, June 28, 2018). The results of a large survey of parents that assessed who contributes more to various activities with children is reported in Figure 10–4 and indicates that mothers' involvement exceeds fathers' involvement. In particular, most mothers have the primary responsibilities for managing children's schedules. The activity that comes closest to being shared equally is playing or doing activities with children.

routine household labor

Household work that is repetitive and less able to be postponed than are other tasks.

Table 10–2 Average Time Spent on Selected Household Chores Per Day, by Sex, 2017 (in Minutes)

	Men	Women
Housework	23 minutes	85 minutes
Food Preparation/Cleanup	36	83
Lawn/Garden	25	11
Consumer Goods Shopping	27	42
Household Management	12	14

SOURCE: Bureau of Labor Statistics. June 28, 2018. "American Time Use Survey Summary." Retrieved 4 September 2018 (https://www.bls.gov/news.release/tus.nr0.htm).

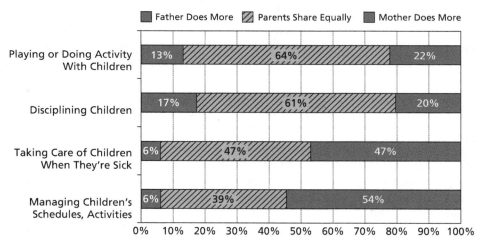

Figure 10–4 Who Does More? Assessments from Parents in Two-Parent Families Who Both Work Full-Time, 2015

SOURCE: Pew Research Center. 2015. "Raising Kids and Running a Household: How Working Parents Share the Load." Social & Demographic Trends. 4 November. Retrieved 3 August 2016 (www.pewsocialtrends.org/2015/11/04/raising-kids-and-running-a-household-how-workingparents-share-the-load/).

Despite the continuing imbalance in the division of housework and childcare, many families are renegotiating how this family labor is performed. The amount of time both fathers and mothers spend with their children has grown considerably since 1965, but fathers' time has increased threefold from 2.5 hours per week to 7.3 hours per week (Parker and Livingston, 2018). In 2015, fathers reported spending, on average, seven hours a week on childcare—almost triple the time they provided back in 1965. Fathers also spend more time doing household chores than they did in the past.

Despite the increased involvement of fathers, they still have several more weekly leisure hours than do their wives (Sayer, 2016). With the lack of leisure and the high demands of children, home, and work, mothers experience more stress and burnout than do their husbands. In particular, when women value equality in the home but end up doing the majority of household labor themselves, their sense of fairness is violated and happiness with their marriage declines (Chong and Mickelson, 2016; Gordon and Mickelson, 2018). Men may compare themselves to what their fathers did, and therefore believe "Wow, I am doing a lot," whereas many women compare their partners to what they are doing and say, "This isn't fair."

Researchers have been studying the ways that work and family influence each other (Nomaguchi and Milkie, 2015; Thebaud and Padulla, 2016; Wayne, Butts, Casper, and Allen, 2017). Out of this research have come several important concepts that help us begin to understand the reciprocal relationship between work and family life.

One such concept is **work–family conflict**, which is the tension people feel when the pressures from paid work and family roles are incompatible (Boyd, Sliter, and Chatfield, 2016; Creary and Gordon, 2016; Henderson, 2016). The conflict can go both ways: Work is made more difficult by virtue of participation in family activities (e.g., it is difficult to work the expected overtime at one's job because of needing to pick up one's children from day care), and participation in family activities is made more difficult by work (e.g., it is difficult to get to one's son's baseball practice every Wednesday afternoon because of a 4:00 department meeting). Work–family conflict has increased for both men and women in recent decades.

Another concept, **role overload**, is the feeling of being overwhelmed by many different commitments and not having enough time to meet each commitment effectively (Creary and Gordon, 2016; Ee, Teoh, and Yen, 2017). *Perception* of overload is key. What appears to make the difference in role overload is not how many hours a person has worked, but how much support a person has. Role overload can lead to

What Do You Think?

Compare your attitudes toward the division of household labor with those of your parents or grandparents. Are your attitudes and expectations different? If so, what accounts for this change?

work–family conflict

The tension people feel when the pressures from paid work and family roles are somehow incompatible.

role overload

The feeling of being overwhelmed by many different commitments and not having enough time to meet each commitment effectively.

stress and depression. Mothers with higher incomes (who can, presumably, hire more help), people with happier marriages, and those with higher-quality jobs were least likely to feel role overload.

Another related concept, **spillover**, refers to the negative (or sometimes positive) moods, experiences, and demands involved in one sphere that carry over or "spill over" into the other sphere (Du, Derks, and Bakker, 2017). How does someone purge the rushed and hectic mood at work when he or she now has to grocery shop with a toddler? How does a parent play with his or her children after work, when a boss is still sending him or her e-mails in the evening? With the invention of computers, cell phones, and other important technology, work increasingly encroaches on family time.

spillover

The negative (or sometimes positive) moods, experiences, and demands involved in one sphere that carry over or "spill over" into the other sphere.

Parenting Contexts

10.5 Review different types of parenting contexts.

Most adults become parents one day, although not all adults do, as you can see in the feature, *A Personal View: "Children? No Thanks."* It is estimated that close to one in five women will not have children, sometimes because of infertility, but also because of personal choice. However, for the other four in five adults, children loom on the horizon, and there are different types of parenting contexts.

A Personal View

"Children? No Thanks."

Dmitriy Shironosov/Alamy Stock Photo

My husband Michael and I just returned last week from Christmas with the family—mom, dad, grandma, my Aunt Sandra and Uncle Bob, and my older brother and his family. What a depressing experience! Don't get me wrong; I love each and every one of them, but I cannot stand the constant snide comments about the fact that Michael and I don't have children. We've been married for nine years, and the first years were okay because we were in graduate school. No one really expected us to have kids while in school. But after we graduated, the comments started coming in, like "So, when are you going to have a family?" or "Any buns in the oven yet?" I really hate that expression. We just smiled and politely said no, even though I was tempted to say "None of your business, if you don't mind!" They probably thought infertility was the issue. But, last week

we did it. Michael and I told them straight out that we were not going to have children because we really did not want them. Aunt Sandra shrieked! My mom started to cry. My brother told me that we were going to miss the best part of life. He and his wife have two preschool-age kids, and, personally, I don't think their life looks so great. Let me be clear. I honestly do enjoy my nieces in short doses. I can play horsey, use crayons, and push them on the swings as well as anyone can. I'm looking forward to having them spend the weekend when they are a bit older. It's just that I don't want to do those things on a full-time basis. Please don't think I'm heartless! I volunteer for Meals on Wheels and help deliver food to seniors twice a month. Last month Michael and I volunteered for the annual cleanup of the wonderful large park in our city. I donate money for a lot of local causes, and I voted yes on the last school levy. However, I also value my privacy, my work, and my relationship with Michael. I am afraid that I would have to compromise on these values if I had children. I just wish people would support my right to choose whether or not to be a mother.

Critical Thinking

An increasing number of women and men are opting to be childfree. Why do you think they are choosing this path? What social changes have taken place in American culture that might explain this new phenomenon?

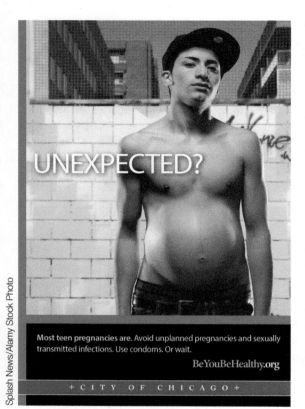

An eye-catching teen pregnancy ad campaign features teen boys mocked-up to look like they have pregnant bellies. The teen pregnancy prevention campaign in Chicago displayed the ads on public transit buses, trains, platforms, and bus shelters. The image was aimed at getting across the message that unexpected pregnancies is a massive responsibility for boys, not just girls.

10.5.1 Teen Parents

About 225,000 teenagers ages 15–19 had babies in 2016, representing 20 births for every 1,000 adolescent girls (Martin et al., 2017). The good news is that the teen pregnancy rate has declined substantially over the past two decades, after reaching its all-time high in 1991 of nearly 62 births per 1,000 girls (Martin et al., 2015). The decline has been large among all racial and ethnic groups, but it has been steepest among blacks, as shown in Figure 10–5.

The negative biological, social, and economic consequences of early parenting in the United States have been well documented (Centers for Disease Control and Prevention, May 9, 2017; National Campaign to Prevent Teen and Unplanned Pregnancy, 2018). Teen mothers are 2.5 times as likely to die in childbirth as are older mothers, their infants are twice as likely to be of low birth weight, and the babies are nearly 3 times more likely to die within the first month of life. Many of these biological problems have social roots; teen mothers are more likely to be poor and lack proper nutrition and prenatal care.

Other repercussions are more social and economic in nature. Teen mothers are more likely to drop out of school than are other teens, are considerably poorer, and more likely to receive welfare. Adolescent mothers are also less knowledgeable about child development, are less prepared for childrearing, and are more likely to be depressed than are other mothers. Children born to teen mothers have lower math and reading skills and increased behavioral problems, although many of these differences may be related to the mother's background rather than to her teen pregnancy per se. It is therefore not surprising that social workers, health professionals, educators, researchers, and parents remain alarmed at the number of teens—both young women and men—involved in adolescent pregnancies. It has been estimated that teen childbearing costs

Figure 10–5 Teenage Birth Rates per 1,000 Women Aged 15–19 by Race and/or Ethnicity for 1991 and 2015

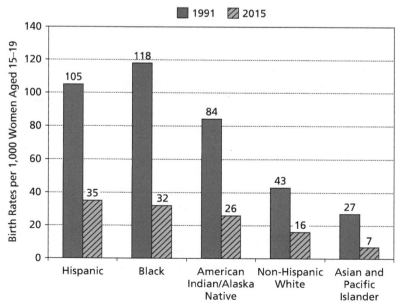

SOURCE: Martin, J. A., Hamilton, B. E., Osterman, J. K., Driscoll, A. K., & Matthews, T. J. "Births: Final Data for 2015." *National Vital Statistics Reports*, vol. 66, no. 1 (January 5, 2017), Centers for Disease Control and Prevention.

taxpayers at least $11 billion each year for health care and child welfare, plus revenues (National Campaign to Prevent Teen and Unplanned Pregnancy, 2018).

10.5.2 Single Parents

Single-parent families used to be referred to as *broken homes*. Today, many people take exception to that term. The vast majority of single-parent families are single-mother families, and the terms are often used interchangeably; if you say "single parent," people typically think of a single mother. These families have been maligned for causing a wide range of social ills, including poverty. The concern with such a sweeping generalization is that (1) there are different kinds of single-parent families with different kinds of circumstances (a teenager vs. a 40-year-old executive); (2) there are different paths to becoming a single parent (never marrying, divorce, or widowhood); (3) the cause-and-effect relationship is unclear (e.g., does poverty cause single parenthood or does single parenthood cause poverty?); and (4) single parenthood is less problematic in other developed nations because of a wide number of social supports provided to all families, which are largely unavailable in the United States.

The number of single parents has risen in recent generations. In 1950, only 6 percent of households with children were maintained by a mother; in 2017 it was 23 percent. Only 1 percent of households in 1950 were maintained by single fathers, but that number has increased to 4 percent by 2017 (U.S. Census Bureau, May 4, 2018). Black children are far more likely to live with a single parent than are children in other racial or ethnic groups. For example, more than half of black children live with a single parent, as compared with just 13 percent of Asian/Pacific Islander children.

There are many different paths to single parenthood. Some women have babies outside of marriage. Some are teenagers and others are older adults. Others become single parents because of divorce or widowhood. Data allow for some generalizations about single parents. They are more likely to be poor or nearly so (Semega, Fontenot, and Kollar, 2017). They are less likely to own a home and they have lower levels of education (Vespa, Lewis, and Kreider, 2013). Yet, you should guard against sweeping generalizations because the different routes to single parenthood do produce different results.

Much of the concern surrounding single parents is targeted toward young women who forgo education when they have babies outside of marriage. However, a growing number of single mothers have a bachelor's degree or higher, and many are at least 30 years old. If you think about it, unmarried women in their thirties and forties offer a substantially different portrait of single parenthood: They are likely to have completed their education and have jobs, perhaps even well-paying careers.

Single parenthood does not have to be synonymous with poverty. Research from other countries makes this point clear. For example, using data from government agencies, social scientists, and researchers worldwide, a recent study of 16 high-income countries shows that single mothers in the United States—most of whom either are separated or were previously married—work more hours, but also have much higher poverty rates than their peers in other high-income countries (Kaufmann, 2012). Why is poverty so much higher in the United States among single mothers than in peer nations? Most high-income developed nations offer universal family or child cash allowances and an assortment of other cash programs and social policies such as childcare and health insurance specifically designed to help families with children. These programs and policies lift families out of poverty (Maldonado and Nieuwenhuis, 2015; Smeeding and Thévenot, 2016).

10.5.3 Lesbian, Gay, Bisexual, and Transgender Families

Lesbian, gay, bisexual, and transgender (LGBT) women and men are fighting for a basic human right: to be recognized and accepted as families. Because same-sex couples have only recently been allowed to marry in all states, their family relationships have

What Do You Think?

If you were given the task of developing a program to prevent teen pregnancy, what would that program look like? Who would you target it to? How would you structure it? What kind of opposition might it face and how would you deal with that?

historically been ignored or trivialized, and even less is known about transgender families. The small amount of research on same-sex families tends to focus on lesbians, furthering the stereotype that gay men are not interested in committed relationships or nurturing relationships with children (Biblarz and Stacey, 2010). However, these stereotypes are untrue. Many gays and lesbians are partnered and now married, now that same-sex marriage is legal in all states, and 17 percent of these families are raising children in the household (U.S. Census Bureau, May 4, 2018). Overall, at least 6 million children (and adults) have an LGBT parent.

For the most part, same-sex parents have a great deal in common with heterosexual parents: They struggle to get their children to school on time, they take their children to soccer practice after school, and they get involved in the local PTA. Their children grow up as well adjusted and happy as do those in heterosexual families (Biblarz and Stacey, 2010; Manning, Fettro, and Lamidi, 2014; Potter and Potter, 2017). One team of researchers reviewed 79 studies that met solid research critieria contributing to knowledge about the wellbeing of children with gay or lesbian parents. Of those 79 studies, 75 concluded that children of gay or lesbian parents fare no worse than other children. While many sample sizes were small, and some studies lacked a control group, researchers regard such studies as providing the best available knowledge about child adjustment. Four studies concluded that children of gay or lesbian parents face added disadvantages. However, these four research studies used samples of children who endured family break-ups, a cohort known to face added risks. Therefore, these four studies have been criticized by many scholars as unreliable assessments of the wellbeing of LGBT-headed households. Taken together, there appears to be an overwhelming scholarly consensus that having a gay or lesbian parent does not harm children. Yet, although most aspects of raising children are similar, a few differences do arise:

- The decision to parent among gay and lesbian couples is generally a deliberate choice that reflects a strong commitment to raising children. Studies tend to show either no difference among homosexuals and heterosexuals in their fitness to parent or give a slight advantage for same-sex couples. For example, lesbian mothers exhibit more parenting skills and awareness of child development than heterosexual couples, and there is greater similarity between partners' parenting skills. Likewise, compared with heterosexual fathers, gay fathers go to greater lengths to promote their children's cognitive skills, are more responsive to their children's needs, and are more involved in activities with children.

- LGBT families are more likely to be affected by loss. Lacking institutional constraints and support such as legalized marriage in all states, their relationships are somewhat more likely to dissolve than are heterosexual ones. However, because same-sex couples have only recently been allowed to marry anywhere in the United States, their trauma may not be publicly recognized or as easily supported. U.S. society acknowledges the tremendous disruption caused by a divorce; however, a "breakup" may be trivialized.

- Lesbian and gay families must cope with homophobia and discrimination. Although attitudes are shifting, same-sex relationships are stigmatized in some circles, and living openly as a family leaves them vulnerable to ridicule or discrimination. Violence against gays and lesbians is a possibility: One large-scale national survey found that 30 percent of LGBT respondents said that they had been threatened or physically attacked (Pew Research Center, 2013). Just as racial and ethnic minorities must teach their children about racism, gay and lesbian parents, too, must teach their children about prejudice and discrimination.

fictive kin

Friends in a close network who provide support.

Lesbians and gay men often have a close network of friends whom they regard as **fictive kin** who provide emotional and social support. Social support is crucial from family and friends as a way to ward off oppression and to create a safe and supportive environment for lesbians, gay men, and their children. They often have developed a close network of friends whom they regard as a sort of extended family. These friends are there to celebrate birthdays; participate in commitment ceremonies; babysit when needed; and in countless ways, offer the love and support that are needed to keep a household and a family running smoothly.

10.5.4 Grandparents Raising Grandchildren

My grandchildren, Caleb and Helen, came to live with my wife and I when they were 11 and 8 years old. We really didn't know what to do, but there was no other choice. Their mother was just up to no good. She'd leave them home alone when she went out partying. I'm not even sure that she came home at night. I think she's using drugs. And their dad, our son, he's so messed up. He ain't around much. So, I just told their mother, the kids gotta live with us. And she dropped them off one day and didn't even put up a fuss. (William, age 61)

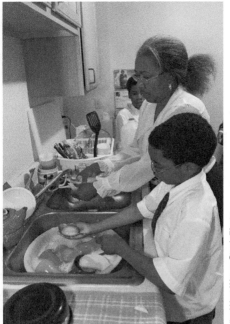

Jim West/Alamy Stock Photo

Roughly 8 million children (about 1 in 10) live with their grandparents (U.S. Census, May 4, 2018). Sometimes the child's parent(s) also live with the grandparent, but the greatest growth has occurred among children living with grandparents on their own, without a parent present. Several million children, like Caleb and Helen, live only with their grandparents and are cared for by those grandparents.

Where are these children's parents? Mothers and fathers may be absent for many reasons, including incarceration, drug or alcohol problems, physical or mental illnesses, employment difficulties, child abuse or neglect, desertion, or even death. There are often multiple problems in the homes of the grandchildren's parents that led the grandparents to take over their grandchildren's care. When parents are unable or unwilling to care for their children, grandparents often step in. Most arrangements are done privately, but in about one in six cases, child welfare agencies have intervened on behalf of the child.

Many of these grandparent-headed families experience considerable strain and challenges (Baugh, Taylor, and Bates, 2016; Ellis and Simmons, 2014; Hayslip, Fruhauf, and Dolbin-MacNab, 2017). First, grandparents face physical exhaustion trying to keep up with their grandchildren. Nearly half of grandparents who take care of their grandchildren are 55 years or older, and 15 percent are 65 or older. More than half are single grandparents, yet many are caring for young children who require considerable energy. Second, the grandparents often have physical or mental health problems, which could make caring for a child difficult. Third, many of these families are poor, have difficulty paying housing bills, or are on public assistance (Ellis and Simmons, 2014).

Despite these challenges, a growing number of grandparents continue to assume the responsibilities of caring for their grandchildren. As William, the grandfather in the earlier account, said, "There was no other choice." Out of love and out of duty, grandparents step in when parents fall short of their own responsibilities.

Most grandparents report having loving and fun relationships with their grandchildren. Some grandparents go one step further and are the primary caretakers of their grandchildren. When parents are unable to care for their own children, perhaps because of drugs, incarceration, or child neglect, it is grandparents who often step in to help.

Family Problems and Challenges

10.6 Explain two types of family problems or challenges: violence and divorce.

Families face many difficulties over their life course. This next section will discuss two difficulties that plague many families: The first is violence, and the second is divorce.

10.6.1 Violence

What do former talk show host Oprah Winfrey, singer Rihanna, and actress Pamela Anderson have in common? In addition to being celebrities, they all have had the frightening experience of being abused within their families or close relationships.

Rihanna and Pamela Anderson were victims of violence by their intimate partners; Oprah Winfrey revealed that several members of her extended family sexually abused her as a child. People find violence in families to be particularly abhorrent because they like to idealize families as safe havens. Yet, for many people, especially women and girls, this safe haven is not the case.

Violence has touched the lives of millions of families. **Violence among intimates**, defined as violence among family members or intimate partners, takes many forms, including intimate partner violence, child abuse, and elder abuse. As you will see, violence is more than simply a personal problem of "he just has a bad temper." Violence among intimates is a *social* problem. First, it affects large numbers of people. Second, violence is not completely random—it is possible to detect particular patterns and risk factors for both victims and perpetrators. Third, the causes, consequences, and solutions of violence must address social, cultural, and economic factors.

Human Rights Watch and the United Nations, both international organizations dedicated to protecting the human rights of people around the world, report that many countries have horrendous records on addressing violence against women and girls, as you learned in Chapter 5, and much of this violence occurs within families and intimate relationships. The following sections will examine violence against partners and children and will consider what might explain it.

INTIMATE PARTNER VIOLENCE Intimate partner violence (IPV) refers to violence between those who are physically and sexually intimate, such as spouses or partners. The violence can encompass physical, economic, sexual, or psychological abuse, and many abusive situations include more than one type. But just as important as the type of violence is the underlying premise of that violence. Family violence researcher Michael Johnson distinguishes between four general premises:

- *Common couple violence (CCV)* arises out of a specific argument in which at least one partner lashes out physically. It is less likely to escalate or involve severe injury; yet, it is this type of violence that is usually captured in research studies.
  - *Intimate terrorism (IT)* is motivated by a desire to control the other partner. It is more likely than CCV to escalate over time and to cause serious injury, although some cases of IT involve relatively little injury. The primary feature of this type of abuse is the general desire for control.
  - *Violent resistance (VR)* is the nonlegal term associated with self-defense. Research on VR is scarce, and it is conducted almost entirely by women. Engaging in violent resistance may be an indicator that a person will soon leave the abusive partner.
  - *Mutual violent control (MVC)* refers to a pattern of behavior in which both partners are controlling and violent; they are battling for control. Again, this pattern is an understudied phenomenon.

Until the 1970s, what people knew about spousal and partner abuse was based on small samples from the isolated case files of social workers, psychologists, and police. These data can be very biased because only certain types of abuse and abusers come to the attention of these professionals.

However, since that time, family and social scientists have been using large and representative samples to understand how often spousal and partner violence occurs, who is likely to be a victim, and what are its causes and consequences. Early surveys by Murray Straus and colleagues (Straus, Gelles, and Steinmetz, 1980) showed an alarming rate of IPV in the United States, and more recent studies confirm this, as you can see in Figure 10–6. This national survey is based on nearly

violence among intimates

Violence among family members or intimate partners.

intimate partner violence (IPV)

Violence between those who are physically and sexually intimate, such as spouses or partners.

Intimate partner violence is a serious social problem causing injury and disability to thousands of people (mostly women) throughout the country each year. Issues of power and control are usually involved.

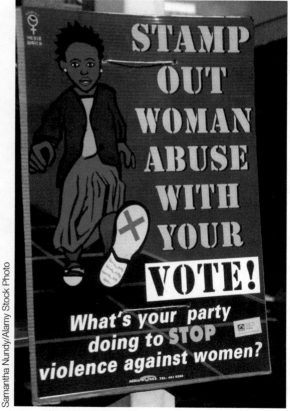

Figure 10-6 Lifetime Prevalence of Physical Violence Victimization by an Intimate Partner, 2010–2012

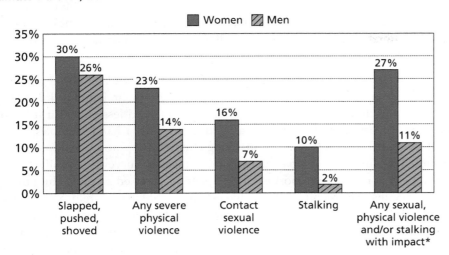

* Includes experiences with any of the following: being fearful, concerned for your safety, any PTSD symptoms, injury, need for medical care, need for housing or legal services, missed at least one day of work or school, contacted a crisis hotline, contracted an STI, or having become pregnant.

SOURCE: Smith, S. G., et al. 2017. "The National Intimate Partner and Sexual Violence Survey (NISVS): 2010–2012 State Report." April. National Center for Injury Prevention and Control. Atlanta, GA: Centers for Disease Control and Prevention.

13,000 interviews with both men and women and sheds light on a wide variety of violent experiences. The figure examines the percentage of women and men who have experienced different forms of IPV over the course of their lives (so far). Women are much more likely than men to say they have experienced contact sexual violence (e.g., rape or other sexual assault), stalking, and severe physical violence, such as beating, choking, being slammed against something, or having a weapon used on them. Only with respect to more "minor" types of violence is the sex difference not large (Smith et al., 2017).

IPV can have tragic results, both emotionally and physically. Approximately 41 percent of female IPV victims and 14 percent of male IPV victims experience some form of physical injury related to their experience of relationship violence (Niolon et al., 2017). Minor forms of bruises, scratches, and welts are most common, but broken bones, severe bruising, or head trauma are other consequences of violence. In general, victims of repeated violence over time experience more serious consequences than victims of one-time incidents (Breiding et al., 2014).

Other consequences are not as visible, but just as real. The stress from IPV can wreak havoc on the immune and endocrine systems, causing conditions such as fibromyalgia, gynecological disorders, irritable bowel syndrome, or gastrointestinal problems (Centers for Disease Control and Prevention, 2017; Smith et al., 2017). Because physical violence is typically accompanied by emotional or psychological abuse, many victims are depressed and have anxiety, disturbed sleep, and low self-esteem. They often are socially isolated and have thoughts of suicide (Breiding et al., 2014). Victims of IPV are more likely to behave in unhealthy ways, such as engaging in high-risk sexual behavior (e.g., having unprotected sex, trading sex for food or money); using harmful substances (e.g., smoking cigarettes, abusing drugs); or having unhealthy diet-related behaviors (e.g., bingeing and purging food).

Despite the clear need for mental health care, many women, especially minority women, often experience barriers to getting this care. Barriers include cultural or language differences, or a lack of services and providers in poor or ethnic communities (O'Neal and Beckman, 2017).

What Do You Think?

Most victims of intimate partner violence eventually leave the situation, but for many people, leaving is a long process. Why do you think leaving takes so long? Why would someone stay in an abusive situation? Be sure to identify both cultural and personal characteristics.

In addition to the consequences to the individual, there are also societal consequences. In other words, you are affected by intimate partner violence even if you do not know anyone who is a victim or perpetrator (which is highly unlikely). Victims lose nearly 8 million days of paid work a year, the equivalent of more than 32,000 full-time jobs. Costs exceed $8 billion, most of which goes to medical and mental health care.

CHILD ABUSE   Child abuse is an attack on a child that violates social norms and may result in an injury. Sometimes these social norms are ambiguous; for example, is hitting your child a form of child abuse? Does it sound less violent if it is called "spanking"? Does it matter whether a child is hit with a hand or a baseball bat? About two-thirds of adults believe spanking children is appropriate, representing a substantial decline over the past generation. However, surveys generally find that over 90 percent of parents report having slapped or spanked a young child over the past 12 months. Meanwhile, others suggest that spanking is child abuse because spanked children are more likely to be depressed, to abuse animals, and to exhibit other anti-social behaviors. In a review of 111 studies involving over 160,000 children, the researchers found that all the studies found a link between spanking and adverse child outcomes (Gershoff and Grogan-Kaylor, 2016).

But often, the abuse is so egregious that there is little doubt, and government agencies become involved to protect the child. According to the U.S. government, 676,000 children were determined to be victims of abuse or neglect in 2016, more than 1,700 of whom died as a result. In fact, more children under the age of 4 die from abuse and neglect than from falls, choking, drowning, fires, or motor vehicle accidents. Abuse occurs in all income, racial, religious, and ethnic groups, and in all types of communities (U.S. Department of Health and Human Services, Administration on Children, Youth, and Families, 2018). The good news, if there is any, is that substantiated abuse cases have declined significantly over the past 20 years.

There are several different types of child abuse:

- *Neglect* is the most common form of abuse and involves the failure to provide for the child's basic needs, such as failing to provide adequate food, clothing, shelter, a safe environment, supervision, or medical care to a dependent child.
- *Physical abuse* involves inflicting physical injury and harm on a child and may include hitting, shaking, burning, kicking, or in other ways physically harming a child. Among substantiated child abuse cases, nearly one in six involved physical abuse. The most extreme cases may result in the death of a child. The most common forms of death were skull fracture and internal bleeding.
- *Sexual abuse* involves inappropriate sexual behavior with a child for sexual gratification. It could include fondling a child's genitals, making the child fondle the perpetrator's genitals, and progressing to more intrusive sexual acts such as oral sex and vaginal or anal penetration. Sexual abuse also includes acts such as exhibition or in other ways exploiting the child for sexual purposes.
- *Psychological maltreatment* includes verbal, mental, or psychological maltreatment that destroys a child's self-esteem. Abuse of this nature often includes threatening, degrading, or humiliating the child and extreme or bizarre forms of punishment, such as confinement to a dark room or being tied to a chair for long periods of time. It is likely that emotional abuse occurs far more frequently than what can be substantiated.
- *Medical neglect* represents a small but important type of abuse, and involves delaying or forgoing a child's needed medical, dental, or prescription care.

There are also other types of abuse, of course, such as congenital drug addiction or threats of harm. Abuse occurs in all income, racial, religious, and ethnic groups and in all types of communities. Female victims outnumber male victims, especially in

Figure 10-7 Who Are the Child Abuse Perpetrators? 2016

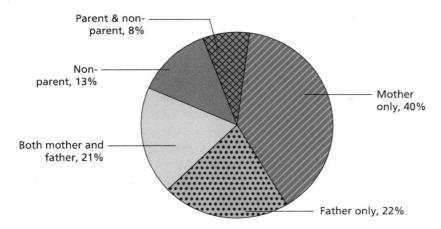

NOTE: Analysis counts every relationship for each report; therefore, the percentages total more than 100 percent.

SOURCE: U. S. Department of Health & Human Services, Administration for Children and Families, Administration on Children, Youth and Families, Children's Bureau. (2018). Child maltreatment 2016. Retrieved 6 September 2018 (https://www.acf.hhs.gov/cb/research-data-technology/statistics-research/child-maltreatment).

cases of sexual abuse. Black children have the highest rates of victimization, and Asian Americans have the lowest. Most people who abuse children are not strangers, but are biological family members, as shown in Figure 10–7. The vast majority of child abusers are family members (most often the mother).

Child abuse can have serious consequences for the child. In its most extreme forms, it can result in death. Each year, more than 1,500 children die as a result of abuse and neglect; 60 percent were age 1 year or younger, and 80 percent were under age 4 (U.S. Department of Health and Human Services, Administration on Children and Families, 2015). Annually, more children under the age of 4 die from abuse and neglect than from falls, choking, drowning, fires, or motor vehicle accidents.

Perhaps even more insidious are the emotional scars left behind. Abuse is trauma. Physically abused children tend to be more aggressive and more likely to get involved in delinquent activities, have difficulty in school, and be involved in early sexual activity, which can result in teen pregnancy. However, not all physically abused children have these outcomes. One study reviewed the findings of 21 published reports on child abuse to note any trends in children's behavior. The researchers found that the number of abused children having difficulty in educational, behavioral, or emotional domains varied greatly and that a child may do poorly in one domain, but excel in another. About one in five abused children had difficulty and functioned poorly in all domains (Walsh, Dawson, and Mattingly, 2010). The emotional trauma can be long-lasting. Even as adults, children who have been abused are more likely to suffer nightmares, depression, panic disorders, and have suicidal thoughts, and this abuse can also affect their relationship with their own children, increasing the likelihood of poor attachment, neglect, and further abuse (Allen, Tellez, Wevodau, Woods, and Percosky, 2014; Somers, Ibrahim, and Luecken, 2017). The costs of child abuse are far too great to ignore.

WHAT EXPLAINS VIOLENCE? A quick survey of your classmates would probably show that virtually everyone abhors violence in families and intimate relationships. Why then is it so widespread? Three factors contribute to violence: (1) intergenerational transmission of violence; (2) stress; and (3) cultural factors, including patriarchy, cultural tolerance for violence, and norms of family privacy.

- *Intergenerational Transmission of Violence.* Drawing on Bandura's (1977) social learning theory, the idea of intergenerational transmission suggests that people learn norms and behaviors, including violence, by observing others. There is a tendency toward intergenerational transmission of violence: Children who witness or experience abuse are more likely to be in abusive relationships as an adult than are other children. For example, a study based on 45,000 responses to a Web-based survey, the "Relationship Evaluation Questionnaire" (RELATE), found that 10 percent of couples without any reported violence in their family of orientation were violent in their current relationship compared with 32 percent of couples who reported that they had either witnessed or experienced violence in their home as children (Busby et al., 2008). Granted, although the sample is large, it is not based on a representative sample because people who completed RELATE may have been part of a class or workshop, or they may have found the questionnaire on their own search of the Web. Nonetheless, it provides some degree of evidence of the intergenerational transmission of violence. However, the study also found that more than two-thirds of people who witnessed or experienced violence as children were *not* in an abusive relationship as an adult. Therefore, it is very important to note that the intergenerational transmission of violence refers to a greater likelihood of engaging in violence; it does not refer to determinism. Many people who witnessed or experienced abuse as children grow up to be caring and supportive partners and parents.

- *Stress.* Inordinate amounts of stress such as chronic under- or unemployment, economic issues, health problems, or other job or family difficulties also may play a role in violent relationships (Straus, 1980). Many stressors are highly correlated with income. Moreover, lower-income families have fewer opportunities available to help them ward off the impact of the stressors, for example, fewer savings or assets. Lower-income families are also more likely to engage in coping mechanisms that jeopardize their health (e.g., drinking, smoking, or eating poorly nutritious foods), whereas wealthier people have other options. Not surprisingly then, violence is more likely to occur in lower-income households, although it does occur at all income levels.

- *Cultural Factors.* Observations about intergenerational transmission of violence and stress help explain why some people are violent, but they do not place individual actions in their social context. Murray Straus, in the study of stress just described, argued that stress by itself does not necessarily lead to violence, but rather, researchers should look at social and cultural attitudes that perpetuate violence as a response to stressors (Straus, 1980). Three of these attitudes, patriarchy, cultural support for violence, and norms of family privacy help to further explain violence.

  - In many patriarchal cultures, violence against women is not only tolerated but also holds a wide degree of support (Crittenden and Wright, 2013). For example, 56 percent of men in Turkey stated on a survey that they accepted "wife beating" (Rani and Banu, 2009). Interestingly, because women are socialized in the same patriarchal culture as men, they often support the violence. One study interviewed 450 women living in three cities in the West Bank to assess their attitudes toward "wife beating." Overall, the women perceived violence against wives to be justified if a wife insults her husband (59 percent), if she disobeys her husband (49 percent), if she neglects her children (37 percent), if she goes out without telling her husband (25 percent), if she argues with her husband (11 percent), and if she burns the food (5 percent). Sixty-five percent of the women agreed with at least one reason for wife beating, and those who have less education, who have more than one child, who make few household decisions, and who have been married less than 10 years agreed most strongly (Dhaher et al., 2010).

  - A second cultural explanation focuses on the fact that some cultures are more tolerant of violence in general than are others. For example, in the United

States, violence is very public, readily seen on television or in theaters. Football, hockey, rugby, wrestling, and race car driving are notoriously violent sports, and those who watch these events expect nothing less, all in the name of fun. Yet at other times, similar aggression is completely inappropriate: Your professor cannot slap you because you failed to read the assigned material. The difficulty lies in the fact that sometimes these lines get blurred. When is it okay to hit, and when is it not okay? Or, when does hitting turn into abuse?

- A third cultural explanation has to do with the level of privacy expected across cultures. You have probably heard the saying, "a man's home is his castle." It refers to the idea that a man is dominant in his home, and what occurs there is no one else's business (Berardo, 1998). The structure of modern society reinforces this sense of privacy. In urban areas, families know few, if any, of their neighbors well, and therefore, are increasingly isolated (Nock, 1998). Moreover, many people genuinely believe that violence is a private matter between family members. Neighbors, coworkers, or even friends and other kin can be hesitant to get involved, perhaps saying, "I didn't want to say anything because it's really none of my business."

Although individual and cultural explanations focus on different factors that contribute to violence, both levels of analysis suggest that perpetrators are exerting their domination, power, and control over their victims. The Power and Control Wheel shown in Figure 10–8 depicts behaviors and privileges that batterers use to dominate and control their partners.

Figure 10–8 Power and Control Wheel

bramgino/Fotolia

Married couples in the United States are more likely to divorce than are couples in any other country except for Russia. Why do you think that is the case?

10.6.2 Divorce

A divorce decree may be granted in a matter of minutes by a judge. However, behind those few tense minutes usually lies a long period in which a couple has analyzed, redefined, and reorganized virtually all aspects of their relationship and their lives. Divorce is not simply the ending of a relationship between two people; it alters or even severs many personal and legal ties. A divorce can end relationships with family members; with friends who find themselves taking sides; with neighbors if one or both of the former couple have moved away; and with community groups of which an ex-spouse is no longer a member or can no longer afford to join. If you are like many college students, you have seen divorce up close.

FREQUENCY OF DIVORCE We commonly hear that "half of all marriages end in divorce." This phrase, however, is somewhat misleading. Some people interpret it to mean that if 100,000 couples married last year, 50,000 divorces were also granted; on the surface, it looks as though 50 percent of marriages ended in divorce. But this comparison does not really make sense because the 100,000 marriages took place in only one year, whereas the divorces are from marriages that may have continued over many years. Therefore, this comparison is misleading and not very useful.

A better measure is called the crude divorce rate, which examines the frequency of divorce per 1,000 people. In the United States, this rate amounts to about 3.1 divorces per 1,000 people in 2015 (Centers for Disease Control and Prevention, 2017).

However, the crude divorce rate is still problematic. Not all people have married; therefore, why should unmarried people be included in a divorce statistic? A more useful way to measure the frequency of divorce is to talk about the number of divorces that occur out of every 1,000 married women, which is called the refined divorce rate. Using the refined divorce rate, there were 16.9 divorces per 1,000 married women in the United States in 2015 (Anderson, 2016). Thus, within a year, less than 17 out of 1,000 married women, or less than 2 percent, received a divorce.

These divorce rates are cross-sectional, meaning that they reflect rates at only one point in time. So, even though a married woman had nearly a 2 percent chance of divorcing last year, she has a far higher chance of divorcing over the course of her married life. If only 17 out of 1,000 married women get divorced this year and the remaining 983 do not, those women could get divorced the following year, or the year after that, or 15 years later. However you measure it, the United States has one of the highest rates of divorce in the world.

THE IMPACT OF DIVORCE ON ADULTS Divorce, even when desired by both partners, is almost always accompanied by considerable emotional and financial strain. One or both partners may feel angry, resentful, sad, depressed, or rejected, and divorced people tend to have more health problems than those who are married (Symoens et al., 2013). Generally, one spouse initiates the breakup of the marriage (Hewitt, Western, and Baxter, 2006). A common pattern is that an initiator expresses general discontent at first, but without attributing it to the marriage per se. He or she may try to alter the relationship or the other spouse's behavior by suggesting such remedies as a new job, having a baby, or some other substantial change to the nature of the relationship. He or she may even use the threat of leaving as a way to demand change. The other spouse's reaction—anger, resentment, sadness, resolve, or rejection—shapes his or her emotional response.

Men and women often have distinctive challenges after divorce. According to feminist theory, society offers men and women different opportunities and constraints that help explain their gendered experiences. For example, women are more likely than men to have financial problems after a divorce. In contrast, men often have a more difficult time emotionally after a divorce, and in some cases, this stress is so extreme that it can lead to increased illness or an early death. One reason for this emotional difficulty is that men tend to have a weaker network of supportive relationships. Additionally, most men lose custody of their children; more than 80 percent of children live with their mother following a divorce (Grall, 2016). For many fathers, moving away from their children is devastating (Kamp Dush, 2013).

With respect to finances, those couples who divorce when young, who are without children, and who have high levels of education and job prospects may fare just fine. However, female-headed families with children are nearly twice as likely as male-headed families, and five times as likely as married-couple families, to live in poverty (Semega, Fontenot, and Kollar, 2017). Most single mothers are unable to support themselves to the level they had while married. Also, because single mothers usually have children living with them, they may have to restrict the type of job they can take (e.g., one that requires no overtime or travel). Most husbands do not support their children after divorce at the level decreed by the courts. According to data from the U.S. Census Bureau, in a recent year, only 46 percent of custodial parents (usually mothers) received the full child support payment that was due to them, 29 percent received a partial payment, and 26 percent received no payment at all (Grall, 2016).

Because of all the decisions a divorcing couple faces—for example, who gets the house, should alimony be paid, how the assets should be divided, where will the children live—a couple may hire a mediator to help them. The goal of a mediator is to be a neutral force (unlike an attorney) who helps couples negotiate before having to go to court.

THE IMPACT OF DIVORCE ON CHILDREN Some people try to brush off the effects of their parents' divorce saying, "Hey, I turned out just fine …," but the truth is that many children are deeply affected by their parents' divorce and remain so for many years (Amato, 2007; Arkes, 2015; Baker and Brassard, 2013). The first year or two after a divorce can be particularly tough for children. During this time, children grieve the loss of their intact family and are dealing with new feelings and fears. They may feel guilty or depressed, suffer from sleep difficulties, and act out aggressively (Guinart and Grau, 2014). In particular, young children are egocentric and often feel that they are responsible for their parents' conflict and divorce—that if they had just behaved better, their parents would not have divorced. During this crisis period, children face many situations with which they must learn to cope, including (1) handling parental conflict; (2) weakened parental bonds, especially to their fathers; (3) coping with a reduced standard of living; and (4) adjusting to many transitions such as a new neighborhood and school.

Although most children adjust adequately over time to the transitions in their lives, some children continue to be plagued by problems (Soria, Morrow, and Jackson, 2018). Children whose parents divorce are more likely to become pregnant before marriage or impregnate someone, drop out of school and have lower academic achievement, experience more behavioral problems and aggression toward peers, use alcohol or drugs, have poor health, be more likely to suffer from depression, and tend toward being idle or unemployed. One recent study looked at whether there were any differences in college students' achievement or their persistence at staying in college in terms of whether or not their parents had divorced. Collecting data from a large public university, the research team found that students whose parents were divorced were significantly less likely to continue into their second year of college than their peers. They also had lower cumulative grade point averages. These differences remained after controlling for demographic characteristics or academic indicators before coming to college (Soria and Linder, 2014).

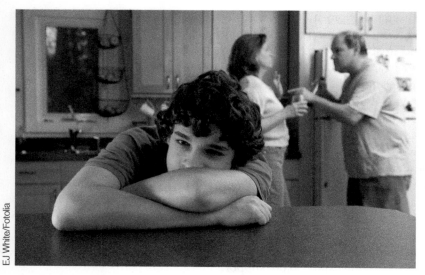

EJ White/Fotolia

Matt's parents have been arguing for years. Their arguments are not violent physically, but they occur frequently, and his parents call each other terrible names. Matt tries to tune them out, but it is difficult to do so, and his own schoolwork is starting to suffer as a result. Do you think Matt would be better off if his parents divorced?

stepfamilies

Families in which one or both of the adult partners have at least one child, either residing with them or living elsewhere.

These findings certainly do not mean that all children from divorced households experience these negative outcomes. Many children whose parents have divorced lead happy, well-adjusted, and successful lives; these studies simply show that children of divorced parents are more likely to have these problems than are children from families in which parents have not divorced.

The question that people usually want answered is: Are children better off when their unhappily married parents remain married or are children better off when their parents divorce? The answer depends on many things, particularly the severity of the conflict in the marriage. Children do not fare well when there is tremendous conflict and when they are put in the middle of their parents' struggles (Bannon, Barle, Mennella, and O'Leary, 2018; Bi, Haak, Gilbert, and Keller, 2017; Gager, Yabiku, and Linver, 2016; Moed, Dix, Anderson, and Greene, 2017)—regardless of whether the parents divorce or remain married. In fact, many researchers suggest that it is the amount of conflict rather than a divorce *per se* that causes the most harm to children.

For example, a pioneering study by Amato and Booth (1997), which was based on telephone and in-person interviews conducted in 1980 and 1992 with a nationally representative sample, found that children who were in families with high marital conflict in 1980 were doing *better* in 1992 if their parents had divorced than if they had stayed together. However, Amato and Booth also found that children from relatively low-conflict families were *worse* off if their parents divorced than if their parents had remained together. These findings suggest that the worst situations for children are to be in either (1) a high-conflict marriage that doesn't end in divorce or (2) a low-conflict marriage that does end in divorce.

STEPFAMILIES   Most people remarry or cohabit after a divorce. Sometimes one or both of these people have children from a previous relationship. Sometimes they have children together. **Stepfamilies** are families in which one or both of the adult partners have at least one child, either residing with them or living elsewhere. Stepfamilies can create an intricate weave of complex relationships. For example, children in stepfamilies can be referred to as (1) siblings (biologically related to same parents); (2) stepsiblings (not biologically related, but parents are married to each other); (3) half-siblings (share one parent biologically); (4) mutual child (a child born to the remarried couple); (5) residential stepchildren (live in the household with the remarried couple more than half of the time); and (6) nonresidential stepchildren (live in the household less than half of the time). There are also multiple part-time and full-time living arrangements.

Despite the prevalence of stepfamilies, the expectations, obligations, and rules within them are ambiguous (Coleman, Ganong, Russell, and Frye-Cox, 2015; DeGreef and Burnett, 2017). No socially prescribed script explains how family members are expected to relate to one another. Should a stepparent behave like a biological parent, like a friend, like an aunt or uncle, or like someone else entirely? To what extent can stepparents discipline their stepchildren? How are stepparents and stepchildren supposed to feel about one another? What names do children call their stepparent? Indeed, do stepparents and their stepchildren even include one another as part of their "family"? For example, if your father remarries when you are an adult and living away from home, and you see his wife once a year or so, would you consider her as "your stepmom" or simply "my dad's wife"? Would you think of her grown children, whom you may have never met, as your "stepsiblings" or are they "her children"?

Nonetheless, stepfamilies can be an enriching experience (Amato, King, and Thorsen, 2016). Children living in stepfamilies gain exposure to new behavior patterns and lifestyles. Children may also benefit from an increased standard of living made possible by two incomes and their parents' greater happiness at being involved in another relationship. Stepfamily adoptions are the most common type of adoption in the United States, a testament to the love and commitment that many stepparents and children feel toward one another.

Social Policy

10.7   Discuss family policy, using the example of paid family leave.

The government regulates many aspects of families. For example, the government prohibits certain people from marrying each other, requires people who intend to marry to have a blood test, and requires two witnesses for a legal wedding ceremony. The government also touches the lives of families by an absence of certain policies. For example, U.S. adults have no guaranteed paid family or maternity leave, national health insurance, or subsidized childcare. These family policies (or the lack thereof) reflect historical, cultural, political, and social factors in the United States, including norms that favor personal over collective responsibility. The United States has little in the way of a comprehensive and collective vision for families, unlike other developed nations (Dey and Wasoff, 2013).

There are many family policy issues worthy of discussion, but due to space limitations we will focus on just one here: maternity leave. An important way to invest in families is by providing paid maternity (and paternity) leaves after the birth of a child. In 2016, 14 percent of civilian workers had access to paid family leave, according to the National Compensation Survey, conducted annually by the Federal Bureau of Labor Statistics (March, 2017). The feature, *A Closer Look: "What a Difference Location Can Make"* examines the maternity leave policy of the United States versus that of our Canadian neighbor.

Why are maternity leaves so important? Lengthy maternity leaves are associated with better maternal and child health and with lower family stress. Moreover, with extended leave benefits, women are likely to breastfeed for longer periods, which improves children's immunity and reduces their later risk of obesity. The benefit of longer parental leaves also extends to employers. Women are more likely to return to work after childbirth in those countries that have longer leaves. It is more cost-effective for a company to develop a well-planned parental leave policy than it is to rehire and retrain new employees.

Even fathers want time off to help bond with and care for a newborn. One-third of fathers stay home more than two weeks, but generally, these fathers work in professional jobs with a higher degree of flexibility and must use their vacation time or take unpaid leave.

The United States has, by far, the least generous family leave policy of any nation in the world, including poor and developing nations, as you can see in Table 10–3. The Family Medical Leave Act of 1993, signed by President Clinton, requires employers with more than 50 employees to offer 12 weeks of *unpaid* leave for maternity or to care for a sick family member. Many women take only a few weeks off from work after having a baby because they cannot afford unpaid leave (Pew Research Center, March 23, 2017). They return to work soon after exhausting any short-term disability, vacation, or sick pay they may have. Among women who worked during their pregnancy, 58 percent returned to work within three months after giving birth, and 72 percent returned within six months.

A Closer Look

What a Difference Location Can Make

Wavebreak Media/Alamy Stock Photo

Melinda and Dave, who live in Seattle, Washington, are excited to welcome their first child, a daughter, to their family. They have dreamed of having a child for several years. Melinda works for a mid-sized corporation that, like most corporations, does not offer a paid maternity leave policy. Luckily for her she has two weeks of sick-leave saved, two weeks of paid vacation she can use, and her company agreed to give her another two weeks off of work, unpaid, to care for her baby. Legally she could stay home another six weeks without pay and not fear losing her job, but her family cannot live on Dave's salary alone. So Melinda goes back to work, still sleep-deprived and anxious over their new baby, not to mention the angst of an $1,100-a-month childcare bill. She takes her breast pump with her to work and uses it in the women's restroom on her breaks. This effort allows her to

save her breast milk to feed it to her daughter while she is away at work.

Meanwhile, Janine, across the border in Vancouver, Canada, is enjoying four months of maternity leave, at 55 percent of her pay. She is also considering taking additional time off, knowing that her job is guaranteed for her when she returns. She rests assured knowing that when she does, the cost of childcare will be subsidized by the government, and she will be eligible for a family allowance to help offset the cost of raising her son. There is no stigma in taking maternity leave in Canada. No one will accuse her of not being "serious" about her job. Virtually all women take maternity leave, and the program is held in very high regard in Canada. Likewise, there is no stigma attached to a family allowance. Children are considered a "public good" because all Canadians benefit by having children who are well-tended to. Therefore, the government gives a small sum of money to help the new family with the costs of raising a child. It is available to all families, regardless of income, and is not considered welfare.

The United States and Canada—two countries that are located right next to one another—could not be further apart.

Critical Thinking

Why do you think that neighboring countries have such different views of what is needed after the birth of a baby? Now compare and contrast how a functionalist and conflict theorist would answer this question.

By way of contrast, consider what other countries offer for maternity leave:

- France offers 16 weeks of paid maternity leave to women at 100 percent of their salary.
- In Denmark, women receive 52 weeks of paid maternity leave at 100 percent of their salary.
- Cuba offers women 18 weeks of leave at 100 percent of their salary.
- The United Kingdom allows maternity pay at 90 percent for 6 weeks and a flat rate after that for up to 1 year.
- Brazil provides 120 days of maternity benefits at 100 percent of the mother's salary (United Nations Statistics Division, 2013).

It is odd to think that a country as wealthy as the United States offers so little to new parents.

10.7.1 Future Prospects

Both former President Obama and current President Trump have reminded Americans that the United States is the only nation without paid family leave. In State of the Union speeches in 2015 and 2018, both asked joint sessions of Congress to pass measures that would assist workers in juggling work and family obligations. Former President Obama pushed an idea allowing workers to earn up to six weeks of paid sick

Table 10–3 A Comparison of Maternity Leave Benefits in Developed and Developing Nations

	Length of Maternity Leave	Percentage of Wages Paid in Covered Period
Less Developed Countries		
Afghanistan	90 days	100%
Bangladesh	16 weeks	100%
Cuba	18 weeks	100%
Egypt	90 days	100%
Guatemala	84 days	100%
India	12 weeks	100%
Kenya	3 months	100%
Mozambique	60 days	100%
Republic of Korea	60 days	100%
Developed Countries		
Canada	17–18 weeks	55% for 15 weeks
Denmark	52 weeks	100%
Finland	105 days	80%
Ireland	28 weeks	80% or fixed rate
Italy	5 months	80%
Japan	14 weeks	67%
Netherlands	16 weeks	100%
Spain	16 weeks	100%
Sweden	480 days	80% for 390 days; flat rate afterwards
Switzerland	98 days	80%
United Kingdom	52 weeks	90% for 6 weeks; flat rate afterwards
United States	12 weeks[a]	0%

a. Applies only to workers in companies with 50 or more employees.

SOURCE: Data from United Nations Statistics Division. 2013. "UN Data: Maternity Benefits." Retrieved 5 March 2015 (data.un.org/DocumentData.aspx?id=344).

time a year that could be used as paid family leave. This proposal, while representing a major change in policy, would still leave Americans with one of the weakest family leave laws in the world. In contrast, President Trump's idea would allow parents to draw from their Social Security benefits early to fund their parental leave, then require them to delay the collection of retirement benefits by some yet-to-be-calculated period of time. Participation would be strictly voluntary. Some fear that this proposal would penalize bigger families more than smaller ones; couples with more children would face later retirement ages before receiving benefits. Moreover, it would likely mean that lower-wage workers would end up putting off retirement longer than wealthier workers who have more generous retirement pensions.

Going Beyond Left and Right

As the social institution that organizes intimate relationships among adults and socializes new generations, the family is frequently singled out as the source of many social problems. Americans hear endless debates about how to restore faltering "family values" or about which policies will best support and enhance the family as a social institution.

These debates are not likely to disappear in the foreseeable future, especially as the diversity of family forms in the United States and throughout the world continues to increase. Politics is becoming more polarized than ever. Americans have trouble even agreeing on which family issues constitute social problems. Is the lack of paid family leave a social problem? Do Americans tend to support or oppose paid family leave, and if they support it, who should pay for it? These are not really Republican or Democratic issues since family issues affect us all, regardless of political persuasion.

Summary

10.1 Define the term *family* and explain why it is important.

Families are defined here as relationships by blood, marriage, or affection, in which members may cooperate economically, may care for any children, and may consider their identity to be intimately connected to the larger group. The definition used has important consequences with respect to informal and formal rights.

10.2 Identify the functions of families.

Functions of the family include regulation of sexual behavior; reproduction and socializing children; property and inheritance; economic cooperation; social placement status and roles; and care, warmth, protection, and intimacy.

10.3 Compare and contrast three perspectives on family change.

Conservatives express grave concern that changes in family structure put children at risk. They suggest that many challenges families face are linked to gross cultural and moral weakening. Liberals suggest that these problems experienced by families result from economic and structural adjustments that place new demands on families without offering additional social supports. Feminists ask for policies that place higher value on the quality of human relationships. They work for reforms that build and strengthen neighborhoods and volunteer groups, support caregiving activities, and encourage education and employment among both women and men.

10.4 Discuss the changing norms of marriage and intimate relationships.

Norms surrounding marriage and intimate relationships are changing. For example, fewer people are married today than in the past, including a delay in the age at which they marry; more couples cohabit before or instead of marrying; same-sex couples fought for and won the right to marry; and the division of household labor has become somewhat more equitable.

10.5 Review different types of parenting contexts.

Most adults have children at some point in their lives. There are different types of parenting contexts, including a declining number of teenage parents, a growing number of single parents, an increase in gay and lesbian families, and an increase in grandparents raising their grandchildren. Although parenting across these contexts has many similarities, it also has significant differences.

10.6 Explain two types of family problems or challenges: violence and divorce.

Families face a number of problems, and two are discussed here. The first is violence, including intimate partner violence and child abuse. The second problem discussed is divorce. The number of divorces has declined steadily since the peak in the 1980s, but the United States still has one of the highest divorce rates in the world. Divorce has a variety of negative consequences for adults and children.

10.7 Discuss family policy, using the example of paid family leave.

The government regulates many aspects of families by the policies it creates. The government also touches the lives of families by an absence of certain policies. For example, U.S. adults have no guaranteed family or maternity leave.

Chapter 11
Problems of Education

WavebreakMediaMicro/Fotolia

 ## Learning Objectives

11.1 Describe the history of the American education system.

11.2 Summarize why education is a social problem.

11.3 Compare and contrast the sociological perspectives on education.

11.4 Identify the educational attainment and achievement of different groups in society.

11.5 Evaluate how students in the United States compare to students in other countries in terms of educational achievement.

11.6 Discuss some of the current social problems facing schools.

11.7 Evaluate access to higher education in the United States.

It's Monday morning, and Mason is just entering his classroom. He is a happy-go-lucky fourth grader and loves school, although he would never admit that to his friends, which include the other 16 students in his class. But he secretly knows that they also enjoy school. When the bell rings, he knows the drill—he goes to his personal computer and begins working on a paper that he saved yesterday in Google Docs. Once his file is up and he rereads his work, he combs the Internet for more information for his paper. He knows that if he has any problems finding what he needs, his teacher or the classroom aide can offer individual help. Likewise, if he has any problems with his computer itself, the school's technology department will have it fixed in no time or they will issue him another. Mason works on his project quietly until his teacher informs the class that the science specialist has just walked into the classroom. Mason saves his work, and eagerly awaits what they will do in science today. His favorite classes are science, art, music, and P.E., all taught by specialists with expertise in their fields. What school is this, you ask, where class size is 17 students, each student has his or her own computer, and the school's curriculum is so enriching? Where can you sign your child up? Mason attends a private school with tuition costs of $25,000 a year, and your child will likely have to be put on the waiting list to get in.

What Do You Think?

How would you rate the quality of your K–12 education, and why? What, if anything, would you like to change? Are the changes realistically possible?

No Child Left Behind Act of 2001

A major legislative initiative of the Bush administration to improve education in four clearly defined ways: (1) accountability for results; (2) emphasis on doing what works based on scientific research; (3) expanded parental school choice options; and (4) expanded local control and flexibility.

Unlike with many private schools that cater to the wealthy, the issues that affect public schools in the United States are staggering. At present, there is a debate about national education standards; school choice; school privatization; prayer in school; weapons in schools; standards for teachers; the impact of technology; classroom and school size; and much more. School reform figures prominently in presidential and gubernatorial elections, and will no doubt be an issue in every local election for years to come. Yet, the irony in all of the controversies swirling around schools, including in higher education, is that people tend to like their own schools, even if they do not think highly of public schools in general, as shown in Figure 11–1 (Gallup, 2018).

The **No Child Left Behind Act of 2001**, a major legislative initiative of President Bush's administration, was designed to improve education in four clearly defined ways: (1) accountability for results; (2) an emphasis on doing what works based on scientific research; (3) expanded parental school choice options; and (4) expanded local control and flexibility.[1] According to the Act's accountability provisions, states must describe how they will close achievement gaps and make sure all students, including those who are disadvantaged or in special education classes, achieve academic

Figure 11–1 Overall, How Satisfied Are You with the Quality of Education? 2018

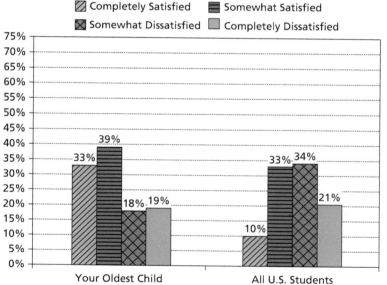

SOURCE: Based on Gallup, 2018. "Americans' Satisfaction with Quality of K-12 Education in U.S. (Trends)." Retrieved from (https://news.gallup.com/poll/241658/americans-satisfaction-quality-education-trends.aspx?g_source=link_newsv9&g_campaign=item_241652&g_medium=copy).

---

[1]No Child Left Behind Act of 2001, U.S. Congress.

proficiency. Schools that do not make progress must provide supplemental services such as free tutoring or after-school assistance; take corrective actions; and, if still not making adequate annual progress after five years, make substantial changes in the way the school is run. Many educators complain, however, that under these strict guidelines schools suffer unfairly by being labeled as failing when they really are not.

President Obama and his administration tried to improve the legislation by making more resources available to the public schools. The **Race to the Top** approach encourages state school systems to institute creative reforms. President Trump's administration is more oriented toward school choice, although at the time of this writing no new large initiatives have been implemented.

History of American Education

11.1 Describe the history of the American education system.

Education is the social institution through which a society teaches its members the skills, knowledge, norms, and values they need to learn to become good, productive participants in society. *Formal* education is often referred to as *schooling*, and as this term implies, it occurs in schools under teachers, principals, and other trained professionals. In contrast, *informal* education may occur almost anywhere: at home, on a walk in the woods, or as you read a good book.

In early American history, education was largely informal. Boys and girls usually learned what they needed to know at home or on the family farm. During the colonial period, the Puritans in Massachusetts required parents to teach their children to read and required larger towns to have an elementary school. However, in general, schooling was not required in the colonies, and only about 10 percent of children, usually just boys from the wealthiest families, went to school. Boys who were not rich or not white were excluded from formal school. Girls were also excluded because their education revolved around homemaking skills and took place informally at home (Urban and Wagoner, 2008).

To help unite the nation after the Revolutionary War, educators created textbooks to standardize spelling and pronunciation. The books were also designed to unify cultural and political views, including patriotism, religion, and distrust of Native Americans. However, school continued to be largely a pastime of boys from wealthy white families.

It took another 75 years, or roughly until the mid-1800s, for people to begin calling for free and compulsory elementary and secondary education, and another 50 years for it to become the law. By the beginning of the twentieth century, most communities of size had schools, and schooling was considered an important development for all children, regardless of sex or social class. Note that blacks were still generally barred from government-subsidized schools that whites attended. Despite this important fact, compulsory education was intended to further national unity and to teach the swarm of new immigrants about "American" values. This period was also the time of the "Industrial Revolution." An industrial economy demanded reading, writing, and math skills at a higher level than was the case in an agrarian society.

Today, schools are open to all young people, regardless of race, ethnicity, sex, and social class. However, you will see that these statuses continue to affect both educational achievement and the type of learning that occurs in schools.

Education as a Social Problem

11.2 Summarize why education is a social problem.

The concerns over the U.S. educational system are complex issues that different groups in society define differently, depending on the specific goals of each group. For example, parents at all social-class levels demand that the schools do a better job of preparing students to work and live in a technologically sophisticated society. Various minority groups

Race to the Top

President Obama and his administration had been trying to improve the No Child Left Behind legislation by making more resources available to the public schools for creative ventures.

Table 11–1 Percent of Parents Responding to Survey Questions, "How Often Did You ____ This Past Year?"

	Daily/ Weekly	Monthly	Once or Twice a Semester	Never
Help your child with his or her homework?	80%	7%	7%	6%
Review your child's grades?	57%	27%	15%	1%
Take on a leadership role in any of your child's extracurricular activities?	18%	16%	32%	34%
Meet with your child's teachers?	17%	22%	55%	5%
Volunteer in your child's classroom?	10%	15%	35%	40%
Donate supplies for the school?	7%	21%	55%	17%
Donate money to the school?	5%	20%	53%	22%

SOURCE: Tompson, T., J. Benz, and J. Agiesta. 2013. "Parents' Attitudes on the Quality of Education in the United States." The Associated Press–NORC Center for Public Affairs Research. Retrieved 15 April 2015. (www.apnorc.org/PDFs/Parent%20Attitudes/AP_NORC_Parents%20Attitudes%20on%20the%20Quality%20of%20Education%20in%20the%20US_FINAL_2.pdf).

What Do You Think?

How involved were your parents in your school when you were a child? Do you think they volunteered too little, too much, or about the right amount? What social factors, including income, jobs, and attitudes affected their level of involvement?

want schools to prepare their children to compete in American society, yet at the same time, not strip them of their cultural identity—or of the language they learn at home. Educational policymakers believe that schools must do more to increase the overall level of student achievement. Many teachers, in contrast, believe that parents should play a greater role in their children's education. Table 11–1 shows what parents are doing in their children's schools, at least from their point of view.

In the face of severe state and federal budget deficits, many school boards have been cutting back on hiring teachers and even laying off some administrators and teachers. This crisis situation does not change the basic debates about school reform, but it does postpone some of the more heated debates as administrators scramble to find ways to retain their programs and staffs. Should schools be more open to new ideas and teaching methods, or should they focus on the traditional curriculum—"the basics"? Indeed, what are the basics? Do they consist simply of reading, writing, and arithmetic, or do they include learning how to get along with others and how to communicate effectively? Are the basics the same for all students? These questions are only some of the fundamental questions being asked about public education in the United States today. There are many others. Should more qualified and effective teachers receive merit pay? Should the school year be longer? Should there be a standardized national curriculum? The United States has led the world in establishing free public education for its people. Per capita public expenditures on education in the United States are among the highest in the world (National Center for Education Statistics, 2017c). A comparison of the countries in the Organisation for Economic Co-operation and Development (OECD), an organization of 24 countries whose purpose is to promote trade and economic growth, shows that the United States is near the top in primary and secondary education funding at roughly $11,000 per full-time-equivalent (FTE) for primary students and $13,000 for secondary students (OECD, 2018).

Although the United States ranks near the top internationally in spending, the amount spent varies considerably from state to state as indicated in Map 11-1 (Cornman, Zhou, Howell, and Young, January, 2018). The District of Columbia spends $27,810 per student, meanwhile, Idaho spends $7,858. While some of these spending differences reflect the cost of living across the country, the differences also reflect the value placed on education and the willingness (and ability) of people to pay taxes for schools.

Education is compulsory in the United States; the requirements differ from one state to another, but usually children must attend school by age 7 until age 16. As a result, 98 percent of all U.S. children between the ages of 7 and 9 are enrolled in school, as are 94 percent of 16- and 17-year-olds (U.S. Census Bureau, 2017). Moreover, the number of students enrolled in higher education increased rapidly in the twentieth century.

Map 11–1 U.S. Expenditures Per Pupil by State, 2015

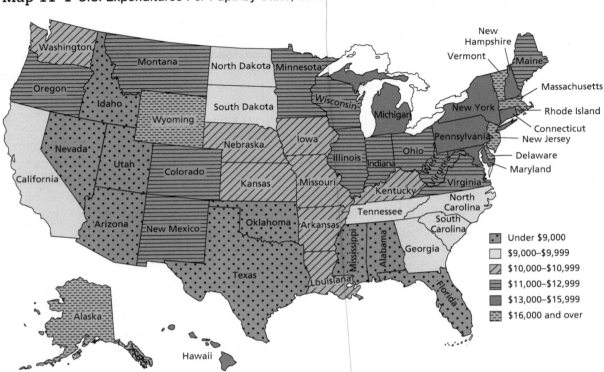

Legend:
- Under $9,000
- $9,000–$9,999
- $10,000–$10,999
- $11,000–$12,999
- $13,000–$15,999
- $16,000 and over

SOURCE: Data from Cornman, S. Q. et al. (January 2018) "Revenues and Expenditures for Public Elementary and Secondary Education: School Year 2014–15 (Fiscal Year 2015)," NCES, U.S. Department of Education.

So, what is wrong? Why is the educational system under attack? How does this impressive record constitute a "failure"? These questions can be answered in different ways, depending on the sociological perspective from which they are viewed.

Sociological Perspectives on Education

11.3 Compare and contrast the sociological perspectives on education.

In democratic nations, education is a primary method of addressing several social problems and needs. The schools are expected to prepare new generations of good citizens and reliable, capable workers who can enter the labor force with the necessary skills in literacy, computation, and written expression. Higher education in colleges, universities, and professional training institutions is expected to produce young adults who can become scientists, professionals, and leaders in business and other social institutions.

These ambitious goals hardly exhaust the list of demands placed on educators. Schools and institutions of higher education are expected to address and solve problems of inequality. They are not expected to make everyone equal (all societies recognize that people are born with differing interests and abilities), but they are expected to provide equal opportunities to learn and to gain the skills and experiences that society requires. And, as if these demands were not enough, the schools are also expected to address other social problems such as racism, sexism, and violence.

As might be expected, there are vast differences in the analyses of public education by sociologists who approach the subject from different theoretical perspectives. Functionalists stress stability and consensus; in their view, education is, or should be, one of several interdependent parts that work together to create a smoothly functioning society whose members all share the same basic values and beliefs. Conflict theorists argue that schools reproduce the society's system of inequality and class stratification in new generations of children. They see society as divided into dominant and subordinate groups, with education being used as a tool to promote the interests of the dominant group while teaching the subordinate groups to accept their situation. Symbolic Interactionists take still another approach: They examine how expectations of students' performance determine that performance and how these expectations can result in labels that shape the students' future. Each of these perspectives gives rise to different approaches to the study of public education and are summarized in Table 11–2 and discussed below.

11.3.1 Functionalist Approaches

Functionalists view education as an important social institution because it can lead to the smooth functioning of society and can provide individuals with opportunities for work, fulfillment, and upward social mobility. **Manifest functions** are those that are direct and the most obvious, such as the teaching of academic subjects and the imparting of new knowledge (e.g., reading, writing, and arithmetic). Other manifest functions include:

manifest functions

Those societal functions that are direct and the most obvious.

- *Socialization, which involves enabling students to absorb dominant cultural norms, values, and attitudes.* In the United States, these norms, values, and attitudes include respect for authority (e.g., raise your hand for the teacher to call on you), patriotism (e.g., reciting the Pledge of Allegiance), punctuality (e.g., the ringing of school bells), time management (e.g., homework, deadlines), and competition (e.g., report cards, sports).
- *Social Placement, which involves assigning, or tracking, students into programs based on individual ability and achievement, and providing credentials.* Early on in school, teachers identify students as bright and motivated or as less so. Depending on how they are identified, children are taught at a level that teachers decide suits them best. For example, high schools may offer both a college "prep" curriculum and a trade school curriculum. In this way, students are presumably prepared for their later station in life.
- *Social Control and Integration, which involves imparting to students the knowledge that society shares.* School is compulsory, and the curriculum is relatively standardized from one school to another. A geometry course in Maine will cover the same material as a geometry course in Oregon, and the course is required for graduation, even though these high schools are located 3,000 miles apart. Schools help prepare students for the workforce and integrate them into American life.
- *Social Change and Innovation, which involves learning new information and technologies as they emerge.* Educational programs are designed to train new scientists, artists, and intellectuals who will make new discoveries, solve social problems, and impart that knowledge to a new generation of students.

Table 11–2 Perspectives on Education

Theoretical Perspective	Major Assumptions
Functionalism	• Education serves several manifest functions for society, including (a) socialization, (b) social integration, (c) social placement, and (d) social and cultural innovation. • Latent functions include reduced crime, child care, the establishment of peer relationships, and lowering unemployment by occupying high school students. • Problems in the educational institution harm society because all these functions cannot be completely fulfilled. • Schools are poorly equipped to help students who come from disorganized backgrounds.
Conflict Theory	• Education promotes social inequality of gender, race, and class through tracking and standardized testing and the impact of its "hidden curriculum." • Schools differ widely in their funding and learning conditions, and this type of inequality leads to learning disparities that reinforce social inequality. • Those with wealth and power try to ensure that their children get high-quality education by going to private schools.
Symbolic Interactionism	• This perspective focuses on social interaction in the classroom, on the playground, and in other school venues. • Specific research finds that social interaction in schools affects the development of gender roles and that teachers' expectations of pupils' intellectual abilities affect how much pupils learn. • Certain educational problems have their basis in social interaction and expectations. Schools label students as "achievers," "underachievers," or "rebels," which lead students to fulfill those expectations.

In addition to these manifest functions, education also provides latent functions. **Latent functions** are the indirect by-products of education rather than a direct effect of the education itself. For example, schooling reduces crime by keeping children and teenagers busy and off the street; it reduces the costs that parents pay for childcare; it lowers the unemployment rate by occupying teenagers; and it establishes peer relationships and assists with mate selection by integrating young men and women in a variety of social activities such as sports, dances, and parties. Can you think of any other latent functions of education?

latent functions

Indirect by-products of some phenomenon that are less obvious.

From a functionalist perspective, problems in the educational system are a symptom of social disorganization. The educational system is geared to students from stable homes and communities. It is not well equipped to handle the problems of students from disorganized homes—for example, where there is a difficult divorce, extreme poverty, or other challenging circumstances. Such students may be depressed and angry, have trouble concentrating on their schoolwork, and therefore have more difficulty achieving in school (Breger, 2017; Guinart and Grau, 2014; Soria and Linder, 2014). According to social-disorganization theorists, these students are more likely to join deviant peer groups, such as gangs, that reinforce their negative attitudes toward school.

Additionally, a functionalist perspective sees schools as mechanisms to reinforce society's values and to control deviance through discipline. Educational problems arise when schools fail to do these tasks. Perhaps schools inadequately teach students the values that our society holds dear, or perhaps schools are weak on disciplining those who do not learn the rules. In a multicultural school with large numbers of students, these tasks become more difficult.

Functionalism may also analyze the difficulties experienced by schools when they attempt to change their organization or procedures to improve student performance. How can schools organize themselves to meet the demands of students with special learning needs? How can schools with high levels of student failure on standardized tests recruit better teachers and administrators? How can school systems offer parents and children more choices of schools and educational approaches? These are all issues that hinge largely on how schools, or entire school systems, are performing as they try to meet the demands placed on them. The No Child Left Behind legislation seeks to make schools accountable for students' performance on nationally distributed standardized tests of reading and math achievement. It also imposes penalties on schools and school districts when they fail to meet minimum standards of achievement. This legislation is a functionalist approach to improving the schools because it is based on performance measurements, but many would point out that the initiative does not provide adequate resources to help schools improve teaching and student performance (Klenk, 2005; Ladd, 2017).

11.3.2 Conflict Approaches

Conflict theory does not dispute the manifest and latent functions described by functionalists. However, it does give these functions a different slant by emphasizing how education also perpetuates social inequality (Ballantine, Hammack, and Stuber, 2017; Schmidt et al., 2015).

One example of this process involves socialization. Conflict theorists point out that compulsory schooling began in part to teach immigrants how to be "American" and prevent immigrants' values from corrupting "American" values. That approach is an example of **ethnocentrism** (the belief that one's own group is superior to another group). Early schools were also designed to teach students the skills they needed to work in the "new" industrial economy of the mid-nineteenth century. Education was not designed to teach students to be managers, leaders, or entrepreneurs, but to be compliant and obedient workers (Cole, 2008). Therefore, compulsory education served the interests of the upper class much more than it served the interests of workers. In a classic statement of this position, Samuel Bowles wrote that compulsory education in the United States developed to meet the needs of a capitalist economy

ethnocentrism

The belief that one's own group is superior to another group.

for skilled and disciplined workers and, while doing so, to justify the unequal social status of workers and capitalists (Bowles, Gintis, and Groves, 2005).

Conflict theorists believe that schooling continues to teach a set of values and beliefs, such as conformity and obedience to authority, that support the status quo and perpetuate the existing social hierarchy. This effect is called the hidden curriculum (Booher-Jennings, 2008). Although no one plots this curriculum behind closed doors, our schoolchildren learn obedience and respect for authority from the books they read and from various classroom activities.

Theorist Pierre Bourdieu suggests that education reproduces social class inequities because students come to school with differing amounts and types of **cultural capital** that they bring from home. This resource may include forms of knowledge, skills, education, and other advantages a person has that give him or her a certain status in society (Bourdieu, 1986). One example of this cultural capital is language. White middle and upper class families are more likely to teach their children to speak **Standard American English (SAE)** and to avoid slang or poor grammar. They learn to "speak *well*" (not "speak *good*"). Blacks sometimes "code-switch" to sound less black when they are at work or in other settings. Even former President Obama is linguistically flexible, giving speeches with two different linguistic styles: one for a mostly upper-middle-class white audience in which he closely followed SAE, and one for an audience comprised of black working-class "brothers," in which his accent, word choice, and tone all differed (Alim and Smitherman, 2012).

An example of these differences in language is shown in the box, *A Personal View: "Learning to Speak SAE."*

Social placement is another aspect of education on which conflict theorists focus. Beginning in grade school, students who are thought by their teachers to be bright are placed in the faster tracks (especially in reading and arithmetic), while other students are placed in the slower tracks. Tracking may affect not only test scores but also the likelihood of college attendance (Jennings et al., 2015). Tracking students does have its advantages; it helps ensure that bright students learn as much as their abilities allow them, and it helps ensure that slower students are not taught over their heads. But conflict theorists believe that tracking perpetuates social inequality by locking students into faster and slower tracks. Worse yet, several studies show that students' social class, race, and ethnicity affect the track into which they are placed, even though their intellectual abilities and potential should be the only things that matter. White middle-class students are more likely to be tracked "up," while poorer students and students of color are more likely to be tracked "down."

Once they are tracked, students learn more if they are tracked up and less if they are tracked down. The latter tend to lose self-esteem; they begin to think they have little academic ability and thus do worse in school because they were tracked down (Chmielewski, Dumont, and Trautwein, 2013; Dumont et al., 2017; Stanley and Chambers, 2018).

Conflict theorists add that standardized tests are culturally biased and thus also help perpetuate social inequality (Grodsky, Warren, and Felts, 2008). They suggest that these tests favor white middle-class students whose socioeconomic status and other aspects of their backgrounds have afforded them various experiences that help them answer questions on the tests.

11.3.3 Interactionist Approaches

Symbolic interaction focuses on micro-level social interactions. Interactionists see education as a vital part of socialization and therefore tend to focus not only on the dynamics of the school or classroom but also on the interactions between students and

cultural capital

The resource that a person brings from his or her family, which may include forms of knowledge, skills, education, and other advantages that a person has, and which give him or her a certain status in society.

Standard American English (SAE)

A speaking style that avoids slang or poor grammar, used by upper-class people.

A Personal View

Learning to Speak SAE

Okay, here's the deal: I'm a working-class girl done good. Please allow me to rephrase that. I would like to share that I am a highly successful woman who has roots in the working class. Do you see the difference in these two ways of speaking? My words, syntax, tones, even gestures change depending on the group I'm with. It hasn't always been that way.

I was raised in a working-class family with notoriously bad grammar. Around them parts we said "ain't," as in "I ain't hungry no more," and "fixin'," as in "Hey Janey, you fixin' to get to the store soon?" We all spoke this way in my family, as did most people within my community, so I really wasn't aware that my grammar was incorrect. I don't even remember my teachers calling me on it.

Things changed drastically when I went to college. Because I did well in high school, I had the fortunate opportunity to attend a prestigious college in the northeast. I would like to say that I loved the experience, but the culture shock was so overwhelming that I might as well have landed on Mars. I especially noticed that people did not speak the same way I did. They didn't have my accent, they used different words, and they used those words in a different pattern. I immediately felt inadequate.

One incident stands out in particular: In one of my math classes I wanted to ask the professor to expand on his explanation, so I simply asked, "How come?" He stared at me. "*How come*?" he repeated. Then he said it again more loudly than the first, "HOW COME?" At first, I didn't catch what they were laughing about. But then it came to me, "I mean, why?" I gulped. Later that day I withdrew from the class.

That same day I also went to the English department and asked the secretary if the department offered any English tutors, "for, you know, people who talk different." She was a sweet lady, "Oh, you mean for people who have English as a second language? Sure, honey, let me give you a list." I didn't dare tell her that I was looking for a tutor for myself. But I contacted the first name on the list, Darcy, and I am forever grateful. She taught me to speak "Standard American English," as she called it. We met twice a week for an entire year, and I practiced daily. The drills included verbal and nonverbal communication.

Gilles Paire/Fotolia

I can now easily pass as an upper-middle-class student at my college. I know how to "talk the talk." However, when I go back home to see my mama and pa, I'm just one of the working-class girls "done good."

By the way, I think I'll stop by to see my old math professor just to say "hey."

—Janey, Age 20

Critical Thinking

What is it about social class that contributes to different speech patterns? Can you think of specific issues that would cause these differences? Why is an upper-middle-class speech pattern more valued than other speech patterns? How would a conflict theorist answer this question?

---

teachers, teachers and administrators, and among students themselves. What are the norms around interaction, and what labels are used?

According to the interactionist perspective, schools label students, and these labels follow them for years (Kirk and Sampson, 2013). Through the formal structure of grades, testing, and tracking, along with the social aspects of cliques, students develop a self-identity, either positive (e.g., "I am a smart person with a talent for basketball") or negative (e.g., "I'm just not good at math"). Self-fulfilling prophecies can become a substantial part of education. That is, when students are labeled in any way—dumb, loser, smart, slut, friendly, jock, cute, learning disabled—they may come to view themselves that way and behave accordingly (Shifrer, Callahan, and Muller, 2013).

According to labeling theorists, teachers form expectations about students early in the school year, and these are communicated to the students in varying ways. The students tend to perform in ways that meet the teacher's expectations, thereby reinforcing them. Sometimes these labels have little to do with reality. An early research study (Rosenthal and Jacobson, 1968) tested this theory by assessing a group of students at the beginning of the school year and telling their teachers which students were smart and which were not. The researchers then tested the students again at the end of the school year. As you might guess, the smarter students had learned more during the year than those students who were not as smart. The truth is, however, that the researchers randomly selected which students would be called smart, and these labels had nothing to do with reality. What would account for these so-called "smart" students to have learned more during the school year, given that they were not necessarily smarter at all? The answers can be found in the teachers' behavior. The teachers of the "smart children" spent more time with them and praised them more often than was true for the "less bright" group.

What Do You Think?

What theoretical perspective do you find most intriguing with respect to education, and why?

Educational Attainment and Achievement

educational attainment

The number of years of school completed.

11.4 **Identify the educational attainment and achievement of different groups in society.**

Today, ever-greater proportions of U.S. students are finishing high school and going on to college. As shown in Figure 11–2, from 1940 to 2016, the nation underwent a transformation in which high school completion, rather than leaving (i.e., dropping out), became the norm (National Center for Education Statistics, 2018a). Only 38 percent of people age 25 to 29 in 1940 had at least a high school diploma; today, that figure is 92 percent. Likewise, those with at least four years of college have also increased significantly. In 1940, only 6 percent of adults age 25 to 29 had earned at least a bachelor's degree, but today, over a third have done so.

Nonetheless, much work remains in helping young people to finish high school and encouraging them to attend college. For members of most minority groups, these educational issues continue to be especially pressing, as shown in Figure 11–3 (National Center for Education Statistics, 2017b). Although the large majority of Asian/Pacific Islander (90 percent) and white (88 percent) high school students graduated from high school in the 2016 school year, only about three-quarters of Hispanic (78 percent) and black (75 percent) students graduated. The rate for American Indian/Alaska Native youths was even lower (72 percent). The good news, however, is that the gap in **educational attainment** (number of years of school completed) between most minority groups and whites has narrowed considerably since the turn of the century. A generation ago, in 1980, 25 percent of whites between the ages of 25 and 29 had completed a bachelor's degree or higher, compared with only 12 percent of blacks, and 8 percent of Hispanics, as shown

These young people did not complete high school. Their job options are very limited, and they have suffered bouts of unemployment. They now work in a packing company, earning $10.50 an hour, with no fringe benefits. It is unlikely that their pay or working conditions will improve significantly; consequently, few people stay at the packing plant for the long term.

Monkey Business/Fotolia

Figure 11–2 Percentage of Persons 25–29 Years Old By Educational Attainment, 1940–2016

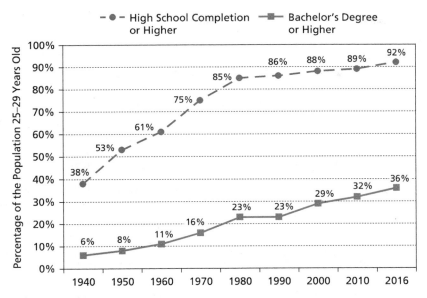

SOURCE: Data from National Center for Education Statistics. 2018a. "Digest of Education Statistics: 2016." February. Retrieved 14 April 2018 (nces.ed.gov/programs/digest/d16/tables_1.asp).

in Figure 11–4 (unfortunately, no data are available for Asian/Pacific Islanders or American Indian/Alaska Natives for that year). However, all groups have seen significant increases over the years. Today, 51 percent of young Asian/Pacific Islanders have at least a bachelor's degree, followed by whites (37 percent), blacks (24 percent), American Indian/Alaska Natives (17 percent), and Hispanics (16 percent).

Why is it so important to close the gap in educational attainment? People with higher levels of education tend to earn more money than those with less education. Figure 11–5 reveals the average earnings of young adults between the ages of 25 and 34 who work full-time (all year). As you can see, educational credentials have a linear effect on earnings. People with a high school diploma (or GED) earn more than those who have not completed high school. People with an associate's two-year degree earn more than those who have completed high school. Those with a bachelor's degree earn more than do those with an associate's degree, and those with an advanced

Figure 11–3 Graduation Rate for Public High School Students, by Race/ Ethnicity: School Year 2016

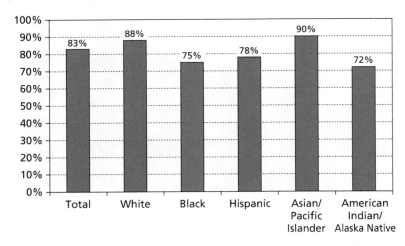

SOURCE: Data from National Center for Education Statistics. 2017b. "Public High School Graduation Rates." April. Retrieved 10 April 2018. (nces.ed.gov/programs/coe/indicator_coi.asp).

Figure 11–4 Percentage of Persons Ages 25–29 Who Have Achieved a Bachelor's Degree or Higher by Race/Ethnicity, 1980 and 2016

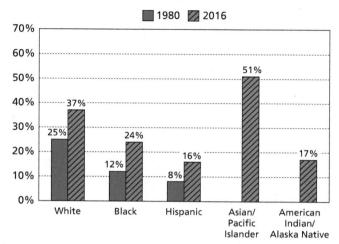

SOURCE: Data from National Center for Education Statistics. 2018a. "Digest of Education Statistics: 2016." February, Table 104.10. Retrieved 14 April 2018 (nces.ed.gov/programs/digest/d16/tables_1.asp).

degree earn the most of all. However, you will also note that men earn considerably more than women do at all education levels. For example, women with a high school diploma earn about the same, on average, as men who have dropped out of high school. Disparities persist even at the most advanced educational levels. Women with a master's degree or higher earn about the same as men with only a bachelor's degree (Ma, Pender, and Welch, 2016).

11.4.1 Blacks

Before World War I, about 90 percent of all blacks in the United States lived in the southern states (Orfield and Eaton, 1996). Although there has been tremendous migration since then, today black students remain disproportionately concentrated in

Figure 11–5 Median Annual Earnings of Full-Time Year-Round Wage and Salary Workers Ages 25–34, by Educational Attainment

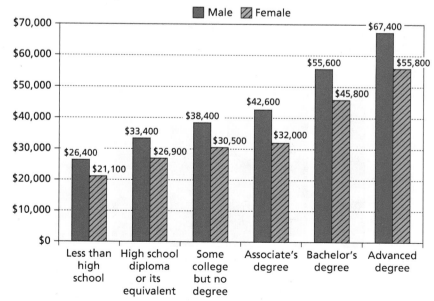

SOURCE: Data from Ma, J., Pender, M., & Welch, M., (2016) "Education Pays 2016: The Benefits of Higher Education for Individuals and Society." *Trends in Higher Education Series,* The College Board.

the South, where blacks (and southern whites) receive only about 60–70 percent of the amount of schooling dollars received by whites in more advantaged areas of the nation (as shown earlier, in Map 11-1).

In the North, educational opportunities for blacks and whites are more equal, but inequalities between schools in poor black communities and those in more affluent white suburbs tend to perpetuate differences in educational attainment. At the beginning of the twentieth century, northern-born blacks were rapidly closing the educational gap between themselves and whites, but the gap widened again after 1915. The reasons for this reversal are complex. An important factor was the competition between black children and the children of European immigrants, who tended to come from better-educated families and thus enjoyed an advantage over blacks, whose parents had migrated from the South. Another factor, beginning in the Great Depression and continuing to the present, was the higher rate of unemployment among blacks. The employment status of parents has a great deal to do with the educational attainment of their children because children in low-income households are more likely to drop out of school. A third factor was segregation, which tends to increase disparities between groups.

11.4.2 Hispanics

Another minority group that has faced difficulties in education are Hispanics. The educational attainment of Hispanic students is lower than among whites and Asians (National Center for Education Statistics, 2018a). But this difference should not be interpreted to mean that Hispanics do not care about education. A study based on telephone interviews of over 1,000 Hispanics (conducted in English and Spanish), asked them to evaluate whether five issues for President Trump and Congress should be a "top priority," an "important but lower priority," or "not too important or it should not be done." The results are found in Figure 11-6, and show that improving education is most commonly listed as a "top priority," while immigration is least likely of the five issues to be listed as a "top priority" (Pew Research Center, 2017).

An especially important factor in the lower educational attainment of Hispanic students to date is that they, like blacks, have experienced the effects of de facto segregation and poor schools. This problem is particularly acute in large metropolitan areas, yet this issue has received minimal attention (Orfield, 2004/2005).

Figure 11–6 Percentage of Hispanic Registered Voters Who Say This Issue Should be a Top Priority for President Trump and Congress in 2017

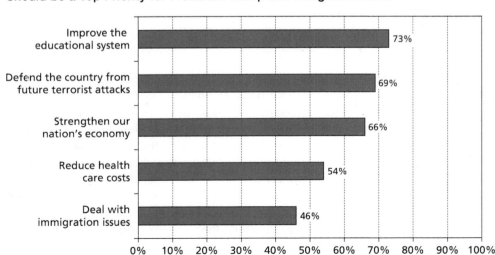

SOURCE: Data from "Latino priorities for the Trump administration and Congress in 2017," Pew Research Center, February 23, 2017.

Figure 11–7 Language Spoken at Home and English Speaking Ability by Age Among Hispanics

SOURCE: Based on Brown, A., & E. Patten. 2014. "Statistical Portrait of Hispanics in the United States, 2012." Pew Research Center. 29 April. Retrieved from (www.pewhispanic.org/2014/04/29/statistical-portrait-of-hispanics-in-the-united-states-2012/).

Another factor that receives greater attention is that some Hispanic students do not speak English at all or do not speak it well enough to succeed in an English-speaking school. A large nationally representative sample of Hispanics in the United States showed that 13 percent of children between the ages of 5 and 17 "speak English less than very well," although the percentage of older Hispanics who do not speak English very well is three times larger (39 percent), as illustrated in Figure 11–7 (Brown and Patten, 2014). If researchers were to look only at young children who are just beginning school, they would likely see that more than 13 percent need substantial help with English to prevent them from falling behind in school.

Since the late 1960s, a primary goal of education for Hispanic students has been to improve their ability to use English without allowing them to fall behind in other subjects. One technique for achieving this goal is bilingual/bicultural education in which students are taught wholly or partly in their native language until they can function adequately in English, and in some cases, longer. This approach has received the support of the federal Office of Civil Rights, which requires that schools take "affirmative steps" to correct minority students' deficiencies in the English language to receive federal funds.

11.4.3 Asian Americans and Pacific Islanders

Students from Chinese, Korean, East Indian, Pacific Islander, and other Asian backgrounds face different problems in American schools. Due to their higher achievement on most measures of school performance, Asian students and their parents are proud of their scholastic achievements but often feel that they are treated as the "model minority" who are expected to be uniformly high achievers and extremely well behaved in schools (Chou and Feagin, 2015; Poon et al., 2016). Asian Americans make up 4 percent of the U.S. population, but represent 20 percent of the students attending elite U.S. Ivy League schools. However, because so many Asian Americans apply, their acceptance rates are much lower than for other racial and ethnic groups (Hernandez, 2017). This representation has led some to ponder whether Ivy League schools may be putting a quota or limits on the number of Asians admitted (Klein, 2014).

Asian Americans have been nicknamed the "model minority." Why is this?

Table 11–3 Results of Youth Risk Behavior Survey of High School Students

Survey Question, "In the past 12 months, have you ..."	Asian Youth	Total U.S. Youth
Had serious thoughts of suicide	19%	16%
Made suicide plans	14%	13%
Attempted suicide	11%	8%
Gotten medical attention for a suicide attempt	5%	2%

SOURCE: Suicide Prevention Resource Center. 2014. "Suicide Among Racial/Ethnic Populations in the U.S.: Asians, Pacific Islanders, and Native Hawaiians." Retrieved 2 February 2015 (www.sprc.org/sites/sprc.org/files/library/API%20Sheet%20August%2028%20 2013%20Final.pdf).

But for Asian students who do not outperform their peers or do not behave according to cultural stereotypes, the extremely high expectations of their families and the larger society can present severe problems. Asian American teenagers and college students experience more stress, harbor more suicidal thoughts, and attempt suicide at higher rates than other racial or ethnic groups, as you can see in Table 11–3 (Suicide Prevention Resource Center, 2014).

11.4.4 American Indians and Alaska Natives

There are nearly 650,000 American Indian and Alaska Native youths enrolled in public schools in the United States (National Indian Education Association, 2018). A much smaller number, about 50,000 students, attend one of the 183 schools funded by the Bureau of Indian Education (BIE). The BIE school system was created to meet the federal government's commitment to provide for the education of American Indian and Alaska Native children. The goal of the BIE is "to provide quality education opportunities from early childhood through life in accordance with a tribe's needs for cultural and economic well-being, in keeping with the diversity of Indian tribes and Alaska Native villages as distinct cultural and governmental entities" (Bureau of Indian Education, 2018a).[2] The BIE schools consider the spiritual, mental, physical, and cultural aspects of the students within their family and tribal or village context. They strive to contribute to the development of quality American Indian and Alaska Native communities (Converse, 2014).

Of the 183 BIE-funded schools, 53 are operated by the BIE and the remaining 130 are tribally controlled. The Bureau also operates two postsecondary schools: Haskell Indian Nations University and Southwestern Indian Polytechnic Institute (Bureau of Indian Education, 2018b).

How do the students in BIE-funded schools compare with other students across the country? A large-scale evaluation was conducted for the BIE by the educational research center, the Northwest Evaluation Association (Converse, 2014). Researchers found that student achievement in both math and reading was below average at all grade levels. In only 29 percent of the BIE-funded schools did students have test scores near the national average. However, a review of data over the four years prior showed that student achievement had improved, particularly among younger students. Math gains were also notable. Therefore, proponents of BIE-funded schools suggest that these improvements, coupled with the social and cultural advantages available to students, indicate the successes and strengths of Indian education.

11.4.5 Can We Find Any Common Themes?

Lower-income persons, blacks, Hispanics, and American Indian/Alaska Native youths are less likely to finish high school and less likely to attend college than are their Asian American/Pacific Islander and white counterparts. Whatever the cause,

What Do You Think?

Identify the specific personal and structural factors that shaped your educational attainment to date (and your plans for the future). Personal factors might include intelligence or personal initiative, while structural factors might include your family's educational background or issues related to your culture, social class, or race or ethnic identity.

[2]Bureau of Indian Education. 2015. Home page. Retrieved 31 March 2015 (www.bie.edu/index.htm).

dropping out has serious economic consequences. Those who have less education earn significantly less than people who have completed more years of school.

We have briefly reviewed some unique characteristics of these minority groups that could account for some of the educational disparities. But can we find any common themes that could offer us more clues? The following seven ideas offer potential leads in better understanding the disparities. Some of these ideas are structural and others represent individual-level factors:

- *Lack of Cultural Capital:* Students bring their own personal history to school with advantages or disadvantages. For example, if a child was raised by parents who did not read well, chances are these parents had a more limited vocabulary than other parents, they did not have a lot of books in the home, and they may not have valued reading as an activity. Therefore, the child begins school at a distinct disadvantage that can continue throughout a child's educational career, unless schools work to equalize cultural capital by providing enriching material and field trips (Kisida, Greene, and Bowen, 2014; Silva, 2017). The lack of cultural capital can hinder higher education as well because parents may not be familiar with college admission procedures, entrance exams, or financial aid.

- *Inferior Teachers:* The first large study of American schools was commissioned by the U.S. Congress and conducted by James Coleman in the 1960s (Coleman, 1966). He noted the factors that contribute to a student's academic performance, including family and neighborhood experiences and, to a lesser degree, school resources. Yet, research suggests that among school-related factors, the quality of teachers matters most (Poulou, 2017; Sadler et al., 2013). When it comes to student performance on reading and math tests, a teacher is estimated to have two to three times the impact of any other school factor, including services, facilities, and even leadership (Rand Education, 2012). Yet classrooms are often segregated into achievement levels, racial composition, and socioeconomic composition, and it is the teachers with less experience who tend to be assigned to the most challenging classes (Grissom, Kalogrides, and Loeb, 2015; Harris, 2017; Kalogrides, Loeb, and Béteille, 2013).

- *Inferior Schools:* Traditionally, schools reflected the socioeconomic and racial profile of the surrounding neighborhood and were most often segregated. Desegregation effectively began with the Supreme Court's 1954 ruling in *Brown v. Board of Education of Topeka, Kansas*, which found that segregation had negative effects on black students even when their school facilities were "equal" (which they rarely were). Segregation continued, however, because many white or upper-income families transferred to private schools (i.e., "white flight") and politicians gerrymandered districts to change school attendance boundaries (Richards, 2014). In 2007, the Court reversed the 1954 landmark decision, and ruled that policies that selected students based on race to achieve more integrated classrooms are unconstitutional. Consequently, today's typical minority student attends school with fewer whites than his or her counterpart did in 1970 (Fiel, 2013), despite the fact that high-poverty schools and racially segregated schools tend to result in lower educational attainment for the poor and racial minorities (Berkowitz et al., 2017; Karner, 2017; Mickelson, Bottia, and Lambert, 2013; Wolf, Magnuson, and Kimbro, 2017).

- *Lack of Parental Engagement:* Parental engagement in their child's schooling is an important factor in student achievement (Hornby and Blackwell, 2018; Majo and Siraj, 2015; Wilder, 2014). Parental involvement is especially important for more disadvantaged students (Benner, Boyle, and Sadler, 2016). However, many low-income and minority parents are less involved in their child's schooling than are other parents (Graves and Wright, 2011; Toldson and Lemmons, 2013). This might include less help with homework, infrequent communication with teachers, and fewer school visits. There are a variety of reasons for this—language barriers, work hours, a lack of understanding educational materials because of their own low level of education, and a general sense of not belonging or feeling different from the school culture.

- *Peer Groups:* Peer groups take on increasing importance as children become teenagers and young adults (Butler-Barnes et al., 2015). Some low-income students, as well as students who are black, Hispanic, and American Indian/Alaska Native, may not have access to a large peer network of high-achieving and college-bound peers because they are overrepresented in underperforming schools. If you do not have very many friends who are finishing high school or considering college, it is not surprising that you may also have limited educational aspirations.

- *Multiple Obligations:* Although the primary cause of dropping out is poor academic performance, students often drop out of high school because of the difficulties they encounter in trying to cope with school, family, and work roles (Doll, Eslami, and Walters, 2013). They may be married and/or pregnant or working at a job, all of which increases the likelihood of dropping out of school.

- *Lack of Financial Resources:* Cutbacks in federally funded assistance, particularly the emphasis on loans rather than outright grants, place a college education out of reach for many minority or poor students. Moreover, since many are first-generational college students, they may not have the cultural capital to understand how to best utilize financial services for their education. A study that looked at students at six large public research universities found that low-income students are more likely to make financial decisions that could negatively impact their immediate academic experience, serve as disruptive barriers to success, delay or prolong graduation, or lead to increased debt upon graduation (Soria, Weiner, and Lu, 2014).

An egalitarian society has a responsibility to provide equal access to high-quality education for all its citizens. Critics claim that U.S. society has failed to meet this responsibility, particularly for persons who are low-income or from minority groups.

David Grossman/Alamy Stock Photo

Low-income and minority students are more likely than others to be in crowded classrooms lacking basic resources such as textbooks, as shown here in a science class in New York.

How U.S. Students Measure Up in International Comparisons

11.5 **Evaluate how students in the United States compare to students in other countries in terms of educational achievement.**

Throughout the world, education runs in two extremes: Some children receive excellent education, at least as evidenced by their high scores on standardized tests. In contrast, other children receive little or no education at all. This pattern is especially the case for girls, who are often excluded from school because of religious, cultural, economic, or sometimes even legal grounds.

These high school students in Singapore are among those with the highest test scores in the world. How would sociologists explain this? Why does the United States rank so comparatively low?

What Do You Think?

What might explain why students in so many other countries have higher test scores than students in the United States? Compare and contrast our culture and American education system with those found in other countries.

11.5.1 Education in Developed Nations

One issue that motivates the clamor for educational reform in the United States is the fact that on standardized tests administered throughout the world, the United States lags other advanced industrialized nations. One piece of evidence for this claim is to compare the average score of 15-year-olds taking the Program for International Student Assessment, which is a very large cross–national test that measures math, science literacy, and other key skills among 15-year-olds in dozens of developed and developing countries. The United States placed a paltry 38th out of 71 countries in math and placed 24th in science and reading (DeSilver, 2017).

The standing of American students is a bit better in other international measures, but not by much. For example, in the assessment known as the Trends in International Mathematics and Science Study (TIMSS), which tests children in grades four and eight every four years (since 1995), American students fare better. In the most recent test, among the fourth graders, the U.S. ranked 11th in math and 7th in science out of 48. Among 8th graders the United States ranked eighth in both math and science, out of 37 countries (DeSilver, 2017). These results are certainly better, but given what our country spends on education, we should expect even stronger outcomes.

There are a few important things to note with respect to these comparisons, however. First, because of the great diversity of U.S. students and schools, the U.S. students' scores vary quite a bit. Much of this variation is explained by whether the students attend segregated schools in which high proportions of students are of poor or of very low income (often measured by whether students are eligible for free lunch in school, a reflection of their family's financial need). The lower the income of students, and the greater the number of low-income students in the schools, the less well they do on standardized international tests.

The second point to note is that American test scores are improving, as shown in Figure 11–8. An assessment of the U.S. Department of Education, the National Assessment of Educational Progress, has found that U.S. students have made substantial gains in their math scores since 1990. Scores have increased slightly every year, although fourth-grade scores have leveled off in recent years (DeSilver, 2017). For example, in 1990, 50 percent of fourth graders scored below a "basic" level in math; by 2015 only 18 percent did so. Likewise, the percentage of eighth graders who scored below "basic" dropped from 48 percent to 29 percent.

These recent national assessments of educational achievement have shown some encouraging improvement in students' math scores. Nevertheless, the level of student achievement remains a subject of widespread debate. In a study of inequalities in educational achievement in the United States, researchers with the McKinsey consulting company concluded that:

> The underutilization of human potential as reflected in the achievement gap is extremely costly. Existing gaps impose the economic equivalent of a permanent national recession— one substantially larger than the deep recession the country is currently experiencing. For individuals, avoidable shortfalls in academic achievement impose heavy and often tragic consequences via lower earnings, poor health, and higher rates of incarceration.[3]

> (McKinsey and Company, 2010)

---

[3]McKinsey & Company. 2010. "How the World's Most Improved School Systems Keep Getting Better."

Figure 11–8 Math Proficiency Slowly Growing Among U.S. Fourth and Eighth Grade Students, 1990 and 2015

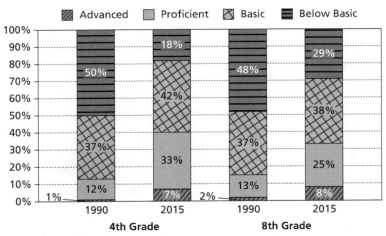

SOURCE: Data from DeSilver, D. (February 15, 2017) U.S. Students' Academic Achievement Still Lags That of Their Peers in Many Other Countries. Pew Research Center.

11.5.2 Education in Less Developed Nations

Many children around the world do not share in the educational successes noted above. Instead, it is not uncommon for them to attend crowded, underfunded schools with teachers who may have little education themselves. Students' attendance may be sporadic, they may have few books for their lessons, and they often quit school after a few years because of the long travel distance from home, the cost of school, or because they are needed to work at home. For example, in Afghanistan, only 21 percent of girls and 55 percent of boys complete primary school, as do only 34 percent of girls and 55 percent of boys in Niger (Population Reference Bureau, 2015).

Investing in education is important because education gives people the skills they need to help themselves out of poverty and into prosperity, which includes the following benefits (Center for Global Development, 2018):

- *Improved health:* With education, people are better prepared to prevent disease and to use health services effectively. For example, young people who have completed primary education are less than half as likely to contract HIV as those with little or no schooling.
- *Delayed marriage and childbearing.* Educated mothers marry later, and have fewer and healthier children.
- *Higher wages and economic growth:* In many poor countries, with each additional year of schooling, people earn ten percent higher wages. These earnings, in turn, contribute to national economic growth. No country has ever achieved continuous and rapid growth without reaching an adult literacy rate of at least 40 percent.
- *Democracy and political stability:* Education supports the growth of civil society, democracy, and political stability, allowing people to learn about their rights and acquire the skills and knowledge necessary to exercise them.[4]

Girls are particularly disadvantaged when it comes to schooling and often do not have the same opportunities and resources as boys do to attend school. This issue is explored in the slideshow, *"Education for Girls."*

---

[4]"Education and The Developing World: Why is education essential for development?," (2018) Center for Global Development.

Education for Girls

Globally, girls are often absent from schools. The local culture, religious customs, or economic circumstances may contribute to the opinion that education for girls is unnecessary. Some parents may see it as a waste of time and money, since their daughter will marry young and move to another household. In other regions, education for girls is viewed as dangerous and a threat to "normal" family functioning. Educated girls may start making demands for change. In other regions, educating girls is considered immoral and contrasts with religious views about right and wrong. But often, the reason comes down to simple economics. Families need the labor of girls. The slideshow provides insight about girls and education in the developing world.

In many countries girls and boys attend separate schools. But separate is not equal. Funding for girls' education lags that spent on boys. Girls' schools may close to maintain a higher educational standard for boys.

Some girls are not able to go to school because they are busy taking care of younger brothers and sisters. It is not unusual for a family to contain five or six children, a result of inadequate access to birth control and traditional customs that promote large families as beneficial.

Many communities in developing nations lack access to clean drinking water. Family members, usually girls and women, often spend nearly an entire day walking to a water source and walking back home carrying up to 50 pounds on their backs, only to do it again later that day. In addition to keeping them out of school, the walk for water also makes the girls and women vulnerable to predators, both animal and human. Girls are raped on their way to and from their water source.

Some girls do not go to school because they are expected to earn money for their family. They may be required to beg on the street, to steal from shop vendors, or to sell themselves sexually to men. Girls are considered valuable only insofar as what resources they can bring to the family.

Girls and women work very hard in developing nations. This 8-year-old girl already is responsible for gathering firewood for her family. This task takes up much of her day because firewood is used for cooking, bathing, and boiling drinking water. Meanwhile, her younger sister helps her mother clean the house while her two older brothers are at school.

Critical Thinking

Reflecting on the four themes of this text—the importance of using an empirical approach, linking individual experiences with social structure, understanding that social inequality contributes to social problems, and acknowledging that understanding social problems requires a comparative perspective—devise a program in the developing world to help girls attend school. What social, personal, economic, and political factors must be addressed?

Current Social Problems in Education

11.6   **Discuss some of the current social problems facing schools.**

There are many contentious issues in education. In the following section, you will read about a few of these, such as the need for quality preschool and early childhood education programs; language problems in schools; the growing problem of school violence and issues surrounding it; issues surrounding school choice; and educational biases based on sex and gender.

11.6.1 Preschool and Early Childhood Education

Thomas is a high-spirited 4-year-old who lives with his mother, father, and 2-year-old sister. He is happy, healthy, and very much loved by his family. He and his sister have a playroom of toys, including many books, puzzles, and interactive videos. His mother and father read to Thomas daily, knowing that this activity will increase his vocabulary and help him learn to read. Thomas has been attending a preschool five mornings a week for almost two years. He knows his alphabet, can sound out letters and count to 100, and he can do simple addition such as 2+2. When he begins kindergarten next year, he will have a smooth transition because he likes school, is eager to learn, and already has mastered a strong foundation.

Bobby, in contrast, is a high-spirited 4-year-old who lives with his mother, father, and 2-year-old sister. He is happy, healthy, and very much loved by his family. His family is poor, so Bobby has only a few toys, and many of them are broken or have pieces that have been lost. Neither his mother nor his father reads well, and therefore there are no books around the house and neither parent cares much for going to the library across town. Bobby has never been to preschool because his parents cannot afford it. He has been taught the alphabet song, but he does not yet know that it describes letters, nor does he know what letters even are. He can count to ten, but stumbles after that. He heard that he will begin kindergarten next year, but he is nervous about that because he's never been away from his mother for long periods. He cries at the thought of leaving home.

These two contrasting case studies illustrate why, for many families, access to high quality preschool and early childhood education programs are so important. Early education is a key element in preventing educational deficits, not only among children from disadvantaged backgrounds but also for all children. Yet, these programs are very expensive and out of reach of many low- and even moderate-income families at roughly $10,000 per year (Bivens et al., 2016; Business Brokers.net, 2018). A study from the Economic Policy Institute, a think tank created to give low-income people a voice in policy, examined the costs of childcare versus college and found that the in-state public college tuition in 23 states was lower than the cost of full-time childcare for a 4-year-old (Bivens et al., 2016).

Because of the importance of childcare, and its high costs, the federally funded program **Head Start** was created for low-income families. Head Start offers a comprehensive program that would provide health and nutritional services to preschool children while also developing their cognitive skills and engaging parents (Head Start, 2015). In addition, educational programs for parents are usually included covering such topics as child development and nutrition. Many programs are integrated to include children with special physical or cognitive needs. The problem, however, is that there are not nearly enough Head Start spots for eligible families.

The United States ranks below almost all the advanced economies of the European Economic Union in funding for early childhood education and care (ECEC) (Organisation for Economic Co-operation and Development, 2013). ECEC has become an important issue in many parts of the world because of the rise in labor force participation of mothers, the push for single mothers to work rather than receive public aid, and a growing interest in ensuring that all children begin elementary school with basic skills and are ready to learn. ECEC programs enhance and support children's cognitive, social, and emotional development. A 3-year study of 12 developed nations compared the availability and

Head Start

The federally funded preschool program for low-income children and their families.

structure of ECEC programs. Several interesting points were noted. To begin with, access to ECEC is a statutory right in all countries except the United States. Although compulsory school begins at age 6 or 7, ECEC availability begins at age 1 year in Denmark, Finland, and Sweden (after generous maternity and family leave benefits are exhausted); at age 2.5 years in Belgium; at age 3 years in Italy and Germany; and at age 4 years in Britain. Most countries have full coverage of education for 3- to 6-year-olds (Clearinghouse on International Developments in Child, Youth, and Family Policies, 2005).

In contrast, in the United States there is no statutory entitlement until ages 5 to 7, depending on the state. Access to publicly funded ECEC programs such as the Head Start program is generally restricted to at-risk children, usually defined as poor or near-poor. Furthermore, the demand for these programs among vulnerable groups far outstrips their availability.

In most of the 12 countries reviewed, government pays the largest share of the costs, with parents covering only 25–30 percent. Countries may also make arrangements for sliding-scale payments for low-income families to help make programs affordable. Most countries require staff to complete at least three years of training at universities or other institutes of higher education. Their earnings reflect their levels of education. The box, *A Global View: "Raising My Children in France,"* describes the French way of delivering early childhood education.

In contrast, U.S. parents pay an average of 60–80 percent of ECEC costs. Some of these costs can be recouped through tax benefits, but many low-income families find the tax system confusing and therefore end up using informal or unregulated childcare. In the United States, there is also no agreed-on set of qualifications for staff. Their status and pay are low, and turnover is high. Other countries make a clear investment in their ECEC. Sweden devotes roughly 1.6 percent of its gross domestic product (GDP) to ECEC, with Denmark, France, and Norway close behind. In contrast, the United States devotes less than half of 1 percent of its GDP to early childhood services (OECD, 2016). Ironically, the United States is a leader in research on child development but has not developed the programs that research suggests are needed and that are increasingly available in other developed nations.

What Do You Think?

Respond to the person who says, "Why should I pay higher taxes to pay for you to educate your young child? S/he is *your* child; therefore, you should pay for his or her early education yourself."

11.6.2 Bilingual/Bicultural Education

Roughly 4.6 million children participate in English Language Learner programs in school each year, which is almost one of every 10 children (National Center for Education Statistics, March, 2017a). Most of these children are in elementary school. As you can see in Map 11-2, the states with the largest number of English Language Learners are in the Southwest United States, and include California, Nevada, Texas, and New Mexico (National Center for Education Statistics, 2017a).

The desirability of teaching non-English-speaking pupils in their native language is a subject of intense debate, particularly in California and other states with large Hispanic populations. On one side are those who believe that preserving the language and culture of minority groups is a worthwhile, even necessary, goal of public education. On the other side are those who believe that minority students must be "immersed" in English-language instruction if they are to be prepared to compete effectively in American society.

Bilingual education has a long history in the United States, shifting between tolerance and repression depending on politics, the economy, and the size of the immigrant population (Gandara and Escamilla, 2017). It was used to help immigrants learn English in the nineteenth century (National Association for Bilingual Education, 2014). In 1839, Ohio was the first state to pass a law requiring bilingual education if parents requested it from the schools. Many other states and communities gradually followed suit. In 1968, the U.S. Congress passed Title VII of the Elementary and Secondary Education Act, known informally as "the Bilingual Education Act," which mandated bilingual education to give immigrants access to education in their "first" language.

A Global View

Raising My Children in France

My sister and I were born and raised in France, but she moved to the United States for college, met an American who she later married, and now has two children. In contrast, I went to university here in France, later married a native Frenchman, and also have two children, roughly the same age. Although I am separated from my sister by thousands of miles, Skype allows us to share the ups and downs of parenting on a weekly basis. What a difference we are having raising our children!

Each time after I had my babies, my employer gave me four months off, completely paid, so that I could stay at home to bond. A newborn turns your world upside down, so I appreciated this time at home with him. We could sleep, eat, relax, and play whenever we needed to and not have to worry about getting on a tight schedule while I went back to work right away. Law in France requires maternity leave, so every woman has 16 weeks of paid time off. I then decided to stay home for another two months without any pay, and my job was held for me.

France also provides a helper to come to the house for two weeks after a baby is born to check on us and help us out. My helper did the laundry for me and cooked some meals. She also watched the baby, so I could go for a walk and have some quiet time, or have lunch with friends. This service was all free.

When my baby was 6 weeks old, I could take him to a childcare center and they would watch him for a very small charge, the equivalent of about a dollar an hour. Since I wasn't yet back to work, I usually just took him there for a couple of hours a day so that I could go to the gym or run my errands. However, after 6 months, I went back to work full-time, and he stayed there from 8:00 until 5:30, and, again, it was just a nominal charge. I felt that he was in good care because all the childcare workers have a university degree and seem to love their jobs. They are paid well. Also, my husband and I receive a Family Allowance from the government for my child, and that helps with incidental costs. Three years later when I had my second baby, my Family Allowance was even higher.

At the same time, I watched my sister in the United States when she had her baby, and her experience was very different. She had only 6 weeks off work and it was completely unpaid other than some saved up vacation pay. How can you heal and bond with a new baby in only 6 weeks? She said that legally she could have taken up to 12 weeks off, but since it was all unpaid, she could not afford it. She also had no helper. I think it would be lonely and very difficult to handle a brand-new baby all by yourself. When she went back to work after 6 weeks, she had to pay over a thousand dollars a month for childcare! My sister also does not get a Family Allowance from her government. Wow, in France, we think of children as a benefit to our entire society, so the government gives us a little money to offset the costs of raising them. I don't know; I guess the United States doesn't see it that way.

—Sylvie, Age 32

Critical Thinking

The French government provides many services to new parents that are paid for by taxes. Would Americans be willing to pay for higher taxes to provide these services? Why or why not? Are there specific groups of Americans that might be more or less likely to support these types of services? Are children a "public" good? Why or why not?

Bilingual education was implemented in all needed schools by the 1970s and 1980s by teaching children primarily or even exclusively in their native language and then transitioning at some point in elementary school to English-only instruction. Proponents argue that the more schools develop children's native-language skills, especially in reading, the higher the children score academically over the long term in English. It may sound counterintuitive, but they claim that proficiency in a second language does not develop separately in the brain, but builds on the proficiency of the native language.

Parents and teachers who believe bilingual education is helpful in keeping their children from falling behind in substantive fields such as math and science face intense pressure from those in the growing English-only movement. Beginning in the 1990s, the political tide shifted, and many people wished to eliminate any use of other languages in government, schools (other than specific world language classes), and

Map 11–2 Percentage of Public School Students Who Were English Language Learners, by State: School Year 2014–15

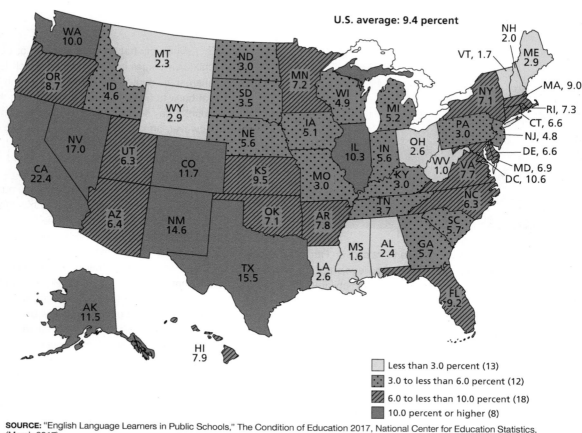

U.S. average: 9.4 percent

Legend:
- Less than 3.0 percent (13)
- 3.0 to less than 6.0 percent (12)
- 6.0 to less than 10.0 percent (18)
- 10.0 percent or higher (8)

SOURCE: "English Language Learners in Public Schools," The Condition of Education 2017, National Center for Education Statistics, (March 2017).

other public institutions. They argued that bilingual education programs are expensive, that native language instruction interferes with or delays English development, and that these programs segregate children to a second-class status.

Several states, including California, Massachusetts, and Arizona, enacted policies to greatly curb bilingual education. However, in 2016, voters in California officially ended the era of English-only instruction in public schools and lifted the restrictions on bilingual education that had been in place for 18 years. Proposition 58, voter-initiated legislation, passed by a 73-27 percent margin.

Often, the discussion about bilingual education deteriorates into political attacks, with opponents arguing that bilingual education threatens our national identity, divides us along ethnic lines, and sends the message to immigrants that they can live in the United States without learning English (Gandara and Escamilla, 2017). In Arizona in 2010, this reasoning allowed Arizona's legislature to ban ethnic studies classes in high school. However, careful research on how students with limited English proficiency can best learn English while keeping up with their other studies indicates that bilingual programs in the early grades, and instruction in English as a second language in the primary and middle grades, result in the high levels of achievement by non-English-speaking students (Bialystok, 2016; Genesee et al., 2005).

The Bush administration's No Child Left Behind initiative insists that all students, regardless of their native language or how recent their arrival in U.S. classrooms, must take the standardized proficiency tests. These test scores must be included in calculating school performance scores. This requirement has placed even more pressure on school districts, many of which have increasing numbers of non-English-speaking children registering each year, to create special programs, including bilingual classes and intensive English instruction for nonnative speakers.

11.6.3 School Violence

In February 2018, a mass shooting occurred at Marjory Stoneman Douglas High School in Parkland, Florida. Seventeen people were killed and 17 more were wounded, making it one of the deadliest school massacres. The 19-year-old perpetrator was identified by witnesses and arrested shortly afterward; he soon confessed.

In December 2012, a young man walked into Sandy Hook Elementary School in Newtown, Connecticut, and gunned down 20 children ages 6 and 7, and 6 school faculty and staff, before committing suicide. Investigating police later found the shooter's mother dead from a gunshot wound. The final count was 28 dead, including the shooter.

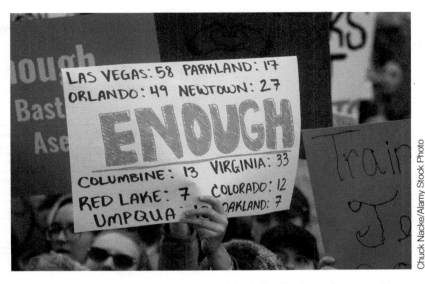

March For Our Lives demonstrations took place around the country in early 2018 to draw attention to the danger of guns in schools.

These events brought school violence into homes throughout the world. Yet, this tragedy was only one of a series of devastating episodes of violence; the story continued into schools in Nevada, Colorado, Oregon, Washington, and elsewhere. In fact, there have been 306 school shootings in the United States between 2013 and February, 2018 (Everytown for Gun Safety, 2018). These senseless acts add to the already long list of violent events within our schools that have shaken Americans' confidence in the security of their children in schools once thought to be safe havens for learning and social development.

To explain why extremely violent episodes are occurring in schools, social scientists and others have cited, among many possible causes: (1) violence in the media, including video games; (2) access to guns and other lethal weapons; (3) mental illness; (4) harassment of students who are nonconformists; (5) the influence of religious cults and "outsider" groups; (6) low self-esteem brought on by social isolation; and (7) the failure of parents to supervise their children. Proposed solutions to school gun violence vary, depending on what is seen as the leading cause of that violence. For example, many students at Marjory Stoneman Douglas High School in Parkland, Florida, are now leading figures in the gun control movement. Yet other people focus instead on increasing mental health treatment, seeing mental illness as a primary culprit.

Although the most extreme forms of school violence grab the media attention, smaller but insidious types of violence such as bullying or fistfights are far more common. Fortunately, most of these types of violence are on the decline, as shown in Table 11–4. In a nationally representative sample of youth in grades 9–12 between 1997 and 2015, the likelihood of carrying a weapon on school property declined from 9 to 4 percent; the likelihood of being threatened with a weapon on school property fluctuated, with a high of 10 percent in 2001 to 6 percent in 2015; the likelihood of being in a physical fight declined from 15 to 8 percent; the percent who missed school because they felt unsafe increased from 4 to 6 percent, and the likelihood of being bullied at school remained constant at 20 percent (Centers for Disease Control and Prevention, March 22, 2018).

Solutions such as installing metal detectors and hiring additional security guards have been attempted, and these measures may help prevent violence by outsiders, but they do not convey authority to teachers. Educators are searching for ways to empower teachers. Several possibilities have been suggested: creating smaller high schools, or

Table 11–4 Trends in Violent Behaviors on School Property: National Youth Risk Behavior Survey, 1997–2015

	1997	2001	2005	2009	2013	2015
Carried a weapon on school property (such as a gun, knife, or club at least once during the 30 days before the survey)						
	9%	6%	7%	6%	5%	4%
Were threatened or injured with a weapon on school property (such as a gun, knife, or club at least once during the 12 months before the survey)						
	7%	10%	8%	8%	7%	6%
Were in a physical fight on school property (at least once during the 12 months before the survey)						
	15%	13%	14%	11%	8%	8%
Did not go to school because they felt unsafe at school or on their way to or from school (at least once during the 30 days before the survey)						
	4%	7%	6%	5%	7%	6%
Were bullied on school property (during 12 months before the survey)						
	-	-	-	20%	20%	20%

SOURCE: Centers for Disease Control and Prevention. 2018. "Youth Risk Behavior Surveillance System (YRBSS)." 22 March.

What Do You Think?

What are your views about arming some teachers with guns at schools to protect students in case of another shooting? Do you think it is a good idea? Why or why not?

"schools within schools"; expecting more from students than mere attendance; and encouraging dropouts to return to school as adults. The last suggestion is especially attractive because adult high school students often become role models for younger students, and their presence tends to reduce the amount of disorder in the schools they attend. Since the shooting in Parkland, Florida, there has been talk of arming teachers; however, nearly two-thirds of teachers strongly disagree with this approach (63 percent). Only 11 percent of teachers say they strongly favor this approach, with the remainder somewhere in between these views (Brenan, March 16, 2018).

11.6.4 School Choice

Efforts to create smaller schools, schools with special approaches to learning, or schools that promote a particular religious orientation invariably become entangled in the ongoing debate over school choice. People who are dissatisfied with the public schools or seek special educational opportunities for their children are often attracted to proposals for expanding the array of parental choices, including parochial and secular private schools.

CHARTER SCHOOLS   U.S. Secretary of Education Betsy DeVos is a committed fan of charter schools. These are special schools that are innovative in their use of resources and yet are funded as public schools. As choices within the public-school system widen, supporters argue, there will be more pressure on the conventional schools to become more competitive and to improve their educational methods. Critics, in contrast, claim that charter schools divert badly needed public school dollars to wealthier families that are more likely to have the ability to forgo attending the neighborhood school to attend a charter school. Charter schools can also discriminate in a number of ways against those students who are less advantaged. For example, they draw students citywide, so providing any type of school buses for transportation becomes difficult. Therefore, it is primarily children who have parents who can drive them to school (i.e., more privileged children) who can attend. Also, parents are often required to volunteer time to the schools, which, again, many low-income families cannot easily do.

Nationwide, about 7,000 charter schools are in operation, serving 3 million students (National Alliance for Public Charter Schools, 2018; National Center for

Education Statistics, 2018b). These schools are most likely to be found in the western or southern states. California has the largest *number* of charter school students (about 600,000), although Arizona has the highest *proportion* of students in charter schools (16 percent).

Most charter schools are small, with fewer than 300 students. They are usually units of a local school system, but each charter school reflects its founders' educational philosophies, programs, and organizational structures.

Research evaluating the effectiveness of charter schools in improving student academic outcomes shows mixed results. Some studies find that students in charter schools do not perform measurably better on reading and math tests than do students in regular public schools with similar student populations. Others show more positive effects (Bluestone, Sjoquist, and Warner, 2016). The differing results likely stem from the fact that charter schools are very diverse. Some serve the urban poor, others the rural poor, and others have more economically advantaged students. It has been noted that there appear to be more positive impacts for more disadvantaged schools and students and more negative impacts for the more advantaged (Clark et al., 2015).

These mixed results are disappointing for advocates of charter schools, but the demand for greater school choice and parents' desire for alternatives to some of the public schools in their communities will continue to stimulate the growth of charter schools and other alternatives to public schooling, such as homeschooling.

While most students in charter schools may not perform better than other students, on average, there are important exceptions. The Knowledge Is Power Program (KIPP) Academy educates 200 middle-school students, mostly poor black and Latino children, and has the highest test scores in the Bronx, New York. To achieve these impressive results, students attend school for nine-and-a-half hours a day, including Saturdays and throughout the summer, and get two hours of homework a night.

SCHOOL VOUCHERS   Proponents of school vouchers ask that parents be allowed to choose among public and private schools that offer all kinds of educational options. The theory is that increased competition among schools to attract students would improve the schools' efficiency or cost-effectiveness while stimulating a more open market for educational practices. The main criticism of voucher plans is that they are likely to be used most effectively by more highly educated and affluent parents, leaving the poorer public schools to less well-equipped parents; this possibility would worsen the existing situation of stratification and inequality in education.

An alternative to school vouchers is reform of the property tax system for funding schools in the United States. Most public-school systems are funded through a levy on residential property known as the school tax. In municipalities throughout the nation, property owners have become increasingly loath to pay higher taxes on their homes to fund increases in teachers' pay or improvements in the local schools. Meanwhile, renters may eagerly vote for education taxes, but do not have to contribute to them. In large cities, where revenues from property taxes are lower, this system is largely responsible for inequities in funding between suburban and urban schools and explains why urban schools often lack the art, music, athletic, and science programs usually found in suburban schools. In the past, state education budgets were used to offset these differences, but as states cut back on public spending, the schools in poorer central-city communities suffer inordinately.

HOMESCHOOLING   Homeschoolers are students whose parents report that their children are taught at home rather than in a public or private school. Although many parents in the homeschooling movement are motivated by religious principles and want to include specific religious instruction in their teaching or wish to avoid the secular aspects of public schooling, many others simply believe that they can do a better job teaching their children than the schools can or wish to emphasize specific language or other skills in their home teaching. Approximately 1.8 million students are homeschooled in the United States (Redford et al., 2017). Homeschooling is facilitated by the wealth of educational materials and resources now available on the Internet.

Students who are homeschooled perform, on average, at least as well as those graduating from public schools. Critics of the movement often argue, however, that while withdrawing students from the public schools may be a good solution to what parents perceive as problems of those schools, homeschooling also takes students out of the school community, perhaps to the detriment of that community, which loses access to the students' talents (and tax dollars). For their part, homeschooling parents argue that their children should be allowed to participate in the school community, even on school grounds (e.g., sports teams, school band), because they pay taxes. Some school districts have complied with these requests.

11.6.5 Sex and Gender Influences in Schooling

Girls do better in school than boys and complete more years of education. For example, from primary school through college, girls average higher grades on all subjects, including math and science. This difference is not just a recent phenomenon, and it occurs in many countries, not just the United States. A large meta-analysis of 369 different studies published between 1914 and 2011 examined the academic grades of over one million boys and girls in more than 30 countries. The analysis found that girls earn higher grades in every subject, even the science-related fields where boys are assumed to surpass them, and girls' higher grades have been consistent over time (Voyer and Voyer, 2014). Therefore, the authors of this study suggest that the recent claim of the "boy crisis" with boys suddenly lagging girls' achievements is false. Other cross-cultural studies also show that girls tend to outperform boys in school in a wide variety of subjects (Heyder, Kessels, and Steinmayr, 2017; Stoet and Geary, 2015).

However, what *has* changed in recent years is young women's likelihood of enrolling in and graduating from college. For example, in 1990 slightly more men than women (age 25–29) had achieved at least a bachelor's degree. But today, women have blown past men. In 2016, 40 percent of young women had at least a bachelor's degree, compared to only 36 percent of young men (National Center for Education Statistics, 2018a). The largest increases in women's college enrollment have been among black and Hispanic women.

Why do girls and women perform better in school than boys and men, on average? We can only speculate. Social, cultural, and economic factors likely operate together. Some parents continue to assume that boys are smarter, especially in math and science and therefore encourage their girls to put more effort into their studies. Differences in studying styles may also affect outcomes; research shows that girls tend to study to understand the material, which tends to produce higher grades, whereas boys emphasize the final performance. Structural conditions are also an important consideration (Lopez and Gonzalez-Barrera, 2014). As labor market barriers to women have been lowered, the benefits of a college education are more obvious for women than they might be for men. In contrast, boys' aspirations may be leveled because of their higher incidence of behavioral and disciplinary problems.

Women have made great strides in advancing their education. Yet, something is amiss; many fields of study remain segregated. For example, fewer women major in "STEM" fields (science, technology, engineering, and mathematics) that can be quite lucrative financially. Why? Is it simply that women do not want to be engineers, mathematicians, or scientists?

A slew of research studies gives us important insights into why women remain poorly represented in STEM fields. Sex and gender bias by schools, teachers, and professors may play a role beginning in elementary school and then continue through college (Blackburn, 2017; Lavy and Sand, 2015). One recent study using data from the

National Education Longitudinal Study found that high schools with highly gendered extracurricular activities (e.g., sports, clubs) had fewer girls enroll in STEM education programs (Legewie and DiPrete, 2014).

Another study examined the opinions of college science faculty toward women in STEM fields. Yale researchers contacted professors in physics, chemistry, and biology at six major research universities (both public and private) and asked them to evaluate an application (fake) from a recent graduate seeking a position as a laboratory manager. All professors received a one-page application from a candidate who was designed to be "promising," although not particularly stellar. Half of the applications were listed as being from "John," while the other half were from "Jennifer." On a scale of 1 to 7, with 7 being the highest, the professors gave John an average score of 4 for competence, while Jennifer received only a 3.3. The professors described John more favorably as someone they might hire for their labs or would be willing to mentor. They also offered John a starting salary that was 15 percent higher than that offered to Jennifer (Moss-Racusin et al., 2012). Remember, these applications were identical.

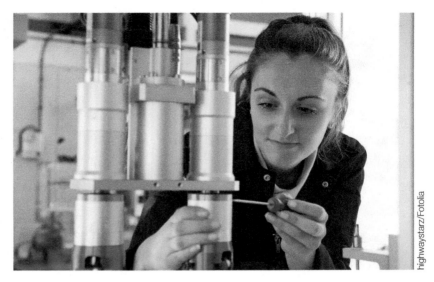

highwaystarz/Fotolia

Despite the fact that women earn the majority of college degrees, college majors remain highly segregated by sex. Few men major in fields traditionally held by women, such as social work or nursing, and it remains that few women major in STEM fields, which tend to pay much higher than average wages. Some schools are brainstorming ways to make these fields more attractive to women.

Should it surprise us that faculty evaluate the applications differently? Sex and gender biases permeate all aspects of our society, including education. In fact, in an interesting twist that looks not at how faculty evaluate students, but rather *how students evaluate faculty*, this bias is clear. A researcher examined 14 million comments on the website "Rate My Professor" in 25 different disciplines in the Humanities, Social Sciences, Physical Sciences, and STEM fields (Schmidt, 2015). He found that students in all disciplines were far more likely to say that male professors, as compared with female professors, were "brilliant," "smart," "intellectual," "knowledgeable," "important," "funny," "interesting," and students referred to them as "professor." Meanwhile, female professors were more often referred to as "biased," "unfair," "moody," "unhappy," "strict," having "busywork," and were called "teacher." To female professors' credit, they were also described more often as "friendly," "helpful," "caring," and "nice," although they were also more likely to be described as the opposite of these: "unfriendly," "unhelpful," "uncaring," and "mean." Clearly, students tend to focus on female professors' interpersonal skills, and think less of their brilliance or intellect.

What Do You Think?

Sex biases in education can go both ways. Why do you think that there are so few men in the fields of nursing, social work, and early childhood education?

Social Policy

11.7 Evaluate access to higher education in the United States.

Of all American social institutions, education may be the easiest to change through social policy, if only people could agree on what they want schools to do. Those who believe American society has become too secular may advocate prayer in the schools. Others, who believe that schools have a responsibility to steer children away from the dangers of AIDS or early pregnancy, may advocate more thorough sex education. Still others, who lament the supposed failure of the schools to produce adequately trained students, may come up with proposals for educational reform in both K–12 and higher education. One issue pertinent to reform has to do with access. While access to K–12 is guaranteed, this cannot be said with respect to higher education. With college tuition costs soaring, many people wonder if attending college is even a possibility.

Tuition costs have soared at both private and public universities. Yet, college remains attractive because graduates earn significantly more than do those who have not graduated from college. This photo of Vanderbilt University shows the allure of the college environment.

Pell Grant

The nation's primary student grant aid program.

11.7.1 Access to Higher Education

The rising cost of college tuition threatens access to public state universities. Taxpayer support for public universities has fallen precipitously over the last decade and legislators look to tuition, grant funding, and private donations to make up the difference. Several prominent university presidents have stated that the decline amounts to privatization of the institutions that played a crucial role in the creation of the American middle class. During the years after World War II, the United States built the world's greatest system of public higher education. "We're now in the process of dismantling all that," said John D. Wiley, chancellor of the University of Wisconsin–Madison.[5]

He has a point. The share of all public universities' revenues derived from state and local taxes hovered around 50 percent, down from 74 percent in 1991. These changes translate to significantly higher tuition costs for students and their parents. Tuition has increased by 35 percent since the 2007–2008 school year, even after adjusting for inflation (Mitchell, Leachman, and Masterson, 2017). The decline in government spending on higher education not only results in high tuition, but is also responsible for drastic spending cuts at colleges and universities that could diminish the quality of education available to students at a time when a highly educated workforce is more crucial than ever to the nation's economic future. For example, many public colleges and universities have cut faculty positions, eliminated course offerings, increased class sizes, closed campuses, shut computer labs, decreased the number of advisors and student support staff, and reduced library services.

Since the recession lifted, only a few states are reinvesting in higher education once more—South Dakota, Wyoming, Montana, and to a very small extent, Nebraska and Indiana. For all other states, higher education funding remains well below pre-recession levels. In fact, per-student funding in Arizona, Louisiana, Illinois, Pennsylvania, Alabama, Oklahoma, and South Carolina is down by more than one-third since the start of the recession, as shown in Figure 11–9 (Mitchell, Leachman, and Masterson, 2017).

As tuition has soared at public state universities, financial aid has grown, too, although it does not come close to meeting the demand. Between the 2007–2008 and 2012–2013 school years, **Pell Grants**—the nation's primary student grant aid program—more than doubled from $16 billion to nearly $36 billion but has since dropped down to $27 million for the 2016–2017 school year (College Board, 2018). Likewise, the number of people receiving Pell Grants jumped from 1.2 million to 9.4 million between 2007–2008 and 2012–2013, but, again, has declined to 7.1 million in 2016–2017. Moreover, because tuition varies so much from one state to the other, and the Pell Grant does not, at $5,800 many students in those states with higher tuition found college to be simply unaffordable. In the 1980s, the Pell Grant covered more than half of the cost of a four-year degree from a public college; now it covers less than a third of that cost (Mayotte, 2014).

11.7.2 Future Prospects

Students' families may try to chip in for the cost of college, but incomes have not risen significantly in recent years while tuition has skyrocketed, so families cannot easily absorb these costs. The bottom line is:

---

[5]Quoted from Dillon, S. "At Public Universities, Warnings of Privatization," by Sam Dillon, *New York Times,* 16 October 2005.

- *More students are working and going to school part-time*, which prolongs their schooling and delays entry into their career of choice, often at considerable hardship.
- *Students are taking on greater debt.* Average student debt at graduation in 2016 ranged from $20,000 in Utah to $36,350 in New Hampshire, and new graduates' likelihood of having debt ranged from 43 percent in Utah to 77 percent in West Virginia. The government earns interest (i.e., makes a profit) on student loans.
- *College dropout rates are increasing* as students find they cannot continue to pay tuition costs.
- *Tuition costs are keeping some students from enrolling, particularly low-income students.* Young people with family incomes in the top 25 percent of incomes (the top quartile) go to four-year colleges at almost twice the rate of equally qualified students from the bottom quartile.

Figure 11–9 Percent Reduction in Higher Education Spending Since the Recession

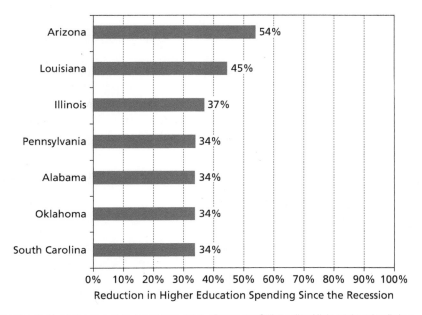

SOURCE: Mitchell, M., V. Palacios, & M. Leachman. 2014. "States Are Still Funding Higher Education Below Pre-Recession Levels." Center for Budget and Policy Priorities. 1 May. Retrieved from (www.cbpp.org/crns/?fa=view&id=4135).

Reforms slated for higher education must keep access as a top priority. One of the primary ways to increase access is to increase spending, especially for financial aid programs. The data show that, in other than a few states, spending on higher education has been cut drastically since the recession, and it has never rebounded.

Going Beyond Left and Right

So many hopes are pinned on education, and schools are asked to do so many things, from assisting in the socialization of young children, to teaching the creativity and skills needed for the 21st century workforce, all the while contending with mental illness and policing. It is little wonder that education is such a contested area of life in democratic societies. There are, however, some areas of convergence between people on the left and right sides of the debate over school issues. For example, there is increasing consensus that schools need to raise their standards, although there is still little consensus about whether the federal or state governments should be the proper enforcers and monitors of these standards. But consensus on the issues has waned, especially with respect to higher education.

Summary

11.1 Describe the history of the American education system.

In early U.S. history, boys and girls usually learned what they needed to know at home or on the family farm. To help unite the nation after the Revolutionary War, educators created textbooks to standardize spelling and pronunciation and to unify cultural and political views such as patriotism, religion, and distrust of Native Americans. It took until the mid-1800s for people to begin calling for free and compulsory elementary and secondary education, and another 50 years for it to become the law.

11.2 Summarize why education is a social problem.

Many people believe that our schools are failing. Parents want the schools to do a better job of preparing students to work and live in a technologically sophisticated and multicultural society. Educational policymakers believe that schools must do more to increase the overall level of student achievement. Many teachers, in contrast, believe that parents should play a greater role in their children's education. Overall, many segments are concerned that schools are failing to teach students adequately. This may be, at least in part, a function of money. Although the U.S. ranks near the top internationally in spending on schools, the amount spent varies considerably from state to state.

11.3 Compare and contrast the sociological perspectives on education.

Functionalists view education as an important social institution because it can lead to the smooth functioning of society. They see education as providing individuals with opportunities for work, fulfillment, and upward social mobility. Conflict theorists emphasize how education perpetuates social inequality and supports the status quo. Interactionists see education as a vital part of socialization and, therefore, tend to focus on the dynamics of the school or classroom and the interactions between students and teachers, between teachers and administrators, or among students themselves.

11.4 Identify the educational attainment and achievement of different groups in society.

Today, ever-greater proportions of U.S. students are finishing high school and going on to college. Nonetheless, much work remains in helping young people to finish high school and in encouraging them to attend college. For members of minority groups, these educational issues continue to be especially pressing. People with higher levels of education tend to earn significantly more money than those with less education.

11.5 Evaluate how students in the United States compare to students in other countries in terms of educational achievement.

The United States has a relatively low ranking on key educational assessments in math and science literacy compared to students in other developed countries. However, it is important to keep in mind that U.S. scores vary signficantly, reflecting greater socioeconomic diversity as compared to most peer countries. In less developed countries, school is often less accessible and resources are minimal.

11.6 Discuss some of the current social problems facing schools.

There are many contentious issues in education. This chapter discussed a few of them, including the need for quality preschool and early childhood education programs, the growing problem of school violence, issues surrounding school choice, biases based on sex and gender, and declining access to higher education.

11.7 Evaluate access to higher education in the United States.

Taxpayer support for public universities has fallen substantially over the last decade. Instead, legislators look to tuition, grant funding, and private donations to make up the difference. However, these deep cuts have affected access to higher education by way of reducing the availability of financial aid for low-income students.

Chapter 12
Problems of Work and the Economy

Justin Sullivan/Getty Images

 Learning Objectives

12.1 Compare and contrast Americans' subjective views on the economy with the objective data.

12.2 Describe the principles underlying key trends in the American system of free enterprise.

12.3 Identify the consequences of global markets and corporate power.

12.4 Assess the consequences of globalization for the American worker.

12.5 Evaluate the problems associated with work today.

12.6 Explain the importance of consumerism, credit, and debt in American society.

12.7 Construct an argument about why the minimum wage should be raised.

I climb and inspect cellular phone towers for a living. This means that I climb up a cell tower, maybe 400 feet in the air and do maintenance like changing out transmission lines or antennas or even just fixing light bulbs on the tower, that sort of thing. It's a good job. I made almost $50,000 last year, but I work pretty long hours too—usually 55 or 60 hours a week. Being up that high takes some getting used to. I've seen new hires say how they are mountain climbers and not scared of heights, and then they don't last a day because they can't do it. It's different. When you climb a mountain, you have it in front of you, but when you climb a tower, you can see right through it and everything below you. That can take some getting used to, especially in the winter when it's cold, wet, and sometimes windy. I swear it's ten times colder up there than on the ground. No thunder though; we aren't allowed to climb in the thunder. I've been doing this for a few years now, but last year, we had to have some new training on account of the number of guys falling. OSHA (Occupational Safety and Health Administration) has been spreading the word that 13 workers died in 2017. I knew one of the guys; it was a real shame. He had a wife and two kids. I heard that four more people died in the first few months of 2018. OSHA said they weren't properly trained. Maybe they were, maybe they weren't. I think it all depends on the specific carrier because they're all pretty different. No doubt about it though, it's dangerous up there.

Because people work for so much of their lives, it is important to understand the social problems related to work and the economy, and how these problems affect our health and well-being. So far, the twenty-first century has been a tumultuous time for the United States economically (Bureau of Labor Statistics, March 2018b; Wolf, 2014). During the first 18 years of the new century, there were a major terrorist attack, a housing foreclosure disaster, a severe economic recession beginning in earnest in 2008, near record-high unemployment, a significant downturn in the U.S. stock market, and disastrous hurricanes and fires that cost the U.S. government billions of dollars in aid. Household net worth dropped by more than $10 trillion during the recession—the largest loss of wealth since the federal government started keeping records of wealth accumulation 50 years ago—and has not yet rebounded to previous levels (Wolff, 2017).

Despite the worst economic times since the Great Depression, however, there has been significant growth and renewed economic activity in the last decade or so. Are these hopeful signs enough to inspire confidence? How do Americans feel about the economy?

Americans' Views on the Economy

12.1 **Compare and contrast Americans' subjective views on the economy with the objective data.**

When a 2018 Gallup Poll was conducted with a nationally representative sample of adults asking them to identify the most serious problem facing America, the second largest single response was "the economy," chosen by 14 percent of respondents (Gallup, 2018). By way of comparison, however, a 2009 Gallup Poll, taken during the throes of the recession, found that the economy was far and away number one, with 86 percent of respondents saying that the economy was the most serious problem, as illustrated in Figure 12–1. This change in only nine years represents a remarkable decline and a growing optimism in the economy.

"The economy," however, is a very broad topic. Of those who claim that the economy is the most important problem today, the majority cite "the economy in general," or "unemployment/jobs" as the primary problem (Gallup, 2018). Far fewer refer to the federal debt, the gap between rich and poor, or taxes as the most problematic. This distinction is interesting because national elections often focus on tax issues, yet most Americans do not see taxes as the most serious issue. In fact, slightly more people today say that their taxes are "about right" than say their taxes are "too high" (Newport, April 16, 2018).

Figure 12–1 Percentage of Americans Mentioning Economic Issues as the Nation's Most Important Problem, 2007, 2009, 2018

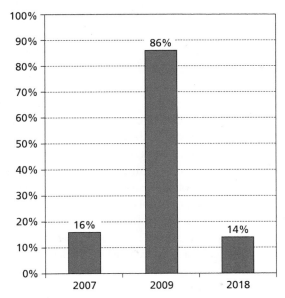

SOURCE: Gallup. 2018. "Most Important Problem." Retrieved 17 April 2018 (news.gallup.com/poll/1675/most-important-problem.aspx).

Other indicators suggest that Americans are growing more confident in the economy. Figure 12–2 examines the degree of financial worry that people report. These data are from another Gallup Poll, again based on a nationally representative sample of American adults (McCarthy, April 28, 2016; May 19, 2017). The survey offered a list of seven personal economic issues that many people face, including not having enough money for retirement; not having enough money to pay the medical costs of a serious accident or illness; not being able to maintain the standard of living that they enjoy; not being able to pay medical costs for normal health care; not having enough money to pay monthly bills; not being able to pay their rent,

Figure 12–2 American's Top Financial Concerns, 2003–2017

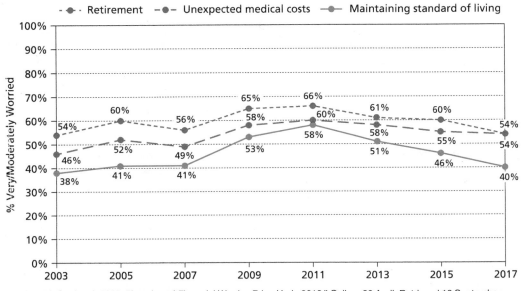

SOURCE: McCarthy, J. 2016. "Americans' Financial Worries Edge Up in 2016." Gallup. 28 April. Retrieved 10 September 2018 (https://news.gallup.com/poll/191174/americansfinancial-worries-edge-2016.aspx).; McCarthy, J. 2017. "Americans' Financial Anxieties Ease in 2017." Gallup. 19 May. Retrieved 17 April 2018 (news.gallup.com/poll/210890/americans-financial-anxietiesease-2017.aspx).

mortgage, or other housing costs; and not being able to pay the minimum amount on their credit cards. Respondents were asked to indicate the degree to which they worried about these things. The most common worries involved retirement savings, unexpected medical costs, and ability to maintain a standard of living. Figure 12–2 shows the percentage of people who report that they are "very worried" or "moderately worried" about these three issues between 2001 and 2017. As you can see, by 2017 the degree of worry is now reduced to pre-recession levels (McCarthy, April 28, 2016; May 19, 2017).

The decline in financial worry is likely related to the fact that fewer Americans feel that their jobs are vulnerable (Riffkin, 2015). Another Gallup Poll asked adults about the likelihood that they would lose their job or be laid off in the next 12 months. As illustrated in Figure 12–3, only 13 percent report that it is "very" or "fairly" likely that they would experience job loss, declining substantially from the percentage who were worried about losing their job during the recession. Americans' fear of losing their job has returned to pre-recession levels.

Yet, despite the improved economic outlook of most Americans, not to mention data that show the economy has indeed improved over the past several years, the social class that many Americans assign themselves to has declined (Newport, 2015). As reported in Figure 12–4, the percentage of people who classify themselves as "upper-middle" or "middle" class has declined from 66 percent in 2008 immediately before the recession to only 51 percent in 2015. Correspondingly, those who identify themselves as "working" or "lower" class increased from 41 percent to 48 percent during this period. Many people during the recession dipped into their savings and retirement accounts (or exhausted them), and had trouble paying mortgages and other bills. They are only now beginning to climb out of debt and replenish their savings, and this might explain the decline in self-perceived social class. It will be interesting to watch whether, over the next few years, social class identification eventually begins to trend toward pre-recession levels, as has been the case for the other indicators presented here.

The next few sections move to a broader discussion of the U.S. economic system. Moving away from Americans' opinions about the economy, especially how it affects them personally, these sections review some of the key trends and features of the American free enterprise system and its connection to the global marketplace.

Figure 12–3 Americans' Concern (Rated as "Very Likely" or "Fairly Likely") for Losing Their Job, 2001–2015

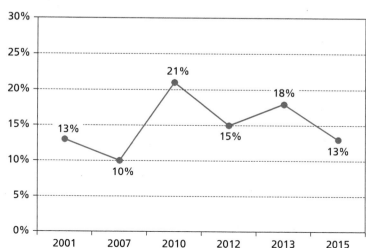

SOURCE: Riffkin, R. 2015. "U.S. Workers Job Loss Fears Down to Pre-Recession Levels." Retrieved 25 May 2015 http://www.gallup.com/poll/182840/workers-job-loss-fears-back-pre-recession-levels.aspx.

Figure 12–4 Social Class Self-Identification, April 2003, 2008, 2012, 2015

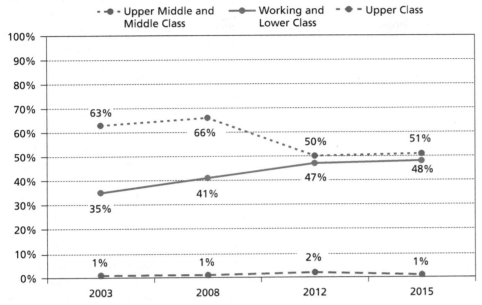

SOURCE: Newport, F. 2015. "Fewer Americans Identify as Middle Class in Recent Years." Gallup. 28 April. Retrieved 3 May 2015 (www.gallup.com/poll/182918/feweramericans-identify-middle-class-recent-years.aspx).; Clifton, J. 2016. "The Invisible American." Gallup. 20 September. Retrieved 17 April 2018 (news.gallup.com/opinion/chairman/195680/invisible-american.aspx).

Principles Underlying Key Trends in the American Free Enterprise System

12.2 **Describe the principles underlying key trends in the American system of free enterprise.**

While the U.S. economy remains by many measures the strongest on Earth, its institutions are undergoing rapid and dramatic changes that can be grouped into a few master trends:

- Globalization of markets and the rise of major multinational corporations that compete for power on the world stage
- Growth in service-sector jobs in the advanced economies and continued export of manufacturing jobs to regions with lower wage rates
- Increasing reliance of families on the incomes of multiple workers, especially of women and formerly retired people
- Increased reliance on innovations in technology and specialization to increase the productivity and competitiveness of companies and their employees

To better understand these trends shaping the economies of the United States (and other developed nations), it is important to clarify the basic principles underlying the system of corporate capitalism as it exists in the United States today.

When people refer to the American free enterprise system, they are talking about an economic system known as **capitalism**. Capitalism is characterized by *private* ownership of the means of production. This means that individuals are free to privately own various kinds of income-producing properties, businesses, or factories and, essentially, buy other people's labor so that they can maximize their personal profit. You may have heard of the slogan, "trickle-down theory." The assumption is that high profits will benefit not only the owner, but that these profits will be shared (will trickle down) to all the workers as well. Capitalism is wary of government intervention. Instead, capitalism suggests that competition in a free marketplace is the most appropriate way to regulate prices for goods and wages for workers. For example,

capitalism

A particular type of economic system found in the United States (and elsewhere); sometimes known as a free enterprise system, characterized by private ownership of the means of production.

nuvolanevicata/Alamy Stock Photo

The idea of capitalism is that the benefits of profits are to "trickle down" to the worker, such as job creation or higher pay. What would a conflict theorist say about this? What do *you* think?

markets

Institutions that regulate the worldwide flow of an almost infinite array of goods and services. Almost all markets in nations throughout the world are regulated by acts of governments, including the United States.

capital

Both the money used to purchase resources (e.g., raw materials) and the physical assets (e.g., buildings and equipment) used to produce goods and services. Capitalists are people who combine capital with the labor of workers to produce goods and services in the hope of making a profit—that is, selling their product or service at a market price higher than the costs of the equipment and labor used to create it.

entrepreneur

A capitalist who creates a new business venture.

limited liability

A protection by which the assets of the corporation are liable to seizure in the case of economic failure or wrongdoing, but the entrepreneur's personal assets are not liable if the corporation fails.

many early capitalists opposed the creation of the minimum wage in 1938. Critics of capitalism, however claim that it is exploitive. They say profits are kept by the rich to enhance their own wealth, and very little actually trickles down to the worker.

The central social institutions of capitalism are **markets**, which regulate the worldwide flow of an extensive array of goods and services. Theoretically, markets in a pure free enterprise system are regulated by the demand for specific goods and services and by the competition among suppliers to furnish them at a price that is attractive to buyers. This is referred to as "supply and demand."

In fact, however, almost all markets in nations around the world are regulated by acts of governments, including in the United States. These regulations usually attempt to protect buyers in terms of the safety of products (e.g., rules about food and drug purity and airline maintenance) or to protect workers (e.g., occupational safety regulations). Other regulations seek to ensure that markets remain competitive and are not dominated by a handful of giant companies in markets, known either as oligopolies (only a few sellers) or monopolies (one seller).

In other cases, governments may try to affect the prices charged for various goods by imposing import taxes, known as tariffs. These levies usually seek to give locally made products a price advantage over products imported from outside the nation. The North American Free Trade Agreement of 1993 (NAFTA), for example, is an arrangement in which the United States, Mexico, and Canada agree not to impose tariffs on goods and services flowing among these countries.

The goal of NAFTA was to make it easier for companies in the three countries to do business across borders. The argument was that—by boosting economic integration—there would be increased economic prosperity in all three countries. Today the future of NAFTA is uncertain. President Trump believes that it represents a bad deal for the United States resulting in job losses in the manufacturing sector, with jobs moving to Mexico where labor is cheaper. Many economists counter by saying that manufacturing jobs were in decline before NAFTA. Instead, they argue much of the decline in manufacturing jobs can be attributed to automation in U.S. industry. Automation allows companies to increase output with fewer workers. Most Americans tend to agree with the economists and believe that new technology is a bigger threat to jobs than is immigration and offshoring, as shown in Table 12–1. President Trump has imposed tariffs on steel and aluminum. Some countries, such as China and the European Union, have responded in kind, by imposing tariffs on pork, soybeans, blue jeans, and motorcycles—all of which are designed to financially hurt President Trump's most ardent supporters.

Capital refers to both the money used to purchase resources (e.g., raw materials) and the physical assets (e.g., buildings and equipment) used to produce goods and services. Capitalists combine capital with the labor of workers (whether hourly or salaried) to produce goods and services in the hope of making a profit—that is, selling their product or service at a market price higher than the costs of the equipment and labor used to create it. A capitalist who creates a new business venture is known as an **entrepreneur**. In the pure form of free enterprise capitalism, the entrepreneur assumes all the business risks and expects to make as much profit as possible with as little regulation as possible. However, in actual practice, most entrepreneurs try to minimize their risks in many ways.

Formation of a corporation is one major way of minimizing risk. Corporations are chartered by governments to conduct business with limited liability to the owners of the business. **Limited liability** means that only the assets of the corporation are liable

Table 12–1 Americans' Perceptions of Threats to Jobs Over the Next Decade

Which of the following do you believe is a greater threat to jobs in the U.S. in the next 10 years: job loss due to immigration and offshoring, that is, jobs or companies moving overseas, or job loss due to new technology, automation, robots, or artificial intelligence?

	New technology	Immigration and offshoring
	%	%
All Americans	58	42
Age		
18–35	61	39
36–50	57	43
51–65	57	43
Education		
Less than a bachelor's degree	57	43
Bachelor's degree or higher	61	39
Job type		
White collar	62	38
Blue collar	59	41
Political party affiliation		
Republican	48	52
Independent	57	43
Democrat	67	33

SOURCE: Data from Reinhart, R. J. "AI Seen as Greater Job Threat Than Immigration, Offshoring," Gallup, Mar. 9, 2018.

to seizure in the case of economic failure or wrongdoing. The entrepreneur's personal assets are not liable if the corporation fails. This protection is vital to the existence of corporations and makes it possible for them to raise funds for expansion by selling shares of their business in the financial markets (stocks and bonds). As shareholders become part owners of the corporation, they are not liable for what the corporation does beyond the risk of losing their investment in the business. The fact that governments grant limited liability to corporations is one way in which the public, through its elected representatives, can try to hold corporations responsible for their actions. Governments can revoke the charters of corporations if they violate federal or state laws.

Not all corporations sell shares to the public, but those that do are among the largest and most powerful economic entities in the world. Indeed, the global reach of large corporations, and their increasing power throughout the world, is often associated with social problems such as environmental pollution, sudden unemployment in specific regions, the use of child labor in poor nations, and many others. It is also true that corporations often create opportunities for economic development and new jobs in formerly impoverished regions.

In contrast to capitalism, **socialism** is a type of economy in which there is *public* ownership of the means of production. The government imposes some degree of limits on the rights of individuals and corporations to own productive property. It deliberately plans and organizes production so that all members of society benefit more equally than with capitalism. Socialism is concerned with the collective good of its citizens.

As it turns out, no economy is purely capitalist or purely socialist; instead, economies are situated somewhere along a continuum. Sweden's place on the continuum leans more toward socialism, while the United States leans toward capitalism. However, each country contains features of both types of economies. Sweden does have some private ownership, and wages range substantially for different kinds of jobs. However, the Swedish government is more involved in providing low- or no-cost services for all residents (e.g., health care, childcare), paid for by higher taxes on the

socialism

A type of economy in which there is *public* ownership of the means of production. The government imposes some degree of limits on the rights of individuals and corporations to own productive property.

wealthy. This level of taxation for the wealthy is a deliberate strategy to reduce the degree of social inequality. Likewise, the United States is not purely capitalistic. Americans have many socialistic features, including a free K–12 education system funded by taxes, a government-run postal service, and a minimum wage for workers.

Some people confuse socialism with communism. Inspired by the Marxian dream of a classless society, nations like Cuba or North Korea loosely follow the tenets of **communism**. This means they attempt to abolish free enterprise, competitive markets, and profits and replace them with a planned economy in which the central government determines the flow of goods and services. As an alternative, they envisioned a classless society, without hierarchy, currency, or personal property; where people work in harmony, resolve their problems in friendly discussions, produce enough goods and services, and where each contributes according to his abilities and receives according to his needs (Kowalczyk, 2016). However, communism as a political system has never really been implemented anywhere, and Karl Marx would probably not be pleased with its attempts in Cuba and North Korea.

Although most Americans tout capitalism as the preferred economic model, capitalist business practices are by no means free of problems, including corruption and exploitation of the powerless. Even when they are successful in generating economic growth and new employment opportunities in a global marketplace, success in one region may come at the expense of workers in another.

communism

A system of government that controls a planned economy, determining the flow of goods and services.

Global Markets and Corporate Power

12.3 **Identify the consequences of global markets and corporate power.**

The effects of globalization are receiving a lot of attention today, but the term and its meanings are often not defined. By **economic globalization**, social scientists refer to the growing tendency for goods and services to be produced in one nation or region and consumed in another. Companies that produce those goods and services engage in business activities in many different regions of the world.

Although most Americans tout capitalism as the preferred economic model, capitalist business practices are by no means free of problems, including corruption and exploitation of the powerless. Even when businesses are successful in generating economic growth and new employment opportunities in a global marketplace, success in one region may come at the expense of workers in another.

This trend is not new. Commodities such as sugar, coffee, tobacco, and tea were early entrants in the global marketplace of the eighteenth and nineteenth centuries. Sugarcane, for example, was produced on slave plantations in the Caribbean, made into raw sugar and rum, and traded in the northern colonies of what is now the United States and Canada for lumber and other products, which were brought back to the rapidly industrializing nations of Europe. Much of the early economic growth of England, France, and Holland, as well as their competition to establish colonies, was stimulated by this global trade.

In today's global economy, the major changes from older patterns of worldwide economic activity are due to the far greater speed of modern communications and transport. Fish produced in massive salmon farms in Chile, for example, can be on American dinner tables the next day.

economic globalization

The growing tendency for goods and services to be produced in one nation or region and consumed in another.

Amazon.com is an example of a company doing business in today's global market.

Alex Segre/Alamy Stock Photo

Information about prices and investment opportunities can travel with electronic speed over computer networks. The Internet can make a corporation such as McDonald's, which has ventures everywhere, lose vast sums of money when there is a health scare about tainted beef from suppliers in Japan and China (Riley, 2014).

Many social problems associated with globalization are due to the overwhelming influence of multinational corporations, both in their home countries and the less developed countries (LDCs), where they increasingly do business (Derber, 2014; Ruggie, 2013; Schrempf-Stirling and Wettstein, 2017).

12.3.1 Multinational Corporations

Few aspects of globalization are more controversial than the operations and even the existence of **multinational corporations**. The definition of these entities is extremely broad. They may produce many different kinds of goods and services, but they are all large corporations (often with many subsidiary corporations) that have their headquarters in one country but pursue business activities and profits in one or more foreign nations (Smelser and Swedberg, 2005). In this sense, multinationals have existed at least since the days of the international banking houses of the Italian Renaissance. American firms such as Singer, United Fruit, and Firestone have had extensive foreign operations—and political influence—since the late nineteenth century. For the most part, however, these early multinationals were national companies with secondary foreign operations.

The sharp rise in foreign investments and the concentration of financial resources that followed World War II led to the development of transnational corporations. These companies are international organizations that operate across national boundaries, whatever their country of origin may be. Their size, wealth, influence, and diversity of operations have grown enormously. The annual sales of companies such as Microsoft, Walmart, Toyota, Apple, Nike, and the major petroleum corporations exceed the gross national product of many nations—not just the poorer LDCs but also highly industrialized countries such as Switzerland and South Africa. In fact, of the world's largest 200 economic entities, 153 were corporations, squeezing out entire countries (Inman, 2016; Global Trends, 2015). Increasingly, therefore, the term *multinational* is used to emphasize the fact that these corporations operate outside national boundaries almost as if they were nations unto themselves.

For decades, the multinational auto companies, such as General Motors and Ford, have been producing thousands of cars in Europe for sale in the expanding European markets. They have had less success in the growing Asian markets, which are dominated by Japanese manufacturers. Now, the Japanese multinational manufacturers, especially Toyota and Honda, produce cars in the United States, using Japanese methods and parts. These and other multinational companies try to create an image of themselves, not as Japanese or American, but as world companies that are above nationalistic sentiments.

Although the multinationals will certainly continue to grow and to account for an increasing share of the world's production of goods and services, they are also widely criticized for operating outside the control of any nation. One way in which multinational corporations are a source of social problems is that they tend to move quickly to areas where labor costs, regulations, and environmental standards are lowest, often to the detriment of workers left behind in the nations where they began their operations (Boehm, Flaaen, and Pandalai-Nayar, 2017; Derber, 2014; Kobrin, 2017).

12.3.2 Global Factories

Multinational corporations are transforming the world's economy by focusing on rapidly developing markets and on labor forces in the LDCs, which have an oversupply of workers in their manufacturing sectors and an undersupply of highly skilled workers with technological training. No longer confined to generating their products in just one country, the multinationals have created a "global factory" that is made possible

multinational corporations (or transnational corporations)
Corporations that have their headquarters in one country but pursue business activities and profits in one or more foreign nations.

by two kinds of technology: high-speed transportation and component production (Martin and Torres, 2004). The first type of technology, high speed transportation, enables companies to get raw materials, finished products, communications, and so on from one point to another anywhere in the world. The second, component production, divides the production process into components that can be carried out anywhere, thereby allowing multinational companies to take advantage of the worldwide supply of cheap labor. For example, U.S. baseball manufacturers send the materials for their product—leather covers, yarn, thread, and rubber cement—to Haiti, where the baseballs are assembled for wages far below those paid for similar work anywhere in the United States.

12.3.3 24/7 Economy

U.S. industries have undergone rapid restructuring in the past few decades in response to technological changes and global competition. The widespread use of personal computers (virtually unheard of just a generation ago, believe it or not), smartphones, fax machines, and pagers has changed the way people do business and the way they conduct their personal life. You can buy e-tickets for your flights, order groceries over the Internet, check e-mail on your smartphones, text your friends to see what is on the agenda for the weekend, post your latest happenings on Facebook or Instagram, and Skype your mom when you are on vacation. The first consequence of this restructuring due to technological changes is that many companies use these technologies to conduct business 24 hours a day, 7 days a week. One study found that three-quarters of people in the UK expect online queries to be dealt with on the same day, while half of us expect a reply within just one hour (Bennett, 2017). This puts extra pressure on companies to be open for business at all times, and to find ways to better serve the needs of their increasingly demanding customers—it's no longer acceptable to pull down the shutters and shut up shop at weekends and evenings.

A second consequence is that more people can do their "work" from just about anywhere, including the dining room table as their children romp in the living room. Work enters the home. Likewise, home life enters the work arena. Thus, for many people, the boundaries between work and family are blurring, as work can occur any time of the day or night. Sometimes this situation works out well (e.g., possibly reducing childcare costs among those who work at home). However, for others, the burst of technology has increased stress levels as work encroaches on other dimensions of their lives.

A third consequence of rapid restructuring is that many jobs are being outsourced to other countries, especially India, Indonesia, and China, as companies search for cheaper labor costs and fewer government regulations (Peck, 2017; Peralta, 2014). Manufacturing jobs, sales, and service are being shipped overseas.

12.3.4 Outsourcing

outsourcing

Locating businesses that produce goods for American (or other Western) markets in poor, developing nations where the firm can take advantage of lower wage rates and fewer environmental restrictions.

Critics of U.S. multinationals have been especially vocal in condemning the practice known as **outsourcing**—locating businesses that produce goods for American markets in poor countries where the firm can take advantage of lower wage rates and fewer environmental restrictions. This practice in effect "exports" jobs from the United States to LDCs, greatly reducing the number of jobs available for American workers (Peck, 2017). The jobs lost by outsourcing may have originally been in manufacturing, but now the lost jobs are often service profession positions. Is your computer on the blink? When you telephone a call center for help, it is quite possible that someone in India will answer the phone. Consumers appreciate the 24/7 economy, and they benefit from the lower cost of goods and services, but outsourcing contributes to widespread job losses in this country. For example, in early 2015, the Walt Disney Company laid off hundreds of information technology workers, outsourcing their positions to

A Closer Look

Disney: The Happiest Place on Earth?

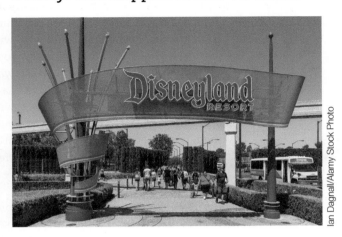

Up to several hundred information technology (IT) workers at Walt Disney Parks and Resorts were called into the conference room one by one to receive notice of their layoffs. The workers were shocked, tearful, and angry. The company decided to restructure its IT department, according to Disney, claiming that it had nothing to do with displacing workers, but rather to shift more resources to projects involving innovation. The laid-off workers were free to reapply for these jobs. However, from the perspective of workers themselves, they knew few co-workers who had landed one of these new jobs. Disney cut well-paid and longtime staff members and shifted work to contractors who use foreign labor, primarily from India. Known as H-1B or "visa" workers, Disney's CEO claims that "H-1B workers complement—instead of displace—U.S. workers."[1] Disney also claims that, as more employers use foreign workers to fill more technical and low-level jobs, firms are able to expand and allow U.S. workers "to assume managerial and leadership positions."

The American workers are upset at losing their jobs and feel that a sense of loyalty on the part of Disney had been breached as a cost-saving measure. As one worker said about the new foreign workers, "Some of these folks were literally flown in the day before to take over the exact same job I was doing." He trained his replacement and is angry over the fact that he had to train someone from India "on site, in our country."

Amid pressure, Walt Disney Parks and Resorts cancelled its plans to replace employees with workers from an agency known for outsourcing jobs to immigrants on temporary work visas.

SOURCE: Based on Thibodeau, P. "Fury Rises at Disney Over Use of Foreign Workers," *Computerworld*, (April 29, 2015).

Critical Thinking

Should a company be allowed to hire and fire whomever they want? What does a company owe its workers, if anything?

[1]Thibodeau, P. "Fury Rises at Disney Over Use of Foreign Workers," *Computerworld*, (April 29, 2015).

other countries (Thibodeau, 2015). They since hired them back due to the negative publicity Disney received. This issue is described more fully in the box, *A Closer Look: "Disney: The Happiest Place On Earth?"*.

In recent years, however, there has also been a countertrend: Multinational firms are increasing their investments in the United States (Dollar, 2017). Sony of Japan has purchased CBS Records; Italy's Fiat owns the Chrysler automobile company; Japanese and German automobile manufacturers have opened plants in the United States to assemble their cars, often using parts manufactured abroad. These arrangements are considered preferable to outsourcing because they keep jobs in the United States. But many foreign-based multinationals resist union contracts and the resulting higher wages and benefits (Dupuis, 2017; Martin and Torres, 2004).

12.3.5 Global Sweatshops

In addition to engaging in outsourcing, multinational corporations attempt to sell their products in the markets of LDCs. As the populations of those countries increase and their standard of living also begins to slowly rise, they represent a vast untapped

Employees dine in a canteen in the Tata Consultancy Services, which provides computer services and back-office support to companies, including Citigroup Inc. and Scandinavian Airline Systems. These jobs have been outsourced to India because of lower labor costs.

sweatshops

Factory-type arrangements, especially in developing nations, with working conditions that would not be tolerated in affluent nations (e.g., crowded, hot spaces; minimal breaks; dangerous work).

source of profits. For example, Coca-Cola is marketed in even the poorest of nations. However, unlike many other corporations, their marketing strategy is to do "good works" in these poor areas, such as investing in infrastructure, providing clean water, providing residents with jobs, and making investments in women's economic empowerment (Westaway, 2014). But it is unlikely that Coca-Cola is turning into a social service agency with a bleeding heart. Rather, they see that a more constructive, organic investment in developing markets is a more cost-effective business strategy than the old way of muscling their way in.

However, most multinationals produce high-technology products and services intended for markets with much greater buying power than that available in poor LDCs. The workers are employed for low pay in **sweatshops**, highly unpleasant factory-like working conditions in which they are essentially forced to endure crowded, hot, and dangerous working conditions with few breaks, conditions that would not be tolerated in affluent nations. Sweatshops are the norm in the global garment industry (International Labor Rights Forum, 2018).

On occasion, usually after a disaster, the world takes note of the condition of sweatshops and fights for their workers. For example, there was headline news around the world when over 1,500 garment workers died in two disasters within one year in 2013. The first incident was a fire that broke out in a sweatshop in Pakistan, and the second involved the collapse of a sweatshop in Bangladesh. In the wake of the disasters, companies, trade unions, and workers' rights groups agreed to make the buildings safer and improve conditions for employees within five years; in many factories, this meant things like adding sprinkler systems or emergency exits. As the five-year agreements' end date arrived in 2018, many factories were still far away from adhering to the new safety measures outlined (White, 2017).

Sometimes American workers and consumers take to the streets in protest. For example, the Nike Corporation subcontracts with overseas employers for about 75,000 Asian workers to make Nike shoes. In some cases, 11-year-old workers who earn about $2.20 a day are producing sneakers at a cost of about $6 a pair. The sneakers are then sold in the United States for $80 or more. Revelations that Nike, McDonald's, and other major global corporations were purchasing goods made by sweatshop labor stimulated the anti-sweatshop movement and forced these powerful corporations to take strong positions against the use of such labor (Bartley and Child, 2014; McDonnell, King, and Soule, 2015; Powell, 2014).

Some people argue that the United States should apply trade sanctions such as import duties against nations that exploit their workers. They believe that wages in Latin America, Asia, and the Middle East will increase only if the rights of workers are protected from repression by their governments and powerful businesses. Workers must have the right to bargain collectively for wages, pensions, and health and other benefits. But representatives of China, Pakistan, India, and many other LDCs where multinationals are active argue that insistence on workers' rights and other protections would drive labor costs up and diminish one of the few advantages poor nations have in the global marketplace.

A Chinese Sweatshop

This slide show depicts a sweatshop in the Chinese province of Guangdong on the southern coast, where one town, Xintang, nicknamed the "denim jeans center of the world," claims to produce 60 percent of the global output of jeans. Who works here, and why do they tolerate low wages and such poor working conditions?

Liu Xiao (left) and Zhu Cheng pose by the lights of the city that lured them to reach for a better life in Xintang. Both boys are from the rural countryside in interior China, and they are very poor. Neither boy finished high school; most children from their village complete only eighth grade. They did not want to be farmers like their parents—"peasant work," Liu claimed—but other opportunities for work do not exist nearby. He saw a flyer advertising "good jobs" and "good pay" in a garment factory far from home. Together with his friend Zhu, they decided to make the trek.

Men and women do different work in the garment industry. The female workers sew blue jeans. They are at their sewing machines for 14 hours a day, six days a week. They receive two 20-minute meal breaks, and two 10-minute rest breaks, all unpaid. All workers receive one day off work; the day rotates because the factory is open seven days per week. The room in which they sew has little ventilation. It is very cold in the winter and stifling hot in the summer months. Song Li chooses to work without a mask that protects her lungs from the damage caused by the cloth fibers. She says that the costs of the masks are deducted from her pay, and she would rather keep the money.

Males do not sew blue jeans, but they prepare the cloth beforehand and iron the newly manufactured jeans afterwards. They, too, work long hours for very little pay; however, they are allowed to move around as they work. The female workers are required to sit at their station and can get up only during their breaks. Most people in the factory say that the men's jobs are better for this reason.

The workers live in small dorms located on the company grounds. There are two beds in each room, and each bed sleeps three women. There is a washbasin in the room that the six workers share, and a community bathroom down the hall. Rooms do not have a window or closet. Mei Xiouyun shows off her room. It is crowded when all six young women are there at the same time, although that is rare because of their different shifts. Mei and her roommates have fixed up the room with posters to make it feel like home. Most workers stay at a factory for only a short time and then move on to a new factory in hopes of a better job or higher pay. In the seven months that Mei has lived here, she has gone through nine different roommates.

Bao Huang, the CEO of the factory, poses in his office. He is a very wealthy man by Chinese standards. He does not feel that his company is exploiting workers. "They come very willingly," he says. "There is nothing for them at home. Here they can earn some money and send it back to their family. Life is better for them here."[2]

---

[2]Bao Huang, CEO.

Critical Thinking

How often do you think of the person(s) who made your clothes? How about the person who picked the fruit or vegetables that you eat? Why are Americans so removed from the clothes they wear and the food they eat?

Effects on American Workers

12.4 **Assess the consequences of globalization for the American worker.**

For the American worker, the growth of multinationals, global factories, and outsourcing of jobs means that a steadily decreasing number of employers have come to dominate the labor market. This trend has had several effects. Chief among them is the tendency to export capital and jobs overseas, where labor is cheaper and more plentiful, and environmental regulations are laxer. U.S. manufacturing workers have been most seriously affected by this trend. In 1960, over 28 percent of all U.S. workers were employed in manufacturing jobs. By 2016, this figure had dropped to under 8 percent (Bureau of Labor Statistics, October 24, 2017c).

There has been a sharp decline in manufacturing jobs in the United States. Many of these jobs have been replaced by service jobs, which tend to have significantly lower pay and fewer job benefits.

jimkruger/Getty Images

The early part of the twentieth century experienced a manufacturing boom as people around the world desired products made in the United States. However, beginning in earnest in the 1970s and 1980s, U.S. plants, factories, mills, and other industrial facilities began to suffer losses as capital was diverted abroad. Unable to maintain their competitive edge, many manufacturing facilities closed. Especially hard hit were plants in the nation's older, single-industry cities, such as Gary, Indiana, once the nation's most important producer of steel.

Over the past generation, there have been three unprecedented changes in the U.S. labor force, largely because of transformations in the global economy. First is the shift from manufacturing to service employment. Second is the large increase in contingent nonstandard work schedules. Third is the enormous increase in the number of women working outside the home—women of all ages and from all kinds of family backgrounds.

12.4.1 From Manufacturing to Services

As manufacturing jobs have declined over the past generation, jobs in the service sector and in sales have increased. These job categories are broad. For example, sales jobs include the clerk at the mom and pop store down the street as well as a high-paid pharmaceutical salesperson with a Ph.D. However, it is fair to say that many service and sales jobs are low-paying and may not provide important fringe benefits such as sick leave, vacation pay, retirement, or health insurance. The growth in these low-paying jobs goes a long way in explaining why educational leaders constantly emphasize the importance of staying in school and gaining the educational credentials required for better-paying positions.

The momentous shift from an economy dominated by manufacturing employment to one dominated by service jobs has improved some work-related social problems and at the same time has created new ones. In terms of an improvement, it should be noted that accidents and deaths on the job are far less prevalent today than they were when the economy was dominated by manufacturing, agriculture, and extractive industries such as mining and lumbering. For example, the rate of accidental deaths at work in 1960 was 21 per 100,000 workers, but by 2016, with the rise of service work as the leading form of employment, that rate had declined to 3.6 per 100,000 workers (U.S. Department of Labor, Occupational Health and Safety Administration, 2018).

moodboard/Alamy Stock Photo

UNIONIZATION One of the down sides of the switch to a service-oriented economy is the decline in union membership. The origin of labor unions dates to the eighteenth century and the industrial revolution in Europe. During this time there was a huge surge of new workers into factories and businesses. Workers were subject to grueling working conditions, exploitation, and workplace dangers.

Industrialization came somewhat later to the United States, but when it did during the nineteenth century, the conditions were largely the same. As small family farms increasingly lost the ability to stay afloat and either folded, or were bought out by large commercial farming companies, there was considerable movement to urban areas in search of jobs. During the early part of the Industrial Revolution, families were often separated because men moved to cities for work, leaving the rest of the family behind. However, as the new industries grew and needed large numbers of laborers, they began to look to women and children to fill jobs alongside men. Industries could pay women and children lower wages and often considered them "better" workers because they were less demanding, more docile, and obedient.

Working conditions in the factories could be exceedingly dangerous, unsanitary, and inhumane. Upton Sinclair wrote of the harrowing conditions that crippled or killed many people, as he described a fictional family working in a meatpacking plant in Chicago in the famous book, *The Jungle*, which was originally published in 1906:

> Of the butchers and floorsmen, the beef-boners and the trimmers, and all those who used knives, you could scarcely find a person who had the use of his thumb; time and time again the base of it had been slashed, till it was a mere lump of flesh....The hands of these men would be criss-crossed with cuts, until you could no longer pretend to count them or to trace them. They would have no nails—they had worn them off pulling hides; their knuckles were swollen so that their fingers spread out like a fan. There were men who worked in the cooking rooms, in the midst of steam and sickening odors, by artificial light; in these rooms the germs of tuberculosis might live for two years, but the supply was renewed every hour. There were the beef-luggers, who carried two-hundred-pound quarters into the refrigerator cars; a fearful kind of work, that began at four o'clock in the morning, and that wore out the most powerful men in a few years. There were those who worked in the chilling rooms, and whose special disease was rheumatism; the time limit that a man could work in the chilling rooms was said to be five years. (Sinclair, 1981, p. 98).[3]

This is a sanitized version of a meat-packing plant discussed in the book *The Jungle*, by Upton Sinclair. In what ways does this photo differ from his description? Why do you think there is such a difference in the visual and the written word?

The labor movement in the United States, just like in Europe, grew out of the need to protect the common interests of workers. Labor unions fought for better wages, reasonable hours, and safer working conditions. They led efforts to stop child labor, give health benefits, and provide financial assistance to workers who were injured or retired.

In 1960, at the height of union influence in the United States, about 27 percent of employees in the private sector were members of unions. Today, only 11 percent are union members (Bureau of Labor Statistics, January 19, 2018c). This change reflects the shift away from manufacturing work, which was always more heavily unionized. The rate of unionization varies from one state to another. New York has the highest proportion of their workers unionized, at 24 percent, while South Carolina has the lowest rate of unionization (2.6 percent).

These differences in union membership are extremely important because unions help workers obtain higher pay, as shown in Figure 12–5. The financial benefits are particularly strong for unionized women; they average $200 more a week than non-unionized women workers (Bureau of Labor Statistics, January 19, 2018c). Unions also are more likely to provide fringe benefits that many nonunion workers often do not have. For example, the

Chronicle/Alamy Stock Photo

---

[3]Sinclair, U. (1906/1981). *The Jungle.* Ann Arbor, MI: Bantam Classics.

Figure 12–5 Median Weekly Earnings of Full-Time Workers, by Union Affiliation and Sex, 2017

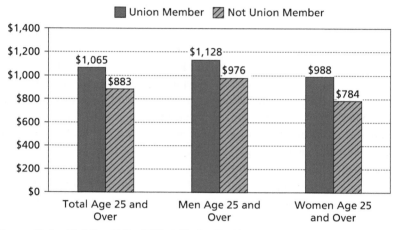

SOURCE: Bureau of Labor Statistics. 2018c. "Table 2. Median Weekly Earnings of Full-Time Wage and Salary Workers by Union Affiliation and Selected Characteristics." Economic News Release. 19 January. Retrieved 19 April 2018 (www.bls.gov/news.release/union2.t02.htm).

proportion of families with health insurance is higher for union families than for non-union ones. Indeed, the loss of union jobs to global manufacturing sites outside the United States is one of the primary reasons the number of Americans without health insurance skyrocketed to 50 million before the Affordable Care Act was passed, as shown in Chapter 2.

12.4.2 Contingent Nonstandard Work

Another aspect of the shift from manufacturing to services is the growing importance of what is known as **contingent nonstandard work**, work that does not have a written employment contract, is only temporary, or has irregular hours. Employees working in these types of jobs represent the fastest-growing category of workers in the United States (George and Chattopadhyay, 2015; Su and Dunifon, 2017). Millions of women and men begin the workday not knowing whether, or for how long, their jobs are likely to continue. Women are overrepresented in these arrangements, particularly in those characterized by lower wages and fewer benefits.

Some contingent nonstandard workers prefer this arrangement, especially highly paid professionals who value their freedom and independence on the job, or mothers with young children who would prefer to work only sporadically. However, most Americans do not work such schedules out of personal choice, but because these are the required working conditions of their jobs as cashiers, maids, nursing aids, cooks, and waiters. They prefer the assurance of a steady job with prearranged hours, an established pay scale with fringe benefits, and daytime hours.

Families with nonstandard work schedules may find it difficult to organize childcare because most childcare facilities are open only between 7 A.M. and 6 P.M. Furthermore, childcare usually requires a paid commitment to a set schedule such as Monday through Friday or Monday, Wednesday, Friday. When a parent works

contingent nonstandard work

Employment that does not have a written employment contract, is only temporary, has irregular hours, or is some combination of these elements.

Non-standard jobs in the United States usually do not provide benefits and the pay is often low. This situation is not necessarily the case in other countries, where the government prohibits employers from treating part-time workers less favorably.

Revelpix/Fotolia

full-time one week, three days the next week, and four half days the next, it wreaks havoc on childcare arrangements, school schedules, and parenting tasks, creating stress (Craig and Brown, 2017; Prickett, 2018; Rachidi, 2016). Children whose parents work evening or nonstandard hours have, on average, more behavioral problems, lower cognitive development, and higher rates of obesity (Kaiser, Li, and Pollmann-Schult, 2017; Li et al., 2014).

Turnover rates in contingent nonstandard jobs are high. Sometimes, people quit work in hopes of finding something better, and other times they are laid off; they are an expendable workforce. To management, people in these largely unskilled or semi-skilled jobs are interchangeable. A high turnover rate is not seen as problematic, and in fact, may even be considered desirable to avoid offering pay raises or fringe benefits. These disposable workers earn less than those on the regular payroll and must live with the uncertainty that their jobs may permanently end today when they clock out at 5:00 P.M. Their anxiety is high, and for many, unemployment insurance is not an option.

"Rhonda" is one of many people looking for a stable job with good pay (Seccombe, 2015). She has a high school diploma but has not gone to college. She is a poor single mother and would like to raise her young son Bobby without relying on welfare assistance. She wants a permanent full-time job, but she has been stymied by the increase of temporary positions with irregular hours (Seccombe, 2015):

> Hopefully I can get me a job. A permanent job. My sister's trying to get me a job where she works. I put my application in last week. And it would be a permanent job. When you go through those agencies, it's just temporary work. It's just whenever they need you, and it's unfair too. Every job I've found is through this temporary agency, like Manpower, but it's only temporary. And they cut my check and my food stamps, and when my job ends, it's like you're stuck again. So I'm trying to find a permanent steady job. But it's hard around here. I've been out looking for work, and hoping that something comes through. (p. 177)[4]

Rhonda may be surprised to learn that temporary agencies are booming. Manpower is one of the largest private employers in the United States, ranking 144 in the *Fortune* 500 list of large companies, with revenues approximating $20 billion worldwide. They serve over 400,000 employer clients worldwide and placed 3.4 million workers within more than 80 countries (ManpowerGroup, 2015).

12.4.3 Women in the Labor Force

The labor force, as defined by the federal government, consists of all people ages 16 years or over (excluding those in institutions) who worked one hour for pay during one survey week (the employed) plus those who did not work during the survey week, do not have a job, and are actively seeking work (the unemployed). As the shift occurred from manufacturing to service work, one of the most significant changes in the labor force was the enormous increase in the number of married women, especially those with children, as paid workers.

> You can really see how women's opportunities have changed by looking at my family. My grandmother, who never worked outside the home, is pretty adamant that mothers should not be working. She talks about that a lot and is worried about the state of families today. Meanwhile, my mom thinks it's okay for mothers to work as long as their children are in school. That's what she did—she waited until my brother and I were in first and third grade. Today, I feel differently. I'm planning to go to medical school, and I just assume that I'll be working when I have my children. I think women can have a fulfilling career and have children at the same time.
>
> — *Abby, Age 22*

As revealed in Chapter 8, most married women with children did not work outside the home until recently. Work during and after the Industrial Revolution

---

[4]Seccombe, K. 2015, p.177. *"So You Think I Drive A Cadillac?" Welfare Recipients' Perspective on the System and Its Reform.* 4th ed. Boston, MA: Pearson.

in the late 1800s was often done in factories, and this work was considered dirty and dangerous. Only women in difficult circumstances took jobs there, most likely immigrant women, poor women, and minority women who needed the wages to survive. This situation created and perpetuated a class- and race-based division among women—those who worked, and those who did not work.

Middle-class white women, especially those who were married with children, largely stayed out of the labor market throughout the early twentieth century except during extreme events like World War II when their labor was sought after. But after the war, most women returned to lives of domesticity, pitying their lower-income counterparts who remained employed (Friedan, 1963).

However, beginning in the 1970s, the tide began to change, and women began to see work more favorably. This shift has been due to a variety of cultural events, including the Women's Movement, which helped to expand job and educational opportunities for women; the invention of the birth control pill, which allowed women greater freedom to control their fertility; and the outsourcing of higher-paying manufacturing jobs overseas, which required many families to now earn two paychecks instead of just one. Thus, work became, for some, more available and desirable and, for many others, a sheer necessity.

Today, over two-thirds of married mothers are employed outside the home for pay, as are three-quarters of unmarried mothers. These trends have remained relatively stable over the last decade and show no signs of significant change in the future. Women work for a variety of reasons: to put food on the table, to provide housing, to pay for vacations, or for personal fulfillment.

Women's employment is not a social problem. The social problem occurs when policies and programs do not keep pace with the changing social structure. Many women and men in the United States scramble because of the lack of paid maternity leaves, the high cost of childcare, the low number of subsidized preschool slots, extended summer vacations from school, and the limited availability of part-time jobs with benefits that would allow families to more easily combine work and family. This dearth of programs and policies affects the quality of life of both adults and their children.

CATCH 22: INFLEXIBLE FULL-TIME WORK OR PART-TIME PENALTY Part of parents' tension over balancing work and family is due to an increasing work week with little control over working conditions—when they work, how long of a day they work, or whether they can take time off. Work is demanding more time of employees: The average American works about 150 more hours per year—more than three weeks a year—than did Americans just a generation ago (Mishel, 2013).

Some parents opt to reduce their work hours to part-time or wish that they could. However, they pay a steep price: Workers who go part-time or to a nonstandard (temporary, contract) route earn much less than regular full-time workers. They are also less likely to receive a pension, health insurance, or other benefits (Bureau of Labor Statistics, July 21, 2017d).

SOLUTIONS IN OTHER COUNTRIES These drawbacks to part-time work have been decreased in many other countries. For example, as far back as 1997, the European Union drafted a directive "to eliminate discrimination against part-time workers and improve the quality of part-time work" (Official Journal of the European Communities, 1998).[5] The directive prohibits employers from treating part-time workers less favorably than comparable full-time workers (unless they can demonstrate that the differential treatment is justified). It addresses issues of pay equity, Social Security, job benefits, training and promotion opportunities, and collective bargaining rights.

How does this directive work? Germany grants the right to work part-time in firms that have more than 15 workers; Belgium grants employees the right to work at

---

[5]*Official Journal of the European Communities.* 1998. "Council Directive 97/81/EC of 15 December 1997 Concerning the Framework Agreement on Part-Time Work Concluded by UNICEF, CEEP and the ETUC."

80 percent of full-time for five years; the United Kingdom allows employees the right to request flexible and part-time work to care for a child under age six or a disabled child under age 18; and Sweden allows parents to work six hours a day until their children turn eight (Gornick, Heron, and Eisenbrey, 2007). All parents in these nations, rich or poor, have these legal rights. The Netherlands, which consistently ranks as one of the best places to live, has taken part-time work to new heights: 27 percent of men and 77 percent of women work part-time (The Economist, May 12, 2015).

What Do You Think?

How do you think your life has been affected by globalization and its effects on American workers? Have these changes been good or bad for you personally? Are they good or bad for society? Why is it that sometimes what is good for you is at odds with what is good for society (and vice versa)?

Problems with Work

12.5 Evaluate the problems associated with work today.

As the economy steadily improves, it remains that several social problems continue to plague the work environment. This section will discuss several of these problems: unemployment, insecurity about the decline of "good" jobs, job discrimination, and occupational health and safety.

12.5.1 Unemployment

Until the recession began in 2008, the United States experienced many years of low unemployment. The economy was strong, inflation was low, and people were working. Some level of unemployment is generally considered "normal" because people change jobs and spend time looking for new ones for a variety of reasons. Economists argue about the precise meaning of the term "full employment," but the consensus is that an unemployment rate between 4 percent and 4.5 percent is to be expected in a thriving economy. However, during the recession, unemployment rates in the United States soared, peaking at 10 percent in 2010. Unemployment rates were particularly high among black and Hispanic people, at nearly 17 percent and 13 percent, respectively.

In response, the Obama administration and Congress used billions of federal dollars to prop up major economic institutions in banking, insurance, and the major auto companies, General Motors and Chrysler—a set of funding priorities commonly known as the stimulus package. The state of the economy began to slowly improve. By 2018, the unemployment rate declined to 3.8 percent, even less than pre-recession rates, as shown in Table 12–2. However, unemployment remains somewhat higher for blacks and Hispanics, at 6.9 and 5.1 percent, respectively, and rates varied by location. These low rates are impressive, but it is always important to keep in mind that unemployment statistics are a bit misleading because they do not include those persons who have given up and are no longer looking for work.

These unemployment figures mean that during the recession many breadwinners lost their jobs or had their income reduced, contributing to the rise in home

Table 12–2 Unemployment Rate, by Age, Sex, and Race, March 2005, 2010, 2018

	2005	2010	2018
Total Age 16 and Over	5.2%	9.9%	3.8%
Adult Men Age 20 and Older	4.6%	10.2%	3.7%
Adult Women Age 20 and Older	11.6%	8.1%	3.7%
White	4.5%	8.9%	3.6%
Black	10.5%	16.8%	6.9%
Asian	3.9%	7.6%	3.1%
Hispanic	5.8%	12.9%	5.1%

SOURCE: Data from Bureau of Labor Statistics. 2018b. "The Employment Situation." News Release. USDL-18-0508. March.

foreclosures, drained savings accounts, and personal bankruptcies. Unemployment also affected personal relationships (Rao, 2017). For example, high unemployment tends to lower marriage rates: People are less likely to marry if they or their potential partner cannot find a job (Edin and Kefalas, 2005).

Although more people are employed today than just a few years ago, it is important to realize that bouts of unemployment can have long-term effects. When people lose an income, especially for long periods of time, they likely need to dip into savings, retirement accounts, or their children's college funds. Many people also use their credit cards for basic living expenses. During the recession, some people exhausted their savings, maxed out their credit cards, filed for bankruptcy, and still lost their

A Personal View

Unemployment Up Close and Personal

designer491/Alamy Stock Photo

I grew up in a typical middle-class family, if there is such a thing. My dad worked as a manager for a medium-sized company, and my mom was a teacher's aide. We had the basic trappings, you know, a three-bedroom house in the suburbs, two cars, and a vacation to the beach every summer. Our lifestyle wasn't fancy, but I never had to worry about whether we had enough money to buy some new school clothes every fall, or whether we would get enough to eat. My parents always stressed that my brother and I would go to college, and they saved a little money toward that goal to help with tuition. In other words, life was secure.

All that changed when I was in high school and my dad lost his job. They gave him a few months of severance pay, but that was it. I remember the frightened look on his face when he came home from work one day and asked my brother and me to leave the room so he could talk to my mom alone. I could hear them talking softly, and then I heard my mother cry. I was dying to know what was wrong.

About 30 minutes later, they called my brother and me back into the room and told us that, after this week, my dad would no longer be working at his company. I didn't really understand what that meant financially. I even thought, "Cool, he'll be home more. Maybe he can go to more of my soccer games." I didn't understand what it meant to be unemployed.

I learned quickly, however. To save money, my parents immediately cut our cable television, and most after-school activities and summer camps. They let me continue the

soccer season, since it was already paid for, but the rest had to go. My brother was really upset about giving up his art lessons because art has always been important to him, and he's really pretty good.

There were also no more allowance, dinners out, or 10 dollars here and there when I wanted to go to the movies. I heard, "no, we can't afford it" daily, and it got old real quickly. By the third month, my parents began to sell some of our possessions—mostly things stored out in the garage that we didn't use, but still, it felt weird to be selling stuff off.

But even more unsettling than the financial issues were the changes I saw in my parents. My father spent the first few months of his unemployment actively seeking work, not finding any, and then it was like he just gave up. He would just sit around the house watching TV and sometimes not even shave or get dressed. He didn't come to my soccer games either, "Sorry son, I just don't feel like it today," he would say. My mom would get upset because when she would come home from her job, the house would be a mess. My brother and I had chores of course, but we didn't think it was our job to clean the whole house! My dad wouldn't even fix dinner most nights. Obviously, this made my mom even more upset and they began to argue a lot. I remember her calling him a "pig" once, and it really broke me up because they never used to talk like that to each other. I'm sure he was depressed, but no one knew what to do about it.

After about 8 months, my father did finally get another job. But things weren't automatically rosy then either. I don't know all the details, but I sense that his bout with unemployment caused them to go into debt. You know, credit cards, home equity loans, and that sort of thing. And our college savings account? That disappeared too. I think their marriage is getting back on track though. Whew, things were rough for a while.

Critical Thinking

Compare and contrast how a functionalist, conflict theorist, and symbolic interactionist would see the issue of unemployment, including its cause and consequence.

homes to foreclosure. It takes these people many years to pull themselves out of this crisis and rebuild their financial and personal lives. This difficulty is part of the reason why many people continue to list the economy as the second most important social problem facing Americans today, even though the economy has regained considerable strength. For a closer look at what unemployment can do to a family, review the box, *A Personal View: "Unemployment Up Close and Personal."*

12.5.2 Insecurity about the Decline of "Good Jobs"

Although many people are now back at work, *where* are they working? If you were offered a full-time service job in the private sector without health benefits, a retirement plan, or paid time off, would you consider it a "good job"? Probably not, yet employers are offering workers more jobs like that one every year, according to data from the U.S. Department of Labor survey of employee benefits. They show that worker (and family) benefits are on the wane, even as the economy has improved, as indicated in Table 12–3 (Bureau of Labor Statistics, September, 2017b).

Table 12–3 Percent of Private Industry Workers Who Have Benefits Provided by Employer, 2010, 2017

Benefit	2010	2017
Defined Benefit Retirement Plan	28%	18%
Any Retirement Plan	69%	66%
Health Care Benefits	74%	68%
Paid Sick Leave	67%	68%
Paid Holidays	76%	77%
Paid Vacation	74%	76%

SOURCE: Data from Bureau of Labor Statistics. 2017b. "Employee Benefits Survey." September. Retrieved 19 April 2018 (www.bls.gov/ncs/ebs/#bulletin_coverage).

12.5.3 Job Discrimination

Several laws exist to protect the rights of workers from job discrimination. For example, in 1963, the Equal Pay Act was passed, which makes it illegal to pay different wages to men and women if they perform equal work in the same workplace. The law also makes it illegal to retaliate against a person because of a complaint about discrimination.

More sweeping, the 1964 Civil Rights Act was passed, which makes it illegal to discriminate against someone based on race, color, religion, national origin, or sex (after one of the longest debates in congressional history). Retaliation for filing a complaint is illegal. The law also requires that employers reasonably accommodate employees' religious practices, unless doing so would impose an undue hardship on the operation of the business.

Other protective laws were passed to prevent discrimination on age, disabilities, pregnancy status, and genetic information. However, there is no federal law that consistently protects lesbians, gays, bisexual, or transgender (LGBT) individuals from employment discrimination. On a state-by-state basis, as of April 2018, as this chapter is written, there are no laws in 28 states that explicitly prohibit discrimination based on sexual orientation and no laws in 32 states that prohibit discrimination based on gender identity. And while the 7th Circuit Court of Appeals recently found Title VII of the Civil Rights Act of 1964 encompasses discrimination based on sexual orientation, the U.S. District Court for the Southern District of Georgia ruled differently. Consequently, in many states, LGBT people can be denied a promotion or fired from their jobs. Yet, more than two-thirds of voters, including a majority of Republican voters, support a federal law protecting LGBT people from discrimination in the workplace (Human Rights Campaign, 2015).

What Do You Think?

How serious of a problem do you think that discrimination in the workplace is today? Is there any evidence that it continues to exist?

While equality in the workplace is an important social justice issue, it is important to remember that laws on the books do not automatically end discrimination. Employers sometimes find ways to circumvent the intent of the law. For example, the 1963 Equal Pay Act requires equal pay for equal work, but some employers assign highly similar jobs a different title, classification, and pay scale. It is not always completely clear whether the jobs are equal or not. How much similarity is needed for jobs to be truly equal?

12.5.4 Occupational Safety and Health

People have long been concerned about the physical toll exacted by work. Medical writings reveal that even in ancient Rome physicians recognized an unusually high frequency of lung disease among metalworkers, miners, and weavers of asbestos cloth. During the Renaissance, each craft was known to have its unique maladies. But the Industrial Revolution created a new wave of deadly occupational hazards. From the beginning, the American labor movement made safety one of its top priorities at the urging of rank-and-file workers and union activists, yet despite this long history of concern and awareness, occupational health remains a serious problem.

Nearly 5,200 workers were killed on the job in 2016, a 10 percent increase over the past several years (U.S. Department of Labor, Occupational Safety and Health Administration, 2018). Figure 12–6 presents the most dangerous occupational categories, some of which have fatality rates 10, 20, or even 30 times that of the

Figure 12–6 Occupations with the Highest Work–Related Fatality Rates (per 100,000 Full–Time Workers), 2016

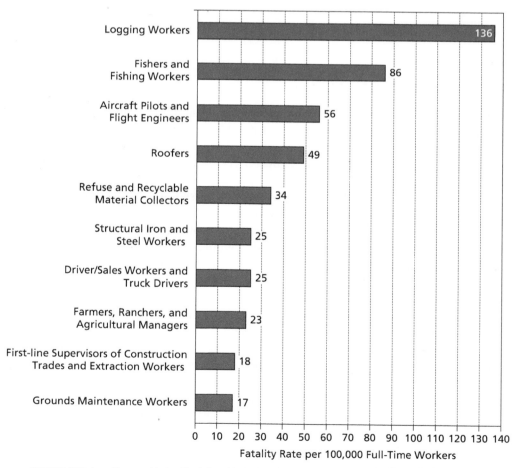

Fatality Rate per 100,000 Full-Time Workers

SOURCE: Data from Bureau of Labor Statistics. 2017a. "National Census of Fatal Occupational Injuries in 2016." News Release. USDL-17-1667. 19 December.

average worker. These occupations tend to be male-dominated, which explains why about 90 percent of those killed on the job are men. As the graph shows, loggers, fishing workers, aircraft pilots and flight engineers, roofers, refuse and recyclable material collectors, structural iron and steel workers, truck drivers and driving sales workers, farmers and agricultural workers, first-line supervisors of construction workers, and grounds maintenance workers have the highest fatality rates (Bureau of Labor Statistics, December 19, 2017a).

But fatalities are only part of the problem. In 2016, over 2.1 million people experienced injuries or illness from their jobs that did not kill them but caused serious pain and suffering (Bureau of Labor Statistics, November 9, 2017e). This amounts to about 3 cases per 100 workers. Some of these are relatively mild, even though a report must be filed. However, 900,000 workers had injuries or illnesses that were severe enough to cause them to miss days of work. These events might include falls, contact with objects, injury from fires, and exposure to harmful substances. These workers miss an average of 8 days of work annually due to these incidents.

Cultura Creative/Alamy Stock Photo

More people die in logging accidents than in any other occupation. What should be done about this, if anything?

Industrial accidents are only part of the problem. The field of occupational health has widened to include illnesses as well as accidents and is concentrating on preventing work-related diseases rather than merely treating or compensating workers for them. Perhaps the greatest health hazards come from the chemical industry. Chemicals, which are involved in the manufacture of almost every product we use, can also produce cancer. Workers who are exposed to certain chemicals have an unusually high rate of malignancies. They also frequently suffer from other health problems, such as nervous disorders and sterility; their children may suffer from birth defects.

Occupational health is an issue loaded with moral, medical, and economic questions. Some industries claim that further safeguarding the workplace will be expensive and costs will be passed along to consumers in the form of higher prices. Other industries argue that compulsory adherence to proposed health regulations will put them out of business or force them to relocate to other countries. Some workers, more fearful of imminent unemployment than of future illness, side with their employers and agree to take their chances in the workplace. Others, realizing that their interests as consumers and citizens may outweigh their economic stake, join the ranks of consumer activists.

As workers in the United States and other industrialized nations organize to deal with occupational safety issues, there is more incentive for industries to locate in low-wage regions of the world whose impoverished citizens are far less capable of recognizing dangers and are less likely to complain to employers about dangerous working conditions. That even more American workers do not question the conditions in which they work or the desirability of what they produce is perhaps attributable, in part, to their high level of indebtedness, which has resulted from extensive use of consumer credit.

Consumers, Credit, and Debt

12.6   Explain the importance of consumerism, credit, and debt in American society.

The United States is a consumer society, one with an economy that depends on the disposable income, or buying power, of consumers. A consumer society requires a large middle and upper class with enough leisure time to enjoy the use of many goods and services that are not strictly necessary (although they may be perceived as such).

Americans are proud of their access to an abundance of consumer goods and often contrast that abundance with the scarcities common in many other nations, especially those in less developed regions of the world.

There are several drawbacks to a consumer-based economy, however. Among these are the dominance of large corporations and franchise operations and the unplanned spread of shopping malls. Smaller businesses find it extremely difficult to compete with chain businesses that are better financed, more efficient, and highly profitable. Indeed, franchise chains such as McDonalds, KFC, and Burger King—the top three global franchises (Franchise Direct, 2018)—have come close to wiping out the mom-and-pop restaurant and the roadside stand, traditional symbols of business independence. These chains have dominated through heavy advertising. Another drawback is that the push to consume encourages some people to spend far beyond their means, sometimes resulting in people losing what they have and filing for bankruptcy. Each of these drawbacks is discussed in the sections that follow.

12.6.1 Advertising and the Consumer Society

The activities of franchise operations and major corporations are accompanied by massive advertising campaigns. "Early to bed, early to rise, Advertise, Advertise, Advertise" is the advice of McDonald's former advertising director.[6] The media are inundated by advertising messages, so much so that advertising slogans have become part of our everyday conversation. "Getting there is half the fun," an executive may comment ruefully as she arrives late for a meeting. "Don't leave home without it," a father may say to his son as he hands him an umbrella. "Because I'm worth it," a woman may say to justify spending money on things that she may not need. Advertising plays a crucial role in a consumer society (Ansarsi and Riasi, 2016; Ritzer, 2012), but some observers are also concerned about its effects on other aspects of social life. For example, to what extent does the dependence of the media on advertisers influence the content of the news and other information they broadcast?

What Do You Think?

Direct-to-consumer pharmaceutical advertisements on television have been legal only since 1985, but did not really appear regularly until 1997. What are the pros and cons of these types of ads?

Advertising is the foundation of a consumer-based society. Advertisers try to create a demand for their products, be it a new car or a Big Mac sandwich.

urbanbuzz/Alamy Stock Photo

A consumer society leads to excessive materialism, a tendency to judge people by their possessions, waste, and other negative consequences. Another serious flaw of a consumer society is that it requires the ready availability of credit. Large-scale production of consumer goods depends on a steady flow of profits, which in turn requires that purchases be made constantly, not just whenever the consumer has a windfall or can accumulate enough through savings—hence the widespread use of consumer credit in the United States.

Since the 1950s the United States has been transformed from a cash to a credit society. As credit companies compete fiercely to lend money to credit seekers, they grant more and more loans to individuals. In total, Americans were a little over $13.15 trillion in debt in early 2017, which is up over 10 percent from just three years ago. As shown in Table 12–4, the typical credit card user has a debt of over $15,900. Student loan debt averages about $47,000, a typical mortgage holder carries about $178,000 in debt. The average auto loan is nearly $28,000 (El Issa, 2018).

---

[6]Ray Kroc, founder of McDonald's.

Table 12–4 American Debt, 2017

Type of Debt	Amount
Average credit card debt	$15,983
Average mortgage debt	$178,037
Average student loan debt	$47,047
Average auto loan	$27,755

SOURCE: Data from El Issa, E. 2018. "Household Debt Climbs, Led by Mortgages, Credit Cards." *Nerdwallet.*

12.6.2 Personal Bankruptcy

Although the enormous increase in consumer credit has been a boon to the U.S. economy, it has given rise to a new and pervasive social problem: debt entanglement and bankruptcy. Each year, more than a million workers have their wages garnished to meet their unpaid debts; many others are sued by their creditors for defaulting.

Personal bankruptcies rose substantially during and after the recession and reached a peak in 2013, at 1.1 million. Why would bankruptcies occur several years *after* the recession? First, bankruptcy has significant consequences, not to mention the stigma associated with it and therefore, people tend to hold on financially as long as possible. They will liquidate their retirement savings and max out their credit cards to avoid filing for bankruptcy. Second, there is generally a lag between failure to make payments and bankruptcy, as the formal process can take some time. In 2008, during the early years of the recession there were about 700,000 personal bankruptcies. By 2017, personal bankruptcies had declined to about 800,000, still higher than before or even during the recession (United States Courts, 2017). In other words, people are still suffering from the effects of unemployment even though they may be back to work. This debt is another reason why, even though the economy has improved significantly by objective measures, subjectively people still consider the economy to be the second most serious social problem.

Social Policy

12.7 **Construct an argument about why the minimum wage should be raised.**

The economy continues to improve, and much of the thanks is due to new key policies that helped stimulate the economy and helped individuals who were suffering from home and job losses. One idea has been floating around to help the economy—raising the minimum wage—and people are lining up to support or oppose this proposal. The next section explores this issue in depth—should we raise the minimum wage?

12.7.1 Minimum Wage

Some U.S. workers earn only the minimum wage or even less. The federal minimum wage in the United States stood at $7.25 per hour in mid-2018 (as this chapter is being written), and has not been increased since 2009, despite inflation during this period (Bureau of Labor Statistics, April, 2018a). This wage comes nowhere near to lifting even a small family out of poverty. At $7.25 per hour, working 40 hours per week yields $290 per week before taxes (yes, people working at minimum wage still pay taxes). Working 52 weeks a year, without any vacation time, a full-time employee would average around $15,080 per year. How does a person or a family pay for rent, utilities, food, clothing, and other incidentals on a federal minimum wage?

Because this rate is so low, 29 states (and the District of Columbia) have adopted state minimum wages that are higher than the federal wage. Washington D. C. and Washington state have the highest state minimum wages in the nation at $12.50 and $11.50 per hour, respectively (U.S. Department of Labor, January 1, 2018). However, in

Table 12–5 Characteristics of Persons Earning the Federal Minimum Wage or Less, 2017 (Age 16 and Older)

Age	
16–24	49%
25 and Over	51%
Sex	
Male	37%
Female	63%
Race/Ethnicity	
White	75%
Black	17%
Asian	4%
Hispanic	17%
Work Status	
Full-Time	35%
Part-Time	65%

SOURCE: Data from Bureau of Labor Statistics. 2018a. "Characteristics of Minimum Wage Workers, 2017." Report 1072. March. Retrieved 20 April 2018 (www.bls.gov/opub/reports/minimum-wage/2017/home.htm).

Georgia, the state minimum wage is $5.15. Employees covered under the federal Fair Labor Standards Act (FLSA) are subject to the federal minimum wage of $7.25, but those not covered under the FLSA (such as many part-time domestic workers) may be paid the state minimum wage of $5.15.

About 1.2 million workers earn the minimum wage or even less (Bureau of Labor Statistics, April, 2018a). Teenagers and young adults are overrepresented among low-wage workers; however, as indicated in Table 12–5, half of these workers are adults age 25 and over. Females are nearly twice as likely as men to earn the minimum wage or less. The racial and ethnic breakdown roughly parallels their distribution in the population with no one group singled out as being more likely than others to hold this distinction. Most low-wage workers are part-time, and nearly a quarter of them reside in only two states: Texas and California (Bureau of Labor Statistics, March, 2018a).

The purchasing power of the minimum wage has eroded substantially over the past decades, controlling for inflation. At its high point in 1968, the federal minimum wage was equal to $9.63 in today's dollars. That means that workers at the minimum wage today are paid roughly 25 percent less than their counterparts 48 years ago (Cooper, 2016). There is not one community in the U.S. in which the federal minimum wage comes close to a living wage for even one person, let alone a small family (Glasmeier and Massachusetts Institute of Technology, 2017).

12.7.2 Future Prospects

Recognizing that the purchasing power of the minimum wage has eroded, and is far too low to support a family, in the 2014 State of the Union Address President Obama called on Congress to raise the federal minimum wage to $10.10 an hour. It did not happen. President Trump has voiced support for raising the minimum wage to $10 at the federal level, but believes states should set the minimum wage as appropriate for their state.

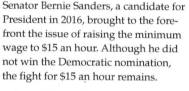

Senator Bernie Sanders, a candidate for President in 2016, brought to the forefront the issue of raising the minimum wage to $15 an hour. Although he did not win the Democratic nomination, the fight for $15 an hour remains.

Philip Scalia/Alamy Stock Photo

Some people feel that a raise in the minimum wage to $10.10 does not go far enough. U.S. Senator Bernie Sanders from Vermont, a candidate for U.S. President in 2016, is an outspoken supporter of raising the minimum wage to $15 an hour. This boost in the minimum wage has received some national traction. For example, the city council in Seattle, Washington, passed an ordinance to raise the minimum wage to $15 an hour. The increase will be phased in over a few years; large firms with greater than 500 workers began in January 1, 2017, while smaller firms have several years longer to phase up to $15 an hour (Office of the Mayor, 2015). The University of California, the County of Los Angeles, Washington D.C., and some businesses in New York City have also agreed to raise the minimum wage to $15 an hour.

Not everyone supports raising the minimum wage, and they argue that if the cost of low-wage labor rises, employers will lay off workers and hire fewer workers in the future (Mourdoukoutas, 2018; Saltsman, 2017). However, there are numerous ways to accommodate wage increases without layoffs. These methods include more efficient production, higher prices, and lower profits. But opponents also rally against paying higher prices.

What do the data suggest? In a review of over 60 studies that look for statistical linkages between minimum-wage increases and job losses, some studies find that raising the minimum wage has a small negative effect on employment, a smaller number find that it has a small positive effect, and most find no significant effect at all (Schmitt, 2013). These findings suggest there could likely be some job losses with an increase in the minimum wage. Nonetheless, advocates of raising the minimum wage say that it is a matter of social justice. People should be paid a livable wage for their work.

Going Beyond Left and Right

The current minimum wage of $7.25 an hour was implemented in 2007 with support from both Republicans and Democrats, and the action is an example of how perceptions of fairness cut across ideological lines. In the face of a widening gap between the haves and the have-nots, Congress raised the minimum wage from $5.15 to $7.25 per hour many years ago. It remains to be seen what will happen as the fight to raise the minimum wage to $10.10, or even $15, intensifies. What do you think about raising the minimum wage?

Summary

12.1 Compare and contrast Americans' subjective views on the economy with the objective data.

Objective data indicate that the U.S. economy is recovering from the recession that plagued the country beginning in 2008. Americans are more optimistic than they were a few years ago. Unemployment has declined, there is less financial worry, and fewer Americans are worried about losing their jobs. However, although there has been significant objective and subjective improvement, Americans are still more likely to rate the economy, as compared with anything else, as the most important social problem.

12.2 Describe the principles underlying key trends in the American system of free enterprise.

A number of key trends in America's capitalist system of free enterprise include the globalization of markets and the rise of major multinational corporations that compete for power on the world stage; growth in service-sector jobs in the advanced economies and continued export of manufacturing jobs to regions with lower wage rates; increasing reliance of families on the incomes of multiple workers; and increased reliance on innovations in technology and specialization to increase the productivity and competitiveness of companies and their employees.

12.3 Identify the consequences of global markets and corporate power.

Multinational corporations are transforming the world's economy by focusing on rapidly developing markets and on labor forces in the less-developed nations. Labor is often done 24 hours a day, seven days a week, and many jobs are outsourced to other countries where the labor is cheaper, working conditions are poor, and environmental policies are weak.

12.4 Assess the consequences of globalization for the American worker.

Over the past generation, there have been three unprecedented changes in the U.S. labor force, largely because of transformations in the global economy. First is the shift from manufacturing to service employment. Second is the large increase in contingent nonstandard work schedules. Third is the enormous increase in the number of women working outside the home—women of all ages and from all kinds of family backgrounds.

12.5 Evaluate the problems associated with work today.

As the economy steadily improves, several social problems continue to plague the work environment. These include unemployment, especially among minority groups; insecurity about the decline of "good" jobs that provide important benefits; job discrimination, especially among groups currently not covered by anti-discrimination legislation; and health and safety in the workplace.

12.6 Explain the importance of consumerism, credit, and debt in American society.

The United States is a consumer society. One drawback to being a consumer society is the dominance of large corporations and franchise operations and the near elimination of small mom-and-pop businesses. Large corporations have used the power of advertising to increase their dominance. Another drawback to consumerism is the push to consume, which encourages some people to spend far beyond their means, often leading to filing for bankruptcy.

12.7 Construct an argument about why the minimum wage should be raised.

Some U.S. workers earn only the minimum wage of $7.25 an hour or even less. This wage comes nowhere near to lifting even a small family out of poverty. The purchasing power of the minimum wage, controlling for inflation, has declined significantly over the years. There is a movement under way to increase the minimum wage to $15 an hour. Critics fear that the minimum wage will cause job cuts.

Chapter 13
Population and Immigration

Sean Pavone/Alamy Stock Photo

 Learning Objectives

13.1 Describe the growth in the world's population.

13.2 Explain the demographic transition and its relevance in the world today.

13.3 Analyze the indicators of rising expectations in the less developed world.

13.4 Compare and contrast governments' involvement in population control efforts.

13.5 Sequence and differentiate the history of immigration in the United States.

13.6 Explore the issue of illegal immigration and its consequences for Americans and the immigrants themselves.

13.7 Consider the controversy and the policies associated with those who were brought to the United States illegally when they were children.

Last July, I landed at the Shanghai airport in mid-afternoon after a long flight from Seattle. When I walked off the plane and headed toward the baggage claim I couldn't believe my eyes. I have not seen this many people jammed together since… well, probably never! It was so crowded, noisy, and chaotic. People shoved their way through, determined to get where they were going, and not let the thousands of people in the room get in their way. It struck me as rude—all this pushing—but no one seemed to mind. In fact, it seemed that this was the only way to actually move forward. I'm not sure how families with children managed to stay together in the crowd. The room was pulsing with noise; and it was oh, so hot and difficult to breathe. If there was any air conditioning, the sheer number of people in the room absorbed it all, and what remained was hot and stale. I finally made it through customs and stumbled outside, only to find the situation repeating itself. How crowded and chaotic can it possibly be outside, you ask? If you have to ask, you clearly haven't been to the airport in Shanghai. I finally made my way to the taxi area. Queuing up is a new concept here. Most people just shoved forward, knowing that if they didn't, they'd be waiting all day. There are not enough cabs for all of us who want one. The sea of people behind me pushed, and I ended up stumbling to the front of the crowd. This is the only way I was able to secure a cab. I knew the taxi driver would not speak English, and unfortunately my Mandarin is minimal, but I was prepared—I had a friend from home write the name of my hotel in Chinese characters. The drive took nearly three hours to get to my hotel. The traffic was unbelievable, and Shanghai just seems to go on, and on, and on. Even with all the high-rise housing, it takes a lot of space to house 25 million people. But, despite my initial culture shock and wondering what I had gotten myself into, I found the city mesmerizing. It's crowded any time of the day or night. The restaurants, clubs, and parks were alive 24/7, and there is something tantalizing about that. By the time I had to leave ten days later, I was firmly committed to returning.

Why study population? Population growth can lead to major social problems such as war, famine, political instability, and infanticide. About 7.6 billion people live in the world today (U.S. Census Bureau, 2018c). There may be room for everyone; in fact, all the world's population standing side by side could fit into the Los Angeles area (Gupton, 2011). However, the issue is about *resources*. How many people can Earth really sustain, and how does our behavior affect that number?

Population changes can be related to high birthrates, low death rates, emigration, or immigration. In the United States, population concerns tend to revolve around immigration, which accounts for much (but by no means all) of the overall growth of the U.S. population. It can be difficult to assimilate new immigrants into U.S. society. The newcomers require education, health care, and other services that may strain already tight local budgets. Yet, if not for immigration, nations like the United States would have growing labor shortages.

In other parts of the world, however, population issues are less related to immigration and are more likely due to large numbers of women giving birth to many children. In this chapter, you will look at some of the patterns of world population. In particular, you will be able to compare some of the key differences between less developed countries (LDCs) and those that are more developed, such as the United States. Understanding the dynamics of population is important because population shifts can cause many different social, health, and environmental problems and tensions.

The World's Population

13.1 Describe the growth in the world's population.

The world's population is currently growing at a rapid rate, but this has not always been the case, as shown in Figure 13–1. Although humans have flourished for around 200,000 years, the rapid and problematic rise in population that concerns us in this chapter is a feature of the last 300 years. The population did not reach 1 billion people until about the year 1800. Then, it increased to 1.6 billion only 100 years later. Today, after another century, the world's population as of late 2018 was about 7.6 billion and, depending on the projection used, could be around 9.8 billion by 2050 (Population Reference Bureau, August 14, 2017; United Nations, June 21, 2017).

Figure 13–1 World Population Change

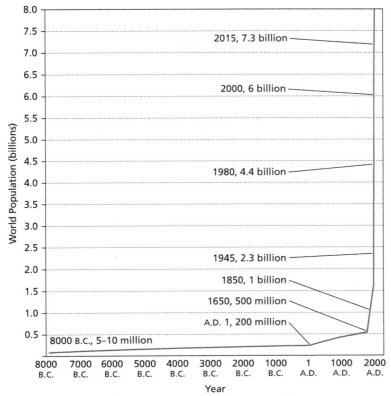

SOURCE: Roser, M. and E. Ortiz-Ospina. 2017. "World Population Growth." *Our World In Data*. Retrieved 14 November 2018 (https://ourworldindata.org/world-population-growth).

If the concept of a billion is difficult to comprehend, consider the following:

- If you were 1 billion seconds old, you would be 31.7 years old.
- The circumference of the earth is 25,000 miles. If you circled the earth 40,000 times, you would have traveled 1 billion miles.

Now, multiply this information by seven or nine, and you'll have a good grasp on what we are talking about for today's population and that of the future. Consider another way to think about population growth: The average population growth rate before 1650 is thought to have been about two-thousandths of 1 percent per year. By 1900, the annual growth rate had reached one-half of 1 percent. Between 1900 and 1940, the rate rose to 1 percent, and by 1960, to 2 percent.

13.1.1 Measures of Population Growth

A few definitions might help you better understand the significance of these population growth numbers. Several terms are used to describe population changes:

- ***Total birth (or fertility) rate.*** The term total birth (or fertility) rate refers to the average number of children born to a woman during her lifetime. This indicator is a direct measure of the level of fertility since it refers to births per woman. It shows the potential for population change in the country. A rate of two children per woman is considered the replacement rate for a population, resulting in relatively stable total numbers. Rates above two children indicate growing populations. This measure allows for useful historical and international comparisons.

- ***General birth (or fertility) rate.*** The term general birth (or fertility) rate means the number of children born per 1,000 women ages 15–44 (some countries use 49 as the cutoff age). This refined method allows international or historical comparisons because it relates birth to the age of females likely to give birth.

total birth (or fertility) rate

Average number of children born to a woman during her lifetime.

general birth (or fertility) rate

Number of children born per 1,000 women ages 15–44 (some countries use 49 as the cutoff age).

crude birth (or fertility) rate

The number of children born per 1,000 of the population.

rate of population growth (natural increase)

The differential between the crude birthrate and the death rate.

What Do You Think?

How would life in the United States be different if our population doubled in 35 years? Think of our social institutions, for example, our schools, economy, families, health care, education, and political system. What kinds of changes would we see?

- *Crude birth (or fertility rate)*. This measure refers to the number of children born per 1,000 of the population. Note that this measure doesn't account for the age of the population. A crude birthrate of 20, for example, means that each year a given group of 1,000 people will produce 20 babies. This figure does not tell what percentage of the population is of childbearing age or are women. Obviously, if the average age of the population is young (e.g., in Kenya), there will be more children born than if the average age of the population is old (e.g., in Japan).

The differential between the crude birthrate and the death rate is called the **rate of population growth (natural increase)** and is usually expressed as a percentage. (In a hypothetical 1,000-person group in which 20 people are added by birth and 10 removed by death, the total population at the end of the year is 1,010—a growth rate of 1 percent.) Note that this figure does not consider immigration patterns.

Most nations have population growth rates of 0.1 percent to 3.0 percent. If a nation's population growth rate is negative, more people are lost through death than are gained through birth and immigration, and the total population can be expected to decline over time. This negative rate could be a problem economically because it is likely that the population is old, with fewer young adults and children. On the flip side, a nation's population growth rate that reaches 2 percent or more is considered "explosive" population growth. If it were to continue unabated, such a rate would cause the population to double in 35 years or less. As you can imagine, this quick increase would be a problem.

13.1.2 Uneven Population Growth: Developed and Less Developed Countries

Population growth occurs unevenly around the world, as shown in Figure 13–2. Growth is particularly pronounced in Africa, where today, a typical woman has about five children. The good news? Fertility has declined in all regions of the world. Only a generation ago, a typical woman in Africa had about seven children.

Less developed countries (LDCs), which include Africa but also parts of South America and Southern Asia, contain about 81 percent of the world's population. In many of these countries, population growth exceeds 2 percent. And, if we look to the future it is likely that their population will continue to grow explosively. Why? In some countries such as Niger, the median age of the population is only 15 years;

Figure 13–2 Total Fertility Rates, 1970–2018

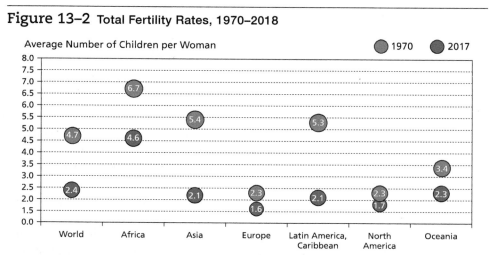

SOURCE: Based on Population Reference Bureau. August 24, 2018. "2018 World Population Data Sheet." Retrieved 14 September 2018 (https://www.prb.org/wp-content/uploads/2018/08/2018_WPDS.pdf).

therefore, the population is likely to grow rapidly because so many people are, or will soon be, of childbearing age. In other words, lots of young women will be having lots of babies. Although women are having fewer children in LDCs, the massive numbers of young people in the early stage of their childbearing age means that many babies will continue to be born.

In contrast, Russia and many other European nations have been experiencing extremely slow or even negative rates of natural population increase. According to estimates by the United Nations, these nations have such low birthrates that they are experiencing population declines. Japan has the oldest median age—47 years (Central Intelligence Agency, 2018). Fewer people there are at the age where they want to (or can) have babies, and the country is concerned about significant population decline and the costs of taking care of all the elderly people.

The median age of a population is important because it allows a glimpse into the future to see what is ahead. A low median age means the population will grow significantly, whereas a high median age means the population has stabilized or may decline. The median age reflects two important trends that occur at opposite ends of the lifespan, and both have important implications for population size. First, the median age reflects birth (fertility) rates. Second, it reflects mortality (death) rates.

Map 13–1 shows birthrates throughout the world using the total birth (fertility) rate, which calculates the average number of children born to a woman during her lifetime. Looking at this map, note that South Korea, Japan, Taiwan, and much of Western and Eastern Europe have fertility rates below 1.5, well below replacement level. Countries with fertility rates this low must rely on immigration to maintain their population, or else the population will decline (Population Reference Bureau, April 14, 2017).

Generally, the fertility rate in developing nations far exceeds the rate in developed nations. In Niger, for example, women have an average of 6.5 children, whereas in Taiwan, women have only 1.1 (Central Intelligence Agency, 2018). One reason for this difference is that, in some LDCs such as Cambodia, Kenya, Liberia, Sierra Leone, and Yemen, less than half of married women ages 15–49 use some sort of contraceptive, as shown in Table 13–1 (Population Reference Bureau, 2017). This limited contraceptive use may be due to obstacles such as inadequate funds for supplies and the lack of comprehensive programs to educate couples on their options. Moreover, large families are often valued culturally as a means of social security. With few government aid programs, large numbers of children (especially sons) are believed to be important social, economic, and political resources that can help maintain and provide for families. However, having many children is more likely to keep families impoverished.

In addition to indicating fertility rates, the median age also reflects a country's mortality (death) rates. You would think that countries with a high mortality rate (i.e., a greater number of people dying) would grow their populations slowly. However, fertility and mortality rates are often positively related to one another; that is, those countries that have the most births also tend to have the most deaths (e.g., most of Africa). But their births surpass their deaths, and so the population grows rapidly. Conversely, those countries with the lowest fertility rates tend to have lower death rates (e.g., the United States, Canada).

Fertility rates are significantly higher in less developed countries than they are in more developed ones. These six Brazilian children pose in their living room with their mother, while their father is away at work.

Homer W Sykes/Alamy Stock Photo

Map 13–1 Total Fertility Rates, 2017

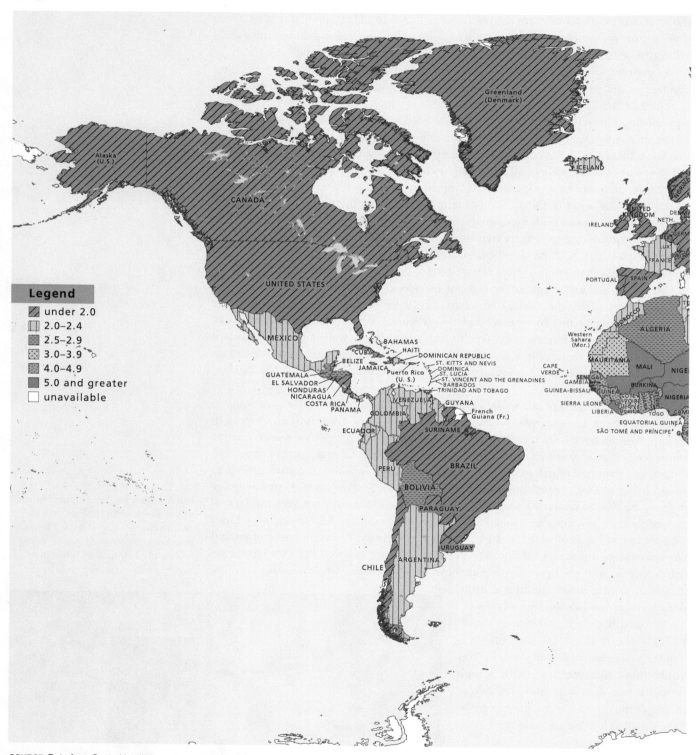

Legend
- under 2.0
- 2.0–2.4
- 2.5–2.9
- 3.0–3.9
- 4.0–4.9
- 5.0 and greater
- unavailable

SOURCE: Data from Central Intelligence Agency. 2018. "The World Factbook." Retrieved 23 April 2018 (www.cia.gov/library/publications/resources/the-world-factbook/docs/notesanddefs.html).

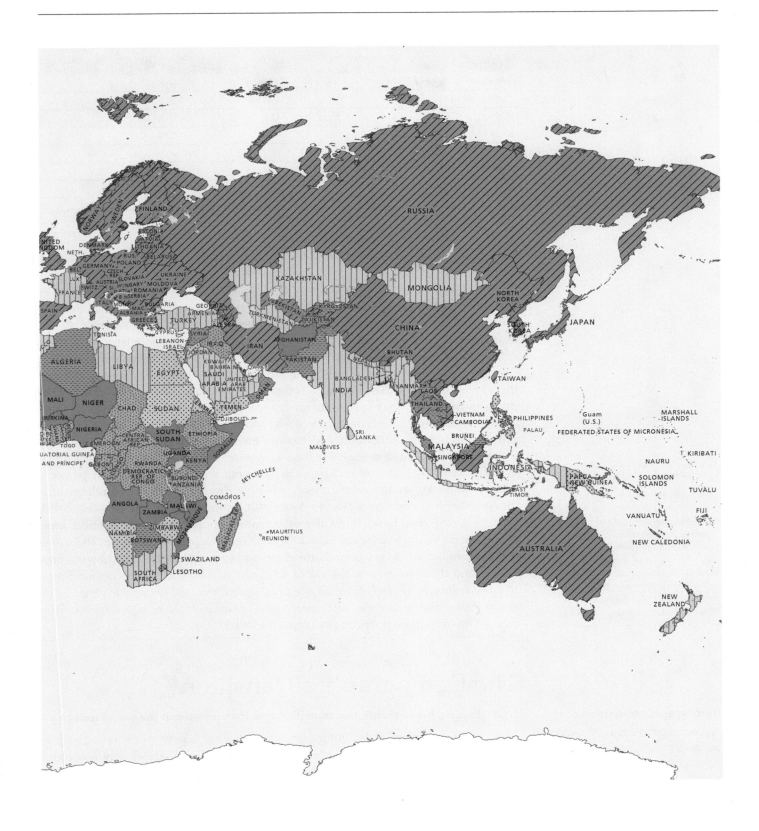

Table 13–1 Percentage of Married Women of Childbearing Age Who Use Modern Contraceptives, Selected Countries, 2018

Contraceptive Use	
Mexico	65%
Bangladesh	54%
Cambodia	39%
Haiti	32%
Liberia	31%
Pakistan	26%
Sierra Leone	16%

SOURCE: Data from Population Reference Bureau. August 24, 2018. "2018 World Population Data Sheet." Retrieved 14 September 2018 (https://www.prb.org/wp-content/uploads/2018/08/2018_WPDS.pdf).

In these countries, birth and death rates are more balanced; therefore, the population grows slowly.

However, some interesting exceptions exist. Some countries with low fertility rates also have high death rates, reflecting an aging population (e.g., Japan and much of Europe). Moreover, some countries have high fertility rates but also surprisingly low death rates, reflecting the youthfulness within a relatively healthy population (e.g., much of Central America). In these countries, population grows rapidly, as you might imagine.

The good news is that, overall, both fertility rates and mortality rates are declining all over the world. The real issue is that more people are living longer. Instead of dying in childhood, they survive to an age when they have babies themselves, and, in fact, are living well beyond these years. More people have been exposed to improved vaccinations, sanitation, and modern medicines and have learned new ways to combat the spread of disease. We have also increased the ability to compensate for excessive cold, heat, and other dangers to life in our environment. And our power to prevent or quickly counteract the effects of famine, drought, flood, and similar natural disasters has improved considerably. As a result, people are living longer. This development is very good news, but it also exacerbates population growth. In effect, more babies are surviving to produce babies themselves, thus posing significant challenges for food production. Many nations are struggling to feed their rapidly growing population and therefore rely on the aid of wealthier nations such as the United States. In other words, as we look forward, *the world's population will continue to grow, but the primary cause will be declining death rates, not necessarily continued high birthrates.* This forecast has important policy implications, doesn't it?

What Do You Think?

Pretend that you work for a nongovernmental organization that has humanitarian issues as a top concern. Your board of directors believes that overpopulation is the root of many social and health problems in the developing world. They ask you to develop a policy that would control population growth. What would your policy look like?

The Demographic Transition

13.2 Explain the demographic transition and its relevance in the world today.

What is the impact of a declining number of deaths? Lower death rates, such as those found in developed countries like the United States, are closely associated with the spread of technological change and higher living standards. This transformation is part of a process known as the **demographic transition**. In this process, a population moves through several stages: an original equilibrium in which a high birthrate is largely canceled out by a high death rate, then through a stage in which the birthrate remains high but the death rate declines, to a final equilibrium in which the birth and death rates are lower but the population is much larger. The first stage is characteristic of peasant and primitive populations before large-scale improvement in sanitation, health care, and other improvements. After this stage comes a period of rapid population growth as traditional values about family size,

demographic transition

A process by which a population moves through several stages: An original equilibrium in which a high birthrate is largely canceled out by a high death rate, then through a stage in which the birthrate remains high but the death rate declines, to a final equilibrium in which the birth and death rates are lower, but the population is much larger.

together with the lack of birth control techniques, keep the birthrate high while technological advances produce a steady decrease in the death rate, especially of infants. Most LDCs are in this stage. In the final stage, which is characteristic of developed industrialized societies, values change, the birthrate declines, and rates of natural increase slow down.

The demographic transition first occurred in northwestern Europe. During a period of about 100 years in the eighteenth and nineteenth centuries, death rates decreased by about 60 percent while birthrates remained at traditionally high levels. Then, toward the end of the nineteenth century, fertility began a long-term decline. Wherever industrial technology has taken hold on a local level, the third stage of the demographic transition has followed—from Western Europe to North America, Australia, and New Zealand and, later, through the rest of Europe. Today, the populations of Japan, Singapore, Taiwan, Hong Kong, and two or three other such areas have reached the final phase, and they have tended to reach it much more quickly (in about 30 years) than the northern European nations did. However, large areas of Asia, Africa, and Latin America remain in the middle phase. Their birthrates, although declining, are still relatively high, and people are living longer. In these societies, population growth often outstrips economic and social development, producing poverty and social unrest.

Rising Expectations in the Developing World

13.3   Analyze the indicators of rising expectations in the less developed world.

There are rising expectations in many LDCs. When some people have access to an improved standard of living naturally, there is the expectation among others that if conditions have begun to improve, everyone should be able to share in its benefits. But will that expectation hold true?

This process of rising expectations began in the late 1950s and early 1960s, when many LDCs, particularly in sub-Saharan Africa and Southeast Asia, gained independence from the former colonial powers (Geertz, 2005). Turning their attention to efforts to improve the lives of people in isolated rural populations, governments embarked on campaigns for favorable terms of trade and direct aid from developed nations. Ever greater sums were invested in education, health care, transportation, and communication. These investments ultimately resulted in changing expectations among the populations of the LDCs as newly educated and healthier masses were exposed to the media and all the information about culture and standards of living that they convey.

It is important to distinguish between the **standard of living** of a population, which is what people want or expect in the way of material well-being, and the **level of living**, which is what people actually obtain. In many LDCs, there is a wide gap between the two, which produces frustration, conflict, and political instability. These problems make economic and social development in the world's poor regions even more problematic, as countries squabble over water rights, borders, and critical resources.

standard of living

What people want or expect in the way of material well-being.

level of living

The level of material well-being that people actually obtain.

13.3.1 Literacy Rates

Literacy rates are a good indicator of the likelihood that traditionally poor and powerless groups are gaining some ground. Literacy has been increasing steadily, from an estimated 68 percent of the total world population in 1970 to 86 percent today. These figures, of course, do not show the tremendous disparities in literacy that persist, as reported in Table 13–2. For example, Cuba enjoys virtually a 100 percent literacy rate, whereas the figure for Chad, a country in Africa, is 22 percent (Central Intelligence Agency, 2018).

Table 13–2 Comparison of Literacy Rates in Selected Less Developed Countries

Literacy Rate	
Cuba	100%
China	96%
Syria	86%
Iraq	80%
Egypt	74%
India	71%
Afghanistan	38%
Chad	22%

SOURCE: Data from Central Intelligence Agency. 2018. "The World Factbook." Retrieved 23 April 2018 (www.cia.gov/library/publications/resources/the-world-factbook/docs/notesanddefs.html).

Significant discrepancies in literacy also exist between women and men, sometimes by a spread of 20 percent or more. Yet, women are also gaining ground. In 1980, just a generation ago, about 62 percent of women worldwide could read and write, but that figure has risen to 83 percent today (CIA World Factbook, 2018). But as discussed in Chapter 11, in many countries educating girls to read and write is steeped in controversy. In highly patriarchal countries, education is considered the prerogative of boys and schools for girls are scarce. Even today in many parts of the world, families who send their daughters to school may face substantial risk of attack. Girls have been sexually assaulted, have had acid poured on their faces, or have even been killed, as they walk to or from school. In April 2014, the militant Islamic group Boko Haram kidnapped 270 girls from a boarding school in Nigeria. Believing that Western education is a sin, the soldiers, dressed in camouflage, shot up the school in the middle of the night and abducted the girls. In the first few days, 57 girls managed to escape from their captors. But hundreds remain missing and are feared to have been sold into marriage or slavery. Their abduction sparked global outrage and a huge campaign calling for their rescue, partly propelled by the hashtag #BringBackOurGirls (Alfred, 2014). As of this writing in 2018, only some of these girls have been returned to their families.

In Pakistan, one young woman, a 17-year-old named Malala Yousafzai, who faced her own grave risks attempting to receive an education, has become an outspoken advocate for the educational rights of women and girls throughout the world. Surviving an attempted assassination attempt, she continues to speak out internationally. For her work, she was awarded the Nobel Peace Prize and is the youngest person ever to win this esteemed award. Her story can be found in the feature box, *A Global View: "Malala's Story."*

Meanwhile, teachers are also at risk of physical violence against them. The situation is so dire and widespread that many international organizations, such as the United Nations and the World Bank, have entire programs designed to intervene on behalf of the teachers, as well as to educate and assist national governments as they fulfill their responsibilities toward ensuring the right to education for all children.

The education of girls is an important human rights issue. But it is more. It is also a critical population control issue. Girls and young women who receive an education are likely to marry later and to have fewer children. They also are more likely to educate their own daughters and sons equally. Educating girls has a domino effect: It is a gift that keeps on giving (Pereznieto, Magee, and Fyles, October, 2017; The World Bank, April 13, 2016).

A Global View

Malala's Story

Brazil Photo Press/Alamy Stock Photo

She's barely an adult, really. Now 21, she's also the youngest person ever to win the Nobel Peace Prize. Her name is Malala. Malala Yousafzai. She's become a household name, and a bit of a rock star among preteen and teenage girls. Who is she? She's a girl who fights for the rights of other girls to receive an education.

In many parts of the world, girls are routinely denied access to schools, or if allowed an education, are harassed by others in the community. Educating girls is considered dangerous and against God's will. With education, girls may start speaking out, demanding rights, and disobeying the men in their families. Girls, like their older sisters and mothers, should be kept at home, inside, illiterate, powerless.

The Taliban, a ruling political organization in parts of the Middle East, fervently holds these views, and when its members come into power, they ban education for girls. The Taliban savagely destroys schools and may maim or kill girls who try to circumvent the law. Malala is a girl who spoke up when the Taliban took control of the area in Pakistan where she lived.

Malala's father was a teacher and political activist, and his daughter was his pride and joy. She went to school and had dreams of becoming a doctor. Meanwhile, her father encouraged her to become a politician, believing that she could change the world. When the Taliban took control, they destroyed schools and mandated that women and girls stay indoors. Malala claims that she prayed for a magic wand so she could make the Taliban disappear. But she soon realized that it would take more, much more, than a magic wand.

After her school was closed, at the age of 11 she gave a public speech titled, "How Dare the Taliban Take Away My Basic Right to an Education?" The next year, when she was 12, she began blogging for the BBC about living under the Taliban's threats to deny her an education. To hide her identity, she used a fake name. However, within months, she was revealed to be the BBC blogger. With a growing public platform, Malala continued to speak out about the right of all girls to an education and was awarded Pakistan's National Youth Peace Prize.

The Taliban considered Malala a threat to their mission, and when she was 14, the Taliban issued a death threat against her. However, Malala's family didn't really believe that the Taliban would harm a child; her family was more concerned that the Taliban would harm Malala's father.

Nonetheless, on her way home from school, a man boarded the bus she was riding and demanded to know which girl was Malala. When her friends looked toward Malala, her location on the bus was given away. The gunman fired at her, hitting Malala in the left side of her head; the bullet then traveled down her neck. Malala was flown to a military hospital in critical condition. A portion of her skull was removed to treat her swelling brain. She was then flown to England to receive further care, which included multiple surgeries to fix the paralyzed left side of her face. Miraculously, Malala suffered no brain damage.

The shooting resulted in an outpouring of support for Malala and her cause. She gave a speech at the United Nations on her sixteenth birthday and published an autobiography, *I Am Malala: The Girl Who Stood Up for Education and Was Shot by the Taliban.* Malala and her family have remained in England where she continues to speak out for the rights of girls to receive an education. The United Nations Secretary-General Ban Ki-moon described Malala as "a brave and gentle advocate of peace who through the simple act of going to school became a global teacher."[1]

Critical Thinking

Why do you think Malala was so intent on getting an education? In what ways would an education change her life? Why do you think the Taliban are so intent on keeping girls uneducated? What is it that the Taliban fear about educating girls?

---

[1]Statement of the Secretary-General on the Awarding of the Nobel Prize for Peace to Malala Yousafzai and Kailash Satyarthi (10 October 2014).

13.3.2 Energy Consumption

As standard of living expectations rise, so does energy consumption. People want to use energy to heat their homes, cook their food, and, increasingly, drive their cars. Per capita (i.e., per person) energy consumption is a good indication of the quality of life of a population, and by this measure, stark disparities remain. Table 13–3 shows average oil consumption per capita in selected countries in 1990 and in 2014 (The World Bank, 2018). As you can see, oil consumption has declined in developed nations such as the United Kingdom, Switzerland, and the United States, although the reduction in the United States, at 10 percent, is among the smallest reductions among developed nations. In contrast, the use of oil has increased in LDCs, sometimes quite substantially. China represents the most extreme case of all: Oil consumption has increased nearly 300 percent during this period, while the population has grown relatively slowly.

Yet, despite the increase in oil consumption in LDCs and the decline in developed countries, the consumption imbalance remains striking. People in developed countries use five to ten times as much oil as do people in LDCs. Americans consume extremely large quantities of oil, reflecting the nature of American lifestyles. The typical middle-class suburban lifestyle consumes considerable gasoline, but also consumes large quantities of paper, steel, synthetic chemicals, aluminum, and so forth, all of which require high levels of oil (and other forms of energy) for their production.

Oil is just one of many forms of energy. Some types of energy are "dirty," such as coal and oil, and others are "clean," such as wind or solar energy, because they do not pollute the earth. These clean forms of energy are also renewable.

Table 13–3 Oil Use in Selected Countries: Kg of Oil Per Capita, 1990 and 2014

	1990	2014
Less Developed Countries:		
Haiti	219	393
India	357	637
Kenya	461	513
China	767	2,237
Developed Countries:		
United Kingdom	3,626	2,777
Switzerland	3,628	3,060
United States	7,770	6,957

SOURCE: Data from World Bank. 2018. "Energy Use (kg of oil equivalent per capita)." Retrieved 24 April 2018 (data worldbank.org/indicator/EG.USE.PCAPKG.KG.OE?end=2010&start=1960&year_high_desc=false).

Thirty years ago, Chinese streets were full of bicycles. Today they are full of cars. There are over 300 million cars in China, which is about one-quarter of all cars worldwide. Ten of the 25 most congested cities globally are in China.

Table 13–4 Carbon Dioxide Emissions, Total and Per Capita

2015 Total Emissions Country Rank	Country	2015 Total Carbon Dioxide Emissions from Fuel Combustion (million metric tons)	2015 Per Capita Carbon Dioxide Emissions from Fuel Combustion (metric tons)
1	China	9,041	6.6
2	United States	4,998	15.5
3	India	2,066	1.6
4	Russia	1,469	10.2
5	Japan	1,142	9.0

SOURCE: Data from Union of Concerned Scientists. 2017. "Each Country's Share of CO_2 Emissions." Retrieved 24 April 2018 (www.ucsusa.org/global-warming/science-and-impacts/science/each-countrys-share-of-co2.html).

Perhaps a better way to compare energy consumption among countries is to examine their level of carbon emissions, primarily carbon dioxide (CO_2). Scientists note that carbon emissions have increased more than 50 percent since 1990, and these emissions have a grave impact on air pollution and climate change. The largest carbon emitting regions were China (28 percent), the United States (15 percent), India (6 percent), the Russian Federation (5 percent), and Japan (4 percent) (Union of Concerned Scientists, 2017).

China and the United States are the largest carbon emitters as you can see in Table 13–4. China produces 9,041 million metric tons of carbon dioxide, and the United States is second at 4,998 million metric tons. However, it is important to note that while China produces twice as much carbon dioxide as the United States, they have five times the population. Therefore, if we look at the per capita (i.e., per person) level, as we did earlier with respect to oil, we see that the United States comes out on top at 15.5 metric tons. Russia and Japan rank second and third, respectively. China comes in fourth, and India trails behind. In other words, the United States still leads the world in carbon emissions per capita, by far (Union of Concerned Scientists, 2017). However, it is striking how quickly Chinese emissions have grown over the past generation.

Naturally, other countries want to emulate the United States. They think, "If Americans can heat or cool their houses, have washing machines, dishwashers, and drive cars, then why shouldn't we?" While all these items are nice, the social problem is that the world's population is too large for everyone to have these things—it would tax our resources and contribute to pollution and climate change beyond what humankind has ever known. But the question remains and is an important one: If Americans can have these things, then why shouldn't the rest of the world? Or maybe the question should be rephrased, "Should Americans have unlimited access to these things?"

13.3.3 Food and Hunger

As population increases, hunger abounds. It is almost impossible to fathom, but the United Nations claims that 815 million people in the world today do not get enough food to eat to lead a healthy and active life (Food and Agriculture Organization of the United Nations, 2017). After steadily declining for over a decade, global hunger appears to be on the rise, up from 777 million in 2015. This hunger affects 11 percent of the global population, or about one person in every nine. Look around you; if your classroom was the world, how many people would be chronically undernourished? In Western Europe and North America, the average person's diet supplies over 3,500 calories a day. In much of Africa south of the Sahara and in South Asia, average daily caloric intake is much lower, between

What Do You Think?

Think about the ways that you used energy over the last week. What would you have to change to reduce your level of energy consumption by one-half to compare with the European Union? Is this reduction feasible? Why or why not?

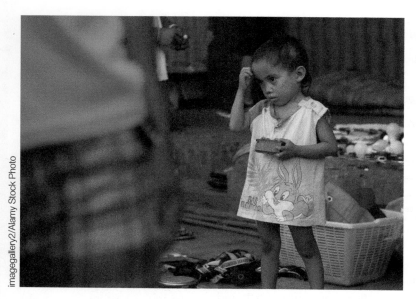

This girl is one of the 815 million persons in the world who suffers from hunger and food insecurity. She does not get enough food to eat to have a healthy, active life. Instead, she is malnourished, which has resulted in stunted growth, hair loss, frequent illness, and possibly cognitive delays.

2,000 and 2,500 calories a day, or even less. These people are chronically undernourished and experience lowered resistance to diseases that comes with semi-starvation. Every four seconds someone, somewhere in the world, dies of hunger-related causes; children account for 75 percent of these deaths.

The food security situation has worsened in parts of sub-Saharan Africa, Southeast Asia, and Western Asia. This was related to severe weather events such as droughts or floods linked, in part, to the El Niño phenomenon and climate change, and were further compounded by the presence of conflict in the region (World Health Organization, September 15, 2017). Over the past ten years, the number of violent conflicts around the world has increased significantly, especially in countries already facing food insecurity, hitting rural communities the hardest and having a negative impact on food production and availability (Food and Agriculture Organization of the United Nations, 2017).

The sad irony of this situation is that food is actually plentiful in the world today, and there is enough food to feed everyone (Portfield, 2018; World Food Programme, 2014). The fundamental problem is the uneven distribution of available food. In most countries around the world food is plentiful, but in some countries, or even areas of countries, it is extremely scarce. There are several reasons for this uneven distribution of food:

- *Hungry people are poor, lacking the money to buy food that will nourish them.* Farmers cannot afford to purchase seeds to produce food for their families. As they get hungrier, their bodies weaken, which further affects their ability to earn a living or farm to feed themselves.
- *Hungry people often live in areas that do not invest in agricultural infrastructure.* They may lack adequate roads for transportation or irrigation to water the crops. There may be limited storage facilities, so food that is produced may go to waste.
- *Hungry people often live in regions where the climate is at odds with food production.* Natural disasters such as droughts, tropical storms, and floods are on the increase, and these events can have catastrophic consequences on food production. For example, droughts are widespread in Africa and directly contribute to crop failures and livestock losses. Moreover, climate change is exacerbating already dire conditions.
- *Wars and conflicts can disrupt farming and food production.* Conflict forces millions of people to leave their homes, and the displaced lack food and a way to feed themselves. Soldiers also use food as a weapon by burning crops, killing livestock, or contaminating water wells. Recent examples of the effect of war on hunger can be seen in Syria, Somalia, and the Democratic Republic of the Congo.
- *Food prices are often unstable.* Roller-coaster prices make it difficult for those who are poor to have consistent access to food. When prices spike upward, food may be out of reach, or people may be forced to shift to cheaper and less nutritious foods, increasing the likelihood of malnutrition.

Hopefully it is becoming clear that population growth is not a space problem per se, but it is a problem of resources. How many people can Earth sustain, given the level of resources that people want or feel that they need for a higher standard of living and a decent quality of life? The slideshow *"Overpopulation"* illustrates some of the challenges facing the roughly 7.6 billion people of the world today.

imagegallery2/Alamy Stock Photo

Overpopulation

Overpopulation has less to do with simply the number of people, than with the number of people who are using precious resources. People require, at a minimum, food, clean water, clothing, and shelter, but certainly most humans want much more than the minimum.

The world contains about 7.6 billion people. It's easy to say "Oh, what's one more," but each beautiful, sleeping, bundle of joy taxes the earth's resources.

Many cities in less developed countries are crowded and do not supply proper sanitation facilities. Infectious diseases easily spread in this environment, including cholera, typhoid, hepatitis, respiratory infections, diarrhea, and tuberculosis.

As developing countries attempt to modernize, they are usually lax about pollution standards. Their goal is to industrialize, at whatever the cost. In China, one of the costs of their rapid development is polluted air. It is not uncommon to see people wearing masks to protect themselves from the fine particles that make up the pollution.

Clean drinking water is a precious commodity and one that is rare in many developing countries. People use the same water to drink as they do to wash clothes, clean the dishes, and relieve themselves. Animals may use the same water source as humans, resulting in a variety of bacteria and diseases. Is it any surprise that the leading cause of death in many developing nations is diarrhea?

The lack of adequate food is a serious social problem in the world affecting 815 million people. This child is one of the lucky ones, however, and is receiving food assistance from aid workers.

Critical Thinking

If the world now contains about 7.6 billion people, what changes might you see if the population reaches 9 billion, or even higher? Will the lifestyles of people in developed countries like the United States change, and if so, what type of changes could occur? What about those who live in less developed countries (LDCs); what changes would they likely see?

Government Involvement in Population Control

13.4 **Compare and contrast governments' involvement in population control efforts.**

As an outsider looking at the plight of poorer LDCs, it is easy to say that they should simply reduce their birthrates to offset their declining death rates. That is, if people are going to live longer, then LDCs must have fewer of them.

Efforts to control population growth differ in severity according to the three basic approaches:

1. Reduce the rate of growth of the population,
2. Control fertility to achieve a zero rate of population growth, or
3. Achieve a negative rate of growth and thus reduce the size of the population.

Obviously, all three of these approaches involve reduction of the birthrate; however, *how much* should births be reduced? And even when it is agreed that births should be limited to some degree, there is much less agreement on how fast and to what extent limits should be imposed—indeed, on whether they should be imposed at all (i.e., whether limits on family size should be voluntary or involuntary). Efforts to limit births raise several moral and ethical questions, but the costs of not making such efforts could be catastrophic.

Family-planning programs have been introduced in LDCs, but the programs have only limited success in rural regions where traditions remain strong. China was a notable exception and provides an interesting example of the extent to which a government will go to achieve a negative rate of growth and reduce the size of the population. Since the late 1970s until 2015, through incentives, deterrents, and punishments, China strongly encouraged families to have only one child. Although the Chinese government now allows families to have two children (and no more), it is worth examining the steps that a country may take to control population growth.

Billboards in China advertised the benefits of having only one child. The billboards usually displayed a family that is wealthy and prosperous, trying to show the advantages of having only one child.

计划生育 强国之本

Keren Su/Getty Images

13.4.1 China's One-Child Policy

The grandmother wrestled the baby girl from the mother's arms, after hours of arguments that were going nowhere. The decision had been made. Both women were sobbing, but the baby girl slept peacefully, not knowing what was in store for her. The grandmother put several layers of clothing on her granddaughter, despite the warmth on this June night. She then laid the one-week-old girl in a box lined with blankets, a bottle, and an extra package of formula, and carried her off into the night. The grandmother could hear the wails of the baby's mother, her own daughter, as she headed down the road to a nearby village. "My baby, my baby, bring back my baby …," the mother cried, although she felt too, deep in her heart, that this relinquishing must be done. The grandmother quickly scurried with her bundle toward the park, which was eerily deserted in the late night. In the light of the moon she kissed her granddaughter for the very last time, propped up the bottle next to the sleeping baby, and set the baby and her makeshift bed on a bench located in a popular area of the park. The grandmother looked up above with tears in her eyes and prayed to her god that the child be found safely and quickly in the early dawn light. With that, she disappeared alone into the night, never to see or hear of her granddaughter again.

This story is one that occurred tens, if not hundreds of thousands of times in China. What would prompt a grandmother to take her granddaughter away from her parents and abandon her in a public place? The answer lies in a complex interweaving of government policy and cultural traditions.

China, like many countries, had a population that was rapidly rising, and the government worried about its people: Would there be enough resources to feed and house everyone sufficiently? To combat tremendous population growth, the Chinese government implemented in the late 1970s what is known as the **one-child policy**. It consisted of three main points: (1) delayed marriage and delayed childbearing, (2) fewer and healthier births, and (3) one child per couple (with a few exceptions, such as instances when the first child is disabled). The policy was slowly modified over time. For example, by the year 2000, a couple living in rural China could have a second child if their first child was a girl.

Families who followed the one-child policy and agreed to be sterilized were rewarded with extra salary, larger houses, better jobs, or some other incentive. The official sanction for violating the one-child policy was a stiff fine. Second or subsequent children might not be eligible for social, educational, and health care benefits.

The government actively promoted the one-child policy through massive media efforts that included newspapers, radio, television, theater, music, local performances, and schools; by a thorough set of laws and policies that governed marriage and fertility; and by strategically placing compliance officers in workplaces and in neighborhoods. For example, each city, county, and township had a family-planning station focused on publicity and education. Most Chinese willingly complied with the policy and saw it as good for the country.

The one-child policy has been both praised and condemned around the world (Hall, 2017; Jian, 2013; Johnson, 2016). It has been applauded as an effective tool for ensuring that China will be able to support and feed its people, increase their standard of living, and combat widespread poverty. In this regard, it has been highly successful. China's population is about 400 million people less than what it would have been without the policy, relieving some of the obvious stresses of overpopulation. Families are more able to concentrate their limited resources on one child, thereby leading to higher standards of living, higher levels of education, and increased income. However, China's one-child policy has also been criticized as an abuse of human rights because of the disappearance of girls, both before and after birth. The sex ratio is highly imbalanced, with at least 35 million more

one-child policy

This Chinese policy had three main points: (1) delayed marriage and delayed childbearing; (2) fewer and healthier births; and (3) one child per couple (with some exceptions).

males than females (Denyer and Gowen, 2018). Naturally, there are 105 boys for every 100 girls, but in parts of China, the ratio is 130 or even 150 boys per 100 girls. Nothing like this has ever happened in history, and the consequences are and will continue to be severe. The family is the bedrock of Chinese society, yet Chinese men will be competing with one another to marry.

What has happened to all these girls? Some were hidden—not recorded in the birth statistics and are therefore uncounted in the census (Johnson, 2016). These girls are "noncitizens," ineligible for any government benefits. Others were abandoned because there was no formal mechanism in China to put a child up for adoption. Still others were killed in utero or quickly after birth. Why is it that girls, rather than boys, disappeared? In China, when only one child was allowed, girls were viewed as an economic liability, and parents saw boys as a better investment. The traditional culture of China favors boys over girls to such a degree that many couples believe they must have a male child at all costs. Sons are expected to carry on the family lineage and take care of their aging parents. When a woman marries, she turns her focus to her husband's family. Customs like these reinforced the preference for sons; daughters are seen as costing more, wasting precious resources, and providing little or no security for parents in old age.

In October 2015, the Chinese government reassessed the one-child policy, noting both the shortage of young women and the growing elderly population with fewer young people to care for them. The one-child policy officially ended, and married couples are now allowed to have two children.

13.4.2 Japan's Quest for Growth

In contrast to China, in which the government is involved in trying to limit births, the Japanese government is trying to *increase* the country's birthrate (Centre for Public Impact, 2017; Lee and Lee, 2013). One-third of Japan's population is age 65 or older (United Nations, Department of Economic and Social Affairs, Population Division, 2017). The rapidly aging population, coupled with a birthrate of under 1.5 births per woman—far below replacement level—shows a declining population, amounting to a 300,000-person decrease between 2017 and 2018 alone. Projections are that Japan's population will decline by about one-third between now and 2065, from about 127 million to 88 million by 2060 (Demetriou, 2017). One reason that women in Japan have so few children is because they have the near exclusive responsibility for taking care of them rather than sharing the workload with their partners, as is increasingly the case in other developed nations. Japan's gendered norms are more traditional than in other developed countries (Nagase and Brinton, 2017; Yoshida, 2017). Japanese fathers, especially those who work on salary, spend very little time with their children. This practice is due in part to the demands made on employed men to work very long hours and in part because of the cultural ideas that childcare is women's work. Other reasons for the low birthrate are that many young adults are postponing marriage or remaining single, in part due to increasing job insecurity (Piotrowski, Kalleberg, and Rindfuss, 2015).

However, hoping to encourage more births, the government instituted the "Angel Plan" in 1994 to help couples raise their

What Do You Think?
What do you personally think of China's policy of requiring families to have just one child? Do you think a model like this one could be implemented in other countries that are also facing tremendous population growth?

Japan is a country with a very low birthrate and high death rates, reflecting an aging population. The population is becoming increasingly older. This is the first time in the world that this has happened, and this unprecedented demographic change has wide consequences. Who will provide economic and social support to all these elderly people?

David Smith/Alamy Stock Photo

children. The government reasoned that if it can encourage fathers to become more involved in the lives of their children, then families might choose to have more births. Their campaign profiled a well-known Japanese celebrity playing with his son, with a slogan claiming "A man who doesn't raise his children can't be called a father" (Ishii-Kuntz, 2003; Ishii-Kuntz et al., 2004).[2]

Nevertheless, fertility rates remained low; so, in 2009 Japan introduced a much broader version of the Angel Plan, called the "Plus One Policy" (Centre for Public Impact, 2017). The government recognized that people feel frustrated because jobs are so demanding that they must often choose between work and having children. In Japanese surveys, over 90 percent of couples said that they did want to marry and would like to have at least two children (Haub, 2010). Therefore, the new program worked to change some aspects of Japanese culture that encourage people to become "workaholics." The goal is to make society more conducive to sharing childrearing and household chores, which also allows mothers to work outside the home. Specifically, the policy includes the following goals (Centre for Public Impact, 2017; Lee and Lee, 2013):

- Enhancing the number of childcare facilities
- Encouraging workers to use 100 percent of their paid annual leave (as opposed to the current 47 percent)
- Reducing by half the number of employees who work 60 hours or more per week, currently at 11 percent
- Increasing the amount of time husbands spend on childcare and housework from the current 1 hour per day to 2.5 hours per day
- Increasing the proportion of people of ages 60–64 who are working to 60 percent, currently at 53 percent
- Reducing the number of so-called "freeters," or youths who skip from one part-time job to another to 1.5 million or less, from the current 1.9 million, by helping them find permanent employment

So far, the policies have not encouraged many more births, and concern lingers about whether Japan will be able to support their large number of elderly persons. Japan's demographic future does not look very promising in this regard.

13.4.3 Family Planning and Population Growth in the United States

Voluntary efforts to limit births are common in the United States and customarily take the form of personal family planning that allows couples to have the number of children they want, when they want them. The American family planning movement owes much to the energy and dedication of Margaret Sanger, a nurse who hoped to free women from the burdens of unplanned childbearing. In 1916, she opened the nation's first birth control clinic, and was jailed for doing so. Later, court decisions allowed physicians to prescribe birth control for health reasons; these were the first in a series of decisions that eventually permitted the sale and advertisement of contraceptive materials and the dissemination of information about birth control. By 1965, some 85 percent of married women in the United States had used some method of birth control (Ehrlich, Ehrlich, and Holdren, 1977).

As a cautionary note, we should be reminded that family planning and population control are not synonymous. Family planning has historically dealt with the needs of individuals and families, not those of societies. Early sociologist Kingsley

---

[2]Ishii-Kuntz, M. (2003). "Balancing Fatherhood and Work: Emergence of Diverse Masculinities in Contemporary Japan." In J. E. Roberson & N. Suzuki (eds.) *Men and Masculinities in Contemporary Japan: Dislocating the Salaryman Doxa.* New York: Routledge.

Davis (1971) pointed out some fundamental weaknesses of the family planning approach as a means of large-scale population control. Chief among them is its basic assumption that the number of children couples *want* is the actual number they *should* have. Families may want four or five children, but is that number desirable for the health of society, and for the world?

The U.S. population is growing at a rate of about 1 percent per year, far slower than those of the LDCs, but faster than the rate of most other highly developed nations. There are two important sources of this growth: (1) natural increase, owing to more births than deaths, and (2) migration, because more people are immigrating to the United States than are leaving it. By 2050, the populations of most other developed nations may decline, while that of the United States is likely to continue to increase, perhaps to as many as 400 million residents (Kochhar, 2014). This estimate assumes that immigration to the United States will continue over the next two or three decades and that these immigrant populations will have higher birthrates than older, native-born populations.

Steady population growth means that people are continuing to settle in new communities to raise their families, and many migrate in search of new opportunities. Recent decades have seen increased migration to the Sunbelt and warm-weather western states (U.S. Census Bureau, 2018a). In 1950, for example, 26 percent of the population lived in the Northeast, whereas today, only 17 percent live there. Instead, people have moved to sunnier climates. Figure 13–3 shows that many of the fastest-growing metropolitan areas—that is, those with the largest numeric increase—are located in the Southwest and West (U.S. Census Bureau, 2018b). Note that Seattle, Washington, with its rapidly growing technology industries, which include Microsoft and Amazon, is experiencing quite rapid growth even though it is not in the Sunbelt.

The next section explores immigration, including its history, recent trends, and its political, social, and economic implications.

Figure 13–3 Ten Metro Areas with the Largest Numeric Increase in Population, 2016–2017

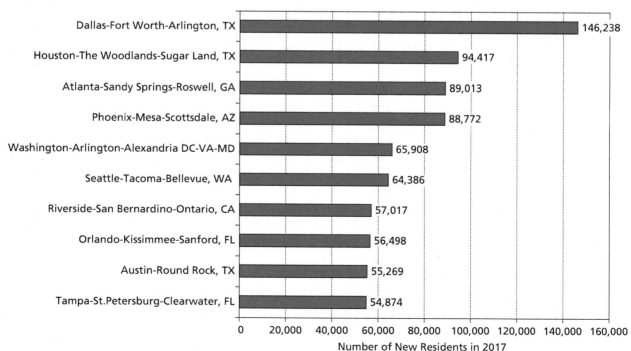

SOURCE: Data from U. S. Census Bureau. 2018b. "New Census Bureau Population Estimates Show Dallas-Fort Worth-Arlington Has Largest Growth in the United States." Newsroom. 22 March. CB18-50.

Immigration

13.5 **Sequence and differentiate the history of immigration in the United States.**

Throughout the world, people in poor nations dream of moving to richer ones. Most often, they do not wish to uproot themselves entirely but hope to be temporary sojourners, working at better-paying jobs temporarily. If they can save and send money home, they reason, then they may someday be able to return to a better life in their homeland.

Data on the birth origin of the U.S. population were first collected in the 1850 census. That year, there were 2.2 million immigrants in the United States, which represented almost 10 percent of the total population. Between 1860 and 1920, immigrants as a share of the total population fluctuated between 13 and 15 percent, peaking at 15 percent in 1890, mainly due to high levels of European immigration. Restrictive immigration legislation of 1921 and 1924, coupled with the Great Depression and World War II, led to a sharp drop in new arrivals in the United States. As a result, the foreign-born share of the U.S. population continued to decline between the 1930s and 1970s, reaching a record low of only 5 percent in 1970 (9.6 million). Since 1970, however, the share and number have increased, this time mainly due to large-scale immigration from Latin America and Asia made possible by changes to admission rules adopted by Congress in 1965 (Nwosu, Batalova, and Auclair, 2014). Today, immigration to the United States has reached levels unmatched since early in the twentieth century, at 13 percent of the American population (45 million).

But immigration is not just an American phenomenon; people seeking refuge from war and conflict, and the movement of people from poorer to richer lands is also occurring in other countries. There has been an influx of Syrian people into Europe (a topic discussed at length in Chapter 15). In the Middle East, there has been a great movement of temporary workers from Egypt to the richer and underpopulated nations of Saudi Arabia and Kuwait. In Japan, there are Korean immigrants, and in Australia, there are immigrants from many Asian nations. It is often said that the United States is a nation of immigrants. Since the earliest days of settlement by Europeans, North America has brought people together from all over the world. Some, like the black slaves from Africa, were brought against their will. Many other groups came in search of new opportunities and freedom from oppression, bringing together people of different races, different religions, different cultures, and different political views to these shores. This diversity has become one of the most important aspects of U.S. culture.

But immigration (although not necessarily immigrants themselves) has also contributed to social problems that plague U.S. society. Beginning with the exclusion of Native Americans from their original lands, immigration has led to ethnic and racial conflict; competition among nationality groups for a "piece of the pie"; debates about immigration policy, illegal immigration, and the exploitation of illegal immigrants; and the stresses and costs associated with educating and caring for newcomers.

The summary of the major periods of immigration to the United States in the next section will help you begin to understand the varying contexts in which immigration has occurred in this country.

13.5.1 Immigration to the United States: A Brief History

THE EARLY COLONIAL PERIOD (TO 1790) During the colonial period, the major population groups in North America, other than Native Americans, came from Europe. Most traveled from England and accounted for 77 percent of the total population. African and native-born slaves of African origin accounted for 19 percent, German immigrants for 4 percent, Irish immigrants for 3 percent, and Dutch immigrants for 2 percent (Bogue, 1985; Portes, 2001). There were many other immigrant groups in the population, but their numbers were much smaller and, consequently, so was their influence.

OLD NORTHWEST EUROPEAN MIGRATION (1820–1885) Large-scale immigration to the new nation known as the United States began again in 1820 and was dominated by people from England and other areas of northwestern Europe until about 1885. In this wave of immigrants, the largest groups came from northern and western Europe, especially Germany, Ireland, and England. The proportion of immigrants from Ireland reached high levels in the 1840s and 1850s because of severe famine and economic catastrophe in Ireland. German immigration reached a peak in the years after 1848, when popular revolutions in Germany failed and many Germans sought asylum or greater political freedom in the United States.

The most significant nonwhite immigrant group during this period were the Chinese, many of whom settled on the West Coast or in the Rocky Mountain states. Labor contractors who were seeking low-wage workers for the construction of railroads brought in many Chinese immigrants.

THE INTERMEDIATE MIGRATION FROM SOUTHERN AND EASTERN EUROPE (1885–1945) Because of the breakup of the Austro-Hungarian and Ottoman empires and the resulting political upheavals, many thousands of people from southern and eastern Europe found their way to the United States. The major immigrant groups during this period were Italians, Poles, Hungarians, Serbians, Croatians, Greeks, and Jews from all these nations and from Russia. During this period, waves of **nativist** feeling (anti-immigrant or anti-foreigner sentiment) swept across sections of the United States. Among other things, nativism gave rise to the Asian exclusion movement, which flourished between 1882 and 1907. It resulted in sporadic violence against Chinese and Japanese Americans and the passage of legislation in some states that stopped further immigration of Asians.

At the same time, large numbers of Mexican immigrants began moving into the Southwest, the West, and portions of the Midwest. These immigrants often joined relatives and friends in parts of California and the Southwest, where Mexicans had been living long before these regions became part of the United States.

During this period, there had been no specific limits on immigration to the United States, and well over 20 million immigrants had arrived since the early nineteenth century. However, concerned about immigration, Congress passed the Immigration Act of 1921, which for the first time in American history established quotas and strict controls over the admission of new immigrants. An overall quota of 150,000 immigrants per year was imposed, which curtailed the United States as a realistic destination for most of those persons fleeing the horrors of Nazi Germany.

THE POST–WORLD WAR II REFUGEE PERIOD (TO 1968) By the end of World War II, hundreds of thousands of Europeans had lost their homes and property, and many were refugees. Some, like Jews and Roman Catholic activists, were fleeing religious persecution. In 1945, Congress agreed to admit 185,000 immigrants per year, many of whom would be European refugees. This count remained a very small number of immigrants allowed into the United States, given the millions of people needing resettlement.

THE NEW IMMIGRATION (1968 AND BEYOND) In 1968, Congress again voted to increase immigration quotas, establishing totals of 170,000 per year from the Eastern Hemisphere and 120,000 from the Western Hemisphere. Priority would

nativist

Anti-immigrant or anti-foreigner sentiment.

Ellis Island was the primary destination for immigrants coming from Europe. Immigrants were not welcomed with open arms. They had to pass rigid medical checkups to be allowed to stay.

Omikron/Getty Images

be given to immigrants who were political or religious refugees or who had close relatives living in the United States—known as the principle of family unification. Between 1975 and 1980, refugees and refugee-related issues dominated immigration more than they had since the years following World War II. Beginning with the fall of Vietnam and Cambodia in April 1975, this five-year period saw the admission of more than 400,000 Indochinese refugees. The Refugee Act was passed in 1980 and made provision for both a regular flow and the emergency admission of refugees. In addition, the law authorized federal assistance for the resettlement of refugees. Shortly after the enactment of the Refugee Act of 1980, an estimated 125,000 Cubans entered the United States through southern Florida, along with continuing smaller numbers of Haitians. There have been many tweaks to immigration policy since then. The increases in immigration quotas in recent decades have given rise to a new pattern of immigration to the United States, with the largest flows of people coming from Asia and Latin America.

13.5.2 Recent Trends in Immigration to the United States

Yue Lin Wang. Jose Gonzalez. Min Nguyen. Diego Molina. What do these four people have in common? They have all immigrated to the United States in recent years. Their circumstances vary. Yue Lin Wang was adopted by an American family when she was 9 months old because of China's one-child policy. Jose Gonzalez, a journalist from Cuba, came to the United States two generations ago seeking political asylum. Min Nguyen and her family escaped the ravages of the Vietnam War when she was only 8, after surviving for a year in a refugee camp in Laos. Diego Molina walked many days through the desert from Mexico trying to evade detection. *A Personal View: "Immigrants' Stories"* provides a close-up experience of immigration.

About 45 million immigrants live in the United States today—they were not born in the U.S. but immigrated from elsewhere. Of these persons, 34 million are lawful immigrants, and a clear majority hold citizenship (44 percent) or have lawful permanent residence (27 percent). The remainder of lawful immigrants have temporary visas, such as student visas (Lopez, Bialik, and Radford, 2018).

In 1900, most persons immigrating to the United States came from Europe; however, by 1980, four times more Hispanics and Asians migrated to the United States than did Europeans, as they fled persecution in their war-torn countries. The largest number of immigrants today come from Asia and from Mexico or other Latin American countries. The percentage of Europeans immigrating to the United States is now a relatively small component of the total.

Characteristics of immigrants vary by their country of origin, length of time in the United States, and the personal circumstances surrounding their immigration. For example, many Asians arriving from Cambodia and Vietnam in the 1980s were poor, and they brought with them young children. These children were exposed to U.S. culture early on and have since attended college in large numbers. Their experiences in the United States may be vastly different from today's migrant farmworkers from Mexico. Nonetheless, some generalizations can be made: Immigrants are more likely than native-born residents to be young adults in their childbearing years; they live in larger family households; they earn less money in their jobs; they are more likely to live in poverty; and they tend to reside in central cities within a metropolitan area (López, Bialik, and Radford, 2018; Zong, Batalova, and Hallock, 2018).

Some groups in U.S. society oppose immigration, and the resulting tensions can be a problem for immigrants and for the regions or cities that receive them. Because new immigrants tend to settle near other immigrants, these tensions can run especially high in regions with large immigrant populations.

What Do You Think?

Describe the influence that immigrants have had on American culture in the last century. Can you think of both positive and negative influences?

A Personal View

Immigrants' Stories

Joshua Resnick/Fotolia

When I was younger, I decided I was going to be president of the United States, but my friend laughed at me and told me I couldn't be the president. I didn't understand. I went home and asked my mom, and she said she wasn't sure, but it was a great question.

I was born in China. My birth parents felt that they couldn't keep me. My mom explained to me that families in China could have only one child, and that Chinese parents often prefer a son. Personally, I think that's crazy because girls are cool, too. As the story goes, I lived in an orphanage for almost a year, and then my parents adopted me and brought me here to California. I have a younger sister who was also adopted from China, but we didn't know each other. In fact, she lived in the northern part of China and I lived in the southern part. But now she's my sister. We hang out a lot after school, but she also gets on my nerves because she likes rock instead of pop, and doesn't even like to watch *Riverdale* or *Grey's Anatomy.* Really? I didn't think that was even possible.

—Kate, age 17

****

Four years ago, I came to America from Greece for holiday—"vacation" as you call it. I was 18 and just graduated from school. This trip was my present before I began college. I got a three-month visa. I planned to return to Greece afterwards; I had no thought that I might overstay my visa. However, life sometimes takes you in new directions. I met the love of my life in Boston and didn't want to go back to Greece. So, I overstayed, figuring how would anyone really know? I thought we would marry and everything would be okay because I could emigrate as his wife. But, we broke up about a year later. As it turned out,

he was a bit of a jerk. I'm still here—I like America—although it's sometimes difficult to find good work. I'm 22 now, and figure I'll probably stay another four or five years if I can afford it. Then I'll head back to Greece when I'm ready to settle down.

—Cinda, age 22

****

My mom left our small village in Mexico when I was 8 and my younger brother was 3, and we went to live with my grandmother. My mom said that she was going to the United States and get a good job to earn enough money to bring us there to live with her. I didn't really know what she meant; I was only 8, and I didn't understand that "going to the United States to get a good job" was against the law, and that my mother could be killed trying to get there. She left quietly one night, and my brother and I cried for many days afterwards. We lived with my grandmother for nearly two years and heard nothing from my mother. Grandma spoke of my mother often, wondering if she made it and what she was doing, but my mother seemed dead to me. Then, suddenly one day Grandma received some cash from my mother. It was enough to smuggle only one of us to America, and since I was the oldest, now 10, I could go. My uncle arranged it all, and the details scared me. I was to leave next month with a small group of other men and boys. We had a leader—a gruff man with piercing eyes—but he said he could get us to the United States, so I forced myself to trust him. He was right. Most of us made it to the United States, but there were many times on the trail that I didn't think we would. One dad and his son turned back because they had bad luck—the dad was robbed, and the son got very sick—but after more than a month of walking, hitching, waiting, wading, and belly crawling, I made it to the United States. It took another couple of weeks to be reunited with my mom, but now we are a family. She works in a factory, pressing fruit. I go to school. I like America, but I miss my family in Mexico so much. I don't know if I'll ever see them again.

—Arturo, age 12

Critical Thinking

Compare and contrast these stories about immigration. How are they similar, and how are they different? Of the two illegal immigration stories, do either of them seem more compelling than the other? If so, why?

13.5.3 Urban Concentration of Immigrants

The most popular states in which immigrants land include California, Texas, New York, Florida, and Illinois. Many congregate in key cities and regions, including New York City, Los Angeles, Miami, and Chicago (Migration Policy Institute, 2018). Immigrants from Mexico and Central America also tend to live in major cities such as Houston and Dallas-Fort Worth.

The concentration of new immigrants in a few metropolitan regions can pose challenges to both immigrants and nonimmigrants in those areas. This concentration leads to the formation of large non-English-speaking enclaves, where education becomes more challenging and the economic and social assimilation of the newcomers may create difficulties for native-born citizens. Increasingly, frequent attacks against immigrants and members of minority groups and the rise of nativist and anti-immigrant feelings in many parts of the United States are another consequence of the concentration of immigrants in certain localities.

The phenomenon of **chain migration**, the primary cause of this urban concentration, refers to the tendency of immigrants to migrate to areas where they have kin and others from their home communities. Most prefer to be around other people who share their culture and language and who can help them adjust to their new social environment.

The uneven distribution of immigrants greatly adds to the costs of education and health care in the cities in which they become concentrated. Because many new immigrants arrive without any form of health insurance and do not speak English well, schools and adult education programs are needed to help them. The federal government does not usually compensate the expenses incurred by the cities, even though the entry of immigrants is regulated by federal legislation.

A problem that affects the immigrants in these urban centers is the intense competition and, at times, direct hostility they encounter from nonimmigrants or other immigrants who have lived there for longer periods. For example, Arabs often establish businesses in segregated minority communities where costs are lower. They thus become a new ethnic and racial group in those communities. They may encounter anger and hostility from residents who are suspicious of Arabs and their Muslim faith (Fadda-Conrey, 2015; Pew Research Center, July 26, 2017; Welch, 2016). Elsewhere in the nation—along the Gulf Coast of Texas, where Vietnamese shrimp fishermen have come into conflict with native-born fishermen, or in the Southwest, where Mexican immigrants are often discriminated against because of language differences—the difficulties of life as a stranger in a strange land are amplified by prejudice and discrimination.

In response to the hostility they can encounter, children and adolescents in the new groups sometimes form defensive groups or gangs. But some immigrant groups, notably the Chinese and Koreans, attempt to shelter their children from the problems of urban street life by imposing a strict set of values and high expectations for achievement in school. Children of Asian immigrants make rapid strides in U.S. schools, often achieving the highest honors in their high schools and on standardized achievement tests. Indeed, the school achievement of Asian Americans is now so high that many of the brightest Asian students have come to believe they are being penalized by admission quotas in private universities, an experience exactly analogous to that of high-achieving children of Jewish immigrants two generations ago (Lipman, 2017; Saffran, 2017).

Not all immigrants are in the United States legally. This next section explores illegal immigration and its consequences.

chain migration

The tendency of immigrants to migrate to areas where they have kin and others from their home communities.

Undocumented Illegal Immigrants

13.6 Explore the issue of illegal immigration and its consequences for Americans and the immigrants themselves.

No one knows exactly how many illegal (undocumented) immigrants actually live in the United States, but it is estimated to be about 11 million, down from 12 million before the recession (Krogstad, Passel, and Cohn, April 27, 2017). More than half of illegal immigrants live in just six states: California, Texas, Florida, New York, New Jersey, and Illinois. About half come from Mexico—a proportion that has been declining in recent years, and most of the other half come from Central America or Asia, where they face extreme poverty and limited job prospects in their countries. Roughly two-thirds of illegal immigrants are working; those who are not are primarily children. A large share of illegal immigrants are long-term residents; two-thirds of the adults have lived in the United States for at least ten years (Krogstad, Passel, and Cohn, April 27, 2017). Forty percent of immigrants lived with their children, some of whom are also immigrants and others who were born in the United States, and these children make up a small but increasing proportion of elementary school children. The issue is that these children, who have a variety of costly needs, are concentrated in just a few states. For example, although nationwide only 7 percent of school children have at least one parent who is an immigrant, this jumps to 18 percent in Nevada, 13 percent in Texas, and 12 percent in California (Passel and Cohn, November 17, 2016).

13.6.1 Modes of Entry into the United States

Nearly half of all illegal immigrants arrived legally as visitors to the United States, passing through ports of entry where they were processed by the U.S. Immigration and Naturalization Service. They begin as legal visitors but become *illegal* immigrants when they exceed the time allocated to them to visit or reside in the United States. This group is referred to as **overstayers**.

The remainder, just over half, entered the United States illegally by hiding in vehicles such as cargo trucks, trekking through the desert or northern plains, wading across the Rio Grande, or otherwise eluding the U.S. Border Patrol. We usually associate illegal immigration with the southwestern border states such as Texas, New Mexico, Arizona, and California, but untold numbers of evaders also arrive over the Canadian border and through ports like New York City through various forms of human smuggling.

These illegal immigrants face many horrific and dangerous situations in their trek to the United States to find work and a better life, and many do not make the journey successfully. Ruthless individuals exploit them because they know that immigrants cannot readily go to the authorities when they have been victimized. Immigrants are robbed, raped, and otherwise taken advantage of by guides, or **coyotes**. The U.S. Border Patrol then captures many of those who do make it to the border. As two men who were detected trying to come into the United States from Mexico emotionally explained in their native Spanish: "The Border Patrol treats us like animals, like dirt, like we don't matter. We know we are doing something wrong, but it is not to hurt anyone but to feed our families. We have nothing to eat [at our homes]" (Arditti, 2006).[3]

Those who do make it into the United States and make it past U.S. Border Patrol agents find jobs in a variety of occupations, including service industries, construction, or agriculture. Their status is quite precarious because employers must report workers who are discovered not to have proper documents. Thus, employers who continue to hire immigrants without documentation or who disregard forgery of their documents can exploit them by paying pitifully low wages and expecting inordinate amounts of work.

One group that has gained attention over the past several years are the children who cross the border as they escape violence in their home countries in Central America—Honduras, Guatemala, and El Salvador in particular. These children often flee their countries on their own, but with the encouragement of their families who fear for their children's lives. Drug and gang violence abound and children are murdered or go missing regularly. In desperation, families encourage their children to head for the United States. The question that is posed, and discussed in the feature box, is, are these children immigrants, or refugees?

overstayer

Someone who starts out as a legal visitor but becomes an *illegal* immigrant when he or she exceeds the time allocated to visit or reside in the United States.

coyotes

Guides who help people immigrate illegally to the United States.

Do illegal immigrants take jobs away from American citizens, or do they do the work that American citizens do not want to do? This woman stoops in the sun for many hours a day and earns the equivalent of the minimum wage on a good day.

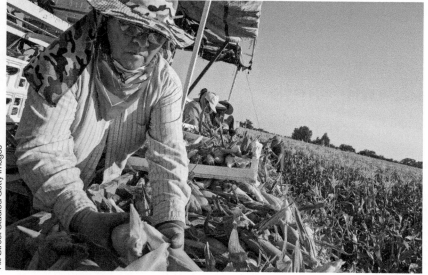

Hill Street Studios/Getty Images

---

[3] Arditti, J.A. 2006. "Editor's Note." *Family Relations, 55,* 263–65.

A Closer Look

Central American Children: Immigrants or Refugees?

Per-Anders Pettersson/Getty Images

Juan, as usual, was walking three miles home after the school day ended at 3:30 in his small town in Honduras. His mother knew to expect him no later than 4:30. He was always prompt, but on this day he never arrived. His parents, aunts and uncles, and neighbors searched for him all night. The next morning his body was found partially buried in a field outside of town. He had been stabbed several times in the chest and his head had been severed. Juan was 14 years old and in the eighth grade. He was a whiz at math and excelled in art. He also enjoyed playing sports with the other boys in the neighborhood. The police investigated the murder but had no real leads. The police assumed that Juan was killed and beheaded by gang members because he refused to join them. This killing was the ninth of this type by gang members over the past year in this small town, yet Juan's murder was not widely reported within the country. It was simply another act of violence—one of many. Meanwhile, Juan's parents are actively encouraging their other sons, ages 10 and 16, to leave Honduras and find their way to the United States to live with their cousin who is in Texas illegally. There, they pray, their remaining sons will be safe from the drug cartels and gangs that proliferate in their country.

The United Nations identifies Honduras as the most violent country in the world, with 90 murders per 100,000 people. El Salvador and Guatemala are not far behind (Labrador and Renwick, 2018). For context, note that the United Nations considers a rate of 10 murders per 100,000 people to be an epidemic. Just as striking as these statistics themselves is the consistently young age of the victims. Nearly 40 percent of those murdered in Honduras every year are between the ages of 15 and 24, and a growing number are even younger (Martinez, 2014). The gangs recruit young children, even as young as 8 or 9, to work as messengers or drug runners because young children are better able to evade detection by police. Refusal to work with the gangs can result in death, usually a grisly one to make maximum impact on the community and to instill maximum fear in other young boys.

To avoid being victims of gang violence, tens of thousands of unaccompanied children, mostly boys, have fled to the United States looking for freedom, safety, and a chance to work (Clemens, 2017; Sawyer and Márquez, 2017). U.S. Customs and Border Protection took more than 60,000 unaccompanied children under 18 into custody in 2017 (Office of Refugee Resettlement, 2018).

What should be done with these children fleeing horrible violence in Central America? Immigration is a controversial political topic. With all the political clamor focusing on securing our borders and deporting those who sneak in, relatively little attention is given to the horrific conditions these children are fleeing and the fate they face if sent home. Are these children *illegal immigrants* or are they *refugees*? Is this situation an *immigration problem* or a *humanitarian crisis*? Should these children be immediately deported, detained for a period, or allowed to seek asylum in the United States? Given the polarity in today's politics, you would think the answers to these questions would be evenly split along party lines. However, they are not (Pew Research Center, 2014).

What is the best way to deal with these unaccompanied children? Advocates call for increasing the number of centers to care for the children and ensure that the United States offers humanitarian protection to children who would truly be in danger if they returned to their home countries. Others suggest quick deportation is in order.

Under President Obama, a multi-strategy approach was conducted, which included launching the 2014 "Dangers Awareness" campaign in the form of billboards, radio, and television advertisements throughout these countries to convince those considering migration that such a trip was not worth the risk. In 2015, these efforts continued under the new name of the "Know the Facts" campaign. The idea was to spread the word among potential migrants that the dangers of such a trip were high and the chances of success were low (Hiskey et al., 2016). President Obama also created makeshift temporary detention centers, necessitated by the bottleneck created from transferring the children to the Office of Refugee Resettlement. Most of those children who had relatives in the United States were released to them. However, under President Trump, the U.S. Department of Homeland Security terminated a program that allowed minors fleeing violence in El Salvador, Guatemala, and Honduras to settle in the United States, ending travel hopes for more than 2,700 children awaiting approval.

Critical Thinking

If Juan, the boy featured in the vignette, was your son, would you encourage his siblings to try to escape to the United States? Why or why not?

13.6.2 Illegal Immigration and the Economy

Until 1986 it was not against the law to employ illegal immigrants. This situation changed when Congress passed the Immigration Reform and Control Act. Under this law, employers are subject to civil penalties that range from $250 to $10,000 for each illegal immigrant they hire.

It is not clear exactly what effect illegal residents have on the U.S. economy, and passionate arguments exist on both sides. They may take some jobs away from native-born residents, but they also perform functions that citizens are reluctant to do—"dirty work" or stoop labor on row crops, for example—and they help maintain some industries by accepting lower wages and inferior working conditions. Their willingness to accept these conditions may hold back progress on wages and working conditions for others, but the survival of such industries stimulates growth in associated services, creating more jobs. Indeed, it appears that illegal immigrants—who can generally be laid off or discharged more easily than citizens—play a vital, if equivocal, role in many advanced nations, cushioning the native-born population from economic uncertainty. And when an increasing proportion of adults are retired—as an estimated 20 percent of U.S. adults will be in 2035—the taxes paid by employed illegal immigrants may become extremely important. A little recognized fact is that millions of undocumented workers do indeed pay taxes—taxes that approach nearly $12 billion (Gee, Gardner, and Wiehe, 2016). Many researchers suggest that these taxes offset, or closely offset, the extra costs associated with providing education, health care, and other services to these workers and their families. Moreover, many undocumented workers also pay into Social Security, but will not receive any benefits from that program when they age.

What Do You Think?

What are the jobs that many illegal immigrants take? Do you think they are taking away jobs from Americans? Do most Americans want these jobs? Do you?

13.6.3 Increased Deportations

As the number of illegal immigrants in the United States grew from about 3 million in 1980 to 11 million today, pressure on government agencies resulted in new waves of enforcement of existing immigration laws, including those that bar undocumented persons from working in most jobs. The Department of Homeland Security reports that it "removed" 226,000 individuals in 2017, including 82,000 within our borders, and 144,000 individuals who were trying to enter the United States illegally (U.S. Department of Homeland Security, December 13, 2017). Under President Trump the number of deportations from within our borders increased by 25 percent; however, the number of individuals detained trying to enter the U.S. actually declined. There has been a substantial increase in the number of deportations to Honduras, El Salvador, and Guatemala.

One method proposed by President Trump to control illegal immigration is to build a secure "wall" across the southern United States. During the 2016 Presidential race he made his position clear: "When Mexico sends its people, they're not sending their best. They're sending people that have lots of problems... They're bringing drugs. They're bringing crime. They're rapists."[4] President Trump initially insisted that Mexico would pay for this wall, "I would build a great wall, and nobody builds walls better than me. I'll build a great, great wall on our southern border, and I'll have Mexico pay for that wall. Mark my words."[5] Nonetheless, it appears that Mexico has no intention of paying for a wall separating the two countries, and President Trump has largely backed down from that claim.

How do most Americans feel about building a wall to curb immigration? Building a wall appears to be out of sync with most Americans—only 35–37 percent claim to support the idea (Newport, June 20, 2018; Quinnipiac Poll, February 6, 2018; Suls, February 24, 2017).

---

[4]Reilly, K. "Here Are All the Times Donald Trump Insulted Mexico," *Time* (August 31, 2016).

[5]Quoted in "Here's Donald Trump's Presidential Announcement Speech," *Time* (June 16, 2015).

Table 13–5 Opinions of Immigration Proposals

	U.S. Adults	Democrats	Independents	Republicans
Allowing immigrants living in the United States illegally the chance to become U.S. citizens if they meet certain requirements over a period of time				
Favor	84%	91%	85%	76%
Oppose	15%	8%	14%	24%
Building a wall along the entire U.S.-Mexico border				
Favor	33%	12%	33%	62%
Oppose	66%	88%	66%	38%
Deporting all immigrants who are living in the United States illegally back to their home country				
Favor	32%	16%	33%	50%
Oppose	66%	83%	65%	48%

SOURCE: Data from Jones, J. M. "More Republicans Favor Path to Citizenship Than Wall," Gallup (July 20, 2016).

13.6.4 Public Attitudes toward Illegal Immigration

Despite a lot of media attention, only about a third of Americans say that they worry a great deal about illegal immigration, a figure that has remained relatively steady for many years. However, there is a small but growing minority who are very concerned: a Gallup Poll conducted in April 2018 found that 11 percent of adults believed that illegal immigration was the most important social problem facing the nation (Gallup, 2018). These Americans are very vocal, and dominate the airwaves with respect to immigration.

The reason that two-thirds of Americans do not worry a great deal about illegal immigration may be because many people are unsure what to do about it. In fact, most people favor a path to citizenship, as shown in Table 13-5. Despite what we may hear in the media, Republicans favor a path to citizenship over building a wall or deporting all illegal immigrants back to their home country (Jones, July 20, 2016).

SANCTUARY CITIES/COUNTIES/STATES   Some cities, counties, or states choose not to cooperate with federal immigration enforcement agents to protect immigrants from deportation. These regions have enacted laws or policies that obstruct the federal government from enforcing their current immigration efforts. In retaliation the federal government has threatened to withhold law-enforcement money from so-called "sanctuary" cities, counties, or states. While California is most prominently in the administration's cross hairs—"California better hold on tight," said Thomas Homan, the acting director of Immigration and Customs Enforcement, in early 2018—California is only one of many targets.[6] Other sanctuary states include Colorado, Illinois, New Mexico, Oregon, and Vermont, and there are nearly 200 cities and counties at risk of losing federal law enforcement funds. Chilling headlines like a recent one in a local newspaper in New Haven, CT—"ICE (Immigration and Customs Enforcement) Lies in Wait at Elm Street Courthouse"—are appearing all over the country as federal agents seek and capture undocumented immigrants.

Social Policy

13.7   Consider the controversy and the policies associated with those who were brought to the United States illegally when they were children.

Immigration is a hotly contested political issue. Most Americans see immigration as a good thing for society (Gallup, 2018), but feelings about illegal immigration are more mixed. One area of concern is over what to do about children. You have learned about the dilemma of children fleeing violence in Central America—are they illegal

---

[6]Greenhouse, L. "The Supreme Court and the New Civil War," *The New York Times* (April 26, 2018).

immigrants or refugees? Another set of children are also of focus—those who were brought to the United States illegally by their parents when they were young children. Because of their youth they had no say in their parents' decision to come to the United States. Yet, they have now lived in the United States for most of their lives, attending schools, worshiping in churches, and fully participating in social and economic life. Should these young people be granted special dispensation?

13.7.1 Deferred Action for Childhood Arrival

In 2012, the Secretary of Homeland Security announced that certain unauthorized immigrants who entered the United States as children would be able to apply for the Deferred Action for Childhood Arrival (DACA) program, granting relief from deportation and work authorization for two years. The authorization could be renewed as the program continued and the applicant remained in good standing. The undocumented immigrants who participate in the program are referred to as "Dreamers."

Prospective beneficiaries must meet a series of requirements, including the following:

- Entered the United States before the age of 16
- Have continuously resided in the United States since June 15, 2007
- Are currently in school, have graduated from high school or earned a GED, or are honorably discharged veterans of the U.S. armed forces (including the Coast Guard)
- Have not been convicted of a felony, significant misdemeanor, or three or more misdemeanors or do not otherwise pose a threat to public safety or national security

Over a million unauthorized youths and young adults were eligible to apply because they met both age and education criteria and had no criminal background. Between 2012 and 2017, 800,000 young, unauthorized immigrants received work permits and protection from deportation through DACA (Lopez and Krogstad, September 25, 2017). Although DACA recipients come from around the world, more than 90 percent were born in Latin America. Nearly half of DACA recipients live in just two states: California and Texas.

President Trump cancelled the DACA program in 2017 and the status of many young persons is now in limbo. Yet, his comments about DACA have not been consistent. He has called the program unlawful, but has also said about DACA recipients, "Tell them not to worry about it. We're going to solve the problem. Now, it's up to the Democrats, but they should not be concerned" (Kopan, 2018).[7]

In April 2018, a federal judge ordered President Trump to reinstate DACA. Judge Bates, who was nominated by President George W. Bush in 2001, described the Trump administration's decision to phase out DACA as "arbitrary and capricious because the department failed adequately to explain its conclusion that the program was unlawful" (Jordan, 2018).[8]

The DACA program has both supporters and opponents (Newport, June 20, 2018). Supporters argue that deporting these children and young adults would be cruel. They were brought to the United States through no fault of their own and the United States is likely the only country that they know. Supporters also point to the fact that those who are eligible for DACA represent the best educated and the highest skilled among all illegal immigrants. In contrast, opponents say that DACA only encourages more illegal immigration. Amnesty should not be given to lawbreakers (ProCon.org, 2018).

---

[7]Kopan, T. "Trump Says He's Open to Pathway to Citizenship 'Incentive' on DACA," *CNN Politics* (January 25, 2018).

[8]Jordan, M. "U.S. Must Keep DACA and Accept New Applications, Federal Judge Rules," *The New York Times* (April 24, 2018).

13.7.2 Future Prospects

Although the world's population is growing rapidly, especially in LDCs, other more developed countries face a population decline unless they can rely on immigration to offset declining birth rates. But immigration policy is controversial, even in those countries that may need immigrants to keep their populations stable. What *type* of immigrant is best? Where should they be from? How will they assimilate? What issues are likely to occur?

The United States has long been thought of as a nation of immigrants. However, attitudes toward immigrants throughout history have often been negative—fraught with prejudicial attitudes and discrimination. Policies toward immigrants have reflected these values.

Despite the wave of anti-immigrant feeling that has arisen in the United States in recent years, it is by no means clear what, if any, new policies will emerge in the future. Will deportations continue to increase? Will children fleeing violence in Central America be sent back to their homes? Will DACA recipients be allowed to stay in the United States? Although President Trump has taken a harder line on immigration than his predecessors, not all Americans take his side on the issue.

Looking into the future is always a tricky proposition, but it has been estimated that if we look at the United States in the year 2065, we would see a nation with 117 million more people in it. About one in three would be an immigrant or have immigrant parents, compared to one in four today (Cohn, October 5, 2015). Immigration is here to stay. Trends in illegal immigration are less clear.

Going Beyond Left and Right

Immigration has become intertwined with politics, and therefore attitudes toward immigration policy and immigrants themselves have become increasingly polarized. Yet it is important to understand your own opinions, and the values that shape your opinions. Think about the social factors that likely shape your views—for example, how your opinions may be shaped by your social class, your age or sex, the state in which you live, and your experience (or the lack thereof) with immigrants. In other words, think like a sociologist.

Summary

13.1 Describe the growth in the world's population.

The world's population is approaching 7.5 billion, and continues to grow rapidly, especially in LDCs. There are several ways to measure population growth: total, general, and crude birth (fertility) rates. The differential between the crude birthrate and the death rate is the rate of population growth, or natural increase. Today, more people are living to childbearing age and fewer are dying, so the world's population is growing faster than in the past and putting increased pressure on resources and the environment.

13.2 Explain the demographic transition and its relevance in the world today.

The demographic transition is a process that consists of three stages: (a) a high birthrate canceled out by a high death rate, (b) a high birthrate coupled with a declining death rate, and (c) low birth and death rates. The process began in northern Europe in the eighteenth century and has occurred in all areas where industrial technology has taken hold on a local level. Today, large areas of Asia, Africa, and Latin America remain in the middle phase of the demographic transition.

13.3 Analyze the indicators of rising expectations in the less developed world.

Currently, expectations in LDCs are rising; people have increasing expectations for their own future and that of their children. Literacy rates serve as an indicator of rising expectations. Although literacy rates have increased in many countries, the gaps in living standards between rich and poor societies have widened. Hunger and malnutrition are persistent problems in the less developed regions of the world.

13.4 Compare and contrast governments' involvement in population control efforts.

Governments can and sometimes do get involved in fertility matters. The Chinese government actively sought to reduce births, while the Japanese government is trying to grow their population. The population of most industrialized nations is growing at a relatively slow rate, and it appears likely that this rate can be maintained through voluntary population control (e.g., family planning).

13.5 Sequence and differentiate the history of immigration in the United States.

The United States is often described as a nation of immigrants; since the earliest years of European settlement, it has attracted people from all over the world. Today, the largest numbers of immigrants have come from Asia and Latin America. A problem related to immigration is the uneven distribution of immigrants among cities and regions in the United States. Immigrants in urban centers encounter intense competition and, at times, direct hostility.

13.6 Explore the issue of illegal immigration and its consequences for Americans and the immigrants themselves.

Millions of undocumented immigrants are currently residing in the United States by either overstaying their visas or sneaking into the country illegally. Undocumented immigrants are easily exploited by employers and others. Their effect on the U.S. economy is not clear, but it appears that they cushion the native-born population from economic uncertainty. Americans are not in agreement about how to address immigration, and popular opinion does not fall neatly along political party lines.

13.7 Consider the controversy and the policies associated with those who were brought to the United States illegally when they were children.

One issue of current interest is what to do about the flood of children fleeing gang violence in their homes in Central America. Are these children immigrants or refugees?

Chapter 14
The Environment

Marcovarro/Fotolia

 Learning Objectives

14.1 Discuss the link between technology and the environment.

14.2 Summarize different types of stressors on the environment.

14.3 Assess the significance of climate change and its consequences.

14.4 Identify the health and economic effects of air pollution.

14.5 Describe the problems related to water pollution.

14.6 Explain the hazards of solid waste disposal and why it is an issue of social justice.

14.7 Identify the role of the United States in the world's environment.

14.8 Critique social policy on climate change.

Jackson was 17 years old and looking forward to buying his first car. He passed driver's education class with flying colors last summer. "Driving," he said, "now that's just plain cool." Up until now he walked or rode his bike the mile and a half to school most days unless his mom could give him a lift on her way to work. But usually she went to work early, and so it just didn't work out for him to ride with her. But now, after working to save money, he would be on the way to having wheels! His big plans went beyond driving to school, and included cruising at night with his friends, driving to the lake with his girlfriend, and offering to drive for every errand for his mother, no matter how close by. Yes, soon he would be driving! Not once did he stop to think about the effects his driving has on the community or the world. After all, his car will be just one of the 1.2 billion cars that are now on the road. How large an effect can his little car possibly have? He didn't realize that, if he drove in a typical American fashion, each year he would spew 9,700 pounds of carbon dioxide into the air, along with 278 pounds of carbon monoxide, 28 pounds of hydrocarbons, 27 pounds of volatile organic compounds, and 10 pounds of nitrogen oxide. The good news? At least he is not driving a truck.

Of the many ways in which technology has changed our lives, probably none has more far-reaching consequences than its impact on Earth's environment. The problems of climate change, toxic waste disposal, and water and air pollution are direct consequences of technological advances. The way we use energy has an enormous effect on Earth's ecological systems. The technologies of production, climate control, transportation, and agriculture transform the physical shape of the planet and lead to environmental stress. The United States is the world's greatest consumer of natural resources, especially carbon-based energy from fossil fuels (coal, oil, and natural gas). It is also the world's leader in the production and use of technological systems of all kinds. The U.S. government and the nation's citizens therefore bear much of the responsibility for seeking ways to reduce the negative effects of pollution due to energy consumption.

Environmentalists claim that in recent years the United States has shifted its concerns away from environmental protection—especially in relation to such crucial issues as climate change—in favor of deregulation and pro-growth policies that have the effect of increasing pollution. As in any dispute, there are arguments on both sides of this debate (Climate Debate Daily, 2015); these debates are discussed in detail in this chapter.

Energy technologies, including petrochemicals, electricity, nuclear power, hydroelectricity, and others, are basic to everyday life throughout the world, so much so that we often take their availability for granted. But we make that presumption at our peril. The contemporary world has become entirely dependent on energy technologies, but we cannot assume that they will always be at our disposal or that we can recover them after disasters such as earthquakes and hurricanes. To better understand the meanings of technologies and their relation to modern science, we turn to some basic social-scientific definitions.

Technology and the Natural Environment

14.1 Discuss the link between technology and the environment.

technology

The use of science in industry, engineering, etc., to invent useful things or to solve problems.

The dictionary definition of **technology** is "the use of science in industry, engineering, etc., to invent useful things or to solve problems."[1] In this sense, technology is a way of solving practical problems; indeed, it is often viewed as the application of scientific knowledge to the problems of everyday life.

Some technological changes have revolutionary significance in that they alter the basic institutions of society. Thus, the Industrial Revolution—that is, the development of factories and mass production—radically altered the organization of many noneconomic institutions, including the family, religion, the military, and science itself.

Not all technological change is revolutionary, however. Some innovations spur only minor adjustments in other sectors of society or among small numbers of people.

---

[1]"Technology." Merriam-Webster.com. Merriam-Webster, n.d. Web.

Nor does technological change always consist of a single major invention. After all, the technological revolution that took place in American agriculture from the end of the nineteenth century to World War II involved hundreds of major inventions and the skills and organization to support them. The combination of all these factors allowed the United States to make the transition from an agrarian society to an urban industrial society in less than one century.

The term **technological dualism** refers to the fact that advances in technology can have both positive and negative impacts. This idea is not new; the ancient Greeks believed the god Apollo embodied this dualism because he could bring them new techniques of healing but could also use those techniques to cause death. More recently, over the last century, automotive technology has changed almost every aspect of how we live and has opened travel, but it has also contributed immensely to the problem of global climate change.

technological dualism

The idea that advances in technology can have both positive and negative impacts.

14.1.1 Technology and Social Institutions

Sociologists who study technology and the effects of technological change most often concern themselves with the adaptation of social institutions to changing technology or, conversely, the adaptation of technology to changing social institutions. The best-known statement of these relationships is William F. Ogburn's **cultural lag** theory, first stated in the 1920s. According to Ogburn (1957), "a cultural lag occurs when one of two parts of culture which are correlated changes before or in greater degree than the other part does, thereby causing less adjustment between the two parts than existed previously" (p. 167).[2] In other words, one aspect of culture changes, but a related part of that culture lags and causes problems.

cultural lag

A delay that occurs when one aspect of a culture changes more rapidly than another, causing some maladjustment between the two aspects.

A classic example of cultural lag during the nineteenth century involves the introduction of the Industrial Revolution, coupled with the failure of social welfare legislation to protect workers who were using the new and dangerous industrial machinery. The frequency of industrial accidents was increasing during that period because operators were not adequately protected from the rapidly moving wheels of the new machines. The loss of life and limb generally meant financial disaster for workers' families because, under existing law, employers could not easily be held liable. As a result, compensation was meager and slow to come. Only when worker's compensation and employer liability were introduced early in the twentieth century was this maladjustment, which had led to much impoverishment and suffering, finally corrected (Ogburn, 1957).

Ogburn's (1957) theory of cultural lag is often used to show that technological innovation dictates changes in social institutions and culture. But Ogburn also demonstrated that in many instances, cultural change occurs long before technological change.

An example of Ogburn's ideas can be found in the way American culture has come to depend on the availability of relatively cheap fossil fuels, even as supplies dwindle and become more difficult to secure for political reasons. The United States (among other countries in the world) has the know-how to harness the wind and rays of the sun to produce "green" renewable energy sources, and these forms of energy receive overwhelming

Wind turbines flank electricity pylons and a coal-fired power plant. Cultural change—the desire for clean energy—occurred long before the technological change, according to Ogburn's theory.

Sean Gallup/Getty Images

[2]Ogburn, W. F. 1957. "Cultural Lag as Theory." Sociology and Social Research, 41, 167–74.

Table 14–1 Environmental and Energy Proposals, 2014, 2018

Percent favoring this proposal...	2014	2018
Spending more government money on developing solar and wind power	67%	76%
Setting higher emissions and pollution standards for business and industry	65%	74%
More strongly enforcing federal environmental regulations	64%	73%
Imposing mandatory controls on carbon dioxide emissions/other greenhouse gases	63%	67%
Setting higher auto emissions standards for automobiles	62%	66%
Opening up land owned by the federal government for oil exploration	58%	43%
Setting stricter standards on the use of techniques to extract natural gas from the earth, including "fracking"	58%	58%
Expanding the use of nuclear energy	47%	45%

SOURCE: Moore, B., and S. Nichols. 2014. "Americans Still Favor Energy Conservation over Production." Gallup. 2 April. Retrieved 15 March 2015 (www.gallup.com/poll/168176/americans-favor-energy-conservation-production.aspx).; Newport, F. 2018. "Americans Want Government to Do More on Environment." Gallup. 29 March. Retrieved 7 May 2018 (news.gallup.com/poll/232007/americans-want-government-more-environment.aspx).

support, as shown in Table 14–1 (Moore and Nichols, 2014; Newport, 2018). This table shows the percentage of adults who favor specific environmental and energy proposals, and how views have changed between 2014 and 2018. Most people support spending more government funds on alternative energy, setting higher standards, and strictly enforcing them. These views have only intensified between 2014 and 2018. Yet, these technologies have been quite slow to evolve and have yet to become mainstream. In other words, America has the will and the capabilities, but green energy outputs remain paltry. Ogburn's theory is played out today: Cultural change occurs before technological change.

Human civilization has been changing and becoming more complex at an accelerating rate. The ideas, facts, and procedures that make up science and technology at any given time serve as a platform for future progress. A single technological advance such as the wheel, the internal combustion engine, or the semiconductor may form the basis of an enormous range of inventions. As the ability of humans to exploit Earth's resources has grown, so has the size of human populations.

These two developments—accelerated technological and scientific change and rapid population growth—are causing pollution and depletion of the natural environment as never before. Natural cycles of purification can absorb only a limited amount of certain artificial substances before ecological damage is done. Water pollution occurs when streams, rivers, lakes, and oceans can no longer purify themselves. When wind, rain, and snow can no longer remove the particles deposited in the air by machines of various kinds, pollution is the result. In these cases, the speed at which technology creates pollutants exceeds the pace at which nature can absorb them.

Sometimes technologies that seem benign and that we take for granted as part of everyday life have unanticipated consequences. Earlier in this century, pesticides and herbicides revolutionized agriculture, making it much more productive. Subsequent research has linked many of these chemicals to the destruction of fish and birds and to certain cancers in humans. Along the same lines, for years people used aerosol containers for purposes ranging from personal hygiene to applying whipped cream to ice cream sundaes. In the mid-1970s, the suspicion that a propellant used in aerosol cans was eroding the atmospheric ozone layer, which protects us from harmful radiation, led to the use of different propellants.

Perhaps the central question is this: Can we control such harmful effects before it is too late? In many cases, the technology exists to control environmental damage, but powerful interests do not wish to shoulder the cost of doing so. Here, the problem becomes one of creating a political consensus around a solution. In other cases, the technology that is needed to get us out of jams that earlier inventions have helped put us into does not yet exist. Thus, advanced economies around the world are consuming energy in the form of oil, which is becoming depleted and for which an adequate substitute has not yet been found. Any technological solution to this and other problems will almost inevitably contribute to a whole new generation of crises.

Environmental Stress

14.2 Summarize different types of stressors on the environment.

An investigation of winter fish deaths in Wisconsin lakes led to the unexpected conclusion that they were caused by snowmobiles. Heavy snowmobile use on a lake during the winter compacts the snow and makes the ice opaque. The opaque ice reduces the amount of sunlight that reaches underwater plants, which need it for photosynthesis. As the plants' oxygen production declines, they die, and their decomposition consumes considerable amounts of the oxygen left in the water. As a result, the fish are asphyxiated.

The term **environmental stress** refers to pressure on the environment caused by human activities or by natural events. As this example suggests, we can best understand environmental stress as the interaction and conflict of three systems: (a) the natural environment; (b) the technological system; and (c) the social system. The fish, ice, oxygen, and plants are all elements of the natural system. The snowmobile is an element of the technological system. That this vehicle is produced, marketed, and used is a product of the social system—as is the fact that no one is held responsible for the fish deaths.

We can define the natural system as containing the following elements and their interrelationships: air, water, earth, solar energy, plants, animals, and mineral resources. Our technological system includes transportation, farming, electricity-generating facilities, manufacturing processes and plants, various methods for extracting mineral resources, and the actual consumption and disposal of the products of these processes. Our social system includes attitudes, beliefs and values, and institutional structures.

It is difficult to reduce environmental stress when our attitudes, beliefs, and values do not recognize the importance of it and the role of humans in creating that stress. Figure 14–1 illustrates the percentage of adults between 2001 and 2018 who say they "worry a great deal" about our environment. These responses are the results of a survey for Gallup, which is based on a large and nationally representative sample. As you can see, the percentage of adults who say that they worry a great deal fluctuates, but since 2017 concern has been at or near an all-time high. Still, fewer than half of the respondents say the environment causes great worry (Gallup, 2018).

What Do You Think?
Can you provide other examples of Ogburn's idea of cultural lag?

environmental stress
Pressure on the environment caused by human activities or by natural events, which includes the interaction and conflict of three systems: the natural environment, the technological system, and the social system.

Figure 14–1 Percentage of Americans Who "Worry a Great Deal" About the Environment, 2001–2018

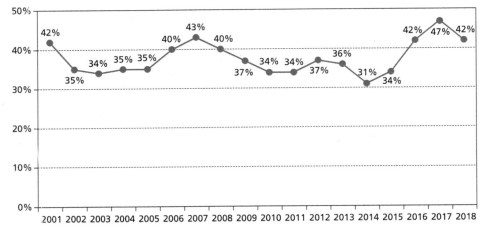

SOURCE: Data from Gallup. 2018. "Environment." Retrieved 7 May 2018 (news.gallup.com/poll/1615/environment.aspx).

Table 14–2 Percentage of Americans Concerned "a Great Deal" About Specific Environmental Problems, 2015, 2017

	2015	2017
Pollution of drinking water	55%	63%
Pollution of rivers, lakes, and reservoirs	47%	57%
Air pollution	38%	47%
Global warming or climate change	32%	45%
The loss of tropical rain forests	33%	44%
Extinction of plant and animal species	36%	44%

SOURCE: McCarthy, J. "In U.S., Water Pollution Worries Highest Since 2001," Social & Policy Issues, Gallup (March 31, 2017).

Specifically, what are people most worried about? Table 14–2 (McCarthy, 2017) indicates that people are most concerned about water pollution. They are concerned about polluted drinking water and polluted rivers, lakes, and reservoirs. Air pollution ranks third, with climate change, the loss of tropical rain forests, and plant and animal extinctions following that. The table also shows that the level of concern with each of these issues has grown over the last couple of years.

14.2.1 Origins of the Problem

Examples of environmental stress abound and include discharging substances into the air, water, and soil; producing heat, noise, and radiation; removing plants and animals; and physically transforming the environment through drilling, damming, dredging, mining, pumping, and so on (Brown, 2015; Worldwatch Institute, 2017). Environmental stress is not synonymous with pollution, although pollution is perhaps its most familiar form. Webster's dictionary defines **pollution** as "the action or process of making land, water, air, etc., dirty and not safe or suitable to use."[3]

Four concepts are basic to understanding environmental stress: interdependence, diversity, limits, and complexity (Ophuls, 1977).

- *Interdependence*, which literally means that everything is related to and depends on everything else; there is no beginning or end to the web of life.
- *Diversity*, which refers to the existence of many different life and life-support forms. A basic principle of ecology is that the greater the diversity of species, the greater the probability of survival of any given one.
- *Limits*, which includes several kinds. First, there is a finite limit to the growth of any organism. Second, there is a limit to the numbers of a given species that an environment—including other organisms—can support. Finally, there is a finite limit to the amount of materials available in Earth's ecosystem.
- *Complexity*, which refers to the intricacy of the relationships that constitute the web of life. Because of this complexity, interventions in the environment frequently lead to unanticipated and undesired consequences.

Use of the chemical DDT (dichlorodiphenyltrichloroethane) is an example of complexity. DDT was the first widely used synthetic pesticide and is extremely persistent in both the environment and the human body. The pesticide was once repeatedly sprayed over large areas of land to eliminate various disease-carrying or crop-destroying insects. To an impressive degree, it succeeded. But DDT is a long-lasting chemical, and its effects are not limited to insects. Much of it was washed

pollution

The action or process of making land, water, air, etc., dirty and not safe or suitable to use.

---

[3]"Pollution." Merriam-Webster.com. Merriam-Webster, n.d. Web.

from farmlands and forests into rivers and oceans, where it was taken up by smaller organisms at the bottom of the food chain. Eventually, as small creatures consumed tiny plants and larger creatures consumed smaller ones, several species of fish-eating birds accumulated so much of the poison that their eggs developed very thin shells, which consistently broke before hatching. These species were in grave danger of extinction, although the users of DDT never intended such a result (Ehrlich and Ehrlich, 2004). Only federal restrictions on the use of DDT prevented the elimination of these bird species.

Although the environmentally harmful effects of widespread DDT use became well-known following Rachel Carson's *Silent Spring* (1962), its human health effects have more recently become clearer. High-level exposure may cause cancer and abnormalities of liver function, skin, and the reproduction and nervous systems (Longnecker, Rogan, and Lucier, 1997). Recent work shows that DDT may also have transgenerational effects, harming a generation that was never directly exposed to DDT (Kabasenche and Skinner, 2014).

A ban on the use of DDT has been in place for over 30 years in the United States and many other countries have banned it as well. However, when a global ban on DDT was proposed in 2001, several countries in sub-Saharan Africa objected, claiming that DDT was still needed as a cheap and effective means for malaria control. Its use for malaria control remains widespread today, despite the health risks (Haberman, 2017; van den Berg, Manuweera, and Konradsen, 2017). In other words, in an attempt to reduce one health problem—malaria—people are exposed to a variety of other health problems.

One of the major difficulties in dealing with environmental stress, therefore, is the number of problems involved and the extent to which they are interrelated. This complexity will become clear as you explore specific problems, particularly climate change, air pollution, water pollution, and solid-waste disposal, and the efforts that have been made to combat them.

Scientist Rachel Carson (1907–1964) appeared before a Senate Government Operations subcommittee studying pesticides in 1963. The author of the best-selling book *Silent Spring* established the harm caused to animals by the pesticide DDT.

What Do You Think?

Can you identify the different ways functionalists, conflict theorists, and symbolic interactionists would think about environmental stress?

Climate Change and Global Warming

14.3   Assess the significance of climate change and its consequences.

Today, terms such as *global warming* and *climate change* have become politicized and controversial. **Global warming** refers to the long-term warming of the planet. Global temperature shows a well-documented rise since the early twentieth century and most notably since the late 1970s. Since 1880, the average worldwide surface temperature has gone up by about 1.0°C (2°F) since the late nineteenth century (NASA, 2018).

Climate change encompasses global warming but refers to the broader range of changes that are happening to our planet. These changes include rising sea levels; shrinking mountain glaciers; accelerating ice melt in Greenland, Antarctica, and the Arctic; extreme weather events; and shifts in flower and plant blooming times. These developments are all consequences of the warming, which is caused mainly by people burning fossil fuels and emitting heat-trapping gases into the air. Earth's climate has changed throughout history, according to NASA; however, the current warming trend is of particular significance because most of it is extremely likely (greater than 95 percent probability) to be the result

global warming

The long-term warming of the planet.

climate change

A type of environmental change that encompasses global warming but refers to the broader range of changes that are happening to our planet, including rising sea levels; shrinking mountain glaciers; accelerating ice melt in Greenland, Antarctica, and the Arctic; and shifts in flower and plant blooming times.

Greg Wood/Getty Images

Americans have been concerned about water and air pollution for decades. The concern about climate change is much more recent. However, climate change is a problem that must be addressed immediately or the other issues are almost moot.

of human activity since the mid-20th century and is proceeding at an unprecedented rate (NASA, 2018).

The two terms are often used interchangeably, although climate change is a more accurate description because the changes involve far more than just an increase in temperatures. Some places will be noticeably hotter or even colder, others will be wetter, and others drier.

14.3.1 What Is Climate Change?

Of all the many aspects of pollution and environmental stress, perhaps none alarms scientists and environmental groups at present as much as climate change—the dangerous warming of the planet, and the consequences associated with this warming. These changes are due to the continued high levels of greenhouse gases released into the atmosphere from (a) carbon dioxide (CO_2), primarily from burning fossil fuels including coal, oil, and gas; (b) breeding vast numbers of methane-producing livestock; and (c) cutting down forests that naturally absorb carbon dioxide from the air (World Wildlife Fund, 2015). Carbon-based gases such as carbon dioxide and methane are natural gases and essential for life on Earth—in the right amounts. However, the extra carbon dioxide and methane in the atmosphere traps more of the sun's heat, creating a "greenhouse effect," and raising global temperatures. That is, these gases trap heat near Earth's surface, raising the average temperature of the atmosphere. Sixteen of the 17 hottest years recorded occurred since 2001 (NASA, 2018).

Such overheating, even by a few degrees, could melt the polar ice caps, with calamitous results. Some scientists believe that globally, the temperature today is 1.0°C above pre-industrial times and that a warming of close to 1.5°C above pre-industrial times is already locked into Earth's atmosphere by past and predicted emissions. Everyone will feel the impact of this warming (World Bank Group, 2018).

Scientists estimate that a rise of just 2°C would cause severe storms and floods in some countries and crippling droughts in others; would cause seas to become more acidic, killing coral and krill and thus disrupting food chains; and would reduce Arctic ice to little or none in the summer, which not only is bad news for polar bears, but also means that Earth would warm even faster because there would be less polar ice to deflect sunlight (Union of Concerned Scientists, 2018; United Nations, 2018; World Wildlife Fund, 2018).

A rise beyond 2°C could lead to dying rain forests, increased melting of the ancient ice sheets of Greenland and Antarctica, dramatic sea level rises, and untold suffering among people and animals. Such a rise in temperature could cause mass human (and animal) migration, as the oceans would rise and cause flooding in coastal cities and islands, deserts would become unbearably hot, and droughts would cause crops to perish (Rigaud et al., 2018). The World Bank projects that without concrete climate and development action, over 143 million people in sub-Saharan Africa, Southeast Asia, and Latin America could be forced to move within their own countries to escape the impacts of climate change (Rigaud et al., 2018). Scientists predict that the temperature could rise to 6°C in this century if the world's people do not drastically cut greenhouse gas emissions.

Until recently, the United States has been the largest energy consumer and the largest contributor to the production of these gases. In recent years, the United States has been eclipsed by China. Figure 14–2 reports the world's top 10 consumers of

Figure 14–2 World's Top 10 Energy Consumers, 2016

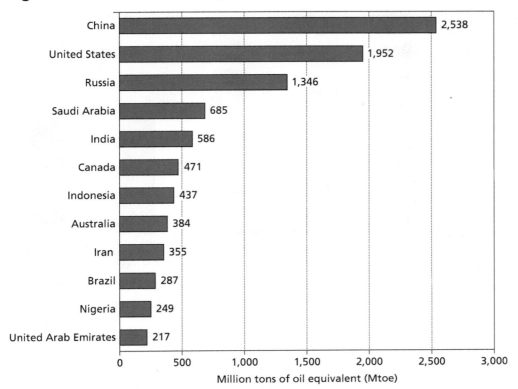

NOTE: Mtoe (Million Tons of Oil Equivalent). Energy consumed includes coal, gas, oil, electric, heat, and biomass.

SOURCE: Data from Enerdata. 2018. "Total Energy Production." Retrieved 7 May 2018 (yearbook.enerdata.net/total-energy/).

energy, which includes the use of coal, gas, oil, electric, heat, and biomass (organic material that comes from plants and animals). China is now ranked first, using 2,538 **million tons of oil equivalent (Mtoe)**, which is a standard method of converting different types of energy units into one measure. The United States uses 1,952 Mtoe units. However, China's population is five times that of the United States, so Americans still use a large majority of the world's energy per person.

Less developed countries (LDCs) burn fossil fuels at far lower rates than developed nations, but many LDCs meet their energy needs by burning wood, straw, and similar fuels, which also emit carbon. The felling and burning of forests in tropical countries add between 1 billion and 2 billion tons of carbon emissions to the worldwide total. Growing populations and the associated demand for energy, land, and other resources will lead to carbon emissions—and hence the amount of carbon dioxide in the atmosphere—that will likely increase for the foreseeable future.

million tons of oil equivalent (Mtoe)

A standard method of converting different types of energy units into one measure.

14.3.2 An Inconvenient Truth

At present, there is widespread consensus among scientists that global warming is a real and present danger (Union of Concerned Scientists, 2018). Nonetheless, there is continued debate about it among laypeople. Two-thirds of adults surveyed acknowledge that climate change is occurring and is caused by human activities; 60 percent of people say it has already begun, but less than half (45 percent) believe it will pose a serious threat in their lifetime, as shown in Figure 14–3 (Brenan and Saad, March 28, 2018). Less than half of adults worry a great deal about global warming, similar to the number who say they worry a great deal about the environment more generally, as reported earlier.

Figure 14–3 Summary of Americans' Views on Global Warming

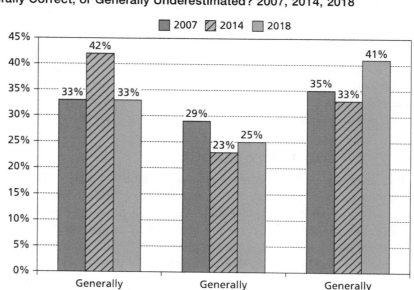

	66%	64%	60%	45%	43%

Categories:
- Say most scientists believe global warming is occurring
- Believe global warming is caused by human activities
- Believe effects of global warming have already begun
- Think global warming will pose a serious threat in their lifetime
- Worry a great deal about global warming

SOURCE: Brenan, M. & Saad, L. "Global Warming Concern Steady Despite Some Partisan Shifts," Politics, Gallup (March 28, 2018).

In other words, most people are aware that climate change is happening, but far fewer are worried about it affecting themselves personally. This mindset may signal that many people do not understand climate change and feel that its seriousness as presented in the news is exaggerated, as shown in Figure 14–4 (Gallup, 2018). One-third of the population believes that the seriousness of global warming is generally exaggerated. Yet most scientists agree that the consequences of climate change are already here and are having significant and costly effects on our communities and our health. As former Vice President and Nobel Prize winner Al Gore has said, climate change is "an inconvenient truth."

Figure 14–4 Is the Seriousness of Global Warming Generally Exaggerated, Generally Correct, or Generally Underestimated? 2007, 2014, 2018

Legend: 2007, 2014, 2018

	Generally exaggerated	Generally correct	Generally underestimated
2007	33%	29%	35%
2014	42%	23%	33%
2018	33%	25%	41%

SOURCE: Data from Gallup. 2018. "Environment." Retrieved 7 May 2018 (news.gallup.com/poll/1615/environment.aspx).

Who are the people who defy the scientific evidence? They run the gamut, of course, but they are most likely to be older men who identify as Republicans. Interestingly, level of education matters very little (Brenan and Saad, March 28, 2018). In fact, political affiliation seems to be, by far, the largest predictor of concern over climate change and global warming. Sixty-six percent of Democrats say they worry a great deal about climate change, as compared to only 18 percent of Republicans (Norman, March 17, 2017).

The gap between Republicans and Democrats became even larger since the election of President Trump. In April 2016, the United States joined 195 other countries in signing the Paris Agreement on climate change—the most comprehensive international agreement to date on combatting global warming. It had been a long-standing goal of Democratic President Barack Obama, who said of the day the agreement was signed: "History may well judge it as a turning point for our planet."[4] But in November, only four days after the agreement went into effect, Republican Donald Trump was elected president on a campaign that included a vow to cancel U.S. involvement in the treaty, and he came through on that promise.

Former U.S. Vice President Al Gore has been an outspoken leader on climate change, stressing the urgency of acting now to control it. His documentary and best-selling book, *An Inconvenient Truth*, published in 2006, brought discussions of climate change into the mainstream.

PARIS CLIMATE AGREEMENT   Climate change is inherently global in nature, as shown in the slide show, *"Some Effects of Climate Change."* The emission of long-lived greenhouse gases into the atmosphere from sources anywhere on the globe will alter atmospheric concentrations that affect everyone. Although some parts of the world will feel the consequences sooner or more significantly than those living elsewhere, ultimately the effects of climate change will affect us all. Therefore, there is a need for collective global action that calls for decision making at many levels: international, national, and local (United Nations Framework Convention on Climate Change, 2018).

The Paris Climate Agreement, also referred to as the Paris Climate Accord, or simply the Paris Agreement, is a pact sponsored by the United Nations to bring the world's countries together in the fight against climate change. In 2015, 195 countries gathered in the French capital to create the first truly universal climate treaty aimed at preventing the worst-case scenarios of global warming. The United States, under President Obama and the other nations, agreed to voluntarily reduce their greenhouse gas emissions to keep the global temperature increase this century to well below 2 degrees Celsius (4 degrees Fahrenheit) above pre-industrial levels, and to work to limit the rise to 1.5 degrees Celsius. To accomplish this 2-degree goal, the Agreement states that countries should strive to reach peak emissions "as soon as possible."

Each country agreed to put forth and meet nationally determined contributions that would help keep global temperature levels down. But the agreement doesn't detail exactly how these countries should do so. Instead it provides a framework for getting momentum going on greenhouse gas reduction, with some oversight and accountability. For the United States, the pledge involves 26 to 28 percent reductions by 2025.

---

[4]Remarks by the President on the Paris Agreement. Office of the Press Secretary, The White House (October 05, 2016).

Some Effects of Climate Change

Climate change is not some far-off prophecy. It is real and happening today, as these images reveal.

This is an aerial view of the town of Ilulissat, Greenland. Even though the disappearing ice cap could lead to higher sea levels all over the world, Greenland's Inuit population will be among the first to feel the effects of climate change. Records show that the average air temperature has risen by 4°C over the past decade while the water temperature has climbed by two degrees. Fishermen and hunters now avoid the fjords where the ice has become too thin to travel on. For the first time, they are now beginning to catch cod, which prefer warmer water.

This woman wades through a flooded street in Miami, Florida, to catch a bus. Some of the streets in Miami Beach were flooded because of unusually high tides due to rising sea levels connected with global warming and climate change. Florida ranks as the state most vulnerable to sea-level rise, with millions of people living on the coast at risk.

Climate change will increase the number and intensity of wildfires, especially in the western United States. Here, a house burns in San Marcos, California. Because of the prolonged and continuing record drought in California, fire agencies are scrambling to prepare for the next season.

The year 2017 emerged as the third hottest year on record. Here you see thousands of New Yorkers at Brighton Beach in April, for the hottest Easter day ever recorded.

One woman distributes drinking water to neighbors as water wells supplying hundreds of residents remain dry in the central California community of East Porterville during the recent drought. Many residents filled water tanks with free nonpotable water for flushing toilets, bathing, and laundering. Bottled water was used for drinking, cooking, and washing dishes. Many wells in the county stopped flowing during the summer due to the drought. In 2015, in the throes of the drought, some scientists believed that California had only enough water in reservoirs to last about one more year. Things may have improved since then, but the possibility of a severe drought in California, and the entire Southwest, is always a threat.

Critical Thinking

Think about where you live. How is climate change and global warming affecting you today? How do you think it will affect you in ten years? What parts of the United States are most vulnerable to climate change and global warming, and why? What does the rest of the country owe the people in these regions, if anything?

The Agreement also has a provision to assist in funding responses to climate change's effects on more vulnerable, developing countries. There is a fundamental inequality when it comes to global emissions. Rich countries have burned very large amounts of fossil fuels and have become rich from them. Poor countries seeking to grow their economies are now discouraged from using the same fuels. Many low-lying poor countries also will be among the first to bear the worst impacts of climate change. Therefore, rich countries are expected to provide funding to help developing countries make the costly shift to cleaner energy sources and to shore up defenses against the impacts of climate change. The United States pledged $3 billion to the Green Climate Fund.

Soon after taking office, President Trump pulled out of the Paris Climate Agreement. He believed that it would cripple U.S. economic growth, and if forced to choose between limiting carbon emissions and economic growth, growing the economy should win. He also ended remaining payments into the Green Climate Fund. The United States now joins the two other U.N. member countries that are not part of the Agreement: Nicaragua and Syria. Nicaragua believes that the Agreement does not go far enough, and that voluntary reductions are a path to failure. Syria is in the midst of a civil war. It is estimated that Syria is responsible for only 0.19 percent of global emissions as compared to the United States at 15 percent.

Trump complained about the Paris Climate Agreement early in his campaign for presidency. He is not a supporter of strong environmental protections on the federal level, calling climate change a hoax created by the Chinese to hurt the U.S. economy. Since taking office, Trump's policies have favored delaying or rolling back rules that would limit carbon emissions by U.S. companies. He appointed Scott Pruitt as the head of the Environmental Protection Agency (EPA). Like President Trump, Pruitt has stated that scientific conclusions on global warming and climate change are exaggerated. While in office (he resigned in July 2018), Pruitt rescinded environmental regulations of previous administrations.

Steve Skjold/Alamy Stock Photo

President Trump pulled the United States out of the Paris Climate Agreement in June 2017. "I was elected to represent the citizens of Pittsburgh, not Paris," he said, referring to Pittsburgh's longstanding history of coal mining, a notorious contributor to greenhouse gases.[5] The mayor of Pittsburgh was not pleased that his city was used to justify pulling out of the Agreement, and noted that Pittsburgh is moving forward with clean energy.

14.3.3 Consequences of Climate Change

What are the serious consequences of climate change? Looking only at the United States, we are likely to see (Union of Concerned Scientists, 2018):

- **Accelerated sea level rise and increased coastal flooding.** The average sea level has increased eight inches since 1880 and is rising the fastest in the East Coast and Gulf of Mexico regions, increasing flooding risks to low-lying communities and coastal properties. This increase is due to the rising temperature in the planet's polar regions, which is causing most of the world's glaciers to melt faster than new snow and ice can replenish them.
- **More frequent and intense heat waves.** Dangerously hot weather is already occurring more frequently in much of the United States, and the last few summers have had record heat. Scientists expect heat waves to become more frequent and severe as global warming intensifies. The heat creates serious health risks, including heat exhaustion, heat stroke, and aggravations of other medical conditions.
- **Longer and more damaging wildfire seasons.** Rising temperatures lead to a longer wildlife season and an increase in the number of wildfires. Spring arrives 10 days earlier on average in the Northern Hemisphere. Higher temperatures and early spring snowmelt cause forests in the West to be drier for longer periods, priming conditions for wildfires to ignite and spread.
- **Heavier precipitation and flooding.** As temperatures increase, more rain falls during the heaviest downpours, increasing the risk of flooding. "Very-heavy" rainfalls, defined as the heaviest 1 percent of storms, now drop 67 percent more

[5]Quoted from Gambino, L. "Pittsburgh Fires Back at Trump: We Stand with Paris, Not You," *The Guardian* (June 1, 2017).

precipitation in the Northeast, 31 percent more in the Midwest, and 15 percent more in the Great Plains than they did 50 years ago. Snow accumulations are also increasing; Boston recently had its highest snowfall ever recorded in one season.

- **More severe droughts in some areas.** Climate change affects many factors associated with droughts, and has increased the drought risk in the West and Southwest. California recently experienced the most serious drought ever recorded.
- **More extreme weather events.** In addition to increased heat waves, climate change causes a wide variety of extreme weather events. This can include record cold temperatures and snowfall, and increased frequency and intensity of hurricanes and tornadoes.
- **Disruption to food supplies.** Rising temperatures and the lack of water in the West and heavier precipitation in other areas has significant implications for crop and meat production. Global warming has the potential to seriously disrupt the American food supply, drive costs upward, and affect the availability and quality of most foods, from coffee to cattle.
- **Plant and animal range shifts.** A changing climate affects the range of plants and animals, causing disruptions throughout the food chain. The range of warm-weather species will expand, but the range of those requiring cooler environments will face shrinking habitats and possible extinction.

As serious as these consequences are for Americans, they pale in comparison to other parts of the world where they are likely to occur in more extreme forms. For example, record high temperatures of between 100 and 105 degrees (Fahrenheit) occurred in several European cities in a recent summer. The year 2017 was the first time in known history that the Atlantic had two storms with 150+ mile per hour winds raging at the same time: Irma and Jose. April 2018 was the coldest on record in the United States in more than twenty years, and many regions broke snow records. The monthly precipitation over the Pacific side of western Japan in a recent year was 301 percent above normal—the highest since area-averaged statistics began in 1946. At the same time, northeast China and parts of the Yellow River basin did not reach half of the summer average rainfall, causing severe drought. Africa is one of the most vulnerable continents to climate change, already suffering from droughts, arid land unsuitable for farming, and severe water shortages. Climate change will intensify these issues, and its poor state of economic development, its high levels of poverty, and its political instability will further worsen this situation (Munang and Andrews, 2014; United Nations, 2015).

As just one example, climate change will have strong effects on agriculture, thereby disrupting the world's food supply (Springmann et al., 2016; Zimmerman et al., 2017). Studies have shown that the combination of increased levels of carbon dioxide in the atmosphere, rising temperatures, and changes to precipitation may result in significantly lower yields for staple crops such as corn and wheat, particularly in tropical areas, where food production is normally high (Miller, 2017). Even the quality of food will be affected, as certain foods grown with high levels of carbon dioxide in the atmosphere lose some of their nutritional value (Diettrich et al., 2015; Myers et al., 2014). As the world's population continues to soar, and food output and its nutritional value begins to decline, the future could look grim unless dramatic action against climate change begins immediately.

All these issues raise the specter of social and political conflict as people try to adapt to changing conditions. When food and water run short, conflict is inevitable. Will the poor suffer more than the rich, or will the challenges be equally shared? The head of the Catholic Church, Pope Francis, raises this question.

California, which recently experienced its worst drought in perhaps 1,000 years, provides an interesting test case of the way that social inequality weaves its way through limited resources. When water, a precious resource, is in short supply, how is it distributed and used? The box, *A Closer Look: "Who's Using the Water? Social Class and Water Usage in California,"* indicates that not all people are conserving equally.

A Closer Look

Who's Using the Water? Social Class and Water Usage in California

Citizen of the Planet/Alamy Stock Photo

California recently experienced a drought that is considered the worst in recorded history. This region, with a dry Mediterranean climate, is used to little rainfall. However, over the last decade the winter rains have been unusually light, snowfall in the mountains has been well below average, and water usage by farmers, industry, and private individuals continues to drain the reservoirs.

After a couple of years of exceedingly dry weather, the state began to take serious notice of the low levels of water in the reservoirs and the dreaded "D" word—drought—became a common part of everyday conversations. Many people considered the drought a short-term inconvenience. Scientists, however, know that there have been multiple droughts in California, often lasting hundreds of years. The two most severe droughts that we know of include a 240-year-long drought that started in 850 AD. Fifty years after its conclusion, another one began that stretched at least 180 years. So, it may be wishful thinking to assume that this one will be over quickly.

As the water crisis continued, tempers began heating up. Governor Brown asked households for a voluntary reduction of water use by 20 percent. The state established rules that allowed communities to fine excessive water-wasters up to $500, but enforcement was rare. In Los Angeles, for instance, only two $200 fines were issued in a service area of about 4 million people. Without serious consequences, many people continued to water lawns, take long showers, wash their cars, and go on day to day as if water were unlimited. Therefore, water usage declined on average only 10 percent. However, by 2015, the governor imposed stricter policies in hopes of cutting use by 25 percent.

Should we be surprised to learn that wealthy people and wealthy communities in California used considerably more water than poorer people and poorer communities?

The California Department of Water Resources noted that, for example, working-class residents in the community of Bellflower used an average of 128 gallons of water a day. Per capita, water use in surrounding low-income suburbs was similar. In contrast, water use in nearby posh Palos Verdes and Beverly Hills was markedly higher at 282 and 284 gallons per day, respectively.

What accounts for income differences in water usage? If you don't mind a large water bill, what is the incentive to conserve? As one man in tony Rancho Santa Fe, a wealthy suburb of Los Angeles, said, "I know I am not supposed to be watering my yard so much, but I think brown grass is ugly. Go ahead, fine me if you have to, but I want to keep things looking nice."

This is one of the reasons that Governor Brown ordered mandatory water use restrictions for the first time in California's history. In an executive order, he directed the State Water Resources Control Board to impose a 25 percent reduction over the coming year in California's local water supply agencies, which serve 90 percent of California's residents. This order imposed cutbacks on water use across the board, affecting homeowners, farms, and businesses, regardless of income; however, the size of cuts varied from community to community, reflecting that some communities had already been better at reducing their water use than other communities. Furthermore, the State Water Resources Control Board had the power to impose fines on local water suppliers that fail to meet the reduction targets.

"People should realize we are in a new era," Governor Brown said at a news conference, as he stood on a patch of brown and green grass that would normally be under snow at that time of year. "The idea of your nice little green lawn getting watered every day, those days are past."[6] Although the drought officially ended in 2017 and "state of emergency" measures were lifted after unusual heavy winter rains that year, California will never really be out of the clear for long. By 2018, much of the state was back to being listed as either "abnormally dry" or listed as being in some level of drought. This is likely to be the new normal in California.

Critical Thinking

How would a conflict theorist analyze water usage in California? Would a conflict theorist support or oppose mandatory water rationing, and why? What approach to conserving water do you think is best?

SOURCES: Drought.gov, 2018; Worland, 2015.

---

[6]Semeniuk, I. "'People should realize we are in a new era': California's Drought Enters a Critical Stage," *The Globe and Mail* (April 2, 2015).

Air Pollution

14.4 Identify the health and economic effects of air pollution.

If the atmosphere is not overburdened, natural processes will cleanse it and preserve its composition. Through photosynthesis, for example, green plants combine water with the carbon dioxide that we and other organisms exhale, and they produce oxygen. But these natural processes, like other resources, have limits. They can remove only a limited quantity of harmful substances from the air; if pollution exceeds their capacity to do so, the air will become progressively more dangerous to those who breathe it.

Human activities are overtaxing the atmosphere. Although the specific nature of air pollution varies from one locality to another (as a function of geography, climate, and type and concentration of industry), we can identify some of the common components, including organic compounds (hydrocarbons); oxides of carbon, nitrogen, and sulfur; lead and other metals; and particulate matter (soot and fly ash).

Nearly one half of all Americans—an estimated 150 million—live in areas that do not meet federal air quality standards. The Clean Air Act requires the EPA to set national air quality standards for pollutants considered harmful to public health and the environment. The Clean Air Act identifies two types of national air quality standards. *Primary standards* provide public health protection, including protecting the health of "sensitive" populations such as asthmatics, children, and the elderly. *Secondary standards* provide public welfare protection, including protection against decreased visibility and damage to animals, crops, vegetation, and buildings.

Air Quality Index (AQI)

A way of categorizing levels of daily air quality that indicates how clean or polluted the air is.

Table 14–3 shows the **Air Quality Index (AQI)**, which is an index of daily air quality that indicates how clean or polluted the air is (Environmental Protection Agency, 2016). The EPA calculates the AQI for five major air pollutants regulated by the Clean Air Act: ground-level ozone, particle pollution (also known as particulate matter), carbon monoxide, sulfur dioxide, and nitrogen dioxide. Think of the AQI as a measuring stick that runs from 0 to 500. The lower the AQI value, the better the air quality.

As you can see in Table 14–3, a value of less than 50 indicates good air quality, while a value between 301 and 500 indicates hazardous air quality that would trigger a health warning of emergency conditions.

Eight of the ten cities with the highest year-round concentration of particulate matter in 2015 were in California. Many of these are farming communities that are hot and dry in the summer months. The most polluted metropolitan regions by average particulate matter are (Schlanger, 2017):

- Visalia-Porterville-Hanford, CA
- Bakersfield, CA
- Fresno-Madera, CA
- San Jose-San Francisco-Oakland, CA
- Los Angeles-Long Beach, CA

Table 14–3 Current EPA Air Quality Index (AQI)

AQI Range	EPA Color Scale	EPA Descriptor
0 to 50	Green	Good
51 to 100	Yellow	Moderate
101 to 150	Orange	Unhealthy for Sensitive Groups
151 to 200	Red	Unhealthy
201 to 300	Purple	Very Unhealthy
301 to 500	Maroon	Hazardous

SOURCE: Environmental Protection Agency. 2016a. "Air Quality Index (AQI) Basics. Retrieved 16 September 2018 (https://cfpub.epa.gov/airnow/index.cfm?action=aqibasics.aqi).

- Modesto-Merced, CA
- El Centro, CA
- Pittsburgh-New Castle-Weirton, PA-OH-WV
- Cleveland-Akron-Canton, OH
- San Luis Obispo-Paso Robles-Arroyo Grande, CA

California is also home to seven of the ten American cities with the worst ozone pollution. The most polluted cities by ozone pollution are (Schlanger, 2017):

- Los Angeles-Long Beach, CA
- Bakersfield, CA
- Fresno-Madera, CA
- Visalia-Porterville-Hanford, CA
- Phoenix-Mesa-Scottsdale, AZ
- Modesto-Merced, CA
- San Diego-Carlsbad, CA
- Sacramento-Roseville, CA
- New York-Newark, NY-NJ-CT-PA
- Las Vegas-Henderson, NV-AZ[7]

Pollution is particularly severe in parts of the world where regulations still permit the use of leaded gasoline and where large populations still rely on firewood or other combustibles for cooking. Over parts of China, the air quality has reached hazardous levels. Just a few years ago the air in Beijing, China, reached unhealthy, very unhealthy, or hazardous levels roughly 70 percent of the time. In 2014, 24 days were recorded as hazardous, having an index higher than 301—often much higher. In fact, the U.S. Embassy recorded one day in 2013 when the pollution reached an index of 755! Because the air in Beijing is so polluted and registered above 500 on the index with some frequency, the U.S. Embassy has created a new category exclusively for China—above 500—and warns everyone to stay indoors with filtered air conditioning turned on high during those days. To their credit, the Chinese have become more concerned about the air quality and have imposed more stringent requirements for factories and automobiles. Consequently, there is some evidence that the air in Beijing, and other parts of China, is beginning to improve somewhat overall (Zheng, 2018).

What causes all of this air pollution? It comes from many sources, of course. However, cars and heavy-duty trucks are the main sources of this pollution, which includes ozone, particulate matter, and other smog-forming emissions (Union of Concerned Scientists, 2018). The EPA says motor vehicles account for three-quarters of the carbon monoxide in the air (Brinson, 2015). The remainder comes from the burning of fossil fuels (oil and coal) in power-generating plants, airplanes, and homes; airborne wastes from manufacturing processes; and the burning of municipal trash. Certain chemical processes frequently render these pollutants more dangerous after they reach the atmosphere. In the presence of sunlight, the emission of hydrocarbons and nitrogen oxides (primarily from cars) produces the photochemical soup called smog that envelops many of our cities, and various oxides combine with water vapor in the atmosphere to produce corrosive acids that eventually become what is known as acid rain, which eats away the surfaces of many buildings.

Since vehicles are a primary culprit, it makes sense to address the pollution they emit. The Obama administration implemented standards to reduce emissions by increasing fuel economy from 27.5 miles per gallon (mpg) to the equivalent of 54.5 mpg for cars and light-duty trucks by model year 2025. This increase in fuel

---

[7]Schlanger, Z. "California Is Home to Eight of the 10 Cities in America Where Air Pollution is Worst," *Quartz* (April 19, 2017).

Beijing and other cities in China have the most polluted air in the world. President Obama and China's President Xi Jinping met in late 2014 and agreed on a plan to limit carbon emissions by their countries, which are the two biggest polluters. More recently, President Trump has rolled back rules on carbon emissions.

economy would reduce greenhouse gas emissions by 6 billion tons over the lifetime of new vehicles and save 2 million gallons of oil per day by 2025 (Milman, 2017). "The fuel efficiency standards the administration finalized today are another example of how we protect the environment and strengthen the economy at the same time," said Obama's EPA Administrator Lisa P. Jackson. "Innovation and economic growth are already reinvigorating the auto industry and the thousands of businesses that supply automakers as they create and produce the efficient vehicles of tomorrow. Clean, efficient vehicles are also cutting pollution and saving drivers money at the pump" (The White House, August 28, 2012).[8]

President Trump, however, opposes the fuel efficiency standards established by the Obama administration. "These standards are costly for automakers and the American people," said Scott Pruitt, former head of the EPA under President Trump.[9] His plan would freeze fuel economy targets at the levels required for vehicles sold in 2020 and leave those in place through 2026. Instead of average vehicle fuel economy ratcheting up to 54.5 mpg, as it would have under former President Obama, it would stall out at 42 mpg (Tabuchi, Plumer, and Davenport, 2018).

Environmental groups and California policymakers have vowed to fight the administration in court (Halper, 2018; Puko, 2018). Under federal law, California has long been allowed to set tougher tailpipe emission rules than the federal government. Other states can adopt California's standards, and a dozen currently do. Those states account for more than a third of cars and trucks in the country. But, under the Trump policy, these states would no longer be allowed to set their own fuel efficiency standards.

Nonetheless, most Americans support setting higher emission standards, as indicated in Table 14–4. In 2018, two-thirds of adults favor setting higher emission standards for automobiles, which is a slight increase from 2012, although a significant decline from 2001.

Table 14–4 Opinions Toward Higher Emission Standards for Automobiles

"I am going to read some specific proposals. For each one, please say whether you generally favor or oppose it. How about—Setting higher emissions standards for automobiles?"

	Favor	Oppose
2018	66%	33%
2012	62%	37%
2006	73%	25%
2001	75%	23%

SOURCE: Data from Gallup. 2018. "Environment." Retrieved 7 May 2018 (news.gallup.com/poll/1615/environment.aspx).

[8]"Obama Administration Finalizes Historic 54.5 MPG Fuel Efficiency Standards," Office of the Press Secretary, The White House (August 28, 2012).
[9]Tabuchi, H., Plumer, B., & Davenport, C. "E.P.A. Readies Plan to Weaken Rules That Require Cars to Be Cleaner," *The New York Times* (April 27, 2018).

14.4.1 Effects on Human Health

The health effects of air pollution can range from headaches, coughs, and dizziness to asthma, cancer, birth defects, nervous system damage, and death (EPA, February 22, 2018; Kinney, 2018; Panis et al., 2017). Clearly, effects of chronic air pollution are of great significance for human health in the long run.

Scientists do not exactly know how much air pollution for how long a period will cause these most extreme effects. Research that tests the effects of air pollution on humans is difficult to conduct for ethical reasons. Instead, scientists usually conduct studies on laboratory animals such as rats and expose them to pollutants at varied concentrations and for varied time periods. Scientists have learned that continued exposure to air pollutants and their accumulation in the body—essentially a slow poisoning process—causes health problems by interfering with normal body functions. Most commonly, pollutants change chemical reactions within individual cells, the building blocks of living things, resulting in impaired cell function, or even cell death.

14.4.2 Economic Effects

Air pollution also has economic effects. It leads to thousands of illnesses each day, lost days at work, and significantly increased hospital spending. A large-scale study of hospital visits estimates that nearly 30,000 hospital admissions and emergency-room visits could have been avoided throughout California alone during a two-year period if federal clean-air standards had been met (Romley, Hackbarth, and Goldman, 2010).

The most worrying and striking impact of air pollution is the large number of premature deaths it causes. The number of premature deaths due to outdoor air pollution is projected to increase from 3 million people globally in 2010 to 6 to 9 million people in 2060 (OECD, June 2016). But short of mortality, air pollution also increases sickness and reduces worker productivity, especially among those who work outdoors.

Air pollution also leads to accelerated deterioration of property; it increases maintenance and cleaning costs; and it blights crops and reduces crop yield, which means lost income for farmers and higher food prices for consumers. The bottom line is that air pollution is expensive, and everyone pays the price.

Water Pollution

14.5 Describe the problems related to water pollution.

Water is emerging as another crisis of our times (Barlow and Clarke, 2005; Black, King, and Lacy, 2009). Water—what so many of us take for granted—is increasingly viewed around the world as "liquid gold." We can no longer take for granted access to fresh water for drinking, for irrigating crops, for cooking or cleaning because it is becoming an increasingly rare commodity. How has this crisis come to be?

Water is constantly moving through what is known as the hydrologic cycle. It is found in the atmosphere as vapor; it condenses and falls to the earth as rain, snow, or dew; it percolates underground or runs off the surface as streams, rivers, and finally oceans; it evaporates into the atmosphere as vapor once again; and the cycle continues. While on the ground, water may be either absorbed into the roots of plants and, through the leaves, eventually evaporate back into the atmosphere or be drunk from streams or other sources by animals or people and excreted or evaporated back into the earth or air. Alternately, it may sink into underground reservoirs and be stored for millions of years.

It is quite possible for water to be used more than once as it passes through a single round of the hydrologic cycle if it is sufficiently purified between uses by natural or artificial means. However, we render much of our water unfit for reuse because of various kinds of pollutants: raw and inadequately treated sewage, oil, synthetic organic chemicals (detergents and pesticides), inorganic chemicals and mineral substances, plant nutrients, radioactivity, and heat. Add to this list the millions of pounds of plastics that have made their way to the water. We therefore face a dual crisis: The amount of water available to us could be insufficient for our demands, and what is available could be polluted.

Just as air can cleanse itself if not overburdened, so too can rivers, lakes, and oceans. But we have been discharging wastes, directly or indirectly, into our waterways in amounts that prohibit natural purification. In fact, nearly 30 percent of the U.S. population is not served by sewage treatment facilities (Center for Sustainable Systems, 2014). The bacteria in untreated sewage render the water unfit for drinking, swimming, and even many industrial uses. Finally, the use of oxygen to decompose the waste reduces the life-support capacity of the water, with a consequent decline in the number and variety of fish. As the human population grows, the problem of waste disposal will become even more acute.

Current farming practices, such as extensive use of nitrate and phosphate fertilizers, also seriously impair water quality. Rain and irrigation cause the runoff of large quantities of these materials into rivers and lakes. The fertilizers work in water much as they do on land, producing algae "blooms"—huge masses of algae that grow very quickly and then die. As with the decomposition of sewage, the decay of these blooms consumes oxygen, thereby killing fish and other animals that have high oxygen requirements. As the algae decay, they settle at the bottom of the water, along with various compounds of nitrogen and phosphorus. At one time, the bottom of Lake Erie, one of the Great Lakes, was covered by a layer of muck from 20 to 125 feet thick. Only intensive efforts by environmentalists to stop pollutants from being discharged into the lake and adjoining waterways saved Lake Erie from destruction.

Long-lasting pesticides and radioactive substances are especially dangerous because they accumulate in the tissues of animals that eat food contaminated with them. One reason this accumulation poses such a serious problem is the process known as biological magnification, whereby the concentration of a given substance increases as it ascends the food chain. This process can be an especially serious danger in the vicinity of nuclear plants, where safe levels of radioactivity in the surrounding waters may still produce high levels of radioactivity in plankton. Those levels, in turn, can multiply to produce extremely high levels of radioactive contamination in birds and fish that eat these microorganisms.

Another form of water pollution is thermal pollution. The effluents of many factories and generating plants—especially nuclear power plants—are warmer than the rivers and lakes into which they flow, and when discharged in quantity, they may raise the water temperature by as much as 10°F to 30°F. Such thermal pollution can be ecologically devastating. Because most aquatic animals are cold-blooded, they are at the mercy of the surrounding water temperature. If the temperature rises beyond an organism's capacity for metabolic adjustment, the animal will die. Because larvae and young animals are far more susceptible than mature organisms to slight temperature variations and because increases in temperature also interfere with the spawning and migratory patterns of many organisms, thermal pollution may exterminate some aquatic populations through reproductive failure.

An important form of water pollution, and one that seems to get the most media attention, is that from oil spills. The Exxon oil spill, which released 11 million gallons of oil in pristine Prince William Sound in Alaska, caught media attention as one of the largest American oil spills to date. However, since that time, there have been dozens of major oil spills in the United States, ranging in size from a few hundred gallons to hundreds of millions. The largest was the Deepwater Horizon oil rig explosion, introduced earlier, which in 2010 killed 11 people and dumped more than 200 million gallons of crude into the Gulf of Mexico. However, America does not win the "prize" with respect to the largest oil spills. That award goes to Kuwait for oil spills related to the Gulf War in 1991 (240–336 million gallons) (CNN Library, February 28, 2018).

One issue that is beginning to receive worldwide attention is the amount of plastics that are polluting our oceans, rivers, and streams. A world without plastic seems almost unthinkable today. Mass production of plastics, which began just six decades ago, has accelerated so rapidly that it has created 8.3 billion metric tons—most of it in disposable products that end up as trash (Parker, 2017). Plastic takes more than 400 years to degrade, so most of it still exists in some form. But where does all this plastic go? Of the 8.3 billion metric tons of plastic, only 9 percent has been recycled and 12 percent incinerated. The large majority—79 percent—is accumulating in landfills or is thrown away in the natural environment as litter (Geyer, Jambeck, and Law, 2017). The bottom line is that much of the plastic makes its way to our waterways. In addition to the visual blight, fish, marine mammals, and birds eat it (it may smell like food) or get tangled in it. According to the National Oceanographic and Atmospheric Administration, plastic debris kills an estimated 100,000 marine mammals annually, as well as millions of birds and fishes (Le Guern, 2018).

Most Americans express some concern over water pollution, particularly the pollution of drinking water, as shown in Figure 14–5. Concern seems to be on an upward trajectory since 2011, as the media highlighted the contaminated drinking water in places like Flint, Michigan, which contained high levels of lead; the drought in Cape Town, South Africa, and the fear of literally running out of water; and the growing crisis of plastics and other garbage in the oceans.

What Do You Think?

Identify at least five ways that you could eliminate the use of plastic in your own life.

Figure 14–5 Americans' Concerns About Water Pollution, 1999–2017

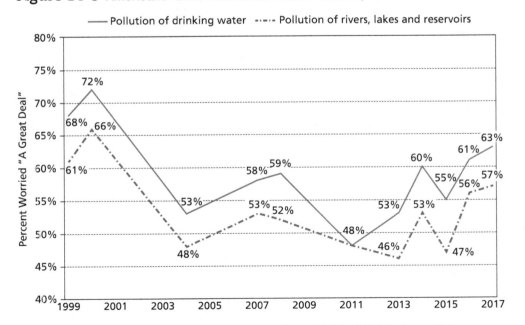

SOURCE: McCarthy, J. "In U.S., Water Pollution Worries Highest Since 2001," Social & Policy Issues, Gallup (March 31, 2017).

Solid-Waste Disposal

14.6 **Explain the hazards of solid waste disposal and why it is an issue of social justice.**

Garbage, too, is a serious environmental problem. Each year Earth's people generate about 1.3 billion tons of waste. That's expected to soar to 4 billion tons by 2100 (Simmons, 2016). The more urbanized and industrialized a country becomes, the more trash it produces. The United States, China, Brazil, Japan, and Germany are the leading trash generators, but the amount of waste will likely increase substantially in lower-income African and Asian cities because of population growth, urbanization, and rising consumption.

Americans do not really "consume" most products, despite our reputation as a consumer society. It is more accurate to say that we buy things, use them, and then throw them away. Americans produce about 259 million tons of municipal solid waste—more commonly known as trash or garbage—to dispose of each year (Environmental Protection Agency, 2016). This amount of solid waste represents a nearly threefold increase since 1960, as illustrated in Figure 14–6. This garbage includes food, paper, glass, plastic, wood, abandoned cars, yard clippings, cans, metals, paints, dead animals, and a host of other things. However, because our population has increased since 1960, it stands to reason that the amount of our garbage would, too. Therefore, another useful way to measure solid-waste output is by looking at how much each individual produces. Here we see better news. The amount of waste generated per capita (per person) has been slowly declining since 2000.

There is another piece of good news. The amount of this waste that gets recycled is on the increase, as shown in Figure 14–7. In 2014, about 89 million tons of the solid waste were recycled (out of the 259 million tons produced). The percentage of the population that recycles is also increasing, although it still represents only about a third of households (35 percent).

When someone throws something away, he or she rarely thinks of where it goes next. But trash does not just disappear. Most often, it goes into a landfill, which is a discrete area of land or excavation that receives household waste.

Figure 14–6 Number of Tons of Total Municipal Solid Waste (MSW) Generated and the Amount of Waste Per Person (Per Capita), 1960–2014

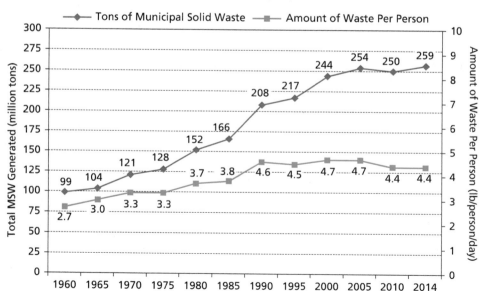

SOURCE: Data from Environmental Protection Agency. 2016b. "Advancing Sustainable Materials Management: 2014 Fact Sheet." November. Retrieved 12 May 2018.

Figure 14–7 Number of Tons of Municipal Solid Waste (MSW) Recycled and Percentage of Households That Recycle, 1960–2014

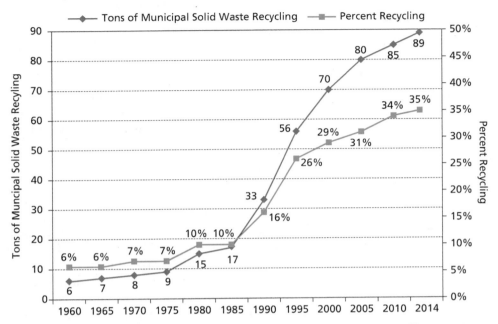

SOURCE: Data from Environmental Protection Agency. 2016b. "Advancing Sustainable Materials Management: 2014 Fact Sheet." November. Retrieved 12 May 2018.

In the last few decades, the waste disposal problem has taken on new urgency as many landfill sites have filled up and fears of groundwater contamination caused many communities to forbid the opening of new sites on their land. Even as early as 1987, a barge filled with garbage from Long Island became a notorious illustration of the seriousness of the problem as it spent several weeks searching the East Coast for a site that would accept its load of waste. In 2015, there were over 2,400 active landfills in the United States, and another 650 under construction or in the planning stage (Environmental Protection Agency, 2015). Landfills are monitored by the EPA and have been redesigned in recent years to reduce the health hazards associated with them, but nonetheless, no one wants to live near a landfill.

The large-scale introduction of plastics and other synthetics has produced a new waste disposal problem: Whereas organic substances are eventually decomposed through bacterial action, plastics remain in their original state when they are buried or dumped. If they are burned, they become air pollutants in the form of hydrocarbons and nitrogen oxides. The EPA estimates that plastics now make up nearly 13 percent of our solid waste (Environmental Protection Agency, 2014).

In addition to plastics, another new disposal problem has to do with metals, which now represent 9 percent of solid waste. Every piece of electronic waste, from fluorescent lights to computer parts, contains some kind of metal, possibly lead. For example, lead is found in most batteries and in the tubes used in television screens and computer monitors. When these items are dumped into landfills, their lead can be absorbed into the

This aerial view is of a former landfill in West Covina, California. The former landfill site now houses a sports complex, commercial space, and a nature preserve. However, according to the EPA, the landfill accepted hazardous wastes from 1972 to 1984. A multimillion dollar lawsuit filed by nearby residents was settled in 1986.

soil and groundwater. Exposure to high levels of lead is a serious health hazard. It can lead to cancers, brain disorders, and death.

The EPA encourages all people to reduce the amount of waste needing to be disposed of. They suggest three broad measures:

What Do You Think?

Design a campaign to increase recycling in your community. Be sure to consider what neighborhood or area you want to focus on and target your campaign specifically to this area. What are some challenges you will face? How will you try to overcome them?

- *Source reduction.* Choose products that are designed and packaged to reduce the amount of waste that will be thrown away.
- *Recycle.* Separate materials that can be recycled, such as paper, glass, plastic, and metals, from the trash. These materials can be used to make new products.
- *Compost organic wastes.* Compost food scraps and yard trimmings and use the result as a natural fertilizer. In a landfill environment, these materials emit large doses of methane, a contributor to climate change.

14.6.1 Toxic Wastes

Toxic wastes or residues from the by-products of manufacturing, construction, laboratories, hospitals, and other systems, including the production of plastics, pesticides, and other products, are a particularly serious problem. These residues have typically been buried in ditches or pits, but they can spread easily into the land and water resources and cause many serious health problems. The waste can harm humans, animals, and plants if they encounter these toxins buried in the ground, in stream runoff, in groundwater that supplies drinking water, or in floodwaters, as happened after Hurricane Katrina. Some toxins, such as mercury, persist in the environment and accumulate. Humans or animals often absorb these toxins when they eat fish.

The famous case of Love Canal, near Niagara Falls, brought toxic waste hazards to national attention (Kleiman, 2018). From 1942 to 1953, the Hooker Chemical Company began using the partially dug canal as a chemical waste dump. By the end of this period, around 21,000 tons of toxic chemicals were dumped into the canal, including at least twelve that are known carcinogens. Hooker capped the 16-acre hazardous waste landfill in clay and sold the land to the Niagara Falls School Board, attempting to absolve itself of any future liability by including a warning in the property deed (Kleiman, 2018).

The crisis arose when the toxic residues that had been dumped into the unfinished canal seeped into the surrounding area and contaminated both the soil and the water, causing cancers, leukemia, birth defects, and other health issues for residents. In 1978, Love Canal was declared an environmental disaster area, and more than 200 families were evacuated from the neighborhood. In early 1985, after more than six years of litigation, 1,300 former residents were awarded payments totaling $20 million in compensation for health problems suffered because of the contamination of their neighborhood by toxic wastes.

The Love Canal saga was a "warning signal" for other communities that could experience the same types of exposures and similar effects on children's health (Clapp, 2009). Because of the evacuation at Love Canal, and other such instances in contaminated communities around the United States, the Senate Environment and Public Works Committee and other legislative committees held hearings that led to the passage of the Superfund legislation in 1980. The EPA's Superfund program is responsible for cleaning up some of the nation's most contaminated land and responding to environmental emergencies, oil spills, and natural disasters. The EPA and state environmental departments now oversee the rules that regulate hazardous waste, requiring extra precautions and disposal at a special facility rather than the landfill. Some communities have collection day events, where people are encouraged to bring their paint, motor oil, batteries, or other hazardous materials.

In 1991, 13 years after the discovery of the contamination and the beginning of cleanup efforts, some houses in the Love Canal area were declared habitable again.

However, it wasn't until 2004 that the EPA announced that the area was clean enough to be taken off the Superfund list.

In another high-profile case, the worst industrial disaster on record, which occurred in Bhopal, India, shows just how dangerous toxic chemicals can be. An accident at the Union Carbide pesticide plant in Bhopal, India, released at least 30 to 40 tons of a highly toxic gas into the air. The pesticide plant was surrounded by poor villages and towns, leading to more than 600,000 people being exposed to the deadly gas cloud. The gases stayed low to the ground, causing victims' throats and eyes to burn, inducing nausea, abdominal pain, respiratory distress, and many deaths. Estimates of the death toll vary from as few as 3,800 to as many as 16,000, but government figures now refer to an estimate of 15,000 killed over the years

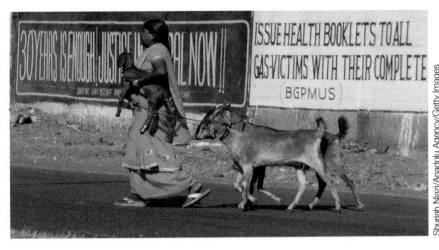

An Indian woman passes by the Union Carbide plant in Bhopal, India. On a night in December 1984, deadly gas leaked from the plant, instantly killing at least 3,800 people and thousands more over subsequent months. Tens of thousands of people were injured. Thirty-five years after one of the world's worst industrial disasters, the Union Carbide plant still stands.

(Broughton, 2005; Taylor, 2014). Toxic material remains and, 30 years later, many of those who were exposed continue to suffer long-term effects of the gas and have given birth to physically and mentally disabled children.

The Bhopal disaster, as it is often referred to, drew international attention to the need for improved safety at chemical facilities. Yet no U.S. federal law adopted since the tragedy requires companies to fully assess and substantiate whether the toxic chemicals they use or store are truly necessary—or whether safer alternatives could be used instead.

This lax oversight has led to many more catastrophic chemical hazards in communities. In the United States, there are toxic chemical releases every week, most of which do not hit the news. However, in 2012, an explosion at the Chevron refinery in Richmond, California, sent 15,000 people to hospitals seeking treatment. In 2013, a fertilizer storage facility explosion in West, Texas, killed 15 people and leveled an entire neighborhood. In a typical year, the U.S. Chemical Safety Board screens more than 250 high-consequence chemical incidents involving death, injury, evacuation, or serious environmental or property damage, and these are only the very worst incidents (Orum et al., 2014).

14.6.2 Radioactive Wastes

The United States currently produces about 20 percent of its electricity in nuclear power plants (U.S. Energy Information Administration, 2018). These plants pose a problem because the radioactive fuel in the reactor's core must be replaced periodically. The spent fuel must be deposited somewhere under extremely well-protected conditions because it is highly dangerous and can contaminate surrounding water and lands. In the last two decades, as tons of nuclear waste have accumulated in temporary storage sites, the U.S. government has spent several billions of dollars on efforts to create a system for permanent storage. The United States has about 65,000 metric tons of spent nuclear fuel and other nuclear wastes (Nuclear Energy Institute, 2015).

Radioactive wastes must be stored safely for up to 1,000 years before they become harmless. During that time, any alteration in the seismological conditions of the burial site could disturb the radioactive material and contaminate the area. A large facility under Yucca Mountain in Nevada is ready, but disputes about its safety (e.g., in an earthquake), transportation of radioactive wastes, and protests by environmentalists caused President Obama to eliminate federal funding for the site. Most people who think about the problem want the wastes to be disposed of properly, but few are willing to have trucks or trains carry these hazardous materials through their communities.

This is because there have been nuclear accidents, and the consequences can be severe. In 2011, when an earthquake damaged significant quantities of radioactive waste material stored at a Japanese nuclear plant, people around the world were reminded of the growing danger posed by these wastes in a world hungry for energy. The incident was also a reminder of how much radioactive material is stored at locations throughout the world.

14.6.3 Environmental Racism/Environmental Justice

environmental racism

The act of disproportionally placing landfills and toxic waste dumpsites near low-income and minority neighborhoods.

environmental justice

Demanding that all people be treated equally with respect to the environment.

Landfills and toxic waste dumpsites are disproportionally located near low-income and minority neighborhoods on the outskirts of metropolitan regions or in rural areas (Bolin and Kurtz, 2018; Grineski et al., 2017; Mohai and Saha, 2015). Many local activists and residents of these neighborhoods label such dumping **environmental racism**. Demanding that all people be treated equally with respect to the environment is called **environmental justice**. This issue is increasingly recognized as a serious social problem. Low-income people—especially blacks and Hispanics who are poor—have far higher levels of illnesses because of contamination of their water, land, and air by toxic chemicals from these dump sites.

One study examined the demographic profile of people living near 3,433 facilities for several common industries that store or use highly hazardous chemicals. There are 134 million people who live within range of a worst-case chemical release. The researchers especially want to know about the 3.8 million people who live at the "fenceline" closest to the chemical plants because these people would face the highest concentrations of poisons and would have the least time to react in a catastrophe. They found that minorities and poor people are greatly overrepresented among this vulnerable group who live closest to the chemical plants (Orum et al., 2014):

- Residents of the fenceline zone have incomes that are 22 percent below the national average.
- The poverty rate for those at the fenceline zone is 50 percent higher than the national average.
- The percentage of blacks at the fenceline zone is 75 percent higher than the percentage of blacks in the United States as a whole.
- The percentage of Hispanics at the fenceline zone is 60 percent higher than for the percentage of Hispanics in the United States as a whole.
- The percentage of adults at the fenceline zone who have less than a high school education is 46 percent higher than the national average, while the percentage of adults with a college diploma is 27 percent lower.[10]

This study reveals that environmental racism indeed exists, and activists suggest that greater justice is warranted.

Environmental justice is also becoming an increasing concern at the global level (Anand, 2017; Klinsky et al., 2017). For example, while climate change will affect everyone, the effects will be felt most strongly in poor nations in Africa. Meanwhile, it is rich nations that are responsible for most of the greenhouse gases that are causing climate change.

---

[10]Orum, P., et al. (2014) "Who's in Danger? Race, Poverty, and Chemical Disasters. A Demographic Analysis of Chemical Disaster Vulnerability Zones." Environmental Justice and Health Alliance for Chemical Policy Reform.

The United States and the World Environment

14.7   Identify the role of the United States in the world's environment.

Americans are among the wealthiest, the most educated, and the most polluting of Earth's peoples. Environmental scientists often argue that Americans bear a large share of the responsibility for the problem, and therefore should lead the way in developing solutions to tame the environmental crisis.

In this chapter we have discussed issues related to climate change, air and water pollution, and solid waste disposal. However, there is another critically important way in which the United States contributes to the world's environmental problems—and could offer solutions—that we have not yet touched upon. It has to do with the *food* we eat. In stark contrast to the hunger that prevails in many poor LDCs, the increased affluence of the United States has made possible a steady increase in per capita consumption of meat and other foods that put the world's environment in peril.

The dominant position of the United States can be seen not only in how much we eat but also in *what* we eat. Americans consume a much larger proportion of meat than do other countries. This is problematic for two reasons. First, vast quantities of grain—one-third of total world production—are fed to livestock in the United States and other developed countries to produce meat. This grain could be used to nourish hungry people elsewhere in the world (Lappé, 1971). It is true that the United States exports large amounts of grain to all parts of the world. Some of these exports are part of international aid programs that help alleviate the problem of hunger in poorer nations; in fact, some of the world's least developed nations depend heavily on this aid. Still, the developed nations, particularly the United States, consume a disproportionate share of the world's food resources, and feeding large quantities of grain to livestock is not a very efficient way of producing food. Moreover, cattle release methane gas as a part of their digestion (this is a polite way of saying cattle fart a lot). Unfortunately, methane is a big contributor to the greenhouse effect, helping to trap heat within Earth's atmosphere and contributing to climate change.

The significance of these facts is twofold. First, the United States consumes a disproportionate share of total food and energy resources, leaving comparatively little for most of the world's population. This imbalance partially explains the desperate plight of people in the least developed nations. The other major effect of the dominant position of the United States is that our food production and consumption contribute to environmental problems both at home and abroad. It turns out that producing half a pound of hamburger for someone's lunch patty of meat the size of two decks of cards releases as much greenhouse gas into the atmosphere as driving a 3,000-pound car nearly 10 miles.

Given these realities, Americans can, and are, changing what they eat. Many people are choosing vegetarian diets (avoiding all meats, and often fish as well), or vegan diets (plant-based). At least 5 percent of Americans are vegetarians, and half of vegetarians are between the ages of 18 and 35 (Reinhart, 2018). About 3 percent of Americans consider themselves vegan.

Americans have a diet that is heavy on meat. However, the grain that is used to feed animals could be used to feed humans throughout the world. Fewer cattle also mean less methane gas, a significant contributor to greenhouse gases that contribute to climate change.

Joerg Boethling/Alamy Stock Photo

Therefore, over time we are likely to see vegetarianism and a vegan diet gain in popularity. There are also many people who do not want to go "all the way," but have chosen to reduce their consumption of beef and pork (although the consumption of chicken has increased overall) (Waite, 2018). These changes can make a real difference in the environment.

Social Policy

14.8 **Critique social policy on climate change.**

As populations increase in size and affluence, the complexity of social organization, the imbalances in energy and food distribution, the depletion of resources, and the difficulty of correcting these problems also increase.

14.8.1 Is It Too Late?

Some people worry that it is too late; they fear that climate change cannot reverse itself. For more on this issue, read the feature box, *A Global View: "Is It Too Late to Prevent Climate Change?"* The consensus among Earth's scientists is that climate change poses

A Global View

Is It Too Late to Prevent Climate Change?

Panther Media GmbH/Alamy Stock Photo

Humans have caused major climate changes that have already occurred, and we have set in motion still more changes. Even if we completely stopped emitting greenhouse gases today, climate change would continue to happen for at least several more decades, if not centuries. The lag occurs because it takes time for the planet and the oceans to respond and because carbon dioxide—the predominant heat-trapping gas—lingers in the atmosphere for hundreds of years. In other words, there is a time lag between what improvements we might make and when we see the results.

In the absence of major action to reduce emissions, global temperature is on track to rise by an average of 6°C (10.8°F) in this century, according to the latest estimates. Some scientists argue that a "global disaster" is already unfolding at the poles of the planet; the Arctic, for example,

could be ice-free in the summer soon. Some express concern that Earth has passed one or more "tipping points"—abrupt, irreversible changes that tip our climate into a new state.

But it may not be too late to avoid or limit some of the worst effects of climate change. Responding to climate change will involve a two-tier approach: (1) "mitigation"—reducing the flow of greenhouse gases into the atmosphere; and (2) "adaptation"—learning to live with, and adapt to, the climate change that has already been set in motion.

The key question is: What will our emissions of carbon dioxide and other pollutants be in the years to come? Recycling and driving more fuel-efficient cars are examples of important behavioral changes that will help, but they will not be enough. Because climate change is a truly global, complex problem with economic, social, political, and moral ramifications, the solution will require both a globally coordinated response (such as strict international policies and agreements between countries and a push to cleaner forms of energy) and local efforts on the city and regional levels (for example, public transport upgrades, energy efficiency improvements, and sustainable city planning). It is up to people themselves as to what happens next.

Source: Based on NASA Global Climate Change and Global Warming: Vital Signs of the Planet website. 2015. http://climate.nasa.gov/vital-signs/.

Critical Thinking

Why has national and global action toward climate change been so slow? How might the reasons for this slow reaction differ across regions of the world?

a genuine threat and needs to be addressed immediately through increased efforts to curb emissions of greenhouse gases. They argue that further study of the situation is always needed, but that it can also represent an effort to delay the responsibility to do anything about the crisis. Climate change is not a vague concern in the far-off future; it is happening right now. Reversing the current effects quickly may be impossible because greenhouse gases stay in the atmosphere for many decades. However, with sufficient and immediate action, the worst aspects of climate change could be avoided or at least minimized.

If the United States is to maintain its position as a world leader, it must take the lead in developing a way to control environmental problems, starting at home. Along with other developed nations, it can use its resources to help control the growth of the world's population and encourage sustainable farming and energy practices. Through its own aid and through cooperation with agencies of the United Nations and the World Bank, the United States can also help to ensure clean water, and help poorer nations develop more adequate and sustainable water supplies. The United States has the capabilities to develop clean energy through wind and solar; nonetheless, it has been slow to react.

However, one interesting example of leadership on the environment can be found in California where, beginning in 2020, all new housing construction must be equipped with solar panels. Critics say that this will increase the cost of new homes by $8,000 to $12,000 in a market that is already one of the least affordable in the nation. However, state officials and environmental supporters say the extra cost to home buyers will be more than made up in lower energy bills. Even the construction industry supports the new legislation and sees solar capability as a selling point for their homes (Penn, 2018). Additionally, California state law requires that 50 percent of its electricity come from noncarbon-producing sources, and solar energy is among the easiest ways to achieve this.

Despite these examples, other nations have a dimming view of environmental leadership in the United States. A survey of 37 countries found that the favorability rating of the United States has declined between 2015 and 2017 in all countries except one: Russia (Wike et al., June 26, 2017). This could be due to a variety of reasons, of course, but the same survey found that 71 percent of respondents in these 37 countries disapprove of the United States withdrawing from international climate change agreements. Only 19 percent approved, with the remainder not having an opinion on the matter. Other countries are far more concerned about environmental issues than the United States, especially Canada, Latin America, Africa, and countries in Western Europe, (Stokes, Wike, and Carle, November 5, 2015). The United States has not emerged as a world leader on fighting climate change and has, in fact, been accused of dragging its feet.

Most experts agree that without U.S. leadership global efforts to reduce emissions will be ineffective. One way to demonstrate leadership is to create markets for emission credits. The most likely policy to achieve lower emissions is what is known as a system of **cap and trade**, a mix of environmentalism with free market principles.

Cap and trade has been referred to "as the most environmentally and economically sensible approach to controlling greenhouse gas emissions" (Environmental Defense Fund, 2018).[11] Companies that pollute could acquire credits from the agency in charge of regulating that particular industry by reducing their emissions below the levels set by the agency. They could then sell the credits to other companies whose emissions exceed regulatory maximums.

This approach rewards industries that clean up their act while allowing those that do not reduce emissions to continue to operate without society, as a whole, exceeding

cap and trade

A program that would create markets for emission credits, representing a mix of environmentalism with free market principles.

---

[11]"How Cap and Trade Works," (2018) Environmental Defense Fund.

global limits on greenhouse gases. In other words, the "cap" sets a limit on emissions, which is lowered over time to reduce the amount of pollutants released into the atmosphere. Meanwhile, the "trade" creates a market for carbon allowances, helping companies innovate to meet, or come in under, their allocated limit. It is an environmental policy tool that can deliver results with a mandatory cap on emissions while providing sources flexibility in how they comply.

Successful cap-and-trade programs can reward innovation, efficiency, and early action and provide strict environmental accountability without inhibiting economic growth. A cap-and-trade approach worked extremely well to reduce chlorofluorocarbons in aerosol sprays that destroy the ozone layer in the atmosphere and for reducing sulfur dioxide emissions that cause acid rain. But energy lobbyists and their allies, many of whom are oil producers, have campaigned effectively to prevent anything but relatively weak voluntary enforcement.

Although a cap-and-trade approach is generally thought to be a more conservative measure to control greenhouse emissions and had the support of former Republican President George W. Bush and former Republican presidential candidate and Senator John McCain, Republicans in Congress have now largely eschewed it (Skocpol, 2013). Most Republicans in the House and Senate have moved away from environmental protections more generally, and some deny the existence of human-generated climate change altogether. When a cap-and-trade bill came before a vote in the U.S. House of Representatives in 2009, Republican opponents demonized the pending legislation as "cap and tax" and proclaimed that, if the bill passed, families would have to spend up to $3,100 more per year for gas and electricity. Opponents also claimed it would be bad for business and discourage job creation. As cap-and-trade supporters in the Senate were making final efforts to assemble votes, American public support also waned. Most people were scared by the claims of it being a tax because few understood the issues. The bill was narrowly passed in the House (although only eight Republicans voted for it); however, it failed in the Senate.

14.8.2 Future Prospects

How do people feel about cap and trade several years later? A meta-analysis, which summarized the results of 25 different surveys of American public opinion on how to best control greenhouse gases, found that about half of people support a cap-and-trade approach (Ansolabehere and Konisky, 2014). However, as you can see in Table 14–5, even more people favor having the EPA regulate greenhouse gases (with no specific details provided), and far fewer people approve of a tax. In other words, people want the EPA to regulate the environment in some vague way, but they are not willing to do the things they would need to do at a personal consumption level, such as pay a higher gas price or pay a higher electricity price.

California began its own cap-and-trade program in 2013 to lower its greenhouse gas emissions. California's program is the fourth largest in the world and provides critical experience in creating and managing a cap-and-trade system that the rest of the United States could follow, if it had the will. California's emissions trading system is expected to reduce greenhouse gas emissions from regulated entities by more than

Table 14–5 How to Best Control Greenhouse Gases

Type of Method	
Favor EPA Regulation	75–80%
Favor Cap and Trade	44–55%
Favor a Carbon Tax	25–44%

SOURCE: Data from Ansolabehere S. & Konisky D. M. (2014) *Cheap and Clean: How Americans Think about Energy in the Age of Global Warming.* Cambridge, MA: MIT Press.

16 percent between 2013 and 2020, and by an additional 40 percent by 2030 (Center for Climate and Energy Solutions, 2018). These regulated entities include large electric power plants, large industrial plants, and fuel distributors (e.g., natural gas and petroleum). Approximately 450 businesses that are responsible for 85 percent of California's total greenhouse gas emissions must comply. One particularly innovative feature to note is that California has linked its program with similar programs in the Canadian provinces of Ontario and Quebec—businesses in one jurisdiction can use emission allowances (or offsets) issued by one of the others for compliance. This effectively broadens the number of businesses under the cap.

What Do You Think?

List all the ways that individuals can reduce their contributions to global warming. Now, from this list, which changes would you personally be willing to make? Which ones would you not make, and why?

Going Beyond Left and Right

This chapter explored a wide range of serious environmental problems that threaten Earth's environment. These environmental problems have become politicized. What is the best way to tackle environmental problems: do we need more research, regulation, and mandates? People on the ideological right and left often have different opinions on vexing questions like these. Those on the right tend to focus on the free market and suggest that government mandates will stagnate our economy. People on the left often say that environmental restoration will add new, less damaging jobs to the economy. In some parts of the country (and the world), these debates are extremely rancorous.

An integrative way to think about environmental problems may be that, no matter what our politics are, humans are the problem and humans can be the solution. Most people who live in affluent nations consume large quantities of gasoline and other consumer goods, and those in LDCs want to do the same. Unless those who live in developed nations begin to understand the global consequences of their consumption, it is argued, the level of stress on the environment will never be sufficiently reduced. This argument is based on facts. It should not really be a right or left debate.

Summary

14.1 Discuss the link between technology and the environment.

Sociologists are concerned with the ways in which social institutions adapt to changing technology or, conversely, how technology adapts to changing social institutions. The best-known statement of these relationships is technological and scientific change and rapid population growth are causing widespread pollution and depletion of the natural environment. Natural cycles of purification can absorb only a limited amount of certain artificial substances before ecological damage is done.

14.2 Summarize different types of stressors on the environment.

Environmental stress is the interaction and conflict of three systems: the natural environment, the technological system, and the social system. There are many different environmental stressors in the world today. This chapter discusses climate change, air and water pollution, and solid waste and its disposal.

14.3 Assess the significance of climate change and its consequences.

The consensus among Earth's scientists is that climate change poses a genuine threat and needs to be addressed immediately through increased efforts to curb emissions of greenhouse gases. Consequences for the United States include accelerated sea level rise and increased coastal flooding; more frequent and intense heat waves; longer and more damaging wildfire seasons; heavier precipitation and flooding; more severe droughts in some areas; disruption to food supplies; and plant and animal range shifts. Results in other parts of the world will be even more serious.

14.4 Identify the health and economic effects of air pollution.

Nearly one half of all Americans—an estimated 150 million—live in areas that do not meet federal air quality standards. Cars and heavy-duty trucks are the main sources of this pollution, which includes ozone, particulate matter, and other smog-forming emissions. The health effects of air pollution can range from headaches, coughs, and dizziness to asthma, cancer, birth defects, nervous system damage, and death. Air pollution reduces worker productivity, causes premature death, leads to accelerated deterioration of property, increases maintenance and cleaning costs, and blights crops, which reduces crop yields.

14.5 Describe the problems related to water pollution.

Rivers, lakes, and oceans can cleanse themselves if not overburdened, but we have been discharging wastes, directly or indirectly, into our waterways in amounts that prohibit natural purification. For example, current farming practices, such as extensive use of nitrate and phosphate fertilizers, impair water quality, as do long-lasting oil spills, pesticides, and radioactive substances. Garbage, especially plastics, also litters our water and poses environmental and health threats.

14.6 Explain the hazards of solid waste disposal and why it is an issue of social justice.

Each year Earth's people generate about 1.3 billion tons of waste. That's expected to soar to 4 billion tons by 2100. Americans produce the most waste: by buying things, using them, and then throwing them away. Most of this waste ends up in landfills, but in the last few decades, the waste disposal problem has taken on new urgency as many landfill sites have filled up and fears of groundwater contamination caused many communities to forbid the opening of new sites on their land. Toxic and radioactive wastes are substantially problematic because of the health dangers they pose. Landfills and toxic waste dumpsites are disproportionally located near low-income and minority neighborhoods on the outskirts of metropolitan regions or in rural areas.

14.7 Identify the role of the United States in the world's environment.

Americans are among the wealthiest, the most educated, and the most polluting of Earth's peoples, and therefore environmental scientists often argue that Americans should not only bear a large share of the responsibility for the problem but should also lead the way in developing solutions. One issue has to do with the food Americans eat, and the harm it causes the world.

14.8 Critique social policy on climate change.

Some people fear that it may be too late to effectively deal with climate change. Most experts agree that Earth is already warming, but the worst effects can be eliminated or reduced with swift action. However, without U.S. leadership, global efforts to reduce emissions will be ineffective. One way to demonstrate leadership is to create markets for emission credits, known as a system of cap and trade, which is a mix of environmentalism with free market principles.

Chapter 15
War and Global Insecurity

John Tlumacki/The Boston Globe/Getty Images

Learning Objectives

15.1 Discuss the direct and indirect effects of war.

15.2 Identify various forms of weapons of mass destruction.

15.3 Review modern-day terrorism in the United States and around the world.

15.4 Explain terrorism's impact on society.

15.5 Compare and contrast sociological theories on war and terrorism.

15.6 Describe policy approaches to dealing with terrorism.

I am a long-distance runner. I started before my children were born, then took a break from it when they were little, but found that I was calmer and less stressed out when I went for long runs. In other words, I was a better mother when I ran. So, my husband James bought me some excellent running shoes for my birthday and took care of the kids when I was off on my own running for a couple of hours. I love the breeze, the sweat, and the endorphins! I ran a couple of local marathons, and then I had a crazy idea about trying to qualify for the Boston Marathon. I wasn't fast enough yet, and it would take some work, but I felt that it was within reach. So, I set up a training program, and my two-hour runs and weekend races became more frequent. After a couple of years of this program, I got a qualifying score! Boston, here I come. I saved money for months so I could afford airfare for James and me, and my sister offered to take the kids for the weekend. The day before the race, I drank lots of water, went for a very short run just to keep the legs moving a bit, and ate all the right foods. I even got a decent night's sleep; I was so nervous I think I just crashed! The day of the race, I woke up early and refreshed. "I am ready for this," I told myself. James told me how proud he was of me.

The race itself is almost a blur as I try to remember it. I paced myself well, but also ran hard. But as I was on the last leg of the run, I heard an incredibly loud, ear-splitting noise. And then another one. Oh my God, what was it, I wondered? I saw smoke up ahead, and there seemed to be a lot of commotion and screaming, but I was too far away to see exactly what was going on. I kept running toward the finish line, but some people were coming toward me shouting at me to hide, to stop, and they were yelling other words that I couldn't understand. Clearly, they were fleeing what was up ahead. Within seconds, large groups of people were running away from the race course, crying in sheer terror. I couldn't make out what they were saying, but it was obvious that something horrible had just happened. I joined them and we ran off the course, away from the finish line. I huddled with a group of people under some bleachers; we were all shaking in fright. It was minutes later that I learned that bombs had just exploded.

A discussion of war and terrorism might seem like a "heavy" way to end a book. Yet, these issues offer an essential opportunity to reexamine the premise of the sociological imagination introduced in Chapter 1. The results of war and terrorism are deeply felt on a personal level. Lives are lost, people are injured, property is destroyed, and immense fear can spread throughout the land.

Yet, war is hardly just a personal issue. C. Wright Mills stressed the importance of understanding the relationship between individuals and the society in which they live (Mills, 1959). The sociological imagination reveals that problems associated with war and terrorism represent far more than personal troubles experienced by a few isolated people. They are issues that affect large numbers of people and originate in society's institutional arrangements.

Using war and terrorism as a case study, this chapter revisits the premise of the sociological imagination and underlines the four themes of the book. The tragic topics of war and terrorism challenge you not only to explicitly see the connections between personal lived experience and broader social problems, but also to understand the importance of these four themes: (Theme 1) using an empirical approach; (Theme 2) linking individual experiences with social structure; (Theme 3) recognizing that social inequality contributes to social problems; and (Theme 4) understanding social problems require a comparative perspective.

War and Its Effects

15.1 **Discuss the direct and indirect effects of war.**

The twenty-first century began on a note of great hope for world peace. The fall of the Soviet Empire and the destruction of the Berlin Wall ended the long period of superpower conflict known as the Cold War. But the spread of advanced weapons around the globe; the rise in racial, ethnic, and religious conflict; and the worsening of environmental problems and limitations of natural resources have increased the threat of wars of all kinds in many parts of the world.

For those who experience its tragic devastation, war is among the most serious social problems one can imagine. The sections that follow discuss both its direct and indirect effects.

15.1.1 Direct Effects of War

Over the centuries, warfare has taken many millions of lives and caused untold suffering. According to one early estimate (Sorokin, 1937), between 1100 and 1925 about 35 million soldiers were killed in some 862 wars in Europe. However, by any standard, the twentieth century was the deadliest in human history. During World War I, eight million soldiers and another one million civilians died. The casualties of World War II were even higher: almost 17 million soldiers and 35 million civilians were killed. In the Soviet Union alone, the generation of men old enough to fight in World War II was nearly decimated. Later, the Korean War, the Vietnam War, the Gulf War (in Kuwait), the war in Iraq, the war in Afghanistan, and so on, caused the death toll to continue to rise. As of July 19, 2016, deaths of U.S. personnel serving in Iraq (since 2003) and in Afghanistan (since 2001) totaled 4,497 and 2,382, respectively (Antiwar.org, 2018). As of April, 2018, those wounded in action in Iraq and Afghanistan totaled 31,957 and 20,095, respectively (Smith, 2018). And, these numbers exclude deaths to noncombatants, such as local citizens, journalists, and military contractors, or "nonhostile" injuries and deaths, such as suicides, vehicle crashes, heat stroke, or respiratory problems.

PHYSICAL INJURIES   Long after peace is declared, many soldiers bear the scars of their battlefield experiences. Using an empirical approach (Theme 1) allows us to fully understand the extent of these physical injuries. For every U.S. soldier who died in battle in World Wars I and II, almost two people were injured. Today in the Middle East, seven men and women are injured for every person killed. About 50,000 people have been injured in recent military conflicts (Wounded Warrior Project, 2018).

Many of the wounded have required medical care for months or years, and many have been so badly injured that they have been unable to hold a job or return to a normal way of life. Almost 4 million veterans are receiving compensation from the U.S. government for war-related disabilities. Of these, over one million have been evaluated as 70 to 100 percent disabled (U.S. Department of Veterans Affairs, 2014). When so many individuals require government assistance for the same reason—war-related injuries—you can see the link between personal experience and social structure (Theme 2).

A wounded U.S. Marine Corps veteran competes in a golf tournament at the St. George's Golf and Country Club during the Invictus Games in Toronto, Canada, in 2017. The Invictus Games is an international Paralympic-style event for injured or sick military personnel and veterans.

MENTAL HEALTH AND PTSD Not all war-related disabilities are physical. War also takes a psychological toll. During and after World War II, Harvard sociologist Samuel Stouffer and his colleagues (1949) conducted the first major study of war stress. They found correlations between psychological stress and several types of combat experience. For example, soldiers stationed close to the front lines—who were constantly exposed to the threat of injury or death to themselves and their friends, to the hardships of life on the battlefield, to the value conflicts involved in killing others, and to the inability to control their own actions—suffered greater psychological stress than others.

In the decades since Stouffer's research, mental-health experts have identified **post-traumatic stress disorder (PTSD)**, a condition in which a person experiences severe stress reactions after a traumatic event; it is a common aftereffect of battle (U.S. Department of Veterans Affairs, 2014). Other factors in a combat situation can add even more stress to an already stressful situation. These factors include what a person does in the war, the politics around the war, where the war is fought, and the type of enemy a soldier faces. For example, the psychological impact of the Vietnam War may have differed from that of earlier U.S. wars because it was a guerrilla war. That is, the enemy blended with the civilian population and therefore seemed to be everywhere and nowhere at the same time. These conditions may have been responsible for the unusually high levels of violence against civilians that characterized the war, as well as for the mistreatment of prisoners and the use of such weapons as napalm, which killed civilians and the enemy indiscriminately. Soldiers who saw or engaged in these forms of violence suffered from psychological disorders more so than those who did not. As one Vietnam veteran said of his experience, fifty years afterwards:

> *I'm shocked at what I did. ... I hurt innocent people. Hurt? What am I saying? I killed them. I killed innocent civilians who didn't even want this war in the first place. I shot a mom with her two young sons because they may have been the enemy. May have ... I don't even know. To this day I see those children's faces, and I hear the mom pleading for their lives. She offered to let us rape her if we would just let her children live. We raped her, and still killed them all. When I think about it I get a panicky feeling inside. I can barely breathe.*

Recent data from the U.S. Department of Veterans Affairs suggest that the number of veterans with PTSD varies by service era (U.S. Department of Veterans Affairs, 2016).

- *Operation Iraqi Freedom (OIF) and Operation Enduring Freedom (OEF):* Between 11 and 20 of every 100 veterans who served in OIF or OEF have PTSD in a given year.
- *Gulf War (Desert Storm):* About 12 of every 100 Gulf War veterans have PTSD in a given year.
- *Vietnam War:* About 15 of every 100 Vietnam veterans were diagnosed with PTSD in the late 1980s at the time of the most recent study, the National Vietnam Veterans Readjustment Study (NVVRS). It is estimated that about 30 of every 100 Vietnam veterans have experienced PTSD in their lifetime.

MILITARY SEXUAL TRAUMA Another cause of PTSD in the military can be **military sexual trauma (MST)**, which is any sexual harassment or sexual assault of military personnel by other military personnel (at any rank). MST can happen to both men and women and can occur during peacetime, training, or war. How common is MST? Data are collected from the national screening program run by the Veterans Administration (VA). Through that program, every veteran seen for health care is asked whether he or she experienced MST. National data from this program reveal that, when screened by their VA provider, about one in four women and one in a hundred men respond that they experienced MST. Although rates of MST are far higher among women, because there are many more men than women in the military, significant numbers of both women and men seen in VA facilities have experienced MST (U.S. Department of Veterans Affairs, 2018).

One rarely discussed aspect of these casualties, injuries, and traumas is the fact that social inequality plays a significant role in who will become a victim, a premise of Theme 3. Men and women who are poor are especially likely to be recruited into

post-traumatic stress disorder (PTSD)

Severe stress reactions after a traumatic event such as war.

What Do You Think?

Using the sociological imagination, can you explain why PTSD is a social problem rather than just a personal issue?

military sexual trauma (MST)

Any sexual harassment or sexual assault suffered by a veteran while serving in the military.

dangerous military roles. Several studies have shown that, during the Vietnam War, battle deaths and injuries were more common among lower-class soldiers than among those from the middle and upper classes (Janowitz, 1978; Moskos, 2005).

15.1.2 Indirect Effects of War

In addition to the killing, wounding, and mental health effects, war disrupts the lives of the veterans themselves and their families. In addition, war disrupts the lives of civilians whose homeland has become a battleground.

INDIRECT EFFECTS ON MILITARY PERSONNEL AND VETERANS Men and women who serve in the military face many significant disruptions in their personal lives, including multiple moves across the country or around the world, long periods away from home, and possibly multiple deployments. Many military personnel are married or partnered and have children, which makes the disruptions in their lives even more complicated. Former First Lady Michelle Obama and Jill Biden, wife of former U.S. Vice President Joe Biden, took on the support of military families as one of their primary roles.

During periods of deployment, family members may have a range of feelings and experiences, including loneliness, sadness, worry, or panic. Coupled with these emotions, the spouse or partner left behind must assume new family responsibilities and may experience financial difficulties, either of which can feel overwhelming.

A growing area of research shows the negative impact on children, youth, and families of U.S. military personnel. Children of military families often experience multiple stressors before and during their parent's deployment and when they come home. They have more school-, family-, and peer-related emotional difficulties (Substance Abuse and Mental Health Services Administration, 2017). Without appropriate mental health support systems, children of military personnel may be at a significant disadvantage compared with their peers in nonmilitary families.

INDIRECT EFFECTS ON CIVILIANS War often leads to mass migrations of people trying to escape from danger or persecution or looking for new opportunities. A look at the causes and consequences of this migration, and social policies around it, using Theme 4 of this text, should be of interest to the United States. The United Nations High Commissioner for Refugees reports that by the end of 2016, 65.6 million people worldwide were international refugees (22.5 million) or internally displaced people. War is the main cause for this displacement, with nearly 60 percent of all refugees coming from six war-affected countries: Syria, Afghanistan, South Sudan, Myanmar, Somalia, and the Democratic Republic of the Congo. Prior to the upsurge in Syrian refugees, Afghanistan had been the world's "top producer" of refugees for 32 years. Over one-half of refugees are children under age 18. At least 75,000 asylum applications were submitted in 2016 from children who were unaccompanied or separated from their parents (United Nations High Commissioner for Refugees, 2017). What is the United States' role in producing so many migrants, and is it the United States' responsibility to help them?

Another major cause of wartime migration is government policy. During and after World War II, several European states forced whole populations to move. During the war, the German government ordered hundreds of thousands of

Men and women in the military, especially those with children, make great personal sacrifices for their country. Here, a father on leave hugs his son whom he has not seen in almost five months.

Peppersmint/Shutterstock

ethnic Germans to move back to Germany from the eastern European nations that Germany had invaded. After the war, under the terms of the Potsdam Treaty, many more Germans were required to move from various eastern European nations to areas within the redrawn borders of Germany.

Some indirect effects of war are not as easy to calculate as the numbers of refugees. For example, it is impossible to measure the economic damage caused by war. Billions of dollars must be diverted from productive uses, first into arms and then into the repair of the damage caused by arms. Even less quantifiable is the impact of war on how people think. The Vietnam War left in its wake widespread disillusionment with traditional values. To many men in the trenches, patriotism lost much of its appeal. After the war, some people were pessimistic about the future of civilization and were alienated from their former way of life.

Liberated Iraq is a good example of the longer-term political and social effects of even a "successful" war. The nation's people remain badly divided in their feelings about what kind of government—secular or religious—should be established. At this writing, Iraq has a prime minister and parliament and is nominally considered a representative democracy. However, Iraq has also been called the most corrupt state in the Middle East and a hybrid between a "flawed democracy" and an "authoritarian regime" (Economist Intelligence Unit, 2018). There are a few hopeful signs as the Iraqi government has recently defeated the Islamic State, thus reasserting sovereignty over parts of the country previously out of its control. Yet, it remains clear that no lasting peace is likely if the many ethnic and religious factions of the Iraqi population cannot work together to ensure peace and the rule of law on their own. What can the United States learn from this experience?

15.1.3 Genocide

Genocide is a term used to describe violence against members of a national, ethnic, racial or religious group with the intent to destroy the entire group. The word came into general usage only after World War II, when the full extent of the atrocities committed by the Nazi regime became known. The word "genocide" was first coined by Polish lawyer Raphäel Lemkin in his 1944 book *Axis Rule in Occupied Europe*. It consists of the Greek prefix *genos*, meaning race or tribe, and the Latin suffix *cide*, meaning killing (United Nations Office on Genocide Prevention and the Responsibility to Protect, 2018).

According to the United Nations Office on Genocide, genocide means any of the following acts committed with intent to destroy, in whole or in part, a national, ethnical, racial, or religious group, such as:

- Killing members of the group;
- Causing serious bodily or mental harm to members of the group;
- Deliberately inflicting on the group conditions of life calculated to bring about its physical destruction in whole or in part;
- Imposing measures intended to prevent births within the group;
- Forcibly transferring children of the group to another group (2018).[1]

Genocide involves both mental and physical elements. Not only are a group of people destroyed, but the *intent* to destroy them is present as well. Victims of genocide are deliberately targeted. Tens of millions of women, men, and children have lost their lives to genocide. Some of the most well-recognized instances of genocide over the past century include (Genocide Education Project, 2014):

- ***Jews in Europe***. It began with a boycott of Jewish shops and ended in the gas chambers of Auschwitz as Hitler and his fellow Nazis attempted to exterminate the entire Jewish population of Europe. The Holocaust took the

---

[1]Genocide Definition. United Nations Office on Genocide, 2018. Retrieved from http://www.un.org/en/genocideprevention/genocide.html.

lives of close to six million Jews during the World War II era. The Nazis also murdered many millions of Poles, Russians, Roma, Sinti, Serbs, Czechs, homosexuals, and political opponents; however, only the Jews were slated for total annihilation.

- *Cambodia*. By 1975, the United States had withdrawn its troops from Vietnam, and Cambodia lost its American military support. Taking advantage of this opportunity, Pol Pot's Khmer Rouge seized control of Cambodia. From 1975 to 1979, Pol Pot led the Khmer Rouge political party in a reign of violence, fear, and brutality over Cambodia. An attempt to form a Communist peasant farming society resulted in the deaths of 25 percent of the population from starvation, overwork, and executions. Different ethnic groups and all those considered to be of the "old society," intellectuals, former government officials, and Buddhist monks, were murdered.

- *Rwanda*. Beginning in April 1994, groups of ethnic Hutu, armed mostly with machetes, began a campaign of terror and bloodshed in the central African country of Rwanda. For about 100 days, the Hutu militias followed a clear and premeditated attempt to exterminate the country's ethnic Tutsi population. The Rwandan state radio, controlled by Hutu extremists, further encouraged the killings by broadcasting non-stop hate propaganda and even pinpointed the locations of Tutsis in hiding. Hutus killed their Tutsi neighbors and friends. By the end of the 100-day massacre, roughly 800,000 Tutsi and Hutu sympathizers were murdered. However, almost as shocking as the genocide itself, but in a positive way, is the sincere progress the country has made in healing and coming together in repentance.

- *Bosnia-Herzegovina*. In the republic of Bosnia-Herzegovina, conflict between the three main ethnic groups—Serbs, Croats, and Muslims—resulted in genocide committed by the Serbs against Bosnian Muslims. In 1992 acts of "ethnic cleansing" started in Bosnia, a mostly Muslim country where the Serb minority made up only 32 percent of the population. The Bosnian Muslims were outgunned, and the Serbs continued to gain ground. They systematically rounded up local Muslims and committed acts of mass murder, deported men and boys to concentration camps, and forced repopulation of entire towns. Over 200,000 Muslim civilians were systematically murdered and 2,000,000 became refugees at the hands of the Serbs.

- *Darfur*. Violence and destruction raged in the Darfur region of western Sudan beginning in 2003 during the country's civil war. Government-sponsored militias known as the Janjaweed conducted a calculated campaign of slaughter, rape, starvation, and displacement in Darfur as they fought the Sudan People's Liberation Army. The war lasted for 22 years, one of the longest civil wars on record. Roughly two million people died from injuries, famine, and disease, one of the highest death tolls from war since WWII.

While there have certainly been other mass killings in recent times, those listed above are ones which clearly meet the United Nations definition of genocide—an intent to destroy a national, ethnical, racial, or religious group. What about the current plight of the Rohingya people living in

A tour guide in Rwanda shows human remains in the national museum. She lost a mother and her children in the Rwandan genocide.

Aurora Photos/Alamy Stock Photo

Myanmar, which was introduced in Chapter 7? As you recall, over 700,000 Rohingya have fled the country to Bangladesh after being targeted by the Myanmar military for systematic killing, torture, arson, gang rape, and other mass atrocities. Several world leaders have declared it "ethnic cleansing" (somewhat short of genocide), while others, including the United Nations, have said that the situation bears the markings of genocide (Kristof, 2018; McCain and Jolie, 2018). They call on world leaders to intervene.

15.1.4 Sexual Violence as a Tactic of War

We saw all of the other women being raped. We screamed and went crazy. And the bastards, you couldn't even tell which one was which. They all wore masks.

Rape and sexual assault of civilians have often been used as weapons of war. It may involve gang rape and rape with objects and weapons. It is often committed in public and with brutal violence, and committed upon women and girls of any age, designed to maximize the humiliation its victims face. Other sexual violence may include sexual slavery, forced prostitution, being held in "rape camps," forced pregnancy, forced sterilization/abortion, sexual mutilation, and sexual torture (Anyangwe, 2018; Dr. Denis Mukwege Foundation, 2018; U.N. Human Rights Council, March 8, 2018).

As you learned in Chapter 8, rape is about power, and rape in the context of war is no different. Rape and sexual assault as weapons of war are first and foremost strategies to demoralize and destabilize an entire community. In patriarchal societies, wives, mothers, and daughters are viewed as the property of men, and therefore rape is considered an attack not only on the woman herself, but on the men in her life whose masculinity is questioned, on her children who are often forced to witness the violence, and on the entire community that was unable to protect her. In other words, sexual violence and humiliation are not just a by-product of war and conflict; they are a feature designed to break combatants and destroy families.

Historically, rape as a weapon of war has been used during conflicts and war around the world in different countries, including Bangladesh, the Democratic Republic of the Congo, Sudan, Syria, Central African Republic, North Korea, Philippines, Rwanda, Sierra Leone, Sri Lanka, Uganda, Liberia, Colombia, Vietnam, Nigeria, and the former Yugoslavia. Rape as a weapon of war was also widespread during World War II in different parts of Europe and Asia.

When conflict ends, the consequences of rape as a weapon of war persist. If their needs are not addressed, victims continue to suffer, physically and mentally. In many cultures, a woman or girl who has been raped has lost her value and may have little place in society anymore. Intense stigma can lead to rejection by families, and even the expulsion of rape victims from their communities. These consequences may also affect children who are born of rape, of which there are many.

Survivors of sexual violence need a variety of services to help them (Dr. Denis Mukwege Foundation, 2018). Medical services and surgical procedures are often required, especially if the victims were young, or the violence was particularly brutal. Besides painful injuries, they suffer from intense emotional and psychological trauma. To heal psychologically, survivors need access to the basics of food, safe shelter, clothing, and psychological services to help them, their families, and their communities process what has happened and to decrease the stigma surrounding it. Finally, one of the main drivers in healing is access to justice. However, most often victims have no recourse to justice; impunity is widespread. When sexual violence goes unpunished, children and young adults learn that sexual violence may be acceptable, and victims are further blamed and stigmatized. The feature box, *A Personal*

A Personal View

"I Am Not Afraid of You Anymore"

Hero Images Inc./Alamy Stock Photo

Hello to you, my Rapist, my Perpetrator,

You will know that I have not forgotten and I never will.

You will pretend it never happened, but if I were you, I would feel ashamed.

You will always be a man without heart or honor.

Know that I am repairing my world, the one you destroyed in the blink of an eye profiting from the war to destroy everything that mattered to me.

Brothers, husbands, children, families remember the moment when you abused their sisters, their wives, and their daughters. You humiliated me, you terrorized me as well as my loved ones; all these screams, these cries were not only coming from me. I am sure you remember it too.

Do you remember destroying the life of that little girl? She cried, she suffered, but you did not stop; you even mutilated her genitals; I don't know whether I can call you a man because for me you have nothing human left in you. Deep inside of you, you do not recognize that women are sacred.

Do you imagine that even years after, they still suffer deep inside of them?

I do not know how to qualify this unbearable, excruciating, devastating, torturing, inconsolable pain that you imposed on me.

At times, every minute, every hour was a living hell.

I could not do anything anymore; I cried, I isolated myself from the world; my life was hanging by a thread, which could break at any moment. I was constantly wondering "what did I do to the world to deserve this?"

There were always a thousand and one reasons to despair, but the only reason to hope was my honor. Deep within my pain, I knew that I was better than you.

I often wonder what place you deserve in this world? None. You don't have the right to exist.

You will know now more than ever, I am not afraid of you anymore, you gave me the courage to fight you. I faced all the pain you inflicted on me, I left the living hell in which you left me.

Unlike you, I can color my world with joy, kindness, justice, and peace because I am not afraid anymore to live and rebuild my life.

Behind my bravery and my strength, there is an immense sadness, humiliation and a deep trauma following what you did to me and to more than three million women in my country. Many of your victims did not survive, however, others now live with chronic diseases.

To me, hope was only a matter of will; this reason to hope was fragile, but the pain taught me how to fight and turned me into a stronger and better person.

Since then, I have decided to face you, you know I already fought to recover my pride, my honor, and my strength. Despite the situation in my country, I am involved in agriculture, animal husbandry, and small trade. I became an active actor in the development of my community, despite all the obstacles I had to overcome.

I am fighting and I will keep fighting so that you can never do again what you did, and if one day you try, I will be here standing in your way with every legal possibility.

SOURCE: "16 Days of Activism campaign: Congo," Dr. Dennis Mukwege Foundation (November 30, 2017).

Critical Thinking

Can you identify the damage this woman experienced that was caused by the sexual violence? Why would writing a letter help this woman repair her world? Chances are that her abuser will never see the letter, but if he did, how do you think he would respond?

View: "I Am Not Afraid of You Anymore," is a letter written from a survivor of sexual violence in the war-torn Democratic Republic of the Congo to her rapist. Her letter represents a path in her healing.

As often as sexual violence is used as a war tactic, there are few scientific studies of the problem (Mpinga et al., 2017). Yet more research could help mobilize local authorities and the international community against this critical human rights violation.

Weapons of Mass Destruction

15.2 **Identify various forms of weapons of mass destruction.**

In the past 100 years, wars have become more intense as military technology has become more lethal. **Weapons of mass destruction**, such as nuclear weapons and biological agents, have the potential to annihilate millions of people quickly.

15.2.1 Nuclear Weapons

The development of nuclear weapons in the 1940s contributed to peace among the major powers because each was fearful of unleashing nuclear devastation on a large scale. However, today, if peace breaks down, a war of almost unimaginable destructiveness could ensue. Eight nations—the United States, Russia, United Kingdom, France, China, India, Pakistan, and North Korea—possess approximately 16,300 nuclear weapons in total. Israel is also believed to possess nuclear weapons. In 2015 the United States, Russia, France, the United Kingdom, Germany, and the European Union reached agreement with Iran on a deal to scale back its own pursuit of nuclear weapons in exchange for the lifting of severe economic sanctions. Although most observers believe that Iran has so far kept its part of the agreement, on May 8, 2018, U.S. President Donald Trump announced that the United States was pulling out of the agreement, which he characterized as a "horrible, one-sided deal." The feature box, *A Global View: "Reneging on the Iran Nuclear Agreement,"* looks at President Trump's decision to leave the agreement in more detail.

How serious of a problem do nuclear weapons pose? Some idea of the nature of the destruction that could occur is provided by accounts of the bombing of Hiroshima and Nagasaki, Japan, during World War II, although today's warheads are far more powerful than those used on Japan. In 1939, President Roosevelt and Congress authorized a secret project to expand research on nuclear fission and use uranium and plutonium to generate nuclear chain reactions as atomic weapons. This project was known as the Manhattan Project. Most of the scientists, civilian leaders, and military officials responsible for the development of the bomb assumed that its military use, however unpleasant, was the inevitable outcome of the project.

Work continued at a variety of locations around the United States throughout World War II, and three bombs were finished by July 1945, then field-tested in the New Mexico desert. By this time, President Roosevelt had passed away (April) and Germany had surrendered (May), but the war in the Pacific continued under President Truman.

American soldiers were weary after years of war, but the Japanese military was a strong opponent and would not give up the fight. Truman issued one final warning to Japan, asking for an immediate unconditional surrender, and stating that refusal would result in total destruction. He did not mention that the United States had nuclear bombs. The Japanese rejected the request for unconditional surrender, although there were some indications that a conditional surrender was possible.

On the morning of August 6, 1945, as the people of Hiroshima were preparing to go to work, a U.S. aircraft called the *Enola Gay* flew over the city. Seconds later, a nuclear bomb exploded 2,000 feet above the center of the city. Even though the 12.5 kiloton device was tiny by modern standards, its effect was devastating. The force and heat of the blast annihilated 70,000 to 80,000 people almost instantly and delivered a deadly dose of radiation to hundreds of thousands of others. Three days later, another bomb was dropped on Nagasaki, immediately killing another 40,000 citizens. Over the course of months and years, the death toll reached at least 100,000 more due to burns and radiation. Japan's Emperor Hirohito announced his country's unconditional surrender in World War II in a radio address on August 15, 1945, citing the

---

weapons of mass destruction
Nuclear weapons and biological agents that have the potential to annihilate thousands or even millions of people quickly.

A Global View

Reneging on the Iran Nuclear Agreement

On May 8, 2018, President Donald Trump pulled the United States out of the 2015 deal brokered by world powers to scale back Iran's nuclear weapons program, formally the Joint Comprehensive Plan of Action, which the President called "decaying and rotten." He reimposed all sanctions and gave foreign firms up to six months to stop doing business with Iran. Other signatories—Britain, France, and Germany—said they would continue to honor the agreement, to which Iran seemed to be adhering. "If we can achieve the deal's goals in co-operation with other members of the deal, it will remain in place," said Iranian President Hassan Rouhani.[2]

The agreement curtails Iran's nuclear program for several years and permanently subjects it to intrusive inspections, in exchange for the lifting of sanctions worth many billions of dollars. President Trump's withdrawal from the agreement honored a campaign promise. In fact, he went beyond his campaign statements by vowing not just to restore sanctions, but extend them, and to punish any firm doing business with Iran wherever it is based. Specifically, President Trump reimposed "secondary" sanctions aimed directly at international banks and other firms doing business with Iran's oil sector. It forces these businesses, and by extension their home countries, to choose between having access to Iran's oil exports or doing business in the enormous U.S. market.

Yet most observers, including even some of the deal's Israeli and Saudi critics, believe that Iran has been honoring the agreement. It has dismantled much of its nuclear program and given international inspectors wide latitude to investigate; by most accounts, Iran is significantly further from a nuclear weapon than it was when the deal came into force. President Trump's case revolved around perceived defects in the deal itself, such as the agreement that restrictions on Iran's nuclear program start to relax about 10 years after the deal was signed (though the agreement not to build a nuclear weapon is permanent). Also, the deal does not cover other problematic activities, including ballistic missile development and Iran's ongoing support for violent militias around the Middle East (like Hezbollah in Lebanon).

The question for all parties is, "What happens next?" The President said that he is "ready, willing, and able" to negotiate a new deal that limits Iran's regional aggression as well as its nuclear weapons, though the structure of that plan is unclear.[3] And, it's unlikely that either Europe or Iran will be willing to renegotiate such a deal, given their belief that the current deal is working. An important question will be how aggressively the U.S. sanctions are imposed by the U.S. Treasury Department, which has some leeway in how stringent the imposed sanctions will be. Less stringent sanctions will ultimately hurt Iran less and give them more incentive to remain in the deal, especially if the Europeans do not re-impose their own sanctions. Of course, the opposite is also true; if European firms stop doing business with Iran to avoid American punishment, then Iran would have little incentive to stay in the deal and would likely resume its nuclear program.

Some observers think that President Trump believes that the re-imposition of heavy sanctions will cause such economic pain among the Iranian people that they will revolt against their leaders. Whether the Iranian leadership would allow this to happen is an open question, however, given their known willingness to use force to maintain power. Perhaps the greatest concern is that the resumption of heavy sanctions will limit future diplomatic options if Iran resumes its nuclear program, leaving military action as the only viable response. In any case, Iran's nuclear future has become much less clear than it was before President Trump's announcement.

SOURCES: Based on *The Economist*, May 12–18, 2018 and Beauchamp, 2018.

Critical Thinking

What repercussions could the United States face for reneging on a deal that seemed to be working? Are these repercussions serious or minor? How might this change of course be viewed around the world? It's also important to look beyond Iran. For example, will this change of course have any implication for future nuclear negotiations? As this book goes to press, negotiations with North Korea to create a nuclear-free Korean peninsula have begun.

---

[2]Iranian President Hassan Rouhani, Quoted in "Iran nuclear deal not dead despite Trump move, France says," BBC (May 9, 2018).

[3]President Donald Trump, Quoted in Aleem, Z. "Trump Just Pulled Out of the Iran Deal. Here's What Happens Next" Vox (May 8, 2018).

Prisma by Dukas Presseagentur GmbH/Alamy Stock Photo

Americans twice used "a new and most cruel bomb" on Japan, which effectively ended their involvement in World War II. Hundreds of thousands of Japanese civilians were killed or seriously injured by the nuclear bombs.

What Do You Think?

The United States is the only country that has ever used a weapon of mass destruction on innocent civilians in another country, and it did so twice. Using the sociological imagination, do you believe that using a nuclear bomb was the right or wrong action to take against Japan? Explain your reasoning. Can you think of a context in which the United States would use it a third time? Would the United States be justified in doing so?

devastating power of "a new and most cruel bomb" (Hall, 2013; History.com, 2015; U.S. History.org, 2014).[4]

Many of those who survived were burned and maimed. One woman, who had been with some junior high school boys about a mile from the center of the blast, was knocked unconscious. "When I came to, I looked around," she said in an interview. "The boys had been so cute before, but now their clothes were burned off and they were nearly naked. Their skin was cut up and ripped off. Their faces were peeling off as well." She herself was so hideously deformed that her own parents urged her to show mercy to her husband and leave him. "At that time, I cried every day, wishing that I had died immediately," she said. She added that she did not seek compensation from the United States. "I just want [Americans] to feel sorry and to try to abolish nuclear weapons" (quoted in Kristof, 1995, pp. 1, 12).[5]

Those who support the bombing argue that both American and Japanese lives may have been saved by ending the war earlier than would have happened with conventional warfare. Surveys conducted in both the United States and Japan in 2015, seventy years after the bombs were dropped, report that 56 percent of Americans and 14 percent of Japanese believe that the bombings were justified (Stokes, August 4, 2015).

In the years since nuclear weapons were developed, war has become much riskier than ever before because local wars fought with conventional weapons can escalate into much wider destruction. The possibility that countries with unstable political regimes could produce nuclear bombs and missiles, and the fear that these and other weapons of mass destruction such as biological agents like the smallpox virus could be sold to terrorist organizations, have become part of the fearful post–9/11 global scene. These scenarios keep the threat of nuclear war alive. Even a limited nuclear war would create human catastrophes on a scale not hitherto experienced, to say nothing of the environmental damage and destruction such wars would cause for years afterward, even in regions beyond the boundaries of the original conflict.

Still, it remains that the United States is the only nation that has ever used nuclear bombs in war, and it has threatened to use nuclear weapons at least 11 times since 1946, including the Berlin crisis of 1961, the Cuban missile crisis of 1962, and twice during the Vietnam War. Because warfare has become so dangerous and the world's military powers have built up huge stockpiles of both conventional and nuclear arms, many people have begun to study the causes of war in the hope of promoting peace.

15.2.2 Biological and Chemical Weapons

Perhaps an even greater threat to the world are biological and chemical weapons that can more easily get into the hands of terrorist groups. Biological weapons include things such as anthrax, botulinum toxins, cholera, smallpox, and ricin, among many other substances.

---

[4]Quoted in The Imperial Rescript on the Termination of the War. Broadcasted in The Gyokuon-hoso, August 15, 1945.

[5]Quoted in Kristof, N. S. "Hiroshima: A Special Report; The Bomb: An Act That Haunts Japan and America," *The New York Times* (Aug. 6, 1995) pp. 1, 12.

The term chemical weapon is applied to any toxic chemical or its precursor that can cause death, injury, temporary incapacitation, or sensory irritation through its chemical action (Organisation for the Prohibition of Chemical Weapons, 2018). Toxic chemicals that have been developed or used as chemical weapons can be categorized as choking, blister, blood, or nerve agents. The most well-known chemicals are chlorine and phosgene (choking agents); mustard gas and lewisite (blister agents or vesicants); hydrogen cyanide (a blood agent); and sarin, soman, and VX (nerve agents).

As one example, botulinum toxins are the deadliest substances known. Because botulinum toxin is so lethal and easy to manufacture, it represents a credible threat as a biological warfare agent. Exposure could occur following inhalation of aerosolized toxin or ingestion of food contaminated with the toxin or its microbial spores. Iraq has admitted to active research on the offensive use of botulinum toxins and to deploying more than 100 munitions with botulinum toxin (Hooker, 2014). The toxin produces similar effects whether ingested, inhaled, or applied to a wound. Symptoms may occur hours to several days after exposure. Initial signs and symptoms include blurred vision, dilated pupils, difficulty swallowing, difficulty speaking, an altered voice, and muscle weakness. After 24 to 48 hours, muscle weakness and paralysis may impede a person's ability to breathe.

The use of chemical weapons has a long history, with the first international agreement limiting their use signed in 1675 between France and Germany, prohibiting poison bullets. Chemical weapons were used on a massive scale during World War I, resulting in more than 100,000 fatalities and a million casualties. Their most recent use has been during the ongoing Syrian civil war. The United States claims that the Syrian government has used chemical weapons, primarily sarin, chlorine gas, and mustard gas, at least 50 times over the seven years of the civil war (Gladstone, 2018). Although the United Nations has confirmed the use of chemical weapons in Syria, the identity of the weapons' users is disputed, especially by the Syrian and Russian governments (BBC.com, 2017).

terrorism

The threatened or actual use of illegal force and violence by a non-state actor to attain a political, economic, religious, or social goal through fear, coercion, or intimidation.

Terrorism, Global and Domestic

15.3 **Review modern-day terrorism in the United States and around the world.**

Terrorism is defined as the threatened or actual use of illegal force and violence by a non-state actor to attain a political, economic, religious, or social goal through fear, coercion, or intimidation (Institute for Economics and Peace, 2017).[6] This definition recognizes that terrorism includes not only the physical attack itself but also the long-term psychological effect it has on society.

Terrorism was a serious social problem in the world long before the suicide bombing of the World Trade Center and the Pentagon on September 11, 2001. One

Carmen Taylor/Getty Images

United Flight 175 flies directly into the World Trade Center Tower 2 during a terrorist attack on September 11, 2001, a day that will always be remembered as "9/11."

[6]"Global Terrorism Index 2015: Measuring and Understanding the Impact of Terrrorism," Institute for Economics and Peace.

need only think of the years of terrorist bombings in Northern Ireland or Sri Lanka, the deadly bombing in Oklahoma City, sniper attacks against abortion clinic doctors, and the episodes of terror attacks in Israel and elsewhere in the Middle East or on the Indian subcontinent or in Russia and Chechnya. But since 9/11 and the declaration by the U.S. government of a "war against terrorism," the world has entered a new era in which terrorism and armed responses against suspected terrorists have become dominant issues. Terrorism in the post–9/11 world has enormous impacts on global economic conditions, on the ability to travel and maintain open borders, on civil rights and the protection of basic freedoms, and much else.

Violent terrorist acts—kidnapping, torture, bombings, beheadings, and the like—are often committed by a nation or a political movement to call attention to its cause and to shake people's faith in their government's ability to eliminate the threat. The movement may be a revolutionary one that seeks far-reaching change in the government or hopes to gain control over the nation. But not all terrorism is revolutionary in nature. The terrorism of cocaine barons in Colombia is designed to take revenge on the authorities and to intimidate them into lax enforcement of the law. Terrorism of governments like that of Nigeria against its own people (known as repressive terrorism or state terrorism) is also not associated with revolutionary movements (Mazrui, 1996).

revolutionary terrorism

Acts of violence against civilians that are carried out by enemies of a government.

But the most common type is **revolutionary terrorism**, which involves acts of violence against civilians that are carried out by enemies of a government. The 1995 bombing of a federal office building in Oklahoma City by Timothy McVeigh and Terry Nichols; the lethal letter bombs mailed to universities and airlines by Ted Kaczynski, the so-called Unabomber, during the 1980s and 1990s; and the 9/11 attacks on the World Trade Center in New York City and on the Pentagon are only a few recent examples of terrorism. Two brothers with extremist Islamic beliefs carried out the 2013 bombings at the Boston Marathon in which three people were killed and over 260 people were injured, as profiled in the opening vignette. These brothers detonated two pressure cooker bombs, set a few hundred feet apart near the finish line of the marathon. In their attempt to escape, they killed a policeman from the Massachusetts Institute of Technology and injured another officer. The older brother was shot by police (and inadvertently run over by his younger brother as he fled in a stolen vehicle) and died at the scene. The younger brother was captured within a few days. Convicted in April 2015, he was given the death penalty.

15.3.1 Modern Terrorist Groups

Since 9/11, terrorism has become among the most dangerous threats to world order. It destabilizes governments, preys on innocent victims, and involves large amounts of financial and human resources. Yet unlike war, which openly pits opponents against each other in a recognized trial of strength, terrorism is covert. It seeks to sway the masses through intimidation and fear.

Four groups—(1) the Islamic State of Iraq and the Levant (ISIL), also called ISIS; (2) Boko Haram; (3) the Taliban; and (4) al Qaeda—"took credit" for 59 percent of all claimed terrorism-related deaths in 2016 (Institute for Economics and Peace, 2017). ISIL is one of the largest active terrorist groups in the Middle East. It was originally a part of al Qaeda in Iraq (AQI), but after the death of AQI's head and after tactical disagreements, ISIL split from AQI. ISIL became known for extreme violence and terror during the Syrian civil war in 2013, rapidly expanding into Syria and then Iraq in 2014. In February 2014, al Qaeda formally broke ties with ISIL, claiming that ISIL disobeyed directions from al Qaeda to kill fewer civilians.

Boko Haram (one translation is "Western education is sin") is a Nigeria-based terrorist group founded in 2002 to create a separatist community within Nigeria under Wahhabi Islamic principles. Originally, the group was not very violent, but since the 2009 death of its leader while in police custody, Boko Haram has been responsible for at least 3,500 civilian deaths. The group is also responsible for the April 2014 kidnapping of 276 female students ages 16 to 18 from a school in northeastern Nigeria. Although over 100 girls have since been freed, a similar number remain missing (Searcey, 2018).

Founded in 1994, the Taliban was originally a mixture of "Mujahedeen," who fought against the 1980s Soviet invasion of Afghanistan, and a group of Pashtun tribesmen. The Taliban took control of Afghanistan in 1996 and ruled until 2001, when they were overthrown by the United States. The Taliban has since regrouped as an insurgency movement to fight the Afghan government and Western security forces. The Taliban strives to retake control of Afghanistan and has rebranded itself an independence movement.

Al Qaeda was formed in 1988 by Osama bin Laden, a Saudi killed by U.S. troops in 2011, and Abdullah Azzam, a Palestinian Sunni scholar who was killed in 1989. Al Qaeda, like the Taliban, arose during the Soviet war in Afghanistan. Its goal is international jihad (i.e., struggle against Islam's enemies), and it is the only group to have successfully conducted large-scale attacks in the West, including the 9/11 attacks in the United States. Many of al Qaeda's leaders have since been killed, and the group now adopts a decentralized structure of regional cells and affiliates. While direct terrorism attributed to al Qaeda has been relatively low since 2011, activity by its affiliated groups has risen.

Although the histories and strategic objectives of these groups differ, they share a focus on religious ideology based on extreme interpretations of Wahhabi Islam and strict adherence to Sharia law. Wahhabism is an austere form of Islam that insists on literal interpretation of the Koran. Strict Wahhabis believe that anyone who does not practice their form of Islam is a heathen and enemy. Sharia law is the body of Islamic law that governs all aspects of daily life from politics and economics to sexual and social issues. Yet, despite the power of religious ideology as a motivation for terrorism among these groups, it is not universal. Outside the Middle East, North and sub-Saharan Africa, and South Asia, terrorism is more likely driven by local separatist, political, or nationalistic movements.

Despite the differing motivations, countries with higher levels of terrorism do seem to share certain characteristics:

- Greater hostilities between different ethnic, religious, and linguistic groups, lack of intergroup cohesion, and high levels of group grievances
- Presence of state-sponsored (i.e., government) violence such as extrajudicial killings, political terror, and gross human rights abuses
- Higher levels of other violence, including deaths from organized conflict, likelihood of violent demonstrations, levels of violent crime, and perceptions of criminality

Contrary to what some may assume, poverty and other economic factors do little to explain the sources of terrorism within a country. Measures such as life expectancy or average levels of education do not matter very much. Instead, weak political systems, a lack of political legitimacy, and government-sponsored violence are much more influential in nurturing terrorism than is the overall economic environment.

15.3.2 Measuring Terrorism

The Institute for Economics and Peace has developed a Global Terrorism Index (GTI), which is the first index to systematically rank and compare 162 countries according to the impact of terrorism (Institute for Economics and Peace, 2017). The GTI uses four indicators to measure the impact of terrorism: number of terrorist incidents, number of deaths, number of casualties, and level of property damage.

On a 0 to 10 scale, with 10 indicating the highest impact of terrorism, the five countries with the highest GTI values in 2017 were Iraq (10.00), Afghanistan (9.44), Nigeria (9.01), Syria (8.62), and Pakistan (8.40), as shown in Table 15–1. For context, 2017 GTI values for selected countries were Saudi Arabia (5.81), China (5.54), United States (5.43), Israel (5.06), Canada (2.96), Honduras (1.56), Guatemala (0.50), United Arab Emirates (0.21), Qatar (0.12), Morocco (0.08), Oman (0.00), and El Salvador (0.00).

These values suggest two interesting issues. First, Honduras, Guatemala, and El Salvador are assigned very low GTIs, much lower than even that of the United States. Yet, few would argue that these Central American countries, which are dealing with the continuing scourge of gang violence, are safer or less violent than the United States. In other words, terrorism's impact in a country may differ quite a lot from the impact of violence from war or other sources. A nation can have a low terrorism score but also be very violent.

Second, the GTIs for the United Arab Emirates, Qatar, Morocco, and Oman are quite low as well. This indicates that the impact of terrorism is not universal across Arab countries, a fact sometimes forgotten. Arab countries should not be lumped together and seen as one large force.

Since 2000, the number of terrorism-related acts worldwide has grown sevenfold, rising from 1,813 to 13,488 in 2016. Terrorism-related deaths have similarly risen from 4,402 in 2000 to 34,676 in 2016. The good news is that both terrorism-related acts and deaths have fallen 20 percent from their 2014 peaks. This represents fewer deaths in Afghanistan, Nigeria, Syria, and Pakistan. In fact, Nigeria saw an 80 percent reduction

Table 15–1 Top Five Countries with Highest Global Terrorism Index Scores, 2017

Highest Scores	Score 0–10
Iraq	10.00
Afghanistan	9.44
Nigeria	9.01
Syria	8.62
Pakistan	8.40
Selected Countries	
Saudi Arabia	5.81
China	5.54
United States	5.43
Israel	5.06
Canada	2.96
Honduras	1.56
Guatemala	0.50
United Arab Emirates	0.21
Qatar	0.12
Morocco	0.08
Oman	0.00
El Salvador	0.00

NOTE: Scale is 0 to 10, with 10 representing the greatest effect of terrorism.

SOURCE: Data from Institute for Economics & Peace. 2017. "Global Terrorism Index 2017." Retrieved 14 May 2018 (visionofhumanity.org/app/uploads/2017/11/Global-Terrorism-Index-2017.pdf).

Table 15–2 Ten Countries with the Most Terrorist Attacks, 2016

Country	Total Attacks	Total Killed	Total Wounded	Average Number Killed per Attack
Iraq	2,965	9,764	13,314	3.44
Afghanistan	1,340	4,561	5,054	3.58
India	927	337	636	0.38
Pakistan	734	955	1,729	1.34
Philippines	482	272	418	0.58
Nigeria	466	1,832	919	4.35
Syria	363	2,088	2,656	6.42
Turkey	363	657	2,282	1.81
Yemen	363	628	793	1.89
Somalia	359	740	943	2.18

SOURCE: Data from National Consortium for the Study of Terrorism and Responses to Terrorism. 2017. "Annex of Statistical Information: Country Reports on Terrorism 2016." July. Retrieved 14 May 2018 (www.state.gov/documents/organization/272485.pdf).

in deaths between 2015 and 2016, reflecting greater military success against Boko Haram combined with declining domestic support for the group. Fewer deaths elsewhere offset the deteriorating situation in Iraq, where deaths increased 40 percent between 2015 and 2016. ISIL has responded to recent military defeats and territorial losses by stepping up localized, individualistic attacks. Moreover, between 2015 and 2016, the number of countries suffering at least one terrorism-related death increased from 65 to 77, a record number of terrorism-affected countries (Institute for Economics and Peace, 2017).

Table 15–2 indicates the 10 countries with the most terrorist attacks in 2016, and reports the total killed, the total wounded, and the average number of people killed per attack. As shown, Iraq, Afghanistan, India, Pakistan, and the Philippines had the largest number of attacks, but attacks in India and the Philippines tended to kill few people. Consequently, it is the terrorist attacks in Nigeria and Syria, along with Iraq, Afghanistan, and Pakistan that killed the most people, nearly 75 percent of lives lost to terrorism in 2016 (National Consortium for the Study of Terrorism and Responses to Terrorism, 2017).

Figure 15–1 illustrates the tactics used in terrorist attacks worldwide in 2016. The use of bombings and explosives were the most common, occurring in over half of terrorist attacks. Armed assaults were the primary method in over one-fifth of attacks around the world.

Terrorism in the United States and throughout the world shows no signs of abating. The number of Taliban fighters is estimated at between 36,000 and 60,000, with ISIL at 20,000, with al Qaeda at between 3,700 and 19,000, and with Boko Haram at

Figure 15–1 Tactics Used in Terrorist Attacks Worldwide, 2016

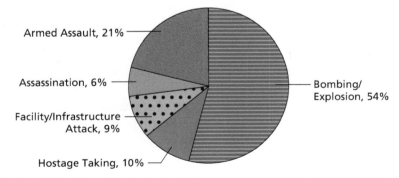

Armed Assault, 21%
Assassination, 6%
Facility/Infrastructure Attack, 9%
Hostage Taking, 10%
Bombing/Explosion, 54%

SOURCE: Data from National Consortium for the Study of Terrorism and Responses to Terrorism. 2017. "Annex of Statistical Information: Country Reports on Terrorism 2016." July. Retrieved 14 May 2018 (www.state.gov/documents/organization/272485.pdf).

between 500 and 9,000. As individuals, terrorists want to save the world, but salvation is based on a few rigid beliefs. The purity of their "end" justifies any means to achieve social change, even at the cost of their own lives, which are essentially meaningless relative to the greater goal (Dershowitz, 2002).

In this process, the victim, who in the terrorist's mind is merely a pawn in the struggle for societal reform, is stripped of human rights and identity. The terrorist wants to punish society, to force it to accept his or her demands. The terrorist preys on both known and unknown victims, convinced that—as representatives of an abhorrent society—the victims are responsible for society's wrongs and are unworthy of compassion. Because any society is the combined achievement of thousands of individuals and many generations, the injustice of terrorist thinking is obvious. Terrorists' victims are innocent people whose lives are destroyed by fanatical intolerance.

15.3.3 Terrorism, Religion, and ISIS/ISIL

That so many terrorist individuals and groups are motivated by extreme religious beliefs and feelings is one of the chief ironies of the present war on terrorism. Religion as a factor in terrorism has grown in importance since 2000 (Arnett, 2014; Institute of Economics and Peace, 2017). All major religions seek peace and understanding among people everywhere. But religions may also have a group of radical segments within them. Some domestic terrorists, such as the anti-abortion organization Army of God, are members of radical Christian groups. Al Qaeda and other contemporary Islamic terrorist groups espouse various forms of fundamentalist Islam—even though, as numerous Islamic leaders have pointed out, terrorism violates basic foundations of Islamic law. But in his analysis of the contribution of religious radicalism to contemporary terrorism, sociologist Amitai Etzioni (2002: 3) notes:

> It is sad but true that Islam, like Christianity and Judaism, has both temperate and virulent strands. Christianity in earlier ages not only had an Inquisition but also those who justified it in religious terms. The Catholic Church supported the mass torture and murder that occurred during military dictatorship in Argentina, deeming them necessary to "excise the cancer of communism." Terrorism in Northern Ireland has religious roots, and Operation Rescue claims religious justifications. Militant Judaism not merely claims a right to the West Bank and finds scriptural support for a still Greater Israel, but also blessed those who assassinated Yitzhak Rabin, the peacemaker.[7]

In other words, just like other world religions, Islam has its aggressive and extreme forms. Wahhabism is the version of Islam that is most dominant in Saudi Arabia and is a leading influence on Muslim fundamentalists elsewhere. Wahhabism pushes for the return to original Islam, rejects innovations, stresses literal belief in the Koran and the Hadith (the sayings or traditions of Mohammad), and calls for the formation of states to be governed strictly according to Islamic law. It rejects all notions of human rights and democratic forms of government as secular and Western notions.

Like many fundamentalist belief systems, extreme forms of Islam tend to be totalitarian in that they seek to control the person's total life: what she or he eats, listens to, wears, and reads. The sight of women in their burkas is a well-defined representation of these views. Extreme Islamists seek to achieve these goals through coercion and the use of fear rather than by persuasion or democratic decision-making. Thus, in trying to distance the U.S. war on terrorism from conflict with Islamic civilization itself, President George W. Bush was correct in stating, "The face of terror is not the true faith of Islam. Islam is peace."[8] Yet extremists of Islam or any other religion can become persuaded that the "end justifies the means" and then may resort to terror or other illegitimate uses of force against innocent civilians.

---

[7]Etzioni, A. (2002). "Opening Islam." *Society, 39*(5), 29–35.
[8]"'Islam is Peace' Says President," Remarks by the President at Islamic Center of Washington, D.C. Office of the Press Secretary, The White House (September 17, 2001).

Victims of Terrorism

Terrorists thrive on anonymity. They want to remain nameless and faceless. Their victims, however, are very real. This slide show introduces you to several victims of terrorism in the United States and abroad.

This picture shows Nazli holding a picture of her son Erdal Elbistan, 26, who died during a battle against ISIL insurgents in the Kurdish Syrian town of Kobane. The city had been under siege from ISIL for months, with brutal abuses against the local population. More than 1,000 people were killed in the fighting. ISIL succeeded in capturing hundreds of Kurdish villages and towns, creating a wave of more than 300,000 displaced Kurds, most of whom fled across the border into Turkey.

Matt Smith (left) of Boston, and Zach Mione of Portland, Oregon, helped Sydney Corcoran on the Boylston Street sidewalk at the scene of the first bomb explosion near the finish line of the 117th Boston Marathon in 2013. These two strangers applied pressure and tried to stop the bleeding of her injured leg. Sydney was standing next to her mother, who lost both legs, as they were waiting for her sister to finish the race when the attack happened. In the opening photo for this chapter, all three women approach the finish line one year later during the 118th Boston Marathon.

A young man carries a young neighbor girl who was injured in a barrel-bomb attack in the northern city of Aleppo, the largest city in Syria. More than 2,000 civilians, including at least 500 children, were killed in regime air strikes in war-torn Aleppo. Thousands more were wounded, often seriously, with limbs blown off or burned.

September 11, 2001, in a coordinated terrorist effort using four airplanes, 2,996 people (including 19 terrorists) were killed and more than 6,000 were injured. The greatest number of casualties (2,606) occurred as planes crashed into the twin towers of the World Trade Center. Perhaps the one image that is forever etched into the minds of those who were nearby are the sounds of bodies smashing into the concrete below. Hundreds of people leapt to their death after the two planes hit the twin towers rather than die in the ensuing inferno.

Congregants of St. Mary Ethiopian Orthodox Church held a vigil for more than 30 Ethiopian Christians who were shot and beheaded by ISIL militants in Libya in 2015. The killings were videotaped for propaganda and show two groups of men, one in orange jumpsuits and one in black, being killed at different locations.

Critical Thinking

Compare and contrast traditional war and terrorism. What are the similarities and differences? Which is more effective, and why? What can be done to stop terrorism?

Those who suffer because of terrorist acts can be divided into two groups. The first are random victims, people who are simply in the wrong place at the wrong time. Bombings, hijackings, and the spontaneous seizure of hostages victimize whoever happens to be available. Other members of society are intimidated by the casualness of this kind of terror, and the terrorist hopes that they will pressure the government to meet his or her demands.

The second category of victims includes individuals who are singled out because of their prominence. They, too, become dehumanized symbols: All politicians are blamed for whatever political injustices the terrorist perceives; all businesspeople are held personally responsible for commercial waste and greed. Civilians who have been killed or injured in bombings by terrorist groups as part of the ongoing Palestinian–Israeli conflict or the four French Jews murdered by Islamic extremists at a Paris kosher market in January 2015 are an example of the first category of random victims (Walt, 2015). The 84 victims killed by a truck intentionally speeding through a crowd celebrating Bastille Day 2016 in Nice, France, are other unfortunate examples (BBC News Europe, 2016). The 11 employees of the prominent French satirical newspaper Charlie Hebdo who were murdered by members of al Qaeda's Yemen branch, also in January 2015, are examples of the second group of victims (BBC News Europe, 2015).

CYBERWARFARE AND CYBERTERRORISM Recent incidents, such as the ongoing investigation into possible Russian interference in the 2016 U.S. Presidential election and the massive 2017 breach of the credit rating agency Equifax's data records, highlight the lack of international consensus on what defines a cyberattack, an act of war in cyberspace, or cyberterrorism. Cyberwar is typically considered a state-on-state action equivalent to an armed attack or use of force in cyberspace that may trigger a military response. Cyberterrorism is considered "the premeditated use of disruptive activities, or the threat thereof, against computers and/or networks, with the intention to cause harm or further social, ideological, religious, political, or similar objectives, or to intimidate any person in furtherance of such objectives."[9] Cybercrime includes unauthorized network breaches and theft of intellectual property and other data; it can be financially motivated, and law enforcement is typically responsible for finding and prosecuting the perpetrators. Within each category, different motivations as well as overlapping intent and methods of various actors complicate response options (Theohary and Rollins, 2015). Cybercrime costs are expected to hit $6 trillion annually by 2021, with cybersecurity spending to hit $1 trillion by then as well. An increased workforce of 3.5 million cybersecurity workers is projected to be needed to clean up the mess (Fruhlinger, 2018).

Terrorism's Impact on Society

15.4 **Explain terrorism's impact on society.**

One reason that terrorism is becoming so common is that terrorism can be extremely effective. As a form of warfare waged by the relatively powerless against powerful states, contemporary global terrorism has had significant effects on world trade and on the institutions of the United States and other nations.

15.4.1 Social, Economic, and Political Impacts

When terrorism strikes, it can be felt in a variety of ways. The effects of recent terrorist activity include the following.

- *Increased fear* of attack and heightened security at airports, ports, and major landmarks and federal buildings
- *Erosion of civil liberties,* including heightened government secrecy, limitations of habeas corpus, and curtailments of freedom of speech in the interests of security

---

[9]Theohary, C. A. & Rollins, J. W. (2015) "Cyberwarfare and Cyberterrorism: In Brief," Congressional Research Service.

- *Economic consequences,* including drastic curtailments in international tourism and trade, especially due to attacks on airlines
- *Health consequences,* such as fear of bioterrorism
- *Political consequences,* including terrorism's threat to polarize the world between Islamic and Christian civilizations, thus increasing the chances of war not only in Iraq but also elsewhere in the Middle East and on the Korean peninsula and increasing tensions between the United States and its European allies who worry that the United States is seeking to extend its power over the Middle East and other regions of the world (Jurkowitz, 2010; Pew Research Center, 2002).

It is too early to fully understand or assess the potential consequences of terrorism or the war on terrorism for people in the United States and elsewhere in the world. While war clouds gather, and threats of major terrorist attacks continue, it is difficult to find anything positive in the current situation. But if the current world crisis yields improvements in the ability of nations to cooperate in combating terrorism, and if the Islamic nations begin to solve some of their problems related to political instability, then the war against terrorism will have had some positive consequences together with the negative ones.

At the same time, the world's major powers, and especially the United States, find their military and logistical resources stretched thin as they struggle to confront threats of terrorism and other sources of violence. Their concerns of overextending leave them less inclined to intervene militarily in situations such as the current presence of ISIL and al Qaeda in Syria. Although the United States has led a multi-national coalition against these groups in Syria since September 2014, U.S. involvement has been limited largely to airstrikes and the training and arming of selected Syrian opposition groups. In the latest example of this, on April 14, 2018, the United States conducted a limited airstrike on Syrian targets in retaliation for a suspected chemical attack on the rebel-controlled town of Douma (AlJazeera.com, 2018). However, there are no current plans for additional strikes. To date, involvement of American soldiers in combat (i.e., "boots on the ground") has been extremely limited in large part because of U.S. weariness after more than a decade of war in Iraq and Afghanistan (Brooks, 2014).

15.4.2 What Do Americans Believe about Terrorism?

Despite few recent terrorist attacks in the United States and reduced government and media alarmism, concern about terrorism among the American public has remained surprisingly high ever since September 11, 2001 (Gallup, 2018; Mueller and Stewart, 2018; Poushter, 2017). Islamic terrorism, in particular, is viewed as a large, international conspiracy with hostile intent toward the United States. As shown in Table 15–3, Americans are far more likely to say that they are very concerned with Islamic extremism than are our neighbors to the north. Although concern about terrorism pervades all demographic groups, it is especially high among persons over age 50 and those on the right of the political spectrum. A 2017 Pew Research Center survey found that 81 percent

Table 15–3 U.S. and Canadian Concern with ISIS

	U.S.	Canada
Not at all Concerned	11%	11%
Not Too Concerned	16%	31%
Somewhat Concerned	30%	31%
Very Concerned	42%	25%

SOURCE: Data from Poushter, J. "Majorities in Europe, North America worried about Islamic extremism," Pew Research Center (May 24, 2017).

of Americans over age 50 were very or somewhat concerned about Islamic extremism (versus 56 percent among persons age 18–29), and 86 percent among those on the political right (versus 57 percent among those on the political left) (Poushter, 2017).

The public has grown somewhat more supportive of U.S. attempts to fight ISIL, as shown in Figure 15–2a–c (Pew Research Center, 2015, 2016). The percentage of surveyed adults who approve of the U.S. campaign against Islamic militants has increased, while the percentage who disapprove has remained constant between 2014 and 2016.

The reaction to the possibility of sending U.S. ground troops to the area is more divisive, with about an equal number favoring and opposing such action by 2016. However, again the numbers who support ground troops have increased significantly between 2014 and 2016. Men, whites and Hispanics, the middle aged, and Republicans are more likely to support the possible use of ground forces than are women, blacks, the young or the elderly, and Independent and Democratic voters. The public is also split over whether using military force is the best way to defeat terrorism or whether military force actually creates more hatred and thus more terrorism.

What Do You Think?

Why do you think that Americans have grown more supportive of U.S. attempts to fight terrorism, including the willingness to send in ground troops? Has there been an objective change in terrorism, is the media more vocal, or is there something else that might affect public opinion?

Figure 15–2a Percentage Saying They Approve or Disapprove of U.S. Campaign against Islamic Militants in Iraq and Syria, 2014, 2016

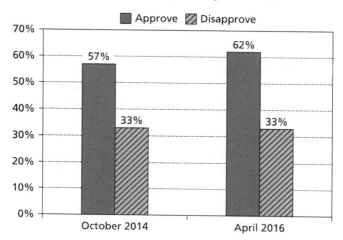

SOURCE: Data from Pew Research Center. 2015. "Growing Support for Campaign Against ISIS—and Possible Use of U.S. Ground Troops." 24 February. Retrieved 12 May 2015 (www.people-press.org/2015/02/24/growing-support-for-campaign-against-isis-and-possible-use-of-u-sground-troops/).; Pew Research Center. 2016. "Public Uncertain, DividedOver America's Place in the World." 5 May.

Figure 15–2b Percentage Saying They Favor or Oppose the Use of Ground Troops to Fight against Islamic Militants in Iraq and Syria, 2014, 2016

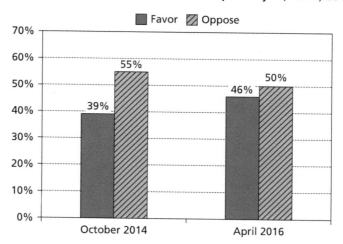

SOURCE: Data from Pew Research Center. 2015. "Growing Support for Campaign Against ISIS—and Possible Use of U.S. Ground Troops." 24 February. Retrieved 12 May 2015 (www.people-press.org/2015/02/24/growing-support-for-campaign-against-isis-and-possible-use-of-u-sground-troops/).; Pew Research Center. 2016. "Public Uncertain, DividedOver America's Place in the World." 5 May.

Figure 15–2c Percentage Who Say That Military Force Is the Best Way to Defeat Terrorism vs. Too Much Reliance on Military Force Creates Hatred and More Terrorism, 2014, 2016

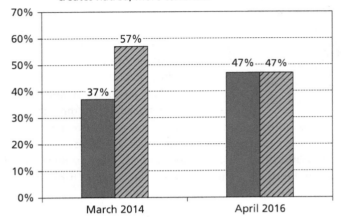

SOURCE: Data from Pew Research Center. 2015. "Growing Support for Campaign Against ISIS—and Possible Use of U.S. Ground Troops." 24 February. Retrieved 12 May 2015 (www.people-press.org/2015/02/24/growing-support-for-campaign-against-isis-and-possible-use-of-u-sground-troops/).; Pew Research Center. 2016. "Public Uncertain, DividedOver America's Place in the World." 5 May.

Sociological Theories about War and Terrorism

· 15.5   Compare and contrast sociological theories on war and terrorism.

No single theory can fully explain any given war or terrorist act. Nevertheless, various sociological perspectives have shed light on some forces that contribute to global conflict and can help us to better understand war and terrorism.

15.5.1 Functionalism

Functionalism is particularly concerned with social organization and the ways in which interconnected parts of a society work together or do not work together. Several early sociologists have examined the functions associated with war (Coser, 1956; Mills, 1958; Park, 1941; Simmel, 1904), including the following functions.

- *The Expansion of Territory*—Countries come into being because of conflicts over boundaries. For example, the United States went to war with France, Spain, Great Britain, and Mexico to establish the borders that currently exist.
- *Economic Benefits*—War can provide economic gains through land, crops, treasures, and natural resources such as oil. War also has an unintended economic benefit; it puts millions of unemployed people to work. For example, World War II was largely responsible for ending the Great Depression in the United States.
- *Advancing Ideology*—Conflict is often about advancing religious or political ideology. The Taliban, Boko Haram, al Qaeda, and ISIL all hope to advance their extremist religious ideology. In these and similar situations, rather than push for peaceful reforms, acts of war and terrorism bond groups of people together in a fever pitch; the outgroup is dehumanized, and revenge is sought. Alternatively, some groups fight to disseminate ideology; the largest wars that the United States have entered have been about defending a democratic form of government.

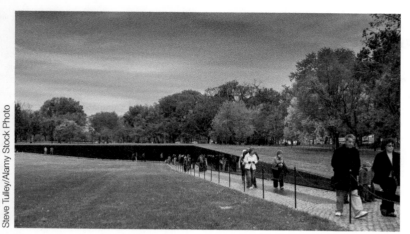

The Vietnam war was particularly unpopular. Service men and women were often booed or ridiculed after returning home from war. The memorial honoring those who died reflects this tense time in American history. Designed by a graduate student from Yale, Maya Lin, the memorial contains two long black walls, sunken partially into the ground, with the names of those who died etched in the stone. Critics opposed its unconventional design and its solemn black color. Some have likened it to a deep scar, gash, or wound. Nonetheless, it has emerged as an often-visited memorial and powerful tribute to those whose lives were lost.

- *Social Change*—Wars are fought in the name of change, but changes also happen to facilitate war itself. For example, our national highway system was developed in the 1950s under President Eisenhower, who pushed to create highways across the United States so that we could move military supplies quickly in case of an attack from the Soviet Union.
- *Social Integration*—Conflicts can bring people together and create a strong sense of nationalism or group solidarity, which can have either negative or positive consequences. The 1994 war in Rwanda pitted two groups against each other, the Tutsi and Hutu. Group identification during the war was so strong that former neighbors, coworkers, and friends turned on members of the other group in a mass slaughter of epic proportions. Within only a three-month span, roughly 800,000 Tutsi and politically moderate Hutu were killed, wiping out roughly three-quarters of the Tutsi population in Rwanda.

Conflicts, war, and terrorism also have many obvious dysfunctions. Innocent people are killed or injured, cities are destroyed, children are orphaned, people are impoverished, and the social fabric is damaged.

15.5.2 Conflict Perspective

Conflict theorists are concerned about tensions and power differentials in society. They suggest that war occurs when interests of nations or groups collide with one another for power, control, resources, and markets. Nations tend to use their military to advance their objectives, while smaller factions may resort to terrorist actions.

Marx predicted that as capitalist economies grew, their need for raw materials, labor, and new markets in which to sell finished goods also would increase. In the early twentieth century, Vladimir Lenin claimed that the competition among Britain, France, Germany, and other major powers to establish colonies around the world during the nineteenth and early twentieth centuries was evidence that Marx's prediction was correct. It was this competition for colonies that led to World War I, according to Lenin. In essence, the war pitted the national ruling classes against one another; the workers had nothing to gain by taking up arms (Rapoport, 1968). According to Lenin, the basis of war is economic competition among national ruling classes.

Marx and Lenin believed that economic interests shape most social phenomena, including warfare, but several social scientists have argued that noneconomic factors must also be considered. These explanations can be grouped into two types. The first takes the individual nation as the unit of analysis and looks inside societies at the relationships among institutions such as the military, government, and business. The second group of explanations focuses on institutions and patterns of behavior that cut across national boundaries. According to this perspective, organizations such as the United Nations, as well as international treaties and trade networks, are among the factors that influence the likelihood of war or peace.

INSTITUTIONAL FORCES WITHIN NATIONS   Most social scientists believe that during much of the twentieth and twenty-first centuries the influence of military leaders on government policy has grown in the United States and elsewhere. This growth may be viewed as a threat to peace. Keeping a large, well-equipped military force at the ready makes it easier for political leaders to choose war rather than negotiation as a tactic for handling international conflicts (Barton, 1981). In contrast, supporters of military interests argue that a powerful military discourages other nations from starting wars.

After World War II, a few critics voiced alarm at the newly won power of the military in the United States. In *The Power Elite*, C. Wright Mills (1956) argued that by the mid-1950s military leaders were "more powerful than they have ever been in the history of the American elite; they have now more means of exercising power in many areas of American life which were previously civilian domains; they now have more connections; and they are now operating in a nation whose elite and whose underlying population have accepted what can only be called a military definition of reality" (198).[10]

In effect, the U.S. economy never returned to its pre–World War II production patterns. Military and industrial leaders have ensured that a significant portion of the national budget is allocated to preparation for war. Today, the defense budget of the United States is three to five times larger than China's, the second largest defense budget. The United States has used this investment to become the world's most powerful military force by far, with weapons that no other nation possesses. With a federal government that intends to maintain this military superiority and use it wherever it believes American security is threatened, defense budgets in the United States are likely to remain extremely high for the foreseeable future, despite tax cuts and increasing levels of federal debt.

In addition to elites, another actor affects the likelihood of war—the public. During the twentieth century, many countries became much more democratic. As a result, political leaders must take public opinion into account in setting foreign policy. In some cases, public opinion favors war, especially when sentiments of **nationalism**—identification with, and exaltation of, the nation's culture and interests above those of all other nations—are strong. During the 1930s and 1940s, powerful nationalistic feelings in Germany helped make peace seem dishonorable and war seem a feasible option.

Today, renewed nationalism in Southeast Asia, Taiwan and China, Russia, and the Middle East poses a serious threat to prospects for world peace because the possibility of civil wars and nationalist movements leads to increased fear of terrorism and greater political instability. Moreover, local wars can draw in the larger nations, as occurred during World War I and could occur again in the Middle East. A more recent area of concern is the East and South China Seas where China has been involved in sometimes tense confrontations with many of its neighbors, including Japan, the Philippines, Taiwan, Malaysia, and Vietnam. Island ownership and other maritime disputes between these countries raise fears that mishandling of even a minor dispute could result in armed clashes that eventually draw in other countries, for example, the United States because of its commitment to Taiwan's defense, which has been intensified under the Trump administration (Westcott and Wang, 2018). In another sense, however, some analysts suggest that tensions in this region may lessen somewhat if only because the United States has apparently chosen not to challenge China over its territorial claims in the South China Sea (Valencia, 2018; McCoy, 2018).

nationalism

Identification with, and exaltation of, the nation's culture and interests above those of all other nations.

Flags wave outside the entrance to the United Nations Building, located in Geneva, Switzerland. The organization was created in 1945 to promote peace and human rights, and currently 193 countries are members.

THE INTERNATIONAL CONTEXT OF WAR AND PEACE Although national institutions and domestic forces can either preserve or threaten peace, no discussion of war and peace would be complete without some attention to the international context.

Gregory Adams/Getty Images

---

[10]Mills, C. W. (1956) *The Power Elite*. New York: Oxford University Press.

The world is composed largely of independent sovereign countries, each with its own interests. Because the supply of natural resources, power, prestige, and other valued commodities is limited, nations inevitably compete with one another. There is no central authority powerful enough to resolve all international conflicts peacefully. Nevertheless, several forces do reduce incentives to wage war.

One such force to promote peace is international cooperation embodied in organizations such as the League of Nations and the United Nations. In 1919, after World War I, the League of Nations was founded and was the first international organization whose principal mission was to maintain world peace. However, despite President Woodrow Wilson's strong support, the United States never joined the League; the American Congress wanted to avoid the United States being drawn into future conflicts because of the League's commitment to mutual defense. Ultimately, the onset of World War II showed that the League had failed in its mission, and it was replaced at the end of the war in 1945 by the United Nations, which now includes 193 member states.

A key function of these organizations is the settlement of disputes. The United Nations, for example, has helped restore peace in three wars between Israel and the Arabs, in the Korean conflict, in the Greek civil war, in Bosnia, and in several other conflicts. It has often failed to resolve clashes that involve the superpowers, however. The United States, Russia, and other major nations are often unwilling to give up some of their power to arbitrators, especially on issues of vital national interest (Raghavan, 2014).

Although the United States and other nations are often drawn into global conflicts in the role of peacekeepers, they usually achieve only limited success. Almost invariably, the peacekeeping force has difficulty withdrawing because of (1) explosiveness of the conflicts themselves; (2) the problems faced by peacekeepers in attempting to maintain neutrality; (3) the difficulty of coordinating in-the-field mediation with diplomacy; and (4) the lack of a workable model for peacekeeping. All these problems were encountered in Bosnia, Rwanda, Somalia, Sierra Leone, Sri Lanka, and the Democratic Republic of the Congo. But the desire to do something to ease bloody conflicts and to provide humanitarian aid continues to motivate third-party peacekeeping efforts and to improve their effectiveness in some instances.

International trade is another force that tends to promote peace. When influential citizens benefit economically from peaceful relations, support for war is diminished. Moreover, trade promotes a common outlook and common interests; trading partners are usually political partners. Today, China, the United States, Germany, Japan, and France are the largest merchandise traders, accounting for 38 percent of world trade in 2016 (World Trade Organization, 2017).

15.5.3 Symbolic Interactionism

The symbolic interactionist perspective looks at the symbols people use in everyday interaction, such as words, gestures, or appearances, and explores the meanings they attach to these symbols. A person's behavior with and among other people (their interaction) is the result of their shared understanding of cultural symbols.

Symbolic interactionist writing on war features several emphases. One theme explores the symbolic meaning behind the military or terrorist attack. According to the symbolic interactionist paradigm, the September 11, 2001, terrorists used the symbols of American power—the World Trade Center, New York City, the Pentagon, Washington, D.C.—to deliver a message to the world concerning their perception that the United States is the cause of the misery of Muslims in the Middle East and throughout the world. The actions of the terrorists were a form of language, a method of communication that was extreme because the message was extreme.

A second emphasis of symbolic interactionists concerns the perceptions and experiences of people involved in war: soldiers, civilians, and others. How are they affected by war? Many moving accounts, for example, both real and fictitious, have been offered of soldiers' lives both on the battlefield and at home after returning from war. A cursory search in May 2015 found 156 entries on the goodreads.com list of best books on the Iraq and Afghanistan wars. In the popular book *The Long Walk*, Brian Castner describes his three tours of duty in the Middle East, two of them in Iraq as the head of an Explosive Ordnance Disposal unit. Whenever bombs were discovered, he and his men would lead the way in either disarming the deadly devices or searching through rubble and remains for clues to the identities of those who made the bombs. Although robots and other remote means were used for safety, when these methods failed, one technician would suit up and take "the long walk" to disarm the bomb by hand. This lethal task expresses the real war in the Middle East. And movies such as American Sniper, The Hurt Locker, and Zero Dark Thirty among many others help shape Americans' current perceptions of the war experience.

A third emphasis concerns the use of symbols to marshal support for war or protest against war. Symbols such as the flag evoke feelings of patriotism, perhaps especially when a nation is at war. The president and other politicians typically display a flag when they give major speeches, and it would be unthinkable for a flag not to be showing when the speech is about war or the threat of war. During the Vietnam War, protesters sometimes flew the American flag upside down (the international symbol of distress) to show their hatred of the war, and some protesters also burned the flag—an act that is almost guaranteed to provoke outrage and hostility from onlookers. Another ubiquitous symbol during the Vietnam War was the so-called international peace symbol, originally designed in the late 1950s to symbolize concern over nuclear weapons. Vietnam War protesters wore this symbol on their clothing, and many put peace symbol decals on their motor vehicles, book bags, and other possessions. More recently, when the United States invaded Iraq in 2003, millions of Americans put magnetic yellow ribbons on their cars, SUVs, and pickup trucks to show their support for the troops.

Another emphasis of symbolic interactionism concerns how concepts related to war and terrorism come to be defined in ways that advance the goals of various parties. For example, a key goal of the military in basic training is to convince trainees that people they may face on the battlefield are "the enemy" and, as such, the killing is justified and is not murder. Similarly, the military often refers to civilian deaths or wounding as "collateral damage" in a conscious or unconscious attempt to minimize public horror at civilian casualties. This attempt backfired in Vietnam where, as a guerilla war, Americans were on the ground fighting for and against people who looked alike. Many innocent victims were shot at, killed, and injured. The My Lai massacre is the most common example of this dissonance. However, in his book *Kill Anything That Moves: The Real War in Vietnam*, author Nick Turse argues that the intentional killing of civilians was common in a war that claimed 2 million civilian lives, left 5.3 million civilians wounded, and generated 11 million refugees. The ongoing conflicts in Iraq, Afghanistan, and Pakistan have continued this legacy, with between 190,000 and 218,000 civilians through July 2016 having died violently because of direct military action. War deaths from malnutrition and a damaged health system and environment likely far outnumber

In this well-known tragedy, 504 defenseless Vietnamese civilians, mostly women and children, were slaughtered by American soldiers during the Vietnam War in what has become known around the world as the My Lai massacre. Before being killed, some of the victims were raped, gang-raped, sodomized, beaten, tortured, maimed, or stabbed. Some of the dead bodies were mutilated. The incident prompted widespread outrage throughout the world and reduced American support at home for the war.

Ronald L. Haeberle/Getty Images

deaths from combat (Watson Institute, 2018). And, according to Human Rights Watch, the Saudi Arabia–led military assault in Yemen has killed 5,295 civilians and wounded 8,873 between March 2015 and November 2017 (Human Rights Watch, 2018).

Social Policy

15.6 Describe policy approaches to dealing with terrorism.

The wars in Iraq and Afghanistan, continuing violence and terrorism in Syria and elsewhere in the Middle East, the continuing instability of the nuclear-armed North Korean government, China's increasing economic and military assertiveness, Russian activities in Ukraine and other former satellites—these and other challenges to peace make the world situation precarious. After an outpouring of sympathy and support for the United States and its people after the 9/11 attacks, the perception in Europe and elsewhere was that the United States pursued a unilateralist, "go-it-alone" set of policies that subverted international bodies such as the United Nations and sought to enhance U.S. control of Middle Eastern oil resources.

The rise of negative feelings about the United States is quite evident from State Department and Pew Research Center international survey results, as shown in Table 15–4. In many nations, the percentage of citizens with favorable views of the United States declined dramatically in the mid-2000s after invading Iraq, including America's closest allies in Western Europe. The most common negative attitude was the belief that the United States did not consider the interests of others outside its borders when making international policies. In most countries where the surveys were conducted, many people saw American policies as contributing to the growing gap between rich and poor nations. Large numbers of people were convinced that the war on terrorism and against Iraq masked American economic and political ambitions and that the United States was not doing enough to solve global problems.

President Obama renounced the unilateral policies of the Bush administration and in his first year as president, went out of his way to speak reassuringly to leaders of other nations, and to the press, about his intentions to seek cooperation and

Table 15–4 U.S. Favorability, 2003–2017 (Percent)

	2003	2005	2007	2009	2011	2013	2015	2017
EUROPE								
France	42	43	39	75	75	64	73	46
United Kingdom	70	55	51	67	61	58	65	50
Germany	45	42	30	64	62	53	50	35
Russia	37	52	41	44	56	51	15	41
Poland	N/A	62	61	67	70	67	74	73
MIDDLE EAST								
Tunisia	N/A	N/A	N/A	N/A	N/A	42	N/A	27
Jordan	1	21	20	25	13	14	14	15
Turkey	15	23	9	14	10	21	29	18
ASIA								
South Korea	46	N/A	58	78	N/A	78	84	75
India	N/A	N/A	N/A	N/A	N/A	56	70	49
NORTH AMERICA								
Canada	63	59	55	68	N/A	64	68	43
Mexico	N/A	N/A	56	69	52	66	66	30

SOURCE: Data from Pew Research Center. 2017. "Build Your Own Chart: Tracking U.S. Favorability and Confidence in the U.S. President, 2002 to 2017." 26 June. Retrieved 15 May 2018 (www.pewglobal.org/interactives/us-image/).

collaboration among nations to address terrorism and nuclear threats. His efforts bore some fruit, as U.S. favorability ratings during his presidency improved in many countries, although they were still low in much of the Middle East and Russia (Pew Research Center, 2017). However, the initial months of the Trump administration have seen a stark decline in the popularity of U.S. policies around the world. In a 2017 Pew Research Center survey of 37 nations, a median of only 22 percent of respondents had confidence in President Trump's ability to direct U.S. affairs. This stood in contrast to President Obama's final years in office when median confidence was 64 percent (Wike, Stokes, Poushter, and Fetterolf, 2017).

15.6.1 Dealing with Terrorism

Terrorist acts, especially suicide bombings, kidnappings, and the holding (and more recently, beheadings) of hostages, often attract worldwide attention. Indeed, terrorists use violence and drastic actions not only to attract media attention to their cause but also to intimidate civilians and show governments that they can exert power. Although public sentiment often favors negotiating with terrorists to win the release of captives, the usual official policy is not to give in to terrorist demands (Clawson, 1988; Spector, 2003). Policies that have proven somewhat effective include the following: imposing boycotts and other measures to put pressure on countries that sponsor terrorism; negotiators making promises but not keeping them after the captives have been released because promises made under threat are not valid; treating terrorists as criminals; enlisting the cooperation of journalists and media personnel in depriving terrorists of media attention; offering substantial rewards for information about and capture of terrorists; and developing an international campaign against terrorists with the help of a network of experts on the subject.

An informed public that will cooperate with antiterrorist policies is extremely important in combating this social problem. Since 9/11, for example, there have been predictions of widespread terrorism, especially against air travelers, and public cooperation with searches and stringent antiterrorist measures at airports was credited with preventing even more violence. However, although these policies may have helped to diminish specific terrorist acts, much larger forces are at work that seem to be increasing the likelihood of terrorism.

Given the rise in terrorist acts, the passage of the Homeland Security Act in 2002 represents the largest reorganization of the federal government in over 50 years. The Department of Homeland Security's mission is to prevent terrorism and enhance security, secure and manage the borders, enforce and administer immigration laws, safeguard and secure cyberspace, and ensure resilience to disasters (U.S. Department of Homeland Security, 2018).

This mission includes preventing terrorist attacks within the United States, reducing America's vulnerability to terrorism, minimizing the damage from attacks that do occur, and aiding in the recovery from such attacks. The Secretary of Homeland Security has jurisdiction over airport security, port security, border surveillance and management, and a wide variety of antiterror initiatives. The Department includes the Coast Guard, the Federal Emergency Management Agency, the U.S. Customs Service, and the Immigration and Naturalization Service.

15.6.2 Future Prospects

What can be done to reduce the likelihood of war and terrorism? No one can answer this question with certainty. Much may depend on how well individual citizens understand its causes and consequences and on how effectively they participate in debates over policies designed to control and limit the use of force in settling national differences.

The continuing political instability in many parts of the world makes it certain that international diplomacy will be a matter of continuing urgency. It is also quite clear that, as they face the continuing threat of international terrorist groups, the United States and other Western targets of terrorist attacks will continue to improve their intelligence capabilities. Strengthening intelligence entails developing more effective undercover operations, hiring agents with world language skills, improving international cooperation, upgrading computer tracking systems, and gaining a more sophisticated understanding of why individuals become motivated to commit acts of suicidal violence.

But going beyond government intelligence, it is important to take a step back and ask why so many people around the world dislike the United States. There is a perception that Americans are rude; they think of themselves as the center of the universe; they believe that money entitles them to everything; they brag; they are greedy and exploit others for their own gain; they are immoral; they spy on other countries; they get involved where they have no business; they fight unfairly (e.g., drones); and they are fanatical.

Before jumping in to say, "What a lie!" perhaps Americans could stop and take stock of their social policies and social and political ethos. Is there a kernel of truth in these allegations? Given America's tremendous resources, more than one person has asked "Why are we dropping bombs on Middle Eastern countries instead of building schools there? Wouldn't that be a more effective way to fight terrorism?"

What Do You Think?

Considering the themes of this text presented in Chapter 1 (using an empirical approach; linking individual experiences with social structure; recognizing that social inequality contributes to social problems; and acknowledging that understanding social problems requires a comparative perspective), describe how these themes help inform your understanding of war and terrorism.

Going Beyond Left and Right

Republicans and Democrats have substantially different views on the best ways to fight terrorism in the world. Most Republicans express the view that force is the best way to defeat terrorism. Many support the use of "enhanced interrogation techniques" that some would refer to as torture (Condon, 2014). They say that the use of harsh interrogation techniques helped bring down Osama bin Laden and disrupt terrorist plots. In contrast, most Democrats disagree with the premise that force is the best way to fight terrorism. Instead, they believe that such force creates hatred that fuels even more terrorism. They suggest that harsh interrogation techniques are tantamount to torture and remind Americans that the United States has long had a record of forbidding torture under any circumstances.

These differences in perspectives between the parties over the right approach to terrorism are hard to reconcile. What do you think about terrorism? Is it something that you worry about? What do you think about using torture?

Summary

15.1 Discuss the direct and indirect effects of war.

The direct effects of war are obvious. Millions of men and women are killed in war, and many more millions are injured. War also takes a psychological toll, and many soldiers and veterans suffer from post-traumatic stress disorder (PTSD). Another cause of PTSD in the military can be military sexual trauma. War also has many indirect effects. Soldiers experience significant disruptions in their personal lives, and war often leads to mass migrations of people trying to escape from danger or persecution or looking for new opportunities.

15.2 Identify various forms of weapons of mass destruction.

In modern times, wars have become more intense as military technology has become more lethal. Nuclear weapons (which are held by at least eight countries) and biological agents have the potential to annihilate millions of people quickly.

15.3   Review modern-day terrorism in the United States and around the world.

Since 9/11, terrorism has become the most dangerous threat to world order. It destabilizes governments, preys on innocent victims, and involves large amounts of financial and human resources. Yet unlike war, which openly pits opponents against each other in a recognized trial of strength, terrorism is covert. It seeks to sway the masses through intimidation and fear. Many terrorist individuals and groups are motivated by extreme religious beliefs, and religion as a factor in terrorism has grown in importance.

15.4   Explain terrorism's impact on society.

The effects of recent terrorist activity include increased fear of attack and heightened security; erosion of civil liberties; economic consequences and curtailments in international tourism and trade; fear of bioterrorism; and polarized Islamic and Christian civilizations. There is a growing concern about terrorism among Americans, with over half of adults surveyed responding that they have a "great deal of concern."

15.5   Compare and contrast sociological theories on war and terrorism.

Several early sociologists have examined the functions associated with war, including the expansion of territory, social integration, social change, advancing ideology, and economic benefits. Conflict theorists suggest that war occurs when interests of nations or groups collide with one another for power, control, resources, and markets. Symbolic interactionist writing on war features several emphases, including the symbolic meaning behind the military or terrorist attack; the war experience by those directly involved; the symbols used to promote or protest the war; and how concepts related to war and terrorism come to be defined in ways that advance the goals of various parties.

15.6   Describe policy approaches to dealing with terrorism.

No one method of dealing with terrorists has universal support. The traditional policy is not to give in to terrorist demands. Other policies that have proven somewhat effective include the following: imposing boycotts and other measures to put pressure on countries that sponsor terrorism; negotiators making promises but not keeping them after the captives have been released because promises made under threat are not valid; treating terrorists as criminals; enlisting the cooperation of journalists and media personnel in depriving terrorists of media attention; offering substantial rewards for information about and capture of terrorists; and developing an international campaign against terrorists with the help of a network of experts on the subject.

Epilogue:
Using the Sociological Imagination

This text has offered an interpretation of social problems through a new lens: the sociological imagination. Problems such as poverty, crime, pollution, racism, mental illness, and drug and alcohol abuse—while probably not new to you—are better understood when we understand their social context. These issues are not just personal problems, although many people experience these problems on a deeply personal level. People feel the sting of hunger associated with poverty, the trauma of being a crime victim, the frustration of discrimination, the pain of mental illness, and the anguish from drug and alcohol abuse.

However, to truly understand these phenomena, we must move beyond seeing these solely as personal problems and recognize the way they are patterned and shaped by our social structure. For example, how do the ways in which society is arranged contribute to poverty? As you have learned in previous chapters, poverty is associated with the government's minimum wage policies, a lack of access to quality medical care, inadequate educational opportunities, race and sex discrimination, inadequate treatment for mental illness, and an eroding safety net, just to name a few topics. A sociological imagination draws attention to the fact that what may at first look like private issues are often public ones requiring public solutions. Giving "Mary" more money will not eliminate poverty when the many social arrangements that contribute to poverty remain intact.

When enough people in a society agree that a condition exists that threatens the quality of their lives and their cherished values, and they agree that something should be done, sociologists refer to this condition as a social problem. However, this does not mean that everyone agrees about the condition's causes, consequences, or solutions. In fact, there is often much disagreement. Some people think the primary cause of poverty lies with individual inadequacy (e.g., laziness, not trying hard enough, unwillingness to defer gratification, poor choices). Others vehemently disagree and point instead to weaknesses of the social structure and safety net programs. Naturally, beliefs about causes of a social problem influence beliefs about its solutions. Should welfare programs, for example, be more difficult to obtain in order to discourage laziness and encourage effort? Or should welfare programs be easier to obtain to provide safety for vulnerable individuals and families, which would then allow them to more easily and safely climb out of poverty?

Perhaps one of the best-known persons today to study sociology is former first lady Michelle Obama. She speaks here in 2017 on behalf of her "Reach Higher" initiative. Interestingly, Barack Obama's Kenyan half-sister Auma also majored in Sociology while in college.

ZUMA Press, Inc./Alamy Stock Photo

462

The Case of Caitlyn

Let me introduce you to Caitlyn, a 23-year-old single mother of a young son, to help answer these questions.

> Caitlyn never expected to be a single mother. She was in what she thought was a loving relationship with a man, Luke, whom she met while attending the local community college. Although they did not live together at first, they spent most of their time together, usually at his apartment. When Caitlyn became pregnant, Luke seemed happy. She herself was somewhat unsure, but Luke, who had recently landed a full-time job, convinced her that having a baby together would be wonderful and that he could take care of them. They even discussed plans to marry, although they didn't set a date.
>
> Unfortunately, as time went on, Caitlyn began to recognize that things were far from wonderful. Because of intense "morning sickness" that lasted most of the day, Caitlyn fell behind in her classes and could not continue going to school. Her financial aid was therefore terminated, and she moved in with Luke to save expenses. Although Luke was enthusiastic about his job at first, it didn't take long for him to change his mind. He often came home in a bad mood and took it out on Caitlyn. He was verbally abusive, and then became physically abusive as well. Once he hit her hard enough to knock her to the floor, hitting her head against a chair. She put up with this treatment, hoping he would change once the baby was born, but deep down, she feared that she had no alternative. She had no money, no education beyond high school and a random set of classes at a community college, no health insurance, and no family that she could turn to.
>
> Luke did not change after the baby, Billy, was born, and the abuse continued. One night in one of their heated arguments, Caitlyn feared that Luke might actually hurt Billy. She knew then that she had to make a plan. The next morning after Luke left for work, she packed a bag with three days' worth of clothing, diapers, and a few miscellaneous items, and fled. She went to a homeless shelter.
>
> Living in a homeless shelter is tough for anyone, but it is especially difficult with a baby. There was little privacy. Being in the family ward, it was noisy. The shelter was closed during the day, and all occupants had to leave the building. She spent the days wandering the streets, sometimes panhandling in hopes of getting enough money for a down payment on an apartment, and sometimes looking for work. But she was caught in the "catch-22" predicament of the homeless. She needed a job to secure a permanent address and phone number, but without a permanent address and phone number, she couldn't land a job. And what about childcare, she wondered.

Caitlyn's quandaries are many. She is poor, but it is not because of her laziness or inadequate parenting. On the contrary, she attended some college until she was too sick to continue, and she left home to protect her son. Instead of placing the blame on Caitlyn as an individual, let's look deeper within her story to see what particular insights a sociological imagination can provide.

Jobs, Income, and Poverty

Poverty is quickly becoming a women's problem, as the popular term "feminization of poverty" suggests. Women are far more likely than men to be impoverished, and single mothers are particularly vulnerable. About 30 percent of single mothers live below the poverty line (Semega, Fontenot, and Kollar, 2017).

Even if Caitlyn were successful at finding a job, would her income be sufficient for a comfortable life for herself and Billy? As shown in earlier chapters, the purchasing power of the minimum wage has eroded, discrimination still exists, and the primary job growth has been in the low-paying service sector. Without job experience or a college degree, Caitlyn's job prospects are limited indeed. While she feels the effects of these issues on a personal level, they certainly are not Caitlyn's fault. They represent social problems rather than personal ones.

Finding adequate childcare is another hurdle Caitlyn, and all parents, face. In a typical week, about 11 million children under age five are in some type of childcare arrangement. People without children often don't realize how expensive childcare can be. It rivals the cost of housing, and can be as expensive as paying for college. For example, in my home state of Washington, care for an infant runs over $13,000 per year, while in-state tuition at a public college runs around $9,000, and average rent is $12,000 (Child Care Aware of America, 2017). This means that infant care for one child would take up nearly 20 percent of a typical family's income in Washington, and would be a significantly larger drain on Caitlyn's budget. When millions of families face this same challenge, we can safely say that it has become a social problem, rather than a personal one.

Housing

Millions of families have critical housing needs just like Caitlyn because they cannot afford to pay rent for safe, sanitary housing. The demand for housing assistance overwhelms the supply. Because of funding limitations, only one in four households that are eligible for public housing receives any form of federal housing assistance. Most agencies have long waiting lists for public housing, and some no longer accept new applications because of the backlog (Fisher and Sard, 2017; Rice, 2018). Unsurprisingly, women and children make up a large and growing segment of the homeless population. According to a 25-city study by the U.S. Conference of Mayors, 40 percent of homeless persons are women, and 36 percent were experiencing homelessness as part of families (U.S. Conference of Mayors, 2016).

Unemployed single mothers without social and financial support can find themselves in precarious situations. Nonetheless, it doesn't have to be this way in a country as wealthy as the United States. Other nations have found ways to better meet the needs of families, including offering a supply of subsidized housing or housing vouchers for those who cannot afford the cost of housing on their own.

Health Insurance

Many millions of Americans are without health insurance, and therefore have difficulty accessing a doctor for their most basic medical needs. They experience unnecessary pain, suffering, disability, and even death.

Caitlyn and Billy are part of the 28 million Americans without health insurance to meet their most basic health care needs (Barnett and Berchick, 2017). Millions more are underinsured; high deductibles or copayments render their insurance virtually useless except in the most catastrophic conditions.

As you've learned, living without health insurance can have serious financial, emotional, and health consequences for the entire family (Kaiser Family Foundation, November 29, 2017). If even one person within a family is uninsured, all share in the anguish of trying to pay medical bills and suffer the consequences when they cannot. Families without health insurance are more likely to delay or forgo seeking needed medical care. They are twice as likely to postpone seeking medical care, over four times as likely to forgo needed care, and are more than twice as likely to have a needed prescription go unfilled. Children may not get needed immunizations as preventative care.

dbimages/Alamy Stock Photo

Is the lack of health insurance a personal issue or a social problem? When so many Americans find themselves in the precarious situation of being uninsured, Americans must examine the social structure to better understand the problem and to seek solutions. The Affordable Care Act (ACA) was designed to help families like Caitlyn's by allowing them to purchase insurance at a discounted price, whether employed or not. Until 2017, when the U.S. Congress under President Trump voted to repeal the individual mandate, families were required by law to have insurance. However, the change in federal law now makes it easier for families to fall through the cracks.

Nonmarital Childbearing and Child Support

Caitlyn has never been married and had her child outside of marriage. It may be tempting to ask: Isn't Caitlyn responsible for creating her own problem?

A simple answer might be "yes." However, a sociological analysis digs deeper to uncover the complexity of common problems and their solutions. After all, Caitlyn is hardly unique in having a baby outside of marriage. Today, over one-third of all births occur outside of marriage, a significant increase from just a decade ago. Some women become pregnant and opt for an abortion rather than carry the child to term. Caitlyn decided against abortion and, in the confines of what she thought was a solid relationship, chose to have her baby instead. Should we criticize her for that decision?

Having a child out of wedlock in other countries generally does not pose the great financial problem that it does in the United States. The reason children in other countries are better off is that they and their single mothers are eligible for many programs to help sustain them, including paid maternity leave, child or family allowances, housing subsidies, health insurance, and free or low-cost childcare. The United States has a laissez-faire approach; parents are expected to assemble their own assistance. However, U.S. programs are limited, income thresholds are extremely low, and the social service maze can be daunting.

Finally, it's easy to judge Caitlyn for the choice she made (either to deliberately have a child outside of marriage or to be lax about using birth control), but let's remember that she did not impregnate herself. Shouldn't we also pose questions for the fathers of their children, most notably, where are they, and why aren't they paying child support?

Caitlyn is among the millions of women who fail to receive support from their children's fathers, and the government takes only limited action on their behalf. Only about half of custodial parents have some type of child support agreement for their children, and of these, many do not receive the full amount regularly (Grall, 2016). Yet, expected child support dollars, which run about $6,000 a year, matter tremendously to families like Caitlyn's, and can pull them out of poverty.

As we review Caitlyn's story, a sociological imagination reveals that many seemingly private struggles are really large-scale social problems. When millions of women are paid poverty-level wages, when childcare is unaffordable, when low-income housing is unavailable, when health insurance is a privilege dependent on the goodwill of employers rather than a right of citizenship, when critical safety nets are missing, and when children receive no or inadequate financial support from their noncustodial parents, these are much more than simply Caitlyn's problems. These are examples of social problems, and their solutions require broad policy changes in U.S. social structure.

Themes Revisited

My goal has been to challenge you not only to see explicitly the connections between personal lived experience and broader social problems, but also to grasp four themes introduced in Chapter 1:

- The importance of using an empirical approach
- Greater understanding comes with linking individual experiences with social structure
- The recognition that social inequality contributes to social problems
- Social problems and their solutions are best understood by using a comparative perspective

Let's review these themes:

The Importance of Using an Empirical Approach

The sociological imagination uses an empirical approach to study families. Most of us probably have strong opinions about the world in which we live. However, sociologists do not rely on so-called common sense, or the sentiment "It's always been that way so it must be right." Instead, they use an empirical approach, in which they answer questions through a systematic collection and analysis of quantitative or qualitative data. Empirical research can shed new light on a topic.

Dating violence on college campuses is a serious public health problem. Approximately 25 percent of dating couples include physical aggression (e.g., punching, slapping, and shoving/pushing), 80 percent include psychological aggression (e.g., threats of violence and derogatory comments) and 20 percent include sexual aggression (e.g., forced/coerced intercourse) each year.

Surveys also indicate that approximately 75 percent of college students report that they consume alcohol, and 35 percent use cannabis. Previous research clearly shows that alcohol use increases the risk for dating violence. In fact, many researchers have concluded that alcohol is a contributing cause of violence between intimate partners.

However, considerably less is known about the role that marijuana may play in dating violence among college students. Some studies report that marijuana promotes feelings of relaxation and calm, which seem at odds with dating violence. Yet, other research finds that users often become irritable or experience anxiety, which could increase the likelihood of violence. What little research there is about the relationship between marijuana use and dating violence is inconsistent and inconclusive. Further research is needed so that programs can be created to address this issue. One especially promising approach is through the use of daily diary designs. This type of methodology allows researchers to determine whether marijuana use precedes dating violence (and how close in time it precedes it), while also reducing recall bias.

Marijuana is now legal in a number of states, and it is a commonly used drug even in those states where it is not legal. However, we know little about the social aspects of drug use. While research has shown a clear link between alcohol use and dating violence, is this the same case with marijuana?

National Geographic Image Collection/Alamy Stock Photo

Greater Understanding Comes with Linking Individual Experiences with Social Structure

Sexual harassment has a long history but received new attention in 2017 as many prominent men were accused of sexual harassment. Leading the way, it was exposed that former Fox News anchor

Bill O'Reilly paid more than $13 million to settle sexual harassment cases with five women by asking them to keep quiet and drop any related legal suits. Several other women spoke about O'Reilly's history of harassment, which included phoning women while apparently masturbating, trying to lure them to his hotel rooms, making lewd remarks to them, trying to kiss them, and hampering their careers when they rebuffed him. After these cases became public, Fox News dropped O'Reilly from their news lineup.

Meanwhile, almost 60 women had accused the once-celebrated comedian Bill Cosby of sexual assault, with some incidents dating back to the 1960s. In the wake of those allegations, numerous organizations had severed ties with the comedian, and previously awarded honors and titles had been revoked.

U.S. Gymnast Aly Raisman, co-captain of the U.S. Women's Gymnastics Squad at the 2012 and 2016 Olympics, competes on the uneven parallel bars. Raisman is one of many U.S. gymnasts who accused former USA gymnastics team doctor Larry Nassar of sexual abuse, and testified at Nassar's sentencing hearing in 2018. Nassar pleaded guilty to 10 counts of sexual abuse.

Then Harvey Weinstein, the motion picture mogul, came under scrutiny for his harassing behaviors toward numerous women, using his power over actresses to try to secure sexual favors. Following Weinstein, the dominoes began to fall: actors, comedians, politicians, and business leaders, among others, stood accused, often forced out of their positions as multiple accusers came forward to tell similar stories and describe the pain they suffered afterwards.

Women often feel very alone when they experience sexual harassment and may not tell anyone about it. They may be plagued with self-doubt, "Did that really just happen? Am I being too sensitive? Did I lead him on somehow?" Victims may initially view it as a personal problem requiring a personal solution, "How can I get him to stop? Should I tell his superior? Should I find a new job?"

Sexual harassment, however, is rooted in a patriarchal culture that offers men greater control and authority in most social realms. It is more about power than lust. It is borne out of the way that gender is constructed in our society. The use of harassment as a tactic to control or frighten women explains why sexual harassment is most frequent in occupations and workplaces where women are relative newcomers and are in the minority. Although sexual harassment can occur in any setting, women who hold jobs traditionally held by men are far more likely to be harassed than women who do "women's work" (AMFCME, 2018).

As prominent cases of harassment were uncovered, the hash tag #MeToo movement was born. It represented the plight of the average woman coming forth to tell her story of harassment, assault, and rape by bosses, colleagues, and others. Twelve million Facebook posts were made in 24 hours. Sexual harassment offers a compelling example of the ways in which personal experience is linked to social structure.

The Recognition that Social Inequality Contributes to Social Problems

Social inequality is pervasive throughout the world. Wars have been fought, homes and communities have been ravaged, families have been torn apart, and ethnic groups have been obliterated in battles over valued resources. The United States is also highly stratified; people with a lot of money have different opportunities from those without.

Much of human progress depends on innovation. It depends on people coming up with a breakthrough idea to improve life. Think about penicillin or cancer treatments, electricity or the silicon chip. For this reason, societies have a great interest in making

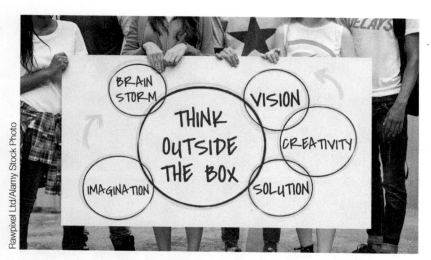

Social inequality is a central organizing feature in society, enhancing the lives of some, but constricting the lives of many. Children with parents in the top 1 percent of the income distribution are much more likely to become inventors than are children with below-average income parents, even if their math scores are lower.

sure that as many people as possible have the opportunity to become inventors, scientists, and entrepreneurs.

Not surprisingly, children who excelled in math were far more likely to become inventors. But being a math standout by itself wasn't enough, according to a recent study by a research team from the Equality of Opportunity Project. Only the top math students who also came from high-income families had a decent chance to become an inventor.

Children with parents in the top 1 percent of the income distribution are ten times more likely to become inventors than children with below-average income parents. In contrast, low-income students who are among the very best math students—those who score in the top 5 percent of all third graders—are no more likely to become inventors than below-average math students from affluent families. This is a clear and compelling example of one of the themes of this text: social inequality is a critical organizing feature in society and contributes to social problems.

Social Problems and Their Solutions Are Best Understood by Using a Comparative Perspective

On October 1, 2017, concertgoers at the Route 91 music festival in Las Vegas were looking forward to good music, food, and dancing. Instead, they were victims of the deadliest mass shooting in U.S. history. From the thirty-second floor of a hotel room across the street, one shooter fired more than 1,100 rounds into the crowd, killing 58 people (including himself) and injuring 546 others. When police stormed his hotel room they found many guns and another 4,000 rounds of ammunition.

The nation mourned, and quickly the issue of gun control legislation resurfaced. Critics of tighter gun laws claimed that the timing was not right—the families and friends of the deceased and wounded needed time to grieve without the massacre being turned into a political event. Those who support tighter gun restrictions argued that the issue should be addressed quickly while the massacre was fresh in our minds. Waiting is simply a stall tactic used by politicians, they said, as the majority of Americans (both Democrats and Republicans) want some restrictions or controls on who can buy guns and what kinds of guns can be purchased.

Is there anything to be learned from the approaches taken by other countries? Australia—the land of rugged individualism—has a relatively high murder rate, and like the United States, has been the site of numerous mass murders. In 1996, in the largest mass murder in Australia's history, a man opened fire in a popular tourist region; 35 persons were killed and 23 were wounded.

In contrast to the United States, Australia decided to take action. The Australian government banned automatic and semiautomatic firearms, adopted new licensing requirements, established a national firearms registry, and instituted a 28-day waiting period for gun purchases. It also bought and destroyed more than 600,000 civilian-owned firearms, in a scheme that cost half a billion dollars and was funded by raising taxes. The entire overhaul took only a few months to implement.

There was widespread opposition to these policies, and the National Rifle Association (NRA) worked to resist any laws that made it more difficult to own guns. Nonetheless, the legislation passed.

What has been the result? Gun-related homicides in Australia dropped by 59 percent. Suicides by gun dropped by 59 percent. Mass shootings in Australia (defined as incidents in which the gunman killed five or more people other than himself) were reduced from 13 in the 18-year period before 1996 to zero (Calamur, 2017). The legislation has been successful.

Of course, the United States is not identical to Australia, culturally, socially, or economically. America has more people, more guns per capita, and, perhaps even more importantly, a constitutional right to bear arms. Nonetheless, Australia provides a thought-provoking example of how a country can successfully deal with gun violence.

This photo is part of a memorial of 58 crosses for those whose who were killed, and one for the strength of the city, in the grounds behind the "Welcome to Las Vegas" sign. Mass shootings continue to plague the United States, unlike in other countries that have more restrictive gun laws.

The Promise of Social Solutions!

A Social Problems course can easily be misinterpreted as a gloomy subject. After all, we have talked about a variety of weighty issues and the controversies that surround various types of solutions. "Don't you get depressed?" a recent student asked me. I was taken aback by the question and had to think for a few moments on how to answer her. In truth, I feel invigorated by the study of social problems. As a sociologist, I know that it is important to understand how social life operates, both the good and the bad. Yes, the problems are real, and I have presented you with many difficult facts. But the solutions are there for us, waiting to be discovered, created, and implemented. This has the potential to be very exciting, indeed.

Glossary

addiction A complex phenomenon that involves the drug user's physical and psychological dependence, the type of drug, and the amount and frequency of use.

advance directive A written statement that explains the patient's wishes for medical care should the person be unable to communicate them to the physician.

affirmative action Controversial policies that require institutions that have engaged in discriminatory practices to increase opportunities for women and members of minority groups.

Affordable Care Act (ACA) Legislation developed by President Obama and passed in 2010 that is the first major overhaul of the U.S. health care system since the creation of Medicare and Medicaid in 1967.

agents of socialization The people, social institutions, and organizations that teach boys and girls their gendered expectations.

Air Quality Index (AQI) A way of categorizing levels of daily air quality that indicates how clean or polluted the air is.

alcoholism The state of being addicted to alcohol with the following four symptoms: craving, loss of control, physical dependence, and tolerance.

Alcohol Use Disorder (AUD) Individuals must meet certain criteria outlined in the Diagnostic and Statistical Manual of Mental Disorders (DSM). The severity of AUD—mild, moderate, or severe—is based on the number of criteria met.

anomie The feeling of being adrift that arises from the disparity between goals and means.

antimiscegenation laws Laws banning marriage between whites and other races.

Any Mental Illness (AMI) A mental, behavioral, or emotional disorder.

assimilation A process through which a racial or an ethnic minority group slowly ceases being "different" by taking on the characteristics of the mainstream culture.

aversion therapy/behavior conditioning A form of treatment that applies nausea-producing drugs or electric shock to condition the patient against alcohol.

baby-boom generation The large number of people who were born between the mid-1940s and the early 1960s who are now reaching retirement age.

binge drinking A pattern of drinking that brings blood alcohol concentration (BAC) levels to 0.08 g/dL. Although the quantity of alcohol required to reach this level can vary, in general it amounts to a consumption of five or more drinks in a single session for males, and to four or more drinks for females.

cap and trade A program that would create markets for emission credits, representing a mix of environmentalism with free market principles.

capital Both the money used to purchase resources (e.g., raw materials) and the physical assets (e.g., buildings and equipment) used to produce goods and services. Capitalists are people who combine capital with the labor of workers to produce goods and services in the hope of making a profit—that is, selling their product or service at a market price higher than the costs of the equipment and labor used to create it.

capitalism A particular type of economic system found in the United States (and elsewhere); sometimes known as a free enterprise system, characterized by private ownership of the means of production.

chain migration The tendency of immigrants to migrate to areas where they have kin and others from their home communities.

civil law Laws that deal with noncriminal acts in which one individual injures another.

class stratification The stratification of individuals and groups according to their access to various occupations, incomes, skills, and opportunities.

climate change A type of environmental change that encompasses global warming but refers to the broader range of changes that are happening to our planet, including rising sea levels; shrinking mountain glaciers; accelerating ice melt in Greenland, Antarctica, and the Arctic; and shifts in flower and plant blooming times.

clitoridectomy A procedure in which the clitoris is cut out of the body.

codependency A relationship pattern in which a person assumes the responsibility for meeting others' needs, often to the detriment of their own needs.

cohabitation Living with a romantic and sexual partner without being married.

communism A system of government that controls a planned economy, determining the flow of goods and services.

community psychology The idea of easily accessible, locally controlled facilities that could care for mentally ill people in their own communities.

comparative perspective A process to learn about other cultures and other historical periods to better understand social problems within one's own culture.

conflict perspective A way of thinking that is based on the belief that social problems arise out of major contradictions in the way societies are organized, contradictions that lead to large-scale conflict between those who have access to the good life and those who do not.

contingent nonstandard work Employment that does not have a written employment contract, is only temporary, has irregular hours, or is some combination of these elements.

coyotes Guides who help people immigrate illegally to the United States.

crime Any act or omission of an act for which the state can apply sanctions.

criminal law The practice wherein society prohibits certain acts and prescribes the punishments to be meted out to violators.

cultural capital The resource that a person brings from his or her family, which may include forms of knowledge, skills, education, and other advantages that a person has, and which give him or her a certain status in society.

cultural lag A delay that occurs when one aspect of a culture changes more rapidly than another, causing some maladjustment between the two aspects.

cyberstalking Stalking and harassment that occurs electronically, such as through e-mail, texts, bulletin boards, chat rooms, or other types of media.

date-rape drugs Drugs such as gamma hydroxybutyrate (GHB), Rohypnol (popularly known as "roofies" or "roofenol"), or ketamine hydrochloride (ketamine), which can immobilize a person to facilitate an assault.

de facto segregation Segregation that is not required by law, but results from housing patterns, economic inequalities, or gerrymandered school districts.

de jure segregation Segregation that is required by law.

deinstitutionalization The act of discharging patients from mental hospitals directly into the community.

dementia   An overall term that describes a wide range of symptoms associated with a decline in memory or other thinking skills severe enough to reduce a person's ability to perform everyday activities.

demographic transition   A process by which a population moves through several stages: An original equilibrium in which a high birthrate is largely canceled out by a high death rate, then through a stage in which the birthrate remains high but the death rate declines, to a final equilibrium in which the birth and death rates are lower, but the population is much larger.

demographic transition   The process in which a society moves from a situation of high fertility rates and low life expectancy to one of low fertility rates and high life expectancy.

detoxify   To keep a person off alcohol or another substance until none shows in blood samples.

differential association   A theory that suggests that criminal behavior is a result of a learning process that occurs chiefly within small, intimate groups—family, friends, neighborhood peer groups, and the like.

discrimination   The differential treatment of individuals considered to belong to a particular social group.

drift hypothesis   A concept that argues that social class is not a cause but a consequence of mental disorder.

drug   Any chemical substance that affects physiological functions, mood, perception, or consciousness; has the potential for misuse; and may be harmful to the user or to society.

drug abuse   The use of socially unacceptable drugs and/or the excessive or inappropriate use of acceptable drugs in ways that can lead to physical, psychological, or social harm.

economic globalization   The growing tendency for goods and services to be produced in one nation or region and consumed in another.

educational attainment   The number of years of school completed.

empirical approach   A method that answers questions through a systematic collection and analysis of data.

enabling behaviors   Behaviors that a codependent person will do to cover for, support, and enable an alcoholic to continue to drink (or to enable another type of abuser to continue toxic behaviors).

entrepreneur   A capitalist who creates a new business venture.

environmental justice   Demanding that all people be treated equally with respect to the environment.

environmental racism   The act of disproportionally placing landfills and toxic waste dumpsites near low-income and minority neighborhoods.

epidemiologists   Social scientists who study the course of diseases in human populations.

ethnic minorities   Groups of people who share cultural features, such as language, religion, national origin, dietary practices, and a common history, and who regard themselves as a distinct group.

ethnocentrism   The belief that one's own group is superior to another group.

euthanasia   The painless killing of a patient suffering from a terminal illness or irreversible coma.

fee-for-service   A type of health care system in which patients are expected to pay directly for their own medical care; the cost is not rolled into taxes.

fetal alcohol spectrum disorders (FASD)   A group of conditions that can occur in a person whose mother consumed alcohol during pregnancy. These effects can include physical abnormalities and problems with cognition, behavior, and learning that last a lifetime.

fictive kin   Friends in a close network who provide support.

functionalist perspective   A way of thinking that considers the way major social institutions such as the family, the military, the health care system, and the police and courts actually operate.

gender   The culturally and socially constructed differences between males and females, which are found in the meanings, beliefs, and practices associated with femininity and masculinity.

gender socialization   A process whereby people learn to behave according to the gendered norms of a culture.

general birth (or fertility) rate   Number of children born per 1,000 women ages 15–44 (some countries use 49 as the cutoff age).

global warming   The long-term warming of the planet.

gun control   Restrictions on what kinds of firearms can be sold and bought, who can possess or sell them, where and how they can be stored or carried, what responsibilities a seller has to vet a buyer, and what obligations both the buyer and the seller have to report transactions to the government. It may also cover related matters, such as limits on types of ammunition and magazines, or other technology.

halfway house   A small, privately run residential community, usually located in an urban area, in which ex-patients are helped to make the transition from the hospital to normal life.

Head Start   The federally funded preschool program for low-income children and their families.

hidden curriculum   An undocumented teaching approach that informally teaches gendered norms.

homogamy   The expectation that one must marry a person like oneself with respect to such characteristics as religion, social class, and race or ethnicity.

hospice   Offers care to a dying person, with the goal of maintaining or improving quality of life; the focus is on caring, not curing.

human trafficking   The illegal and highly profitable business of recruitment, transport, or sale of human beings into all forms of forced labor and servitude.

identity theft   Stolen identity, which can then lead to a misuse of a credit card, bank account, or other theft.

infant mortality   The number of deaths of children in their first year of life, for every 1,000 live births.

infibulation   A procedure in which the clitoris is cut out of the body, the vaginal lips are cut or scraped away, and the outer labia are stitched together, leaving only a miniscule opening for menstrual blood and urine to escape the body.

institution building   A modern version of the functionalist perspective, which attempts to show how people reorganize their lives to cope with new conditions.

institutional discrimination   An unconscious result of the structure and functioning of the public institutions and policies themselves.

internalized racism   The personal conscious or subconscious acceptance of the dominant society's racist views, stereotypes, and biases of one's racial or ethnic group.

intersexed   Individuals with anatomical categories that are not easily identifiable.

intimate partner violence (IPV)   Violence between those who are physically and sexually intimate, such as spouses or partners.

latent functions   Indirect by-products of some phenomenon that are less obvious.

level of living   The level of material well-being that people actually obtain.

life expectancy   How long a person can expect to live; it is usually calculated at birth.

limited liability   A protection by which the assets of the corporation are liable to seizure in the case of economic failure or wrongdoing, but the entrepreneur's personal assets are not liable if the corporation fails.

long-term care   Care for chronic physical or mental conditions that will likely never go away.

lumpenproletariat   Members of capitalist societies who are poor and not in the labor force, according to Karl Marx.

Mothers Against Drunk Driving (MADD)   A nonprofit organization working to protect families from drunk driving and underage drinking through education and support of victims and survivors.

manifest functions   Those societal functions that are direct and the most obvious.

manslaughter   Unlawful homicide without malice aforethought.

markets   Institutions that regulate the worldwide flow of an almost infinite array of goods and services. Almost all markets in nations throughout the world are regulated by acts of governments, including the United States.

Medicaid   The federal-state health care program for certain categories of low-income people.

medical sociology   The subfield of sociology that specializes in research on the health care system and its impact on the public, especially access to health care.

Medicare   A federal health insurance program for people age 65 and older (and for younger people receiving Social Security Disability Insurance payments or suffering from specified conditions).

mental health   A state of well-being in which the individual realizes his or her own abilities, can cope with the normal stresses of life, can work productively and fruitfully, and is able to make a contribution to his or her community.

mental illness   A mental, behavioral, or emotional disorder (excluding developmental or substance abuse disorders), diagnosable currently or within the past year and of sufficient duration to meet diagnostic criteria specified within the fifth edition of the *Diagnostic and Statistical Manual of Mental Disorders (DSM-V)*.

military sexual trauma (MST)   Any sexual harassment or sexual assault suffered by a veteran while serving in the military.

million tons of oil equivalent (Mtoe)   A standard method of converting different types of energy units into one measure.

modernization   Contains three characteristics: (1) the transformation of societies to urbanized and industrialized ways of life based on scientific technologies, (2) individualized rather than communal or collective roles, and (3) a cosmopolitan outlook that values efficiency and progress.

multinational corporations (or transnational corporations)   Corporations that have their headquarters in one country but pursue business activities and profits in one or more foreign nations.

multiple jeopardy   Having multiple minority statuses that include being old, female, and black (or Hispanic or Native American), which may cause more hardships than a person would face if he or she were in just one or two of these categories.

multiple partner fertility   Having children with multiple partners.

murder   Unlawful killing of a human being with malice aforethought.

nationalism   Identification with, and exaltation of, the nation's culture and interests above those of all other nations.

nativist   Anti-immigrant or anti-foreigner sentiment.

natural history approach   The idea that social problems develop in a series of phases or stages.

net worth   For a person or entity, the value of savings and checking accounts, real estate, automobiles, stocks and bonds, and other assets (minus debts).

No Child Left Behind Act of 2001   A major legislative initiative of the Bush administration to improve education in four clearly defined ways: (1) accountability for results; (2) emphasis on doing what works based on scientific research; (3) expanded parental school choice options; and (4) expanded local control and flexibility.

nonconsensual pornography (NCP)   The nonconsensual distribution of private, sexually explicit images, which can be distributed through social media networks, messaging platforms, and websites. It is often referred to as "revenge porn."

one-child policy   This Chinese policy had three main points: (1) delayed marriage and delayed childbearing; (2) fewer and healthier births; and (3) one child per couple (with some exceptions).

outsourcing   Locating businesses that produce goods for American (or other Western) markets in poor, developing nations where the firm can take advantage of lower wage rates and fewer environmental restrictions.

overstayer   Someone who starts out as a legal visitor but becomes an *illegal* immigrant when he or she exceeds the time allocated to visit or reside in the United States.

patriarchy   A form of social organization in which men dominate and have power and authority over women.

Pell Grant   The nation's primary student grant aid program.

pollution   The action or process of making land, water, air, etc., dirty and not safe or suitable to use.

post-traumatic stress disorder (PTSD)   Severe stress reactions after a traumatic event such as war.

prejudice   An emotional, rigid attitude toward members of the subordinate group.

projection   The act of attributing the unwanted traits of oneself onto others.

psychotherapy   Interaction between a patient and a therapist or among patients in groups that is intended to foster insight and change.

qualitative methods   A research strategy that focuses on narrative description with words rather than numbers to analyze patterns and their underlying meanings.

quantitative methods   A research strategy in which data can be measured numerically.

Race to the Top   President Obama and his administration had been trying to improve the No Child Left Behind legislation by making more resources available to the public schools for creative ventures.

racial minorities   Groups of people who share certain inherited characteristics.

racial/ethnic/cultural socialization   Teaching children about their cultural heritage, and providing children with the coping skills necessary to develop and maintain a strong and healthy self-image in the face of possible prejudice and discrimination.

racism   Behavior, in word or deed, motivated by the belief that human races have distinctive characteristics that determine abilities and cultures.

rape   Penetration, no matter how slight, of the vagina or anus with any body part or object, or oral penetration by a sex organ of another person, without the consent of the victim.

rate of population growth (natural increase)   The differential between the crude birthrate and the death rate.

recidivism   The tendency that a former inmate will break the law after release and be arrested again.

revolutionary terrorism   Acts of violence against civilians that are carried out by enemies of a government.

role   The performance of a certain set of behaviors that go with a status.

role overload   The feeling of being overwhelmed by many different commitments and not having enough time to meet each commitment effectively.

routine household labor   Household work that is repetitive and less able to be postponed than are other tasks.

rude birth (or fertility) rate   The number of children born per 1,000 of the population.

sandwich generation   Adults who are caring for an aging parent while also caring for their own children under age 18.

secondary deviance   A state in which a person who is labeled "deviant" may then adopt elements of what is popularly viewed as a deviant lifestyle.

selection effect   An effect that occurs when the sample is not random and leads to biased inferences about social processes, such as the relationship between cohabitation and divorce.

sex   Biological differences and one's role in reproduction.

Serious Mental Illness (SMI)   A mental, behavioral, or emotional disorder resulting in serious functional impairment, which substantially interferes with or limits one or more major life activities.

sexual assault   An act that may include rape, but which also includes other types of behavior, such as unwanted physical contact or non-contact, unwanted sexual experiences.

sexual coercion   Unwanted vaginal, oral, or anal sex after being pressured in ways that include being worn down by someone who repeatedly asked for sex or showed they were unhappy, feeling pressured by being lied to, being told promises that were untrue, having someone threaten to end a relationship or spread rumors; and sexual pressure due to someone using their influence or authority.

single-payer   A healthcare system that is financed by taxes and covers the costs of essential healthcare services.

social construction   The process by which some claims about social problems become dominant and others get little or no attention; these claims develop through the activities of actors and institutions in society that shape our understanding of the social world more generally.

social control   The capacity of a social group, which could be an entire society, to regulate itself according to a set of higher moral principles beyond those of self-interest.

social disorganization   The result when rules break down; it is manifested in three major ways: normlessness, culture conflict, and breakdown.

social institution   A more or less stable structure of statuses and roles devoted to meeting the basic needs of people in a society, for example, the health care system.

social norm   A commonly accepted standard that specifies the kind of behavior appropriate in a given situation.

social policies   Formal procedures designed to remedy a social problem; can be designed by officials of government at the local, state, or federal level or by private citizens in voluntary associations, by corporations, and by nonprofit foundations.

social problem   Widespread agreement that a condition threatens the quality of life and cherished values and that something should be done to remedy that condition.

social stratification   A pattern in which individuals and groups find themselves in different positions in the social order, positions that enjoy varying amounts of access to desirable goods and services.

social structure   The organized arrangements of relationships and institutions that together form the basis of society.

socialism   A type of economy in which there is *public* ownership of the means of production. The government imposes some degree of limits on the rights of individuals and corporations to own productive property.

spillover   The negative (or sometimes positive) moods, experiences, and demands involved in one sphere that carry over or "spill over" into the other sphere.

spurious   A type of apparent relationship between two variables that is really caused by a third factor.

stalking   Obsessive contact or tracking of another person—attention that is unwanted and causes a reasonable concern for one's safety.

Standard American English (SAE)   A speaking style that avoids slang or poor grammar, used by upper-class people.

standard of living   What people want or expect in the way of material well-being.

status   A social position.

stepfamilies   Families in which one or both of the adult partners have at least one child, either residing with them or living elsewhere.

stereotyping   Attributing a fixed, and usually unfavorable or inaccurate, conception to a category of people.

sweatshops   Factory-type arrangements, especially in developing nations, with working conditions that would not be tolerated in affluent nations (e.g., crowded, hot spaces; minimal breaks; dangerous work).

symbolic interactionist perspective   A way of thinking that offers an explanation that gets closer to the individual level of behavior by looking at the symbols people use in everyday interaction—words, gestures, appearances—and how these symbols are interpreted by others. People's interactions with others are based on how symbols are interpreted.

technological dualism   The idea that advances in technology can have both positive and negative impacts.

technology   The use of science in industry, engineering, etc., to invent useful things or to solve problems.

terrorism   The threatened or actual use of illegal force and violence by a non-state actor to attain a political, economic, religious, or social goal through fear, coercion, or intimidation.

total birth (or fertility) rate   Average number of children born to a woman during her lifetime.

total institution   A place of residence and work where a large number of like-situated individuals are cut off from the wider society for an appreciable period of time and together lead an enclosed life.

Uniform Crime Reports (UCR)   A national database of nearly 18,000 city, university and college, county, state, tribal, and federal law enforcement agencies voluntarily reporting data on crimes brought to their attention.

violence among intimates   Violence among family members or intimate partners.

weapons of mass destruction   Nuclear weapons and biological agents that have the potential to annihilate thousands or even millions of people quickly.

welfare state   A type of country in which a significant portion of the GDP is taken by the government to provide certain minimum levels of social welfare for those who are poor, elderly, or disabled, among others.

work–family conflict   The tension people feel when the pressures from paid work and family roles are somehow incompatible.

working poor   Individuals who, within a year, spent at least 27 weeks in the labor force (working or looking for work), but whose incomes fell below the official poverty level.

References

Chapter 1

Berger, P. 1963. *Invitation to Sociology*. New York: Doubleday.

Brenan, M., and L. Saad. 2018. "Global Warming Concern Steady Despite Some Partisan Shifts." Gallup. 28 March. Retrieved 30 March 2018 (news.gallup.com/poll/231530/global-warming-concern-steady-despite-partisan-shifts.aspx).

Caplan, R. 2005. "Political Institution-Building." In *International Governance of War-Torn Territories*, Ch. 6. New York: Oxford University Press.

Centers for Disease Control and Prevention. 2016. "National Suicide Statistics." 19 July. Retrieved 30 March 2018 (www.cdc.gov/violenceprevention/suicide/statistics/).

Chang, A. 2018. "We Can Draw School Zones to Make Classrooms Less Segregated. This Is How Well Your District Does." Vox. 8 January. Retrieved 28 March 2018 (www.vox.com/2018/1/8/16822374/schools-segregation-gerrymander-map).

Cohn, D. and Passel, J. S. 2018. "A record 64 million Americans live in multigenerational households." Pew Research Center. 5 April. Retrieved 10 July 2018 (http://www.pewresearch.org/fact-tank/2018/04/05/a-record-64-million-americans-live-in-multigenerational-households/).

Coontz, S. 2005. *Marriage, a History: From Obedience to Intimacy, or How Love Conquered Marriage*. New York: Penguin.

Durkheim, É. 1897/1951. *Suicide, a Study in Sociology*. New York: Free Press.

Edin, K., and M. Kefalas. 2005. *Promises I Can Keep: Why Poor Women Put Motherhood Before Marriage*. Berkeley, CA: University of California Press.

Edwards, L. P. 1927. *The Natural History of Revolution*. Chicago: University of Chicago Press.

Fiel, J. E. 2013. "Decomposing School Resegregation: Social Closure, Racial Imbalance, and Racial Isolation." *American Sociological Review*, 78, 828–48.

Funk, C., and B. Kennedy. 2016. "The Politics of Climate." 4 October. Pew Research Center.

Gallup. 2018. "Most Important Problem." Retrieved 27 March 2018 (news.gallup.com/poll/1675/most-important-problem.aspx).

Garcia-Moreno, C., A. H. Jansen, F. M. Ellseberg, L. Heise, and C. Watt. 2015. WHO Multicultural Study on Women's Health and Domestic Violence Against Women. Retrieved 21 May 2015 (http://www.who.int/gender/violence/who_multicountry_study/Introduction-Chapter1-Chapter2.pdf).

Goldhaber, D., L. Lavery, and R. Theobald. 2015. "Uneven Playing Field? Assessing the Teacher Quality Gap Between Advantaged and Disadvantaged Students." *Educational Researcher*, 44, 293–307.

Gramlich, J. 2017. "Far More Americans Say There Are Strong Conflicts Between Partisans Than Between Other Groups in Society." Pew Research Center. 19 December. Retrieved 28 March 2018 (www.pewresearch.org/fact-tank/2017/12/19/far-more-americans-say-there-are-strong-conflicts-between-partisans-than-between-other-groups-in-society/).

Griswold, W. 2012. *Cultures and Societies in a Changing World*, 4th ed. Thousand Oaks, CA: Pine Forge Press.

Jones, J. M. 2014. "In U.S., Most Do Not See Global Warming as Serious Threat." Gallup. 13 March. Retrieved 15 March 2015 (www.gallup.com/poll/167879/not-global-warming-serious-threat.aspx).

Kalogrides, D., and S. Loeb. 2013. "Different Teachers, Different Peers: The Magnitude of Student Sorting within Schools." *Educational Researcher*, 42, 304–16.

Kalogrides, D., S. Loeb, and T. Béteille. 2013. "Systematic Sorting: Teacher Characteristics and Class Assignments." *Sociology of Education*, 86, 103–23.

Kiley, J. 2017. "In Polarized Era, Fewer Americans Hold a Mix of Conservative and Liberal Views." Pew Research Center. 23 October. Retrieved 28 March 2018 (www.pewresearch.org/fact-tank/2017/10/23/in-polarized-era-fewer-americans-hold-a-mix-of-conservative-and-liberal-views/).

Larana, E., H. Johnston, and J. R. Gusfield, eds. 1994. *New Social Movements: From Ideology to Identity*. Philadelphia: Temple University Press.

Lasswell, H. D. 1941. "The Garrison State." *American Journal of Sociology*, 46, 455–68.

Leeder, E. 2004. *The Family in Global Perspective: A Gendered Journey*. Thousand Oaks, CA: Sage Publications.

Marx, K. 1867/1971. *Das Kapital* (*Capital*). New York: International Publishers.

Marx, K., and F. Engels. 1848/1971. *Manifesto of the Communist Party*. New York: International Publishers.

Mills, C. W. 1959. *The Sociological Imagination*. New York: Oxford University Press.

Mindfully.org. 2015. "Consumption in the United States." Retrieved 28 April 2015 (http://www.mindfully.org/Sustainability/Americans-Consume-24percent.htm).

Mintz, S. 2004. *Huck's Raft: A History of American Childhood*. Cambridge, MA: Belknap Press.

National League for Nursing. 2018. "Biennial Survey of Schools of Nursing, Academic Year 2015–2016." Retrieved 27 March 2018 (www.nln.org/newsroom/nursing-education-statistics/biennial-survey-of-schools-of-nursing-academic-year-2015-2016).

Norman, J. 2017. "Democrats Drive Rise in Concern About Global Warming." Gallup. 17 March. Retrieved 30 March 2018 (news.gallup.com/poll/206513/democrats-drive-rise-concern-global-warming.aspx).

Park, R. E. 1955. "The Natural History of the Newspaper." In *Society: The Collected Papers of Robert Ezra Park, Vol. III*. New York: Free Press.

Pew Research Center. 2017. "The Partisan Divide on Political Values Grows Even Wider." 5 October. Retrieved 30 March 2018 (www.people-press.org/2017/10/05/the-partisan-divide-on-political-values-grows-even-wider/).

RAND Education. 2012. "Teachers Matter: Understanding Teachers' Impact on Student Achievement." Retrieved 9 February 2015 (www.rand.org/education/projects/measuring-teacher-effectiveness/teachers-matter.html).

Richards, M. P. 2014. "The Gerrymandering of School Attendance Zones and the Segregation of Public Schools: A Geospatial Analysis." *American Educational Research Journal*, 51, 1119–57.

Riffkin, R. 2015. "Americans Name Terrorism as No. 1 U.S. Problem." Gallup. 14 December. Retrieved 27 March 2018 (news.gallup.com/poll/187655/americans-name-terrorism-no-problem.aspx).

Saad, L. 2017. "Global Warming Concern at Three-Decade High in U.S." Gallup. 14 March. Retrieved 30 March 2018 (news.gallup.com/poll/206030/global-warming-concern-three-decade-high.aspx).

Seccombe, K. 2015. *"So You Think I Drive a Cadillac?" Welfare Recipients' Perspectives on the System and Its Reform*, 4th ed. Boston: Pearson.

Semega, J. L., Fontenot, K. R., and Kollar, M. A. 2018. *Income and Poverty in the United States: 2016*. U.S. Census Bureau, Current Population Reports P60–259, U.S. Government Printing Office, Washington, DC.

Shaw, C. R. 1929. *Delinquency Areas: A Study of the Geographic Distribution of School Truants, Juvenile Delinquents, and Adult Offenders in Chicago*. Chicago: University of Chicago Press.

Smith, M., and L. Saad. 2016. "Economy Top Problem in a Crowded Field." Gallup. 19 December. Retrieved 27 March 2018 (news.gallup.com/poll/200105/economy-top-problem-crowded-field.aspx).

Smith, S. G., J. Chen, K. C. Basile, L. K. Gilbert, M. T. Merrick, N. Patel, M. Walling, and A. Jain. 2017. "The National Intimate Partner and Sexual Violence Survey (NISVS): 2010–2012 State Report." April. National Center for Injury Prevention and Control. Atlanta, GA: Centers for Disease Control and Prevention.

Spector, M., and J. Kitsuse. 1987. *Constructing Social Problems*. Hawthorne, NY: Aldine de Gruyter.

Thomas, W. I., and F. Znaniecki. 1922. *The Polish Peasant in Europe and America*. New York: Knopf.

Wilson, W. J. 1987. *The Truly Disadvantaged: The Inner City, the Underclass, and Public Policy*. Chicago: University of Chicago Press.

Wilson, W. J. 1996. *When Work Disappears: The World of the New Urban Poor*. New York: Knopf.

Wirth, L. 1927. "The Ghetto." *American Journal of Sociology*, 23, 57–71.

World Health Organization. 2017. "Media Centre: Violence Against Women." November. Retrieved 28 March 2018 (www.who.int/mediacentre/factsheets/fs239/en/).

Chapter 2

Administration on Aging. 2017. "A Profile of Older Americans: 2017." Retrieved 23 March 2018 (www.aoa.acl.gov/Aging_Statistics/Profile/2016/docs/2016_Profile.pdf).

Agency for Healthcare Research and Quality. 2014. "The Number of Practicing Primary Care Physicians in the United States: Primary Care Workforce Facts and Stats No. 1." Retrieved 3 April 2018 (www.ahrq.gov/research/findings/factsheets/primary/pcwork1/index.html).

Altman, D. 1987. *AIDS in the Mind of America*. New York: Anchor Press/Doubleday.

Altman, D. 2014. "Health Cost Growth Is Down, Or Not. It Depends Who You Ask." Kaiser Family Foundation Perspectives. 5 March. Retrieved 16 April 2014 (kff.org/health-costs/perspective/health-cost-growth-is-down-or-not-it-depends-who-you-ask/).

American Cancer Society. 2018. "Tobacco and Cancer." Retrieved 5 April 2018 (www.cancer.org/cancer/cancer-causes/tobacco-and-cancer.html).

American Lung Association. 2018. "10 of the Worst Diseases Smoking Causes." Retrieved 5 April 2018 (www.lung.org/our-initiatives/tobacco/reports-resources/sotc/by-the-numbers/10-worst-diseases-smoking-causes.html).

Barnett, J. C., and E. R. Berchick. 2017. "Health Insurance Coverage in the United States: 2016." Current Population Reports. P60–260. September. Washington, DC: U.S. Census Bureau.

Blumenthal, D. 2006. "Employer-Sponsored Health Insurance in the United States—Origins and Implications." *New England Journal of Medicine*, 355, 82–88.

Brenan, M. 2017. "Affordable Care Act Approval Slips After Record Highs." Gallup. 27 November. Retrieved 15 May 2018 (news.gallup.com/poll/222734/affordable-care-act-approval-slips-record-highs.aspx).

Centers for Disease Control and Prevention. 2016. "Defining Adult Overweight and Obesity." 16 June.

Centers for Disease Control and Prevention. 2017. "Economic Trends in Tobacco." 16 November.

Centers for Disease Control and Prevention. 2018a. "Current Cigarette Smoking Among Adults in the United States." 15 February.

Centers for Disease Control and Prevention. 2018b. "Fast Facts: Tobacco." 20 February.

Centers for Disease Control and Prevention. 2018c. "Adult Obesity Causes & Consequences." 5 March.

Centers for Disease Control and Prevention. 2018d. "Youth and Tobacco Use." 26 March.

Centers for Medicare & Medicaid Services. 2018. "National Health Expenditure Data: Historical." 16 February. Retrieved 4 April 2018 (www.cms.gov/Research-Statistics-Data-and-Systems/Statistics-Trends-and-Reports/NationalHealthExpendData/NationalHealthAccountsHistorical.html).

Clemens, M. 2017. "Technology and Rising Health Care Costs." Forbes Technology Council. 26 October. Retrieved 3 April 2018 (www.forbes.com/sites/forbestechcouncil/2017/10/26/technology-and-rising-health-care-costs/#5b26c01a766b).

DiJulio, B., A. Kirzinger, B. Wu, and M. Brodie. 2017. "Data Note: Americans' Challenges with Health Care Costs." Henry J. Kaiser Family Foundation. 2 March. Retrieved 3 April 2018 (www.kff.org/health-costs/poll-finding/data-note-americans-challenges-with-health-care-costs/).

Dropp, K., and B. Nyhan. 2017. "One-Third Don't Know That Obamacare and Affordable Care Act Are the Same." *New York Times*. 7 February.

Dugan, A. 2015. "In U.S., Support Up for Doctor-Assisted Suicide." Gallup. 27 May. Retrieved 5 April 2018 (news.gallup.com/poll/183425/support-doctor-assisted-suicide.aspx).

Ferdinand, A. O., J. P. Epane, and N. Menachemi. 2014. "Community Benefits Provided by Religious, Other Nonprofit, and For-Profit Hospitals: A Longitudinal Analysis 2000-2009." *Health Care Management Review*, 39, 145–153.

The Fistula Foundation. 2018. "Fistula Fast Facts and Frequently Asked Questions." Retrieved 2 April 2018 (www.fistulafoundation.org/what-is-fistula/fast-facts-faq/).

Foutz, J., E. Squires, and R. Garfield. 2017. "The Uninsured: A Primer-Key Facts about Health Insurance and the Uninsured Under the Affordable Care Act." Henry J. Kaiser Family Foundation. 14 December. Retrieved 2 April 2018 (www.kff.org/uninsured/report/the-uninsured-a-primer-key-facts-about-health-insurance-and-the-uninsured-under-the-affordable-care-act/).

Fryar, C. D., M. D. Carroll, and C. L. Ogden. 2016. "Prevalence of Overweight and Obesity Among Children and Adolescents Aged 2–19 Years: United States, 1963–1965 Through 2013–2014." Health E-Stats. National Center for Health Statistics. July.

Gallagher Healthcare. 2017. "How Much Does Medical Malpractice Insurance Cost?" 12 December. Retrieved 11 July 2018 (www.gallaghermalpractice.com/blog/post/how-much-does-medical-malpractice-insurance-cost).

Gallup, 2018. HealthCare System. Retrieved 8 April 2018. (http://news.gallup.com/poll/4708/healthcare-system.aspx).

Garfield, R., and K. Young. 2015a. "Adults who Remained Uninsured at the End of 2014." The Henry J. Kaiser Family Foundation. Executive Summary. 29 January. Retrieved 25 February 2015 (kff.org/health-reform/issue-brief/adults-who-remained-uninsured-at-the-end-of-2014/).

Garfield, R., and K. Young. 2015b. "How Does Gaining Coverage Affect People's Lives? Access, Utilization, and Financial Security among Newly Insured Adults." The Henry J. Kaiser Family Foundation. 19 June. Retrieved 7 April 2018 (www.kff.org/health-reform/issue-brief/how-does-gaining-coverage-affect-peoples-lives-access-utilization-and-financial-security-among-newly-insured-adults/).

Greenwald, L., C. Copeland, and J. VanDerhei. 2017. "The 2017 Retirement Confidence Survey: Many Workers Lack Retirement Confidence and Feel Stressed About Retirement Preparations." No. 431. 21 March. Employee Benefit Research Institute.

Health Canada. 2018. "Latest News." Retrieved 6 April 2018 (www.canada.ca/en/health-canada.html).

Henry J. Kaiser Family Foundation. 2012. "Health Care Costs: A Primer." May. Retrieved 3 April 2018 (kff.org/health-costs/issue-brief/health-care-costs-a-primer/).

Henry J. Kaiser Family Foundation. 2015. "ACA 101: What You Need to Know." Retrieved 29 April 2015 (kff.org/health-reform/event/aca-101-what-you-need-to-know-2015/).

Henry J. Kaiser Family Foundation. 2017a. "The U.S. Government and International Family Planning & Reproductive Health Efforts." 10 July. Retrieved 2 October 2017 (www.kff.org/global-health-policy/fact-sheet/the-u-s-government-and-international-family-planning-reproductive-health-efforts/).

Henry J. Kaiser Family Foundation. 2017b. "2017 Employer Health Benefits Survey." 19 September. Retrieved 2 April 2018 (www.kff.org/health-costs/report/2017-employer-health-benefits-survey/).

Hirst, E.J. 2014. "Generic Drug Prices Skyrocket in Past Year." Retrieved 28 April 2015 (www.huffingtonpost.com/2014/09/03/health-care-spending-2013_n_5759800.html).

Hubert, C., P. Reese, and J. Sanders. 2013. "Nevada Buses Hundreds of Mentally Ill Patients to Cities Around Country." Sacramento Bee. 14 April. Retrieved 11 July 2018 (www.sacbee.com/news/investigations/nevada-patient-busing/article2577189.html).

Jilani, Z. 2017. "Single-Payer Opponents Say the Transition Process Would Be Too Difficult. But 10,000 People Do It Every Day." The Intercept. Retrieved 8 April 2018 (https://theintercept.com/2017/10/09/new-medicare-recipients=bernie-sanders-health-care/)

Kesselheim, A.S., J. Avorn, and A. Sarpatwari. 2016. "The High Cost of Prescription Drugs in the United States: Origins and Prospects for Reform." Journal of the American Medical Association, 316, 858–871.

Kutscher, B. 2014. "For-Profit Hospitals: More Cost-Cutting…Acquisitions to Build Scale or Diversify…Robust Environment for IPOs." Modern Healthcare, 44, 16–17.

Linkins, J. 2017. "News Flash! Obamacare and the Affordable Care Act Are the Same Thing." Huffpost. 17 January. Retrieved 3 April 2018 (huffingtonpost.com/entry/Obamacare-affordable-care-act_us_587ea7f6e4b0c-f0ae880af9a).

National Center for Health Statistics. 2017. "Health, United States, 2016: With Chartbook on Long-Term Trends in Health." Hyattsville, MD.

National Rural Health Association. 2018. "About Rural Health Care." Retrieved 3 April 2018 (www.ruralhealthweb.org/about-nrha/about-rural-health-care).

Newport, F. 2017. "Majority Want Government to Ensure Healthcare Coverage." Gallup. 8 December. Retrieved 15 May 2018 (news.gallup.com/poll/223391/majority-government-ensure-healthcare-coverage.aspx).

Physicians for a National Health Program. 2016. "What is Single Payer?" Retrieved 8 April 2018. (http://www.pnhp.org/facts/what-is-single-payer).

Pollitz, K., C. Cox, K. Lucia, and K. Keith. 2014. "Medical Debt Among People With Health Insurance." Henry J. Kaiser Family Foundation. 7 January. Retrieved 27 February 2015 (kff.org/report-section/medical-debt-among-people-with-health-insurance-incidence-of-medical-debt/).

Population Reference Bureau. 2018. "2017 World Population Data Sheet With Focus on Youth." Retrieved 2 April 2018 (www.prb.org/2017-world-population-data-sheet/).

Proctor, R. N. 2012. Golden Holocaust: Origins of the Cigarette Catastrophe and the Case for Abolition. Berkeley, CA: University of California Press.

Rainwater, L. 1974. "The Lower Class: Health, Illness, and Medical Institutions." In L. Rainwater, ed., Inequality and Justice. Hawthorne, NY: Aldine.

Rosenthal, E. 2014. "Even Small Medical Advances Can Mean Big Jumps in Bills." New York Times. 5 April. Retrieved 17 April 2014 (www.nytimes.com/2014/04/06/health/even-small-medical-advances-can-mean-big-jumps-in-bills.html).

Stanford Research into the Impact of Tobacco Advertising. 2014. "Slogans." Retrieved 17 April 2014 (tobacco.stanford.edu/tobacco_main/slogans.php).

Starr, P. 2010. "A Health Insurance Mandate with a Choice." New York Times. March 4. Retrieved 15 May 2018 (www.nytimes.com/2010/03/04/opinion/04starr.html).

Sulmasy, L. S., and P. S. Mueller. 2017. "Ethics and the Legalization of Physician-Assisted Suicide: An American

College of Physicians Position Paper." *Annals of Internal Medicine*. 17 October. Retrieved 5 April 2018 (annals.org/aim/fullarticle/2654458/ethics-legalization-physician-assisted-suicide-american-college-physicians-position-paper).

Ungar, L., and J. O'Donnell. 2014. "Health Care Grows at Lowest-Ever Rate." Retrieved 29 April 2015 (www.huffingtonpost.com/2014/09/03/health-care-spending-2013_n_5759800.html).

United Nations Development Programme. 2018. "Good Health and Well-Being." Retrieved 5 April 2018 (www.undp.org/content/undp/en/home/sustainable-development-goals.html).

Wangsness, L. 2009. "Health Debate Shifting to Public vs. Private." *Boston Globe*. June 21.

Weiss, G. L., and L. E. Lonnquist. 2015. *The Sociology of Health, Healing, and Illness*, 8th ed. Boston: Pearson.

Weitz, R. 2017. *The Sociology of Health, Illness, and Health Care: A Critical Approach*, 7th ed. Boston: Cengage.

World Bank. 2018. "Life Expectancy at Birth, Female (Years)/Data." Retrieved 2 April 2018 (data.worldbank.org/indicator/SP.DYN.LE00.FE.IN?end=2015&start=1970).

World Health Organization. 2018a. "10 Facts on Obstetric Fistula." January. Retrieved 2 April 2018 (www.who.int/features/factfiles/obstetric_fistula/en/).

World Health Organization. 2018b. "Media Centre: Tobacco." March. Retrieved 5 April 2018 (www.who.int/mediacentre/factsheets/fs339/en/).

Wouters, O. J., P. G. Kanavos, and M. McKee. 2017. "Comparing Generic Drug Markets in Europe and the United States: Prices, Volumes, and Spending." *Milbank Quarterly*, 95, 554–601.

Chapter 3

Abelson, R. 2017. "In Clash Over Health Bill, a Growing Fear of 'Junk' Insurance." New York Times. 15 July. Retrieved 23 February 2018 (www.nytimes.com/2017/07/15/health/senate-health-care-obamacare.html).

Albert, P. R. 2015. "Why Is Depression More Prevalent in Women?" *Journal of Psychiatry & Neuroscience*, 40, 219–221.

Alzheimer's Association. 2018. "What Is Alzheimer's?" Retrieved 22 February 2018 (www.alz.org/alzheimers_disease_what_is_alzheimers.asp).

American Psychiatric Association. 2015. "DSM-5 Implementation and Support." Retrieved 11 April 2015 (www.dsm5.org/Pages/Default.aspx).

American Psychological Association. 2018. "Different Approaches to Psychotherapy." Retrieved 23 February 2018 (www.apa.org/topics/therapy/psychotherapy-approaches.aspx).

Beam, A. 2003. *Gracefully Insane: Life and Death Inside America's Premier Mental Hospital*. New York: PublicAffairs Publisher.

Boyle, K. M. 2017. "Sexual Assault and Identity Disruption: A Sociological Approach to Posttraumatic Stress." *Society and Mental Health*, 7, 69–84.

Brown, R. A., G. N. Marshall, J. Breslau, C. Farris, K. C. Osilla, H. A. Pincus, T. Ruder, P. Voorhies, D. Barnes-Proby, K. Pfrommer, L. Miyashiro, Y. Rana, and D. M. Adamson. 2015. "Far from Care: Increasing Access to Behavioral Health Care for Remote Service Members and Their Families." RAND Corporation Research Brief. Retrieved 11 April 2015 (www.rand.org/content/dam/rand/pubs/research_briefs/RB9700/RB9790/RAND_RB9790.pdf).

Centers for Disease Control and Prevention. 2015. "Suicide Prevention." Retrieved 11 April 2015 (http://www.cdc.gov/violenceprevention/pub/youth_suicide.html).

Centers for Disease Control and Prevention. 2018. "Autism Data & Statistics." 26 April. Retrieved 24 July 2018 (https://www.cdc.gov/ncbddd/autism/data.html).

Chiles, C., E. Stefanovics, and R. Rosenheck. 2017. "Attitudes of Students at a U.S. Medical School Toward Mental Illness and Its Causes." *Academic Psychiatry*, 41, 320–325.

Clark, T. T., C. P. Salas-Wright, M. G. Vaughn, and K. E. Whitfield. 2015. "Everyday Discrimination and Mood and Substance Use Disorders: A Latent Profile Analysis with African Americans and Caribbean Blacks." *Addictive Behaviors*, 40, 119–25.

Cockerham, W. C. 2014. *Sociology of Mental Disorder*, 9th ed. Boston: Pearson.

Curtis, W. R. 1986. "The Deinstitutionalization Story." *Public Interest*, 85, 34–49.

Faris, R. E. L., and H. W. Dunham. 1938. *Mental Disorders in Urban Areas*. Chicago: University of Chicago Press.

Giang, V. 2012. "Untreated Mental Illnesses Are Costing American Companies Billions Every Year." *Business Insider*, September 29. Retrieved 20 July 2018 (http://www.businessinsider.com/you-dont-even-know-how-many-mentally-ill-people-youre-working-with-2012-9).

Goffman, E. 1961. *Asylums: Essays on the Social Situation of Mental Patients and Other Inmates*. Garden City, NY: Doubleday.

Harvey, S. B., S. Øverland, S. L. Hatch, S. Wessely, A. Mykletun, and M. Hotopf. 2018. "Exercise and the Prevention of Depression: Results of the HUNT Cohort Study." *American Journal of Psychiatry*, 175, 28–36.

Hendryx, M., C. A. Green, and N. A. Perrin. 2009. "Social Support, Activities, and Recovery from Serious Mental Illness: STARS Study Findings." *Journal of Behavioral Health Services Research*, 36, 320–29.

Henry J. Kaiser Family Foundation. 2017. "Facilitating Access to Mental Health Services: A Look at Medicaid, Private Insurance, and the Uninsured." 27 November. Retrieved 23 February 2018 (www.kff.org/medicaid/fact-sheet/facilitating-access-to-mental-health-services-a-look-at-medicaid-private-insurance-and-the-uninsured).

Hoven, C. W., C. S. Duarte, C. P. Lucas, P. Wu, D. J. Mandell, R. D. Goodwin, M. Cohen, V. Balaban, B. A. Woodruff, F. Bin, G. J. Musa, L. Mei, P. A. Cantor, J. L. Aber, P. Cohen, and E. Susser. 2005. "Psychopathology Among New York City Public School Children 6 Months After September 11." *Archives of General Psychology*, 62, 545–51.

Hudson, D. L., H. W. Neighbors, A. T. Geronimus, and J. S. Jackson. 2016. "Racial Discrimination, John Henryism, and Depression Among African Americans." *Journal of Black Psychology*, 42, 221–243.

Hurst, C. 2013. *Social Inequality: Forms, Causes, and Consequences*, 8th ed. Boston: Pearson.

Keene, Michael T. 2013. *Mad House: The Hidden History of Insane Asylums in 19th-Century New York*. Fredericksburg, VA: Willow Manor Publishing.

Kessler, R. C., M. B. Stein, M. V. Petukhova, P. Bliese, R. M. Bossarte, E. J. Bromet, C. S. Fullerton, S. E. Gilman, C. Ivany, L. Lewandowski-Romps, A. Millikan-Bell, J A. Naifeh, M. K. Nock, B. Y. Reis, A. J. Rosellini, N. A Sampson, A. M. Zaslavsky, R. J. Ursano, and Army STARRS Collaborators. 2017. "Predicting Suicides After Outpatient Mental Health Visits in the Army

Study to Assess Risk and Resilience in Servicemembers (Army STARRS)." *Molecular Psychiatry,* 22, 544–551.

Kozol, J. 1988. "The Homeless and Their Children." *The New Yorker.* 25 January, pp. 65ff; 1 February, pp. 36ff.

Kugelmass, H. 2016. "'Sorry, I'm Not Accepting New Patients': An Audit Study of Access to Mental Health Care." *Journal of Health and Social Behavior,* 57, 1–16.

Leupp, K. 2017. "Depression, Work and Family Roles, and the Gendered Life Course." *Journal of Health and Social Behavior,* 58, 422–441.

Madsen, I. E. H., S. T. Nyberg, L. L. Magnusson Hanson, and J. E. Ferrie. 2017. "Job Strain as a Risk Factor for Clinical Depression: Systematic Review and Meta-Analysis With Additional Individual Participant Data." *Psychological Medicine,* 47, 1342–1356.

Mays, V., A. L. Jones, A. Delany-Brumsey, C. Coles, and S. Cochran. 2017. "Perceived Discrimination in Health Care and Mental Health/Substance Abuse Treatment Among Blacks, Latinos, and Whites." *Medical Care,* 55, 173–181.

McCash, J. A., and S. Abraham. 2018. "Effects of Aerobic Exercise on Patients with Mental Illness in a Veterans Inpatient Psychiatric Unit: A Review of the Literature." *International Journal of Studies in Nursing,* 3, 34–41.

McEwen, C. 1988. "Continuities in the Study of Total and Non-total Institutions." In: *Annual Review of Sociology.* Newbury Park, CA: Sage.

Mental Health America. 2018. "Housing." Retrieved 23 February 2018 (www.mentalhealthamerica.net/housing).

Messia, E. L. Chen, C. Y. Eaton, W. W. "Epidemiology Of Schizophrenia: Review of Findings and Myths." *The Psychiatric Clinics Of North America,* 30, 323–338.

Meyer, O. L., L. Castro-Schilo, and S. Aguilar-Gaxiola. 2014. "Determinants of Mental Health and Self-Rated Health: A Model of Socioeconomic Status, Neighborhood Safety, and Physical Activity." *American Journal of Public Health,* 104, 1734–1741.

National Alliance on Mental Illness. 2015. "Mental Health Medications." Retrieved 11 April 2015 (www.nami.org/Learn-More/Treatment/Mental-Health-Medications).

National Alliance on Mental Illness. 2018. "Mental Health Treatment & Services." Retrieved 23 February 2018 (www.nami.org/Learn-More/Treatment).

National Council for Behavioral Health. 2017. "The Psychiatric Shortage: Causes and Solutions." 28 March. Retrieved 23 February 2018 (www.thenationalcouncil.org/wp-content/uploads/2017/03/Psychiatric-Shortage_National-Council-.pdf).

National Institute of Mental Health. 2015. "Statistics." Retrieved 11 April 2015 (www.nimh.nih.gov/health/statistics/index.shtml).

National Institute of Mental Health. 2017a. "Mental Illness." November. Retrieved 23 February 2018 (www.nimh.nih.gov/health/statistics/mental-illness.html).

National Institute of Mental Health. 2017b. "Suicide." Retrieved 22 February 2018 (www.nimh.gov/health/statistics/suicide.shtml#part_154969).

National Institute of Mental Health. 2018. "Mental Health Information." Retrieved 23 February 2018 (www.nimh.gov/health/topics/index.html).

Payne, C. 2009. *Asylum: Inside the Closed World of State Mental Hospitals.* Cambridge, MA: MIT Press.

RAND Center for Military Health Policy Research. 2008. "Invisible Wounds: Mental Health and Cognitive Care Needs of America's Returning Veterans." RB-9336. Retrieved 11 April 2015 (http://www.rand.org/content/dam/rand/pubs/research_briefs/2008/RAND_RB9336.pdf).

Romo, V. 2018. "Trump Calls For Mental Health Action After Shooting; His Budget Would Cut Programs." NPR: The Two-Way. 15 February. Retrieved 23 February 2018 (www.npr.org/sections/thetwo-way/2018/02/15/586095437/trump-calls-for-mental-health-action-after-shooting-his-budget-would-cut-program).

Rosenhan, D. L. 1973. "On Being Sane in Insane Places." *Science,* 179, 250–58.

Rubin, M, and R. Stuart. 2018. "Kill or Cure? Different Types of Social Class Identification Amplify and Buffer the Relation Between Social Class and Mental Health." *Journal of Social Psychology,* 158, 236–251.

Rueger, S. Y., C. K. Malecki, Y. Pyun, C. Aycock, and S. Coyle. 2016. "A Meta-Analytic Review of the Association Between Perceived Social Support and Depression in Childhood and Adolescence." *Psychological Bulletin,* 142, 1017–1067.

Russell, D. W., F. D. Clavel, C. E. Cutrona, W. T. Abraham, and R. G. Burzette. 2018. "Neighborhood Racial Discrimination and the Development of Major Depression." *Journal of Abnormal Psychology.* (lib.dr.iastate.edu/cgi/viewcontent.cgi?article=1098&context=hdfs_pubs).

Salize, H. J., H. Schanda, and H. Dressing. 2008. "From the Hospital into the Community and Back Again—A Trend towards Reinstitutionalization in Mental Health Care?" *International Review of Psychiatry,* 20, 527–34.

Scheff, T. J. 1963. "The Role of the Mentally Ill and the Dynamics of Mental Disorder." *Sociometry,* 26, 436–53.

Schoenbaum, M., R. C. Kessler, S. E. Gilman, L. J. Colpe, S. G. Heeringa, M. B. Stein, R. J. Ursano, and K. L. Cox. 2014. "Predictors of Suicide and Accident Death in the Army Study to Assess Risk and Resilience in Servicemembers (Army STARRS)." *JAMA Psychiatry,* 71, 493–503.

Scull, A. T. 1988. "Deviance and Social Control." In: *The Handbook of Sociology,* edited by N. J. Smelser. Newbury Park, CA: Sage.

Sheehan, S. 1982. *Is There No Place on Earth for Me?* New York: Scribner.

Sperry, L. 1995. *Pharmacology and Psychotherapy: Strategies for Maximizing Treatment Outcomes.* New York: Brunner/Mazel.

Squire, S. 1987. "Shock Therapy's Return to Respectability." *New York Times Magazine.* 22 November. Pp. 78ff.

Srole, L., T. S. Langner, S.T. Michael, P. Kirkpatrick, M. K. Opler, and T. A. C. Rennie. 1978. *Mental Health in the Metropolis: The Midtown Manhattan Study,* rev. ed. New York: New York University Press.

Szasz, T. S. 2003. *The Myth of Mental Illness: Foundations of a Theory of Personal Conduct,* rev. ed. New York: Perennial.

Torrey, E. F. 2016. "A Dearth of Psychiatric Beds." Psychiatric Times. 25 February. Volume 33.

Toussaint, L., G. S. Shields, G. Dorn, and G. M. Slavich. 2016. "Effects of Lifetime Stress Exposure on Mental and Physical Health in Young Adulthood: How Stress Degrades and Forgiveness Protects Health." *Journal of Health Psychology,* 21, 1004–1014.

Treatment Advocacy Center. 2015. "Consequences of Nontreatment." Retrieved 15 April 2015 (http://www.treatmentadvocacycenter.org/problem/consequences-of-non-treatment).

Treatment Advocacy Center. 2018. "How Many People with Serious Mental Illness Are Homeless?" Retrieved 23

February 2018 (www.treatmentadvocacycenter.org/fixing-the-system/features-and-news/2596-how-many-people-with-serious-mental-illness-are-homeless).

U. S. Department of Housing and Urban Development. 2017. "The 2017 Annual Homeless Assessment Report (AHAR) to Congress." December. Retrieved 23 February 2018 (www.hudexchange.info/resources/documents/2017-AHAR-Part-1.pdf).

U.S. Department of Veterans Affairs. 2017. "What Is PTSD?" Retrieved 22 February 2018 (www.ptsd.va.gov/public/PTSD-overview/basics/what-is-ptsd.asp).

Villatoro, A. P., V. M. Mays, N. A. Ponce, and C. S. Aneshensel. 2018. "Perceived Need for Mental Health Care: The Intersection of Race, Ethnicity, Gender, and Socioeconomic Status." *Society and Mental Health*, 8, 1–24.

Werner-Seidler, A., M. H. Afzali, C. Chapman, M. Sunderland, and T. Slade. 2017. "The Relationship Between Social Support Networks and Depression in the 2007 National Survey of Mental Health and Well-Being." *Social Psychology and Psychiatric Epidemiology*, 52, 1463–1473.

Wheaton, B. 2001. "The Role of Sociology in the Study of Mental Health... and the Role of Mental Health in the Study of Sociology." *Journal of Health and Social Behavior*, 42, 221–234.

World Health Organization. 2012. "Media Centre: Depression." Fact Sheet No. 369. October. Retrieved 11 April 2015 (www.who.int/mediacentre/factsheets/fs369/en/).

World Health Organization. 2017. "Media Centre: Mental Disorders." April. Retrieved 22 February 2018 (www.who.int/mediacentre/factsheets/fs396/en/).

World Health Organization. January 31, 2018. "Suicide." Retrieved 20 July 2018 (http://www.who.int/en/news-room/fact-sheets/detail/suicide).

World Health Organization and the Calouste Gulbenkian Foundation. 2014. "Social Determinants of Mental Health." Retrieved 20 July 2015. (http://www.who.int/mental_health/publications/gulbenkian_paper_social_determinants_of_mental_health/en/)

Yucel, D. 2017. "Work-Family Balance and Marital Satisfaction: The Mediating Effects of Mental and Physical Health." *Society and Mental Health*, 7, 175–195.

Zschucke, E., K. Gaudlitz, and A. Ströhle. 2013. "Exercise and Physical Activity in Mental Disorders: Clinical and Experimental Evidence." *Journal of Preventive Medicine & Public Health*, 46, S12–S21.

Chapter 4

Alcoholics Anonymous. 2017. "Estimates of A. A. Groups and Members as of January 1, 2017." June. Retrieved 2 March 2018 (www.aa.org/assets/en_US/smf-53_en.pdf).

Baker, Al. 2017. "When Opioid Addicts Find An Ally in Blue." New York Times. 12 June. Retrieved 7 March 2018 (www.nytimes.com/2017/06/12/nyregion/when-opioid-addicts-find-an-ally-in-blue.html?smid=tw-share&_r=1).

Becker, H. S. 1963. "Becoming a Marijuana User." In: *Outsiders: Studies in the Sociology of Deviance*. New York: Basic Books.

Behnken, M. P. 2017. "Contextualizing the Role of Alcohol in Sexual Violence." *Journal of Adolescent Health*, 61, 1–2.

Brick, J., ed. 2004. *Handbook of the Medical Consequences of Alcohol and Drug Abuse*. New York: Haworth Press.

Campbell, E. 2005. "Injection Drug Use, Global HIV/AIDS, and Human Rights." *Journal of Ambulatory Care Management*, 28, 286–87.

Centers for Disease Control and Prevention. 2013. "Alcohol Related Disease Impact (ARDI) application." Retrieved 2 March 2018 (nccd.cdc.gov/dph_ardi/default/default.aspx).

Centers for Disease Control and Prevention. 2014a. "Unintentional Drowning: Get the Facts." 15 May. Retrieved 15 April 2015 (www.cdc.gov/HomeandRecreationalSafety/Water-Safety/waterinjuries-factsheet.html).

Centers for Disease Control and Prevention. 2017a. "Fact Sheets—Binge Drinking." 7 June. Retrieved 28 February 2017 (www.cdc.gov/alcohol/fact-sheets/binge-drinking.htm).

Centers for Disease Control and Prevention. 2017b. "Impaired Driving: Get the Facts." 16 June. Retrieved 28 February 2018 (www.cdc.gov/Motorvehiclesafety/impaired_driving/impaired-drv_factsheet.html).

Centers for Disease Control and Prevention. 2017c. "Information for Women." 6 June. Retrieved 28 February 2018 (www.cdc.gov/ncbddd/fasd/women.html).

Centers for Disease Control and Prevention. 2017d. "About Drugs and Addiction." 25 January. Retrieved 28 February 2018 (www.cdc.gov/pwud/addiction.html).

Chartier, K. G., K. J. Karriker-Jaffe, C. R. Cummings, and K. S. Kendler. 2017. "Review: Environmental Influences on Alcohol Use: Informing Research on the Joint Effects of Genes and the Environment in Diverse U.S. Populations." *The American Journal on Addictions*, 26, 446–460.

Dayton, T. 2011. "What is an ACOA?" *Huffington Post*. 13 February. Retrieved 20 April 2015. (www.huffigtonpost.com/dr-tian-dayton/what-is-an-acoa_b_822493.html).

Filbey, F. M., S. Aslan, V. D. Calhoun, J. S. Spence, E. Damaraju, A. Caprihan, and J. Segall. 2014. "Long-Term Effects of Marijuana Use on the Brain." *Proceedings of the National Academy of Sciences*, 111, 16913-16918.

Glaser, G. 2013. *Her Best-Kept Secret: Why Women Drink-And How They Can Regain Control*. Simon and Schuster.

Green, K. M., E. E. Doherty, H. S. Reisinger, H. D. Chilcoat, and M. Ensminger. 2010. "Social Integration in Young Adulthood and the Subsequent Onset of Substance Use and Disorders among a Community Population of Urban African Americans." *Addiction*, 105, 484–93.

Han, B., J. C. Gfroerer, and J. D. Colliver. 2010. "Associations between Duration of Illicit Drug Use and Health Conditions: Results from the 2005–2007 National Surveys on Drug Use and Health." *Annals of Epidemiology*, 20, 289–97.

Ingraham, C. 2014. "Think You Drink a Lot? This Chart Will Tell You." *Washington Post*. 25 September. Retrieved 15 April 2015 (www.washingtonpost.com/blogs/wonkblog/wp/2014/09/25/think-you-drink-a-lot-this-chart-will-tell-you/).

Johnston, L. D., Miech, R. A., O'Malley, P. M., Bachman, J. G., Schulenberg, J. E., and Patrick, M. E. (2018). *Monitoring the Future National Survey Results on Drug Use, 1975–2017: Overview, Key Findings on Adolescent Drug Use*. Ann Arbor: Institute for Social Research, The University of Michigan.

Kaplan, L. M., M. B. Nayak, T. K. Greenfield, and K. J. Karriker-Jaffe. 2017. "Alcohol's Harm to Children: Findings from the 2015 National Alcohol's Harm to Others Survey." *Journal of Pediatrics*, 184, 186–192.

Krebs, C. P., C. H. Lindquist, T. D. Warner, B. S. Fisher, and S. L. Martin. 2009. "College Women's Experiences with Physically Forced, Alcohol- or Other Drug-Enabled, and Drug-Facilitated Sexual Assault Before and Since Entering College." *Journal of American College Health*, 57, 639–649.

Lopez, G. 2017. "When a Drug Epidemic's Victims Are White." Vox.com. 4 April. Retrieved 7 March 2018 (www.vox.com/identities/2017/4/4/15098746/opioid-heroin-epidemic-race).

McCarthy, J. 2017. "Record-High Support for Legalizing Marijuana Use in U.S." Gallup. 25 October. Retrieved 28 February 2018 (news.gallup.com/poll/221018/record-high-support-legalizing-marijuana.aspx).

National Council on Alcohol and Drug Dependence, Inc. 2015a. "Alcohol and Crime." Retrieved 20 April 2015 (ncadd.org/learn-about-alcohol/alcohol-and-crime/202-alcohol-and-crime).

National Council on Alcohol and Drug Dependence, Inc. 2015b. "Drugs and Crime." Retrieved 20 April 2015 (ncadd.org/learn-about-drugs/drugs-and-crime).

National Council on Alcohol and Drug Dependence, Inc. 2015c. "Alcohol, Drugs, and Crime." 27 June. Retrieved 28 February 2018 (www.ncadd.org/about-addiction/alcohol-drugs-and-crime).

National Highway Traffic Safety Administration. "Traffic Safety Facts 2016 Data: Alcohol-Impaired Driving." U.S. Department of Transportation, 2017. Washington, DC; Retrieved 16 April 2018 (https://crashstats.nhtsa.dot.gov/Api/Public/ViewPublication/812450).

National Highway Traffic Safety Administration. 2018. "State Alcohol-Impaired-Driving Estimates." January. U.S. Department of Transportation. DOT HS 812 483. Retrieved 28 February 2018 (crashstats.nhtsa.dot.gov/Api/Public/ViewPublication/812357).

National Institute on Alcohol Abuse and Alcoholism. 2015. "Alcohol's Effects on the Body." Retrieved 20 April 2015 (www.niaaa.nih.gov/alcohol-health/alcohols-effects-body).

National Institute on Alcohol Abuse and Alcoholism. 2017. "Alcohol Facts and Statistics." June. Retrieved 28 February 2018 (www.niaaa.nih.gov/alcohol-health/overview-alcohol-consumption/alcohol-facts-and-statistics).

National Institute on Drug Abuse. 2016a. "What is MDMA?" October. Retrieved 28 February 2018 (www.drugabuse.gov/publications/drugfacts/mdma-ecstasymolly).

National Institute on Drug Abuse. 2016b. "What is Cocaine?" June. Retrieved 28 February 2018 (www.drugabuse.gov/publications/drugfacts/cocaine).

National Institute on Drug Abuse. 2016c. "What are Hallucinogens?" January. Retrieved 28 February 2018 (www.drugabuse.gov/publications/drugfacts/hallucinogens).

National Institute on Drug Abuse. 2017a. "What are Inhalants?" February. Retrieved 28 February 2018 (www.drugabuse.gov/publications/drugfacts/inhalants).

National Institute on Drug Abuse. 2017b. "What is Methamphetamine?" February. Retrieved 28 February 2018 (www.drugabuse.gov/publications/drugfacts/methamphetamine).

National Institute on Drug Abuse. 2017c. "Trends & Statistics: Costs of Substance Abuse." April. Retrieved 28 February 2018 (www.drugabuse.gov/related-topics/trends-statistics).

National Institute on Drug Abuse. 2018a. "What are Prescription Opioids?" January. Retrieved 28 February 2018 (www.drugabuse.gov/publications/drugfacts/prescription-opioids).

National Institute on Drug Abuse. 2018b. "What is Heroin?" January. Retrieved 28 February 2018 (www.drugabuse.gov/publications/drugfacts/heroin).

National Institute on Drug Abuse. 2018c. "CommonlyAbused Drugs Charts." January. Retrieved 28 February 2018 (www.drugabuse.gov/drugs-abuse/commonly-abused-drugs-charts).

Newcomb, M. E., M. Birkett, H. L. Corliss, and B. Mustanski. 2014. "Sexual Orientation, Gender, and Racial Differences in Illicit Drug Use in a Sample of US High School Students." *American Journal of Public Health*, 104, 304–310.

Park, S., and K. G. Schepp. 2015. "A Systematic Review of Research on Children of Alcoholics: Their Inherent Resilience and Vulnerability." *Journal of Child and Family Studies*, 24, 1222–1231.

Prescott, C. A. 2003. "Sex Differences in the Genetic Risk for Alcoholism." National Institute on Alcohol Abuse and Alcoholism. Retrieved 15 April 2015 (pubs.niaaa.nih.gov/publications/arh26-4/264-273.htm).

Savage, C., and J. Healy. 2018. "Trump Administration Takes Step That Could Threaten Marijuana Legalization Movement." *New York Times*. 4 January. Retrieved 28 February 2018 (www.nytimes.com/2018/01/04/us/politics/marijuana-legalization-justice-department-prosecutions.html).

Sellers, C. M., K. H. McManama O'Brien, L. Hernandez, and A. Spirito. 2018. "Adolescent Alcohol Use: The Effects of Parental Knowledge, Peer Substance Use, and Peer Tolerance of Use." *Journal of the Society for Social Work and Research*, 9, 69–87.

Substance Abuse and Mental Health Services Administration. 2017. "Key Substance Use and Mental Health Indicators in the United States: Results from the 2016 National Survey on Drug Use and Health (HHS Publication N. SMA 17-5044, NSDUH Series H-52). September. Rockville, MD: Center for Behavioral Health Statistics and Quality.

Swift, A. 2017. "In U.S., 45% Say They Have Tried Marijuana." Gallup. 19 July. Retrieved 28 February 2018 (news.gallup.com/poll/214250/say-tried-marijuana.aspx).

Szasz, T. S. 1992. "The Fatal Temptation: Drug Prohibition and the Fear of Autonomy." *Daedalus*, pp. 161–65.

Tawa, E. A., S. D. Hall, and F. W. Lohoff. 2016. "Overview of the Genetics of Alcohol Use Disorder." *Alcohol and Alcoholism*, 51, 507–514.

Testa, M., and M. J. Cleveland. 2017. "Does Alcohol Contribute to College Men's Sexual Assault Perpetration? Between- and Within-Person Effects Over Five Semesters." *Journal of Studies on Alcohol and Drugs*, 78, 1–13.

Tyler, K. A., R. M. Schmitz, and S. A. Adams. 2017. "Alcohol Expectancy, Drinking Behavior, and Sexual Victimization Among Female and Male College Students." *Journal of Interpersonal Violence*, 32, 2298–2322.

United Nations Office on Drugs and Crime. 2017. "World Drug Report 2017." (United Nations publication, Sales No. E.17.XI.6).

U.S. Department of Health and Human Services. 2018. "About the U.S. Opioid Epidemic." Retrieved 7 March 2018 (www.hhs.gov/opioids/about-the-epidemic?).

Verhulst, B., M. C. Neale, and K. S. Kendler. 2015. "The Heritability of Alcohol Use Disorders: A Meta-Analysis of Twin and Adoption Studies." *Psychological Medicine*, 45, 1061–1072.

Volkow, N. D., J. M. Swanson, A. E. Evins, L. E. DeLisi, M. H. Meier, R. Gonzalez, M. A. Bloomfield, H. V. Curran, and R. Baler. 2016. "Effects of Cannabis Use on Human Behavior, Including Cognition, Motivation, and Psychosis: A Review." *JAMA Psychiatry*, 73, 292–7.

Wechsler, H., and T. F. Nelson. 2008. "What We Have Learned From the Harvard School of Public Health College Alcohol Study: Focusing Attention on College Student Alcohol

Consumption and the Environmental Conditions That Promote It."*Journal of Studies on Alcohol and Drugs*, 69, 481–90.

Wilsnack, S. C., R. W. Wilsnack, and L. W. Kantor. 2014. "Focus On: Women and Costs of Alcohol Use."*Alcohol Research: Current Reviews*, 35, 219–28.

Chapter 5

Anderson, E. 1992. *Streetwise*. Chicago: University of Chicago Press.

Bales, W. D., C. Clark, S. Scaggs, D. Ensley, P. Coltharp, A. Singer, and T. G. Blomberg. 2015. "An Assessment of the Effectiveness of Prison Work Release Programs on Post-Release Recidivism and Employment." 1 December. National Institute of Justice, Office of Justice Programs, U.S. Department of Justice.

Black, P. 2014. "Subcultural Theories of Crime." *The Encyclopedia of Criminology and Criminal Justice*. 1–3. Oxford: Blackwell Publishing Ltd.

Breiding, M. J., S. G. Smith, K. C. Basile, M. L. Walters, J. Chen, and M. T. Merrick. 2014. "Prevalence and Characteristics of Sexual Violence, Stalking, and Intimate Partner Violence Victimization – National Intimate Partner and Sexual Violence Survey, United States, 2011." *Morbidity and Mortality Weekly Report*, 63, 1–18.

Brenan, M. 2017. "Americans' Perceptions of Local Crime Slightly Improved." Gallup. 2 November. Retrieved 8 March 2018 (news.gallup.com/poll/221222/americans-perceptions-local-crime-slightly-improved.aspx).

Brown, M. K. 1988. *Working the Street: Police Discretion and Dilemmas of Reform*. New York: Russell Sage.

Burt, C. H., M. K. Lei, and R. L. Simons. 2017. "Racial Discrimination, Racial Socialization, and Crime Over Time: A Social Schematic Theory Model." *Criminology*, 55, 938–979.

Chambliss, W. 1973. "The Saints and the Roughnecks."*Society*, 2, 24–31.

Chambliss, W. J. 2000. *Power, Politics, and Crime*. Boulder, CO: Westview Press.

Coccia, M. 2017. "A Theory of General Causes of Violent Crime: Homicides, Income Inequality and Deficiencies of the Heat Hypothesis and of the Model of CLASH." *Aggression and Violent Behavior*, 37, 190–200.

Cohen, A. K. 1971. *Delinquent Boys*. New York: Free Press.

Conklin, J. E. 2007. *Criminology*, 9th ed. Boston: Pearson/Allyn & Bacon.

Daly, M. 2016. *Killing the Competition: Economic Inequality and Homicide*. London: Routledge.

Dobrow, J. A. 2015. "Differential Association Theory." *The Encyclopedia of Crime and Punishment*. 1–4. New York: John Wiley & Sons.

Dunaway, R. G., F. T. Cullen, V. S. Burton, Jr., and T. D. Evans. 2000. "The Myth of Social Class and Crime Revisited: An Examination of Class and Adult Criminality." *Criminology*, 38, 589–632.

Egan, M. 2017. "Wells Fargo Uncovers Up to 1.4 Million More Fake Accounts." CNNMoney. 31 August. Retrieved 5 March 2018 (money.cnn.com/2017/08/31/investing/wells-fargo-fake-accounts/index.html).

Enamorado, T., L.-F. López-Calva, C. Rodriguez-Castelán, and H. Winkler. 2014. "Income Inequality and Violent Crime: Evidence from Mexico's Drug War." World Bank Policy Research Working Paper 6935. June.

Federal Bureau of Investigation. 2017. "About the Uniform Crime Reporting Program." Uniform Crime Reporting Statistics. January. Retrieved 4 March 2018 (www.bjs.gov/ucrdata/abouttheucr.cfm).

Federal Bureau of Investigation. 2018. "Transnational Organized Crime." Retrieved 5 March 2018 (www.fbi.gov/investigate/organized-crime).

Federal Bureau of Investigation, Uniform Crime Reports. 2017a. "2016 Crime in the United States." Retrieved 6 March 2018 (ucr.fbi.gov/crime-in-the-u-s/2016/crime-in-the-u.s.-2016/topic-pages/tables/table-21).

Federal Bureau of Investigation, Uniform Crime Reports. 2017b. "Hate Crime Statistics, 2016." Retrieved 5 March 2018 (ucr.fbi.gov/hate-crime/2016).

Findlaw, 2018. "Revenge Porn Laws By State." Retrieved 16 April 2018 (https://criminal.findlaw.com/criminal-charges/revenge-porn-laws-by-state.html).

Gallup. 2017. "Crime." Retrieved 8 March 2018 (www.gallup.com/poll/1603/crime.aspx).

Garland, D. 2005. "Cruel and Unusual: Punishment and U.S. Culture." *Social and Legal Studies*, 14, 299–302.

Garrett, B. L. 2014. *Too Big to Jail: How Prosecutors Compromise with Corporations*. Cambridge, MA: Harvard University Press.

Human Rights Watch, 2013. *Rape Victims as Criminals: Illegal Abortion After Rape in Ecuador*. Retrieved 29 March 2015 (www.hrw.org/sites/default/files/reports/ecuador0813_ForUpload_1.pdf).

Human Rights Watch, 2014. *Here Rape is Normal: A Five Point Plan to Curtail Rape in Somalia*. Retrieved 29 March 2015 (www.hrw.org/sites/default/files/reports/somalia0214_ForUpload.pdf).

James, N. 2015. "Offender Reentry: Correctional Statistics, Reintegration into the Community, and Recidivism." Congressional Research Service. Retrieved 29 April 2018 (https://fas.org/sgp/crs/misc/RL34287.pdf).

Janowitz, M. 1978. *The Last Half Century: Societal Change and Politics in America*. Chicago: University of Chicago Press.

Kobrin, S. 1959. "The Chicago Area Project—A 25-Year Assessment." *Annals of the American Academy of Political and Social Sciences*, 322, 20–29.

Kristof, N. D., and S. WuDunn. 2009. *Half the Sky: Turning Oppression into Opportunity for Women Worldwide*. New York: Knopf.

Kristof, N. D., and S. WuDunn. 2014. *A Path Appears: Transforming Lives, Creating Opportunity*. New York: Random House.

Lee, H., M. S. Vaughn, and H. Lim. 2014. "The Impact of Neighborhood Crime Levels on Police Use of Force: An Examination at Micro and Meso Levels." *Journal of Criminal Justice*, 42, 491–99.

Markman, J. A., M. R. Durose, R. R. Rantala, and A. D. Tiedt. 2016. "Recidivism of Offenders Placed on Federal Community Supervision in 2005: Patterns from 2005 to 2010." Bureau of Justice Statistics. NCJ 249743. 21 June.

Martinson, R. 1972. "Planning for Public Safety." *New Republic*. 29 April, pp. 21–23.

Matthews, R. 2015. "Female Prostitution and Victimization: A Realist Analysis." *International Review of Victimology*, 21, 85–100.

Matulich, S., and D. M. Currie, eds. 2008. *Handbook of Frauds, Scams, and Swindles: Failures of Ethics in Leadership*. Boca Raton, FL: CRC Press.

Menaker, T. A., and C. A. Franklin. 2018. "Prostitution Myth Endorsement: Assessing the Effects of Sexism, Sexual Victimization History, Pornography, and Self-Control." *Psychology of Women Quarterly*, doi. org/10.1177/0361684318754790).

Merton, R. K. 1968. *Social Theory and Social Structure*, 3rd ed. New York: Free Press.

Metz, N., and M. Burdina. 2018. "Neighbourhood Income Inequality and Property Crime." *Urban Studies*, 55, 133–150.

Miczek, K.A., S. C. Maxson, E. W. Fish, and S. Faccidomo. 2001. "Aggressive Behavioral Phenotypes in Mice." *Behavioural Brain Research*, 125, 167–181.

Miller, W. B. 2001. *The Growth Of Youth Gang Problems in the United States: 1970–98 Report*. Darby, Pa: Diane Pub. Co.

Morgan, R. E., and G. Kena. 2017. "Criminal Victimization, 2016." Bureau of Justice Statistics. NCJ 251150. December. U.S. Department of Justice.

Morris, C. 2017. "Revenge Porn Law Could Make It A Federal Crime to Post Explicit Photos Without Permission." November 28. *Fortune*. Retrieved 10 May 2018 (http://fortune.com/2017/11/28/revenge-porn-law/).

Murphy, S. L., J. Xu, K. D. Kochanek, S. C. Durbin, and E. Arias. 2017. "Deaths: Final Data for 2015." National Vital Statistics Reports. Vol. 66, No. 6. Centers for Disease Control and Prevention.

National Institute of Justice. 2017. "Rape and Sexual Violence." 21 March. Retrieved 20 July 2018 (https://www.nij.gov/topics/crime/rape-sexual-violence/Pages/welcome.aspx).

Nelkin, D. 1995. "Biology Is Not Destiny." *New York Times*. 28 September, p. A27.

Parker, K., J. Menasce Horowitz, R. Igielnik, B. Oliphant, and A. Brown. 2017. "Views of Guns and Gun Violence." Pew Research Center. 22 June. Retrieved 8 March 2018 (www.pewsocialtrends.org/2017/06/22/views-of-guns-and-gun-violence/).

Pérez-Peña, R. 2015. "Gun Control Explained." New York Times. 7 October. Retrieved 8 March 2018 (www.nytimes.com/interactive/2015/10/07/us/gun-control-explained.html).

Petrosky, E., J. M. Blair, C. J. Betz, K. A. Fowler, S. P. D. Jack, and B. H. Lyons. 2017. "Racial and Ethnic Differences in Homicides of Adult Women and the Role of Intimate Partner Violence – United States, 2003–2014." *Morbidity and Mortality Weekly Report*, 66, 741–746.

Pew Research Center. 2017. "Public Views About Guns." 22 June. Retrieved 8 March 2018 (www.people-press.org/2017/06/22/public-views-about-guns/#total).

Planty, M., L. Langton, and C. Barnett-Ryan. 2014. "The Nation's Two Crime Measures." Bureau of Justice Statistics. Retrieved 4 March 2018 (www.bjs.gov/content/pub/ascii/ntcm_2014.txt).

Radzinowicz, L. R., and J. King. 1977. *The Growth of Crime: The International Experience*. New York: Basic Books.

Reiss, A. J., Jr., and J. A. Roth, eds. 1993. *Understanding and Preventing Violence*. Washington, DC: National Academy of Sciences Press.

Salinger, L. M., ed. 2004. *Encyclopedia of White Collar and Corporate Crime*. Thousand Oaks, CA: Sage.

Sanchez-Jankowski, M. 2008. *Cracks in the Pavement: Social Change and Resilience in Poor Neighborhoods*. Berkeley: University of California Press.

Schaible, L. M., and I. Altheimer. 2016. "Social Structure, Anomie, and National Levels of Homicide." *International Journal of Offender Therapy and Comparative Criminology*, 60, 936–963.

Smith, S.G., J. Chen, K. C. Basile, L. K. Gilbert, M. T. Merrick, N. Patel, M. Walling, and A. Jain. 2017. "The National Intimate Partner and Sexual Violence Survey (NISVS): 2010–2012 State Report." Atlanta, GA: National Center for Injury Prevention and Control, Centers for Disease Control and Prevention.

Stewart, J. B. 2015. "In Corporate Crimes, Individual Accountability is Elusive." February 19. *New York Times*. Retrieved 29 March 2015 (nyti.ms/1zRG1BJ).

Sutherland, E. H., and D. R. Cressey. 1960. *Principles of Criminology*. Philadelphia: Lippincott.

Suttles, G. 1970. *The Social Order of the Slum*. Chicago: University of Chicago Press.

Sweet, K. 2017. "Wells Fargo Says 3.5 Million Accounts Involved in Scandal." US News.com. 31 August.

Sykes, B. L., A. R. Piquero, and J. P. Gioviano. "The Prejudice Paradox: Perceptions of Discrimination Among Adolescents in Safe Neighborhoods and Schools." *Sociological Forum*, 32, 952–974.

Unicef. 2017. "The State of the World's Children 2016: A Fair Chance for Every Child." June.

United Nations Office on Drugs and Crime. 2013. "Homicide Counts and Rates, Time Series 2000–2012." Global Study on Homicide. Retrieved 25 March 2015 (www.unodc.org/gsh/en/data.html).

United Nations Office on Drugs and Crime. 2018a. "Organized Crime." Retrieved 5 March 2018 (www.unodc.org/unodc/en/organized-crime/intro.html).

United Nations Office on Drugs and Crime. 2018b. "UNODC on Human Trafficking and Migrant Smuggling." Retrieved 20 July 2018 (https://www.unodc.org/unodc/en/human-trafficking/index.html).

United Nations Population Fund. 2017. "Gender-Based Violence: Overview." 18 September. Retrieved 20 July (https://www.unfpa.org/gender-based-violence).

U.S. Department of Justice. 2015. "Victims of Identity Theft, 2014." Office of Justice Programs, U.S. Department of Justice. NCJ248991. September.

U.S. Department of State. 2017. "Trafficking in Persons Report 2017." Retrieved 5 March 2018 (www.state.gov/j/tip/rls/tiprpt/2017/index.htm).

Violence Policy Center. 2015. "States with Weak Gun Laws and Higher Gun Ownership Lead Nation in Gun Deaths, New Data for 2013 Confirms." Retrieved 25 March 2015 (www.vpc.org/press/1501gundeath.htm).

Walker-Rodriguez, A., and R. Hill. 2011. "Human Sex Trafficking." FBI Law Enforcement Bulletin. March. Retrieved 14 May 2013 (leb.fbi.gov/2011/march/human-sex-trafficking).

Wilkinson, R., and K. Pickett. 2010. *The Spirit Level: Why Greater Equality Makes Society Stronger*. New York: Bloomsbury Press.

Wilson, J. Q. 1977. *Thinking About Crime*. New York: Vintage Books.

Wilson, J. Q. 1993. *The Moral Sense*. New York: Basic Books.

Wilson, J.Q. and R. J. Herrnstein. 1985. *Crime and Human Nature*. Simon and Schuster.

Wilson, W. J. 1996. *When Work Disappears: The World of the New Urban Poor*. Chicago: University of Chicago Press.

Winking, J. 2018. "Exploring the Great Schism in the Social Sciences: Confirmation Bias and the Interpretation of Results Relating to Biological Influences on Human Behavior and Psychology." *Evolutionary Psychology*, 16(1), (https://doi.org/10.1177/1474704917752691).

World Economic Forum. 2016. "Organized Crime." Retrieved 5 March 2018 (reports.weforum.org/global-competitiveness-index-2017-2018/competitiveness-rankings/#series=EOSQ035).

World Health Organization. 2017. "Media Centre: Violence Against Women: Intimate Partner and Sexual Violence Against Women." November. Retrieved 8 March 2018 (www.who.int/mediacentre/factsheets/fs239/en/).

Chapter 6

Bell, M., N. Fosse, M. Lamont, and E. Rosen. 2015. "Beyond the Culture of Poverty." *The Wiley Blackwell Encyclopedia of Race, Ethnicity, and Nationalism*, p. 1–16. New York: Wiley.

Blumberg, D. 1980. *Inequality in an Age of Decline*. New York: Oxford University Press.

Bogenschneider, K. 2014. *Family Policy Matters: How Policymaking Affects Families and What Professionals Can Do, 3rd ed.* New York: Lawrence Erlbaum.

Bor, J., G. H. Cohen, and S. Galea. 2017. "Population Health in an Era of Rising Income Inequality: USA, 1980–2015." *The Lancet*, 389, 1475–1490.

Brooks-Gunn, J., and G. J. Duncan. 1997. "The Effects of Poverty on Children." *The Future of Children (Children and Poverty)*, 7, 55–71.

Burgard, S. A., and M. M. King. 2014. "National Report Card: Health Inequality." Stanford Center on Poverty and Inequality. January.

Bywaters, P., Bunting, L., Davidson, G., Hanratty, J., Mason, W., McCartan, C., and Steils, N. 2016. "The relationship between poverty, child abuse, and neglect: An evidence review." Retrieved 29 June 2018 (https://jrf.org.uk/report/relationship-between-poverty-child-abuse-and-neglect-evidence-review).

Cancian, M., K. S. Slack, and M. Y. Yang. 2010. "The Effect of Family Income on Risk of Child Maltreatment." Discussion Paper No. 1385–10. August. Madison, WI: Institute for Research on Poverty.

Centers for Disease Control and Prevention. 2015. "Child Maltreatment Prevention." Retrieved 5 March 2015 (www.cdc.gov/violenceprevention/childmaltreatment).

Child Care Aware of America. 2017. "What Does Childcare Cost in Your State?" Retrieved 9 February 2018 (usa.childcareaware.org/advocacy-public-policy/resources/research/costofcare/).

Child Trends Data Bank. September 2016. "Child Maltreatment: Indicators of Child and Youth Well-Being." Retrieved 29 June 2018 (https://www.childtrends.org/wp-content/uploads/2016/09/40_Child_Maltreatment.pdf).

Children's Defense Fund. 2005. "Defining Poverty and Why It Matters for Children." Retrieved 6 July 2007 (www.childrensdefensefund.org).

Children's Defense Fund. 2014. "The State of America's Children 2014 Report." Retrieved 11 August 2014 (www.childrensdefense.org/child-research-data-publications/state-of-americas-children/).

Cohen, Y., M. Krumer-Nevo, and N. Avieli. 2017. "Bread of Shame: Mechanisms of Othering in Soup Kitchens." *Social Problems,* 64, 398–413.

Coleman-Jensen, A., M. P. Rabbitt, C. A. Gregory, and A. Singh. 2017. "Household Food Security in the United States in 2016." ERR–237. Washington, DC: U.S. Department of Agriculture, Economic Research Service.

Conger, R. D., and K. J. Conger. 2008. "Understanding the Processes Through Which Economic Hardship Influences Families and Children." *Handbook of Families and Poverty*, edited by D. R. Crane and T. B. Heaton, 64–81. Thousand Oaks, CA: Sage Publications.

Credit Suisse, 2017. Global Wealth Report 2017. Retrieved 29 June 2018 (http://publications.credit-suisse.com/tasks/render/file/index.cfm?fileid=168E2808-9ED4-5A5E-19E43EA2A731A4ED).

Crosnoe, R., T. Leventhal. R. J. Wirth, K. M. Pierce, R. C. Pianta, and NICHD Early Child Care Research Network. 2010. "Family Socioeconomic Status and Consistent Environmental Stimulation in Early Childhood." *Child Development*, 81, 972–87.

Dean, S. 2017. "The Future of SNAP." Center on Budget and Policy Priorities. 28 March. Retrieved 12 May 2018 (www.cbpp.org/food-assistance/the-future-of-snap).

Edin, K., and M. Kefalas. 2005. *Promises I Can Keep: Why Poor Women Put Motherhood Before Marriage*. Berkeley, CA: University of California Press.

Elgar, F. J., G. Gariépy, T. Torsheim, and C. Currie. 2017. "Early-Life Income Inequality and Adolescent Health and Well-Being." *Social Science & Medicine*, 174, 197–208.

Elger, T. 2015. "Dual Labor Markets." *The Blackwell Encyclopedia of Sociology*.

Ermisch, J., M. Jäntti, T. Smeeding, and J. Wilson. 2012. "Thinking about Cross-National Research on the Intergenerational Transmission of Advantage." In *From Parents to Children: The Intergenerational Transmission of Advantage*, edited by J. Ermisch, M. Jäntti, and T. Smeeding, Chapter 1. New York: Russell Sage Foundation.

Federal Interagency Forum on Child and Family Statistics. 2014. "At A Glance: America's Children: Key National Indicators of Well-Being." Washington, DC: U.S. Government Printing Office. Retrieved 20 March 2015 (http://www.childstats.gov/pdf/ac2014/ac_14.pdf).

Fernald, A., V. A. Marchman, and A. Weisleder. 2013. "SES Differences in Language Processing Skill and Vocabulary Are Evident at 18 Months." *Developmental Science*, 16, 234–248.

Fisher, J., D. Johnson,, J. Latner, T. Smeeding, and J. Thompson. 2016. "Inequality and Mobility Using Income, Consumption, and Wealth for the Same Individuals." *RSF Journal of the Social Sciences*, 2, 44–58.

Floyd, I., L. Pavetti, and L. Schott. 2017. "TANF Reaching Few Poor Families." Center for Budget and Policy Priorities. 13 December. Retrieved 30 January 2018 (www.cbpp.org/research/family-income-support/tanf-reaching-few-poor-families).

Fowler, K. A., L. L. Dahlberg, T. Haileyesus, C. Gutierrez, and S. Bacon. 2017. "Childhood Firearm Injuries in the United States." *Pediatrics*. 140: e20163486.

Friedman-Krauss, A., W. S. Barnett, and M. Nores. 2016. "How Much Can High-Quality Universal Pre-K Reduce Achievement Gaps?" Center for American Progress. 5 April. Retrieved 27 January 2018 (nieer.org/wp-content/uploads/2017/01/NIEER-AchievementGaps-report.pdf).

Galbraith, J. K. 1958. *The Affluent Society.* Boston: Houghton Mifflin.

Gans, H. J. 1995. *The War Against the Poor: The Underclass and Antipoverty Policy.* New York: Basic Books.

Gershoff, E. T., and A. Grogan-Taylor. 2016. "Spanking and Child Outcomes: Old Controversies and New Meta-Analyses." *Journal of Family Psychology*, 30, 453–469.

Gilbert, D., and J. A. Kahl. 1993. *The American Class Structure: A New Synthesis, 4th ed.* Belmont, CA: Wadsworth.

Godfrey, E.B. and Wolf, S. 2016. "Developing critical consciousness or justifying the system? A qualitative analysis of attributions for poverty and wealth among low-income racial/ethnic minority and immigrant women." *Cultural Diversity and Ethnic Minority Psychology*, 1, 93–103.

Grall, T. S. 2016. "Custodial Mothers and Fathers and Their Child Support: 2013." Current Population Reports. U.S. Census Bureau. P60–255. January. Retrieved 18 August 2016 (www.census.gov/content/dam/Census/library/publications/2016/demo/P60-255.pdf).

Gundersen, C., and J. P. Ziliak. 2015. "Food Insecurity and Health Outcomes." *Health Affairs*, 34, 1830–1839.

Hair, N. L., J. L. Hanson, B. L. Wolfe, and S. D. Pollak. 2015. "Association of Child Poverty, Brain Development, and Academic Achievement." *JAMA Pediatrics*, 169, 822–829.

Hart, B., and T. R. Risley. 1995. *Meaningful Differences in the Everyday Experience of Young American Children.* Baltimore, MD: Paul H. Brookes Publishing Company.

Haushofer, J., and E. Fehr. 2014. "On the Psychology of Poverty." *Science*, 344, 862–867.

Homan, P., Valentino, L., and Weed, E. 2017. "Being and becoming poor: How cultural schemas shape beliefs about poverty." *Social Forces*, 95, 1023–1048.

Internal Revenue Service. 2018. "2017 EITC Income Limits, Maximum Credit Amounts and Tax Law Updates." Retrieved 12 May 2018 (www.irs.gov/credits-deductions/individuals/earned-income-tax-credit/eitc-income-limits-maximum-credit-amounts).

International Monetary Fund World Economic Outlook Database. "World Economic Outlook Update: January, 2018." Retrieved 12 May 2018 (www.imf.org/en/Publications/WEO/Issues/2018/01/11/world-economic-outlook-update-january-2018).

Jackman, M. R., and R. W. Jackman. 1983. *Class Awareness in the United States.* Berkeley: University of California Press.

Jackson, G. L., T. E. Trail, D. P. Kennedy, H. C. Williamson, T. N. Bradbury, and B. R. Karney. 2016. "The Salience and Severity of Relationship Problems Among Low-Income Couples." *Journal of Family Psychology*, 30, 2–11.

Jansson, B. S. 2012. *The Reluctant Welfare State: A History of American Social Welfare Policies, 7th ed.* Boston: Cengage Learning.

Johnson, A. D., and Markowitz, A.J. 2018. "Associations between household food insecurity in early childhood and children's kindergarten skills." *Child Development*, 89, e1–e17.

Jusko, K., and K. Weisshaar. 2014. "National Report Card: Safety Net." Stanford Center on Poverty and Inequality. January.

Kaiser, T., J. Li, and M. Pollmann-Schult. 2017. "Evening and Night Work Schedules and Children's Social and Emotional Well-Being." *Community, Work & Family.* doi.org/10.1080/13668803.2017.1404443.

Kane, J. B., T. J. Nelson, and K. Edin. 2015. "How Much In-Kind Support Do Low-Income Nonresident Fathers Provide? A Mixed-Method Analysis." *Journal of Marriage and Family*, 77, 591–611.

Landry, S. H., T. A. Zucker, H. B. Taylor, P. R. Swank, J. M. Williams, M. Assel, A. Crawford, W. Huang, J. Clancy-Menchetti, P. Lonigan, M. Barnes, P. Starkey, and A. Klein. 2014. "Enhancing Early Child Care Quality and Learning for Toddlers at Risk: The Responsive Early Childhood Program." *Developmental Psychology*, 50, 526–541.

Laughlin, L. 2013. "Who's Minding the Kids? Child Care Arrangements: Spring 2011." Household Economic Studies, 70–135. April. Washington, DC: U.S. Census Bureau.

Lewis, O. 1968. *The Study of Slum Cultures—Backgrounds for La Vida.* New York: Random House.

Li, J., S. E. Johnson, W. J. Han, S. Andrews, G. Kendall, L. Stradzins, and A. Dockery. 2014. "Parents' Nonstandard Work Schedules and Child Well-Being: A Critical Review of the Literature." *The Journal of Primary Prevention*, 35, 53–73.

Lopez, G., and Radford, J. "Facts on U.S. Immigrants." Pew Research Center. Retrieved 29 June 2018 (http://www.pewhispanic.org/2017/05/03/facts-on-u-s-immigrants-trend-data/).

López, G., N. G. Ruiz, and E. Patten. 2017. "Key Facts About Asian Americans, A Diverse and Growing Population." Pew Research Center. 8 September. Retrieved 23 October 2017 (www.pewresearch.org/fact-tank/2017/09/08/key-facts-about-asian-americans/).

Maldonado, L. C., and R. Nieuwenhuis. 2015. "Family Policies and Single Parent Poverty in 18 OECD Countries, 1978–2008." *Community, Work & Family*, 18, 395–415.

Market Data Enterprises. 2017. The U.S. Weight Loss and Diet Control Market. Retrieved 29 June 2018 (http://www.marketresearch.com/Marketdata-Enterprises-Inc.-v416/Weight-Loss-Diet-Control-10825677/).

McClam, E. 2013. "Americans Blame Poverty on 'Too Much' Welfare, NBC/WSJ Poll Shows." thegrio.com. 6 June. Retrieved 1 March 2015 (thegrio.com/2013/06/06/americans-blame-poverty-on-too-much-welfare-nbcwsj-poll-shows/).

Midgley, J., E. Dahl, and A. C. Wright, eds. 2017. *Social Welfare: International and Critical Perspectives.* Northampton, MA: Edward Elgar Publishing.

Mitchell, T., and L. Pavetti. 2018. "Life After TANF in Kansas: For Most, Unsteady Work and Earnings Below Half the Poverty Line." 23 January. Center for Budget and Policy Priorities. Retrieved 30 January 2018 (www.cbpp.org/research/family-income-support/life-after-tanf-in-kansas-for-most-unsteady-work-and-earnings-below).

Murray, C. 1984. *Losing Ground: American Social Policy, 1950–1980.* New York: Basic Books.

National Center for Health Statistics, 2017. *Health, United States, 2016: With Chartbook on Long-term Trends in Health.* Hyattsville, MD.

National Conference of State Legislatures. 2017. "State Minimum Wages: 2018 Minimum Wage by State." Retrieved 27 January 2018 (www.ncsl.org/research/labor-and-employment/state-minimum-wage-chart.aspx#Table).

National Conference of State Legislature. January 2, 2018. "NCSL in the News, January 2018." Retrieved 29 June 2018 (http://www.nesl.org/press-room/nesl-in-the-news-january-2018.aspx).

Nores, M., and W. S. Barnett. 2014. "Access to High Quality Early Care and Education: Readiness and Opportunity Gaps in America." Center on Enhancing Early Learning Outcomes. May. Retrieved 4 February 2018 (ceelo.org/wp-content/uploads/2014/05/ceelo_policy_report_access_quality_ece.pdf).

Office of Family Assistance. 2017. "TANF Caseload Data 2017." Administration for Children & Families, U.S. Department of Health and Human Services. Retrieved 4 February 2018 (www.acf.hhs.gov/ofa/resource/tanf-caseload-data-2017).

Reich, R. B. 1998. "Broken Faith: Why We Need to Renew the Social Compact." *Generations.* Winter, 19.

Riesman, D., N. Glazer, and R. Denney. 1950. *The Lonely Crowd.* New Haven, CT: Yale University Press.

Sauter, M. B., A. E. M. Hess, and T. C. Froelich. 2013. "America's Richest (and Poorest) States." 247wallst.com. 19 September. Retrieved 1 March 2015 (247wallst.com/special-report/2013/09/19/americas-richest-and-poorest-states/).

Schott, L., and I. Floyd. 2017. "Policy Brief: How States Use Funds Under the TANF Block Grant." Center on Budget and Policy Priorities. 10 January. Retrieved 30 January 2018 (www.cbpp.org/research/family-income-support/policy-brief-how-states-use-funds-under-the-tanf-block-grant/).

Seccombe, K. 2015. *So You Think I Drive a Cadillac?: Welfare Recipients' Perspectives on the System and Its Reform, 4th ed.* Boston: Pearson.

Seccombe, K. 2016. *Families and Their Social Worlds, 3rd ed.* Pearson.

Semega, J. L., K. R. Fontenot, and M. A. Kollar, 2017. "Income and Poverty in the United States: 2016." Current Population Reports. P60-259. September. Washington, DC: U.S. Census Bureau.

Shankar, P., R. Chung, and D. A. Frank. 2017. "Association of Food Insecurity with Children's Behavioral, Emotional, and Academic Outcomes: A Systematic Review." *Journal of Developmental & Behavioral Pediatrics, 38, 135–150.*

Sherman, A. 2016. "Citing Poverty's Toll on Children, Pediatricians Call for Stronger Safety Net." Center on Budget and Policy Priorities. 10 March. Retrieved 1 February 2018 (www.cbpp.org/blog/citing-povertys-toll-on-children-pediatricians-call-for-stronger-safety-net).

Sherter, A. 2013. "Millions on Food Stamps Facing Benefits Cuts." cbs.com/moneywatch. 3 November. Retrieved 1 March 2015 (www.cbsnews.com/news/millions-on-food-stamps-facing-benefits-cuts/).

Siebens, J. 2013. Extended Measures of Well-Being: Living Conditions in the United States. U.S. Census Bureau. Report P70–136.

Smith, O. 2017. "The Haven for Honeymooners Where Everyone Gets Divorced." The Telegraph. 18 October. Retrieved 17 January 2018 (www.telegraph.co.uk/travel/maps-and-graphics/mapped-countries-with-highest-divorce-rate/).

Stanford Center on Poverty & Inequality. 2017. "Pathways: State of the Union 2017." Retrieved 4 February 2018 (inequality.stanford.edu/publications/pathway/state-union-2017).

Stein, R. 2010. "Study Finds That Effects of Low-Quality Child Care Last Into Adolescence." *Washington Post.* 14 May. Retrieved 1 March 2015 (www.washington-post.com/wp-dyn/content/article/2010/05/14/AR2010051400043.html).

Stone, C., D. Trisi, A. Sherman, and E. Horton. 2017. "A Guide to Statistics on Historical Trends in Income Inequality." Center on Budget and Policy Priorities. 11 October. Retrieved 26 January 2018 (www.cbpp.org/research/poverty-and-inequality/a-guide-to-statistics-on-historical-trends-in-income-inequality).

Strong-Jekely, L. 2006. Letter to the Editor. *Brain, Child, 2.* Budapest, Hungary, Winter.

Tamborini, C. R., C. Kim, and A. Sakamoto. 2015. "Education and Lifetime Earnings in the United States." *Demography,* 52, 1383–1407.

Tax Policy Center. 2017. "Distributional Analysis of the Tax Cuts and Jobs Act as Passed by the Senate." 4 December. Retrieved 4 February 2018 (www.taxpolicycenter.org/publications/distributional-analysis-tax-cuts-and-jobs-act-passed-senate/full).

Thompson, J., and T. Smeeding. 2014. "National Report Card: Income Inequality." Stanford Center on Poverty and Inequality. January.

Trisi, D., and L. Pavetti. 2012. "TANF Weakening as a Safety Net For Poor Families." Center for Budget and Policy Priorities. 13 March. Retrieved 1 March 2015 (www.cbpp.org/cms/?fa=view&id=3700).

UNICEF. 2018. "A Growing Number of Countries Are Developing National Action Plans for Orphans and Other Vulnerable Children." January. Retrieved 26 January 2018 (data.unicef.org/topic/hivaids/protection-care-and-support-for-children-affected-by-hiv-and-aids/).

UNICEF Innocenti Research Centre. 2013. "Child Well-Being in Rich Countries: A Comparative Overview." Report Card 11. April. Retrieved 26 February 2014 (www.unicef-irc.org/publications/pdf/rc11_eng.pdf).

U.S. Bureau of Labor Statistics. 2017. "A Profile of the Working Poor, 2015." April. Retrieved 29 June 2018 (https://www.bls.gov/opub/reports/working-poor/2015/home.htm).

U.S. Conference of Mayors. 2016. "The U.S. Conference of Mayors' Report on Hunger and Homelessness." Retrieved 8 February 2018 (endhomelessness.atavist.com/mayorsreport2016).

U.S. Department of Commerce, January 26, 2018. "2018 Release Schedule for Economic Indicators." Retrieved 29 June 2018 (https://www.commerce.gov/page/2018-release-schedule-economic-indicators).

U.S. Department of Housing and Urban Development. 2017. "Fair Market Rents." Retrieved 12 February 2018. (www.huduser.gov/portal/datasets/fmr.html).

White, L., and S. J. Rogers. 2000. "Economic Circumstances and Family Outcomes: A Review of the 1990's." *Journal of Marriage and Family,* 62, 1035–51.

Wilson, W. J. 1987. *The Truly Disadvantaged: The Inner City, the Underclass, and Public Policy.* Chicago: University of Chicago Press.

World Bank. 2017. "Poverty Overview." Retrieved 30 January 2018 (www.worldbank.org/en/topic/poverty/overview).

World Bank 2017. "Poverty and Shared Prosperity 2016." Retrieved 26 January 2018 (www.worldbank.org/en/publication/poverty-and-shared-prosperity).

Yeung, W. J., M. R. Linver, and J. Brooks-Gunn. 2002. "How Money Matters for Young Children's Development: Parental Investment and Family Processes." *Child Development,* 73, 1861–79.

Chapter 7

Aljazeera News. 2018. "UN: Myanmar Should Be Investigated for Crimes Against Rohingya." Retrieved 9 March 2018 (www.aljazeera.com/news/2018/03/myanmar-investigated-crimes-rohingya-180309105233347.html).

...ger, E. 2014. "The Rapid Demographic Shift of American Public Schools." Washingtonpost.com. 18 August. Retrieved 15 March 2015 (www.washingtonpost.com/blogs/wonkblog/wp/2014/08/18/the-rapid-demographic-shift-of-american-public-schools/).

Banks, K.H, and J. Stephens. 2018. "Reframing Internalized Racial Oppression and Charting a way Forward." *Social Issues and Policy Review, 12*, 91–111.

Beckett, K., and H. Evans. 2014. "The Role of Race in Washington State Capital Sentencing, 1981-2014." Law, Societies, & Justice Program. University of Washington. Retrieved 3 March 2015 (lsj.washington.edu/sites/lsj/files/research/capital_punishment_beckettevans_10-1.6.14.pdf).

Brewster, Z. W., J. R. Brauer, and M. Lynn. 2015. "Economic Motivations and Moral Controls Regulating Discrimination against Black and Hispanic Diners." *The Sociological Quarterly*, 56, 506–538.

Brooks, R. 2017. "The Retirement Crisis Facing African Americans." Money. 9 March 2017. Retrieved 27 August 2018 (https://www.forbes.com/sites/nextavenue/2017/03/09/the-retirement-crisis-facing-african-americans/#232db32e4f5b).

Bureau of Labor Statistics. 2017. "Employment Projections." 24 October. Retrieved 11 March 2018 (www.bls.gov/emp/ep_chart_001.htm).

Butler, D. M., and D. E. Brockman. 2011. "Do Politicians Racially Discriminate Against Constituents? A Field Experiment on State Legislators."*American Journal of Political Science*, 55, 463–77.

Clouston, S. A. P., M. S. Rubin, J. C. Phelan, and B. G. Link. 2016. "A Social History of Disease: Contextualizing the Rise and Fall of Social Inequalities in Cause-Specific Mortality." *Demography*, 53, 1631–1656.

Colby, S. L., and J. M. Ortman. 2015. "Projections of the Size and Composition of the U.S. Population: 2014 to 2060: Population Estimates and Projections." Current Population Reports, 25–1143. March. U.S. Census Bureau. Retrieved 9 March 2015 (www.census.gov/content/dam/Census/library/publications/2015/demo/p25-1143.pdf).

Colen, C. G., D. M. Ramey, E. C. Cooksey, and D. R. Williams. 2017. "Racial Disparities in Health Among Nonpoor African Americans and Hispanics: The Role of Acute and Chronic Discrimination." *Social Science & Medicine*, 10.1016/j.socscimed.2017.04.051.

Coles, R. 2003. *Children of Crisis*. New York: Back Bay Books.

Conley, D. 1999. *Being Black, Living in the Red: Race, Wealth and Social Policy in America*. Berkeley: University of California Press.

Death Penalty Information Center. 2018. "Facts about the Death Penalty." 23 February.

Derlan, C. L., Umaña-Taylor, A. J., Jahromi, L. and Updegraff, K. A. (2018). "Cultural socialization attitudes and behaviors: Examining mothers' centrality, discrimination experiences, and children's effortful control as moderators." *Cultural Diversity and Ethnic Minority Psychology, 24*, 162–172.

Doleac, J. L., and L. C. D. Stein. 2013. "The Visible Hand: Race and Online Market Outcomes." *The Economic Journal*, 123, F469–92.

Douglass, S., & Umaña-Taylor, A. J. (2016). "Time-varying effects of family ethnic socialization on ethnic-racial identity development among Latino adolescents." *Developmental Psychology, 52*, 1904–1912.

Drake, B. 2014. "Public Strongly Backs Affirmative Action Programs on Campus." Pew Research Center. 22 April. Retrieved 3 March 2015 (www.pewresearch.org/fact-tank/2014/04/22/public-strongly-backs-affirmative-action-programs-on-campus/).

Eckholm, E. 1995. February 24. "Studies Find Death Penalty Tied to Race of Victims." *New York Times*, pp. B1–4.

The Economist. 2013. "Affirmative Action: Is Affirmative Action a Good Idea?" 29 June. Retrieved 29 June 2013 (www.economist.com/debate/overview/251).

Epp, C. R., S. Maynard-Moody, and D. Haider-Harkel. 2014. *Pulled Over: How Police Stops Define Race and Citizenship*. Chicago: University of Chicago Press.

Feagin, J. 2013. *The White Racial Frame: Centuries of Racial Framing and Counter-Framing*, 2nd ed. New York: Routledge.

Federal Bureau of Investigation (FBI). 2013. "Expanded Homicide Data Table 6." Crime in the United States 2013: About Crime in the U.S. (CIUS). Retrieved 3 March 2015 (www.fbi.gov/about-us/cjis/ucr/crime-in-the-u.s/2013/crime-in-the-u.s.-2013).

FEDS Notes. September 27, 2017. "Recent Trends in Wealth-Holding by Race and Ethnicity: Evidence from the Survey of Consumer Finances." L. J. Dettling, J. W. Hsu, L. Jacobs, K. B. Moore, J. P. Thompson, and E. Llanes. Retrieved 15 July 2018 (https://www.federalreserve.gov/econres/notes/feds-notes/recent-trends-in-wealth-holding-by-race-and-ethnicity-evidence-from-the-survey-of-consumer-finances-20170927.htm).

Feltman, C. E., and D. M. Szymanski. 2018. "Instagram Use and Self-Objectification: The Roles of Internalization, Comparison, Appearance Commentary, and Feminism." *Sex Roles*, 78, 311–324.

Frey, W. H. 2015. "Census Shows Modest Declines in Black-White Segregation." Brookings. 8 December. Retrieved 13 March 2018 (www.brookings.edu/blog/the-avenue/2015/12/08/census-shows-modest-declines-in-black-white-segregation/).

Gaylord-Harden, N. K., and J. A. Cunningham. 2009. "The Impact of Racial Discrimination and Coping Strategies on Internalizing Symptoms in African American Youth." *Journal of Youth and Adolescence*, 38, 532–43.

Hanselman, P., and J. E. Fiel. 2017. "School Opportunity Hoarding? Racial Segregation and Access to High Growth Schools." *Social Forces*, 95, 1077–1104.

Innocence Project. 2018. "Report: Exonerations in 2017." 14 March. Retrieved 15 March 2018. "www.innocenceproject.org/report-exonerations-in-2017/).

Kaiser Family Foundation. 2016. "Population Distribution by Race/Ethnicity." Retrieved 9 March 2018 (www.kff.org/other/state-indicator/distribution-by-raceethnicity/?currentTimeframe=0&sortModel=%7B%22colId%22:%22Location%22,%22sort%22:%22asc%22%7D).

Kelley, R. 2010. "Why We Still Need Affirmative Action." Newsweek.com. 17 February. Retrieved 3 March 2015 (www.newsweek.com/hy-we-still-need-affirmative-action-75297).

Kristof, N. 2018. "I Saw a Genocide in Slow Motion." New York Times. 2 March. Retrieved 9 March 2018 (www.nytimes.com/2018/03/02/opinion/i-saw-a-genocide-in-slow-motion.html).

Kwate, N. O., and M. S. Goodman. 2015. "Cross-Sectional and Longitudinal Effects of Racism on Mental Health Among Residents of Black Neighborhoods in New York City." *American Journal of Public Health*, 105, 711–18.

Lamont, M. 2003. "Who Counts as 'Them?': Racism and Virtue in the United States and France." *Contexts*, 2, 36–41.

Lempert, R. 2014. "The Schuette Decision: The Supreme Court Rules on Affirmative Action." Brookings Institution. 25 April. Retrieved 3 March 2015 (www.brookings.edu/blogs/fixgov/posts/2014/04/25-schuette-affirmative-action-supreme-court-comment-lempert).

Lichter, D. T., D. Parisi, and H. De Valk. 2016. "Residential Segregation." Pathways: The Poverty and Inequality Report 2016. The Stanford Center on Poverty and Inequality.

Lieberson, S. 1990. *From Many Strands,* 2nd ed. New York: Russell Sage.

Liptak, A. 2016. "Supreme Court Upholds Affirmative Action Program at University of Texas." *New York Times*. 23 June 2016. Retrieved 5 July 2018 (https://www.nytimes.com/2016/06/24/us/politics/supreme-court-affirmative-action-university-of-texas.html).

Livingston, G., and A. Brown. 2017. "Intermarriage in the U.S. 50 Years After *Loving v. Virginia*." Pew Research Center. 18 May. Retrieved 23 October 2017 (www.pewsocialtrends.org/2017/05/18/intermarriage-in-the-u-s-50-years-after-loving-v-virginia).

Logan, J. R. 2011. "Separate and Unequal: The Neighborhood Gap for Blacks, Hispanics, and Asians in Metropolitan America." US2010 Project. Brown University. July. Retrieved 3 March 2015 (www.s4.brown.edu/us2010/Data/Report/report0727.pdf).

MacDonald, H. 2001. "The Myth of Racial Profiling." *City Journal*. Spring.

Massey, D. S., and J. J. Fischer. 2004. "The Ecology of Racial Discrimination." *City and Community*, 3, 221–24.

Massey, D. S., and J. S. Rugh. 2017. "The Intersections of Race and Class." The Fight for Fair Housing, G. D. Squires, ed. London: Routledge.

McCain, J., and A. Jolie. 2018. "America Should Lead in Saving the Rohingya." New York Times. 8 March. Retrieved 15 March 2018 (www.nytimes.com/2018/03/08/opinion/america-rohingya-myanmar.html).

McFarland, J., J. Cui, and P. Stark. 2018. "Trends in High School Dropout and Completion Rates in the United States: 2014 (NCES 2018-117)." U.S. Department of Education. Washington, DC: National Center for Education Statistics. Retrieved 13 March 2018 (nces.ed.gov/pubsearch).

Merton, R. K. 1949. *Social Theory and Social Structure*. New York: Free Press.

Milkman, K. L., M. Akinola, and D. Chugh. 2014. "What Happens Before? A Field Experiment Exploring How Pay and Representation Differentially Shape Bias on the Pathway into Organizations." Social Science Research Network. 13 December. Retrieved 12 March 2015 (papers.ssrn.com/sol3/papers.cfm?abstract_id=2063742).

Morris, E. W., and B. L Perry. 2016. "The Punishment Gap: School Suspension and Racial Disparities in Achievement." *Social Problems*, 63, 68–86.

Musu-Gillette, L., J. Robinson, J. McFarland, A. KewalRamani, A. Zhang, and S. Wilkinson-Flicker. 2016. "Status and Trends in the Education of Racial and Ethnic Groups 2016 (NCES 2016-007)." U.S. Department of Education, National Center for Education Statistics. Washington, DC. Retrieved 13 March 2018 (nces.de.gov/pubsearch).

National Advisory Commission on Civil Disorders. 1968. *Report of the National Advisory Commission on Civil Disorders*. Washington, DC: U.S. Government Printing Office.

National Association for the Advancement of Colored People (NAACP). 2015. "Criminal Justice Fact Sheet." Retrieved 3 March 2015 (www.naacp.org/pages/criminal-justice-fact-sheet).

National Association for the Advancement of Colored People (NAACP). 2018. "Death Penalty Fact Sheet." Retrieved 13 March 2018 (www.naacp.org/latest/death-penalty-fact-sheet).

National Association of School Psychologists. 2012. "Racism, Prejudice, and Discrimination." Position Statement. Retrieved 15 March 2015 (www.nasponline.org/about_nasp/positionpapers/RacismPrejudice.pdf).

National Center for Education Statistics. 2014. "Rates of High School Completion and Bachelor's Degree Attainment Among Persons Age 25 and Over, by Race/Ethnicity and Sex: Selected Years, 1910 through 2013." Table 104-10. Digest of Education Statistics. February. Retrieved 15 March 2015 (nces.ed.gov/programs/digest/d13/tables/dt13_104.10.asp).

National Center for Education Statistics. 2018. "Digest of Education Statistics: 2016." February. Retrieved 15 March 2018 (nces.ed.gov/programs/digest/d16/).

National Coalition to Abolish the Death Penalty. 2018. "Exonerations of Innocent Men and Women."

National Conference of State Legislatures. 2014. "Affirmative Action: Overview." 7 February. Retrieved 15 March 2015 (www.ncsl.org/research/education/affirmative-action-overview.aspx).

Newport, F. 2008. "Americans See Obama Election as Race Relations Milestone." Gallup.com. 7 November. Retrieved 15 March 2015 (www.gallup.com/poll/111817/americans-see-obama-election-race-relations-milestone.aspx).

Newport, F. 2016. "Most in U.S. Oppose Colleges Considering Race in Admissions." Gallup. 8 July. Retrieved 15 March 2018 (news.gallup.com/poll/193508/oppose-colleges-considering-race-admissions.aspx).

Oliver, M. L., and T. M. Shapiro. 2006. *Black Wealth/White Wealth: A New Perspective on Racial Inequality*, 2nd ed. New York: Routledge.

Ore, T. E. 2006. *The Social Construction of Difference and Inequality: Race, Class, Gender, and Sexuality*, 3rd ed. Boston: McGraw-Hill.

Orfield, G., J. Ee, E. Frankenberg, and G. Siegel-Hawley. 2016. "*Brown* at 62: School Segregation by Race, Poverty, and State." Civil Rights Project. 16 May.

Owens, A. 2018. "Income Segregation between School Districts and Inequality in Students' Achievement." *Sociology of Education*, 91, 1–27.

Pager, D., B. Western, and B. Bonikowski. 2009. "Discrimination in a Low-Wage Labor Market: A Field Experiment." *American Sociological Review*, 74, 777–99.

Parrillo, V. N. 2016. *Understanding Race and Ethnic Relations*, 5th ed. Boston: Pearson.

Parrillo, V. N. 2019. *Strangers to These Shores*, 12th ed. Boston: Pearson.

Pew Research Center. 2016. "On Views of Race and Inequality, Blacks and Whites Are Worlds Apart." 27 June.

Pierce, G. L., and M. L. Radelet. 2005. "Impact of Legally Inappropriate Factors on Death Sentencing for California Homicides, 1990–1999, The Empirical Analysis." 46 *Santa Clara Law Review* 1. 1 January. Retrieved 3 March 2015 (digitalcommons.law.scu.edu/cgi/viewcontent.cgi?article=1174&context=lawreview).

.ce, G. L., and M. Radelet. 2011. "Death Sentencing in East Baton Rouge Parish, 1990–2008." *Louisiana Law Review*, 71, 647–73.

Quillian, L., D. Pager, O. Hexel, and A. H. Midtbøen. 2017. "Meta-Analysis of Field Experiments Shows No Change in Racial Discrimination in Hiring Over Time." *Proceedings of the National Academy of Sciences*, 114, 10870–10875.

Reardon, S. F., and A. Owens. 2014. "60 Years After *Brown*: Trends and Consequences of School Segregation." *Annual Review of Sociology*, 40, 199–218.

Schaefer, R. T. 2019. *Race and Ethnicity in the United States*, 15th ed. Boston: Pearson.

Sears, D. O., J. Sidanius, and L. Bobo, eds. 2000. *Racialized Politics: The Debate About Racism in America*. Chicago: University of Chicago Press.

Seccombe, K. 2015.*"So You Think I Drive a Cadillac?" Welfare Recipients' Perspectives on the System and Its Reform*, 4th ed. Boston: Pearson.

Semega, J. L., K. R. Fontenot, and M. A. Kollar. 2016. "Income and Poverty in the United States: 2017 Current Population Reports." P60–259. U.S. Government Printing Office.

The Sentencing Project. 2017. "Trends in U.S. Corrections." June.

Simpson, G. E., and J. M. Yinger. 1985. *Racial and Ethnic Minorities: An Analysis of Prejudice and Discrimination*, 5th ed. New York: Plenum.

Snyder, T. D., C. de Brey, and S. A. Dillow. 2018. "Digest of Education Statistics 2016 (NCES 2017-094)." National Center for Education Statistics, Institute of Education Sciences, U. S. Department of Education.

Swift, A. 2017. "Americans' Worries About Race Relations at Record High." Gallup. 15 March. Retrieved 9 March 2018 (news.gallup.com/poll/206057/americans-worry-race-relations-record-high.aspx).

Syzmanski, D.M., and C. Henrichs-Beck. 2014. "Exploring Sexual Minority Women's Experiences of External and Internalized Heterosexism and Sexism and Their Links to Coping and Distress." *Sex Roles*, 70, 28–42.

U.S. Census Bureau. 2017. "Quarterly Residential Vacancies and Homeownerships, Second Quarter 2017." Release Number: CB17-110. 27 July.

U.S. Commission on Civil Rights, Ohio Advisory Committee. 2001. "Briefing on Civil Rights Issues Facing Muslims and Arab Americans in Ohio Post–September 11." 14 November.

U.S. Department of Housing and Urban Development, Office of Policy Development and Research. 2013. "Housing Discrimination Against Racial and Ethnic Minorities 2012." Retrieved 12 March 2015 (www.huduser.org/portal/Publications/pdf/HUD-514_HDS2012.pdf).

U.S. Equal Employment Opportunity Commission. 2018. "Statistics." Retrieved 15 March 2018 (www.eeoc.gov/eeoc/statistics/index.cfm).

U. S. Holocaust Memorial Museum. 2018. "Is the Worst Yet to Come? Ongoing Mass Atrocity Risk in Syria."

Vaillancourt, T. 2013. "Do Human Females Use Indirect Aggression as an Intrasexual Competition Strategy?" *Philosophical Transactions of the Royal Society B: Social Sciences*, DOI: 1098/rstb.2013.0080.

Watson, E. D. 2014. "Interracial Couples and Marriage More Accepted Among Americans." Huffington Post/Black Voices. 27 January. Retrieved 11 March 2015 (www.huffingtonpost.com/elwood-d-watson/interracial-couples-and-m_b_4663479.html).

West, C. 1994. *Race Matters*. New York: Vintage.

Williams, D. R., and R. Wyatt. 2015. "Racial Bias in Health Care and Health: Challenges and Opportunities." *Journal of the American Medical Association*, 314, 555–556.

Zambrana, R. E., A. H. Wingfield, L. M. Lapeyrouse, B A. Dávila, T. L. Hoagland, and R. B. Valdez. 2017. "Blatant, Subtle, and Insidious: URM Faculty Perceptions of Discriminatory Practices in Predominantly White Institutions." *Sociological Inquiry*, 87, 207–232.

Chapter 8

Abathun, A. D., A. A. Gele, and J. Sundby. 2017. "Attitude towards the Practice of Female Genital Cutting among School Boys and Girls in Somali and Harari Regions, Eastern Ethiopia." *Obstetrics and Gynecology International*, doi:10.1155/2017/1567368.

Adelufosi A., B. Edet, D. Arikpo, E. Aquaisua, and M. M. Meremikwu. 2017. "Cognitive Behavioral Therapy for Post-Traumatic Stress Disorders in Women and Girls Living with Female Genital Mutilation: A Systematic Review." *International Journal of Gynecology & Obstetrics*, 136, doi.org/10.1002/ijgo.12043.

American Bar Association. 2017. "A Current Glance at Women in the Law." January. Retrieved 17 March 2017 (www.americanbar.org/women).

American Society of Plastic Surgeons. 2017. "2016 National Plastic Surgery Statistics." Retrieved 3 October 2017 (www.plasticsurgery.org/documents/News/Statistics/2016/plastic-surgery-statistics-full-report-2016.pdf).

Association of American Medical Colleges. 2016. *2016 State Physician Workforce Data Book*.

Bandura, A. 1977. *Social Learning Theory*. New York: General Learning Press.

Becker, J. B., K. J. Berkley, N. Geary, E. Hampson, J. P. Herman, and E. A. Young, eds. 2008. *Sex Differences in the Brain: From Genes to Behavior*. New York: Oxford University Press.

Bernard, J. 1987. *The Female World from a Global Perspective*. Bloomington, Indiana: Indiana University Press.

Bramble, M. S., A. Lipson, N. Vashist, and E. Vilain. 2017. "Effects of chromosomal sex and hormonal influences on shaping sex differences in brain and behavior: Lessons from cases of disorders of sex development." *Neuroscience Research*, 95, 65–74.

Bureau of Labor Statistics. 2017. "Highlights of Women's Earnings in 2016." BLS Report 1069. August. Retrieved 15 March 2017 (https://www.bls.gov/opub/reports/womens-earnings/2016/pdf/home.pdf).

Bureau of Labor Statistics. 2018. "Usual Weekly Earnings of Wage and Salary Workers: Fourth Quarter 2017." 17 January. USDL-18-0079.

Bureau of Labor Statistics. 2017. "Women's and Men's Earnings by Age in 2016." August 25. Retrieved 18 March 2018 (https://www.bls.gov/opub/ted/2017/womens-and-mens-earnings-by-age-in-2016.htm).

Bussey, K., and A. Bandura. 1999. "Social Cognitive Theory of Gender Development and Differentiation." *Psychological Review*, 106, 676–713.

Camera, L. 2017. "Trump Administration Rescinds Obama-Era Campus Sexual Assault Guidance." US News. 22 September. Retrieved 8 January 2018 (www.usnews.com/news/education-news/articles/2017-09-22/trump-administration-rescinds-obama-era-campus-sexual-assault-guidance).

Centers for Disease Control and Prevention. 2012. "Sexual Violence: Facts at a Glance." National Center for Injury Prevention and Control, Division of Violence Prevention.

Clinton, H. R. "Remarks to the U.N. 4th World Conference on Women Plenary Session." Retrieved 20 March 2018 (www.americanrhetoric.com/speeches/hillaryclintonbeijing-speech.htm).

Connell, R. W. 1995. *Masculinities.* Berkeley: University of California Press.

Cook, N. K., and T. L. Messman-Moore. 2018. "I Said No: The Impact of Voicing Non-Consent on Women's Perceptions of and Responses to Rape." *Violence Against Women,* 24, 507–527.

Coontz, S. 2000. *The Way We Never Were: American Families and the Nostalgia Trap.* New York: Basic Books.

Donde, S. D. 2017. "College Women's Attributions of Blame for Experiences of Sexual Assault." *Journal of Interpersonal Violence,* 32, 3520–3538.

Donde, S. D., S. K. A. Ragsdale, M. P. Koss, and A. N. Zucker. 2018. "If It Wasn't Rape, Was It Sexual Assault? Comparing Rape and Sexual Assault Acknowledgment in College Women Who Have Experienced Rape." *Violence Against Women,* doi.org/10.1177/1077801217743339.

Duggan, M. 2017. "Online Harassment 2017." Pew Research Center. 11 July.

Eliot, L. 2009. *Pink Brain, Blue Brain: How Small Differences Grow Into Troublesome Gaps—And What We Can Do About It.* New York: Houghton Mifflin.

Endendijk, J. J., M. G. Groenveld, S. R. van Berkel, E. T. Hallers-Haalboom, J. Mesman, and M. J. Baker-mans-Kranenburg. 2013. "Gender Stereotypes in the Family Context: Mothers, Fathers, and Siblings." *Sex Roles,* 68, 577–90.

Entertainment Software Association, 2018. "Essential facts about the computer and video game industry." Retrieved 27 August 2018 (http://www.theesa.com/about-esa/essential-facts-computer-video-game-industry/).

Equal Employment Opportunity Commission. 2017. "Sex-Based Discrimination." Retrieved 16 March 2018 (https://www.eeoc.gov/eeoc/statistics/enforcement/sex.cfm).

Etaugh, C. A., and J. S. Bridges. 2013. *Women's Lives: A Psychological Exploration,* 3rd ed. Boston: Pearson.

Feltman, C. E., and D. M. Szymanski. 2013. "Instagram Use and Self-Objectification: The Roles of Internalization, Comparison, Appearance Commentary, and Feminism." *Sex Roles,* 78, 5–6; 311–324.

Fine, C. 2010. *Delusions of Gender: The Real Science Behind Sex Differences.* London: Icon Books Ltd.

Fine, C. 2017. *Testosterone Rex: Myths of Sex, Science, and Society.* New York: W. W. Norton.

Flores, A. R., J. L. Herman, G. J. Gates, and T. N. T. Brown. 2016. "How Many Adults Identify as Transgender in the United States?" Williams Institute. June. Retrieved 3 October 2017 (williamsinstitute.law.ucla.edu/wp-content/uploads/How-Many-Adults-Identify-as-Trans-gender-in-the-United-States.pdf).

Forger, N. G., G. J. Rosen, E. M. Waters, D. Jacob, R. B. Simerly, and G. J. de Vries. 2004. "Deletion of Bax Eliminates Sex Differences in the Mouse Forebrain." *PNAS,* 101, 13666–71.

Geiger, A., and K. Parker. 2018. "For Women's History Month, A Look At Gender Gains—And Gaps—In The U.S." Pew Research Center. 15 March. Retrieved 21 March 2018 (www.pewresearch.org/fact-tank/2018/03/15/for-womens-his-tory-month-a-look-at-gender-gains-and-gaps-in-the-u-s/).

Gerding, A., and N. Signorielli. 2014. "Gender Roles in Tween Television Programming: A Content Analysis of Two Genres." *Sex Roles,* 70, 43–56.

Halpern, H. P., and M. Perry-Jenkins. 2016. "Parents' Gender Ideology and Gendered Behavior as Predictors of Children's Gender-Role Attitudes: A Longitudinal Exploration." *Sex Roles,* 74, 527–542.

International Monetary Fund. 2016. "Women's Empowerment: An Economic Game Changer." 14 November. Retrieved 17 March 2018 (www.imf.org/en/News/Articles/2016/11/14/SP111416-Womens-Empower-ment-An-Economic-Game-Changer).

Jirout, J. J., and N. S. Newcombe. 2015. "Building Blocks for Developing Spatial Skills: Evidence From a Large, Representative U.S. Sample." *Psychological Science,* 26, 302–310.

Kågesten, A., S. Gibbs, R. W. Blum, C. Moreau, V. Chandra-Mouli, A. Herbert, and A. Amin. 2016. "Understanding Factors that Shape Gender Attitudes in Early Adolescence Globally: A Mixed-Methods Systematic Review." *PLoS One,* 11, e0157805.

Kenney-Benson, G. A., E. M. Pomerantz, A. M. Ryan, and H. Patrick. 2006. "Sex Differences in Math Performance: The Role of Children's Approach to Schoolwork." *Developmental Psychology,* 42, 11–26.

Kimmel, M. S., and M. A. Messner. 2013. *Men's Lives,* 9th ed. Boston: Pearson.

Kimura, D. 2002. "Sex Differences in the Brain." *Scientific American.* 15 May. Retrieved 23 June 2006 (www.sciam.com/print_version.cfm?articleID=00018E9D-879D-1D06-8E49809EC5).

Koss, M. P., and S. L. Cook. 1993. "Facing the Facts: Date and Acquaintance Rape Are Significant Problems for Women." In *Current Controversies in Family Violence,* edited by R. J. Gelles and D. R. Loseke. Newbury Park, CA: Sage Publications.

Koss, M. P., C. Gidycz, and N. Wisniewski. 1987. "The Scope of Rape: Incidence and Prevalence in a National Sample of Higher Education Students." *Journal of Consulting and Clinical Psychology,* 55, 162–70.

Kristof, N., and S. WuDunn. 2010. *Half the Sky: Turning Oppression into Opportunity for Women Worldwide.* New York: Vintage Books.

Kristof, N., and S. WuDunn. 2014. *A Path Appears: Transforming Lives, Creating Opportunity.* New York: Alfred A. Knopf.

Lee, S., and Clark, N. 2014. "The Normalizing of Cosmetic Surgery in Women's Magazines from 1960–1989." *Journal of Magazine and New Media Research,* 15, 1–22.

Maccoby, E. E. 1998. *The Two Sexes: Growing Up Apart, Coming Together.* Cambridge, MA: Harvard University Press.

Marken, Stephanie. 2016. "Fewer in U.S. Say Men and Women Have Equal Job Opportunities." Gallup. 28 July. Retrieved 21 March 2018 (news.gallup.com/poll/194036/fewer-say-men-women-equal-job-opportunities.aspx).

Martin, J. A., B. E. Hamilton, M. J. K. Osterman, A. K. Driscoll, and T. J. Mathews. 2017. "Births: Final Data for 2015." National Vital Statistics Reports, Vol. 66, No. 1. 5 January. Centers for Disease Control and Prevention.

Mascaro, J. S., K. E. Rentscher, P. D. Hackett, M. R. Mehl, and J. K. Rilling. 2017. "Child Gender Influences Paternal Behavior, Language, and Brain Function." *Behavioral Neuroscience,* 131, 262–273.

McCarthy, M. M., A. P. Arnold, G. F. Ball, J. D. Blaustein, and G. J. De Vries. 2012. "Sex Differences in the Brain: The Not So Inconvenient Truth." *The Journal of Neuroscience,* 32, 2241–47.

..en, B. S., and T. A. Milner. 2017. "Understanding the Broad Influence of Sex Hormones and Sex Differences in the Brain." *Journal of Neuroscience Research, 95,* 24–39.

Miller, C. C. 2018. "Americans Might No Longer Prefer Sons Over Daughters." *New York Times.* 5 March.

Miller, C. C., and D. Willis. 2015. "Maiden Names, on the Rise Again." *New York Times.* 27 June.

Miller, D. I., and D. F. Halpern. 2014. "The New Science of Cognitive Sex Differences." *ScienceDirect,* 18, 37–45.

Mills, V. K. 1972. "The Status of Women in American Church-es." *Churches and Society*, 63, 50–55.

Mo, C. 2012. "What? Me Sexist?" 5 November. Gender News. The Clayman Institute for Gender Research. Retrieved 31 March 2015 (gender.stanford.edu/news/2011/what-me-sexist).

Mosley, M. 2014. "Is Your Brain Male or Female?" BBC News. 29 September. Retrieved 15 April 2015 (http://www.bbc.com/news/science-environment-29405467).

Mulvey, K. L., and M. Killen. 2014. "Challenging Gender Stereotypes: Resistance and Exclusion." *Child Development.* doi: 10.1111/cdev.12317.

Münzer, A. M., J. Fegert, H. G. Ganser, S. Loos, A. Witt, and L. Goldbeck. 2016. "Please Tell! Barriers to Disclosing Sexual Victimization and Subsequent Social Support Perceived by Children and Adolescents." *Journal of Interpersonal Violence,* 31, 355–377.

Murdock, G. 1949. Social Structure. New York: Macmillan.

Murdock, G. 1957. "World Ethnographic Sample" *American Anthropologist,* 59, 664–87.

National Center for Education Statistics. 2013. "Enrollment, Staff, and Degrees/Certificates Conferred in De-gree-Granting and Non-Degree-Granting Postsecondary Institutions, by Control and Level of Institution, Sex of Student, Type of Staff, and Level of Degree: Fall 2010, Fall 2011, and 2011–12." Digest of Education Statistics 2013, Table 301.10. Retrieved 26 November 2014 (nces.ed.gov/programs/digest/d13/tables/dt13_301.10.asp).

National Center for Health Statistics. 2017. *Health, United States, 2016: With Chartbook on Long-term Trends in Health.* Hyattsville, MD.

National Institute on Media and the Family. 2009. "Fact Sheet: Media's Effect on Girls: Body Image and Gender Identity." Retrieved 16 April 2010 (www.mediafamily.org/facts/facts_mediaeffect.shtml).

National Institute of Mental Health. 2013. "Statistics." Retrieved 23 June 2013 (www.nimh.nih.gov/statistics/index.shtml).

Near, C. E. 2013. "Selling Gender: Associations of Box Art Rep-resentation of Female Characters With Sales for Teen- and Mature-rated Video Games." *Sex Roles*, 68, 252–69.

Newport, F. 2011. "Americans Prefer Boys to Girls, Just as They Did in 1941." Gallup. 23 June. Retrieved 31 March 2015 (www.gallup.com/poll/148187/americans-pre-fer-boys-girls-1941.aspx).

Onion, A. 2005. "Scientists Find Sex Differences in Brain." *ABC News: Technology & Science,* 19 January. Re-trieved 23 June 2006 (abcnews.go.com/Technology/Health/story?id=424260&page=1).

Orenstein, P. 1994. *School Girls.* New York: Anchor Books.

Parker, K., J. M. Horowitz, and R. Stepler. 2017. "On Gender Differences, No Consensus on Nature vs. Nurture." Pew Research Center. 5 December. Retrieved 21 March 2018 (www.pewsocialtrends.org/2017/12/05/on-gender-differences-no-consensus-on-nature-vs-nurture).

Parker, K., and G. Livingston. 2017. "6 Facts About American Fathers." Pew Research Center. Retrieved 29 September 2017 (www.pewresearch.org/fact-tank/2017/06/15/fathers-day-facts/).

Panet, S. 2013. "Rising Up for Rights for Women and Girls: Abandoning Female Genital Mutilation and Cutting in the Fouta of Senegal." United Nations Population Fund. Retrieved 23 June 2013 (www.unfpa.org/public/home/publications/pid/13042).

Pew Research Center. 2016. "Religion in Everyday Life." 12 April.

Platt, L. F., and K. S. Bolland. 2017. "Relationship Partners of Transgender Individuals: A Qualitative Explanation." *Journal of Social and Personal Relationships* (https://doi.org/10.1177/0265407517709360). 22 May.

Population Reference Bureau. 2018. "2017 World Population Data Sheet." Retrieved 17 March 2018 (www.prb.org/Publications/Datasheets/2017/2017-world-population-data-sheet.aspx).

Rogers, L. O., and A. N. Meltzoff. 2017. "Is Gender More Im-portant and Meaningful Than Race? An Analysis of Racial and Gender Identity Among Black, White, and Mixed-Race Children." *Cultural Diversity and Ethnic Minority Psychology,* 23, 323–334.

Roudsari, B. S., M. M. Leahy, and S. T. Walters. 2009. "Cor-relates of Dating Violence Among Male and Female Heavy-Drinking College Students." *Journal of Interpersonal Violence*, 24, 1892–2905.

Safilios-Rothschild. 1974. *Women and Social Policy.* Englewood Cliffs, NJ. Prentice Hall.

Schilt, K., and D. Lagos. 2017. "The Development of Transgender Studies in Sociology." *Annual Review of Sociology,* 43, 425–443.

Schmitt, D. P. 2017. "The Truth About Sex Differences." *Psychology Today.* Retrieved 17 March 2018 (www.psychologytoday.com/articles/2017/11/the-truth-about-sex-differences).

Shafer, A., R. R. Ortiz, B. Thompson, and J. Huemmer. 2018. "The Role of Hypermasculinity, Token Resistance, Rape Myth, and Assertive Sexual Consent Communication Among College Men." *Journal of Adolescent Health,* 62, S44–S50.

Shipherd, J. C., K. E. Green, and S. Abramovitz. 2010. "Trans-gender Clients: Identifying and Minimizing Barriers to Mental Health Treatment." *Journal of Gay & Lesbian Mental Health*, 14, 94–108.

Sifferlin, A. 2015. "How American Women Fought to Keep Their Maiden Names After Marriage." *Time.* 17 December. Retrieved 17 March 2018 (time.com/4153417/how-american-women-fought-to-keep-their-maiden-names-after-marriage).

Sink, A. and Mastro, D. 2017. "Depictions of Gender on Prime-time Television: A Quantitative Content Analysis." *Mass Communication and Society*, 20, 3–23.

Sinozich, S., and L. Langton. 2014. "Rape and Sexual Assault Victimization Among College-Age Females, 1995–2013." NCJ 248471. December. Washington, DC: Bureau of Justice Statistics, U.S. Department of Justice.

Slocumb, P. D. 2015. *Boys in Crisis, Revised Edition 4th.* High-lands, TX: Aha! Process, Inc.

Smith, S. G., J. Chen, K. C. Basile, L. K. Gilbert, M. T. Merrick, N. Patel, M. Walling, and A. Jain. 2017. "The National Intimate Partner and Sexual Violence Survey (NISVS): 2010-2012 State Report."April. National Center for Injury Prevention and Control, Centers for Disease Control and Prevention Atlanta, Georgia.

Stansell, C. 2010. *The Feminist Promise: 1792–Present*. New York: Modern Library.

Starr, S. B. 2012. "Estimating Gender Disparities in Federal Criminal Cases." University of Michigan Law and Economics Research Paper, no. 12-018. Retrieved 31 March 2015 (papers.ssrn.com/sol3/papers.cfm?abstract_id=2144002##).

Stevens, J. 1999. *Reproducing the State*. Princeton, NJ: Princeton University Press.

Stoiko, R.R. and Strough, J. 2017. "'Choosing' the Patriarchal Norm: Emerging Adults' Marital Last Name Change Attitudes, Plans, and Rationales." *Gender Issues* 34(4). January.

Strum, L. 2016. "Study Tracks 31-Year History of Female Sexualization in Video Games." PBS NewsHour. 8 July. Retrieved 29 September 2017 (www.pbs.org/newshours/rundown/study-tracks-31-year-history-of-female-sexualization-in-video-games).

Sweet, E. 2014. "How Did Toys Get Stereotyped by Sex?" New York Times. 22 December.

Szymanski, D. M., & Henrichs-Beck, C. L. 2014. "Exploring sexual minority women's experiences of external and internalized heterosexism and sexism and their links to coping and distress." *Sex Roles*, 70, 28–42.

Taylor, C. 2015. "Transgender Surgery Can Cost More Than $100,000." *Money*, October 29. Retrieved 27 August 2018 (http://time.com/money/4092680/transgender-surgery-costs/).

UNICEF. 2016. "Female Genital Mutilation/Cutting: A Global Concern." Retrieved 15 March 2018 (https://www.unicef.org/media/files/FGMC_2016_brochure_final_UNICEF_SPREAD.pdf).

UNWomen. 2015. "Progress of the World's Women 2015–2016: Transforming Economies, Realizing Rights." Retrieved 27 August 2018 (http://progress.unwomen.org/en/2015/pdf/UNW_progressreport.pdf).

UNWomen. 2017. "Facts and Figures: Economic Empowerment." July. Retrieved 20 March 2018 (www.unwomen.org/en/what-we-do/economic-empowerment/facts-and-figures).

U.S. Department of Health and Human Services, Office of Women's Health. 2017. "Date Rape Drugs." 28 April. Womenshealth.gov. Retrieved 10 March 2018 (https://www.womenshealth.gov/a-z-topics/date-rape-drugs).

U.S. Department of Labor, Women's Bureau. 2017. "Women in the Labor Force: Data and Statistics." October. Retrieved 14 March 2018 (https://www.dol.gov/wb/stats/stats_data.htm).

Vaillancourt, T. 2013. "Do human females use indirect aggression as an intrasexual competition strategy?" *Philosophical Transactions of the Royal Society B*, 368, 1–7.

Ward, M., and M. Edelstein. 2014. *A World Full of Women*, 6th ed. Boston: Allyn & Bacon.

Winter, S., E. Settle, K. Wylie, S. Reisner, M. Cabral, G. Knudson, and S. Baral. 2016. "Synergies in Health and Human Rights: A Call to Action to Improve Transgender Health." *The Lancet*, 388, 318–321.

World Health Organization. 2011. "An Update on WHO's Work on Female Genital Mutilation (FGM): Progress Report."

World Health Organization. 2018. "Female Genital Mutilation." January. Retrieved 21 March 2018 (http://www.who.int/mediacentre/factsheets/fs241/en/).

Worldwatch Institute. 2016. "Family Planning and Environmental Sustainability: Assessing the Science."

Yount, K. M. 2002. "Like Mother, Like Daughter? Female Genital Cutting in Minia, Egypt." *Journal of Health and Social Behavior*, 43, 336–58.

Zweig, J., and M. Dank. 2013. "Teen Dating Abuse and Harassment in the Digital World: Implications for Prevention and Intervention." Urban Institute. February. Retrieved 26 January 2015 (www.urban.org/UploadedPDF/412750-teen-dating-abuse.pdf).

Chapter 9

Administration on Aging. 2017. "A Profile of Older Americans: 2017." Retrieved 23 March 2018 (www.aoa.acl.gov/Aging_Statistics/Profile/2016/docs/2016_Profile.pdf).

Albom, M. 1997. *Tuesdays with Morrie: An Old Man, A Young Man and Life's Greatest Lesson*. New York: Doubleday.

Alzheimer's Association. 2017a. "What Is Alzheimer's?" alz.org. Retrieved 28 December 2017 (ww.alz.org/alzheimers_disease_what_is_alzheimers.asp).

Alzheimer's Association. 2017b. "2017 Alzheimer's Disease Facts and Figures." Retrieved 28 December 2017 (www.alz.org/facts/overview.asp).

American Foundation for Suicide Prevention. 2018. "Suicide Statistics." Retrieved 26 March 2018 (www.afsp.org/about-suicide/suicide-statistics).

American Society of Plastic Surgeons. 2017. "2016 Plastic Surgery Statistics Report."

AVERT. 2018. "Growing Older and Aging with HIV." 2 July 2018. Retrieved 29 August 2018 (https://www.avert.org/living-with-hiv/health-wellbeing/growing-older-ageing).

Barrett, A. E., and E. L. Toothman. 2017. "Multiple 'Old Ages': The Influence of Social Context on Women's Aging Anxiety." *The Journals of Gerontology: Series B*, doi.org/10.1093/geronb/gbx027.

Bloom, E. 2017. "Here's how many Americans have nothing at all saved for retirement." CNBC. Retrieved 2 April 2018 (https: www.cnbc.com/2017/06/13/heres-how-many-americans-have-nothing-at-all-saved-for-retirement.html).

Brandon, E. 2016. "The 4 Most Important Sources of Retirement Income." 26 June 2016. Retrieved 10 June 2018 (https://money.usnews.com/money/retirement/articles/2016-06-06/the-4-most-important-sources-of-retirement-income).

Capogrosso, P., M. Colicchia, E. Ventimiglia, G. Castagna, M. C. Clementi, N. Suardi, F. Castiglione, A. Briganti, F. Cantiello, R. Damiano, F. Montorsi, and A. Salonia. 2013. "One patient out of four with newly diagnosed erectile dysfunction is a young man—worrisome picture from the everyday clinical practice." *Journal of Sex Medicine*, 10, 1833–41.

Centers for Disease Control and Prevention. 2018. "Fatal Injury Data."

Choi, S. K., and I. H. Meyer. 2016. "LGBT Aging: A Review of Research Findings, Needs, and Policy Implications." August. Los Angeles: The Williams Institute.

Clarke, L. H. 2017. "Women, Aging, and Beauty Culture: Navigating the Social Perils of Looking Old." *Generations*, 41, 104–108.

Cohn, D., and J. S. Passel. 2016. "A Record 60.6 Million Americans Live in Multigenerational Households." Pew Research Center. 11 August. Retrieved 23 March 2018 (http://www.pewresearch.org/fact-tank/2016/08/11/a-record-60-6-million-americans-live-in-multigenerational-households/).

___, J., and T. Neuman. 2017. "The Facts on Medicare Spending and Financing." Henry J. Kaiser Family Foundation. Retrieved 26 March 2018 (www.kff.org/medicare/issue-brief/the-facts-on-medicare-spending-and-financing/).

DeSilver, D. 2015. "5 Facts About Social Security." Pew Research Center. 18 August. Retrieved 26 March 2018 (www.pewresearch.org/fact-tank/2015/08/18/5-facts-about-social-security/).

Durkheim, É. 1897/1951. *Suicide, a Study in Sociology*. New York: Free Press.

Ellis, S. R., and T. G. Morrison. 2005. "Stereotypes of Ageing: Messages Promoted By Age-Specific Paper Birthday Cards Available in Canada."*International Journal of Aging and Human Development*, 61, 57–73.

Elwert, F., and N. A. Christakis. 2006. "Widowhood and Race."*American Sociological Review*, 71, 16–41.

Employee Benefit Research Institute. 2018. "2017 Retirement Confidence Survey-2017 Results." Retrieved 23 March 2018 (www.ebri.org/surveys/rcs/2017/).

File, T. 2017. "Voting in America: A Look at the 2016 Presidential Election." Census Blogs. 10 May.

Fisher, L. L. 2010. "Sex, Romance, and Relationships: AARP Survey of Midlife and Older Adults." Publication D19234. May. Washington, DC: AARP.

Forbes, M. K., N. R. Eaton, and R. F. Krueger. 2017. "Sexual Quality of Life and Aging: A Prospective Study of a Nationally Representative Sample." *The Journal of Sex Research*, 54, 137–148.

Fredriksen-Goldsen, K. 2018. "Shifting Social Context in the Lives of LGBTQ Older Adults." *Public Policy & Aging Report, 2018*, Vol. 28, No. 1, 24–28.

Fredriksen-Goldsen, K. I., A. E. B. Bryan, S. Jen, J. Goldsen, H.-J. Kim, and A. Muraco. 2017. "The Unfolding of LGBT Lives: Key Events Associated With Health and Well-Being in Later Life."*The Gerontologist*, 57, S15–S29.

Friedan, B. 1993.*The Fountain of Age*. New York: Simon & Schuster.

Genworth Financial, Inc. 2017. "Cost of Care."

Gilhooly, K.J., M.L.M. Gilhooly, M.P. Sullivan, A. McIntyre, L. Wilson, E. Harding, R. Woodbridge, and S. Crutch. 2016. "A Meta-Review of Stress, Coping and Interventions in Dementia and Dementia Caregiving."*BMC Geriatrics*, 16, 106 (doi.org/10.1186/s12877-016-0280-8).

Gillespie, B. J. 2017. "Correlates of Sex Frequency and Sexual Satisfaction Among Partnered Older Adults."*Journal of Sex & Marital Therapy*, 43, 403–423.

Hardy, M. A., and K. Shuey. 2000. "Retirement." In *Encyclopedia of Sociology*, 2nd ed., edited by E. F. Borgatta and R. J. Montgomery, pp. 2401–10. New York: Macmillan.

He, W., D. Goodkind, and P. Kowal. 2016. "An Aging World: 2015: International Population Reports." P95/16-1. March. Washington, DC: U.S. Census Bureau.

The Heritage Foundation. 2013. "The Number of Workers Per Medicare Beneficiary Is Falling." Retrieved 30 March 2015 (http://www.heritage.org/multimedia/infographic/2012/05/medicare-at-risk/the-number-of-workers-per-medicare-beneficiary-is-falling).

Hillman, J. 2008. "Sexual issues and aging within the context of work with older adult patients." *Professional Psychology: Research and Practice*, 39, 290–297.

Holmes, T. H., and R. H. Rahe. 1967. "The Social Readjustment Rating Scale." *Journal of Psychosomatic Research*, 11, 213–18.

Hooyman, N., K. Kawamoto, and H. A. Kiyak. 2015. *Aging Matters: An Introduction to Social Gerontology*. Boston: Pearson.

Hooyman, N., and H. A. Kiyak. 2011. *Social Gerontology: A Multidisciplinary Perspective*, 9th ed. Boston: Pearson.

Hospice Foundation of America. 2014. "What Is Hospice?" Retrieved 27 October 2014 (hospicefoundation.org/End-of-Life-Support-and-Resources/Coping-with-Terminal-Illness/Hospice-Services).

Human Rights Campaign. 2018. "Explore Health and Aging." Retrieved 29 August 2018 (https://www.hrc.org/explore/topic/health-and-aging).

Karraker, A., and J. DeLamater. 2013. "Past-Year Sexual Inactivity Among Older Married Persons and Their Partners." *Journal of Marriage and Family*, 75, 142–163.

Kim, M. H., R. E. Dunkle, A. J. Lehning, H.-W. Shen, S. Feld, and A. K. Perone. 2017. "Caregiver Stressors and Depressive Symptoms Among Older Husbands and Wives in the United States." *Journal of Women & Aging*, 29, 494–504.

Klein, E. 2013. "Feds Spend $7 on Elderly for Every $1 on Kids." 15 February. Washingtonpost.com. Retrieved 27 October 2014 (www.washingtonpost.com/blogs/wonkblog/wp/2013/02/15/feds-spend-7-on-elderly-for-every-1-on-kids/).

Kochanek, K. D., S. L. Murphy, J. Xu, and E. Arias. 2017. "Mortality in the United States, 2016." NCHS Data Brief No. 293. December. Centers for Disease Control and Prevention.

Kübler-Ross, E. 1969. *On Death and Dying*. New York: Macmillan.

Levy, B. R. 2017. "Age-Stereotype Paradox: Opportunity for Social Change."*The Gerontologist*, 57, S118–S126.

Lin, X., C. L. Mattson, M. Freedman, and J. Skarbinski. 2017. "Erectile dysfunction medication prescription and condomless intercourse in HIV-infected men who have sex with men in the United States." *AIDS and Behavior*, 21, 1129–1137.

McArdle, F., T. Neuman, and J. Huang. 2014. "Overview of Health Benefits for Pre-65 and Medicare-Eligible Retirees." 14 April. Retrieved 26 October 2014 (kff.org/report-section/retiree-health-benefits-at-the-crossroads-overview-of-health-benefits-for-pre-65-and-medicare-eligible-retirees/).

MedPAC. 2014. "A Data Book: Health Care Spending and the Medicare Program." June. Retrieved 3 March 2015 (www.medpac.gov/documents/publications/jun14databookentirereport.pdf?sfvrsn=1).

Morgan, L., and S. Kunkel. 1998. *Aging: The Social Context*. Thousand Oaks, CA: Pine Forge Press.

National Center for Health Statistics. 2017. "Health, United States, 2017: With Chartbook on Long-term Trends in Health." Hyattsville, MD.

National Hospice and Palliative Care Organization. 2014. "NHPCO's Hospice Facts and Figures: Hospice Care in America: 2014 Edition." Retrieved 3 March 2014 (www.nhpco.org/sites/default/files/public/Statistics_Research/2014_Facts_Figures.pdf).

Paniagua, F.A. 1999. "Commentary on the possibility that Viagra may contribute to transmission of HIV and other sexual diseases among older adults." *Psychological Reports*, 85, 942–944.

Pew Charitable Trusts. 2016. "Extended Family Support and Household Balance Sheets." 2 March. Retrieved 23 March 2018 (www.pewtrusts.org/en/research-and-analysis/issue-briefs/2016/03/extended-family-support-and-household-balance-sheets).

Population Reference Bureau. 2018. "International Data." Retrieved 29 August 2018 (https://www.prb.org/international/indicator/age65-50/snapshot/).

Quadagno, J. S. 2002. *Aging and the Life Course*, 2nd ed. New York: McGraw-Hill.

Riffkin, R. 2014. "Average U.S. Retirement Age Rises to 62." Gallup. 28 April. Retrieved 23 October 2014 (www.gallup.com/poll/168707/average-retirement-age-rises.aspx).

Riley, M. W., and J. W. Riley, Jr. 2000. "Age Integration: Conceptual and Historical Background." *The Gerontologist*, 40, 266–69.

Sage: Advocacy & Services for LGBT Elders. 2017. "Discrimination." Retrieved 26 December 2017 (www.sageusa.org/issues/general.cfm).

Semega, J. L., K. R. Fontenot, and M. A. Kollar. 2017. "Income and Poverty in the United States: 2016." U.S. Census Bureau, Current Population Reports. P60–259. Washington, DC: U.S. Census Bureau.

Social Security Administration. 2017. "Research, Statistics, & Policy Analysis: OASDI and SSI Program Rates & Limits, 2018." November. Retrieved 26 December 2017 (www.ssa.gov/policy/docs/quickfacts/prog_highlights/index.hrml).

Social Security Online. 2018. "Retirement & Survivors Benefits: Life Expectancy Calculator." Retrieved 22 March 2018 (www.ssa.gov/cgi-bin/longevity.cgi).

Tinker, B. 2017. "US Life Expectancy Drops for Second Year in a Row." CNN.com. 21 December. Retrieved 22 March 2018 (www.cnn.com/2017/12/21/health/us-life-expectancy-study/index.html).

Transamerica Center for Retirement Studies. 2015. "The Current State of Retirement: Pre-Retiree Expectations and Retiree Benefits." TCRS 1300-1215. December.

Tucker, J. V., V. P. Reno, and T. N. Bethell. 2014. "Strengthening Social Security: What Do Americans Want?" National Academy of Social Insurance. Retrieved 27 October 2014 (www.nasi.org/sites/default/files/research/What_Do_Americans_Want.pdf).

United Nations, Department of Economic and Social Affairs, Population Division. 2017. "World Population Ageing 2017 – Highlights (ST/ESA/SER.A/397)."

U.S. Census Bureau. "America's Families and Living Arrangements: 2017." 6 April. Retrieved 12 February 2018 (www.census.gov/data/tables/2016/demo/families/cps-2016.html).

U.S. Equal Employment Opportunity Commission. 2018. "Age Discrimination in Employment Act ((Charges filed with EEOC) (includes concurrent charges with Title VII, ADA, EPA, and GINA) FY 1997-FY 2017). Retrieved 26 March 2018 (www.eeoc.gov/eeoc/statistics/enforcement/adea.cfm).

Utz, R. L., M. Caserta, and D. Lund. 2012. "Grief, Depressive Symptoms, and Physical Health Among Recently Bereaved Spouses."*The Gerontologist*, 52, 460–71.

Waid, M. 2014. "Social Security Is a Critical Income Source for Older Americans: State-Level Estimates, 2010–2012." Fact Sheet 300. January. Washington, DC: AARP Public Policy Institute.

Whitbourne, S. K. 2005. *Adult Development and Aging: Biopsychosocial Perspectives*, 2nd ed. Hoboken, NJ: Wiley.

Wright, M. R., and S. L. Brown. 2017. "Psychological Well-being Among Older Adults: The Role of Partnership Status." *Journal of Marriage and Family*, 79, 833–849.

Chapter 10

Adams, J. and R. Light. 2015. "Scientific Consensus, the Law, and Same-Sex Parenting Outcomes." *Social Science Research*, 53, 300–310.

Allen, B., A. Tellez, A. Wevodau, C. L. Woods, and A. Percosky. 2014. "The Impact of Sexual Abuse Committed by a Child on Mental Health in Adulthood." *Journal of Interpersonal Violence*, 29, 2257–2272.

Amato, P. R. 2007. "Divorce and the Well-being of Adults & Children." *National Council on Family Relations Report*, 52, F3–F4, F18.

Amato, P. 2014. "What Is a Family?" National Council on Family Relations Report. Volume 59.2. Summer.

Amato, P. R., and A. Booth. 1997. *A Generation at Risk: Growing up in an Era of Family Upheaval.* Cambridge, MA: Harvard University Press.

Amato, P. R., V. King, and M. L. Thorsen. 2016. "Parent-Child Relationships in Stepfather Families and Adolescent Adjustment: A Latent Class Analysis." *Journal of Marriage and Family*, 78, 482–497.

Anderson, L. R. 2016. "Divorce Rate in the U.S.: Geographic Variation, 2015." National Center for Family and Marriage Research. Bowling Green State University.

Arkes, J. 2015. "The Temporal Effects of Divorces and Separations on Children's Academic Achievement and Problem Behavior." *Journal of Divorce & Remarriage*, 56, 25–42.

Bachman, J. G., L. D. Johnston, and P. M. O'Malley. 2014. *Monitoring the Future: Questionnaire Responses from the Nation's High School Seniors, 2012.* Ann Arbor, MI: Institute for Social Research.

Baker, A. J. L., and M. R. Brassard. 2013. "Adolescents Caught in Parental Loyalty Conflicts." *Journal of Divorce & Remarriage*, 54, 393–413.

Bandura, A. 1977. *Social Learning Theory.* New York: General Learning Press.

Bannon, S. M., N. Barle, M. S. Mennella, and K. D. O'Leary. 2018. "Parental Conflict and College Student Functioning: Impact of Child Involvement in Conflict." *Journal of Divorce & Remarriage*, 59, 157–174.

Baugh, E. J., A. C. Taylor, and J. S. Bates. 2016. "Grandparents Raising Grandchildren." *The Wiley Blackwell Encyclopedia of Family Studies*, 1–9.

Berardo, F. M. 1998. "Family Privacy: Issues and Concepts." *Journal of Family Issues*, 19, 4–19.

Bi, S., E. A. Haak, L. R. Gilbert, and P. S. Keller. 2017. "Children Exposed to Marital Conflict Exhibit More Disordered Eating Behaviors: Child Emotional Insecurity and Anxiety as Mechanisms of Risk." *Journal of Child and Family Studies*, 26, 3112–3122.

Biblarz, T. J., and J. Stacey. 2010. "How Does the Gender of Parents Matter?" *Journal of Marriage and Family*, 72, 3–22.

Bos, H. M., J. R. Knox, L. van Rijn-van Gelderen, and N. K. Gartrell. 2016. "Same-Sex and Different-Sex Parent Households and Child Health Outcomes: Findings from the National Survey of Children's Health." *Journal of Developmental & Behavioral Pediatrics*, 37, 179–187.

Boyd, E. M., M. T. Sliter, and S. Chatfield. 2016. "Double Trouble: Work–Family Conflict and Well-Being for Second Job Holders." *Community, Work & Family*, 19, 462–480.

...M. J., S. G. Smith, K. C. Basile, M. L. Walters, J. Chen, ...d M. T. Merrick. 2014. "Prevalence and Characteristics of Sexual Violence, Stalking, and Intimate Partner Violence Victimization—National Intimate Partner and Sexual Violence Survey, United States, 2011." *Morbidity & Mortality Weekly Report.* 5 September. 63(SS08):1–18. Retrieved 27 February 2015 (www.cdc.gov/mmwr/preview/mmwrhtml/ss6308a1.htm?s_cid=ss6308a1_e).

Brown, S. L., and M. R. Wright. 2016. "Older Adult Attitudes toward Cohabitation: Two Decades of Change." *Journals of Gerontology: Social Sciences,* 71, 755–764.

Bureau of Labor Statistics. March 2017. National Compensation Survey. Retrieved 9 February 2018 (www.bls.gov/ncs/ebs/benefits/2017/ownership/.../table32a.pdf).

Bureau of Labor Statistics. 2018. "American Time Use Survey Summary." Retrieved 28 June 2018 (https://www.bls.gov/news.release/atus.nr0.htm).

Busby, D. M., T. B. Holman, and E. Walker. 2008. "Pathways to Relationship Aggression between Adult Partners." *Family Relations,* 57, 72–83.

Centers for Disease Control and Prevention. 2017. "About Teen Pregnancy." 9 May. Retrieved 11 February 2018 (www.cdc.gov/teenpregnancy/about/index.htm).

Chong, A., and K. D. Mickelson. 2016. "Perceived Fairness and Relationship Satisfaction During the Transition to Parenthood: The Mediating Role of Spousal Support." *Journal of Family Issues,* 37, 3–28.

Coleman, M., L. Ganong, L. Russell, and N. Frye-Cox. 2015. "Stepchildren's Views About Former Step-Relationships Following Stepfamily Dissolution." *Journal of Marriage and Family,* 77, 775–790.

Coltrane, S. 2000. "Research on Household Labor: Modeling and Measuring the Social Embeddedness of Routine Family Work." *Journal of Marriage and Family,* 62, 1208–33.

Coontz, S. 2007. "The Family Revolution." Greater Good: The Science of a Meaningful Life. 1 September. Retrieved 27 February 2015 (greatergood.berkeley.edu/article/item/the_family_revolution).

Copen, C. E., K. Daniels, J. Vespa, and W. D. Mosher. 2012. "First Marriages in the United States: Data from the 2006–2010 National Survey of Family Growth." *National Health Statistics,* 49. Retrieved 22 March 2018 (https://www.cdc.gov/nchs/data/nhsr/nhsr049.pdf).

Cott, N. F. 2002. *Public Vows: A History of Marriage and the Nation.* Cambridge, MA: Harvard University Press.

Creary, S. J., and J. R. Gordon. 2016. "Role Conflict, Role Overload, and Role Strain." *The Wiley Blackwell Encyclopedia of Family Studies,* 1–6.

Crittenden, C. A., and E. M. Wright. 2013. "Predicting Patriarchy: Using Individual and Contextual Factors to Examine Patriarchal Endorsement in Communities." *Journal of Interpersonal Violence,* 28, 1267–88.

DeGreeff, B. L., and A. Burnett. 2017. "Are You My Grandmother?: Constructing and Maintaining Stepgrandparent Identity and Roles." *Communication Quarterly,* 65, 603–623.

DeSilver, D. 2013. "Supreme Court's DOMA Ruling Comes as Majority Now Supports Same-Sex Marriage." 26 June. Pew Research Center. Retrieved 27 February 2015 (www.pewresearch.org/fact-tank/2013/06/26/supreme-courts-doma-ruling-comes-as-majority-now-supports-same-sex-marriage/).

Dey, I., and F. Wasoff. 2013. *Family Policy.* New York: Routledge.

Dhaher, E. A., R. T. Mikolaczyk, A. E. Maxwell, and A. Kramer. 2010. "Attitudes Toward Wife Beating among Palestinian Women of Reproductive Age from Three Cities in West Bank. " *Journal of Interpersonal Violence,* 25, 518–37.

Du, D., D. Derks, and A. B. Bakker. 2017. "Daily Spillover From Family to Work: A Test of the Work-Home Resources Model." *Journal of Occupational Health Psychology,* doi:10/1037/ocp0000073.

Ee, M. J. Y. C., W. M. Y. Teoh, and Y. Y. Yen. 2017. "Role Conflict, Role Ambiguity and Role Overload: The Strains of Work-Family Conflict." *The Social Sciences,* 12, 1566–1576.

Ellis, R. R., and T. Simmons. 2014. "Coresident Grandparents and Their Grandchildren: 2012." *Population Characteristics.* P20-576. October. U.S. Census Bureau. Retrieved 27 February 2015 (www.census.gov/content/dam/Census/library/publications/2014/demo/p20-576.pdf).

Engels, F. 1902, original 1884. *The Origin of the Family.* Chicago: Charles H. Kerr & Co.

Farr, R. H. 2017. "Does Parental Sexual Orientation Matter? A Longitudinal Follow-Up of Adoptive Families With School-Age Children." *Developmental Psychology,* 53, 252–264.

Forehand, R., J. Parent, A. Golub, and M. Reid. 2016. "Positive Parenting of Young Adolescents by Male Cohabiting Partners: The Roles of Coparenting Conflict and Support." *The Journal of Early Adolescence,* 36, 420–441.

Gager, C. T., S. T. Yabiku, and M. R. Linver. 2016. "Conflict or Divorce? Does Parental Conflict and/or Divorce Increase the Likelihood of Adult Children's Cohabiting and Marital Dissolution?" *Marriage & Family Review,* 52, 243–261.

Gershoff, E. T. and A. Grogan-Taylor, A. 2016. "Spanking and Child Outcomes: Old Controversies and New Meta-Analyses." *Journal of Family Psychology,* 30, 453–469.

Gibson-Davis, C., and H. Rackin. 2014. "Marriage or Carriage? Trends in Union Context and Birth Type by Education." *Journal of Marriage and Family,* 76, 506–19.

Giele, J. Z. 1996. "Decline of the Family: Conservative, Liberal, and Feminist Views." In *Promises to Keep: Decline and Renewal of Marriage in America,* D. Popenoe, J. B. Elshtain, and D. Blankenhorn, eds. Lanham, MD: Rowman & Littlefield.

Goodwin, P. Y., W. D. Mosher, and A. Chandra. 2010. "Marriage and Cohabitation in the United States: A Statistical Portrait Based on Cycle 6 (2002) of the National Survey of Family Growth." *Vital Health Stat* 23 (28). Washington, DC: National Center for Health Statistics.

Gordon, A. E., and K. D. Mickelson. 2018. "Couple-Level Predictors of Perceived Fairness During Pregnancy in First-Time Parents." *Journal of Family Issues,* 39, 55–77.

Grall, T. 2016. "Custodial Mothers and Fathers and Child Support: 2013." Current Population Report. P60–255. U.S. Census Bureau. Retrieved 15 May 2018 (www.census.gov/content/dam/Census/library/publications/2016/demo/P60-255.pdf).

Guinart, M., and M. Grau. 2014. "Qualitative Analysis of the Short-Term and Long-Term Impact of Family Breakdown on Children: Case Study." *Journal of Divorce & Remarriage,* 55, 408–22.

Hamplová, D., C. LeBourdais, and É. Lapierre-Adamcyk. 2014. "Is the Cohabitation-Marriage Gap in Money Pooling Universal?" *Journal of Marriage and Family,* 76, 983–97.

Hayslip, B., C. A. Fruhauf, and M. L. Dolbin-MacNab. 2017. "Grandparents Raising Grandchildren: What Have We Learned Over the Past Decade?" *Gerontologist,* doi: 10.1093/geront/gnx106.

Henderson, A. K. 2016. "Jesus Didn't Teach Us to Juggle: Religious Involvement, Work-Family Conflict, and Life Satisfaction Among African Americans." *Journal of Family Issues,* 37, 1558–1584.

Hewitt, B., M. Western, and J. Baxter. 2006. "Who Decides? The Social Characteristics of Who Initiates Marital Separation." *Journal of Marriage and Family,* 68, 1165–77.

Human Rights Campaign. 2018. "Marriage Center." Retrieved 2 February 2018 (www.hrc.org/campaigns/marriage-center).

Kamp Dush, C. M. 2013. "Marital and Cohabitation Dissolution and Parental Depressive Symptoms in Fragile Families." *Journal of Marriage and Family,* 75, 91–109.

Kaufmann, G. 2012. "This Week in Poverty: U.S. Single Mothers—'The Worst Off.'" *The Nation.* 21 December. Retrieved 6 July 2013 (www.thenation.com/blog/171886/week-poverty-us-single-mothers-worst#ixzz2YK8GuGqn).

Kuperberg, A. 2014. "Age at Coresidence, Premarital Cohabitation, and Marriage Dissolution: 1985–2009." *Journal of Marriage and Family,* 76, 352–69.

Laplant, K. M. 2016. "Family Decline Theory." *The Wiley Blackwell Encyclopedia of Family Studies.* 1–5.

Livingston, G., and A. Caumont. 2017. "5 Facts on Love and Marriage in America." Pew Research Center. 13 February. Retrieved 2 February 2018 (www.pewresearch.org/fact-tank/2017/02/13/5-facts-about-love-and-marriage).

Maldonado, L. C. and R. Nieuwenhuis. 2015. "Family Policies and Single Parent Poverty in 18 OECD Countries, 1978–2008." *Community, Work & Family,* 18, 395–415.

Manning, W. D., and S. Brown. 2006. "Children's Economic Well-Being in Married and Cohabiting Parent Families." *Journal of Marriage and Family,* 68, 345–62.

Manning, W., M. N. Fettro, and E. Lamidi. 2014. "Child Well-Being in Same-Sex Parent Families: Review of Research Prepared for American Sociological Association Amicus Brief." *Population Research and Policy Review,* 33, 485–502.

Martin, J. A., B. E. Hamilton, J. J. K. Osterman, S. C. Curtin, and T. J. Matthews. 2015. "Births: Final Data for 2013." *National Vital Statistics Report.* Vol. 64, No. 1. Retrieved 19 July 2015 (www.cdc.gov/nchs/data/nvsr/nvsr64/nvsr64_01.pdf).

Martin, J. A., B. E. Hamilton, M. J. Osterman, A. K. Driscoll, and T. J. Mathews. 2017. "Births: Final Data for 2015." *National Vital Statistics Report.* January. Vol. 67, No. 1. Retrieved 7 February 2018 (www.ncbi.nlm.nih.gov/pubmed/28135188).

Moed, A., T. Dix, E. R. Anderson, and S. M. Greene. 2017. "Expressing Negative Emotions to Children: Mothers' Aversion Sensitivity and Children's Adjustment." *Journal of Family Psychology,* 31, 224-233.

Murray, C. 1984. *Losing Ground: American Social Policy, 1950–1980.* New York: Basic Books.

National Campaign to Prevent Teen and Unplanned Pregnancy. 2018. "Why It Matters." Retrieved 7 February 2018 (powertodecide.org/what-we-do/information/why-it-matters).

Niolon, P. H., M. Kearns, J. Dills, K. Rambo, S. Irving, T. L. Armstead, and L. Gilbert. 2017. *Preventing Intimate Partner Violence Across the Lifespan.* Centers for Disease Control and Prevention. Retrieved 5 September, 2018 (https://www.cdc.gov/violenceprevention/pdf/ipv-technicalpackages.pdf).

Nock, S. L. 1998. *Marriage in Men's Lives.* New York: Oxford University Press.

Nomaguchi, K. M., and M. A. Milkie. 2015. "Gender, Accuracy About Partners' Work-Family Conflict, and Relationship Quality." pp. 159–176 In: *Gender and Work-Family Experience: An Intersection of Two Domains.* Maura J. Mills, ed. New York: Springer.

O'Neal, E.N., and L. O. Beckman. 2017. "Intersections of Race, Ethnicity, and Gender: Reframing Knowledge Surrounding Barriers to Social Services Among Latina Intimate Partner Violence Victims." *Violence Against Women,* 23, 643–665.

Parker, K. and G. Livingston. 2018. "7 facts about American dads." Retrieved 13 June 2018 (http://www.pewresearch.org/fact-tank/2018/06/13/fathers-day-facts/).

Perelli-Harris, B., A. Berrington, N. S. Gassen, P. Galezewska, and J. A. Holland. 2017. "The Rise in Divorce and Cohabitation: Is There A Link?" *Population and Development Review,* 43, 303–329.

Pew Research Center. 2013. "A Survey of LGBT Americans: Attitudes, Experiences and Values in Changing Times." 13 June. Retrieved 27 February 2015 (www.pewsocialtrends.org/files/2013/06/SDT_LGBT-Americans_06-2013.pdf).

Pew Research Center. 2015. "Raising Kids and Running a Household: How Working Parents Share the Load." Social & Demographic Trends. 4 November. Retrieved 3 August 2016 (www.pewsocialtrends.org/2015/11/04/raising-kids-and-running-a-household-how-working-parents-share-the-load/).

Pew Research Center. 2017. "Support for Same-Sex Marriage Grows, Even Among Groups That Had Been Skeptical." 26 June. Retrieved 11 February 2018 (www.people-press.org/2017/06/26/support-for-same-sex-marriage-grows-even-among-groups-that-had-been-skeptical/).

Popenoe, D. 2008. "Cohabitation, Marriage and Child Well-Being: A Cross-National Perspective." National Marriage Project. Piscataway, NJ: Rutgers, The State University of New Jersey.

Potter, D., and E. C. Potter. 2017. "Psychosocial Well-Being in Children of Same-Sex Parents: A Longitudinal Analysis of Familial Transitions." *Journal of Family Issues,* 38, 2303–2328.

Pyke, K. 2000a. "Ideology of 'Family' Shapes Perception of Immigrant Children." Minneapolis, MN: National Council on Family Relations.

Pyke, K. 2000b. "'The Normal American Family' as an Interpretive Structure of Family Life among Grown Children of Korean and Vietnamese Immigrants." *Journal of Marriage and Family,* 62, 240–45.

Rani, M., and S. Banu. 2009. "Attitudes toward Wife Beating." *Journal of Interpersonal Violence,* 24, 1371–97.

Rothwell, D. W., and A. McEwen. 2017. "Comparing Child Poverty Risk by Family Structure During the 2008 Recession." *Journal of Marriage and Family,* 79, 1224–1240.

Sayer, L. 2016. "Trends in Women's and Men's Time Use, 1965-2012: Back to the Future?" In: *Gender and Couple Relationships.* McHale, S., V. King, J. Van Hook, and A. Booth, eds. National Symposium on Family Issues, vol. 6, New York: Springer.

Semega, J. L, K. R. Fontenot, and M. A. Kollar. 2017. "Income and Poverty in the United States: 2016." Current Population Reports. P60–259. Washington, DC: U.S. Census Bureau.

Smeeding, T., and C. Thévenot. 2016. "Addressing Child Poverty: How Does the United States Compare With Other Nations?" *Academic Pediatrics,* 16, S67–S75.

..., J. Chen, K. C. Basile, L. K. Gilbert, M. T. Merrick, . Patel, M. Walling, and A. Jain. 2017. "The National Intimate Partner and Sexual Violence Survey (NISVS): 2010-2012 State Report." April. National Center for Injury Prevention and Control. Atlanta, GA: Centers for Disease Control and Prevention.

Somers, J. A., M. H. Ibrahim, and L. J. Luecken. 2017. "Biological Sensitivity to the Effects of Childhood Family Adversity on Psychological Well-Being in Young Adulthood." *Child Maltreatment*, 22, 236–244.

Soria, K. M., and S. Linder. 2014. "Parental Divorce and First-Year College Students' Persistence and Academic Achievement." *Journal of Divorce & Remarriage*, 55, 103–16.

Soria, K. M., D. J. Morrow, and R. Jackson. 2018. "Parental Divorce and College Students' Persistence and Degree Attainment." *Journal of Divorce & Remarriage*, 59, 25–36.

Straus, M. A. 1980. "Social Stress and Marital Violence in a National Sample of American Families." *Annals of the New York Academy of Sciences*, 347, 229–50.

Straus, M. A., R. J. Gelles, and S. K. Steinmetz. 1980. *Behind Closed Doors: Violence in the American Family*. New York: Anchor Books.

Stepler, R. 2017. "Number of U.S. Adults Cohabiting With a Partner Continues to Rise, Especially Among Those 50 and Older." Pew Research Center. Retrieved 15 May 2018 (www.pewresearch.org/fact-tank/2017/04/06/number-of-u-s-adults-cohabiting-with-a-partner-continues-to-rise-especially-among-those-50-and-older/).

Symoens, S., K. Bastaits, D. Mortelmans, and P. Bracke. 2013. "Breaking Up, Breaking Hearts? Characteristics of the Divorce Process and Well-Being after Divorce." *Journal of Divorce & Remarriage*, 54, 177–96.

Thébaud, S., and D. S. Pedulla. 2016. "Masculinity and the Stalled Revolution: How Gender Ideologies and Norms Shape Young Men's Responses to Work-Family Policies." *Gender & Society*, 30, 590–617.

United Nations Statistics Division. 2013. "UN Data: Maternity Benefits." Retrieved 5 March 2015 (data.un.org/DocumentData.aspx?id=344).

U. S. Census Bureau. 2018. "America's Families and Living Arrangements: 2017." Retrieved 4 May 2018 (https://www.census.gov/data/tables/2017/demo/families/cps-2017.html).

U. S. Department of Health & Human Services, Administration for Children and Families, Administration on Children, Youth and Families, Children's Bureau. 2018. "Child Maltreatment 2016." Retrieved 6 September 2018 (https://www.acf.hhs.gov/cb/research-data-technology/statistics-research/child-maltreatment).

Vespa, J., J. M. Lewis, and R. M. Kreider. 2013. "America's Families and Living Arrangements: 2012." Population Characteristics. P20-570. August. U.S. Census Bureau. Retrieved 27 February 2015 (www.census.gov/prod/2013pubs/p20-570.pdf).

Walsh, W. A., J. Dawson, and M. J. Mattingly. 2010. "How Are We Measuring Resilience Following Childhood Maltreatment? Is the Research Adequate and Consistent? What Is the Impact on Research, Practice, and Policy?" *Trauma, Violence, & Abuse*, 11, 27–41.

Wayne, J. H., M. M. Butts, W. J. Casper, and T. D. Allen. 2017. "In Search of Balance: A Conceptual and Empirical Integration of Multiple Meanings of Work-Family Balance." *Personnel Psychology*, 70, 167–210.

Wilcox, W. B. 2017. "Marriage Matters." American Enterprise Institute. 26 July. Retrieved 2 February 2018 (www.aei.org/publications/marriage-matters-2/).

Wilson, W. J. 1996. *When Work Disappears: The World of the New Urban Poor*. New York: Alfred A. Knopf.

Yavorsky, J., C. M. Kamp Dush, and S. J. Schoppe-Sullivan. 2015. "Production of inequality: Gender division of labor across the transition to parenthood." *Journal of Marriage and Family*, 77, 662–679.

Chapter 11

Alim, S. and G. Smitherman. 2012. *Articulate While Black*. New York: Oxford University Press.

Ballantine, J. H., F. M. Hammack, and J. Stuber. 2017. *The Sociology of Education: A Systematic Analysis*, 8th ed. New York: Routledge.

Benner, A. D., A. E. Boyle, and S. Sadler. 2016. "Parental Involvement and Adolescents' Educational Success: The Roles of Prior Achievement and Socioeconomic Status." *Journal of Youth and Adolescence*, 45, 1053–1064.

Berkowitz, R., H. Moore, R. A. Astor, and R. Benbenishty. 2017. "A Research Synthesis of the Associations Between Socioeconomic Background, Inequality, School Climate, and Academic Achievement." *Review of Educational Research*, 87, 425–469.

Bialystok, E. 2016. "Bilingual Education for Young Children: Review of the Effects and Consequences." *International Journal of Bilingual Education and Bilingualism*. doi.org/10.1080/13670050.2016/1203859.

Bivens, J., E. García, E. Gould, E. Weiss, and V. Wilson. 2016. "It's Time for an Ambitious National Investment in America's Children." Economic Policy Institute. 6 April.

Blackburn, H. 2017. "The Status of Women in STEM in Higher Education: A Review of the Literature 2007–2017." *Science & Technology Libraries*, 36, 235–273.

Bluestone, P., D. Sjoquist, and N. Warner. 2016. "Review of Charter Schools' Effects on Student Achievement and Life Outcomes." The Center for State and Local Finance, Georgia State University. 29 September.

Booher-Jennings, J. 2008. "Learning to Label: Socialisation, Gender, and the Hidden Curriculum of High-States Testing." *British Journal of Sociology of Education*, 29, 149–60.

Bourdieu, P. 1986. "The Forms of Capital." In *Handbook of Theory and Research for the Sociology of Education*, J. Richardson, ed. New York: Greenwood.

Bowles, S., H. Gintis, and M. O. Groves, eds. 2005. *Unequal Chances: Family Background and Economic Success*. New York: Russell Sage.

Breger, L. 2017. "Poverty and Student Achievement in Chicago Public Schools." *The American Economist*, 62, 206–216.

Brenan, M. 2018. "Most U.S Teachers Oppose Carrying Guns in School." 16 March. Gallup. Retrieved 20 April 2018 (news.gallup.com/poll/229808/teachers-oppose-carrying-guns-schools.aspx).

Brown, A., and E. Patten. 2014. "Statistical Portrait of Hispanics in the United States, 2012." Pew Research Center. 29 April. Retrieved 31 March 2015 (www.pewhispanic.org/2014/04/29/statistical-portrait-of-hispanics-in-the-united-states-2012/).

Bureau of Indian Education. 2018a. "Parents and Students." Retrieved 11 April 2018 (www.bie.edu/ParentsStudents/index.htm).

Bureau of Indian Education. 2018b. "Schools." Retrieved 11 April 2018 (www.bie.edu/Schools/index.htm).

Business Brokers.net. 2018. "The Cost of Childcare in Every State." April 12, 2018. Retrieved 7 September 2018 (https://www.businessbroker.net/blog/good-info-for-new-buyers-and-sellers/average-child-care-costs-state-map).

Butler-Barnes, S. T., L. Estrada-Martinez, R. J. Colin, and B. D. Jones. 2015. "School and Peer Influences on the Academic Outcomes of African American Adolescents." *Journal of Adolescence*, 44, 168–181.

Center for Global Development. 2018. "Education and the Developing World." Retrieved 15 April 2018 (www.cgdev.org).

Centers for Disease Control and Prevention. 2018. "Youth Risk Behavior Surveillance System (YRBSS)." 22 March.

Chmielewski, A. K., H. Dumont, and U. Trautwein. 2013. "Tracking Effects Depend on Tracking Type: An International Comparison of Students' Mathematics Self-Concept." *American Educational Research Journal*, 50, 925–57.

Chou, R. S., and J. R. Feagin. 2015. *Myth of the Model Minority: Asian Americans Facing Racism*, 2nd ed. New York: Routledge.

Clark, M. A., P. M. Gleason, C. C. Tuttle, and M. K. Silverberg. 2015. "Do Charter Schools Improve Student Achievement?" *Educational Evaluation and Policy Analysis*, 37, 419–436.

The Clearinghouse on International Developments in Child, Youth, and Family Policies. 2001. "New 12 Country Study Reveals Substantial Gaps in U.S. Early Childhood Education and Care Policies."

Cole, M. 2008. *Marxism and Educational Theory: Origins and Issues*. New York: Routledge.

Coleman, J. S. 1966. "Equality of Educational Opportunity." National Center for Educational Statistics. Report Number OE-38001. Retrieved 31 March 2015 (files.eric.ed.gov/fulltext/ED012275.pdf).

College Board. 2018. "Trends in Higher Education: Total Pell Grant Expenditures and Number of Recipients Over Time." Retrieved 15 May 2018 (trends.collegeboard.org/student-aid/figures-tables/pell-grants-total-expenditures-maximum-and-average-grant-and-number-recipients-over-time).

Converse, J. 2014. "Portrait in Partnership: Map Data Contributes to Three BIE Schools Forward Momentum." Retrieved 8 September 2018 (https://www.nwea.org/blog/2014/portrait-partnership-map-data-contributes-three-bie-schools-forward-momentum/).

Cornman, S. Q., L. Zhou, M. R. Howell, and J. Young. 2018. "Revenues and Expenditures for Public Elementary and Secondary Education: School Year 2014–15 (Fiscal Year 2015)." National Center for Education Statistics. NCES 2018-301. January.

DeSilver, D. 2017. "U.S. Students' Academic Achievement Still Lags That of Their Peers in Many Other Countries." Pew Research Center. 15 February. Retrieved 13 April 2018 (www.pewresearch.org/fact-tank/2017/02/15/u-s-students-internationally-math-science/).

Doll, J. J., Z. Eslami, and L. Walters. 2013. "Understanding Why Students Drop Out of High School, According to Their Own Reports: Are They Pushed or Pulled, or Do They Fall Out? A Comparative Analysis of Seven Nationally Representative Studies." *SAGE Open*, 3, doi.org/10.1177/2158244013503834.

Dumont, H., P. Protsch, M. Jansen, and M. Becker. 2017. "Fish Swimming Into the Ocean: How Tracking Relates to Students' Self-Beliefs and School Disengagement at the End of Schooling." *Journal of Educational Psychology*, 109, 855–870.

Everytown for Gun Safety. 2018. "306 School Shootings in America Since 2013." Retrieved 14 April 2018 (everytownresearch.org/school-shootings/).

Fiel, J. E. 2013. "Decomposing School Resegregation: Social Closure, Racial Imbalance, and Racial Isolation." *American Sociological Review*, 78, 828–48.

Gallup. 2018. "Americans' Satisfaction With Quality of K-12 Education in U.S. (Trends)." Retrieved 7 September 2018 (https://news.gallup.com/poll/241658/americans-satisfaction-quality-education-trends.aspx?g_source=link_newsv9&g_campaign=item_241652&g_medium=copy).

Gándara, P., and K. Escamilla. 2017. "Bilingual Education in the United States." *Bilingual and Multilingual Education*, 1–14.

Genesee, F., K. Lindholm-Leary, W. Saunders, and D. Christian. 2005. "Language Learners in U.S. Schools: An Overview of Research Findings." *Journal of Education for Students Placed at Risk*, 10, 363–86.

Graves Jr., S. L., and L. B. Wright. 2011. "Parent Involvement at School Entry: A National Examination of Group Differences and Achievement." *School Psychology International*, 32, 35–48.

Grissom, J., D. Kalogrides, and S. Loeb. 2015. "The Micropolitics of Educational Inequality: The Case of Teacher-Student Assignments." *Peabody Journal of Education*, 90, 601–614.

Grodsky, E., J. R. Warren, and E. Felts. 2008. "Testing and Social Stratification in American Education." *Annual Review of Sociology*, 34, 385–404.

Guinart, M., and M. Grau. 2014. "Qualitative Analysis of the Short-Term and Long-Term Impact of Family Breakdown on Children: Case Study." *Journal of Divorce & Remarriage*, 55, 408–22.

Harris, K. 2017. *Teachers and Classes: A Marxist Analysis*. New York: Routledge.

Head Start. 2015. "Head Start Program Facts Fiscal Year 2014." Retrieved 16 April 2015 (heclkc.ohs.acf.hhs.gov/hslc/data/factsheets/2014-hs-program-factsheet.html).

Hernandez, M. 2017. "The Ivy League Asian Problem." Huffington Post. 6 December. Retrieved 13 April 2018 (www.huffingtonpost.com/dr-michele-hernandez/the-ivy-league-asian-prob_b_10121814.html).

Heyder, A., U. Kessels, and R. Steinmayr. 2017. "Explaining Academic-Track Boys' Underachievement in Language Grades: Not a Lack of Aptitude But Students' Motivational Beliefs and Parents' Perceptions?" *British Journal of Educational Psychology*, doi.org/10.1111/bjep.12145.

Hornby, G., and I. Blackwell. 2018. "Barriers to Parental Involvement in Education: An Update." *Educational Review*, 70, 109–119.

Jennings, J. L., D. Deming, C. Jencks, M. Lopuch, and B. E. Schueler. 2015. "Do Differences in School Quality Matter More Than We Thought? New Evidence on Educational Opportunity in the Twenty-First Century." *Sociology of Education*, 88, 56–82.

Kalogrides, D., S. Loeb, and T. Béteille. 2013. "Systematic Sorting: Teacher Characteristics and Class Assignments." *Sociology of Education*, 86, 103–23.

Karner, C. 2017. *The Urban School: A Factory for Failure*. New York: Routledge.

, and R. J. Sampson. 2013. "Juvenile Arrest and ⌐₁ateral Educational Damage in the Transition to Adulthood." *Sociology of Education*, 86, 36–62.

Kisida, B., J. P. Greene, and D. H. Bowen. 2014. "Creating Cultural Consumers: The Dynamics of Cultural Capital Accumulation." *Sociology of Education*, 87, 281–95.

Klein, M. C. 2014. "Are Ivy League Schools Biased against Asians?" *Bloomberg View*. 3 April. Retrieved 2 February 2015 (www.bloombergview.com/articles/2014-04-03/are-ivy-league-schools-biased-against-asians).

Klenk, J. 2005. *Choosing a School for Your Child*. Washington, DC: Office of Innovation and Improvement, U.S. Department of Education.

Ladd, H. F. 2017. "No Child Left Behind: A Deeply Flawed Federal Policy." *Journal of Policy Analysis and Management*, 36, doi.org/10.1002/pam.21978.

Lavy, V., and E. Sand. 2015. "On the Origins of Gender Human Capital Gaps: Short and Long Term Consequences of Teachers' Stereotypical Biases." National Bureau of Economic Research. NBER Working Paper No. 20909. January. Retrieved 9 February 2015 (www.nber.org/papers/w20909).

Legewie, J., and T. DiPrete. 2014. "The High School Environment and the Gender Gap in Science and Engineering." *Sociology of Education*, 87, 259–80.

Lopez, M. H., and A. Gonzalez-Barrera. 2014. "Women's College Enrollment Gains Leave Men Behind." 6 March. Pew Research Center. Retrieved 31 March 2015 (www.pewresearch.org/fact-tank/2014/03/06/womens-college-enrollment-gains-leave-men-behind/).

Ma, J., M. Pender, and M. Welch. 2016. "Education Pays 2016: The Benefits of Higher Education for Individuals and Society." Trends in Higher Education Series. College Board.

Mayotte, B. 2014. "Past, Future Pell Grant Changes Offer Hope for Families." USNews.com. 24 September. Retrieved 9 February 2015 (www.usnews.com/education/blogs/student-loan-ranger/2014/09/24/past-future-pell-grant-changes-offer-hope-for-families/).

McKinsey and Company. 2010. "How the World's Most Improved School Systems Keep Getting Better." Retrieved 9 February 2015 (www.mckinsey.com/industries/social-sector/our-insights/how-the-worlds-most-improved-school-systems-keep-getting-better).

Mickelson, R. A., M. C. Bottia, and R. Lambert. 2013. "Effects of School Racial Composition on K–12 Mathematics Outcomes: A Metaregression Analysis." *Review of Educational Research*, 83, 121–58.

Mitchell, M., M. Leachman, and K. Masterson 2017. "State Cuts Have Driven Up Tuition and Reduced Quality." Center for Budget and Policy Priorities. 23 August. Retrieved 16 April 2018 (www.cbpp.org/research/state-budget-and-tax/a-lost-decade-in-higher-education-funding).

Moss-Racusin, C. A., J. F. Dovidio, V. L. Brescoll, M. J. Graham, and J. Handelsman. 2012. "Science Faculty's Subtle Gender Biases Favor Male Students." *Proceedings of the National Academy of Sciences*, 109, 16474–79.

National Alliance for Public Charter Schools. 2018. "Estimated Charter Public School Enrollment, 2016–17."

National Association for Bilingual Education. 2014. "What Is Bilingual Education?" Retrieved 31 March 2015 (www.nabe.org/BilingualEducation).

National Center for Education Statistics. 2017a. "English Language Learners in Public Schools." March. Retrieved 14 April 2018 (nces.ed.gov/programs/coe/indicator_cgf.asp).

National Center for Education Statistics. 2017b. "Public High School Graduation Rates." April. Retrieved 10 April 2018 (nces.ed.gov/programs/coe/indicator_coi.asp).

National Center for Education Statistics. 2017c. "Education Expenditures by Country." May. Retrieved 10 April 2018 (nces.ed.gov/programs/coe/indicator_cmd.asp).

National Center for Education Statistics. 2018a. "Digest of Education Statistics: 2016." February. Retrieved 14 April 2018 (nces.ed.gov/programs/digest/d16/tables_1.asp).

National Center for Education Statistics. 2018b. "Public Charter School Enrollment." March. Retrieved 14 April 2018 (nces.ed.gov/programs/coe/indicator_cgb.asp).

National Indian Education Association. 2018. "Information on Native Students." Retrieved 11 April 2018 (www.niea.org/our-story/history/information-on-native-students/).

OECD. 2016. "Family Database: Public Spending on Childcare and Early Education." Retrieved 7 September 2018 (http://www.oecd.org/els/family/database.htm).

Orfield, G. 2004/2005. "Why Segregation Is Inherently Unequal: The Abandonment of *Brown* and the Continuing Failure of *Plessy*." *New York Law School Law Review*, 49, 1041–52.

Orfield, G., and S. E. Eaton. 1996. *Dismantling Desegregation: The Quiet Reversal of* Brown *v*. Board of Education. New York: Free Press.

Organisation for Economic Co-operation and Development. 2015. Retrieved 7 July 2015 (www.OECD.org).

Organisation for Economic Co-Operation and Development. 2018. "Education Spending." Retrieved 10 April 2018 (data.oecd.org/eduresource/education-spending.htm#indicator-chart).

Pew Research Center. 2017. "Latinos and the New Trump Administration." 23 February. Retrieved 15 May 2018 (www.pewhispanic.org/2017/02/23/latinos-and-the-new-trump-administration/).

Poon, O. Y., D. Squire, C. Kodama, A. Byrd, J. Chan, L. Manzano, S. Furr, and D. Bishundat. 2016. "A Critical Review of the Model Minority Myth in Selected Literature on Asian Americans and Pacific Islanders in Higher Education." *Review of Educational Research*, 86, 469–502.

Population Reference Bureau. 2015. "World Population Data Sheet 2014." Retrieved 16 April 2015 (www.prb.org/Publications/Datasheets/2014/2014-world-population-data-sheet.aspx).

Poulou, M. S. 2017. "An Examination of the Relationship Among Teachers' Perceptions of Social-Emotional Learning, Teaching Efficacy, Teacher-Student Interactions, and Students' Behavioral Difficulties." *International Journal of School & Educational Psychology*, 5, doi.org/10.1080/21683603.2016.1203851.

RAND Education. 2012. "Teachers Matter: Understanding Teachers' Impact on Student Achievement." Retrieved 9 February 2015 (www.rand.org/education/projects/measuring-teacher-effectiveness/teachers-matter.html).

Redford, J., D. Battle, S. Bielick, and S. Grady. 2017. "Homeschooling in the United States: 2012." NCES 2016-096.REV. National Center for Education Statistics. April.

Richards, M. P. 2014. "The Gerrymandering of School Attendance Zones and the Segregation of Public Schools: A Geospatial Analysis." *American Educational Research Journal*, 51, 1119–57.

Rosenthal, R., and L. Jacobson. 1968. *Pygmalion in the Classroom: Teacher Expectation and Pupils' Intellectual Development*. New York: Rinehart and Winston.

Sadler, P. M., G. Sonnert, H. P. Coyle, N. Cook-Smith, and J. L. Miller. 2013. "The Influence of Teachers' Knowledge on Student Learning in Middle School Physical Science Classrooms." *American Educational Research Journal*, 50, 1020–49.

Schmidt, B. M. 2015. "Rate My Professor." Retrieved 16 April 2015 (benschmidt.org/2015/02/06/rate-my-professor/).

Schmidt, W. H., N. A. Burroughs, P. Zoido, and R. T. Houang. 2015. "The Role of Schooling in Perpetuating Educational Inequality: An International Perspective." *Educational Researcher*, 44, 371–386.

Shifrer, D., R. M. Callahan, and C. Muller. 2013. "Equity or Marginalization? The High School Course-Taking of Students Labeled with a Learning Disability." *American Educational Research Journal*, 50, 656–82.

Silva, E. B. 2017. "Cultural Capital." In: *The Wiley-Blackwell Encyclopedia of Social Theory*, B. S. Turner, ed. New York: Wiley.

Soria, K. M., and S. Linder. 2014. "Parental Divorce and First-Year College Students' Persistence and Academic Achievement." *Journal of Divorce & Remarriage*, 55, 103–16.

Soria, K. M., B. Weiner, and E. C. Lu. 2014. "Financial Decisions among Undergraduate Students from Low-Income and Working-Class Social Class Backgrounds." *Journal of Student Financial Aid*, 44, 1/2.

Stanley, D., and T. T. Venzant Chambers. 2018. "Tracking Myself: African American High School Students Talk About the Effects of Curricular Differentiation." *International Journal of Education Policy & Leadership*, 13, doi.org/10.22230/ijepl.2018v13n1a748.

Stoet, G., and D. C. Geary. 2015. "Sex Differences in Academic Achievement Are Not Related to Political, Economic, or Social Equality." *Intelligence*, 48, 137–151.

Suicide Prevention Resource Center. 2014. "Suicide Among Racial/Ethnic Populations in the U.S.: Asians, Pacific Islanders, and Native Hawaiians." Retrieved 2 February 2015 (www.sprc.org/sites/sprc.org/files/library/API%20Sheet%20August%2028%202013%20Final.pdf).

Toldson, I. A., and B. P. Lemmons. 2013. "Social Demographics, the School Environment, and Parenting Practices Associated with Parents' Participation in Schools and Academic Success among Black, Hispanic, and White Students." *Journal of Human Behavior in the Social Environment*, 23, 237–255.

Tompson, T., J. Benz, and J. Agiesta. 2013. "Parents' Attitudes on the Quality of Education in the United States." The Associated Press–NORC Center for Public Affairs Research. Retrieved 15 April 2015 (www.apnorc.org/PDFs/Parent%20Attitudes/AP_NORC_Parents%20Attitudes%20on%20the%20Quality%20of%20Education%20in%20the%20US_FINAL_2.pdf).

Urban, W. J., and J. L. Wagoner, Jr. 2008. *American Education: A History*, 4th ed. New York: Routledge.

U.S. Census Bureau. 2017. "Data: School Enrollment in the United States: October 2015 – Detailed Tables." 8 May.

Valle, R. C., S. Normandeau, and G. R. González. 2015. "Education at a Glance Interim Report: Update of Employment and Educational Attainment." Organisation for Economic Co-Operation and Development. January. Retrieved 31 March 2015 (www.oecd.org/edu/EAG-Interim-report.pdf).

Voyer, D., and S. D. Voyer. 2014. "Gender Differences in Scholastic Achievement: A Meta-Analysis." *Psychological Bulletin*, 140, 1174–204.

Wilder, S. 2014. "Effects of Parental Involvement on Academic Achievement: A Meta-Synthesis." *Educational Review*, 66, 377–397.

Wolf, S., K. A. Magnuson, and R. T. Kimbro. 2017. "Family Poverty and Neighborhood Poverty: Links with Children's School Readiness Before and After the Great Recession." *Children and Youth Services Review*, 79, 368–384.

Chapter 12

Ansari, A., and A. Riasi. 2016. "An Investigation of Factors Affecting Brand Advertising Success and Effectiveness." *International Business Research*, 9, dx.doi.org/10.5539/ibr.v9n4p20.

Bartley, T., and C. Child. 2014. "Shaming the Corporation: The Social Production of Targets and the Anti-Sweatshop Movement." *American Sociological Review*, 79, 653–679.

Bennett, M. 2017. "Why 24/7 Business Is The Future." *The Telegraph*. 10 March. Retrieved 17 April 2018 (www.telegraph.co.uk/business/ready-and-enabled/the-future-of-24-7-business/).

Boehm, C., A. Flaaen, and N. Pandalai-Nayar. 2017. "Multinationals, Offshoring, and the Decline of U.S. Manufacturing." U. S. Census Bureau Center for Economic Studies Paper No. CES-WP-17-22.

Bureau of Labor Statistics. 2017a. "National Census of Fatal Occupational Injuries in 2016." News Release. USDL-17-1667. 19 December.

Bureau of Labor Statistics. 2017b. "Employee Benefits Survey." September. Retrieved 19 April 2018 (www.bls.gov/ncs/ebs/#bulletin_coverage).

Bureau of Labor Statistics. 2017c. "Employment Projections: Employment by Major Industry Sector." Retrieved 19 April 2018 (www.bls.gov/emp/ep_table_201.htm).

Bureau of Labor Statistics. 2017d. "Employee Benefits in the United States–March 2017." News Release. 21 July. USDL-17-1013.

Bureau of Labor Statistics. 2017e. "Employer-Reported Workplace Injuries and Illnesses (Annual) News Release." Economic News Release. 11 September. Retrieved 10 September 2018 (https://www.bls.gov/news.release/osh.htm).

Bureau of Labor Statistics. 2018a. "Characteristics of Minimum Wage Workers, 2017." Report 1072. March. Retrieved 20 April 2018 (www.bls.gov/opub/reports/minimum-wage/2017/home.htm).

Bureau of Labor Statistics. 2018b. "The Employment Situation." News Release. USDL-18-0508. March.

Bureau of Labor Statistics. 2018c. "Table 2. Median Weekly Earnings of Full-Time Wage and Salary Workers by Union Affiliation and Selected Characteristics." Economic News Release. 19 January. Retrieved 19 April 2018 (www.bls.gov/news.release/union2.t02.htm).

Clifton, J. 2016. "The Invisible American." Gallup. 20 September. Retrieved 17 April 2018 (news.gallup.com/opinion/chairman/195680/invisible-american.aspx).

Cooper, D. 2016. "The Federal Minimum Wage Has Been Eroded by Decades of Inaction." Economic Policy Institute. Economic Snapshot. 25 July.

Craig, L., and J. E. Brown. 2017. "Feeling Rushed: Gendered Time Quality, Work Hours, Nonstandard Work Schedules, and Spousal Crossover." *Journal of Marriage and Family*, 79, 225–242.

Derber, C. 2014. *Corporation Nation: How Corporations Are Taking Over Our Lives—and What We Can Do about It*. New York: St. Martin's Press.

.7. "United States-China Two-Way Direct In-
..ent: Opportunities and Challenges." *Journal of Asian
Economics*, 50, 14–26.

Dupuis, M. 2017. "How Do Local Unions Strategize Against
Multinational Corporations' Restructuring Threats? Some
Insights From France." *Economic and Industrial Democracy*, 1
February, doi.org/10.1177/0143831X16684555.

The Economist. 2015. "Why So Many Dutch People Work Part
Time." 12 May. Retrieved 20 April 2018 (www.economist.
com/blogs/economist-explains/
2015/05/economist-explains-12).

Edin, K., and M. Kefalas. (2005). *Promises I Can Keep: Why Poor
Women Put Motherhood before Marriage*. Berkeley: University
of California Press.

El Issa, E. 2018. "Household Debt Climbs, Led by Mortgages, Credit Cards." *Nerdwallet*. 16 April. Retrieved 22
April 2018 (www.nerdwallet.com/blog/credit-cards/
q4-2017-hhd-study-update).

Franchise Direct. 2018. "Top 100 Global Franchise-Rankings
(2018)." Retrieved 19 April 2018 (www.franchisedirect
.com/top100globalfranchises/rankings).

Friedan, B. 1963. *The Feminine Mystique*. New York: Dell.

Gallup. 2018. "Most Important Problem." Retrieved 17 April 2018
(news.gallup.com/poll/1675/most-important-problem.aspx).

George, E., and P. Chattopadhyay. 2015. "Non-Standard Work
and Workers: Organizational Implications." Conditions of
Work and Employment Series No. 61. Geneva, Switzerland:
International Labour Office.

Glasmeier, A. K. and the Massachusetts Institute of Technology. 2017. "Living Wage Calculator." Retrieved 18 December
2017 (livingwage.mit.edu).

Global Trends. 2015. "Corporate Clout 2013: Time for Responsible Capitalism." Retrieved 10 May 2015 (www.
globaltrends.com/knowledge-center/features/
shapers-and-influencers/190-corporate-clout-2013-
time-for-responsible-capitalism).

Gornick, J. C., A. Heron, and R. Eisenbrey. 2007. "The
Work-Family Balance: An Analysis of European, Japanese,
and U.S Work-Time Policies." Technical Report No. Briefing Paper 189. Washington, DC: Economic Policy Institute.

Human Rights Campaign. 2015. "Employment
Non-Discrimination Act." Retrieved 6 May 2015
(www.hrc.org/resources/entry/employment-non-
discrimination-act).

Inman, P. 2016. "Study: Big Corporations Dominate List
of World's Top Economic Entities." *The Guardian*. 12 September. Retrieved 17 April 2018 (www.theguardian.com/
business/2016/sep/12/global-justice-now-study-multina-
tional-businesses-walmart-apple-shell).

International Labor Rights Forum. 2018. "When Workers Rise Up For Change." Retrieved 17 April
2018 (www.laborrights.org).

Kaiser, T., J. Li, and M. Pollmann-Schult. 2017. "Evening and
Night Work Schedules and Children's Social and Emotional Well-being." *Community, Work, & Family*,
doi.org/10.1080/13668803.2017.1404443.

Kobrin, S. J. 2017. "Bricks and Mortar in a Borderless World:
Globalization, the Backlash, and the Multinational Enterprise." *Global Strategy Journal*, 7, 159–171.

Kowalczyk, H. A. 2016. "Capitalism, Socialism, and Communism." *Huffington Post*. 10 November. Retrieved 20 April
2018 (www.huffingtonpost.com/henryk-a-
kowalczyk/capitalism-socialism-and-_b_8523486.html).

Li, J., S. Johnson, W-J. Han, S. Andrews, G. Kendall, L.
Stradzins, and A. M. Dockery. 2014. "Parents' Nonstandard Work and Child Well-Being: A Critical Review of the
Existing Literature." *The Journal of Primary Prevention*, 35,
53–73.

ManpowerGroup. 2015. "What Sets Us Apart." Retrieved 25
May 2015 (www.manpowergroup.com/wps/wcm/con-
nect/manpowergroup-en/home/why-manpowergroup/
what-sets-us-apart/#.VV_NodpVhBc).

Martin, E., and R. D. Torres. 2004. *Savage State: Welfare Capitalism and Inequality*. Lanham, MD: Rowman and Littlefield.

McCarthy, J. 2016. "Americans' Financial Worries Edge Up
in 2016." Gallup. 28 April. Retrieved 10 September 2018
(https://news.gallup.com/poll/191174/americans-
financial-worries-edge-2016.aspx).

McCarthy, J. 2017. "Americans' Financial Anxieties Ease in
2017." Gallup. 19 May. Retrieved 17 April 2018 (news.
gallup.com/poll/210890/americans-financial-anxieties-
ease-2017.aspx).

McDonnell, M. H., B. G. King, and S. A. Soule. 2015. "A
Dynamic Process Model of Private Politics: Activist Tar-
geting and Corporate Receptivity to Social Challenges."
American Sociological Review, 80, 654–678.

Mishel, L. 2013. "Vast Majority of Wage Earners Are Working
Harder, And For Not Much More." Economic Policy Institute. 30 January. Retrieved 23 May 2018 (www
.epi.org/files/2013/ib348-trends-us-work-hours-wag-
es-1979-2007.pdf).

Mourdoukoutas, P. 2018. "The $15 Minimum Wage Movement
Is Winning, And That's Bad News for Cashiers." *Forbes*. 1
January.

Newport, F. 2015. "Fewer Americans Identify as Middle Class
in Recent Years." Gallup. 28 April. Retrieved 3 May 2015
(www.gallup.com/poll/182918/fewer-
americans-identify-middle-class-recent-years.aspx).

Newport, F. 2018. "Slim Majority Now Says U.S. Middle Class
Pays Fair Tax Share." Gallup. 16 April. Retrieved 10 September 2018 (https://news.gallup.com/poll/232484/slim-majori-
ty-says-middle-class-pays-fair-tax-share.aspx).

Office of the Mayor (City of Seattle). 2015. "$15 Minimum
Wage." Seattle.gov. Retrieved 6 May 2015 (murray.seattle.
gov/minimumwage/#sthash.YslR1Cmf.dpbs).

Official Journal of the European Communities. 1998. "Council
Directive 97/81/EC of 15 December 1997 Concerning the
Framework Agreement on Part-Time Work Concluded by
UNICEF, CEEP and the ETUC." Retrieved 5 January 2010.
(Eur-Lex) (eur-lex.europa.eu/LexUriServ/LexUriServ.
do?uri=CELEX): 31997L0081: EN: HTML.

Peck, J. 2017. *Offshore: Exploring the World of Global Outsourcing*.
Oxford University Press.

Peralta, K. 2014. "Outsourcing to China Costs U.S.
3.2 Million Jobs since 2001." *U.S. News and World
Report*. Retrieved 10 May 2015 (www.usnews.
com/news/blogs/data-mine/2014/12/11/
outsourcing-to-china-cost-us-32-million-jobs-since-2001).

Powell, B. 2014. *Out of Poverty: Sweatshops in the Global Economy*. Cambridge, MA: Cambridge University Press.

Prickett, K. C. 2018. "Nonstandard Work Schedules, Family
Dynamics, and Mother-Child Interactions During Early
Childhood." *Journal of Family Issues*, 39, 985–1007.

Rachidi, A. 2016. "Child Care Assistance and Nonstandard
Work Schedules." *Children and Youth Services Review*, 65,
104–111.

Rao, A. H. 2017. "Stand By Your Man: Wives' Emotion Work During Men's Unemployment." *Journal of Marriage and Family*, 79, 636–656.

Riffkin, R. 2015. "U.S. Workers Job Loss Fears Down to Pre-Recession Levels." 23 April. Retrieved 25 May 2015 (www.gallup.com/poll/182840/workers-job-loss-fears-back-pre-recession-levels.aspx).

Riley, C. 2014. "Asia Consumers Shun McDonald's after Food Scare." 10 September. CNN.com. Retrieved 3 May 2015 (money.cnn.com/2014/09/10/news/mcdonalds-food-scare/).

Ritzer, G. 2012. *The McDonaldization of Society*, 7th ed. Thousand Oaks, CA: Sage.

Ruggie, J. G. 2013. *Just Business: Multinational Corporations and Human Rights*. New York: W.W. Norton.

Saltsman, M. 2017. "Why The $15 Minimum Wage Will Cost California 400,000 Jobs." *Forbes*. 15 December. Retrieved 20 April 2018 (www.forbes.com/sites/michaelsaltsman/2017/12/15/why-the-minimum-wage-will-cost-california-400000-jobs/#6f5ecf3943b9).

Schmitt, J. 2013. "Why Does the Minimum Wage Have No Discernible Effect on Employment?" Center for Economic and Policy Research. February. Retrieved 6 May 2015 (www.cepr.net/documents/publications/min-wage-2013-02.pdf).

Seccombe, K. 2015. *"So You Think I Drive a Cadillac?" Welfare Recipients' Perspective on the System and its Reform*, 4th ed. Boston, MA: Pearson.

Schrempf-Stirling, J., and F. Wettstein. 2017. "Beyond Guilty Verdicts: Human Rights Litigation and its Impact on Corporations' Human Rights Policies." *Journal of Business Ethics*, 145, 545–562.

Sinclair, U. 1906, reprinted 1981. *The Jungle*. New York: Bantam.

Smelser, N. J., and R. Swedberg, eds. 2005. *The Handbook of Economic Sociology*, 2nd ed. Princeton, NJ: Princeton University Press.

Su, J. H., and R. Dunifon. 2017. "Nonstandard Work Schedules and Private Safety Nets Among Working Mothers." *Journal of Marriage and Family*, 79, 597–613.

Thibodeau, P. 2015. "Fury Rises at Disney Over Use of Foreign Workers." *Computerworld*. Retrieved 9 May 2015 (www.computerworld.com/article/2915904/it-outsourcing/fury-rises-at-disney-over-use-of-foreign-workers.html).

United States Courts. 2017. "June 2017 Bankruptcy Filings Down 2.8 Percent." 21 July. Retrieved 19 April 2018 (www.uscourts.gov/news/2017/07/21/june-2017-bankruptcy-filings-down-28-percent).

U.S. Department of Labor, Occupational Health and Safety Administration. 2018. "OSHA Data & Statistics: Commonly Used Statistics." Retrieved 25 May 2018 (www.osha.gov/oshstats/commonstats.html).

U.S. Department of Labor, Wage and Hour Division. 2018. "Minimum Wage Laws in the States." 1 January. Retrieved 20 April 2018 (www.dol.gov/whd/minwage/america.htm).

Westaway, K. 2014. *Profit and Purpose*. Hoboken, NJ: Wiley.

White, G. B. 2017. "What's Changed Since More Than 1,110 People Died in Bangladesh's Factory Collapse?" *The Atlantic*. 3 May. Accessed 20 May 2018 (https://www.theatlantic.com/business/archive/2017/05/rana-plaza-four-years-later/525252/).

Wolf, M. 2014. *The Shifts and the Shocks: What We've Learned—and Have Still to Learn—from the Financial Crisis*. London: Penguin.

Wolff, E. N. 2017. "Household Wealth Trends in the United States, 1962 to 2016: Has Middle Class Wealth Recovered?" National Bureau of Economic Research Working Paper No. 24085. November.

Chapter 13

Alfred, C. 2014. "Remember #BringBackOurGirls? This Is What Has Happened in the 5 Months Since." Huffington Post. 19 September. Retrieved 27 February 2015 (www.huffingtonpost.com/2014/09/14/nigeria-girls-kidnapped-5-months_n_5791622.html).

Arditti, J. A. 2006. "Editor's Note." *Family Relations*, 55, 263–65.

Bogue, D. J. 1985. *The Population of the United States: Historical Trends and Future Projections*. New York: Free Press.

Central Intelligence Agency. 2018. "The World Factbook." Retrieved 23 April 2018 (www.cia.gov/library/publications/resources/the-world-factbook/docs/notesanddefs.html).

Centre for Public Impact. 2017. "Tackling the Declining Birth Rate in Japan." 7 April. Retrieved 24 April 2018 (www.centreforpublicimpact.org/case-study/tackling-declining-birth-rate-japan/).

Clemens, M. 2017. "The Root Causes of Child Migration from Central America: Safety vs. Opportunity." Center for Global Development. 1 August. Retrieved 26 April 2018 (www.cgdev.org/blog/root-causes-child-migration-central-america-safety-vs-opportunity).

Cohn, D. 2015. "Future Immigration Will Change the Face of America by 2065." Pew Research Center. 5 October. Retrieved 26 April 2018 (www.pewresearch.org/fact-tank/2015/10/05/future-immigration-will-change-the-face-of-america-by-2065/).

Davis, K. 1971. "Population Policy: Will Current Programs Succeed?" In *American Popular Debate*, edited by D. Callahan. Garden City, NY: Doubleday.

Demetriou, D. 2017. "Japan's Population to Shrink by a Third by 2065." *The Telegraph*. 11 April. Retrieved 24 April 2018 (www.telegraph.co.uk/news/2017/04/11/japans-population-shrink-third-2065/).

Denyer, S., and A. Gowen. 2018. "Too Many Men." *Washington Post*. 18 April.

Department of Homeland Security. 2017. "Immigration Enforcement." 13 December. Retrieved 26 April 2018 (www.ice.gov/removal-statistics/2017).

Ehrlich, P. R., A. H. Ehrlich, and J. P. Holdren. 1977. *Ecoscience: Population, Resources, Environment*. San Francisco: W. H. Freeman.

Fadda-Conrey, C. 2015. "Arab American Stereotypes." In *Ethnic American Literature: An Encyclopedia for Students*, edited by E. S. Nelson, 68–71. Santa Barbara, CA: Greenwood Publishers.

Food & Agriculture Organization of the United Nations. 2017. "How Close Are We to Zero Hunger?" Retrieved 24 April 2018 (www.fao.org/state-of-food-security-nutrition/en/).

Gallup. 2018. "Immigration." Retrieved 24 April 2018 (news.gallup.com/poll/1660/immigration.aspx).

Gee, L. C., M. Gardner, and M. Wiehe. 2016. "Undocumented Immigrants' State & Local Tax Contributions." February. Washington, D.C.: The Institute on Taxation & Economic Policy.

...5. "What Was the Third World Revolution?"*Dis-*...inter, pp. 35–45.

...nhouse, L. 2018. "The Supreme Court and the New Civil War."*New York Times*. 26 April. Retrieved 26 April 2018 (www.nytimes.com/2018/04/26/opinion/su-preme-court-new-civil-war.html).

Gupton, N. 2011. "Quiz: Population 7 Billion—Could We All Fit in One City?" NationalGeographic.com. Retrieved 27 February 2018 (news.nationalgeographic.com/news/2011/10/111031-population-7-billion-earth-world-un-seven/).

Hall, C. February 1, 2017. "How Has the End of Its One-child Policy Affected China?" *Aljazeera*. Retrieved 5 May 2018 (https://www.aljazeera.com/indepth/features/2017/01/child-policy-affected-china-170129130503972.html).

Haub. C. 2010. "Japan's Demographic Future." Population Reference Bureau. Retrieved 16 May 2018 (https://www.prb.org/japandemography/).

Hiskey, J. T., A. Cordova, D. Orces, and M. F. Malone. 2016. "Understanding the Central American Refugee Crisis." American Immigration Council. Retrieved 17 July 2018 (https://www.americanimmigrationcouncil.org/research/understanding-central-american-refugee-crisis).

Ishii-Kuntz, M. 2003. "Balancing Fatherhood and Work: Emergence of Diverse Masculinities in Contemporary Japan." In *Men and Masculinities in Contemporary Japan: Dislocating the Salaryman Doxa*, edited by J. E. Roberson and N. Suzuki, pp. 198–216. New York: Routledge.

Ishii-Kuntz, M., K. Makino, K. Kato, and M. Tsuchiya. 2004. "Japanese Fathers of Preschoolers and Their Involvement in Child Care."*Journal of Marriage and Family*, 66, 779–91.

Jian, M. 2013. "China's Brutal One-Child Policy."*New York Times*. 21 May. Retrieved 19 February 2015 (www.nytimes.com/2013/05/22/opinion/chinas-brutal-one-child-policy.html?_r=0).

Johnson, K. A. 2016. *China's Hidden Children: Abandonment, Adoption, and the Human Costs of the One-Child Policy*. Chicago: University of Chicago Press.

Jones, J. M. 2016. "More Republicans Favor Path to Citizenship Than Wall." Gallup. 20 July. Retrieved 26 April 2018 (news.gallup.com/poll/198317/republicans-favor-path-citizenship-wall.aspx).

Jordan, M. 2018. "U. S. Must Keep DACA and Accept New Applications, Federal Judge Rules."*New York Times*. 24 April. Retrieved 26 April 2018 (www.nytimes.com/2018/04/24/us/daca-dreamers-trump.html).

Kochhar, R. 2014. "10 Projections for the Global Population in 2050." Pew Research Center. 3 February. Retrieved 27 February 2015 (www.pewresearch.org/fact-tank/2014/02/03/10-projections-for-the-global-population-in-2050/).

Kopan, T. 2018. "Trump Says He's Open to Pathway to Citizenship 'Incentive' on DACA."*CNN*. 25 January. Retrieved 26 April 2018 (www.cnn.com/2018/04/24/politics/trump-citizenship/index.html).

Krogstad, J. M., J. S. Passel, and D. Cohn. 2017. "5 Facts About Illegal Immigration in the U.S." Pew Research Center. 27 April. Retrieved 26 April 2018 (www.pewresearch.org/fact-tank/2017/04/27/5-facts-about-illegal-immigration-in-the-u-s/).

Labrador, R. C., and D. Renwick. 2018. "Central America's Violent Northern Triangle." Council on Foreign Relations. 18 January. Retrieved 27 April 2018 (www.cfr.org/backgrounder/central-americas-violent-northern-triangle).

Lee, G. H. Y., and S. P. Lee. 2013. "Childcare Availability, Fertility, and Female Labor Force Participation in Japan." Monash University Department of Economics, ISSN 1441-5429 Discussion Paper 36/13. Retrieved 27 February 2015 (www.buseco.monash.edu.au/eco/research/papers/2013/3613childcareleelee.pdf).

Lipman, S. 2017. "New Spotlight On Admissions Illuminates Old Divisions." *The Jewish Week*. 27 April. Retrieved 26 April 2018 (jewishweek.timesofisrael.com/new-spotlight-on-admissions-illuminates-old-divisions/).

López, G., K. Bialek, and J. Radford. 2018. "Key Findings about U.S. Immigrants." Pew Research Center. Retrieved 14 September 2018 (http://www.pewresearch.org/fact-tank/2018/09/14/key-findings-about-u-s-immigrants/).

López, G., and J. M. Krogstad. 2018. "Key Facts About Unauthorized Immigrants Enrolled in DACA." Pew Research Center. 25 September. Retrieved 26 April 2018 (www.pewresearch.org/fact-tank/2017/09/25/key-facts-about-unauthorized-immigrants-enrolled-in-daca/).

Martinez, O. 2014. "Why the Children Fleeing Central America Will Not Stop Coming."*thenation.com*. 30 July. Retrieved 27 February 2015 (www.thenation.com/article/180837/why-children-fleeing-central-america-will-not-stop-coming).

Migration Policy Institute. 2018. State Immigration Data Profiles. Retrieved 3 June 2018 (https://www.migrationpolicy.org/programs/data-hub/state-immigration-data-profiles).

Nagase, N., and M. C. Brinton. 2017. "The Gender Division of Labor and Second Births: Labor Market Institutions and Fertility in Japan."*Demographic Research; Rostock*, 36, 339-370.

Newport, F. "Americans Oppose Border Walls, Favor Dealing with DACA." Gallup. 20 June. Retrieved 14 September 2018 (https://news.gallup.com/poll/235775/americans-oppose-border-walls-favor-dealing-daca.aspx).

Nwosu, C., J. Batalova, and G. Auclair. April 28, 2014, "Frequently Requested Statistics on Immigrants and Immigration in the United States." Migration Policy Institute. Retrieved 10 July 2018 (https://www.migrationpolicy.org/article/frequently-requested-statistics-immigrants-and-immigration-united-states-3).

Office of Refugee Resettlement. 2018. "Facts and Data." 27 March. Retrieved 27 April 2018 (www.acf.hhs.gov/orr/about/ucs/facts-and-data).

Passel, J., and D. Cohn. 2016. "Children of Unauthorized Immigrants Represent Rising Share of K-12 Students." Pew Research Center. 17 November. Retrieved 26 April 2018 (www.pewresearch.org/fact-tank/2016/11/17/children-of-unauthorized-immigrants-represent-rising-share-of-k-12-students/).

Pereznieto, P., A. Magee, and N. Fyles. 2017. "Evidence Review: Mitigating Threats to Girls' Education in Conflict-Affected Contexts: Current Practice." United Nations Girls' Education Initiative. October.

Pew Research Center. 2014. "Surge of Central American Children Roils U.S. Immigration Debate." 16 July. Retrieved 27 July 2018 (http://assets.pewresearch.org/wp-content/uploads/sites/5/2014/07/07-16-14-Obama-and-Immigration-Policy-Release1.pdf).

Pew Research Center. 2017. "U. S. Muslims Concerned About Their Place in Society, But Continue to Believe in the American Dream." 26 July. Retrieved 23 May 2018 (www.pewforum.org/2017/07/26/findings-from-pew-research-centers-2017-survey-of-us-muslims/).

Piotrowski, M., A. Kalleberg, and R. R. Rindfuss. 2015. "Contingent Work Rising: Implications for the Timing of Marriage in Japan."*Family Relations*, 77, 1039–1056.

Population Reference Bureau. 2017. "World Population Highlights: Focus on Human Needs and Sustainable Middle Eastern Terrorist Stereotypes Resources." 14 August.

Population Reference Bureau. 2018. "2018 World Population Data Sheet." 24 August. Retrieved 14 September 2018 (https://www.prb.org/wp-content/uploads/2018/08/2018_WPDS.pdf).

Porterfield, A. 2018. "We Produce Enough Food on This Planet to Feed Everyone: So Why Do We Need GMOs?" Genetic Literacy Project. 12 January 2018. Retrieved 10 July 2018 (https://geneticliteracyproject.org/2018/01/12/produce-enough-food-planet-feed-everyone-need-gmos/).

Portes, A. 2001. *Ethnicities: Children of Immigrants in America.* Berkeley: University of California Press.

ProCon.org. 2018. "Are DACA and the DREAM Act Good for America?" 23 February. Retrieved 26 April 2018 (www.procon.org/headline.php?headlineID=005384).

Roser, M. and E. Ortiz-Ospina. 2017. "World Population Growth." Our World In Data. Retrieved 14 November 2018 (https://ourworldindata.org/world-population-growth).

Saffran, D. 2017. "When It Comes To College Admissions, Asians Are The New Jews."*Forward*. 10 August. Retrieved 26 April 2018 (forward.com/opinion/national/379610/when-it-comes-to-college-admissions-asians-are-the-new-jews/).

Sawyer, C. B., and J. Márquez. 2017. "Senseless Violence Against Central American Unaccompanied Minors: Historical Background and Call For Help." *The Journal of Psychology*, 151, 69–75.

Suls, R. 2017. "Most Americans Continue to Oppose U. S. Border Wall, Doubt Mexico Would Pay For It." Pew Research Center. 24 February. Retrieved 26 April 2018 (www.pewresearch.org/fact-tank/2017/02/24/most-americans-continue-to-oppose-u-s-border-wall-doubt-mexico-would-pay-for-it/).

Union of Concerned Scientists. 2017. "Each Country's Share of CO2 Emissions." Retrieved 24 April 2018 (www.ucsusa.org/global-warming/science-and-impacts/science/each-countrys-share-of-co2.html).

United Nations, Department of Economic and Social Affairs. 2017. "World Population Projected to Reach 9.8 Billion in 2050, and 11.2 Billion in 2100." 21 June. Retrieved 23 April 2018 (www.un.org/development/desa/en/news/population/world-population-prospects-2017.html).

U. S. Census Bureau. 2018a. "Population Growth by Region." Retrieved 24 April 2018 (www.census.gov/popclock/print.php?component=growth&images=//www.census.gov/popclock/share/images/growth_1498867200.png).

U. S. Census Bureau. 2018b. "New Census Bureau Population Estimates Show Dallas-Fort Worth-Arlington Has Largest Growth in the United States." Newsroom. 22 March. CB18-50.

U.S. Census Bureau. 2018c. "U.S. and World Population Clock." Retrieved 14 September 2018 (https://www.census.gov/popclock/).

Welch, K. 2016. "Middle Eastern Terrorist Stereotypes and Anti-Terror Policy Support: The Effect of Perceived Minority Threat."*Race and Justice*, 6, 117–145.

World Bank. 2016. "World Bank Group to Invest $2.5 Billion in Education Projects Benefiting Adolescent Girls." 13 April. Retrieved 23 April 2018 (www.worldbank.org/news/press-release/2016/04/13/world-bank-group-to-invest-25-billion-in-education-projects-benefiting-adolescent-girls).

World Bank. 2018. "Energy Use (kg of oil equivalent per capita)." Retrieved 24 April 2018 (data.worldbank.org/indicator/EG.USE.PCAPKG.KG.OE?end=2010&start=1960&year_high_desc=false).

World Food Programme. 2014. "What Causes Hunger?" Retrieved 27 February 2015 (www.wfp.org/hunger/causes).

World Health Organization. 2017. "World Hunger Again on the Rise, Driven By Conflict and Climate Change, New UN Report Says." 15 September. Retrieved 24 April 2018 (www.who.int/en/news-room/detail/15-09-2017-world-hunger-again-on-the-rise-driven-by-conflict-and-climate-change-new-un-report-says).

Yoshida, A. 2017. *Unmarried Women in Japan: The Drift into Singlehood.* Abingdon, U. K.: Routledge.

Zong, J., J. Batalova, and J. Hallock. 2018. "Frequently Requested Statistics on Immigrants and Immigration in the United States." Migration Immigration Source. 8 February. Retrieved 27 April 2018 (www.migrationpolicy.org/article/frequently-requested-statistics-immigrants-and-immigration-united-states).

Chapter 14

Anand, R. 2017. *International Environmental Justice: A North-South Dimension.* New York: Routledge.

Ansolabehere, S., and D. M. Konisky. 2014. *Cheap and Clean.* Cambridge, MA: The MIT Press.

Barlow, M., and T. Clarke. 2005. *Blue Gold: The Fight to Stop the Corporate Theft of the World's Water.* New York: New Press.

Black, M., J. King, and C. Lacey. 2009. *The Atlas of Water*, 2nd ed. Berkeley: University of California Press.

Bolin, B., and L. C. Kurtz. 2018. "Race, Class, Ethnicity, and Disaster Vulnerability." In: *Handbook of Disaster Research*, edited by H. Rodriguez, W. Donner, and J. Trainor, 181–203. New York: Springer.

Brenan, M., and L. Saad. 2018. "Global Warming Concern Steady Despite Some Partisan Shifts." Gallup. 28 March. Retrieved 7 May 2018 (news.gallup.com/poll/231530/global-warming-concern-steady-despite-partisan-shifts.aspx).

Brinson, L. C. 2015. "How Much Air Pollution Comes from Cars?" HowStuffWorks. Retrieved 15 March 2015 (auto.howstuffworks.com/air-pollution-from-cars.htm).

Broughton, E. 2005. "The Bhopal Disaster and Its Aftermath: A Review." *Environmental Health*, 4, 6.

Brown, L. R. 2015. *The Great Transition.* New York: W.W. Norton.

Carson, R. 1962. *Silent Spring.* Fawcett World Library.

Center for Climate and Energy Solutions. 2018. "California Cap and Trade." Retrieved 16 May 2018 (https://www.c2es.org/content/california-cap-and-trade/).

Center for Sustainable Systems. 2014. "U.S. Wastewater Treatment Factsheet." No. CSS04-14. University of Michigan. October. Retrieved 20 March 2015 (css.snre.umich.edu/css_doc/CSS04-14.pdf).

Clapp, R. 2009. "The Love Canal Story Is Not Finished." *Environmental Health Perspectives*, 117, A54.

Climate Debate Daily. 2015. Home page. Retrieved 15 March 2015 (climatedebatedaily.com/).

CNN Library. 2018. "Oil Spills Fast Facts." 28 February. Retrieved 9 May 2018 (www.cnn.com/2013/07/13/world/oil-spills-fast-facts/index.html).

I., A. Zanobetti, I. Kloog, P. Huybers, ⌐. Leakey, A. J. Bloom, E. Carlisle, N. Fernando, G. Fitz-ⱪerald, T. Hasegawa, N. M. Holbrook, R. L. Nelson, R. Norton, M. J. Ottman, V. Raboy, H. Sakai, K. A. Sartor, J. Schwartz, S. Seneweera, Y. Usui, S. Toshinaga, and S. S. Myers. 2015. "Impacts of Elevated Atmospheric CO2 on Nutrient Content of Important Food Crops." *Scientific Data*, 2, 10.1038/sdata.2015.36.

Drought.gov. 2018. "Summary of Drought for California." Retrieved 7 May 2018 (www.drought.gov/drought/states/california).

Ehrlich, P. R., and A. H. Ehrlich. 2004. *One with Nineveh: Politics, Consumption, and the Human Future*. Washington, DC: Island Press.

Enerdata. 2018. "Total Energy Production." Retrieved 7 May 2018 (yearbook.enerdata.net/total-energy/).

Environmental Defense Fund. 2018. "How Cap and Trade Works." Retrieved 12 March 2018 (www.edf.org/climate/how-cap-and-trade-works).

Environmental Protection Agency. 2014. "Municipal Solid Waste." 28 February. Retrieved 16 March 2015 (www.epa.gov/epawaste/nohaz/municipal/).

Environmental Protection Agency. 2015. "Landfill Methane Outreach Program." Retrieved 17 March 2015 (www.epa.gov/outreach/lmop/index.html_).

Environmental Protection Agency. 2016a. "Air Quality Index (AQI) Basics. Retrieved 16 September 2018 (https://cfpub.epa.gov/airnow/index.cfm?action=aqibasics.aqi).

Environmental Protection Agency. 2016b. "Advancing Sustainable Materials Management: 2014 Fact Sheet." November. Retrieved 12 May 2018 (19january2017snapshot.epa.gov/sites/production/files/2016-11/documents/2014_smmfactsheet_508.pdf).

Environmental Protection Agency. 2018. "Research on Health and Environmental Effects of Air Quality." 22 February. Retrieved 9 May 2018 (www.epa.gov/air-research/research-health-and-environmental-effects-air-quality).

Gallup. 2018. "Environment." Retrieved 7 May 2018 (news.gallup.com/poll/1615/environment.aspx).

Geyer, R., J. R. Jambeck, and K. L. Law. 2017. "Production, Use, and Fate of All Plastics Ever Made." *Science Advances*, 3, e1700782.

Grineski, S. E., T. W. Collins, J. Chakraborty, and M. Montgomery. 2017. "Hazard Characteristics and Patterns of Environmental Injustice: Household-Level Determinants of Environmental Risk in Miami, Florida." *Risk Analysis*, 37, 1419–1434.

Haberman, C. 2017. "Rachel Carson, DDT, and the Fight Against Malaria." *New York Times*. 22 January. Retrieved 7 May 2018 (www.nytimes.com/2017/01/22/us/rachel-carson-ddt-malaria-retro-report.html).

Halper, E. 2018. "Trump and California Are Set to Collide Head-On Over Fuel Standards." *Los Angeles Times*. 27 April. Retrieved 9 May 2018 (www.latimes.com/politics/la-na-pol-mileage-20180427-story.html).

Kabasenche, W. P., and M. K. Skinner. 2014. "DDT, Epigenetic Harm, and Transgenerational Environmental Justice." *Environmental Health*, 13, 62.

Kleiman, J. 2018. "Love Canal: A Brief History." SUNY Geneseo. Retrieved 10 May 2018 (www.geneseo.edu/history/love_canal_history).

Klinsky, S., T. Roberts, S. Huq, C. Okereke, P. Newell, P. Dauvergne, K. O'Brien, H. Schroeder, P. Tschakert, J. Clapp, M. Keck, F. Biermann, D. Liverman, J. Gupta,

A. Rahman, D. Messner, D. Pellow, and S. Bauer. 2017. "Why Equity is Fundamental in Climate Change Policy Research." *Global Environmental Change*, 44, 170-173.

Lappé, F. M. 1971. *Diet for a Small Planet*. New York: Ballantine Books.

Le Guern. 2018. "When the Mermaids Cry: The Great Plastic Tide." March. Coastal Care. Retrieved 9 May 2018 (http://plastic-pollution.org/).

Longnecker, M. P., W. J. Rogan, and G. Lucier. 1997. "The Human Health Effects of DDT (Dichlorodiphenyltrichloroethane) and PCBS (Polychlorinated Biphenyls) and an Overview of Organochlorines in Public Health." *Annual Review of Public Health*, 18, 211–244.

McCarthy, J. 2017. "In U.S., Water Pollution Worries Highest Since 2001." Gallup. 31 March. Retrieved 7 May 2018 (news.gallup.com/poll/207536/water-pollution-worries-highest-2001.aspx).

Miller, S. 2017. "Climate Change Is Transforming the World's Food Supply." *Live Science*. 16 February. Retrieved 8 May 2018 (www.livescience.com/57921-climate-change-is-transforming-global-food-supply.html).

Milman, O. 2017. "Trump Begins Rollback of Obama's Car Pollution Standards to Curb Emissions." *The Guardian*. 15 March. Retrieved 9 May 2018 (www.theguardian.com/us-news/2017/mar/15/car-pollution-carbon-emissions-obama-trump-epa).

Mohai, P., and R. Saha. 2015. "Which Came First, People or Pollution? Assessing the Disparate Siting and Post-Siting Demographic Change Hypotheses of Environmental Injustice." *Environmental Research Letters*, 10, 1–17.

Moore, B., and S. Nichols. 2014. "Americans Still Favor Energy Conservation over Production." Gallup. 2 April. Retrieved 15 March 2015 (www.gallup.com/poll/168176/americans-favor-energy-conservation-production.aspx).

Munang, R., and J. Andrews. 2014. "Despite Climate Change, Africa Can Feed Africa." AfricaRenewal. Retrieved 15 March 2015 (www.un.org/africarenewal/magazine/special-edition-agriculture-2014/despite-climate-change-africa-can-feed-africa).

Myers, S. S., A. Zanobetti, I. Kloog, P. Huybers, A. D. B. Leakey, A. J. Bloom, E. Carlisle, L. H. Dietterich, G. Fitzgerald, T. Hasegawa, N. M. Holbrook, R. L. Nelson, M. J. Ottman, V. Raboy, H. Sakai, K. A. Sartor, J. Schwartz, S. Seneweera, M. Tausz, and Y. Usui. 2014. "Increasing CO2 Threatens Human Nutrition." *Nature*, 510, 139–142.

NASA. 2018. "Global Climate Change: Facts." Retrieved 12 May 2018 (https://climate.nasa.gov/faq/).

Newport, F. 2018. "Americans Want Government to Do More on Environment." Gallup. 29 March. Retrieved 7 May 2018 (news.gallup.com/poll/232007/americans-want-government-more-environment.aspx).

Norman, J. 2017. "Democrats Drive Rise in Concern About Global Warming." Gallup. 17 March. Retrieved 8 May 2018 (news.gallup.com/poll/206513/democrats-drive-rise-concern-global-warming.aspx).

Nuclear Energy Institute. 2015. "Used Nuclear Energy in Storage." Retrieved 20 March 2015 (www.nei.org/getmedia/1b50e6a4-9da9-44fe-af41-7eb1dc0c4e74/Used-Fuel-Map-2013?width=1100&height=850&ext=.png).

Ogburn, W. F. 1957. "Cultural Lag as Theory." *Sociology and Social Research*, 41, 167–74.

Ophuls, W. 1977. *Ecology and the Politics of Scarcity*. San Francisco: Freeman.

Organisation for Economic Co-Operation and Development. 2016. "The Economic Consequences of Outdoor Air Pollution." June. Retrieved 12 May 2018 (www.oecd.org/environment/indicators-modelling-outlooks/Policy-Highlights-Economic-consequences-of-outdoor-air-pollution-web.pdf).

Orum, P., R. Moore, M. Roberts, and J. Sánchez. 2014. "Who's in Danger? Race, Poverty, and Chemical Disasters. A Demographic Analysis of Chemical Disaster Vulnerability Zones." Environmental Justice and Health Alliance for Chemical Policy Reform. May. Retrieved 16 March 2015 (comingclean-inc.org/assets/media/images/Reports/Who's%20in%20 Danger%20Report%20FINALpdf).

Panis, L., E. B. Provost, B. Cox, T. Louwies, M. Laeremans, A. Standaert, E. Dons, L. Holmstock, T. Nawrot, and P. De Boever. 2017. "Short-Term Air Pollution Exposure Decreases Lung Function: A Repeated Measures Study in Healthy Adults." Environmental Health, 16, 60, doi.org/10.1186/s12940-017-0271-z.

Parker, L. 2017. "Here's How Much Plastic Trash is Littering the Earth." National Geographic. 19 July. Retrieved 17 May (https://news.nationalgeographic.com/2017/07/plastic-produced-recycling-waste-ocean-trash-debris-environment/).

Penn, I. 2018. "California Will Require Solar Power for New Homes." New York Times. 9 May. Retrieved 10 May 2018 (www.nytimes.com/2018/05/09/business/energy-environment/california-solar-power.html).

Puko. T. 2018. "Trump Administration May Eliminate Increases in Fuel-Economy Standards." The Wall Street Journal. 27 April. Retrieved 9 May 2018 (www.wsj.com/articles/trump-administration-may-eliminate-increases-in-fuel-economy-standards-1524859884).

Reinhart, R. J. 2018 "Snapshot: Few Americans Vegetarian or Vegan." Gallup. 1 August. Retrieved 16 September 2018 (https://news.gallup.com/poll/238328/snapshot-few-americans-vegetarian-vegan.aspx?g_source=link_NEWSV9&g_medium=NEWSFEED&g_campaign=item_&g_content=Snapshot%3a%2520Few%2520Americans%2520Vegetarian%2520or%2520Vegan).

Rigaud, K. K., A. de Sherbinin, B. Jones, J. Bergmann, V. Clement, K. Ober, J. Schewe, S. Adamo, B. McCusker, S. Heuser, and A. Midgley. 2018. "Groundswell: Preparing for Internal Climate Migration." Washington, DC: World Bank.

Romley, J. A., A. Hackbarth, and D. P. Goldman. 2010. "The Impact of Air Quality on Hospital Spending." RAND Health Technical Report. Santa Monica, CA: RAND Corporation.

Schlenger, Z. 2017. "California is Home to 8 of the 10 Cities in America Where Air Pollution Is Worst." Quartz. 19 April. Retrieved 16 September 2018 (https://qz.com/963089/california-is-home-to-eight-of-the-10-cities-in-america-where-air-pollution-is-worst/).

Simmons, A. M. 2016. "The Worlds' Trash Crisis, and Why Many Americans are Oblivious." 2 April. Los Angeles Times. Retrieved 22 May 2018 (http://www.latimes.com/world/global-development/la-fg-global-trash-20160422-20160421-snap-htmlstory.html).

Skocpol, T. 2013. "Naming the Problem: What It Will Take to Counter Extremism and Engage Americans in the Fight against Global Warming." Harvard University. January. Retrieved 15 March 2015 (www.scholarsstrategynetwork.org/sites/default/files/skocpol_captrade_report_january_2013_0.pdf).

Springmann, M., D. Mason-D'Croz, S. Robinson, T. Garnett, C. J. Godfray, D. Gollin, M. Rayner, P. Ballon, and P. Scarborough. 2016. "Global and Regional Health Effects of Future Food Production Under Climate Change: A Modelling Study." The Lancet, 387, 1937-1946.

Stokes, B., R. Wike, and J. Carle. 2015. "Global Concern about Climate Change, Broad Support for Limiting Emissions." Pew Research Center. 5 November. Retrieved 10 May 2018 (www.pewglobal.org/2015/11/05/global-concern-about-climate-change-broad-support-for-limiting-emissions/).

Tabuchi H., B. Plumer, and C. Davenport. 2018. "E.P.A. Readies Plan to Weaken Rules That Require Cars to be Cleaner." New York Times. 27 April. Retrieved 27 April 2018 (www.nytimes.com/2018/04/27/climate/epa-emissions-california.html).

Taylor, A. 2014. "Bhopal: The World's Worst Industrial Disaster, 30 Years Later." The Atlantic. 2 December. Retrieved 10 May 2018 (www.theatlantic.com/photo/2014/12/bhopal-the-worlds-worst-industrial-disaster-30-years-later/100864).

Union of Concerned Scientists. 2018. "Global Warming Impacts." Retrieved 7 May 2018 (www.ucsusa.org/our-work/global-warming/science-and-impacts/global-warming-impacts#.WvEMylMVzUI).

United Nations. 2015. "21st Century 'Hottest' on Record as Global Warming Continues – UN." UN and Climate Change. 2 February. Retrieved 15 March 2015 (www.un.org/climatechange/blog/2015/02/21st-century-hottest-record-global-warming-continues-un/).

United Nations. 2018. "Climate Change." Retrieved 7 May 2018 (www.un.org/en/sections/issues-depth/climate-change/index.html).

United Nations Framework Convention on Climate Change. 2018. "The Paris Agreement." Retrieved 8 May 2018 (unfccc.int/process-and-meetings/the-paris-agreement/the-paris-agreement).

U.S. Energy Information Administration. 2018. "Nuclear and Uranium: Current Issues and Trends." Retrieved 24 May (https://www.eia.gov/nuclear/).

Van den Berg, H., G. Manuweera, and F. Konradsen. 2017. "Global Trends in the Production and Use of DDT for Control of Malaria and Other Vector-Borne Diseases." Malaria Journal, 16, 401.

Waite, R. 2018. "2018 Will See High Meat Consumption in the U.S., but the American Diet is Shifting." World Resources Institute. 24 January. Retrieved 11 May 2018 (www.wri.org/print/57991).

White House. 2012. "Obama Administration Finalizes Historic 54.5 MPG Fuel Efficiency Standards." 28 August. Retrieved 9 May 2018 (obamawhitehouse.archives.gov/the-press-office/2012/08/28/obama-administration-finalizes-historic-545-mpg-fuel-efficiency-standard).

Wike, R., B. Stokes, J. Poushter, and J. Fetterolf. 2017. "U. S. Image Suffers as Publics Around World Question Trump's Leadership." Pew Research Center. 26 June. Retrieved 10 May 2018 (www.pewglobal.org/2017/06/26/u-s-image-suffers-as-publics-around-world-question-trumps-leadership/).

Worland, J. 2015. "California May Crack Down Further This Week on Water-Wasters." Time.com. 15 March. Retrieved 16 March 2015 (time.com/3745247/california-drought-water-state-regulators/).

World Bank Group. 2018. "Climate Change." Retrieved 7 May 2018 (www.worldbank.org/en/topic/climatechange/overview).

stitute. 2017. *EarthEd (State of the World)*. Wash-
  DC: Island Press.

Wildlife Fund. 2015. "What Are Climate Change and
  Global Warming?" Retrieved 15 March 2015
  (www.wwf.org.uk/what_we_do/tackling_
  climate_change/climate_change_explained/).

World Wildlife Fund. 2018. "Effects of Climate Change."
  Retrieved 7 May 2018 (www.worldwildlife.org/
  threats/effects-of-climate-change).

Yale Program on Climate Change Communication. 2018. "Beliefs and Attitudes." Retrieved 11 May 2018
  (climatecommunication.yale.edu/visualiza-
  tions-data/americans-oppose-drilling-arctic-national-wild-
  life-refuge/).

Zheng, L. 2018. "Reality Check: Is Beijing's Air Quality Better
  This Winter?" BBC Chinese. 9 January. Retrieved 9 May
  2018 (www.bbc.com/news/world-asia-china-42513531).

Zimmermann, A., H. Webber, G. Zhao, F. Ewert, J. Kros, J. Wolf,
  W. Britz, and W. de Vries. 2017. "Climate Change Impacts
  on Crop Yields, Land Use and Environment in Response
  to Crop Sowing Dates and Thermal Time Requirements."
  Agricultural Systems, 157, 81–92.

Chapter 15

AlJazeera.com. 2018."US and Allies Strike Syria: The Full
  Story." 14 April. Retrieved 14 May 2018 (www.aljazeera
  .com/news/2018/04/allies-strike-syria-chemical-weap-
  ons-sites-180414011901735.html).

AntiWar.org. 2018. "Casualties in Iraq." Retrieved 14 May
  2018 (antiwar.com/casualties/).

Anyangwe, E. 2018. "Rape in the Congo: An Economic War
  on Women's Bodies." CNN.com. 19 January. Retrieved
  15 May 2018 (www.cnn.com/2017/10/19/africa/denis-
  mukwege-congo-doctor-rape/index.html).

Arnett, G. 2014. "Religious Extremism Main Cause of Terrorism, According to Report." *The Guardian*. Retrieved 17
  May 2015 (www.theguardian.com/news/datablog/2014/
  nov/18/religious-extremism-main-cause-of-terrorism-ac-
  cording-to-report).

Barton, J. H. 1981. *The Politics of Peace: An Evaluation of Arms
  Control*. Stanford, CA: Stanford University Press.

BBC News Europe. 2015. "Charlie Hebdo Attack: Three Days
  of Terror." 14 January. Retrieved 17 May 2015 (www.bbc.
  com/news/world-europe-30708237).

BBC News Europe. 2016. "Timeline: Attacks in France."
  26 July. Retrieved 14 May 2018 (www.bbc.com/news/
  world-europe-33288542).

BBC.com. 2017. "Syria Chemical 'Attack': What We Know."
  26 April. Retrieved 20 May 2018 (www.bbc.com/news/
  world-middle-east-39500947).

Beauchamp, Z. 2018. "Trump's Withdrawal From the Iran
  Nuclear Deal, Explained." Vox.com. 8 May. Retrieved
  15 May 2018 (www.vox.com/world/2018/5/8/
  17328520/iran-nuclear-deal-trump-withdraw).

Brooks, R. 2014. "Why Obama's Assurance of 'No Boots on
  the Ground' Isn't So Reassuring." Washington Post.com.
  26 September. Retrieved 15 May 2015 (www.washington-
  post.com/opinions/why-obamas-assurance-of-no-boots-
  on-the-ground-isnt-so-reassuring/2014/09/26/c56d859e-
  44bf-11e4-9a15-137aa0153527_story.html).

Clawson, P. 1988. "Terrorism in Decline?" *Orbis*, 32, 263–76.

Condon, S. 2014. "GOP Report Defends CIA Interrogation Tactics." CBS.com. 9 December. Retrieved 8 May 2015 (www.cbsnews.com/news/
  gop-report-defends-cia-interrogation-tactics/).

Coser, L. 1956. *The Function of Social Conflict*. New York: Free
  Press.

Dershowitz, A. 2002. *Why Terrorism Works*. New Haven, CT:
  Yale University Press.

Dr. Denis Mukwege Foundation. 2018. "Rape and Social Violence Are Widely Used as Weapons of War." Retrieved 15
  May 2018 (www.mukwegefoundation.org).

Economist Intelligence Unit. 2018. "Democracy Index 2017: Free
  Speech Under Attack." Retrieved 14 May 2018 (pages.eiu.
  com/rs/753-RIQ-438/images/Democracy_Index_2017.pdf).

Etzioni, A. 2002. "The Good Society," *Seattle Journal for Social
  Justice*: Vol. 1: Iss. 1, Article 7. (https://digitalcommons.law.
  seattleu.edu/sjsj/vol1/iss1/7).

Fruhlinger, J. 2018. "What is a Cyber Attack? Recent Examples
  Show Disturbing Trends." CSO. 7 March. Retrieved 20
  May 2018 (www.csoonline.com/article/3237324/cyber-at-
  tacks-espionage/what-is-a-cyber-attack-recent-examples-
  show-disturbing-trends.html).

Gallup. 2018. "Terrorism." Retrieved 14 May 2018 (news.gal-
  lup.com/poll/4909/terrorism-united-states.aspx).

Genocide Education Project. 2014. "Modern Era Genocides."
  Retrieved 14 May 2018 (genocideeducation.org/resources/
  modern-era-genocides/).

Gladstone, R. 2018. "U.S. Says Syria Has Used Chemical Weapons at Least 50 Times During War." *New York
  Times*. 13 April. Retrieved 20 May 2018 (www.nytimes.
  com/2018/04/13/world/middleeast/un-syria-haley-
  chemical-weapons.html).

Goodreads.com. 2015. "Best Iraq and Afghanistan
  War Books." May. Retrieved 17 May 2015 (www
  .goodreads.com/list/show/16945.Best_Iraq_and_
  Afghanistan_War_Books).

Hall, Michelle. 2013. "By the Numbers: WW II's Atomic Bombs." Retrieved 20 May 2015 (www.cnn.
  com/2013/08/06/world/asia/btn-atomic-bombs/).

History.com. 2015. "Bombing of Hiroshima and Nagasaki." Retrieved 20 May 2015 (www.history.com/topics/
  world-war-ii/bombing-of-hiroshima-and-nagasaki).

Hooker, E. 2014. "Bioterrorism and Biowarfare Today."
  Emedicinehealth. 3 December. Retrieved 8 May 2015
  (www.emedicinehealth.com/biological_warfare/
  page2_em.htm#bioterrorism_and_biowarfare_today).

Human Rights Watch. 2018. "Yemen: Events of 2017." World
  Report 2018. Retrieved 15 May 2018 (www.hrw.org/
  world-report/2018/country-chapters/yemen).

Institute for Economics & Peace. 2017. "Global Terrorism Index 2017." Retrieved 14 May 2018 (visionofhumanity.org/
  app/uploads/2017/11/Global-Terrorism-Index-2017.pdf).

Janowitz, M. 1978. *The Last Half Century: Societal Change and
  Politics in America*. Chicago: University of Chicago Press.

Jurkowitz, M. 2010. "Terrorism Tops Disasters." 11 May. Philadelphia: Pew Research Center.

Kristof, N. D. 1995. "The Bomb: An Act That Haunts Japan
  and America." 6 August. *New York Times*, pp. 1, 12.

Kristof, N. 2018. "I Saw a Genocide in Slow Motion." *New York
  Times*. 2 March. Retrieved 9 March 2018 (www.nytimes.
  com/2018/03/02/opinion/i-saw-a-genocide-in-slow-mo-
  tion.html).

Mazrui, A. A. 1996. "The New Dynamics of Security: The United Nations and Africa." *World Policy Journal*, 13, 37–42.

McCain, J., and A. Jolie. 2018. "America Should Lead in Saving the Rohingya." *New York Times*. 8 March. Retrieved 15 March 2018 (www.nytimes.com/2018/03/08/opinion/america-rohingya-myanmar.html).

McCoy, R. E. 2018. "Do China's Missiles in the South China Sea Mean War?" *The National Interest*. 15 May. Retrieved 15 May 2018 (www.yahoo.com/news/china-apos-missiles-south-china-112900346.html#Aside).

Mills, C. W. 1956. *The Power Elite*. New York: Oxford University Press.

Mills, C. W. 1958. *The Causes of World War Three*. New York: Simon & Shuster.

Mills, C. W. 1959. *The Sociological Imagination*. New York: Oxford University Press.

Moskos, C. C. 2005. "Saving the All-Volunteer Force." *Military Review*, May–June, pp. 6–7.

Mpinga, E. K., M. Koya, J. Hasselgard-Rowe, E. Jeannot, S. B. Rehani, and P. Chastonay. 2017. "Systematic Review of the Scientific Literature." *Trauma, Violence, & Abuse*, 18, 581–592.

Mueller, J., and M. G. Stewart. 2018. "Why Are Americans Still So Afraid of Islamic Terrorism?" *Washington Post*. 23 March. Retrieved 14 May 2018 (www.washingtonpost.com/news/monkey-cage/wp/2018/03/23/why-are-americans-still-so-afraid-of-islamic-terrorism/?utm_term=.63bd426a768d).

National Consortium for the Study of Terrorism and Responses to Terrorism. 2017. "Annex of Statistical Information: Country Reports on Terrorism 2016." July. Retrieved 14 May 2018 (www.state.gov/documents/organization/272485.pdf).

Organisation for the Prohibition of Chemical Weapons. 2018. "Brief Description of Chemical Weapons." Retrieved 15 May 2018 (www.opcw.org/about-chemical-weapons/what-is-a-chemical-weapon/).

Park, R. 1941. "The Social Functions of War." *American Journal of Sociology*, 46, 551–70.

Pew Research Center. 2002. "What the World Thinks in 2002." December 4. Retrieved 3 June 2018 (http://www.people-press.org/2002/12/04/what-the-world-thinks-in-2002/).

Pew Research Center. 2015. "Growing Support for Campaign Against ISIS—and Possible Use of U.S. Ground Troops." 24 February. Retrieved 12 May 2015 (www.people-press.org/2015/02/24/growing-support-for-campaign-against-isis-and-possible-use-of-u-s-ground-troops/).

Pew Research Center. 2016. "Public Uncertain, Divided Over America's Place in the World." 5 May.

Pew Research Center. 2017. "Build Your Own Chart: Tracking U.S. Favorability and Confidence in the U.S. President, 2002 to 2017." 26 June. Retrieved 15 May 2018 (www.pew-global.org/interactives/us-image/).

Poushter, J. 2017. "Majorities in Europe, North America Worried About Islamic Extremism." Pew Research Center. 24 May. Retrieved 14 May 2018 (www.pewresearch.org/fact-tank/2017/05/24/majorities-in-europe-north-america-worried-about-islamic-extremism/).

Raghavan, S. 2014. "Record Number of U.N. Peacekeepers Fails to Stop African Wars." *Washington Post*. 3 January. Retrieved 26 May 2015 (www.washingtonpost.com/world/record-number-of-un-peacekeepers-fails-to-stop-african-wars/2014/01/03/17ed0574-7487-11e3-9389-09ef9944065e_story.html).

Rapoport, A. 1968. "Introduction." In C. von Clausewitz, *On War*. Harmondsworth, England: Penguin Books.

Searcey, D. 2018. "Kidnapped as Schoolgirls by Boko Haram: Here They Are Now." *New York Times*. 11 April. Retrieved 14 May 2018 (www.nytimes.com/interactive/2018/04/11/world/africa/nigeria-boko-haram-girls.html).

Simmel, G. 1904. "The Sociology of Conflict." *American Journal of Sociology*, 9, 490–525.

Smith, S. 2018. "The Cost Of War Since September 11, 2001." The Balance Careers. Retrieved 14 May, 2018 (www.thebalancecareers.com/the-cost-of-war-3356924).

Sorokin, P. 1937. *Social and Cultural Dynamics: Vol. 3. Fluctuations of Social Relationships, War, and Revolution*. New York: American Book.

Spector, B. I. 2003. "Negotiating with Villains Revisited: Research Note." *International Negotiation*, 8, 613–21.

Stokes, B. 2015. "70 years after Hiroshima, Opinions Have Shifted on Use of Atomic Bomb." Pew Research Center. 4 August. Retrieved 16 June 2018 (http://www.pewresearch.org/fact-tank/2015/08/04/70-years-after-hiroshima-opinions-have-shifted-on-use-of-atomic-bomb/).

Stouffer, S. A., E. A. Suchman, L. C. DeVinney, S. A. Starr, and R. M. Williams. 1949. *The American Soldier*. Princeton, NJ: Princeton University Press.

Substance Abuse and Mental Health Services Administration. 2017. "Veterans and Military Families." 15 September. Retrieved 14 May 2018 (www.samhsa.gov/veterans-military-families).

Theohary, C. A., and J. W. Rollins. 2015. "Cyberwarfare and Cyberterrorism: In Brief." Congressional Research Service. 27 March. Retrieved 20 May 2018 (fas.org/sgp/crs/natsec/R43955.pdf).

United Nations High Commissioner for Refugees. 2017. "Global Trends: Forced Displacement in 2016." 19 June. Retrieved 14 May 2018 (www.unhcr.org/5943e8a34.pdf).

United Nations Human Rights Council. 2018. "'I Lost My Dignity': Sexual and Gender-Based Violence in the Syrian Arab Republic." 8 March. Retrieved 15 May 2018 (reliefweb.int/report/Syrian-arab-republic/i-lost-my-dignity-sexual-and-gender-based-violence-syrian-arab-republic).

United Nations Office on Genocide Prevention and the Responsibility to Protect. 2018. "Genocide." Retrieved 14 May 2018 (www.un.org/en/genocideprevention/genocide.html).

U.S. Department of Homeland Security. 2018. "About DHS." Retrieved 16 May 2018 (www.dhs.gov/about-dhs).

U.S. Department of Veterans Affairs. 2014. "Service-Connected Disabled Veterans by Disability Rating Group: FY1986 to FY2013." Retrieved 8 May 2015 (www.va.gov/vetdata/Utilization.asp).

U.S. Department of Veterans Affairs. 2016. "How Common is PTSD?" 3 October. Retrieved 14 May 2018 (www.ptsd.va.gov/public/ptsd-overview/basics/how-common-is-ptsd.asp).

U.S. Department of Veterans Affairs. 2017. "PTSD Basics." 17 April. Retrieved 16 May 2018 (www.ptsd.va.gov/public/PTSD-overview/basics/index.asp).

U.S. Department of Veterans Affairs. 2018. "Military Sexual Trauma: Overview." 18 April. Retrieved 14 May 2018 (www.mentalhealth.va.gov/msthome.asp).

U.S. History.org. 2014. "The Decision to Drop the Bomb." Retrieved 20 May 2015 (www.ushistory.org/us/51g.asp).

2018. "The South China Sea: Reality Is ...nking In." The Diplomat. 26 April. Re- ...ved 25 May 2018 (thediplomat.com/2018/04/ the-south-china-sea-reality-is-slowly-sinking-in/).

Walt, V. 2015. "Paris Jews Reel after Deadly Kosher-Supermarket Attack." Time.com. 11 January. Retrieved 17 May 2015 (time.com/3663060/paris-terror-attack-jews-kosher-supermarket-siege/).

Watson Institute. 2018. "Human Costs of War: Direct War Death in Afghanistan and Pakistan (Oct. 2001 – July 2016) and Iraq (Oct. 2001 – April 2015)." Retrieved 15 May 2018 (watson.brown.edu/costsofwar/figures/2016/direct-war-death-toll-iraq-afghanistan-and-pakistan-2001-370000).

Westcott, B., and S. Wang. 2018. "Xi Jinping Sends Warning to Taiwan, United States With Live-Fire Drills." CNN.com. 16 April. Retrieved 15 May 2018 (www.cnn.com/2018/04/15/asia/taiwan-us-china-xi-jinping-drills-intl/index.html).

Wike, R., B. Stokes, J. Poushter, and J. Fetterolf. 2017. "U.S. Image Suffers as Publics Around World Question Trump's Leadership." Pew Research Center. 26 June. Retrieved 15 May 2018 (www.pewglobal.org/2017/06/26/u-s-image-suffers-as-publics-around-world-question-trumps-leadership/).

World Trade Organization, 2017. "Highlights in World Trade in 2017." Retrieved 22 June 2018 (https://www.wto.org/english/res_e/statis_e/wts2018_e/wts2018chapter02_e.pdf).

Wounded Warrior Project. 2018. "Who We Are." Retrieved 18 May 2018 (www.woundedwarriorproject.org/mission?gclid=EAIaIQobChMI66rj6LiK2wIVUSOBCh0EnQObE-AAYASABEgIvEPD_BwE).

Epilogue

AMFCME. 2018. "Women in Nontraditional Jobs." Retrieved 13 February 2018 (https://www.afscme.org/members/education-and-training/education-resources/fct-sheets/women-in-nontraditional-jobs).

Barnett, J.C. and E.R. Berchick. 2017. "Health Insurance Coverage in the United States: 2016." Current Population Reports, P60-260, September. Washington, DC: U.S. Census Bureau.

Calamur, K. 2017. "Australia's Lessons on Gun Control." The Atlantic. Retrieved 14 February 2018 (https://theatlantic.com/international/archive/2017/10/australia-gun-control/541710).

Child Care Aware of America. 2017. "What is the Cost of Child Care in Your State?" Retrieved 12 February 2018 (https://usa.childcareaware.org/advocacy-public-policy/resources/research/costofcare/).

Fisher, W. and B. Sard. "Chart Book: Federal Housing Spending is Poorly Matched to Need." Center on Budget and Policy Priorities. Retrieved 13 February 2018 (https://www.cbpp.org/research/housing/chart-book-federal-housing-spending-is-poorly-matched-to-need).

Grall, T. 2016. "Custodial Mothers and Fathers and Child Support: 2013." Current Population Reports. P60-255. Washington, DC: U.S. Census Bureau.

Kaiser Family Foundation. 2017. "Key Facts about the Uninsured Population." Retrieved 14 February 2018 (https://www.kff.org/uninsured/fct-sheet/key-facts-about-the-uninsured-population).

Rice, D. 2018. "Strengthening Federal Rental Aid Should Be 2018 Budget Priority." Retrieved 12 February 2018 (https://www.cbpp.org/blog/strengthening-federal-rental-aid-should-be-2018-budget-priority).

Semega, J. L., Fontenot, K. R., & Kollar, M. A. 2017. "Income and Poverty in the United States: 2016." Current Population Reports. P60-259. September. Washington, DC: U.S. Census Bureau.

U.S. Conference of Mayors. 2016. "The U.S. Conference of Mayors' Report on Hunger and Homelessness." Retrieved 8 February 2018 (https://endhomelessness.atavist.com/mayorsreport2016).

Name Index

Subject Index

Page numbers in *italics* indicate figures and tables.